THE PUBLIC PAPERS OF
THE GOVERNORS OF KENTUCKY

Robert F. Sexton
General Editor

I0576185

SPONSORED BY THE

Kentucky Advisory Commission
on Public Documents

AND THE

Kentucky Historical Society

KENTUCKY ADVISORY COMMISSION ON PUBLIC DOCUMENTS

Jacqueline Bull

Henry E. Cheaney

Thomas D. Clark, *Chairman*

Holman Hamilton

Kenneth Harrell

Lowell H. Harrison

Richard Hill (*deceased*)

James F. Hopkins

Malcolm E. Jewell

Landis Jones

A. D. Kirwan (*deceased*)

Arthur Krock (*deceased*)

George W. Robinson

W. Frank Steely

Wallace J. Williamson III

John D. Wright, Jr.

THE PUBLIC PAPERS OF

GOVERNOR
LOUIE B. NUNN

1967-1971

Robert F. Sexton, *Editor*

Lewis Bellardo, Jr.,
Associate Editor

The University Press of Kentucky

ISBN: 978-0-8131-5410-7

Library of Congress Catalog Card Number: 74–18938

Copyright © 1975 by The University Press of Kentucky

A statewide cooperative scholarly publishing agency serving Berea College, Centre College of Kentucky, Eastern Kentucky University, Georgetown College, Kentucky Historical Society, Kentucky State University, Morehead State University, Murray State University, Northern Kentucky State College, Transylvania University, University of Kentucky, University of Louisville, and Western Kentucky University.

Editorial and Sales Offices: Lexington, Kentucky 40506

CONTENTS

CONTENTS

PUBLIC ADDRESSES [95]

CONTENTS

CONTENTS

CONTENTS

CONTENTS

CONTENTS

CONTENTS

CONTENTS

VALEDICTORY ADDRESS   [567]

APPENDIXES   [571]

INDEX   [605]

THE PUBLIC PAPERS OF
THE GOVERNORS OF KENTUCKY

THIS series is the result of the need to collect and disseminate the official record of the governors of the Commonwealth of Kentucky. During the 1960s this need was recognized by a number of persons interested in Kentucky history, government, and politics, and their efforts culminated in the creation of the Kentucky Advisory Commission on Public Documents. The Commission recommended the publication of a series of volumes, *The Public Papers of the Governors of Kentucky*.

It is hoped that the series will prove useful to all those interested in Kentucky government, including academicians, journalists, public servants, and interested citizens. Not only will the volumes be of contemporary interest, but they will preserve vital materials on past events for future generations. These materials will be presented with scholarly accuracy and objectivity and will be accompanied by scholarly apparatus where needed.

The series includes the papers of past as well as present governors. Approximately every four years the papers of the current governor and one past governor will appear in separate volumes.

EDITORS' PREFACE

EDITORS' PREFACE

THIS volume is designed to preserve and disseminate a record of the Nunn administration. It provides a convenient source of reference material for interested citizens; for the serious students of Kentucky government, politics, or history, it makes available materials which are not otherwise easily accessible. On the other hand, it is not a comprehensive collection of documents emanating from the Governor's Office in the administration of Louie B. Nunn.

A large number of documents was generated during the Nunn years, thus demanding, for the purpose of the volume, careful selectivity. After examining the various types of public papers produced by the governor, we concluded that public addresses best reflected the concerns of the administration. These furnish an overall view of the many facets of the administration and contain Nunn's rationale for his actions as governor. Moreover, they are among the papers that will be most elusive in the future. Consequently, we decided that an extensive, representative sample of these addresses would be most appropriate and that records of other types would be used only when necessary to fill gaps in the administrative record.

Documents such as executive orders, veto messages, proclamations, press releases, and press statements were omitted for several reasons. The most significant groups of documents deleted were executive orders and veto messages, both of which have the force of law. In his four years as governor, Nunn signed 4,644 executive orders, excluding Kentucky Colonelcies. We omitted these from the volume because the orders of Kentucky governors are filed either at the Secretary of State's Office, the Kentucky Historical Society, or the State Archives and Records Center. Significant executive orders are mentioned in the governor's addresses; when they illuminate the meaning of an address we either included them or explained them in notes.

We omitted veto messages because they, too, are part of the preserved public record. They can be found in the published Senate and House *Journals*; the original messages are in the *Enrolled Bills* volumes at the Secretary of State's Office. Moreover, veto messages posed a special editorial problem; the governor wrote his comments in the margin of the vetoed bill itself, and the comments were transferred to the Senate and House *Journals*. These marginal remarks do not always explain the veto. A meaningful explication of the veto messages would require detailed collation with the legislation itself, and the sheer bulk of such annotation would be prohibitive. Finally, the general assumptions which underlie the veto decisions are amply expressed in the addresses. In short, we determined that there was little to be lost by their exclusion.

A total of 650 proclamations were signed by Governor Nunn. We omitted these in part because they, too, are preserved at the Secretary of State's Office, the Kentucky Historical Society, and the State Archives and Records Center, and since, like the gubernatorial proclamations of other states, they are characterized by a general lack of substance.

Press releases, issued by the thousands and not totally retrievable, were not included because they were either largely repetitive of material included in speeches or were secondary to speeches in general importance. The exception to this generalization was the statements concerning the University of Kentucky campus disturbances of May 1970, which have been included. The serious researcher can find the substance and much of the wording of other significant statements in the files of Kentucky newspapers.

Our decisions to exclude these materials will in no way limit the choice of material for future volumes in this series. Within the available space, the total content of each governor's papers, the relative significance and comprehensiveness of each type of document, as well as its public accessibility should determine the scope of subsequent volumes.

To understand fully the nature of this volume, one must consider some of the procedures developed and the difficulties encountered in its preparation. Editorial work on this first volume of the Public Papers of the Governors of Kentucky began only six months before the end of Governor Nunn's term. Consequently we were faced with the need to reorder quickly a filing system not designed for the long-term preservation of materials, but for prompt access to items of current importance. As is the case with all active public officials, the governor and his staff were more concerned with the next speech or the next meeting than with the one just completed. This often meant that speeches were accidentally discarded or misfiled by a clerk or by a researcher seeking ideas for a future speech. Governor Nunn also delivered some speeches extemporaneously, leaving only the barest of notes, if any, for the record.

In many cases, speeches that were on file contained little identifying information about the dates and places of delivery and the audiences being addressed. A few speeches, because of last-minute schedule changes, were read by someone other than the governor or not delivered at all. Finally, documents other than speeches were often placed in the speech file for future reference by staff members. It was, therefore, sometimes difficult to distinguish a speech from research materials or even from a press release. The first order of business was to separate the various types of documents, determine what was missing, and locate those items. Only after this was done did it become possible to determine the scope of the project.

The first requirement was the compilation of a complete list of the governor's speeches. In assembling this inventory, we relied on Governor Nunn's speech and press statement files, his itineraries, and his staff. Two separate speech files, one containing the original speech texts and the other containing copies distributed to the press, provided us with a cross-check. Since press copies of speeches were prepared before delivery, they supplied substitutes for speeches lost after delivery. Unfortunately, none of these sources was comprehensive; however, by checking the one against the other, we were able to compile a virtually complete record of speeches delivered.

Listed are 560 speeches, not including press conference statements, press releases, informal remarks to boards, commissions, and committees in the governor's conference room, and impromptu public remarks. Of these 560 speeches, 166 were printed in this volume; 96 were not located. After extensive searching, we determined that a large proportion of the missing speeches were prepared only in brief outline form or were short, officially scheduled remarks given without notes or text.

In the course of several readings of the speeches, we prepared a cross-index which enabled us to select speeches that provided the fullest possible coverage of the subjects at issue. Those included should give the reader a clear picture of Governor Nunn's position on the most important questions facing Kentucky during his administration. The 298 speeches omitted either duplicated in actual words or in ideas speeches that were included; some of the omissions were fragments or notes which in themselves were not comprehensible. That this was true of a large number of addresses is not surprising, for Governor Nunn's schedule called for an average of one speech every two or three days.

Textual editing was held to a minimum, so that Governor Nunn's words could be conveyed directly. Changes were made only to correct typographical errors or to clarify misleading phraseology. When the governor's handwritten comments or notes could be deciphered and blended into the text, they were included. Occasionally, sections of speeches were deleted when they appeared in speeches elsewhere in the volume. In these cases deletions were noted and cross-referenced to another speech.

Explanatory material was included in notes when important to the meaning of the speech; when possible, quotations used by the governor were cited. It is important to note, however, that we made no effort to substantiate or verify facts as stated by the governor. Neither have we made any attempt to support the governor's positions or opinions nor to express approval or disapproval.

Editorial apparatus in this volume consists of the comprehensive speech list, the contents page, index, individual speech headings, and notes. In cases where the audience identified in the heading may not be well known to the general reader, explanatory notes are provided. Notes are also included where knowledge of the context of a particular speech is necessary for proper understanding. Similarly, notes were added concerning agencies, acts, bills, and executive orders left unexplained by the speech text. Sources for quotations used in the addresses were cited when this information was available.

In the case of biographical notes, we made no attempt to supply information concerning such non-Kentuckians of national prominence as senators, congressmen, presidents, and cabinet secretaries. Other non-Kentuckians were briefly identified. More complete biographical information was provided for Kentuckians, except for prominent historical figures. For all others who are known to have spent at least part of their lives in Kentucky, the following information was supplied when available: birth and death dates; significant nongovernmental positions held; county or city of residence; significant public offices held (if the individual held elective office, political party affiliation was also provided); and offices held in political organizations.

In the process of collecting and editing the papers of Governor Nunn, we were assisted and advised by many individuals. These included members of Governor Nunn's staff, secretaries, reference librarians, and state administrators, and they have our sincere appreciation.

In presenting this first volume of *The Public Papers of the Governors of Kentucky*, we hope that an important step has been taken to preserve for the future the public record of Kentucky's chief executives.

GOVERNOR LOUIE B. NUNN

GOVERNOR LOUIE B. NUNN
December 12, 1967, to December 7, 1971

LOUIE BROADY NUNN, the forty-ninth governor of the Commonwealth of Kentucky, was born March 8, 1924, at Park, Barren County, Kentucky, the fourth son of Mr. and Mrs. Waller H. Nunn, farmers and merchants. Louie Nunn was married to Beula Cornelius Aspley on October 12, 1950. They are the parents of two children, Jennie Lou and Stephen Roberts.

Nunn graduated from Hiseville High School and attended Bowling Green Business University before World War II. Following his military service in the infantry and air force (1943–1945) he attended the University of Cincinnati; he then entered the University of Louisville School of Law, graduating in February 1950 with the Juris Doctor degree. He began the practice of law at Glasgow, Barren County, Kentucky, in 1950.

Active in civic and religious affairs, Nunn served as chairman of the Board of Elders and Deacons of the First Christian Church at Glasgow, where he also taught a Sunday school class. He was active in and served as officer of such organizations as Rotary, Chamber of Commerce, Parent-Teacher Association, American Legion, and the Junior Chamber of Commerce. The Chamber of Commerce selected him as Barren County's outstanding young man and one of the three outstanding young men in Kentucky in 1956. He has also received the thirty-third degree in the Masonic order.

Nunn has been active in statewide Republican politics since 1950. His own political career began in 1953 when he was elected county judge of Barren County. In 1956 he served as the state campaign chairman for Senator John Sherman Cooper, Senator Thruston B. Morton, and President Eisenhower. In 1960 Nunn managed the senatorial campaign of John Sherman Cooper and the Kentucky campaign for presidential candidate Richard M. Nixon; in 1962 he was chairman for the successful Morton campaign for reelection to the United States Senate.

Louie Nunn first ran for statewide office in 1963, losing to Edward T. Breathitt in the general election. As a gubernatorial candidate again in 1967, he won in the Republican primary over Jefferson County Judge Marlow Cook; he won the general election by defeating former Highway Commissioner Henry Ward to become the first Republican governor of the Commonwealth in twenty years.

Active in National Republican party affairs as early as 1956, he was an early supporter of Richard Nixon for the presidential nomination in 1968. He served on the Temporary Platform Committee and as chairman of the Subcommittee on Federal-State Relations at the 1968 Republican National Convention and was chairman of the Kentucky delegation to the convention. While governor, he was active in the Southern, Midwestern, National, and Republican Governors' conferences, serving as chairman of the latter.

Nunn has received honorary degrees of Doctor of Law from the University of Kentucky, Eastern Kentucky University, Murray State University, and Pikeville College, and a Doctor of Letters from Lincoln Memorial University.

INAUGURAL ADDRESS

INAUGURAL ADDRESS
Frankfort / December 12, 1967

SINCE June 4, 1792, the day on which Isaac Shelby took the oath as Kentucky's first Governor, less than half a hundred men have been so highly honored.[1] Six of these men are living and three of them sit upon this platform.[2] I am certain that each of them would agree that the moment when one becomes First Magistrate of this Commonwealth is a moment of high emotion. Pride and humility are strangely intermixed. The elation of political victory is tempered by the certain knowledge of public responsibility.

The stalwart column of my predecessors passes in review. Each in his own way and in his own time and generation has made his contribution—great or small. Each, according to the light which at the time illuminated his path, has left his imprint on the progress of our State for many years after his term of service has ended. With equal clarity, one sees those who will follow him. These are his judges! They will inherit his successes, his failures, his achievements, his errors, and his omissions. For good or ill they will, in the light of history, appraise the quality of his service.

Beyond these stand, and have stood, the people of Kentucky! From those who have gone before we have inherited a great legacy. We drink from wells we did not dig; we reap from vines we did not plant. The people who have elected us to office and generations yet unborn expect, and have the right to expect, that we will, in our turn and in our time, serve them well.

It is the crowning glory of a democracy that government is in the hands of the many and not of the few. It is a heavy burden which democracy casts upon her citizens who are selected for public service. They are not invested with privilege, they are not crowned with power, but rather they have been afforded an opportunity to serve. They are not the masters of those who have selected them, but their servants.

I am persuaded that this is a new era in the political history of our Commonwealth and our nation. The fact that I am here gives eloquent testimony to this conviction. I am not unaware that in the last century only five Governors of my political persuasion have been elected by the people of Kentucky.[3] This means, and must mean, that the people of Kentucky, and particularly the younger ones, look with a jaundiced eye at party labels. It means, and must mean, that the acid, final test of a public person is the quality of his service and not necessarily the precepts of his party.

There are those who have said, and others who will say, that we shall have a divided house and that a house divided against itself cannot stand. This need not be true. It will not be true if each of us who is charged with public responsibility keeps firmly in his mind that there is a common touchstone, a mutual meeting place, where they and all Kentuckians may assemble without division. We may meet, all of us, around the altar of the common good and here we shall find the area of agreement to be very broad and the area of division to be very narrow and very selfish.

Many times in the next four years we shall meet at this altar of common good to fulfill our public responsibility. For my part, I shall extend the hand of friendship. It will be offered in good faith and in good will to all who will accept it. It will be a firm hand and if it is rejected for selfish reasons, I shall at once appeal to the court of last resort, the people of my State. I shall not indulge in partisan politics, nor shall I permit partisan politics to impede the programs and the progress that we shall undertake.

This is neither the time nor the place for me to announce, except in broadest outline, the programs which I shall suggest to the General Assembly. It is enough now for me to say that, in my view, the quality of government may be measured properly by the benefits that it confers upon the governed. If this be a true test, then let it now be said: Young Kentuckians may look forward to a progressively better educational system in all its aspects. The pursuit of knowledge will be readily available and on the best terms that our financial conditions will permit. It is my hope and my prayer that these thousands of young Kentuckians will find a place for their genius in Kentucky. I trust that they will realize a responsibility to provide for those who follow them even better educational opportunities than they have had. If the educational system in Kentucky receives more and more of our substance, it is not unreasonable to expect those who administer it to produce a better product, to instill in those who come under their influence those principles which have been weighed in the balances and found not wanting, and to discourage the idea that liberty is license and that freedom is without responsibility. The future of our Commonwealth and, indeed, the future of our country demands an awareness of the blessings which we enjoy and a determination, at all costs, to keep and defend them. I would be the last to stifle free expression, but I would be the first to defend the institutions which are at the root of our greatness.

For those who have topped the crest of the hill, who find that now the shadows fall behind them, and who have earned the right to be useful and serene, to enjoy "the last of life for which the first was made," we shall try to add a new freedom—the freedom from loneliness. It has been demonstrated that our elder citizens can live in dignity and peace, with adequate medical care and modern comfort, during the latter years of their lives. It is my hope that, four years from now, when another Governor stands in this place to succeed me, there will be entrusted to him facilities across the length and breadth of Kentucky where senior citizens are living in all the comfort that their years of productivity have earned them. Those civilizations have lasted longest which have respected their elders. There may be some correlation between these two historical facts. Is it not written in Holy Writ: "Honor thy father and thy mother that thy days may be long upon the earth"?

Between the young and the old is the productive, vigorous, busy, majority of Kentuckians who, let it be faced, must carry the load of preparing the young for usefulness and providing the old with comfort, for they too, if they live, will join their elders. To them I say that I will spare no effort to provide gainful employment. The emphasis, Governor Breathitt,[4] which you have placed upon bringing new industries to Kentucky will not be lessened; the exertions which you have demonstrated will not diminish. The Kentucky story will be told where it reasonably may be expected to attract new industries to our State. Indeed, it is my hope that before many weeks of the new administration have passed, I shall have important announcements in this significant area of government.

We shall work with communities, we shall work with individuals, and we will join forces under any reasonable circumstances with anyone who shares our view that each of our citizens is entitled to an opportunity to be gainfully employed. We shall expect labor and management, this industrial partnership, to work in harmony, to bargain collectively, and to produce continuously the products for an expanding state and national economy.

The dilemma of our Kentucky farmers must not and will not escape our attention. Perhaps no area of economic policy so cries out for a frank facing of the facts as agriculture. We begin with the basic conviction that a prosperous and efficient agriculture is as important to the city-dwellers as it is to the farm families. The key to a strong agricultural economy is the ability of the individual farmer to utilize capital and managerial ability together with the best equipment and technique available, and to produce by his own work the food and fiber that an expanding economy demands.

The future of Kentucky agriculture is bright if the adjustments required by scientific changes are made, and if the farm family, the farm organizations, and the government join together in a dedicated effort to resolve the problems for which answers have been so long sought. It is our hope that the progress of the Kentucky farmer during these four years will help lead the way for the sagging national farm economy.

Neither shall I be unmindful of the latent possibilities of our mining industries. Here we must look to technology. The day is not far distant when coal will be in competition with nuclear energy. Every resource at our command must be brought to bear on the problem of converting the vast mineral deposits of Kentucky into sources of energy which will find acceptance in the market place. And in so doing, we will provide new products and find new markets for our minerals. We will provide new hope for a section of our Commonwealth which needs new hope and needs it desperately.

I hold the view that, in some manner, the collective genius, the combined and total intellect of the citizens of this Commonwealth, ought to be mobilized in the interest of better government. Those of us who have been elected to public office will need desperately the ingenuity and resourcefulness of every single, solitary Kentuckian. The Kentucky Efficiency Task Force,[5] consisting of outstanding Kentuckians, has commenced its work to aid us in improving your government. It will be the duty of the members of the Kentucky Efficiency Task Force not only to assist us but to search out new and better ways for the government to serve the people. These may be ways that are yet untried but, if they are feasible, we will try them. They may represent dramatic departures from conventional concepts of governmental operations, but this is a new day and we shall not be afraid to try new techniques if they are devised.

I invite your ideas. I pray for your patience and indulgence. I am not unaware of the burdens of the office which I have sought and which tomorrow I shall undertake. Your confidence would bring humility to anyone; your kindness places me forever in your debt. To these things give me one thing more, your sustaining prayers and your cooperation and assistance for the next four years. With these I will not fail, without them I cannot succeed.

Judge Steinfeld, Mr. Ford and I are prepared to take the oath of office.[6]

---

1. Nunn took the oath as forty-ninth governor of Kentucky after a four-hour parade watched by over twenty-five thousand spectators. He was the first Republican governor since Simeon S. Willis in 1943.

2. The six living governors of Kentucky were Edward T. Breathitt (1963–1967), Bert Combs (1959–1963), Albert B. Chandler (1935–1939, 1955–1959), Lawrence Wetherby (1951–1955), Earle C. Clements (1947–1951), and Keen Johnson (1939–1943). Those attending the inauguration were Chandler, Wetherby, and Breathitt.

3. William S. Taylor (1899–1900), Augustus E. Wilson (1907–1911), Edwin P. Morrow (1919–1923), Flem D. Sampson (1927–1931), and Simeon S. Willis (1943–1947).

4. Breathitt (1924–), an attorney from Hopkinsville and a Democrat, preceded Nunn as governor of Kentucky (1963–1967). He has served as state representative from Christian County, Eighth District (1952–1956), and has held numerous other positions.

5. The Task Force was made up of 157 persons representing ninety-three groups including business firms, the state universities, and municipal agencies. For its purpose and objectives see Executive Order 67–35. For its analysis of state government, see *Kentucky Efficiency Task Force, Report* and *Recommendations 1968* (Frankfort, 1968).

6. Samuel Steinfeld (1906–), a Louisville attorney, was judge, Kentucky Court of Appeals, Fourth District, Jefferson County (1967–). Wendell H. Ford, Democrat, Owensboro, was elected as lieutenant governor at the same time Nunn was elected as governor. In Kentucky, voters are permitted to cast separate votes for the gubernatorial and lieutenant gubernatorial candidates, sometimes resulting in significant ticket splitting.

STATE OF THE
COMMONWEALTH ADDRESSES
& LEGISLATIVE MESSAGES

STATE OF THE
COMMONWEALTH ADDRESS
Frankfort / January 2, 1968

BEFORE proceeding with my message, let me congratulate you, members of the General Assembly, on your successful efforts in winning the opportunity to serve your fellow man. The citizens of the Commonwealth have selected you, as they have me, to be their servants and not their masters. No other General Assembly, in the history of Kentucky, has been faced with so heavy a burden for sane, sound, responsible leadership.

In obedience to the mandates of the Constitution of this Commonwealth, it is my duty as the Chief Executive to appear before you, the General Assembly, and to report on the general operations of State Government and its finances, and to make my recommendations dealing with the State's fiscal and legislative policy.

I have learned, as have most governors before me, that the time which elapses between the inauguration of the Governor and his first report to the legislative branch is entirely too short for him to appraise precisely the condition of the Commonwealth, to make appropriate recommendaions for legislative deliberations, and to establish a sound and equitable fiscal policy. It is utterly impossible to conscientiously and intelligently explore the needs of each of the departments and agencies of the Commonwealth and to formulate budget and fiscal policy which would reasonably meet those needs. As a result of changing circumstances and unforeseen conditions, more time will be required than has been available to suggest to you a complete program.

This is a memorable occasion and it is my deepest wish that I could have come before you with the traditional optimism many of you have learned to expect. I wish I could say, as many governors before me have said, that the present is secure, the future bright, the economy vigorous, our financial structure sound, and that we have no worry. I cannot do this. It would not be true. To do so would deceive you, the members of the General Assembly and the citizens of Kentucky, whose affairs are in our trust.

We are here to do the people's work. The privileges of serving are tempered by public responsibility. The hour of decision is now at hand. Our responsibility transcends party affiliation or personal ambitions. The cold hard facts are distressing, but you and the people we represent are entitled to know the truth.

You are well aware of the magnitude of government. The services and the programs are as complex as society itself. Its cost of operation is now over one billion dollars annually. More than twenty-five thousand employees are paid a monthly payroll in excess of eleven million dollars.

As you know, about the middle of November, Governor Breathitt ordered a twenty-four million dollar budget reduction. He directed each department to reduce its budget in order that the Constitutional requirement of a balanced budget be met at the end of this fiscal year. This cut was necessary because fifteen million dollars less revenue was received than had been estimated for the current fiscal year, and nine million dollars less than had been estimated was available to be brought forward from the preceding fiscal year. It is my considered opinion that, had the reduction been instituted as of July, when the shortage became apparent, the present crisis and cutback in services to the people would not have been so pronounced and elimination of services perhaps would not have been at all necessary.[1]

The 1966 General Assembly, of which many of you were members, recognized the need for the funds that were appropriated. Those needs which were recognized in 1966 still exist. Recurring budget costs have not been reduced by the twenty-four million dollar reduction. Much of the so-called budget cut is only a postponement of expenditures which must eventually be funded. Many departments are only delaying expenditures for such things as building maintenance, equipment purchases, and facility replacements. These required, essential, and needed items will have to be met next year.

The obligations and commitments of state government challenge the imagination. For instance, on December 12, when I took the oath of office, this Commonwealth had an outstanding bonded indebtedness totaling in excess of one billion, eighty million dollars. The annual principal and interest payments upon this indebtedness amount to fifty-five million dollars. Over the life of the bonds, the taxpayers of Kentucky will pay out in interest alone approximately seven hundred sixty-seven million dollars.

This is not the only debt obligation of this State. In addition, the State is indebted to the Teachers' Retirement Fund to the extent of one million, two hundred thousand dollars. In the Highway Department, 55 percent of the State Road Fund is committed to debt service—interest and principal payments on bonds issued and outstanding. It is impossible to maintain and operate, much less expand, an adequate road system on the 45 percent of the State Road Fund which is left after payment of debts. And, to make matters worse, I am advised that beginning the second year of the biennium, when the full impact of our borrowing will be felt, the situation will worsen. In addition to this, the completion of the Interstate and Appalachian Highway system will require twenty-five million dollars more than remains in the 1965 bond authority. Prior commitments to which we are obligated would exhaust the existing available funds by the end of 1969. Unliquidated balances on personal service contracts as of December 12, 1967, were approximately thirteen million dollars. These are the unpleasant, bitter facts, but these are the facts.

The school system of Kentucky, at all levels, clamors for improvement. The inherent escalation which is built into our school financing programs, the forces of inflation, the competition from other states, and the progressive increase in student population, place a higher and higher price tag on the kind of school system Kentuckians want. It is probable that the school population in our institutions of higher learning will increase by 12 percent during 1968 and that the school population in our common school system will increase by 10 percent. About school financing, it has been said that we must run very fast to stand still. The budget requests for education are staggering. The entire general fund budget could be devoted to education alone without over-financing it. Of course this cannot be done. But we simply cannot fail to recognize the need of our school children for adequate facilities and proper training for today's competitive society.

The Commissioners of Mental Health and Economic Security have furnished me with most urgent requests for increased financial assistance. These are the departments where government has become the guardian of many Kentuckians who, for one reason or another, are not physically, mentally, or financially able to sustain themselves. Here, in truth, we are our brother's keeper. Consider, if you will how adequately we are "keeping our brother." The Department of Mental Health spends sixty-nine cents per day per patient for food—twenty-three cents per meal, less than half the cost of a sandwich and a cup of coffee at the corner restaurant. It spends eleven cents per day per patient for medicine and about thirty-five dollars per patient per year for clothes.

Sleep does not come easily to me after I have read these reports. I know that you are concerned, as I am concerned. Government, in our age and generation, touches many lives. It is the source of sustenance, the food and shelter and clothes, for many people. They look to us, these unfortunates, and for my part, I cannot look away.

As an emergency measure, I have made available from the Governor's contingency fund three hundred thousand dollars to tide us over the immediate deficiency. However, this is only a small patch on a threadbare garment. The magnitude of the problem in this area is best illustrated by a recent Legislative Research Commission report, which called for a doubling of appropriations to the Department of Mental Health. Here again we must give attention to those people who did not bring about the situation in which they find themselves. Here again is an activity of government which deals with people toward whom we must have compassion. These are only a few of the reports which I have received from responsible department heads. The fact that I have omitted many of them should not be construed to mean that the need is any less great in other areas of government.

I am greatly concerned about the unmet needs in such areas as child welfare, handicapped children, tuberculosis, mental retardation, agriculture, and others. I have omitted them because it would serve no useful purpose to take you further into depressing detail at this time. I shall deal with all these problems, point by point, department by department, when I submit to you the executive budget.

One other thing should be mentioned. Any budget submitted to you, any fiscal recommendations made to you, always must be made in the light of federal influence. For instance, newly enacted federal legislation will require Kentucky to raise benefit payments to public assistance recipients or risk the loss of federal aid funds. The matching of Social Security coverage on the state employees will be an additional expense. Federal participation in the Medicaid program may be cut back to the point where state participation must be greater. Fiscal experts estimate that an increase in federal income taxes, which the President is pressing heavily upon the Congress, may cost Kentucky ten to fifteen million dollars, if enacted, because federal income taxes are deductible on state income tax returns.

I plan to present the executive budget for your consideration in late February. At least four considerations make this timetable advisable. First, the time that will be afforded to me by this schedule will enable me to effect economies which will have a long-range influence on expenditure patterns. In the brief three weeks I have been in office, I have reduced expenditures and attempted to streamline administrative functions, even to the extent of ordering all agencies to use up old stationery from the previous administration before ordering new. We have called in credit cards and ordered all state vehicles to be appropriately marked in order to discourage unauthorized use. We have shortened the holiday vacation time, cancelled most out of state travel, and denied payment for unused vacation time for departing commissioners. By changing the communications system in the Highway Department alone, we are saving about eight hundred dollars per day on just that one item.

Second, the Kentucky Efficiency Task Force, composed of some of the best-informed citizens available for public service, working at no cost to the taxpayer, will make its report in early February. Undoubtedly, some of the Task Force's recommendations will have a direct bearing on my budget proposal. The economy knife will cut deeply. No department agency, or activity will be spared. I intend to pare down the cost of operating the Governor's office, and I would be hopeful that all other elected and appointed State officials will cooperate with me in that regard. I shall not ask more than I am prepared to give.

Third, it may be that by reorganization of the executive branch of state government significant savings can be made. This will be studied, and as specific changes appear feasible they will be taken into account in formulating the budget which I shall submit to you.

Fourth, the impact of of federal legislation on both the income and the expenditure side of the budget can be gauged more accurately by mid-February than it can earlier.

The development, discussion and enactment of a sound financial plan for state government is our priority business. Other recommendations that I will wish to place before you for your consideration must come later. Many of the proposals that you will wish to bring before this General Assembly can be acted upon more effectively after we have, together, faced up to the fiscal facts of life. Such would certainly be the case in regard to appropriation or revenue bills. I am asking, therefore, that the leadership of both parties meet with me tomorrow for the purpose of jointly determining how we can make the best use of our time between now and the introduction of the budget.

You, the members of the General Assembly, carefully selected by the citizens of Kentucky, shall determine the extent to which roads will be constructed, whether cancer tests and care shall continue, whether our streams and air shall be kept free of polution, and whether our mental patients shall receive complete care and treatment. You shall also determine the quality of education of our children and the number of new jobs made available to our young people.

I deeply feel that it is time for us in Kentucky to meet our responsibility and to let each one of our fellow Kentuckians feel no doubt that we will act in a sensible and responsible manner. We have much work to do. Our business is big business and cannot be dealt with easily or lightly or in a partisan manner. We have a joint responsibility which we must jointly discharge.

I recognize and accept my responsibilities to help provide for you leadership that will show a course of direction that will light the way for a better Kentucky for years to come. I know that you come here tonight as the peoples' representatives with the same hopes, aspirations, and desires as I do as their Chief Executive.

It is my privilege, with pride and humility, to stand here as your partner, ready and willing to do all that I can for the common good of all Kentuckians. To stand here without obligation to any special group, with no one to defend and no one to protect, and with no desire to coerce, intimidate, expose, or incriminate. Free to do that which is right, as the One above, the Chief Magistrate of us all, imparts to me the wisdom to determine that which is right. Obligated only to three million Kentuckians without regard to their religious convctions, their party affiliations, their color, their social or economic standing; devoted and determine to give to them the best of my heart and mind, so long as I remain their servant. They should expect no more, they deserve and will receive no less.

————————

1. Estimates of state revenue had been raised in 1966 by $24 million, presumably as a result of increased salary demands by teachers; according to the *Courier-Journal*, these optimistic estimates were made in 1967 to fend off charges that the state budget could not be balanced if the increase was granted. *Louisville Courier-Journal*, November 16, 17, 1967.

BUDGET MESSAGE
Frankfort / February 13, 1968

WE meet here tonight in common cause, the people's business. We meet to consider the condition and the course of their government. What we do here, or what we may fail to do here, will touch the lives and well-being of every citizen of this Commonwealth. We are, for better or worse, part of the life of every Kentuckian. Together, we hold in our hands their welfare; we represent their interests. Together, we must exercise leadership, courage, and compassion in the conduct of their business.

The immediate problems and the compelling issues which face our people are not partisan in nature or solution. There is no time for individual or party politics. The implications are too great for facts to be colored or for games to be played. Those here of goodwill and serious intent know this to be true. So, let us work together, not in partisanship, but in partnership, proper partners in the goal and purpose of every man: comfort for the old, food for the needy, health for the sick, education for the young, and opportunity for all. Kentucky's problems are many and the answers are not easy ones.

The preparation of the Executive Budget rests, by law, upon the Chief Executive. Its review, by law, rests upon this General Assembly. Its fairness and its adequacy will be the measure of our stewardship. The preparation of budget recommendations meet my obligation under the law. But there is the further obligation that I fully explain to you, and to all the people, the programs the budget contains, the decisions it represents, the sacrifices it requires.

The budget I lay before you tonight meets the standard of fairness and equity. It reflects a realistic assessment of the world in which we live. It combines progress with economy. It is testimony to the erosion which inflation imposes upon public services. It reminds us of the high cost of public borrowing. It shows the interrelation of the state and federal government. It is a human investment plan, not just for two years or four, but a long-range plan for Kentucky's future.

In this budget, you will find the human faces of Kentucky. In its pages are the faces of children who depend upon it for their education; the faces of young men and women who depend upon this budget for their university and college education; the faces of our ill and aged who depend upon this budget for the hopes of health and life itself; the faces of those who tremble in fear of those who hold our laws in contempt; and the faces of our mentally ill and retarded who find in this budget the gift of hope. From the richest and most self-sufficient to the poorest and most helpless, each and every Kentuckian has a stake in this human document.

Its major focus is very properly upon education, the promise and future of the young. This is as it should be, as it must be. From vocational schools to the state-supported universities, from the Minimum Foundation Program to the Teachers' Retirement Fund, from educational television to schools for the blind and the deaf, this budget accepts the challenge confronting us. It acknowledges that we must move ahead to keep from falling still further behind. Its major thrust is that there is no economy in retreat. This budget contains the first increase for school operating expenses and capital outlay allowances in the last eight years. It honors our obligations to the Teachers' Retirement System and to appropriate salary increases. It signals the beginning of statewide educational television in the fall of this year. Twelve transmitting stations, spanning the Commonwealth, will enrich the training and instruction of our children. Four and one-half million dollars are required to operate this program during the next two years. This is one of many programs committed but for which no revenue had been provided to pay the cost.

This budget recognizes that the number of college students will continue to grow, and in acknowledgement of the premium we all place on quality higher education, it provides for the increasing costs of increasing enrollments. It recognizes the long-term economy of investing $170 million in the next two years to enable Kentucky's sons and daughters to attend our six major institutions. And it recognizes, too, the need to invest $6 million in the University of Louisville, to assist during the pending merger.

This budget honors Kentucky's commitment to community colleges and special training opportunities. It furnishes low-interest loans to deserving students. It includes funds for long-range planning to meet future community and four-year college needs. And it permits operation of all vocational schools which have been constructed. It strengthens the state library program and enables the department to supply "talking books" and braille literature for some twenty-five hundred blind persons. This budget includes increased funding for the School for the Blind, the School for the Deaf, and the Lincoln School for Exceptional Children. It increases the provision for special training for the handicapped child.

In the field of education, as throughout the entire budget, we have employed a sense of restrained urgency to enable this government to provide these services which are available from no other source. To accomplish these objectives $936 million are required in the next two years. This is approximately 66.5 percent of the total general fund budget.

To meet the needs of welfare and health, the budget continues the public assistance payment programs and meets our estimated obligations in the medical program. And I am certain that you will take pleasure, too, in noting that the increases proposed for our mental health and retardation programs go substantially beyond anything we have done before. Appropriations recommended are 23.2 percent greater than those for the last two years, but surely you will agree that conscience no longer permits us to turn away from the afflicted and the anguished in our institutions.

Funds are included to bring minimum salaries to $285 per month, and salaries for all personnel involved in patient care to a minimum of $300 a month. These modest increases for twenty-one hundred dedicated and devoted employees will show your appreciation for better care and attention to the afflicted. The budget includes funds during the biennium to repair and modernize hospital facilities. It requires $549 million for the biennium to meet our obligations and needs in this area of deep concern without considering construction, renovation and other improvements.

Recommended appropriations for education, health, and welfare amount to 83 percent of the budget. This attests to our deep and troubled concern for the people of Kentucky.

Provisions have been made for Kentucky's continued economic development, for agriculture, for better police protection and security, and for better recreation facilities. Funds are recommended for the industrial development authority. Sixteen new and enlarged airports are suggested, and the Department of Commerce is funded to assure long-range planning and close cooperation with the local communities for industrial expansion. In order that each Kentuckian shall share in the recreational facilities, state funds are recommended to match federal funds to assist local communities in providing better community park facilities of their own. The completion of two new state parks now under construction is included.

In the area of agriculture, the state's largest industry, added funds for soil conservation districts and the equipment loan fund are included in the recommended budget. Additional money must be provided in the Department of Agriculture in order that the Hopkinsville Livestock Laboratory may become fully operative. These investments in Kentucky's future development and growth will pay dividends from today's investments of $66 million for this biennium.

Few investments pay better community dividends than do good roads. Kentucky has made progress, but much remains to be done. Maintenance and debt costs for Kentucky's present roads threaten to cripple the entire road-building schedule within a few months. Rural roads will require twenty-five million dollars during the biennium. Debt on the interstate and toll road bonds will increase twenty-two million dollars during the next two years. Maintenance costs will increase by eleven million dollars. The road construction schedules call for spending $446 million during the next two years.

In recent years, bond funds have been available to match Federal grants for highway construction. However, remaining bonds are insufficient to complete the interstate and Appalachian road systems. The new budget will allocate $36 million in road fund revenue to match the Federal grants and will mark the first time in a decade that tax funds have been utilized for Federal matching to a significant degree. This budget proposes to halt the diversion of $3 million each year from the Road Fund to other agencies. The total road program requires appropriations of $758 million for the next two years. I believe you will hold this to be a wise investment.

Law and order and highway safety are placing new demands upon all law enforcement agencies. Neither dollars nor effort can be withheld if we are to remain protected and secure in our homes and upon our streets. The budget recognizes these demands and provides for an increase of the State Police force by thirty additional troopers in each of the next two years. It contemplates connecting the National Crime Information System to the Regional Troop Headquarters and establishment of a State Bureau of Investigation.

In the area of general government services, appropriations are recommended to allow for improvements in financial management and revenue administration. We recommend improvements in the recruiting services provided by the Department of Personnel to ensure that technically qualified young people are attracted to careers in the public service. A new salary schedule is recommended for our court system to ensure that the highest type individuals can afford to serve the cause of justice.

The recommended appropriation for the legislative branch will allow for needed and worthwhile reform and improvements, which we all desire. The amount contained in the budget bill is precisely the amount the legislative branch suggested for its proper and independent operation. I have placed items appropriating money for the General Assembly and its agencies in the executive budget to assure continued operation of these necessary functions. I have no objection to the Legislature developing its own realistic budget, and even today have shown this by signing House Bill 47.

For the first time in many years, the budget proposed to you makes a modest but realistic provision for the building and maintenance needs of state institutions. The major item recommended is nine million dollars for the construction of a new mental retardation institution. Few needs within this Commonwealth cry out so desperately or so convincingly as the facilities of the Frankfort State Hospital and School. A new education facility is recommended for the School for the Blind and a primary-grade classroom and dormitory building at the School for the Deaf. This is necessary to eliminate the need for the younger children with impaired hearing to cross a busy city street several times daily to get to and from their classes. New facilities for Child Welfare and a modern and complete vocational rehabilitation center are recommended. Six hundred thousand dollars is recommended to continue building highway-fill lakes so important to industrial and community development. Also recommended is an Animal Disease Diagnostic Laboratory to serve the Eastern and Blue Grass livestock producers.

All of the recommendations call for a drastic shift in the direction of more pay-as-we-go financing. While I cannot hope to halt the practice of public borrowing, I am determined with your support to reverse the tide and slow the rate at which the state incurs debt against future generations. The General Fund appropriations recommended for capital improvements total twenty-four million dollars, a minimum amount in terms of agency needs, but a modest amount in terms of recent outlays.

We are and must be committed to operate the government with due and careful regard for the tax dollar. We must establish a sound fiscal base for this government and operate it in a businesslike manner. A task force of businessmen, at no cost to the state, is busy reviewing governmental procedures. I intend to economize wherever possible without impairing needed public services.

I stated, as did others, that I could operate this government within existing revenue. But since then, it has since been revealed that the financial resources, the estimated revenues plus surplus would be twenty-four million dollars less than originally anticipated. More recent estimates reveal the shortage will total approximately twenty-eight million dollars.

As you are aware, there are other problems that bear heavily upon us: Inflation will result in approximately a 4 percent increase in the cost of goods and services purchased by the state. Enactment by the Federal government of increased social security payments will deprive us of taxable income. There are programs committed by other legislatures but not funded by them. Fixed obligations, as well as the increased cost of expanded programs, add to the burden.

It can be said in all honesty that we would need an additional forty million new dollars in order to maintain our present level of services. Without a tax increase, services and programs would have to be reduced or eliminated to that extent. No progressive, concerned, conscientious citizen would want our state to retreat. Surely no one would want less than we now have.

When we compare our state with other states, we embarrassingly find ourselves rated near the bottom in most measurements of human progress. If we want, and if we are to have, the services enjoyed by the citizens of other states, then we the people of the Commonwealth must pay as citizens of the other states pay.

A careful analysis of the state's present revenue structure reveals it can no longer produce the resources necessary to meet the requirements of public programs and services. It is necessary that I recommend certain changes in the tax laws for your consideration and action.

I have, with the best experts available, for many days and long hours, reviewed our tax structure and economic outlook. The facts are these. In only four states is the per capita state and local tax less than in Kentucky. Forty-eight of the fifty states have had one or more tax increases since the last increase in Kentucky. In only eight states is the total state and local tax as small a part of personal income as it is in Kentucky. In only four states is the state and local property tax a smaller percentage of personal income than in Kentucky. In only one state is the auto license fee less than in Kentucky.

Statistics reveal that the gasoline tax, the corporate tax, and the individual income tax in Kentucky are comparable to those in many states. And these taxes must remain constant if we are to compete with other states for greater industrial development and greater economic growth. We must first consider our present position and give immediate attention to the remainder of this fiscal year.

In my first and only appearance before you, I spoke solemnly of our financial crisis. The twenty-four million dollar cutback directed by Governor Breathitt, the cancellation of many personal service contracts, the several improvements suggested by the Efficiency Task Force, and other savings and cutbacks directed by me in the sixty days I have been here, are still not adequate to meet the revenue deficit. We must have several million dollars more than will be realized from present revenues for a balanced budget in this fiscal year as required by law.

For this reason, I am requesting that the revenue measure which I am submitting to you tonight, become effective on April 1st of this fiscal year. Unless this is done and an adequate amount of revenue is made available by that date, I shall have no alternative but to suspend, curtail or possibly eliminate for the balance of this fiscal year the medicaid program, old age benefits, public assistance, educational programs, and, perhaps, other public services. The unfortunate circumstances of many who will lose these services cause them to look to us and, as I have said before, I cannot look away. This is not a crisis created by me, or a crisis created by you, yet it is a most serious and critical condition which you and I must resolve.

In preparing a revenue plan, consideration was given to all forms of taxation. We considered many factors: its effect on the individual, its effect on the economic structure, our competitive position among other states, the balance of the entire revenue system, the convenience and expense of administration, and the extent to which non-residents of Kentucky would bear a part of the burden. And we asked ourselves which plan would provide the amount of revenue necessary to meet the needs of the citizen? Which would do the job most equitably?

After long hours of work, consultation with the best minds available, comparative and analytical research, and deliberate and prayerful consideration, I have concluded that a tax increase is absolutely necessary, and that an increase in the sales tax from three to five cents, would better meet the guidelines than any other plan which I might recommend.

In order to continue an essential and acceptable road program it was determined that funds could best be provided by recommending an increase from five dollars to twelve dollars and a half for motor vehicle licenses. I should also point out that because of possible federal tax enactment stability must be provided in regard to state income tax deductions.

I respectfully ask you to approach this most monumental task with courage and conviction to do that which must be done. These are my recommendations to you. I have now drained the bitter cup. The burden passes from me to you.

Technicians in the Finance Department and the Revenue Department, as well as department heads, are available to you for consultation and advice. They are available to your Committees as you may see fit to use them. I hope and I believe you will exercise the responsibility that is expected of you and all of us by the citizens of our beloved Commonwealth.

My fellow Kentuckians, would you have me do what is politically expedient or would you have me do what is best for the well-being of all our people? I have done what the time, circumstances, and conditions demand I do. To do otherwise, I would not be worthy of the office I hold.

Let us reaffirm to ourselves, let us recommit to those we serve, and let us proudly proclaim to all men everywhere, that we are willing to undertake any labor and to make any sacrifice in order that the future of our Commonwealth may be secure, and that our State and its people will have more productive and happier futures.

May God bless you and help you to do that which appears to you to be right.

STATE OF THE
COMMONWEALTH ADDRESS
Kentucky Press Association
Louisville / January 24, 1969

It was by design, rather than by accident, that we chose this group and this time to propose and launch a program which hopefully will become an established custom for Kentucky governors. We are proposing today that in those years when the General Assembly is not in session, future governors may have an opportunity to come before the Mid-Winter Meeting of the Kentucky Press Association to deliver the traditional State of the Commonwealth Address. Through this proposal, we hope to underscore our confidence in a free and informed press. We also want to demonstrate our appreciation for the significant contribution the Kentucky Press Association and each of its member newspapers has made to the progress and the well-being of the Commonwealth during the hundred years of service just concluded.

Kentucky celebrates another important anniversary this year in addition to marking the end of KPA's first century. Two hundred years ago, in 1769, Daniel Boone blazed a trail through the Cumberland Gap and the arduous task of settling Kentucky began. The first hundred years before the birth of the Kentucky Press Association were mainly consumed by the birth and establishment of our great Commonwealth. Growing pains have characterized Kentucky's efforts during the last hundred years, and we would point out that over the span of the past century, much of Kentucky's growth has resulted from the prodding of newspaper editors who have had the courage and the insight to light the path of the Commonwealth with their words. It is altogether fitting, then, that we would choose this as the site at which plans to inaugurate Kentucky's third century would be announced.

This, ladies and gentlemen of the Kentucky Press Association and my fellow Kentuckians, is the state of the Commonwealth as of January 24, 1969. After two hundred years, Kentucky has now grown into manhood. And today, as we step into the third century of our history, I believe firmly that our beloved Commonwealth is on the threshold of unmatched greatness. Everywhere we look there is promise of unprecedented accomplishment. There is a mature balance in our concern for social as well as economic progress; perhaps now, for the first time, our concern is being matched by our progress in both areas. There is a pervading spirit of confidence in Kentucky's future, a confidence hard-earned but now, hopefully, a confidence ingrained in a new generation of Kentuckians who have seen this state and its people overcome problems basic to growth and fulfillment. This is a challenging time for Kentucky and yet, it is a gratifying time to have the privilege and the responsibility of leadership. It is an era which will challenge all of us, you and I together, to meet the demands of Kentucky's destiny. The partnership between public and private agencies, the working alliance between those charged with public responsibility and those who represent the private sector, will be tested in the days ahead.

Today, then, let us resolve to go forward together, matching our resources, our talents, our energies, and our dedication to the task of building foundations for the future of Kentucky. I pledge the willingness of state government to share an equal part of the burden of the future, and I am proud to report today to the citizens of the Commonwealth that, in my opinion, state government has never been more able to meet the demands of the task that awaits us.

Thirteen months ago, I accepted the reins of state government with one commitment which overshadowed all others. I was and I am fully committed to the belief that the primary obligation of state government is to help construct foundations for the future. This has been the aim of this administration, and it is my most sincere hope that all the changes which have been made have contributed to the fulfillment of that goal. We accepted the mandate of the electorate to revitalize state government, to build on the progress that had been made by past administrations. And in order to keep faith with the people, we determined that it would be necessary to mobilize state government so that its full force could be brought to bear on the problems of the Commonwealth. This effort found shape in two forms. First, we undertook a painful, though necessary, evaluation of the financial foundation on which the State was resting. Next, we began a controversial and sometimes frustrated attempt to improve the service of state government by making changes we felt were necessary in personnel and organization.

One year ago, I told a joint meeting of the State Legislature that the financial state of the Commonwealth was distressing. There was an imminent deficit, then estimated at twenty-four million dollars and which would actually have reached thirty-six million dollars by the end of the last biennium in July of 1968. Principal and interest payments from previously approved bond issues were outpacing our capability to meet these obligations without seriously reducing other vital human services. Projects already committed were stranded helplessly between beginning and completion. Built-in growth of expense in fields such as education, health, and welfare could neither be denied nor ignored.

In the face of these problems, we began an austerity program which touched every department. Services, supplies, and salaries were investigated. Excesses were curbed, the fat was trimmed. In addition, an Efficiency Task Force made a comprehensive study and has since brought forth recommendations which already have saved the taxpayers of Kentucky millions of dollars. But even this was not enough. There was still the need for funds. Educational television was four million dollars away from becoming a reality. Medical services and retirement benefits for the aged demanded more of the state treasury. The alarming need of more care and better facilities for the mentally retarded appealed to the conscience of Kentucky. These and many other programs and services demanded that new revenue measures be passed.

They were, and here are the results: fiscal chaos was averted; sound financial foundations were created. Today, the fiscal soundness of the Commonwealth is unquestioned; our financial health was never better. Our budget of 481 million dollars includes projects of undeniable value and we are precisely on target with revenue collections.

The surplus in the General Fund at the close of fiscal 1967, compared with the surplus at the close of fiscal 1968, is indicative of our present financial position as contrasted with twelve months ago. In 1967, state government carried forward $10.8 million, $6.2 million short of the surplus called for in the executive budget. In the fiscal year closed last July 1, the combined impact of economy and new revenue raised the budgeted surplus of $4 million to $8 million, which the state carried forward in the General Fund.

Meanwhile, the economy of the state has not suffered as some had predicted. Business in the cities which border on neighboring states is as good or better than ever. The leakage which was predicted has not occurred, and figures in the Department of Revenue attest to this fact. There is other evidence of our improved financial condition, and this can be attested in each of the communities you represent. For the first time in the history of the Minimum Foundation Program for education, Kentucky is now able to meet school payments during the month they become due. In the past, many school boards were forced to borrow from local banks to meet current operating expenses, such as teachers' salaries, because of the delay of state payments.

It is because of the new fiscal soundness that the ferment of hope is evident in Kentucky. This secure financial position and a revitalized, responsive state government are underwriting new confidence in our people. More importantly, these two elements have brought forth programs which can become the foundations on which Kentucky will build greatness in the future. For instance, in the field of education, where the determination of a state to achieve new quality and excellence is best measured, Kentucky has taken steps unequalled in its history. Thirty-four million dollars was added to the Minimum Foundation Program. Capital outlay was increased $100 and current expense allotment was increased $200 per classroom unit, the first increases in each category since 1960. Kentucky today has 1,000 new teachers and the state's 32,000 teachers received an average salary increase of $462. The average salary for all instruction personnel is now at an all-time high, $6,750. School construction or renovation is now possible in every one of Kentucky's 195 school districts; 97.3 percent of Kentucky's teachers are fully qualified—another record achievement.

In vocational education, $3 million is being spent to construct a rehabilitation center in Eastern Kentucky. One hundred and eighty-six new vocational education units were allotted to school districts. Five new vocational extension centers were completed, five area schools were expanded, and two new area centers are now under construction. In higher education, a 34 percent increase in funds was made available to Kentucky colleges and universities as we attempt to keep pace with this mushrooming demand. For the first time, our colleges are competitive with other states in attracting and holding talented instructors. A new four-year Northern Kentucky State College will be constructed. Substantial increases in state support were made to the University of Louisville. Operation of four new community colleges began and planning is under way to construct two others.

In the area of mental health, Kentucky has at long last faced its problems with exciting answers. A new 450-bed facility for the mentally retarded will be constructed at Somerset to replace the 107-year old Frankfort State Hospital and Training School. A facility for the severely and profoundly retarded children which would be located near one of the state's medical schools is being planned. The number of trained personnel to care for the mentally ill is at the highest level in the state's history. To deal with the problem of juvenile delinquency, Jewel Manor, a facility for girls under fourteen, was opened. The state has leased Ridgewood here in Jefferson County, and after extensive remodeling this will become a treatment center for girls fifteen to eighteen years old. At Kentucky Village, a surprise inspection trip uncovered disturbing conditions at the state's largest juvenile correction center. Steps have been implemented and definite improvement is already evident.

Kentucky's network of highways and secondary roads is becoming an enviable example for other states. The County Road Aid Fund was increased by $10 million over the current biennium and the rural secondary roads program has been increased by $2 million for this fiscal year. In addition, the midsection of Kentucky which has long been retarded in its development because of inaccessibility, will now benefit from four new toll roads stretching from Bowling Green to Hazard. Our parks system, previously acknowledged as one of the nation's finest, is being enhanced by the construction of a new lodge at Lake Barkley and a new lodge and other facilities at Barren River and Greenbo Lake.

These are dramatic illustrations of Kentucky's quest for progress and our determination to create an environment of quality. In each of these vital areas we now have foundations on which growth can take place. But, so there can be no misunderstanding, let me hasten to add that government alone is not the architect of these foundations. As an instrument of the people, government has perhaps poured the foundation, but this structure and the towering achievements of the past will always stand as a monument to the willingness and the cooperation of all the people of Kentucky.

During 1969, and for the remainder of this administration, we will continue to add to these foundations as new projects bear fruit. We are involved in united efforts to expand the agricultural and industrial economy of the state. We expect to present a wide ranging program of airport development to the next Legislature. A comprehensive plan for state health planning is taking shape. Funds are now available for the establishment of a statewide plan of action against the threat of rising criminal activity. A new, effective arm of government has been added in the establishment of the Kentucky Program Development Office. Already this agency has coordinated the activities of some of your communities with state and federal agencies. Again, I say that the state of the Commonwealth is promising. We will realize that promise with the total effort of the private and the public sector.

I feel that it is my duty, however, to explore with you the two greatest threats which I see to the foundations that have been constructed. The first threat is that of a hostile Legislature when the General Assembly convenes next January. The second danger is that in this era of increased state and federal support local communities may become complacent and fail to supply the initiative and the creativity that is needed to keep our system of government strong. In both these areas we must look to the private sector for strength. Particularly those of you in the newspaper profession share a unique responsibility to the maintenance of progress.

Regarding the next Legislature, I urge you to exercise your full responsibility as editors and handmaidens of public opinion. Sort out those candidates who, regardless of party affiliation, would put narrow personal ambitions above the future of the Commonwealth. Send to Frankfort legislators who will come armed with reason and concern instead of those who will come with political swords drawn. Send to Kentucky's legislative halls men and women responsive to the challenge of our times, aware of the opportunities to be realized and dedicated to the task that is at hand. And upon your return to the communities you represent, I urge you to look carefully from the vantage point of your editorial columns—evaluate your communities, your people, your government, and your schools. Impartially weigh your community's plan for progress, hold it up for public inspection, criticism or praise. And when a viable course has been charted, urge its implementation. When there is complacency, take the advice of one of your colleagues, who said that the mission of a modern newspaper is to comfort the afflicted and afflict the comfortable.

Together, we can maintain the foundations which have been erected during the past two hundred years. This is not the work of one man or one party of the public or the private sector. It is, however, a task to which your talents and your responsibilities as newspapermen are well adapted. I would conclude by paraphrasing Oscar Wilde: In America a president reigns for one or two terms; in Kentucky, governors serve for four years; but in Kentucky and throughout America, journalism governs for ever and ever.[1]

---

1. Governor Nunn paraphrased the following quotation from Oscar Wilde, "In America the President reigns for four years, and journalism governs for ever and ever." Burton Stevenson, ed., *The Home Book of Quotations, Classical and Modern*, 10th ed. rev. (New York, 1967), p. 1602.

STATE OF THE
COMMONWEALTH ADDRESS
Frankfort / January 6, 1970

OUR constitution provides that the Governor shall "give to the General Assembly information of the State of the Commonwealth and recommend their consideration of such measures as he may deem expedient." While complying with this constitutional provision, former Governors have used such glowing phrases as: "the future is bright," "the economy vigorous," and "the state sound." Thanks to the necessary and courageous action of a bipartisan majority of the 1968 legislators, all of these statements can be truthfully repeated tonight. But tonight there is one new, significant, and important difference. For the first time in the history of our Commonwealth, the Governor can stand before you and say that a tax reduction for all the people of Kentucky can be given without shifting the tax burden to other shoulders and without reducing the existing level of services to the people. Of this I am proud. Not because I am the first, but because the state of our Commonwealth is so secure, its financial strength so completely rejuvenated, and its most crucial programs on such a progressive course, that you have an option to give the people needed tax relief, to provide new programs, or to expand existing programs that are desirable and worthwhile.

My purpose tonight is not only to inform you as to the state of the Commonwealth, but to share with you information and ideas on tax relief gleaned from many hours of serious deliberation with noted advisors, revenue experts, budget analysts, and members of both the executive and legislative branches of our government. If it is your desire to give to the taxpayers some relief, you can and you should do so; first, without destroying the fiscal soundness of the state; secondly, without reducing services to the people; and finally, by approving a balanced budget.

To act responsibly you must consider many complex and intricate factors before enacting a plan of tax relief. Some of the significant questions to be considered in the development of a tax reduction plan are: will it provide relief for those whose needs are most critical? will needed services for the people be continued? will the budgetary process be affected? will it increase administrative costs? will compliance work an undue burden upon the citizens? will it harmfully affect the total economy? will it be discriminatory in its application? will it adversely affect our industrial expansion and economic growth?

To answer these questions we studied, analyzed, deliberated, and agonized as to what could or should be done; how it could best be accomplished; and its ultimate effect upon the people we serve. The plan we finally accepted as best will provide the greatest tax relief for the needy, the sick, the blind, the elderly, and the low and fixed income groups. It is the plan that best meets the human and professional criteria. It guarantees that Kentucky will not retreat from its finest hour and its greatest opportunity.

Governor Bert Combs, the father of our modern-day sales tax, addressed this distinguished body in 1962 and said: "Thanks to the sales tax Kentucky has for the first time in this century enough money to make a brave advance in progressive government. . . . without the sales tax we would fall back into the old and desperate pattern of failure and neglect. Even with the tax we have not a dollar to spare as we try to forge a pattern of government sufficient to meet the minimum requirements of our people. Those who would alter our tax structure should, for the sake of Kentucky's welfare, propose an alternate source of equal revenue."[1]

Some members of this General Assembly of 1970 were at that time among the chief architects and administrators of his programs, including the sales tax. Some of you were main supporters of his deeds and applauders of these very words. If you should change your position now, because the people have changed Governors and political parties, then it will be apparent that this Legislature owes its first allegiance to politics rather than to progress for the people. The people of Kentucky are looking. I invite their attention.

In that same address Governor Combs also had something to say on the subject of politics which might be helpful now: "Of course, I am not blind and you are not blind to the facts of political life. You and I know that there are those who want to make this General Assembly a testing ground for missiles designed to be launched in the gubernatorial campaign of 1963. But you and I were not elected to be manipulated and controlled for the personal advantage of ambitious candidates. We were elected to do something constructive for the people of Kentucky and those who will follow us."[2]

But I am aware that almost a third of this General Assembly is made up of members who were not here during the last session. It is particularly for their benefit that I review the grave situation confronting us at that time and enumerate some of the major accomplishments that have been made primarily to illustrate what can be accomplished when the membership of this body dedicates itself to serious, unselfish, courageous, non-partisan action.

On December 12, 1967, we found that commitments had been made and citizens expected the construction and operation of new health, education, correction, and mental care facilities costing millions of dollars. But what neither we nor they knew was that full funding for these projects had not been provided. New revenue anticipated from economic growth would not begin to adequately meet these commitments or to ease the financial chaos that paralyzed almost every vital service. Those commitments are now being kept and the people's expectations fulfilled.

On December 12, 1967, reductions in state services ranging from the education of our youth to the care of the elderly seemed unavoidable. Aid to the needy would have been terminated. We averted that catastrophe.

On December 12, 1967, Kentucky's mental health facilities were in desperate need of repairs and renovation—yes, even food. Some were about to be closed. They were unsafe, inhumane, and deteriorated to the point that they could no longer qualify as hospitals. They were mere warehouses of human suffering. Now, however, fifty renovation and repair projects, costing in excess of $4 million, and increased salaries for psychiatric aides have brought us from that dismally low ebb. We have now reached the highest plateau in Kentucky's history for services and care to the mentally ill. Today, for the first time in our history, every mental hospital in Kentucky is fully accredited.

On December 12, 1967, virtually in the shadow of our Capitol dome, the Frankfort State Hospital and School sat forgotten, run down, antiquated beyond hope, ill equipped, understaffed, and overcrowded—a mockery of all the optimistic oratory of those who in other years had proclaimed a new and better day for Kentucky. Today, we are moving out of the dark ages of mental health and mental retardation, out of the oldest institution of its kind still in use in the United States. Today, we are achieving national leadership not only in the design of our treatment services, but also in the construction of the most modern and comprehensive retardation facility in the country.

In the field of child welfare, two years ago there was not enough money, despite the generous support of the private sector, to open a desperately needed juvenile care center for young delinquent girls. Today this facility, Jewel Manor near Louisville, is in operation and making a constructive impact on the lives of its inhabitants.

Two years ago, young delinquents shivered through the winters in drafty, dirty, dilapidated buildings at Kentucky Village near Lexington, an installation once condemned but now praised by Federal grand juries. The students there were undisciplined, because of inadequate concern and unqualified supervisory personnel; ill clothed and dirty, because others had reneged on their budgetary promises. The youngsters at Kentucky Village were moving further down the road toward a life of crime rather than upward on the intended path toward rehabilitation and useful citizenship.

Today drastic, progressive, creative action has left its mark. Physical, mental, and moral differences are immediately noticeable. The buildings have been repaired, the children are clean, a new comprehensive education program has been initiated, and regular religious training is required. Discipline is being taught and being learned.

A new home for mentally retarded delinquents has been established at Frenchburg and a renovated facility for older delinquent girls will soon be in operation in Louisville. Tonight more than 400 additional children are experiencing a happy and more complete life in foster homes.

Here in yet another vital human service Kentucky has moved from obscurity and shame to a place of national prominence and leadership. This is not my evaluation alone or that of the able staff that has directed this Department to its newfound place of prominence. The National Council on Crime and Delinquency has identified Kentucky as among the nation's top three states in juvenile care and delinquency prevention and we are on the verge of being recognized as number one.

In education Kentucky's generous investment pays visible dividends by affording to all an opportunity for productive participation in our society. Let us turn now to the state of the Commonwealth. Tonight we are able to proclaim *and to prove* that Kentucky is rushing rapidly toward a true destiny of greatness. What a contrast this is to the bleak picture of Kentucky's depressing financial plight that confronted all of us only two short years ago.

On December 12, 1967, state funds were nearly exhausted. Our State was well on its way into bankruptcy. We faced a deficit of $36 million. The state was delinquent by $27.5 million in funds for education. We faced a $3.5 million cutback in medical assistance for the aged and needy. Three hundred thousand dollars were needed immediately just to keep open our mental hospitals. Interstate and Appalachian highways could not be completed. Projects already under way stacked approximately $100 million on top of the existing deficit. Kentucky had been overspent, overcommitted, and undersold. When it came time to pay the bills there was no money in the state purse.

The fact that this challenge has been resolved, financial soundness restored, and a $25 million construction program authorized from current revenues is in itself a tribute to the courage and the dedication of the 1968 Legislature and to the people of Kentucky.

I do not recite the unpleasantries of the past in an effort to fix blame or to criticize. A record $90 million increase in appropriations rescued the hopes of 640,000 students in our local elementary and secondary schools. It provided the first increase in funds for current expenses and capital outlay in eight years and stemmed the outward migration of our teachers by pushing their salaries to record levels. Because of appropriations included in the budget two years ago for classroom construction, $250 million is available today to construct modern, safe, serviceable school buildings, or additions thereto, in every one of our 193 school districts. Funds for our state colleges and universities were increased by 34 percent to a record $177 million so that we might accommodate the record enrollment of 62,600 students. The number of Kentucky's community colleges has been increased by 50 percent. The new Northern Kentucky State College, which you approved and which we have temporarily funded, is well on its way to becoming a reality for a long-ignored region of our Commonwealth. This is the first four-year college established in Kentucky in forty-seven years.

Kentucky was one of the few states to hold the line against rising tuition fees for resident students and actually lowered tuition costs at the University of Louisville. Consequently, both the students and their parents benefited. This plan is a more equitable and helpful method than tax credits for parents of college students. Kentucky became the first state in the nation to welcome a student leader to membership on the boards of regents and trustees at state-supported colleges and universities. The college intern program which we initiated for students, coupled with other demonstrations of our concern for the youth of this state, has fostered a bond of mutual understanding and respect which no doubt has helped to spare our campuses the interruption and destruction witnessed outside of our state. Through several brainstorming seminars attended by members of this Administration, outstanding college educators, and talented student leaders, we are striving to build from this bond of mutuality a productive relationship and a constructive dialogue between state government and the gifted human resources on our campuses.

By doubling our investment and our emphasis on vocational education, four new extension centers have expanded curriculum, nine local centers are now open, four more are scheduled for operation before July, and the construction of five others is now under consideration, bringing vocational education opportunities to within twenty-five miles of every Kentuckian. More than 115,000 Kentuckians benefited during the past two years from our nationally heralded system of vocational training.

Kentucky's educational television network, the largest, most flexible, and most functional in America, is serving young and old alike as it reaches into 170 of our 193 school districts and into countless thousands of Kentucky homes.

With twenty-four construction projects under way, Kentucky is building more public libraries than any other state in the nation. Supplementing this expansion is a fleet of 105 bookmobiles, the largest state-owned traveling library in the United States.

What has been described by educators as the two most progressive and memorable years of educational accomplishment in Kentucky's history will be climaxed this spring with the completion of a $1.3 million training facility at the School for the Deaf and a $900 thousand all-purpose center at the School for the Blind. These two new facilities shall stand for years to come as reminders of our concern and as challenges to broaden the horizon of education for all who are in need of special care and training.

Turning now to other areas of accomplishment and progress: Agriculture, the backbone of Kentucky's economy, is basking in the light of unparalleled attention. The constitutional amendment affecting taxes on farm land was approved by the people at the last election and now awaits your implementation.[3] Discriminatory farm machinery taxes have been eliminated.[4] A meat inspection law to aid small packers and to assure the health of our citizens was enacted during our last session.[5]

The full force and assistance of technology and research from our colleges, universities, county agents, and new diagnostic facilities have been directed to the aid of Kentucky's farmers. The Animal Diagnostic Laboratory for western Kentucky has been made operative. Construction on the Diagnostic Laboratory for eastern Kentucky and establishment of the livestock research center at Lexington will begin shortly.

At a time when Kentucky farms and our major cash crop are both under severe attack, it is my privilege tonight to report, based on estimates now available, that in 1969 for the first time in our history Kentucky's realized gross income from farming has exceeded $1 billion.

Our mining industry continues to surge forward. With the 102 million tons of coal produced in 1968, we passed Pennsylvania to become second in production among the states. With the recent opening of several large new mines, Kentucky will soon be first in the nation.

Production is only one aspect, however. Concern is growing for our environment and for the health and safety of our people. Conservation of both our natural and our human resources has become a necessary and commendable part of the mining operation. I especially commend those who suggested and enacted Kentucky's progressive laws pertaining to surface mining. We have kept faith with the spirit as well as the letter of those laws. Enforcement has been firm but fair. The health and safety of the miners has not gone unnoticed. Kentucky last year became the first state in the nation to use modern scientific equipment to reduce the dangers of black lung. For the first time a concerted effort was made to provide better coverage and benefits for miners under the Workmen's Compensation Act. And for the year 1969 we are thankful for the fewest number of deaths ever recorded in the history of the industry in this Commonwealth.

Nearly all of eastern Kentucky and much of western Kentucky is dependent on the mining industry. Not for the sake of the industry, but for the sake of the people employed and its contribution to the economy, serious consideration should be given to any legislation that would be discriminatory or place this important industry at an economic disadvantage.

Recent months have also witnessed the continuation of our march toward industrialization. With confidence in our broad-based, nondiscriminatory tax structure, and with confidence in the skills and dedication of our people, industry has invested more than $513 million to build and expand manufacturing facilities in the Commonwealth during the past two years; 152 new industries and 214 expanded plants have provided more than 23,000 new jobs for Kentuckians. In view of rising interest rates, national inflation, and the recent ceiling placed upon industrial bonds, these are truly outstanding achievements.

There has been at long last a breakthrough in locating industry in eastern Kentucky. Thirty distinguished companies have demonstrated confidence in the people of the mountains. These new plants, representing a capital investment of more than $27 million will provide more than 2,500 new jobs. We are reasonably certain that nine additional companies plan even larger investments in this area that will create about 4,500 more jobs. We are confident that the success of these pioneers will attract still more companies in the near future.

We have undertaken important, ambitious steps to prepare for the future. In keeping with our goal of total resource development, a plan for scientific development has been formulated to extend through the seventies. This plan focuses on the petrochemical industries and the nuclear industries. New uses for coal in the production of chemicals is one of many forward-looking enterprises we expect to stimulate during the next decade.

Industry is going to the air. The fact that Kentucky is within two hours by air of 70 percent of America's population is a considerable advantage in competing for new industry. That is why we are dedicated to achieving unparalleled growth in the number of airports in Kentucky. Due in part to record appropriations, twelve new, expanded, or improved airport facilities became operative during the current biennium. Six new airport projects are under construction and eight more are planned. Significantly, we have consolidated the state's own force of airplanes at a savings during this administration alone of approximately $350 thousand.

To the political critics of this administration's operation of the Department of Highways, our reply is immediate, straightforward, and factual: Last year Kentucky led all other states with nearly 3,000 miles of new highways let for contract. Kentucky led the entire nation with the completion of 288 miles of modern, four-lane limited access highways last year. Kentucky now leads the thirteen Appalachian states in highway miles completed or under construction under the Appalachian Program. The Toll Road Authority has approved and we have begun construction on a broad corridor of opportunity that will enhance the future of more than a third of the counties in Kentucky along a 254-mile route from Henderson to Hazard. Kentucky was the first state to complete its section of Interstate 65. Increased revenue from updated auto license fees allowed us to maintain approximately 3,000 more miles of county roads. The rural secondary road system was significantly expanded and modernized. Today, more Kentuckians than ever before are traveling to church, to school, and to work on safe, convenient, blacktop roads, roads made possible during the 1968 legislative session.

Collapse of the Silver Bridge in West Virginia within days of my inauguration pointed up the price that other states were forced to pay for neglect. Determined that the same tragedy should not occur in Kentucky, we established a statewide bridge inspection program that uncovered 171 perilous spans in need of emergency repair to make them safe for their posted capacities. It has taken time and money to overcome this neglect. Under an accelerated program, fifty-seven bridges have been repaired, forty-two replaced, forty-nine are in some state of planning, and twenty-three are in need of further action.

Highway construction is among the best of many examples of progressive, prudent, professional stewardship during the past two years. We stand proudly on this undeniable record of achievement as sound builders of Kentucky.

For many years, Kentuckians have been justly proud of their world-famous resort parks and recreational facilities. To remain number one in this field, and to meet the demands created by the record 9.4 million persons who now visit our state parks each year, require far more than a caretaker government. It requires constant improvement and steady progress. These goals are being met by this administration. New resort parks are being developed at Dale Hollow, at Lake Barkley, at Barren River, and at Greenbo Lake. In addition, new parks are being planned at Grayson Reservoir in eastern Kentucky and at Green River Reservoir in central Kentucky. Overnight lodging facilities in the state park system will have been increased by a full 50 percent by the end of this administration.

In view of the fact that tourists spent $510 million in Kentucky in 1969, and provided the state with $38 million in tax revenue, we regard expenditures toward the improvement and expansion of our parks system as prudent and fully justified investments.

Few states have been blessed with as many natural riches as Kentucky, and it is reasonable to assume that few states stand to lose as much as ours if we condone the blight of environmental pollution. Proceeding from this fundamental principle, we are confronted with the demanding, arduous task of writing guidelines to govern the use of Kentucky's clean air, pure streams, wild rivers, and fertile fields. There is no room for quarrel between conservationists and industry or agriculture. We must move with caution. All should have as their over-riding purpose the wisest use and preservation of our natural resources. That is why in constructing anti-pollution and conservation guidelines we must cultivate a common ground on which these forces, industrialists, and conservationists can meet and work together.

Meanwhile, efforts continue to preserve the matchless beauty of our Commonwealth. Since we last met, the breathtaking grandeur of the Red River Gorge has been preserved. And Lilley's Woods in Letcher County is now our gift to present and future generations, in hopes that the quiet majesty of this untainted virgin forest may someday inspire its visitors to a better understanding and appreciation of our land and those who developed it.

Less than two years ago we created the Kentucky Program Development Office. It was designed to be one of the planning arms of state government and was particularly intended as a coordinating agency for projects involving local, state, and federal participation. Here is the remarkable record already established by this infant agency, for which I now ask your confirmation: It brought $93 million in federal grant monies to Kentucky in its first year and that total likely will be surpassed in the current year. The Kentucky Program Development Office also pioneered the concept of multi-county Area Development

Districts designed to facilitate the coordination of comprehensive planning for future growth through local initiative, state technical assistance, and federal funding. Through the work of this agency Kentucky has become the first state in the nation to establish comprehensive health planning councils in every region. Recreation, vocational education and rehabilitation, sewage treatment, public housing, and other projects have been pushed forward in every part of Kentucky by this agency.

We are determined also that good personnel management shall be one of the outstanding hallmarks of this administration. Therefore, I am pleased to report that strict personnel policies, including a freeze on hiring, have enabled us to provide more services at a higher level of efficiency with fewer state workers than were on the payroll at the time of my election in 1967.

The state's unrealistic and wasteful proliferation of holidays has been reduced from 16 paid holidays to 9½. I ask that you confirm this action. Kentucky taxpayers have been burdened too long already by this unnecessary luxury, amounting to $4.5 million in lost work hours.

For the first time in the history of this government, minimum and maximum employment levels have been established in every state agency to assure the greatest economy of operation and the most efficient level of service to the people. Modern personnel management techniques used successfully in business are now being instituted throughout our government. In the delivery of human services to those who seek state aid we have formed the Human Resources Coordinating Commission in an effort to avoid costly duplication and overlapping of social services.

Taxpayers throughout Kentucky owe a debt of gratitude to the volunteer citizen leaders from business, industry, and education who inspected, audited, and analyzed state government as part of the Efficiency Task Force. Their recommendations already have resulted in millions of dollars of savings that can be carried over and multiplied by future administrations.

To meet the complexities that confront government today we constantly require the assistance of computer technology. A plan is being devised to consolidate the state's computer program. Once enacted it has been estimated that the new system can be operated at a savings of approximately $4.5 million over the next four years.

This state's technical resources and research capability have been measurably strengthened by the fact that Spindletop Research has cast aside its chains of indebtedness and ineptitude of two years ago and is now accomplishing its intended and much needed purpose. Private enterprise, showing confidence in this administration, demonstrated its endorsement of this worthwhile project and its concern for the future of our State by investing in excess of $500 thousand in grants to help Spindletop avoid impending bankruptcy. Spindletop has and will continue to make an immeasurable contribution to our quest for new and expanding industry, to social and economic progress, and to the effectiveness of governmental institutions in our State.

At the penal institutions adult offenders entrusted to our care have not been forgotten in our endeavor to make every Kentuckian count. At Eddyville a new farm dormitory for 100 inmates has been opened to relieve overcrowded conditions. A medical clinic with complete surgical facilities is under construction and a psychiatric unit for mentally disturbed inmates is being provided. At LaGrange a modern $628 thousand vocational training and rehabilitation center has been constructed. A key punch operation at both institutions provides service to several governmental agencies, resulting in savings already amounting to more than $100 thousand to Kentucky taxpayers while providing learning opportunities for useful, productive skills. Farm production on institution property is up by 20 percent, resulting in net profits to the State in excess of $26 thousand over the previous fiscal year. At no cost to the state we obtained the Job Corps Center at Frenchburg to be used for the rehabilitation of first offenders, another progressive, pace-setting, advancement in the field of corrections.

The social well-being and the economic progress of our State are directly related to the health of our people. Not only must we strive to eliminate the existing health problems, but we must constantly plan to prevent future dangers. Ours was the first state to initiate a rubella control program and a cervical cancer testing program. Many new and additional health facilities have been added throughout the State during the last two years. Twenty-nine new hospitals providing 1,750 beds have been expanded or constructed, along with 30 nursing homes, 12 public health centers, and 9 community mental health centers with 170 new psychiatric beds.

Through salary increases we have recognized the contribution of public health nurses as the front line of defense against physical affliction. Expenditures for medical assistance have almost doubled since 1967. The employees in this department must of necessity be highly skilled and technically trained individuals. Competing for their skills is one of our major problems in endeavoring to secure for our people the best in medical attention.

Even in the shadow of towering accomplishment and rapid progress much remains to be done. No State of the Commonwealth message is complete, indeed no Governor has performed his whole duty, without also pointing out current issues and problems that confront our people. Great problems of moral, constitutional, economic, and social importance cry out for your attention and your action in the days ahead. I call these matters to your attention because, under our Constitution, you, and only you, can bring about their resolution and give to the people a course of action.

Knowing your concern, being aware of the views many of you have stated publicly, appreciative of your expressed desire for independence, and recognizing your constitutional authority to act, I await your decisions on these matters. Once you have resolved these differences, then I shall fulfill my constitutional duties to the best of my ability.

Chief among these is the "rollback" law that fixes property tax revenue at 1966 levels.[6]

Conflicting positions have been expressed regarding the present interest rates. Inasmuch as this subject affects so many Kentucky families in so many ways, it should have your immediate attention.

Another issue to be acted upon, one that has generated extreme passion in other coal-producing states, is coal workers' pneumoconiosis, or "black lung."

Professional negotiation for teachers is an area of potential conflict that begs legislative deliberation.

Other contemporary problems demanding your attention include: environmental pollution, conflict of interest laws and financial disclosure requirements for public officials and candidates, and consolidation of school and governmental units into multi-county realignment.

Several other issues have thus far escaped satisfactory resolution. As you will recall, the 1968 General Assembly was so closely divided on the question of Daylight Savings Time that it was finally decided by the vote of one man. Now there is a clamor for revision.[7] Sunday closing laws have inspired strong moral and legal questions and have aroused the conscience of many of our people. The people now turn to you for direction.

Many other complex problems are of a financial nature and I shall deal with them in my budget address. Also, from time to time during this session, other matters of great importance and urgency probably will be brought to my attention. In that event, I feel an obligation to communicate them to you and I shall honor that obligation.

Ladies and gentlemen, on these notes of high accomplishment and lingering challenge, we say farewell tonight to Kentucky's second century. Two hundred years ago in 1769 the first settlers came to explore the mountains and the meadows of our great State.

Uniquely, the burden of history and the responsibility for setting a new course for the future were placed on this administration. Our first two years bring down the curtain on two centuries marked by dramatic human effort and great sacrifices, a time in which Kentucky came out of the wilderness to attain statehood and national brotherhood, all the while developing and sending forth men and women of great character and courage, foresight and determination to lead and serve our state and our nation.

Our next two years, the biennium on which we must soon embark, open Kentucky's third century, a new era in which I pray the sacrifices and the contributions of past generations can be joined with the efforts of now and future generations to produce a better life for all our people.

Mindful of the historic implications attendant to this term of office, it has been our principal duty and our supreme goal to write an honorable ending to Kentucky's first 200 years, and at the same time to construct solid, useful foundations for the future.

This I firmly believe we have done. We stand tonight willingly awaiting the judgment of history and our fellow man, confident in the knowledge that our beloved Kentucky is now prepared to enter the new era that awaits us. Inspired by the adventure of progressive programs to ease human suffering, eradicate ignorance, fight poverty, and prevent crime; assisted by our restored financial strength; helped along the way by an increasingly effective government; and urged on by public confidence Kentucky now seeks and no longer shuns the uncertainties, the challenges, and the opportunities of the future.

And now, I conclude with a special request. So that we may proceed as rapidly as possible in serving the future needs of those to whom we have pledged our service, I respectfully ask permission to come before you tomorrow afternoon at one o'clock to present for your approval the executive budget.

At that time I shall lay before you a comprehensive blueprint for the future, a foundation from which together we can launch Kentucky toward new greatness in a new decade and a new century.

---

1. Bert Thomas Combs (1911–   ), governor (1959–1963); candidate for governor (1955, 1959, 1971); judge, United States Court of Appeals, Sixth Circuit (1967–1970); an attorney in Prestonsburg. *Who's Who in American Politics, 1969–1970,* 2d ed. (New York, 1969), p. 232; Department of Public Information biographical files. For the material quoted here, see Kentucky, General Assembly, House of Representatives, *Journal of the House of Representatives of the Commonwealth of Kentucky, 1962,* p. 20.

2. Ibid., p. 23.

3. See Section 172 A of the Constitution of Kentucky; for implementing legislation see an act "relating to revenue and taxation," which provided that land used for agricultural and horticultural purposes be assessed for taxation at a value based on its use rather than on its cash value. The act was signed by Governor Nunn on March 30, 1970. Kentucky, General Assembly, *Acts of the General Assembly of the Commonwealth of Kentucky, 1970*, Chapter 249 (H.B. 442), pp. 868–74.

4. An act "relating to sales tax" exempted farm machinery from the state sales tax. The act was signed by Governor Nunn on March 15, 1968. *Acts of the General Assembly, 1968*, Chapter 36 (S.B. 84), pp. 50–51.

5. An act "relating to meat inspection" provided for inspection by the Kentucky Department of Agriculture of all animals before slaughter; it required postmortem examinations; it required wholesome meat to be labeled and all other meat destroyed. The act was signed by Governor Nunn on March 27, 1968. Ibid., Chapter 205 (H.B. 499), pp. 832–56; and files of Kentucky Legislative Research Commission.

6. See an act "relating to revenue and taxation," which was signed by Governor Edward T. Breathitt on September 16, 1965. *Acts of the General Assembly, Extraordinary Session, 1965*, Chapter 2 (H.B. 1), pp. 3–27.

7. House Bill 39 "relating to standard time in Kentucky," which would have exempted Kentucky from the Federal Uniform Time Act of 1966, was defeated by the Kentucky Senate on March 6, 1968. Kentucky, General Assembly, Senate, *Journal of the Senate of the Commonwealth of Kentucky, 1968*, pp. 795, 1306.

BUDGET MESSAGE
Frankfort / January 7, 1970

LAST evening it was my privilege to present to you an assessment of our past accomplishments and a review of our efforts to construct solid, useful foundations for the future of the people of the Commonwealth. It was my purpose then to apprise you of Kentucky's present position. It is my purpose today to speak of the future, to lay before you programs and policies on which we and others may extend the progress that we have engendered.

Among the most important duties that you and I must share in directing the affairs of the state are the submission and the adoption of a budget. With its presentation to you today, I hereby fulfill my budgetary obligation.

At our pre-legislative conference, I pledged you full cooperation of the executive branch during this session. My reasons for presenting this budget to you at the outset are to demonstrate my desire to cooperate and to extend to you, for the first time in this state's legislative history, the opportunity not only to approve, but to share in the reduction of taxes or the distribution of the funds that are available during the next biennium. I have also chosen to bring the budget to you early so you may have ample time to study, conduct hearings, and act on its passage within the time allotted. Many state funds to be appropriated are matched against federal funds, and the failure to enact a budget could result in a great loss of available revenue and a corresponding loss of services to the people.

The document submitted today represents more than an exercise in arithmetic, much more than paper, ink, and numbers. It underscores the hopes and aspirations of more than three million Kentuckians. It is a sound financial plan for the future, one that continues progress with justice, a carefully conceived extension of that human document so overwhelmingly approved by the General Assembly two years ago.

It does not propose expenditures in excess of the funds available. It leaves no deficit such as we faced two years ago. I would not, under any circumstances, place the people of Kentucky in that perilous financial position for either the appeasement of any political group or the political ambition of any person.

If a simple description can be made of such a complex document, let us say that this is a budget for the people. It recognizes that the people need and deserve a rest from the endless growth of government. This budget reflects our assumption that you will grant tax relief to the people. I will submit to the Appropriations and Revenue Committee a plan of tax reduction that will allow such relief and guarantee a balanced budget.

This plan meets the human and professional criteria outlined to you in the State of the Commonwealth address. It will include: elimination not only of the 2 percent sales tax on prescription medicine endorsed by the General Assembly two years ago, but also elimination of the 3 percent sales tax imposed by the 1960 legislature; elimination of the 5 percent use tax on the transfer of automobiles within a family; an increase in the minimum standard personal deduction and a higher minimum filing requirement for personal income; and extensive relief for the blind and the elderly.

This budget provides for an uncommitted reserve of $18 million to finance the adoption of this tax plan or for other legislative disposition. At this point I would caution you that the fragile balance of the budget will be destroyed by a larger revenue reduction than I have outlined. If it is the will of this legislature to go beyond the provisions of this tax reduction plan, then it is incumbent on you to replace the lost revenue with alternate sources or to justify to the people the destruction or cutback of vital programs that will result from your action.

This budget will receive more careful scrutiny than any budget in the history of the Commonwealth. I neither question nor resent this careful review. On the contrary, I welcome it. The decisions you make here in the next few weeks will have an everlasting effect on the lives of our fellow citizens. Therefore, I feel compelled to commend to your attention some elements within this document that are especially deserving of your careful consideration.

It is impossible to overemphasize the importance and the influence of modern, safe highways. The emerging pattern of industrial development and tourist attractions along our present system stand as undeniable evidence of the progress good roads bring to our people. We plan to continue the construction programs now under way and to increase our efforts to extend these corridors of opportunity to all citizens of the Commonwealth. Our highway program calls for construction expenditures of more than $636 million. It permits the accelerated continuation of the Interstate and Appalachian systems as well as completion of the Henderson to Hazard Parkway. County roads have not been forgotten. Aid to counties for the construction and maintenance of rural roads will be increased to $89.9 million.

In 1968, the General Assembly approved our recommendation that more than $40 million be allocated to match federal funds available for the construction of highways, the first time in more than a decade that borrowed money was not used. Today I am recommending $43 million for this purpose in order that we may utilize available federal funds to Kentucky's fullest advantage.

The rate of crime continues to increase in cities and counties throughout the state. The death toll on our highways continues to mount. To prevent these situations from growing worse, more and better trained police officers are needed. Two years ago available funds enabled us to add only sixty troopers and twelve criminal investigators to the ranks of the Kentucky State Police. This budget contains provisions to add sixty-five troopers.

Funds now available dictated that we allocate far less than was requested by the Department of Public Safety. However, I remain firmly convinced that the safety of our people and their property must be one of the primary concerns of this government. Therefore, I have included and call to your attention a special recommendation that a significant portion of a possible new source of funds be made available for state and local law enforcement.

A bi-partisan Crime Commission, consisting of technical and lay individuals who have devoted much time and study to this problem, will present a crime package costing approximately $9 million. This is not included in the budget because, obviously, funds are not presently available.

However, prior to your convening in 1972, the United States Congress possibly may approve the much-discussed revenue sharing plan. Although no firm, precise estimate of Kentucky's share can be made at this time, and in view of the fact that at least 38 percent is required to be passed onto our cities, I am requesting that if any funds are received, 50 percent of the amount be appropriated to the Department of Public Safety for the following projects: an extensive traffic safety program; additional state troopers; funding of an intensive effort to stop the illegal sale and use of drugs; establishment of a State Bureau of Criminal Investigation; and such other projects as may appear necessary to secure the safety of the people and their property, and to carry out as much of the Crime Commission's program as possible.

I propose that the remaining 50 percent of our federal tax sharing funds, if any, be used in the battle against air and water pollution and in other areas of public health.

To be fully effective, our law enforcement officers must be reinforced by a competent, dedicated, and courageous judiciary. Often overcrowded court dockets cause unnecessary delay in the administration of justice. To ease this situation, we have provided funds to establish three new circuit judgeships.

By far the largest portion of our available resources will again be invested in education; 67.9 percent of the General Fund has been allocated for this purpose, compared with 67.3 percent two years ago. This guarantees that the record high standards achieved for the Minimum Foundation Program in the 1968 biennium will be preserved. For instance, the increases of almost 60 percent for operations and $600 for each classroom unit for capital outlay approved two years ago are continued by this budget.

Keeping abreast of the increases in students in our local grade and high schools requires a substantial increase in funds each year. Therefore, we recommend that $57 million, representing 42 percent of the added revenue from economic growth, be appropriated to the Minimum Foundation Program and the Teachers' Retirement System.

These funds are marked primarily for use in meeting the rapid growth of pupil enrollment, continuation of the free textbooks program, and supplemental support for the teachers' retirement fund.

The growth in number of school age children beyond our estimates and the partial or complete closing of some parochial schools have created the need for a supplemental appropriation of $2 million in the current fiscal year. Fortunately, economy and efficiency in state government have enabled us to realize a surplus from which these necessary funds can be appropriated.

Two years ago I included in the budget $36.7 million to fund a $700 salary increase for teachers. In eight of the last nine years teachers have received substantial increases. In 1960 the average annual salary for teachers in Kentucky was $3,412. Today it has grown to $6,491. Kentucky ranks number one in the nation in percentage of increases in teachers' salaries between 1959 and 1969. I regret that adequate funds are not available for me to include in the budget an increase in teachers' salaries and at the same time offer a proposal for tax relief. However, this does not preclude an increase in teachers' salaries. If you, the legislature, in your collective judgment, assign this a higher priority than tax relief, then I shall not stand in your way.

In the event you do not see fit to exercise your option in favor of the school teachers, I am providing another opportunity for salary increases. Realizing that the quality of our education is directly related to our financial ability to attract the best possible teachers, I am including in the budget bill a provision stipulating that if the actual revenue received by the state during the next fiscal year exceeds the estimate projected by the Department of Revenue and on which this budget is predicated, up to $9 million of that excess, if any, will be allocated to increase teacher salaries. Despite the fact that present revenue expectations force us to take this position, we have offered positive alternatives that clearly demonstrate our sincere concern and commitment to Kentucky's teachers.

Our state colleges and universities, like the elementary and secondary schools, are caught up in population and information explosions. The amounts of money in this budget for higher education reflect the particularly critical point at which our colleges and universities now find themselves. Increased enrollment in the past decade, in some instances as much as four times greater, has forced accelerated construction programs upon the colleges and universities. Although it is not anticipated that the situation of the past decade will continue, this is the most critical budget for higher education in modern Kentucky history. This budget enables our universities to meet the challenge of ever-increasing enrollment with quality education.

Sympathetic to its acute financial position and recognizing its notable contribution to our largest metropolitan area, we recommend that you allocate $8.2 million to the University of Louisville. With the 1970–71 appropriation, support to this university has been increased by 300 percent during my administration.

This budget contains $2.5 million to breathe life into the Northern Kentucky State College—the first four-year state college established since 1922. With the location of this well-deserved facility in one of our largest and most promising regions, we are a significant step closer to the goal of making four years of quality education readily available to all Kentuckians.

Our concern for those among us who are afflicted, infirmed, disadvantaged, or whose lives are otherwise at odds with society, is reflected in the appropriations we are recommending for the development of Kentucky's human resources:

$50 thousand for an Early Childhood Development Project in southeastern Kentucky;

$400 thousand to strengthen the Community Services Program of the Department of Child Welfare;

funds for the full operation of the Ridgewood Center for Girls at Louisville, the Northern Kentucky Diagnostic Center, and boys camps at Pine Mountain and Green River;

funds to establish a Chronic Pulmonary Disease Program, and to establish clinics in Lexington and Louisville for the treatment of cystic fibrosis and chronic asthma;

funds to operate the new first offender camp at Frenchburg, and to increase guard salaries at other correctional institutions;

$500 thousand to eradicate rubella or German measles among mothers-to-be;

$800 thousand for expansion of the community mental health centers which reduce hospital population and more effectively treat patients closer to home;

$700 thousand for more adequate staffing of Kentucky's fully accredited system of mental hospitals;

$400 thousand to begin operations at the $9 million Somerset facility for retarded children;

$1 million for the full cost of nursing home care for disabled citizens.

I call to your attention the $9.4 million in new money required for aid to the aged, blind, disabled, and to dependent children. This brings the state appropriation to a record $56.5 million.

The Medicaid program initiated in 1962 required an appropriation of $1.1 million. This budget requires a state appropriation for $36.2 million.

Changes in federal regulations stifle our attempts to control expenditures in this area. For example, since you approved the 1968–1970 budget, changes in the Medicaid formula have increased the state's share of the total cost from 19 percent to 26 percent. This change resulted in a $4.3 million program deficit in this fiscal year, which will require a supplemental appropriation. Fortunately, the economy and efficiency of this government enables us to meet this need. The new budget is adequate to meet the costs of the Medicaid program as it is now structured. However, at its present rate of growth in terms of benefits and eligibility, it can in the future place an extreme burden on the taxpayers. The next Governor and the next Legislature may be compelled to take drastic action if it continues to escalate, and I encourage you to direct serious attention to this program.

As I indicated earlier, this is the people's budget. Two years ago the long neglect of state buildings and properties demanded immediate attention. Twenty-four million dollars in new construction funds from current revenue was used as a start toward reducing backlog of immediate needs in the areas of mental health, child welfare, corrections, vocational education, and other needs.

I realize and regret that all the needs in these areas cannot be met during my administration. Today, we can go to the people and invite their participation in determining the extent, the desire, and the speed at which they wish to provide these badly needed buildings for the training, treatment, and rehabilitation of those for whom we have and must accept responsibility. I am today proposing for your consideration that a General Obligation Bond issue in the amount of $47.9 million be submitted to the people of this state for their approval or disapproval at the next general election. You surely must realize that these desirable improvements cannot be made during my term of office, but my feelings, hopes, and aspirations for this state and its people will not end with my term of office. As a responsible Governor, I must plan for the future as well as render services at the present. If the people approve this bond issue, proceeds would be used in the vital human areas that I have mentioned. A more detailed proposal will be presented later. Briefly, it will include:

a vocational-technical institute for west Jefferson County;

needed buildings at the School for the Deaf and the School for the Blind;

a new correctional institution;

a new diagnostic center for juvenile offenders;

construction and necessary renovation of Kentucky's mental health hospitals.

I am confident that Kentucky can and will go forward into the seventies in prudent, well-measured, progressive strides if you choose to follow the path and the pace established by this budget. In its present form you will find that we have achieved a true balance on the outside between expenditures and receipts; you will also find that an inner balance has been achieved in the fair and even-handed distribution of funds among the many worthwhile services provided to the people. It is a balance created only after the needs of our citizens were carefully weighed against their weariness of taxes and increased spending. The optimism and aspirations of this document have been tempered by the ability and the willingness of the people to pay the inflated costs of progress at this point in our economic history.

Throughout the budget you will find that it does not vary more than 1.5 percent from the distribution of funds in the last budget that won approval by a majority of 137 to 1. In submitting it for your consideration, I stand ready to accept full responsibility for its excellence or its inadequacies. However, if there is reckless tampering and if political maneuvering is allowed to destroy the delicate balance of this instrument, the responsibility shall pass from me to you.

If you choose to enact legislation creating new programs that require expenditures over the amount budgeted or not included in the budget, you have a moral if not a legal obligation to provide the necessary revenue. Some states, specifically California, prohibit the enactment of any legislation requiring the expenditure of funds unless the source of such funds is provided within the measure or is provided in the budget. Kentucky might do well to consider such a law in view of recent experience. I would cite, for example, the meat inspection law enacted two years ago. This was desirable legislation, but the General Assembly did not provide funds to implement the program. Consequently, ninety thousand dollars had to be taken from the state's emergency fund. Today, that same program requires a budgetary appropriation of twelve times that amount, $1.2 million.

Four years ago the General Assembly created the Capitol Plaza. For the next biennium this project requires $7.1 million for debt service. In other words, the 1966 legislature left the people of Kentucky and us a $10 thousand burden for every day of the next biennium. At all times, we must be aware of the long-range consequences of our every act.

This year a milk inspection program will be proposed for your confirmation. This legislation would no doubt be helpful to our farm economy, but, like the meat inspection bill, it requires additional funds.

Today, many other deserving and worthwhile programs demand your consideration. With $18 million in uncommitted revenue available for your disposal, you will be under tremendous pressure to provide funds for a multitude of projects that touch the lives and the hopes of many Kentuckians. I reiterate that if it is the collective judgment of this Assembly to use the $18 million for all or a portion of these deserving projects and programs, I shall not oppose such action.

These requests must be weighed carefully, because they come from vital segments of our society. For instance:

Kentucky's independent colleges and universities have been rendering invaluable service to the Commonwealth since the beginning of its history. Now, they are requesting public aid. They will come to you with facts and figures that may be as convincing and a plan that may be as deserving of your attention and consideration as the plan presented by the University of Louisville two years ago. Two years ago, by joint resolution, the General Assembly included the University of Louisville as a state institution for budgetary consideration. The $8.2 million included in this budget does not meet their request and perhaps you will give further consideration to their requirements.

The parochial schools, in educating a significant portion of our young people, have relieved to a great degree the burden on public schools. They now face enormous financial difficulties. Many already have closed their doors, and we have felt the impact of these closings in our public school system. Here is a matter that involves not only financial consideration but also constitutional issues of great concern to many.

Throughout Kentucky we have courageous firemen and policemen who have requested state aid. These men are dedicated protectors of life and property. Frequently accused and often abused, underpaid, and overworked, their lives in constant danger, they deserve encouragement.

More effective regulation of the pollution of our air and the fouling of our streams requires more funds than are available in this budget. Private enterprise and other governmental agencies offer high salaries, making it difficult for us to obtain technicians and highly skilled experts, as well as scientific personnel necessary for effective pollution control.

New federal programs have been and will be adopted. No doubt, these will require additional state funds. Provision for this crucial expenditure is made in the revenue sharing plan I have already outlined.

With the presentation of this document, we now move on to another phase of the complex and sometimes controversial process of enacting the executive budget. It is reported that historically the Legislature at its second session during any administration finds great sport in defying the governor and trying to defeat his programs. Surrounding this session have been rumors and overt suggestions that harmful legislation might be enacted simply to test the executive veto and attempt to place the Governor in an embarrassing position. *My only reply is that rather than use the Governor's veto on such legislation, the people's veto, to be stamped on perpetrators of such damaging schemes by an aroused voting public, might far better serve Kentucky's true purpose.*

If given a choice, I prefer to spend the next two years carrying out the constructive good this Legislature can accomplish for Kentucky, rather than being forced to use that time to point the finger of blame in a state perishing amid the ruins of unrealized opportunity and unfulfilled destiny. I am confident that this will not be Kentucky's fate. This is not blind optimism. It is engendered by the fact that perhaps never before in the history of our Commonwealth have so many of such talent and so much to offer sat together in these legislative halls. In carefully examining the backgrounds, qualifications, and accomplishments of each member of this Assembly, one cannot help but be encouraged that the army of light and not the army of darkness shall here prevail.

It has been said and written by the public news media that you and I must do battle. But, were we both not sent here to serve the people. And did we both not take the same oath? Do we both not have a responsibility to serve all of the people, regardless of political persuasion or personal ambition? How can we do battle if we are united, as we should be, in that common cause of public good?

On Inauguration Day, 1967, I said: "There are those who have said—and others who will say—that we shall have a divided house and that a house divided against itself cannot stand. This need not be true. It will not be true if each of us who is charged with public responsibility keeps firmly in his mind that there is a common touchstone, a mutual meeting place, where they and all Kentuckians may assemble without division. We may meet, all of us, around the Altar of the Common Good and here we shall find the area of agreement to be very broad, the area of division to be very narrow and very selfish. Many times in the next four years we shall meet at this altar of common good to fulfill our public responsibility."

I said then and I repeat now: "For my part, I shall extend the hand of friendship. It will be offered in good faith and in good will to all who will accept it. It will be a firm hand and if it is rejected for selfish reasons, I shall at once appeal to the court of last resort, the people of my state. I shall not indulge in, nor shall I permit, partisan politics to impede the programs and the progress that we shall undertake.

CONSUMER PROTECTION
Frankfort / January 20, 1970

I present to the 1970 Kentucky General Assembly a program to protect and further the interests of the Kentucky consumer.[1] It has been observed that while some Kentuckians have their interests protected in Frankfort by special professional groups, it is left to the General Assembly, the Governor, and the Judiciary to speak for every citizen regarding consumer protection.

The Kentucky Consumer Affairs Commission has examined the existing statutes of this state with a special awareness of the major problems confronting the Kentucky consumer. The legislation I am recommending to the General Assembly today is based on their report.

The growth of the consumer movement in this country has been a phenomenon of no small proportion. Until recent years, protection of the consumer was relegated to licensing and regulatory agencies, local trade groups, and industry associations, whose primary goal was to achieve integrity in the business community. Within recent years, however, the pendulum of public concern has swung toward a more consumer-oriented posture. We heartily endorse this trend. We believe that the time has come to accord full recognition and justice to the American consumer.

The solution to consumer problems will not and should not come from federal initiative. Accordingly, thirty-one states have implemented consumer protection programs. Consumer legislation has been introduced in all fifty states during the last five years, and in many cases laws enacted by state legislatures have been more progressive, more specific, and more protective than any legislation attempted at the national level.

In this respect, Kentucky's record in the area of constructive legislation is distinguished. For example, the 1968 Kentucky Legislature enacted two comprehensive insurance laws, the *Unauthorized Insurers Act,* and the *Auto Cancellation Act,* which considerably strengthened the state's protection of the consumer.[2]

The wisdom and foresight of the Kentucky lawmakers also was evidenced by the passage of a state Truth-in-Lending Act and a milestone Meat Inspection Law.[3] These bills are excellent examples of general comprehensive, enforceable legislation that forms the basis for a sound consumer protection program.

Yet, there is much more to be accomplished. Every day, the American marketplace offers more abundance, becomes more impersonal, grows more complex, and demands more buying skills of the consumer.

In addition to the important legislation enacted by the last two General Assemblies, the establishment of the Kentucky Consumer Affairs Commission has been an historic step toward full protection of the public and has enabled Kentucky to attain leadership in this field. The Kentucky Consumer Affairs Commission was established to aid and to represent the buying public of Kentucky and to ensure that the voice of the consumer sounded loud, clear, uncompromising, and effective in the highest councils of this state. They have performed excellently.

During the last 18 months, the Kentucky Consumer Affairs Commission has been continuously and intimately involved in working with and for the consumer in Kentucky. They have taken a close look at the State Departments of Health, Agriculture, Insurance, and Banking in order to discover exactly how the consumer-oriented agencies in state government are really protecting the taxpayer. The commission has worked closely with the business community in an attempt to encourage re-evaluation of practices and policies in the interest of improving responsiveness to consumer demands.

The commission has been able to involve an increasing number of private organizations with vast resources and technical skill in a concerted effort to educate the consumer. It has provided a voice for the Kentucky consumer in the national councils of our nation. It has studied the efforts of other states. And most importantly, it has pioneered a unique, effective program of consumer education, studied and praised by national organizations, and considered as a model for a national effort. This commission has succeeded in humanizing the machinery of government to overcome indifference to consumer problems, and in developing and implementing a comprehensive consumer program for the 1970s.

Today, as we reflect on our efforts, it is evident that much has been accomplished. The Kentucky consumer today has a greater stature in the marketplace, a more powerful voice in the legislative halls, and more protection in our courts of justice. Yet, it is also evident that more remains to be done. The needs of the consumer change as our society changes and legislation must keep pace.

For 1970 I propose to the General Assembly a seven-point program:

1. A *Deceptive Trade Practices Act* to provide Kentucky's law enforcement officials with more effective and speedier remedies to protect Kentucky consumers from thirteen common deceptive trade practices.

2. A *State Credit Card Crime Act* to provide criminal punishment for credit card theft, forgery, and abuse.

3. An *Unsolicited Credit Card Act* to eliminate the proliferation of unsolicited credit cards that are irresponsibly flooding the marketplace.

4. An Act to declare unsolicited goods a gift to the receiver and thereby eliminate this deceptive marketing technique.

5. The strict regulation of debt-pooling agencies.

6. To establish a Poultry and Rabbit Product Inspection System for the protection of every Kentuckian.

7. Strong, strident, and effective opposition to the proposed revision of the Insurance Code that would provide for 'Open Competition' and effectively eliminate any protection for the Kentuckian who purchases insurance.

As we contemplate the need for additional consumer protection, however, we must also recognize that we are interested not only in protecting ourselves as consumers, but also in preserving and strengthening the competitive free enterprise system. Therefore, our approach to the question of consumer legislation is the approach of reason. We feel no substantial and lasting benefit will come to the taxpayer of Kentucky from a crusade based on invective, demagoguery, and emotionalism. No good can come to the consumer if we begin to enact poorly organized, catch-as-catch-can consumer legislation.

The legislation we recommend is sound. It takes account of the practical consideration involved. It is workable. It will give consumers very substantial public enforcement assistance and private remedies they have not had before. We believe it will provide a firm foundation for enforcement and further development.

It is our belief that the Kentucky lawmakers, by enacting the legislation which we have here proposed, can justly and proudly consider themselves leaders in protecting the citizens of the Commonwealth of Kentucky.

Your decisions, your votes, and your actions will determine whether Kentucky continues a progressive program to aid and to protect the Kentucky consumer, or whether the newly discovered political appeal of consumer protection will produce a torrent of inefficacious, unenforceable legislation that will aid no one and will only mislead the individual citizen to believe that he is being protected.

All reasonable forces for years have decried consumer fraud. It is long past time we turned our orations into action, lament into law, and exhortation of fraud into elimination of fraud. This is not a partisan program, not a business program, not a labor program, but a program for all of us—all three million Kentuckians.[4]

Every Spring, when families turn their thoughts to household improvements, the shady operator goes to work. With false and deceptive offers of attractive home repairs or items that are more promise than product, he preys most of all on those who are least able to protect themselves: the poor, the elderly, the untrained.

Crime is crime, whether it be at the tip of a gun or at the tip of a pen and the tip of a tongue of a fradulent sales operator. A recent Report of the Senate Commerce Committee argues that deceptive selling is the nation's "most serious form of theft," accounting for more dollars lost each year than robbery, larcency, auto theft, embezzlement, and forgery combined.

As the law now stands, there is no effective way to stop these unscrupulous practices when they are discovered. The legal machinery may drag on for two or three years before the violator can be ordered to cease and desist. In the meantime, countless more Kentuckians are cheated. In matters so flagrantly deceptive, the consumer and the honest businessman deserve greater—and speedier—protection.

I recommend that the General Assembly enact a Deceptive Trade Practices Act. The purpose of this act is, and its effect will be, to afford consumers substantial additional protection against fraud and deception. It does this by expanding the jurisdiction and powers of the Attorney General, and by making certain defined activities by sellers of goods and services violations of state law. Under this act, the Attorney General would be able to obtain court orders to stop fraudulent and deceptive practices immediately.

This act specifically spells out the thirteen prohibited practices. These are practices which have substantial adverse effects on consumers. They are well known to be unfair and deceptive practices and are prohibited under Section 5 of the Federal Trade Commission Act.

The consumer protection afforded by this legislation is greatly needed. Consumers in all income levels are among the victims of unfair and deceptive practices, including those of us who may consider ourselves sophisticated in the marketplace.

Violence and crime are major concerns of the American people at this hour in our history. Threaded through the reports of the National Commission on Civil Disorders and the President's Commission on Law Enforcement and Administration of Justice was the impact which consumer fraud has on our economy and its impact as a causative factor in the unrest in our society. The National Commission on Civil Disorders' report indicated that consumer frustrations were among the twelve most deeply held grievances which fostered discontent and disorders. The Commission declared that "there can be no higher priority for national action and no higher claim on the nation's conscience" than the need to develop programs to "change the system of failure and frustration that now dominates the ghetto and weakens our society."

Ours is a credit economy. The use of consumer credit has achieved amazing growth in the last twenty years. In 1968, outstanding consumer credit totaled $113 billion, compared to $21 billion in 1950. The auto loan, the installment contract, the revolving charge, the credit card—all have brought a revolutionary change for business.

This new credit society, however, has also encouraged more sophisticated crime. As the number of credit cards in the United States has proliferated—there are more than 300 million currently in consumer wallets and they are used to charge between $40 billion and $60 billion annually—so has their illegal use. Exact fraud loss figures are not known. But the insurance companies that pay some of the losses estimate that more than 1.5 million cards are stolen or lost each year and that fraud losses have jumped from $20 million annually in 1966 to more than $100 million a year today. With so many cards in circulation, it is not surprising that many find their way into the wrong hands.

The proposed Act would provide criminal punishment of not less than $1,000 fine or imprisonment for one year or both, or more than $3,000 fine or three years' imprisonment or both for all types of crimes involving the use of credit cards. Specifically, this Act would punish credit card theft, the purchase or sale of credit cards, forgery of a credit card, or the use of an illegally obtained credit card.

Because of the numerous complaints and public outrage over unsolicited credit cards, I have proposed a bill to bar such mailing or distribution unless the person so solicited has previously made a request for such a credit card in writing. The proliferation of unsolicited credit cards now flooding the marketplace poses a serious threat to the low income consumer and others who are not able to manage credit. It is obvious that the vast majority of consumers of the Commonwealth feel that this public nuisance should be barred.

I propose a bill providing mandatory inspection of the slaughter of poultry and rabbits and the processing of poultry and rabbits and poultry and rabbit products for distribution in this Commonwealth.

The Wholesome Poultry Products Act was passed by the U. S. Congress, August 18, 1968. This statute, administered under Consumer Protection Service, USDA, specified that all states shall be equal to Federal Inspection statutes in the inspection of poultry and poultry products by August 18, 1970. A similar requirement was specified in the Wholesome Meat Act passed by the U. S. Congress in December, 1967. As was the case in the Wholesome Meat Act, the Poultry Products Act likewise allows an additional year if a program is being developed that has a potential of being equal to Federal Requirements. Additional funds and appropriations will not be requested other than those specified for the administration of the Kentucky Meat Inspection Act for fiscal year 1970–72.

The poultry slaughter industry is one of very small volume in the Commonwealth. Only three operators of such establishments slaughter poultry in any significant volume. However, considerable numbers of poultry establishments are processing whole broiler and fryer carcasses for retail and restaurant outlets. This is a growing business and can be easily covered by personnel of the Kentucky Meat Inspection Program, because poultry is processed in most instances in the same establishments as red meat, now covered under the Kentucky Meat Inspection Act. Inspection for this phase of the poultry industry is essential.

Poultry and poultry products are an important source of the nation's total supply of food. It is essential in the public interest that the health and welfare of consumers be protected by assuring that slaughtered poultry and poultry products and slaughtered rabbit and rabbit products distributed to them are wholesome, not adulterated, and properly marked, labeled, and packaged.

Recent federal inspection teams have found that at least one-half of the poultry and rabbit products slaughtering and processing plants in Kentucky do not meet federal standards and will be closed if the state does not take immediate and effective action in this area.

I propose a bill whereby if unsolicited goods are addressed and delivered to a person, he would be permitted to consider the goods a gift, with no obligation to return or pay for the merchandise. This would discourage the common practice of delivering unwanted and unordered goods and then coercing the receiver to pay for them.

The bill to regulate the business of debt-management basically provides for licensing of debt-pooling agencies and their regulation by the Department of Banking. The bill also specifically names certain illegal acts; defines certain areas of responsibility for debt-poolers; provides for annual review of the licensee; and requires annual reports much the same as the statutes regulating small loan and industrial loan companies. These rating statutes were drafted to establish principles of regulation within which administrative authority could exercise a broad discretionary power, and thereby provide flexibility.

The 1968 Kentucky General Assembly, by Senate Resolution No. 51, directed the Legislative Research Commission to prepare a proposed substantive revision of the Kentucky Insurance Code to be presented to the 1970 General Assembly. The most novel feature of this proposed law is that the state adopt an "open competition" rating law in place of the present "all-industry" regulation. Present law requires that rate changes and supporting statistical evidence be filed with the Commissioner of Insurance. If the Commissioner does not disapprove them during a 30-day waiting period, these rates and rating plans become effective at the end of the waiting period. If the Commissioner deems it necessary, he may order open hearings to be held on the rates. The Kentucky rating statutes further require that rates shall neither be excessive nor inadequate nor unfairly discriminatory. These are the same standards found in the majority of states that adopted the all-industry type rating laws.

We feel that the administration of the present regulations has been fair and equitable. During 1969 the Kentucky Department of Insurance approved over 97 percent of the 3,136 requests it received concerning rates.

Insurance is a vital necessity. The State Financial Responsibility Law, for example, requires citizens to be insured and state law also allows for credit life insurance and fire insurance on home mortgages. There is also no substitutability for insurance. It is not the same as purchasing other necessities such as fuel, where one can choose between coal or oil or gas or wood. Secondly, the consumer is limited by a serious lack of knowledge in this field. Insurance is so highly complex that it is almost impossible for the average consumer to fully comprehend the difference between different insurance arrangements.

The question, therefore, is whether to regulate or not to regulate: whether to ensure that the Kentuckian who buys insurance is protected or whether to effectively eliminate insurance regulation, leave the insurance department with no way to protect the public, and leave every Kentuckian to be on his own in the complex insurance marketplace. Other states have experimented with this system and are now reverting to regulation. This speaks for itself.

This law would permit insurance companies to fix their rates at whatever level a customer is willing to pay. It would make the continuance of the state Department of Insurance meaningless and vain. And most of all, it would render the average insurance buyer—the great majority of Kentuckians—defenseless and unprotected. This is neither necessary nor desirable. And it is not in the best interests of the consumers of Kentucky.

---

1. An abridged version of this message was transmitted to the House of Representatives on March 11, 1970.

2. An act "relating to the regulation and control of the conduct of unauthorized insurers, corporations, and persons not authorized to conduct the business of insurance within this state," was signed by Governor Nunn on March 25, 1968. See *Acts of the General Assembly of the Commonwealth of Kentucky, 1968*, Chapter 113 (S.B. 290), pp. 331–43. An act "relating to automobile insurance" specifying that automobile liability policies on private passenger vehicles could not be canceled except for nonpayment of premium or for suspension of license or registration. The act became law without Governor Nunn's signature on March 27, 1968. Ibid., Chapter 158 (S.B. 169), pp. 655–58.

3. An act "relating to disclosure of charges in connection with extension

of credit" became law without Governor Nunn's signature. Ibid., Chapter 188 (H.B. 250), pp. 789–98.

4. The remainder of this address appeared only in the version transmitted to the Senate.

GENERAL OBLIGATION
BOND ISSUE
Frankfort / March 2, 1970

IN presenting the 1971–72 executive budget to the Legislature, I said it was a budget for the people. With the same objective I proposed a general obligation bond issue to provide funds for major capital improvements at certain of the state's institutions—improvements which could not be provided through the biennial budget because of lack of general fund revenue.

These projects could have been funded through the issuance of revenue bonds by the State Property and Buildings Commission. However, I deliberately chose to recommend the issuance of general obligation bonds because this method solicits and requires the approval of not only the representatives of the people, but also the people themselves. Thus, the people are permitted to express their wishes regarding not only the extent, but also the speed at which these badly needed projects are to be pursued.

The proposed bond issue is in the amount of $48.3 million. Without exception the projects contained in the bond package would provide for the training, treatment, rehabilitation, and encouragement of a wide range of Kentucky citizens. These are human projects to meet the real human needs of the people of this Commonwealth.

Specifically, we have proposed:

(1) Eight million dollars for a Vocational Technical Institute for west Jefferson County. This area has the state's largest load of public assistance recipients, the heaviest concentration of unemployment, and ten separate areas of concentrated poverty. An extensive vocational training program would be a long step toward the goal of moving Kentuckians off welfare rolls onto payrolls. There is conclusive proof that industry is attracted to those areas where a broadbased

program of vocational-technical education is available. The facility to be provided by this bond issue would accommodate more than 2,500 students at a time and provide training in up to forty different occupational areas.

(2) Eighteen million dollars for a new correctional institution. At present we are housing approximately 2,900 inmates at Eddyville and LaGrange in institutions designed for only 1,900. If we are to reduce our present recommitment rate, we must find a way to separate first offenders from the influence of the hardened criminals. The 475-bed facility which these funds can provide would be a major step in more effective rehabilitation of those for whom some hope remains.

(3) Kentucky's mental health institutions were, for the most part, constructed in the 19th century and are inadequate as modern hospitals for the treatment and medical rehabilitation of mentally ill persons. Eighteen million dollars of the bond proceeds will be devoted to the construction or reconstruction of mental health facilities. Projects will be included for each of the four psychiatric hospitals located at Danville, Lexington, Louisville, and Hopkinsville. Plans call for facilities which are patient oriented, such as housing and admissions and treatment centers.

Projects will include the construction of new treatment units at the Lexington and Louisville hospitals. These units are designed to meet the needs of newly developed methods requiring short-term, intensive care for increasing numbers of patients. New buildings for housing treatment facilities for emotionally ill children are also planned. Renovation projects at the Danville and Hopkinsville hospitals will provide more livable quarters for patients and facilitate their treatment.

Another priority item, renovation of a building at Outwood State Hospital and School for the retarded at Dawson Springs, could generate for the state about 300 thousand dollars a year in federal funds.

(4) Child Welfare will receive $1.165 million for the construction of a new Regional Diagnostic-Reception Center in Jefferson County. The facility now in use at Lyndon will be converted to a Security Treatment Center for fifty hard-core delinquent boys. Combined with Regional Diagnostic Centers now under consideration in Northern and Western Kentucky, this new facility will be another step toward providing smaller, more manageable, institutions with specialized programs adopted to best deal with the varying problems of young offenders.

(5) A classroom-student center building at the School for the Deaf will receive $2.1 million. This building will provide urgently needed facilities for all the students and faculty.

(6) The School for the Blind will receive $495 thousand for construction of a building to be utilized for music instruction.

(7) Four hundred thousand dollars will stand as the guarantee fund behind loans to Kentucky farmers, as provided in HB 577, the Farm Loan Development Authority Act.[1] This portion of the bond revenues can provide a dramatic lift to Kentucky's record-breaking farm economy by making available $10.5 million for loans to farm families. The state's gross realized farm income is estimated to have passed the one billion dollar mark for the first time in history during 1969, a sure sign that Kentucky's farm economy is alive with promise. At the same time, however, we find that the number of farmers and farm families is decreasing. While there are several reasons for this decline, a major cause appears to be the difficulty which the small farmer has in obtaining a loan for the purchase or improvement of land.

I believe that we can and we must give encouragement to the ownership and operation of small acreage farms. By guaranteeing all, or a portion of farm loans, many of our farmers will be able to continue operations and others to begin farming. This bond provision is another step in our attempts to stem the flow of migration from rural areas to urban centers. It provides the means for many of our citizens to continue to be productive and self-sustaining rather than being forced to join the growing welfare ranks. It presents the opportunity to our farmers to realize the dignity and pride which can come with the tilling of their own land. It should be emphasized that this does not directly involve the government in the mortgage loan business. Rather, it encourages the participation of private lenders by guaranteeing up to $7,500 of any loan made on operating farm land to a qualified applicant. I believe it represents one of the best examples of cooperation between government, private enterprise, and the farm community in the encouragement of individual initiative.

This bond issue is not recommended without due regard for Kentucky's existing obligations. The state Finance Commissioner [Albert Christen] reports that a recently completed analysis shows Kentucky's fiscal position to be sound. When related to total resources and ability to pay, the total of Kentucky's obligations is well within the safety guidelines established by governmental finance experts.

In dealing with human resources, as each of the projects contained in the bond proposal do, we must realize the economy that can be realized by acting, not by postponing, our responsibilities. The people of Kentucky have indicated their increasing awareness and interest in the problems and the opportunities facing their government. I am confident that the people can properly decide the course which they wish to follow. In asking that this question be answered at the ballot box, I can find no reasons why the Legislature should deny the people of Kentucky the privilege of expressing their judgment.

---

1. The Farm Loan Development Authority Act was signed by Governor Nunn on March 30, 1970. For further information see "An act relating to farming and establishing the Kentucky Farm Development Authority," *Acts of the General Assembly of the Commonwealth of Kentucky, 1970,* Chapter 273 (H.B. 577), pp. 933–38.

SPECIAL EDUCATION
Frankfort / March 11, 1970

I COME to you to initiate legislation and to ask your support, as sensitive Kentuckians, for a noble and worthwhile cause—one which, if pursued, would brighten the futures of approximately 285,000 young Kentuckians, to say nothing of their families. This includes 27,435 children with speech handicaps, 4,521 with hearing handicaps, 7,635 with learning disabilities, 730 with visual handicaps, 2,919 who are crippled and have special health problems, 8,317 who are educable mentally retarded, 1,698 who are trainable mentally retarded, 1,593 who are emotionally disturbed. These children are not being served in today's classroom.[1]

Add to this number about 214,000 functionally retarded. These are children who have the mental capacity to function as normal children but cannot because of other handicapping conditions, such as impoverished environment. Most of them are considered underachievers or failures in school. If we then combine about 15,000 gifted youngsters who are inadequately served today, we have a figure equal to 33 percent of the total elementary and secondary school age population in Kentucky.

For this reason I am requesting authorization to implement the program I now present for approval by the General Assembly. My objective is to provide the focus needed for our exceptional children. With your help we can begin to give these youngsters the chance in life that rightfully belongs to them. By definition, *exceptional children* means children who differ in one or more respects from average or normal children in physical, mental, emotional, or social characteristics and abilities to such a degree that it is impractical or impossible for them to benefit from, or participate in, the regular or usual facilities or classroom programs of the public schools.

I propose that this definition be clarified to include, though not being limited to, the neurologically impaired, the intellectually gifted, the emotionally disturbed, the functionally retarded, children with learning disabilities, communications disorders and those who are multiply handicapped.

The history of help for the exceptional child has been bleak. It will remain so unless we dedicate ourselves to its improvement. The transition of our society from agrarian to the urban scene of today, by its very nature, sophisticates life. A more complicated environment has also contributed a greater number of mentally disturbed to whom the state must give attention.

In molding a plan for Kentucky's exceptional children, the programs of other states have been considered and researched. To determine the effectiveness of each state's plan and the feasibility for adoption by Kentucky, a very intensive study was conducted by the Legislative Research Commission and the results were compiled and published (Research Report #56). Contributing to the study and planning related to special needs were six Action Committees for exceptional children, a part of the process of the White House Conference on Children and Youth. The Committees' membership was comprised of fifty-five lay citizens, youth and adult, who were assisted by a team of ninety-three professional consultants. Participation was entirely on a voluntary basis. After studying the programs utilized by other states and after considering recommendations of the six Action Committees, we have assembled a comprehensive and pragmatic plan we feel best fits the temperament and needs of Kentucky's exceptional children. The program is flexible enough to envision future expansion.

A Task Force, to be known as the State Task Force, shall be established as an arm of the Human Resources Coordinating Council, the "Council." The State Task Force shall consist of eleven members with no more than five members drawn from the professional community involved in the problems of exceptional children. It will be required that one member be appointed from the State Department of Education and one member from higher education who is involved in training of teachers of exceptional children.

Incorporated, non-profit organizations with a state-wide membership which endeavor to provide programs for exceptional children may recommend nominees to the Council. Each department representative on the Human Resources Coordinating Commission and the Medical Director for Handicapped Children or their designate shall serve in an advisory capacity to the State Task Force. The members shall serve without compensation, although they shall be reimbursed for all necessary expenses.

The powers and duties of the State Task Force shall encompass:

1. Surveying needs and resources available as they relate to the various facets of education of exceptional children.
2. Recommending regulations to the Department of Education and other departments as they relate to the exceptional child.
3. Employing independent professional organizations and staff for services not immediately available.
4. Making recommendations to the Council, school boards, and others relating to the exceptional child.
5. Establishing Regional Task Forces, setting the terms of service for Regional members, and receiving and evaluating the reports of Regional Task Forces.
6. Serving in advisory capacity to the Department of Education, to the Legislative Research Commission, and to the Human Resources Coordinating Commission and Council.

For expedient implementation of this program, it is felt that by July 1, 1971, each regional task force shall submit plans for accomplishing special educational programs. If a regional task force fails to submit such a plan, it shall be the duty of the State Task Force to prepare a plan and present it to the regional councils and State Council. By December 1, 1971, the State Task Force shall submit its final reports to the Human Resources Coordinating Commission and Council which shall send the report to the Governor, to the State Board of Education, and to the Legislative Research Commission. By July 1, 1974, all county and independent school boards shall operate special education programs as approved by the State Board of Education, after consideration of recommendations of the State Task Force and the Human Resources Coordinating Commission and Council.

Another alarming situation pertains to instructors in the area of special education. In Kentucky we produce only about 150 special education teachers annually. This, too, represents an area of grave concern. If we are to improve Kentucky's special education program, we must endeavor to attract more teachers to this field. We must work to awaken high school and college students, especially, to the possibilities awaiting them in this area.

It is my duty and your duty to see that our children develop to the fullest extent of their capabilities. If some of our children are exceptional or mentally gifted, the responsibility for their development remains with us. Therefore, I ask you to join me in the challenge I have set before you.

———————————

1. This message was transmitted to the House of Representatives only.

EDUCATIONAL REFORM
Frankfort / March 11, 1970

AMERICANS have always valued education. It has been predicted that history will record the public school system, aimed toward educating all at public expense, as America's contribution to civilization. It is a tribute to this unique and great system of education that society is increasingly looking to education to help solve its most complex problems. It seems abundantly clear today that the quality of life in America for all our citizens lies in the kind and quality of education provided. There has developed, because of the fact that education is so important and so crucial, a great outcry for reforms and improvements in the accomplishments of the public school system.

There is the demand to make education more relevant, more meaningful, more up-to-date, and more available to each and every one according to his needs, interests, and talents. Just recently an expert on computer systems speaking to every commissioner and agency head in Kentucky government predicted that by 1980 the labor market will change drastically because the computer will have become so integrated in industry. This means a different kind of education than we have today.

Kentuckians have always valued education. The history of education in Kentucky is exciting. Dramatic improvements have been made during the past decade and a half since the creation of the Foundation Program of Education by the citizens and the profession and enacted into law by the Kentucky General Assembly. Just as we needed to remove some of the barriers that hindered our Minimum Foundation Program, so now we must remove some of the barriers that hinder our children's progress in meeting today's educational challenges.

I became involved in and personally aware of many significant efforts toward innovations, reform, and improvements in our schools during the project I initiated last year, "The Governor's Award for Outstanding Innovations." Those in the teaching profession involved most dramatically and determinedly in making needed improvements want legislative support which will enable them to break barriers of tradition and to pioneer improvements in educational opportunities for Kentucky's youth by using fully Kentucky's staff of more than 36,000 teachers and administrators.

Because of the professional status of Kentucky's teachers, and because of some educational lags of urgent concern, I am proposing enabling legislation which will provide opportunity for new directions and opportunities for Kentucky to break with conventional practices. The traditional ways have resulted in inadequacies which are crying out for new responses. We are at the crossroads of mounting costs and inadequate accomplishments, at a time when both tax relief and educational improvements are being called for. I believe strongly that Kentucky can find its way at this crossroads. I am proposing legislation for experimentation and study which I believe will provide the freedom and the challenge for leadership, through the true Kentucky pioneering spirit, to meet one of the most vital needs.

First, enabling legislation which will provide more freedom and flexibility on the part of classroom teachers and school administrators in selecting the learning material used in our classrooms. A reform is needed in this area so that materials may be more relevant and more current and on the reading level of each child. There was a time when the textbook was the only word or only piece of learning material a child or the teacher had. Now, with mass media—with educational television—with library materials, tapes, films, records—teachers and students too often feel stymied in being bound legally by having to follow an adopted textbook.

My proposal for flexibility has emerged from teachers and administrators who participated in "The Governor's Outstanding Innovation Award" and from our study in preparation for the 1970 White House Conference on Children and Youth. I am convinced that many school systems which are rapidly trying to make needed improvements in education want the flexibility I propose.

In summary, this legislation would allow up to ten local school districts during 1970–72 to receive one-sixth of the amount of free textbook funds designated by the State Department of Education to that district. Such funds could be used in purchase of materials other than the adopted text, which have been prepared by teachers and curriculum consultants, or by professionals, or academic groups locally or on a national basis, provided that the subject and material shall be approved by the State Board of Education. This simply allows teachers and administrators to use one-sixth of the free textbook funds for purchase of learning materials which in their judgment are most suitable.

Second, legislation to allow up to twenty public schools to establish differentiated pay schedules on an experimental basis for teachers according to the professional responsibility they carry and on the basis of differentiated teaching assignment according to a variety of teaching roles. In addition to the current salary schedule based on experience and college degrees, this proposal advocates a third element —the degree of professional responsibility of the teacher in the overall improvement of learning. This means, in addition to actual teaching in the classroom, the excellent teacher might work with other teachers in helping them become better teachers in reading, etc., or more skilled in the whole process of teaching and learning. In this proposal, I do not anticipate that all teachers would receive the top salary in his or her rank, but that the more capable teachers, professionally, would be rewarded because they are willing to share their professional expertise with more children, more teachers, more aids, more student teachers in training, and with the community.

The criteria for administration of the program must be submitted for approval with the application to the State Board of Education to participate in this differentiated pay schedule plan. Under my proposal this plan would break with the traditional salary schedule based on college degrees and experience only. It would allow a local school district to develop a plan of differentiated staffing and a corresponding differentiated salary schedule. Under the plan salary raises during the next two years could be weighted in favor of the teacher who does more professional work including such responsibilities as working as head of a team of teachers, or working with inexperienced teachers, or working with aides and other para-professionals, working with larger groups of children in cooperation with para-professionals, or producing more relevant learning materials, or working with parents and the community, or working beyond the regular school day or beyond the regular school term on those matters which promise improvement in education for Kentucky's children.

Some may say the concept of differentiated staffing and salary is risky when there are few precedents on which to proceed. But, I agree with Dr. Roy A. Edelfelt, Executive Secretary, National Commission on Teacher Education and Professional Standards, "risk-taking is necessary if schools are to begin to meet the great challenges of human progress."[1]

Third, on an experimental basis, enabling legislation to allow use of Foundation Program funds for teacher aides and para-professionals. School districts in Kentucky can successfully improve the learning situation by expanding the professional expertise of a teacher by providing opportunity for her or him to have aides, thereby making it possible for a larger group of children to have the benefit of the teacher. With aides and other non-certificated personnel, a professional teacher may devote her time to professional responsibilities—planning for improvement of learning environments, guiding and counseling children, and directing learning.

There are school systems in Kentucky which want the opportunity and freedom to employ, with Foundation Program funds, a number of these aides and para-professionals in the belief that improvement in the educational situation will follow. I propose enabling legislation which would allow ten districts designated by the State Board of Education to receive Foundation Program funds in an amount equal to 40 percent of the amount for a teacher in rank III with no experience, multiplied by the number of such para-professionals and teacher aides employed in the designated school or schools—provided that the number of such non-certificated aides and para-professionals shall not exceed one-half the number of certificated personnel in the designated school or schools.

This proposed legislation will not require any additional funds, nor any less, but provides freedom for use of the Foundation Program funds for salaries for either teachers or aides within these limits. With the same amount of money a school district may choose to expand the professional responsibility of excellent teachers by employing aides to work with good teachers. This does not anticipate reducing the cost for salaries, but provides freedom for a school district to make use of a plan of utilizing aides—a plan which educators have indicated to me that they want the freedom to use.

Fourth, one of the strengths of our non-tax-supported schools has been their ability to innovate. At present private schools receive no financing from the state, and, so long as this is true, should be freer to make their own judgment of what a good teacher is. We propose to allow private schools to experiment by providing for certification of their teachers with a college degree who are extremely proficient in their subject areas.

Fifth, to broaden the experimentation provided for in the four preceding proposals, I ask that the General Assembly join with me in calling for the creation of a State Task Force on Education Innovation by the State Board of Education. The Task Force will be for the purpose of studying innovations which are being tried as a way of bringing improvement in education, and for the purpose of bringing recommendations to our attention—recommendations for breaking the cycle of traditional school organization, curriculum, and approaches which have resulted in inadequate accomplishments. I would think that such a State Task Force should study the ideas and research in such areas as how to guarantee for every child his "right to read"; fuller utilization of public school resources in preparation of teachers; differentiated staffing and salaries; the open-campus concept; continuing education; offering of mini-courses; liberalization of textbook laws; use of teacher-prepared textbooks; model centers for student teachers and interns; redefinition of the school day and school attendance, substitutions for the Carnegie unit; and centers for innovation, research, and information. I would also suggest that the State Task Force make its report on recommendations by July 1, 1971.

These proposals for experimentation and study are in keeping with the theme of this administration, "Every Kentuckian Counts." These proposals aim toward quality education for each Kentuckian. It is my desire that within the next ten years there will be a marked increase in literacy and a school system responsive to individual needs, ensuring that every child gets the best possible education.

In accord with United States Commissioner of Education James Allen, it is our hope that by the end of the seventies every child will be reading "to the full limit of his capability by the time he leaves school."[2]

---

1. The quoted material is from Roy A. Edelfelt, "Is Differentiated Staffing Worth Risking?" *Connecticut Teacher* 37 (December 1969): 6–7, 27.

2. James E. Allen, Jr. (1911–   ), assistant secretary for education and commissioner of education, United States Department of Health, Education, and Welfare (1969–   ). *Who's Who in American Politics, 1969–1970*, 2d ed. (New York, 1969), p. 16.

WELFARE REFORM
Frankfort / March 11, 1970

KENTUCKY has added 160,000 people to its welfare rolls over the past ten years—the equivalent of putting a city the size of Henderson on welfare every year. This Commonwealth has spent a billion dollars on its poor in that ten years.[1]

Today's federal-state system is being choked by a tangled web of complexities and contradictions. This confuses the taxpayer who finances it and frustrates the needy person it was designed to serve. The present welfare system has overlooked some basic questions about what welfare should do. This administration is prepared to confront those questions. We are asking you, the Kentucky General Assembly, to address these problems with us, and to help us accomplish a major change in state welfare policies.

At the foundation of our proposals are certain beliefs: that the public funds placed in our trust must become not an expenditure, but rather an investment in the rehabilitation of human beings; that we must endeavor to place in the mainstream of society the needy among us who have the potential of becoming productive, wage-earning citizens; that the individual dignity and worth of our disadvantaged can be respected while at the same time we render our administration of the system more economical and efficient; and that individuals and organizations outside of government must be not simply permitted, but actively encouraged, to share the responsibility for attaining these goals.

We must now finally recognize and begin to deal with the fact that there are two distinctly different types of welfare recipients. There are those who are *permanently* dependent, and there are those who are only *temporarily* dependent. A basic failure of the present system is that eventually everyone who gets on the welfare rolls comes to be regarded as permanently dependent. The emphasis has been on *maintenance* only and not on rehabilitation. Only token recognition has been given to the principle that, with the right kind of preparation, many welfare citizens can become working citizens. We propose to commence a meaningful effort to have the welfare Kentuckian take his place among the ranks of working Kentuckians.

Our present system contains no real incentives to work. Unfortunately, the incentive all too often is in the opposite direction. The welfare recipient who has just begun to work at low wages is penalized for his effort. We propose to make self-support attractive by creating incentives to work among those at the lowest income level. We would transfer some of our welfare benefits—at no additional cost to the state —to allow those families which earn the *least* money to retain *more* of the earnings they so desperately need. No longer will the working welfare family be required to exist on less than a minimum subsistence level. At the same time, we would remove from the relief rolls those people who have demonstrated an ability to care for themselves. Under our proposal, all welfare recipients who are workready, or who could become so with adequate training and education, would be required to apply for appropriate work or training.

I have mentioned work training and rehabilitation. In this, as in other areas, there is a limit to what government can and should do. The resources of government are not boundless, and must be carefully distributed in the interest of the taxpayers who support it. But the resources of the private sector, by comparison, are vast. We submit that government should not attempt to do the whole job. We submit that it is a proper function of government—even a primary function— to stimulate a greater involvement by private individuals and organizations in the problems of our time.

In every county and in every community in this state there are enlightened and interested citizens who are looking for a way to help those among us who are disadvantaged. For those citizens, we would offer the opportunity to enlist in a new effort—Community Resources for Employment And Training Effort—CREATE for short.

CREATE would work directly with state government in finding employment for all who qualify. It would advise on training programs. It would help with child care placement. It would call upon community agencies and individuals to help shoulder the burden of preparing our needy for the world of work. It would involve the local community in rehabilitating its own citizens.

CREATE is nothing more complicated than neighbor helping neighbor. In order to work together, CREATE and the welfare recipient must be permitted to talk together. For too many years, an artificial veil of secrecy has hidden the welfare recipient from his fellow citizens. It has created guilt in the mind of the recipient, and suspicion in the mind of the taxpayer. It has created a permanent second class of 300,000 citizens, whose membership is known only to those of us in government. We propose to lift that veil, to the degree necessary to put help-minded citizens in touch with the disadvantaged, without infringing upon the personal dignity or right of privacy of any person.

A continuing criticism of our welfare policy is that it contributes to the breakdown of the family unit—the social unit which has been the basic source of strength of our nation. When the government gives money to a family *only* if the father is absent, then there is the possibility that the father will *make* himself absent so that the family can receive money. Recent studies from other states indicate that this is exactly what has been happening. Our fiscal limitations prevent us from extending benefits to *all* poor families that choose to stay together. However, we can and should discourage the absenteeism of the father. We should require, as a condition of eligibility for his family, that he be located and required to make his financial contribution to his family, whenever and wherever possible. In order to coordinate these efforts we are establishing a parental support unit in the Department of Economic Security to ensure that those who have the legal responsibility for support assume that responsibility.

These proposals to you, the General Assembly, represent a change of emphasis—a change of direction—not a change of the amount of our budget request. Our recommendations can be accomplished with the same amount of money we would otherwise need over the coming biennium even if our welfare system went on unchanged. This is as it should be. Money has proven not to be the final answer to the welfare dilemma.

----

1. This message was transmitted to the House of Representatives only.

VOTING AND
GOVERNMENTAL REFORMS
Frankfort / March 11, 1970

THE American system of government rests upon two basic premises: first, the free and fair participation of the citizenry through the electoral process; and secondly, the ability of government at many levels to serve the people within its constitutionally defined institutions.

Consistent with these underlying principles of representative government, on Monday I shall send to the members of the General Assembly for their consideration a six-point program designed to accomplish three distinct and desirable goals: to foster greater citizen participation in the electoral process, to help local governments develop machinery that meets the challenges of contemporary society, and to stimulate a more creative involvement of the private sector in the vital technical endeavors of government.

The challenges and opportunities of the seventies require Kentucky to improve its governmental procedure and encourage greater participation of her citizens, young and old alike. In gearing government to the future, there must be more responsiveness to the critical needs of our urban and local communities.

Responsive and responsible government demands the participation of every citizen. However, in the election of 1960, an estimated 8 million adults, or 8 percent of those old enough to vote, were excluded from the polls because they could not meet the stringent residency requirements imposed by various state and local governments. This number becomes crucial when one considers that both the 1960 and 1968 presidential races were decided by margins of less than 600,000 votes each.

Most laws on voter residence requirements were enacted in a period when American society was more provincial and people did not move as far and as often as they do today. Moreover, tremendous improvements in the communications media have given citizens a much better understanding of national issues. In light of these contemporary circumstances, unreasonable residency requirements in national elections are obsolete and detrimental to the nation's interest by causing many citizens to forfeit temporarily their vital voting rights. Likewise, the rapidly increasing mobility of Kentuckians has caused a corresponding increase in the number of our citizens unnecessarily disenfranchised by movement from one county to another.

I am therefore recommending that the General Assembly consider an amendment to the Constitution of Kentucky that would reduce the residency requirements for certain Kentuckians and would also allow qualified new residents who have recently moved to Kentucky to vote for the president and vice-president, but for no other offices. This constitutional amendment would make Kentucky's voting laws realistic and return voting rights to those now barred from the voting booth by the mobility of our society. If the General Assembly takes favorable action on this amendment, it would be presented to the voters of the Commonwealth in November 1970.

The first part of the Amendment, *a Voting by New Residents Law, would allow anyone who moves to Kentucky and who would have otherwise been a qualified elector under the constitution of this state*

except that he has been a resident of Kentucky for less than six months
prior to the date of a presidential election, to vote for presidential and
vice-presidential electors but for no other offices, if he applies for a
new resident's voting ballot with the county clerk of the county of his
new residence at least thirty days prior to the election. It would be administered the same as an absentee ballot, and the new resident will
qualify under its terms only if he is ineligible to vote in another state.

The second section of the proposed Amendment would alter Section
145 of the Kentucky Constitution. Presently this section requires the
voter to live in the state one year, county six months, and precinct sixty
days; this amendment would change the requirement to six months'
residency in the state, three months' in the county, and sixty days' in
the precinct.

An even greater threat to our representative form of government is
the danger that the will of the people may be thwarted by election
irregularities. While voting machines and permanent registration have
reduced wholesale fraud at the ballot box, election fraud still exists.
For example, the Honest Ballot Association figured that four million
fraudulent or invalid votes were cast in the 1964 elections, about 5.5
percent of the total. Many races that year were decided by a narrower
margin than 5 percent. Vote fraud is crime just the same as robbery
or murder. In fact, vote fraud is among the worst crimes, for it undermines the process through which we elect those who will enact and enforce our laws.

Good and fair government will be enhanced if the General Assembly tightens the controls on ineligible voting or impersonation. A statutory requirement that a voter sign not only his name but also his present address in the polling books would help eliminate fradulent voting
—as would imposing a stiff penalty for incorrect signing.

We must improve our governments as well as our electoral system.
It is crucial that we begin now to plan for our future and especially to
build the kind of local and urban communities that inspire rather than
crush man's spirit.

For too long the extent to which our towns became cities, and our
cities became expanding urban areas has gone unrealized. In the 1960
census Kentucky was considered a rural state: 55.5 percent of our
population lived on farms. The 1970 census will firmly emphasize
Kentucky's urban face, with more than 50 percent of its population
living in urban areas.

Our cities and local communities, with their suburbs, have the
chance to avoid repeating and indeed learning from the mistakes made
during the rise of our major cities. The challenge today is to enlist the

support and the cooperation of the state, the county, and the local governments to work together with each other and with the private sector to develop realistic programs that will overcome our social problems and improve the quality of life for all Kentuckians.

All major studies dealing with urban and local affairs have agreed on the absolute necessity of governmental planning. Recognizing this, by Executive Order in June 1968, I established the Kentucky Program Development Office to provide a coordinated statewide planning and implementation system which would place the development emphasis on a local and regional level.[1] Two major functions of this office are to coordinate the state technical assistance that is available to the local and urban levels and to help channel appropriate federal and state grants available for their use. *I am, therefore, urging the General Assembly to give full statutory agency powers to the Kentucky Program Development Office, as requested in H.B. 175 and H.B. 176.*[2]

In the first year of its operation, KPDO helped channel over $93 million in federal funds to various local communities throughout Kentucky. This year that figure was increased to over $109 million. It expects over the next two years to channel more than $300 million in federal funds in Kentucky. For a four-year investment of $6 million, Kentucky would receive a return of $500 million. Two widely publicized examples of coordinated technical assistance were the Pikeville project and the Southeastern Kentucky Health Demonstration Project, whereby the resources of local, state, and national public agencies and private enterprise all worked together. KPDO also coordinates planning of "Model Cities" projects, an undertaking that calls for a comprehensive approach to social, economic, and physical problems in the slums and blighted areas.

KPDO will provide imaginative planning and assistance for Kentucky urban areas needing aid in devising policies and programs for orderly growth.

In addition to the helpful role KPDO can play, however, it is still essential that urban and local areas initiate their own problem-solving mechanisms through existing governmental institutions. To facilitate the productive intergovernmental cooperation encouraged by the legislation in this message, it is important that state and local officials be able to serve on intergovernmental bodies so that they may provide responsible and direct representation for the people in matters of concern. *I am therefore proposing for deliberation legislation to reduce unreasonable restrictions in the area of incompatible offices and employments.*

Originally, incompatibility laws (Kentucky Constitution, Section 165 and KRS 61.080) were enacted on the generally sound premise that public officials who serve two masters may be unreasonably impaired from serving the public interest. This premise would seem to be inapplicable and unreasonably confining in those instances where service on intergovernmental bodies is compatible with the public interest. Such officials have valuable current experience and a direct concern for the problems that are likely to call for service on intergovernmental bodies.

No government can adequately develop programs for the future without an awareness of present economic realities and the potential available resources of the public and private sectors. With this need in mind, *I am proposing for consideration by the General Assembly the creation of a Governor's Council of Economic Advisors. This panel is patterned after its namesake in Washington, which for many years has provided creative national economic and technical analysis for the president of the United States.*

The Council will prepare and submit to the executive and legislative branches by November 1, 1971, a report providing long-range projections of the total economy of the state to cover at least the years 1975, 1980 and 1990. These five-, ten-, and twenty-year forecasts would involve socioeconomic activities such as personal income, labor force, employment, unemployment, profits, wages, and population.

Secondly, the Council is to submit yearly reports to the Governor and General Assembly analyzing economic trends during the preceding years and revealing business, industrial, and agricultural prospects and potentialities.

Thirdly, the Council is to help develop significant future growth potential for the Kentucky economy, such as additional agricultural crops and products, increased overseas markets, and new fields for economic expansion.

The Council shall be composed of eight voting members selected from the academic community; from the business, industrial, and labor communities; and from the general public. The Dean of the College of Business and Commerce of the University of Kentucky, the Commissioner of Revenue, the Commissioner of Finance, and the Director of the Budget shall be ex-officio members.

The Council of Economic Advisors can best be summarized as another attempt to activate the talents and resources of the private sector in harmony with state government for the public betterment. Once again we are also seeking the creative involvement of the academic community in a joint effort with state officials to move Kentucky ahead.

1. See Executive Order 68–489 (June 28, 1968), establishing the Kentucky Program Development Office.

2. An act "relating to the coordination of programs concerned with the development of state, intergovernmental cooperation, state planning, and providing for the establishment of the Kentucky Program Development Office" was signed by Governor Nunn on March 27, 1970. For further information see *Acts of the General Assembly of the Commonwealth of Kentucky, 1970*, Chapter 66 (H.B. 176), pp. 297–99.

STATE OF THE
COMMONWEALTH ADDRESS
Kentucky Press Association
Louisville / January 22, 1971

Two years ago I suggested that this mid-winter meeting of the Kentucky Press Association would be an appropriate biennial forum in which the state of our Commonwealth could be discussed. Thank you for allowing me to begin what I believe can be a helpful custom for Kentucky governors and for the people.

The selection of this meeting was not a random choice. It was chosen with care out of a sincere respect for the "Fourth Estate." I am aware of the burdensome responsibilities of your profession and I am impressed with the manner, with few exceptions, in which you carry out those responsibilities.

Ours is a better Commonwealth today, because for 102 years of service through this organization, newspapermen and women have believed their profession to be an instrument of truth and information, rather than distortion and selfish manipulation. And they have had the courage to follow that conviction. Never in our history, as a state, as a nation, has it been more important than now that the news media honor this tradition. These are times when confusion, frustration, and doubt cloud the minds of the public as they view some, if not all, of our basic institutions. As one of our most honored institutions, this could hardly come as a surprise to the newspaper industry. The press has come in for its share of criticism recently. You, like those in government, in religion, in education, in law enforcement, and

other of our basic institutions should not fail to respond to this challenge. This should be a period for honest self-examination, a time for
reappraisal by each of you of the role, the function, and the performance of the press. And above all else, it should be a time to defend
your profession against those who jeopardize it, regardless whether
they are members of the press or outsiders.

Today as we discuss the state of the Commonwealth, it is a time to
speak of success and achievement. For the present state of our Commonwealth is one of achievement; of vigorous, visible progress; of
documented and unconcealed financial stability; and vast social improvement.

This picture of the present takes on added meaning against a backdrop of recent history. The stark reality of Kentucky's economic problems; the depressing state of vital human programs; the stagnation of
planning for physical improvements, were revealed to the people of
this Commonwealth just three years ago. Plans, hopes, promises, and
priorities were drastically altered by the dark circumstances that
greeted a new administration dedicated to constructive change.

What we found was a rapidly crumbling financial foundation; a
foundation jeopardized by an immediate deficit of $36 million and an
impending deficit that could have reached $100 million in the next
biennium. On this foundation lay the aspirations for health and happiness of literally hundreds of thousands of Kentuckians. On this foundation rested the hopes of those who turned to us for assistance. We
could not turn away. On this foundation rested the opportunities of
the young for better education, of the elderly for earned comfort and
deserved freedom from loneliness.

It is against this dramatic backdrop of recent history that we must
today assess Kentucky's present status. Mindful of the crisis from
which we emerged, aware of the courage and the sacrifice required to
bring us to this moment, I tell you: The state of the Commonwealth
today is one of confidence, not despair; one of vigorous advancement,
not retreat; one of financial strength, not fiscal uncertainty; one of
social progress, not social denial; and finally, one of unlimited potential, not hopelessness. And there is brand new, reassuring evidence to
back up that assessment.

You may recall that in July of 1970, the economic situation dictated
a downward revision of the official state revenue estimate on which
Kentucky's General Fund budget is predicated. At that time, the estimate was reduced from $557 million to $553 million for this fiscal year.

Accordingly, the General Fund budget also was immediately reduced.
To avoid a deficit, a 1.1 percent reduction in the level of spending was

put into effect with equal application to all state agencies. The decision to act promptly, rather than hide from reality, reflects the lesson inflicted upon Kentucky in 1967. By immediately reducing the level of spending last summer when the first signs of economic change appeared, state agencies were able to absorb the impact over an eleven-month period. They were spared the agony experienced three years earlier when a cutback four times greater had to be absorbed in half the time. That decision should also underscore our determination and our commitment to do all that is necessary, so that we might entrust to Kentucky's next governor a Commonwealth unencumbered by fiscal misery.

Revenue experts in the government will confirm this afternoon that Kentucky is moving out of a period of economic uncertainty that has been felt throughout the nation in recent months. Results of a careful study of present indicators persuade us that the Kentucky economy is moving ahead to a good 1971. In fact, economists are now forecasting that personal income, the measure of a state's economic activity, will show a solid 6.2 percent increase over fiscal 1970.

Recent actions by the Federal Reserve Bank to ease interest rates, along with the recent announcement by the president to ease depreciation guidelines, add up to a strengthening of confidence in the economy in the months ahead. This augurs well for business investment, stabilization of employment, and increased consumer buying. Accordingly, this augurs well for the Commonwealth's revenue program, the General Fund, and the Road Fund.

In fact, the Department of Revenue now advises that more General Fund revenue may be realized than had originally been estimated during budget preparations in 1969. The original estimate of $172 million for the Road Fund remains unchanged. However, the monthly revenue report to be released this afternoon will show General Fund revenues for the first six months of the current fiscal year running ahead of the official estimate that was revised downward by $4 million at the start of this fiscal year. Therefore, the official revenue estimate is being readjusted to $560 million for the current fiscal year. This welcome news means that the General Fund budget reductions ordered last August can be restored.

Since the general economic picture in Kentucky has improved, I am pleased that we can return to the original expenditure levels set by the Legislature. However, I am also aware of the governmental tendency to spend every available dollar, sometimes simply because it is *available* and not because it is *needed*. Therefore, I have today instructed the state Budget Director to continue his careful examination of the spending patterns of each state agency and to exercise stringent control and vigilance over the funds being restored to be sure that each agency has a genuine need for every dollar invested. This cautious approach takes notice of the fact that revenue expectations for the year are estimates and sound management of the people's revenue dictates that we go slow at this point.

While today's announcement has immediate application to the present, its ramifications are no less crucial to the future of our Commonwealth.

We are encouraged that in a time of economic uncertainty in our nation, Kentucky's economy has shown uncommon stability and its revenue program has shown unusual strength. The reasons are evident. First, we are fortunate in Kentucky to have a diversified economy, an economy bolstered by record growth in both agriculture and industrial development in recent years.

In 1969, Kentucky farmers realized a gross income of over a billion dollars for the first time in history. We are advised that the gross income figure will again reach that level for 1970, despite the heavy toll of the corn blight experienced in Kentucky last season.

At the same time this milestone in agricultural progress was being observed, Kentucky also began to set new marks in industrial expansion. In less than three years, over a billion dollars was invested by industry in Kentucky's new climate of confidence and progress. This new record was achieved despite the loss of industrial bond financing privileges, rising inflation, high interest rates, and scarcity of capital.

The second reason for Kentucky's sound economic position today rests with our broad-based, non-discriminatory tax system, a system carefully developed three years ago when changes were being made in the revenue program.

Both of these elements are essential to any plans or hopes we may have for the prolonged growth and development of this state. They are encouraging signs for the present. But more importantly, they form strong, durable foundations for an even brighter future.

There are other signs of encouragement that lead us to take a positive view of the state of our Commonwealth. We are enthused that state government has responded to innovation and change during the past three years. After three years of sometimes frustrating effort, there are indications today that the tide of bureaucracy has in some instances been stemmed, if not reversed. For instance, during the first eight years of the decade of the sixties, the number of employees on the state payroll increased an average of 5.6 percent each year. We have cut that increase almost in half the past two years, despite the fact that the

Kentucky of today has more state parks to operate, more highways to maintain, more vocational schools to operate, more juvenile facilities to oversee, and far more federally sponsored programs to administer.

Modern personnel practices have been adopted. Employee benefits have been increased and incentives have been added. We are competing for the skilled, trained, and professional manpower that is needed to operate a three-billion-dollar business.

The upgrading of our personnel situation is but one of the necessary tasks we have begun. Throughout the various agencies a broad campaign is being waged to improve and sharpen the management tools of government. The complex demands upon modern-day government, in addition to requiring tremendous financial resources, also require competence of those in government and capability of the instruments of service at the government's disposal.

Again, I want to personally extend my gratitude and my commendations to the Efficiency Task Force for their help at the beginning of this administration. Their findings pointed out areas of weakness in the management of state government. All of us are indebted to this group of concerned citizens who unselfishly gave their time and talent to an effort that will save the taxpayers of Kentucky millions of dollars for each year their suggestions are followed.

The far-reaching impact of their service is best demonstrated when we examine the recommendation to establish an electronic data processing system. The Task Force found that little regard had been given to long-range needs in this highly specialized, technical, and crucial field. Tax dollars had been committed for an extravagant, fragmented, short-sighted, and ineffective computer program. The Task Force noted in its report that, for the most part, "the departments and agencies have built data systems with an eye to accommodate only their own needs."[1]

Today, at their suggestion, and at a predicted savings of over four million dollars the next few years, we are developing a consolidated computer system that will quickly retrieve information vital to efficient management and planning. What we are striving for is a sound management system, better coordination of programs, prevention of waste and duplication, and creation of a planned approach to progress. By the end of this administration, Kentucky will have at its service the most sophisticated data system to be found in state governments anywhere in the nation. It is being called the Kentucky Management Information System and we are proud of the fact that several states as well as a number of federal agencies are now imitating the start we have made.

Accounting experts and management analysts have called this system the most progressive step toward real cost accounting and systemized fiscal management ever taken in the Commonwealth of Kentucky. Its necessity and its application are immediate. For instance, one of the reasons the scope of planning in previous years has been so limited was because so little information was available from which to draw long-range plans. The budget process has been an inexact process in some notable areas, such as higher education. At this moment, there is no common system among our colleges and universities to determine the cost of educating their respective students. If we are to be accountable, and I believe we should be, then we must devise an effective accounting system. The Kentucky Management Information System, for the first time, should give us that capability.

The spin-off effect of such a system has tremendous potential. Without question, it will give Kentucky a leg up in the competition for federal funds. This will take on added significance in view of plans which will be discussed tonight by President Nixon in his State of the Union address. I look forward to his disclosure tonight of the domestic program that will be put before the Ninety-Second Congress.

The president's continued support of a revenue sharing plan is most encouraging to those of us on the state level who are being squeezed between federal preeemption of revenue sources and the constant demand for matching funds in newly created federal programs.

Let me assure each of you that Kentucky is well-equipped to seize the opportunity of revenue sharing. One of the first acts of this administration was to designate the Kentucky Program Development Office as this state's single planning agency. It is the specific liaison agency between state and local communities and the federal government. With the help of this agency, we have been able to generate well in excess of $335 million in federal grants and matching funds in three years. Before the end of this administration, that figure will have risen past the half-billion-dollar mark.

Through better management practices, through constant efforts to maximize our resources by the use of federal funds, through creative innovations in the use of state revenues, and with the assistance and growing confidence of the people of Kentucky, I am pleased to report to you today a series of related developments and accomplishments that have dramatically changed the state of our Commonwealth the past thirty-six months. To recite this record in many specific details would be unnecessary, because the changes already are apparent throughout the state.

Your children perhaps attend one of the new or remodeled schools being built in every one of Kentucky's 193 education districts as the result of the first increase in capital outlay allowances in eight years.

Their teachers are better paid by approximately fifteen hundred dollars. Their learning materials have been improved and expanded by the first increase in classroom operating funds in eight years. They travel to school and you go about your business safer, quicker, and more conveniently today because of the most massive highway construction program in the history of the state.

The rural road program has been increased by 77 percent. The County Road Aid fund has been increased by 78.4 percent. More than 3,000 miles of new, blacktopped roads have been constructed. County roads have been improved and increased by 7,700 miles through state projects. And the road program will be expanded even further during the coming months. A 254-mile parkway system now under construction will provide a corridor of opportunity from Henderson in western Kentucky to Hazard in eastern Kentucky. With the addition of 310 new miles of Interstate Highways, Kentucky has become the "crossroads of America."

As indicated earlier by the report of record growth to billion-dollar levels, both agriculture and industry have responded dramatically to the stimulation of this new and growing system of safe, modern highways. Over 115,000 persons are being trained each year in our expanded system of vocational schools. And a positive plan of welfare reform is being implemented to help Kentuckians escape from the relief rolls and get on payrolls. During the last session of the General Assembly we passed a plan which will provide welfare to those who can't work and deny welfare to those who won't work.

There are other changes which have helped improve the quality of life enjoyed by our citizens. Our natural and human resources are being protected better than at any time in modern history. The air we breathe, the water we drink, the scenic beauty that surrounds us here in Kentucky is being guarded by an enforced policy of protection and correction. The strict, but reasonable application of pollution and surface mining regulations has fostered a new spirit of cooperation between those who guard the land and those who use the land.

In addition, our state has been firmly established as the recreational heartland of mid-America. In three years, the state parks system has been expanded by 50 percent. At the same time, we have embarked upon a comprehensive community recreational plan to keep Kentucky families together. We are concentrating on family recreational needs with the addition of camping facilities at the state parks and establishment of sixty-two new community parks, many of which are located near the urban areas too long neglected in the past.

These are but a few of the changes through which we have endeavored to restore a feeling of confidence and trust in state government. Through these new programs, we have tried to say that government in Kentucky is capable of achievement and is courageous enough to fulfill its responsibilities and its obligations to the people. We have tried to discern between political expediency and public service. We have tried to do not just those things which would guarantee the most personal satisfaction or win the most partisan approval, but those things we felt to be in the greatest public interest.

The complexities and perplexities of our time call for cooperation of government with the people, not alienation of government from the people. It is in that spirit—one of partnership, not partisanship; of achievement, not procrastination—that I have considered the decision to call a special session of the General Assembly to deal with reapportionment.

I have been warned repeatedly over the past year of the political jeopardy to which a governor subjects himself by calling a special session of the Legislature in the face of impending campaigns. And I am well aware of the polluted political atmosphere that is beginning to spread across our state this election year.

But I believe that if we are to keep pace, if we are to preserve our commitments to public service, if we are to continue making progress, if we are to build the people's confidence in the equity and goodness of their government, then we must be willing to look beyond the next election and look past the partisan political battles that some endlessly wage. We must look into the oncoming years and even into the next century. Because future generations will judge us not on the basis of whether we win elections. They will judge us on the courage and the determination with which we discharge the responsibilities imposed on us by the people we serve.

Equal, effective representation is the hope and the implied promise of our system of government. Census figures have clearly proven the need for readjustment if our Legislature is to extend that hope to the people. The courts, likewise, have now spoken on this issue with equal clarity. And as promised a year ago, I will honor my obligation to provide the General Assembly an opportunity to place Kentucky in conformity with the law on reapportionment. As of today it is my intention to call the people's branch of government into Special Legislative Session on February 25. As of now, the sole purpose of the special session will be to consider reapportionment of state legislative districts.

By announcing the anticipated date more than one month in advance, it is our intention to provide the Legislature adequate time to prepare a plan that will hopefully be ready for presentation on the first day of the session. During the past several months, the Legislative Research Commission has been at work preparing the interim committees of both the House and Senate for the task of reapportionment. With the date of the session now fixed, it is my hope that these committees will diligently approach the problem in the time between now and February 25.

In addition to having time to prepare a plan, I am confident that the Legislature also has been given adequate time, once the session begins, to fully consider and pass a fair, equitable, and legal reapportionment law well before the filing deadline for candidates in multi-county legislative districts.

Last year, at the insistence and with the full cooperation of the Executive Branch, the members of the 1970 General Assembly established a new benchmark of legislative independence in Kentucky. During this special session we are providing an opportunity for that branch of government to achieve a new milestone in legislative maturity. How the members of the Legislature respond to this opportunity may well decide, for better or for worse, the course of our government and our Commonwealth for the remainder of this decade.

I invite them, I urge them to seize this opportunity for partnership in the continuing effort to build our Commonwealth up from its present foundation of solid achievement, of dramatic progress, of documented financial strength, and of social improvement to even greater heights in the future.

---

1. Kentucky Efficiency Task Force, *Kentucky Efficiency Task Force Report and Recommendations, 1968* (n.p., 1968), p. 20.

EXTRAORDINARY SESSION
OF THE KENTUCKY
GENERAL ASSEMBLY
Frankfort / February 25, 1971

IN order that the citizens of Kentucky might, as nearly as possible, be equally represented in the affairs of legislative government, our con-

stitution provides that each ten years the General Assembly shall re-
district itself to so secure the populace. The courts have affirmed the
wisdom of that provision.

Despite the clarity of that mandate, the convening of this special
session represents only the second time since 1892 that the Legislature
has been voluntarily summoned to consider the equitable reapportionment of Kentucky's legislative districts.[1] Tonight, for only the second
time since the adoption of the present constitution, the legally complex
and politically quarrelsome task of reapportionment in special session
and as ordained by the constitution is being willingly, openly, and voluntarily undertaken, rather than at the point of a judicial pen or under
the duress of legal action. Your deliberations should be conducted in
that same spirit. I trust that this is your intention, as evidenced so
clearly and so commendably by the efforts which reportedly have been
put forth to prepare for this session.

Let me publicly pay tribute and congratulate those of you who have
made such an impressive effort toward the creation of an acceptable
and workable plan of reapportionment. May I also implore you not
to squander the efforts and dollars invested in this effort toward constitutional compliance. In the interest of the people that you represent,
I ask that you not resort to the desperate patterns of selfish factionalism
and partisanship that some have predicted for this session. Instead,
you are encouraged to put an end, once and for all, to the old political
patterns, and to signal the beginning of an even brighter era of responsible, courageous, enlightened legislative action.

This goal, so long aspired, but so long denied to the people of Kentucky, is now within reach. I have steadfastly believed you could attain
this goal. It was on the strength of that belief that I have endorsed a
number of proposals designed to strengthen the people's branch of
government and free it from the heavy yoke imposed by some of the
previous governors. For example, during the last three years your
interim committees were fully financed for the first time and you were
permitted to draft your own legislative budget.

Clearly, what we have seen in Kentucky the past three years has
been the establishment of a new benchmark of legislative independence
by the General Assembly. In keeping with that progressive trend, tonight I pledge to you and to all Kentuckians that legislative independence without executive interference will be the hallmark of this special
session.

In return, the people of Kentucky have a right to expect that your
time and their money will not be wasted on partisan gerrymandering.

If blatantly political and discriminatory measures are enacted, they will only sabotage the vital mission of this Assembly and needlessly involve the executive and judicial branches of government in a matter that is uniquely yours to resolve.

I believe that you are in a much better position to reapportion your own districts than even the most competent and impartial court. You have at your disposal, and in your midst, sufficient combined legal talent to know the judicial requirements of a fair and equitable reapportionment plan. In addition, certainly you have been advised on the many judicial precedents on redistricting. They should be of help in illuminating your course of action.

It should be perfectly clear that if these guidelines are flagrantly abused, if a plan is devised that is obviously political in nature, and if any group or any section of our state is discriminated against, *that plan will be struck down*. Any miscalculation of this can only be construed as deliberate denial of the right of our people to equal representation.

With diligence in approaching this task, with fidelity to the reassuring pattern of responsible action that has been established thus far, and with courage marking your pursuit of an equitable solution to this difficult problem, I am confident that you can seize this truly unique opportunity to acquit yourselves with honor as servants of the people.

Knowing you are aware of the fact that each day of this special session costs between eight and eleven thousand dollars, and knowing you are anxious to complete this task at a minimum cost and in such time that you can soon return to your families and businesses, I wish you Godspeed in your deliberations.

---

1. On February 22, 1971, Governor Nunn issued the following proclamation:

TO THE MEMBERS OF THE GENERAL ASSEMBLY OF THE
COMMONWEALTH OF KENTUCKY AND TO ALL TO WHOM
THESE PRESENTS SHALL COME:

Pursuant to the power vested in me by Section 80 of the Constitution of Kentucky to convene the General Assembly into Extraordinary Session, I, LOUIE B. NUNN, Governor of Kentucky, do issue this, my proclamation, convening the General Assembly of Kentucky in Extraordinary Session at the seat of government at Frankfort, Kentucky, at 7:00 P.M., E.S.T., on Thursday, February 25, 1971, for the purpose of considering the following subject:

(1) To reapportion the General Assembly of Kentucky in conformity with the Constitution of the United States, the Kentucky Constitution and re-

cent court decisions, using as a basis the population figures resulting from the 1970 census.

The members of the General Assembly in accordance with this proclamation will assemble in Extraordinary Session at the seat of government at Frankfort, Kentucky, on the day, date, and at the time above written, to consider the subject herein mentioned and only said subject and only to the extent mentioned in this proclamation.

PUBLIC ADDRESSES

LEGISLATIVE CONFERENCE
Kentucky Dam Village State Park
Gilbertsville / December 18, 1967

LADIES and gentlemen, I want to be frank with you. I know that what we do in the next three months will be exceedingly important to the future of the people of Kentucky, as well as to the future of you and me. So it is extremely important that we know and understand each other, that I know your problems and desires, that you know mine, and that together we serve the Commonwealth in common purpose.

For myself, I have only one mission, and that is to administer the affairs of Kentucky as wisely and efficiently as it is within my power to do. I have a deep concern for Kentucky and her people, and I know that, if you did not share this concern with me, you would not be here. Many of you I know well, others I soon will know well, and that you are here is comforting to me.

I will not take up your time tonight with trifles. This is not a time for trifles. It is a time, instead, for serious study and statesmanship. Those of you who have been here before know from your own depth of experience that the state is in financial difficulty. Those of you who have not been here before have been told this by your newspapers and radio and television. The reports have not been exaggerated. Kentucky faces a financial crisis, the magnitude of which we still have not fully determined. It was not until late last week that adequate funds became available to meet the December payroll. There is a twenty-four-million-dollar deficit and revenue is fifteen million dollars under estimates. And there are other problems.

The questions raised by an off-again-on-again federal tax increase have a far-reaching effect on our own revenue. No businessman or government official can foretell with any degree of exactness the status of the economy six months from now. Nor can anyone foretell the effect of a federal tax in computing Kentucky income tax or the effect of reduced purchasing power on the sales tax.

On the expenditure side we are making a sincere effort to find areas where savings can be achieved. The Kentucky Efficiency Task Force, which is already functioning, is charged with examining each department of state government with an eye toward potential economy measures. It is enough to say now that we must tighten our belts, that we must take every step possible to economize and to extract the ultimate benefit from each tax dollar. This is not a situation with which any of us should play politics. There is far too much at stake for that.

Without any doubt the resolution of our difficulties and the progress all of us desire for Kentucky will depend on our patient understanding of each other. I cannot emphasize too strongly my desire to work closely with you. It must be evident by this time that I have demonstrated a cooperative attitude and that I have in mind only what is best for the Commonwealth. I am certain that you will respond to your responsibilities in the same fashion.

There will be an open door policy in my office to help implement the closeness and cooperation I so sincerely seek. Mr. Tom Emberton, one of my administrative assistants, will be assigned from the Governor's Office to assist you.[1] At any time before and during the General Assembly, each of you will have priority to my office. If there are other visitors waiting, you will not have to wait with them. Explain your mission to Tom, and he will see that you see me as soon as practically possible.

You are familiar with the 175th anniversary celebration this year of Kentucky's statehood. The philosophy expressed so well in our motto, "united we stand, divided we fall," has resulted in whatever progress we have made through the years. Cooperative endeavor was paramount in the opening of the frontier, in the clearing of the land, and in the establishment of new settlements and in building a new state. This same cooperative philosophy has continued through the years to be a dominant ingredient in the development of progressive advancement. Only when there is cooperation is there real progress.

We all are interested in new and expanded industry. We all are interested in improving agricultural programs, because agriculture still is the biggest business in Kentucky. And we all want to continue to expand and improve the tourist industry.

From public health and public safety to labor and libraries, from mines and minerals to military affairs, and with all the other agencies of state government, our motivation should be what is best for all Kentuckians.

Kentucky's economic development can be much more readily achieved, much more easily attained, by a meeting of minds, by the application of all of our individual talents, and certainly by our sincere cooperation, one with another.

This is not a time for political bickering, for individual greed, or for selfish personal ambitions. This is a time for pulling together, for united effort toward the common good. The areas of agreement are wide; the areas of disagreement are usually narrow and selfish. There will be differences of opinion, of course. But they will be honorable differences, and they will be worked out for the common good, instead of being wrangled over for no one's good. You will on occasion disagree with me, and I will on occasion disagree with you, but if we honestly try to reason things out, the entire Commonwealth will benefit from our efforts.

You represent separate House and Senate districts, of course, but to a larger extent you represent all Kentuckians. And I, too, represent all Kentuckians, Kentuckians of both parties, of all colors and creeds. There is no doubt in my mind that together we can give this state a government of which it can be proud. There is no doubt in my mind but that we will do just that.

---

1. Thomas D. Emberton (1933–   ), Monroe County; executive administrative assistant to Governor Louie B. Nunn (1967–1968); member, Public Service Commission (1968–1970); unsuccessful Republican candidate for governor (1971). Department of Public Information biographical files and Mary Ann Reynolds, Governor Nunn's staff, August 31, 1971.

GOVERNOR'S CONFERENCE
ON TRAVEL AND TOURISM
Louisville / February 6, 1968

It's a real privilege to have you here for this conference and let me thank you personally for coming.[1] I am confident that considerable mutual benefit will come out of our meeting here.

Now we recognize the tourist as a valuable friend and we know that if we treat him properly he will come back. He wants to see our beautiful scenery, visit our points of interest and enjoy our lakes and streams and beaches. It's up to us to get him to come to Kentucky in the first place; to make his visit as thoroughly enjoyable and satisfying as we possibly can; and to send him away so pleased that he will not only want to come back, but he will also tell his friends about Kentucky and urge them to visit us.

Our approach to the potential visitors who live beyond our borders and the way we treat them when they get here are our principal concerns today. In Kentucky we have an infinite variety of attractions, perhaps more than any other state. We don't have to invent legends or indulge in phony promotions. We have the genuine article in abundance. People want to visit us. John Gunther, in his book *Inside USA*, named Kentucky as the state most Americans want to visit. More than one-third of all Americans live within a day's drive of our border. And we must do an even better job of bringing visitors here. We have scarcely scratched the real potential. We can increase out-of-state visitation beyond anything we have dreamed so far. If we all work together we will certainly do it! We must be prepared to utilize our fullest advantages.

This is as good a time as any to point out one of the most important aspects of the new look that is apparent in Kentucky. Kentuckians have worked together to create one of the finest state parks systems in the nation. The vacation resort parks have been well promoted and they are outstandingly successful. But let us not forget that they are really our show windows. They are the bright, glittering signs with which we entice people to visit our state. In other words, I look on them as the means, not the end. You will find in the months to come that, promotionwise, although our parks will not be neglected, there will be a far stronger accent on privately owned facilities. That's part of the new look. You'll find that your state government is 100 percent in favor of private enterprise and that it will do everything in its power to promote private enterprise. For example, and this is a small thing, but it serves to indicate how your state government is now thinking, we have had complaints from motel owners near state parks that they do not get cooperation from that particular park. When that park has to turn people away, they do not suggest trying such and such a motel, perhaps just down the road a way. Well, that will no longer be true. Commissioner Gable has assured me that the desk personnel at every state park lodge will give the disappointed traveler every help in securing accommodations, even to keeping in touch with neighboring motels regarding what rooms they have available.[2] This is plain common business sense. The parks are owned by all Kentuckians, including motel and restaurant owners, and the parks are here, among other reasons, to boost Kentucky's economy.

A healthy, expanding economy is one goal for which all Kentuckians strive. We must look on the state economy in much the same way a physician regards his patient's bloodstream. If it falters, the whole body sickens. And one of the most vital factors in our state economy is the travel industry. The size and importance of the travel industry, and this covers all forms of tourism, of course, is really impressive. It is centered in just under fifteen thousand retail establishments. They include restaurants, hotels and motels, transportation facilities, recreation and automobile services. And, excluding agriculture, they comprise one out of every five business firms in the state.

Now there is one difference in your state government's perspective and that of the private operator. These viewpoints, however, are not in conflict. The owner of a restaurant or a motel or a filling station is not too concerned about from where his customers come. They can all be his neighbors or his near neighbors, and he is perfectly happy as long as he gets the volume and it is profitable.

And this is fine, of course. Every merchant operating at a profit is an economic asset to Kentucky. But we have to survey the horizon behind and beyond that merchant. Your state government has to be concerned with that part of the merchant's prosperity that comes from other states. It's new money that we are after. Money that comes to us from other states is like a transfusion to that vital bloodstream of which I spoke a moment ago.

If I walk into your store and buy a hat for $11.00 you make a fair profit on it and the state gets $.33 in sales tax. The difference is that if I come from another state and buy that hat from you, the economy of Kentucky is actually richer by $11.33. There's $11.33 of new money that wasn't in Kentucky before the purchase. The reason I use the figure $11.33 is that it is just about what each visitor from out of state is worth to Kentucky. Multiply that average by the number of people we can induce to visit us and we begin to get an idea of the size of our travel industry and of its value to the state.

Right here, behind this curtain, is a magic number. It's one that only a handful of people have seen. It's a figure from the brand new Copeland report[3] on Kentucky's travel industry in 1967.

I'll tell you that in 1966 the spending in Kentucky by out-of-state visitors totaled $295 million. That was the biggest such figure for any year in Kentucky's history. Are you wondering what this new figure is? It is $316 million!

That's the spending of twenty-eight million out-of-state visitors, two million more people than came to us in 1966. So it's plain for everyone to see that our travel industry is of major importance to Kentucky. And it benefits every single Kentuckian, not just filling stations and restaurants and motels. This money spreads into every corner of the economy. Of the $316 million that the out-of-state tourists left with us in 1967, $26 million came into the state treasury in the form of taxes. This is a massive transfusion that we desperately need.

I intend to do everything in the power of our state government to increase this tourist influx.

The $26 million that the state treasury received from out-of-state visitors in 1967 is tremendously important, of course. But it is no more important than the distribution of the balance of the $316-million transfusion.

I do not like to spout out a lot of figures and statistics that people cannot remember anyway. But I think you'll be interested in knowing how the tourist's dollar breaks up in its first generation of spending. When the visitor spends a dollar over the counter, the store owner, or whatever the point of sale is, retains about a dime. Ninety cents goes to pay the help, rent, utilities, and other operating expenses. Around thirty-eight cents goes to wholesalers and suppliers of one kind or another. Thirty-four cents is paid out in personal income. That means payrolls and the spendable income of the proprietor. The remaining nine cents goes to state, county, and municipal taxes. Just think what that thirty-four cents means to Kentucky! It adds up to $107 million for 1967 and this year will almost certainly be higher.

That $107 million went into a second generation of spending. It went for groceries, car payments, rent, mortgage payments, clothing, and the thousand and one other expenses of modern life. And wherever one of those dollars is spent, it produces another three cents for the state treasury. It pays wages of other clerks and workers and proprietors, and they in turn spend their disposable income, generating more business and more profit with each turnover.

The reason I am citing these figures and stressing the money aspect of the travel business is that I want each of us to take away from this conference a vivid sense of the importance of our activities to the economic health of Kentucky. I want you to be as aware of your importance as we in state government are.

---

1. Representatives from over 250 businesses and interested groups attended the Governor's Conference designed to increase tourism in Kentucky. Governor Nunn's files.

2. Robert E. Gable (1934–), commissioner, Department of Parks (1967–1970); director, Kentucky Travel Council (1969–1970); member, Association of Southeastern State Park Directors, vice president (1969–1970). Gable, a corporation executive, was born in New York City and resides in Stearns. *Who's Who in the South and Southwest, 1971–72,* 12th ed. (Chicago, 1971), p. 216.

3. The Copeland report was a study of the tourist and travel industry in Kentucky commissioned by the Tourist and Travel Division, Department of

Public Information. The report stated that during 1967 visitors to Kentucky spent $316 million, which was $21 million more than was spent in 1966, a 7 percent increase. Lewis C. Copeland, *Travel Survey in Kentucky, 1967* (Frankfort, 1967).

FARM-CITY COMMITTEE
AND THE KENTUCKY
DEVELOPMENT COMMITTEE
Lexington / February 15, 1968

IT is a pleasant experience for me to visit with you at this combined banquet of the 14th annual Farm-City Committee and the Kentucky Development Committee. Your two groups have a common goal toward building a better Kentucky and I share with you this purpose. Never before in our history has it been so important for us to have better relations and understanding between our rural and urban people as today. There is no longer any real separation between city and country with highways now crisscrossing our state in every direction.

Never before has it been so important and necessary for us to use every means at our command to properly develop and plan how we are going to conserve and wisely use our land and natural resources. I know of no one problem that is greater to mankind today, with its tremendous growth in population, than that of proper planning for the future. Certainly, one cannot travel the highways today or visit our cities and see the growth in subdivisions and apartment housing, and not realize that we must plan ahead for growth of the future.

We in Kentucky are adequately blessed with both human and natural resources, and we must plan how to use both of these resources wisely. One of the greatest blessings of this state is that we are not torn by the many critical problems that plague other sections of the country: water shortage, stifling air pollution, too many people, haphazard growth, racial strife, and lack of convenient recreation opportunities. While some of these problems exist in some measure, they exist on a much smaller scale and are much more manageable than they may be in many other states. And we do have time to prepare to cope with them. But since we do have problems facing us with our growth of the future, and since we in this state are in a position to do some proper planning for the future, it is time for our leaders, singly or in a concerted effort, to lay the groundwork for our future needs.

From the earliest days and extending to the present, we in these United States have fostered the institution of private property, especially the private ownership of homes, farms, and land. Land ownership was a key incentive in the drive of western settlement. The vast empire of land in the public domain was sliced up and federal ownership was reduced as a matter of national policy. American pioneers with axe and plow and cattle moved over the Appalachians, across the prairies and plains, and all the way to the Pacific to stake out and populate the heart of our continent. We became, predominantly, a nation of landowning farmers.

Today, close to three-quarters of all the land in our nation is owned by private citizens. More than the land itself is involved in this ownership pattern. With the land are all the interrelated resources of timber, game, fish, wildlife, and most of the water. The meaning of this is clear. Individual citizens control most of the American countryside, landscape, and natural resources. Here on this privately owned land is where the biggest and most difficult job of stewardship and conservation is being performed, and where, by necessity, it will have to be performed in the future.

If we are to leave to future Kentuckians the kind of state they are entitled to, dedicated men and women must assume leadership in planning how to conserve and develop our natural resources, how to make our towns and cities a better place to live, and how to provide adequate recreation areas. Recreation today is America's second most time-consuming activity, only sleep takes more than the 400 billion man-hours spent annually at play by the United States population. It is also safe to say that tourism today is probably the only universal industry that has the interest and participation of virtually every country of the world, both free and communistic, most certainly every state, and virtually every single area in this nation.

Kentucky can be one of the leading tourist states. We have all the advantages that most tourists look for: good highways; plenty of water for fishing, boating, and swimming; a fine park system, among the best in the nation; and vast areas of open space. Kentucky is within one day's driving distance of more than 90 percent of this nation's population. Tourism, recreation, and leisure are all tied together and they place an even greater demand and give added economic justification for conservation and beautification.

Our recreation system is responsive to an illness in American society: space-starved cities and a job-starved countryside. This is one of the reasons why I have requested of the General Assembly appropriations that will allow us to match federal and local pledges for development of more community parks and recreation areas. We have crowded 140 million Americans, 7 out of 10 persons, on just 1 percent of our land and the result is urban blight. On the other hand, only 57 million people, 3 out of 10, live on 99 percent of our land, with a double share of the nation's poverty. Worse still, if present trends continue in the next 25 years, 100 million additional Americans will be added to the 140 million already in our cities and suburbs, enough more people in the cities to stack 13 more New Yorks on the present New York.

We must plan for better land use in our growing cities in Kentucky. They must have room for outdoor recreation, not only for their own people, but for visitors. They must have trees and grass, and freshly developed lakes and reservoirs. Our cities must have space for the good life. It is a proper function of the state to encourage this. The effectiveness of recreation services is, and will be, determined to a great degree by how many or how few interested persons, groups, communities, and areas are aware of their existence and of their potential.

Outdoor recreation offers a truly exciting opportunity, not only to supply a much needed service for all Kentuckians, both urban and rural, but to contribute markedly to the revitalization of the rural economy. Recreation areas create many jobs, bring new money into the community, and improve the economy of the entire state. In the past we have left all the problems of natural resource development and conservation to government, both state and federal. But the time has come when all citizens must accept their responsibilities to see that our children and our children's children are provided with all the benefits from our natural resources they are entitled to. Public apathy is the greatest enemy of conservation.

Resource stewardship in this final third of the twentieth century is a demanding challenge to all Kentuckians, testing whether we as a State and as individuals are still willing and able to function actively and intelligently for the common good. All of us have high stakes in the outcome. Imposing as this resource stewardship responsibility is, God does not expect the impossible from you and me. He asks and expects only what is reasonable and right. He asks and expects that each among us will use the gifts he has given us, gifts of intellect and energy, and spirit and enterprise, to share in his plan for a more fruitful, better world.

We are provided with a wealth of resources, in trust, to use and develop. Each among us benefits from the lands and waters, the forests, the fish, and wildlife. Together we use them in our search for a fuller life. But each of us, individually, is accountable for his own use, or misuse, of these resources.

We are no longer a state divided into rural people and urban people. What benefits one benefits the other. What hurts one hurts the other. So we must all learn to work together—local, county and state government; businessmen and farmers; and rural and urban citizens—all dedicated to the common goal of building a greater Kentucky.

GOVERNOR'S CONFERENCE ON FORESTRY
Lexington / February 27, 1968

IT gives me great pleasure to meet with this distinguished group of foresters and conservationists. I wish to thank each of your speakers for taking time from their busy schedules to come here and discuss some of the problems we must solve if forestry is to play a more vital role in the State's economic growth.

I am here tonight to tell you that my administration is dead serious about continuing and strengthening the State's forestry program. I have long been convinced of our need to do everything in our power to make Kentucky's nearly twelve million acres of forest land produce to full potential, and I will do what I can to see it done.

Twenty-four years ago today the Kentucky Division of Forestry was operating on a state appropriation of $20 thousand a year. The total budget, including state, private, and federal funds, was less than $75 thousand. With these meager funds token fire protection was provided for about two million acres of forest in parts of sixteen counties. A thirteen acre nursery in Jefferson County, on land reclaimed from a swamp, produced about 500 thousand seedlings a year. Two state forests totaling 16 thousand acres were operated as demonstrations of good forestry.

But then public interest and legislative support began to grow. In 1944 the state appropriation was increased to $50 thousand a year; in 1946 to $75 thousand. In my own budget I have requested more than

$1.7 million for each of the next two years. Fire prevention has been extended to nearly 11 million forested acres, and three modern nurseries can produce up to 40 million seedlings annually for reforestation of idle land. We have undertaken a cooperative Forest Management Program, a Small Watershed Program, and forest insect and disease control. We manage seven state forests, totalling 47 thousand acres.

Typical of the broadening development of the forestry program is the Forestry Rehabilitation Camp at Pineville. This camp is doing an excellent job of rehabilitating some of the inmates from LaGrange. It is much better for these men to be in camps such as these than in a regular prison, and the camp has returned many men to a useful and productive life. While there was some apprehension among the local people when this camp was first established, I understand that they are now proud of the camp and the good work the men are doing.

It seems a shame that our youth must get in trouble in order to have an opportunity to attend a forestry camp. We should have several forestry camps where our children could learn about the outdoors. This need will become even more pressing as more and more of our children are raised in cities without an opportunity to enjoy the forests. Such a camp would develop a strong interest in natural resources and would be a fine influence.

Along this line, we have several tracts of virgin timber in eastern Kentucky. Commissioner Matlick informs me that there are very few remaining tracts of virgin Appalachian timber.[1] Such areas are little changed from the time the white man first came into Kentucky. I hope that either a state agency or a private foundation can obtain such an area and preserve it in its present state for future generations. Such an area would be ideally suited for a conservation education center, where our youth could be brought and taught conservation of our natural resources.

To educate our young people we urgently need to establish a four-year forestry school in Kentucky. For years our youth wishing to study forestry have had to leave the state, and too often they have not returned after completing their education. If we are to attract bright young men into this field, we also must be prepared to offer salaries comparable to other states and private industry.

Kentucky has nearly 12 million acres of forest land, and this is 46 percent of our entire land area. In some counties of eastern Kentucky forests comprise 80 to 90 percent of the total land. In many of these counties, the economy is almost totally dependent on coal mining. We must make every effort to make forestry a part of the economy in these counties, because it is not healthy when the entire economy is based on one industry. The forest is a valuable part of Kentucky's economy. Approximately $30 million worth of rough forest products are being harvested each year. Some 650 primary wood-using establishments are active in Kentucky at this time.

But we must concentrate, too, on secondary manufacturing. As logs and bolts are further processed into lumber, veneer, furniture stock, and other products, the value added in processing, transportation, and marketing increases several fold. According to the U. S. Census Bureau, some forty thousand Kentuckians participate in these timber-based activities, with a payroll of about $220 million.

Of the seven states that border Kentucky, only Virginia and Tennessee harvest more timber. Yet, when we look at the income generated by secondary manufacturing, we find that Kentucky exceeds only West Virginia. The reason is simple. Kentucky still has fewer secondary manufacturing firms than her neighboring states.

Kentucky has made progress in secondary manufacturing, and indications from industrial prospects lead me to believe that this increase will be greatly augmented in the next two years. Even with past increases we need to expand the amount of assistance we are now making available to all phases of the industry. We need not only to provide more assistance to new industry, but to expand our assistance to existing industry.

You are familiar with the various population projections that place the national population for the year 2000 at from 275 to 360 million. Even if we use the lower figure, it is apparent that future demands for all types of forest products will increase substantially. Not only will we have to produce more lumber and pulpwood, but we will have to do it on less land. At the least, we will have to increase the growth rates of sawtimber by 40 percent.

The latest forest survey figures show that approximately 92 percent of Kentucky's nearly 12 million acres of forest land is in small private owners. Kentucky ranks fourth from the top of all states in the number of private, commercial timberland owners, having better than 240,000 separate holdings. This means the average forest landowner owns less than fifty acres. The annual growth on much of this land is only about 100 board feet per acre a year, but it could in many cases be doubled if, and this is a big "if," the owner can be shown that it is possible to make a profit from his timber.

If Kentucky is to maintain its position of leadership in the hardwood lumber market, it must make every effort to improve quality of management on these private ownerships. How do we account for the fact that the land is not more productive? Part of the answer lies in the types of trees growing on the land. More than half of the trees are twenty to fifty years old, and most are fifteen inches and smaller. Past fires have reduced quality. Much of the sawtimber is cut from the good quality trees, whereas most of the growth is on the small low-quality trees. High-value species, such as yellow poplar and black walnut, are being cut more heavily than low-value species, hickory and elm for example.

Many forest landowners are placing their forests under management. But others seem to be unaware of the possibilities open to them. One of the most important approaches to securing better management of small privately owned woodlands is through informational and educational programs conducted by state agencies, forest industries, and interested private individuals. The forest owner must be convinced that better forest practices are desirable.

Let me make one final point. In both eastern and western Kentucky, large areas of land have been disturbed by coal mining. During recent years the coal industry has reforested thousands of acres, and these reforested acres will add to the forest economy in the future. Unfortunately, large areas of old stripping remain in an unproductive state. We must find a way to reclaim these areas, so they too will make a worthwhile coutribution to the State's economy.

As part of the state effort, we plan to experiment with seeding of these decimated areas by airplane. Within the next few days I will be in southeast Kentucky to participate in a demonstration seeding project, seeding by air, that I am hopeful will make a great contribution to conservation and restoration.

In all, I think we all agree that our work is cut out for us. It is important work, important to us, to those who follow us, and to the land itself.

If I can help you in your work, you have only to ask me.

---

1. James O. Matlick (1911–), commissioner, Department of Natural Resources (1960–1968); editor and general manager, *Kentucky Farmer*, *Tennessee Farmer*, and *Indiana Farmer* (1940–1960); and numerous other positions; born in Memphis, residing in Louisville. Press Release files, April 30, 1968, and Mary Ann Reynolds, Governor's Office, September 20, 1971.

CONSUMERS ASSOCIATION
OF KENTUCKY
Louisville / April 5, 1968

I AM happy to be with the Consumers Association of Kentucky this morning. All Kentuckians should have an interest in your association and this meeting because we are all consumers.

I want to begin with a few remarks directed not to you as consumers in the marketplace but rather to you as citizens of Kentucky and consumers of state services. I do this because the budget and revenue programs passed by the Legislature this winter are vitally important to the future of every man, woman, and child in this Commonwealth. The budget for the current fiscal year was prepared by Governor Breathitt and passed by the Legislature in 1966. It called for expenditures from the General Fund of $397 million. But, as you know, last November, Governor Breathitt had to cut state spending by $24 million for this year because actual state revenues were falling short of estimated revenues. The fact is that the total state revenue this fiscal year will be only $361 million—a substantial amount below what Governor Breathitt and the 1966 Legislature appropriated two years ago.

What made the State's revenue crisis even worse was that our tax sources as of the first of this year were only going to be able to produce $390 million *next* fiscal year less than the $397 million which had already been committed for the *present* fiscal year. As if this was not bad enough, the Commonwealth must spend an additional $120 million during the coming two years just to complete construction projects and programs already started, to operate state facilities already finished, to pay for unavoidable increases in existing programs, and so forth.

There was nothing you or I or the Legislature could do about this; the decisions had been made in the past and were beyond our control. For example, there were $4.5 million in new money needed to operate the State's new educational television network, to prevent the closing of recently completed facilities costing $12 million; $17.5 million in new money for the unavoidable caseload growth in the State's welfare program during the next two years; $11 million in new money for normal growth in elementary and secondary school enrollments and $13 million additional for increased enrollment in our state universities and colleges; $8 million for operation of new vocational schools throughout the State; and even $22 million more just for increases in debt service due on our highway bonds.

Bonds valued at $465 million have been issued for the toll roads in Kentucky, not including the Kentucky Turnpike, and not one dollar in principal has been repaid as of this date. Other examples of already committed money include that for the Jewel Manor Treatment Center for Girls, the Daniel Boone Boys' Camp, and the Farm Dormitory at Eddyville. These facilities were started by past administrations, but it was my decision, and that of the Legislature, that they should be funded and utilized rather than allowed to sit uncompleted or empty.

Because we could not look away from our less fortunate citizens, the budget also provides substantial increases for our mental health and mental retardation programs, including a $9 million institution for the retarded, new aid for the schools for the deaf and the blind, and for the state TB hospital. But, in my opinion, the best feature of the budget is its focus on education: 67 percent of the General Fund Appropriations is devoted to education at all levels in Kentucky.

The State's tax structure at the beginning of this calendar year just could not produce the revenue necessary to finance the programs and services to which the State was already committed or could not avoid. We had had no state tax increase for eight years, and during this time, forty-eight of the other forty-nine states had been forced to raise taxes. Certainly, there is no popular way to raise necessary tax revenue, but I submit that the increase in the sales tax was the best approach under the circumstances. Kentucky taxpayers get help from tourists and interstate travelers on the sales tax, $26 million which our people will not have to pay.

An increase in the sales tax will not hurt our economic development program, whereas increases in our income tax would have made Kentucky less attractive as a place for doing business. And, there is no better way to ease the tax burden than by providing more and better jobs. Additional taxes on Kentucky's basic industries, coal, tobacco and alcohol, would only have depressed our State's economy, putting more Kentuckians out of work and creating greater welfare problems. Despite the increase in our sales tax, balance in the tax system affecting Kentuckians is still guaranteed because almost 60 percent of the total taxes paid by our citizens result from income taxes, which require those who make more to pay more.

On the other hand, last year sales tax revenues represented only 10 percent of all tax money paid by our citizens. Even with the increased sales tax, Kentucky's total tax burden still is much lighter than that of other states. In the last published figures, we ranked forty-sixth among the states in tax burden, far below the national average. And the sales tax is the only tax which everyone pays.

Surely it is only fair that all Kentuckians share, to some extent, the cost of government. In fact, the strength of our democratic political system depends in great measure upon all citizens feeling the payment of taxes. Only under such circumstances will our people be conscious of the need for economy and wise spending. Only then will they realize that government cannot give something for nothing and that the more we ask of government, the more we must be prepared to pay.

I have talked about these matters of state because above all else, you are citizens and should know and understand the cold, hard facts of government and public responsibility. Also, as members of this Association, what the State will be doing during the next two years should be important to you because ultimately all state expenditures are in your behalf, and you are a consumer in relation to the state's budget and programming almost as much as you are a consumer in your private actions in the commercial marketplace.

Now, I would like to talk with you for a few minutes about the problems of the consumer in the marketplace. Our country is, in the language of the economist Adam Smith, a people of customers. And, in these affluent times, the voice of the customer, or consumer, is increasingly being heard. Special concern for the consumer dates back to the early twentieth century. It was then that so-called muckraking journalists and writers exposed some of the dangers facing an unaware public. For example, Upton Sinclair wrote *The Jungle* to reveal, among other things, the way certain meat packers tossed rats, sawdust, and garbage into canned ham. President Theodore Roosevelt responded to such disclosures by promptly appointing an investigating committee, and this led to some of the first consumer protection laws. In the past, it has usually taken a public scare, poisoned meat from Chicago's stockyards, a stock market crash, thalidomide babies or the like, to get government concerned with the interest of the consumer. Without some dramatic exposé to prod it, the voice of the consumer has not been heard very much.

However, today's consumer is beginning to insist on more information on, and, where needed, protection from, the sometimes baffling array of goods on the market. The modern supermarket stocks an average 8,000 items. The impersonality of the market place, supermarkets replacing the friendly corner grocer, has encouraged the buyer to look for more help from the government. Then, too, technological advances have placed an overwhelming choice of packaged goods and complicated appliances on the shelves.

Finally, more and more Americans have become affluent consumers in a way that only the extremely wealthy used to be. About one-third of the public's purchasing power can now be spent on things beyond the necessities. Such new forces in society have been responsible for the gradual undermining of the old adage *"caveat emptor,"* or "let the buyer beware." It is also clear that the present concern for the customer arises because the American consumer is the best educated in the world, and he and she are beginning to demand more information on purchasing decisions.

I think that Betty Furness's predecessor, Mrs. Esther Peterson, stated the case well when she said: "As a housewife, I am already functioning with doubtful effectiveness as a chauffeur, mother, PTA executive, housemaid, bookkeeper, and purchasing agent. Now I find that in order to do a good job of buying I have to be a high-speed computer. Help!"[1] Many businesses have gotten the message and, to the credit of our private enterprise system, responded voluntarily to provide relief and assistance. Of course, we have had federal consumer protection laws. But what I have liked is the way that some states have taken the lead over the federal government in consumer legislation. And, I think the record shows that the Kentucky consumer was certainly respected in Frankfort this winter, as evidenced by such new laws as our state meat inspection and truth-in-lending acts.

But, because I believe state government should become more aware of the needs of the consumer and provide him with additional help where needed, I am today creating an eleven member Consumer Affairs Commission. I want to read you a few paragraphs from the Executive Order establishing this body.[2]

Because our consumers are the best educated in the world, I think one of the Commission's main goals should be simply to help the consumer get more specific and easily understandable information so that he can make intelligent choices in his purchases.

In trying to aid the consumer, the Commission would do well to keep in mind the remarks of Senator Jackson of Washington, who said that "The question which should be asked is not too much or too little legislation for the consumer? But, how can we better work together to make certain that consumer legislation will do the job for which it is intended without injuring or unduly burdening business?"

It has been a pleasure to be here with you today, and I look forward to working with you and your association during my administration.

---

1. Betty Furness, special assistant to the president for consumer affairs (1967–1970); executive secretary, Consumer Advisory Council (1967–1970); and President's Commission on Consumer Interests (1967–1970). *Who's Who*

in America, 1970–71 (Chicago, 1971), 36: 787; Esther Peterson, special assistant to the president for consumer affairs (1964–1967); chairman, President's Commission on Consumer Interests (1964–1967); assistant secretary, Department of Labor (1961–1964); and director, Women's Bureau, Department of Labor (1961–1964). *Who's Who in America, 1970–71* (Chicago, 1971), 36: 1779.

2. At this point Governor Nunn read from Executive Order 68–294, the whereas clauses on pages 1 and 2.

KENTUCKY CHAMBER
OF COMMERCE
Louisville / April 10, 1968

I AM here to fulfill an annual tradition of Kentucky's Governor in attending this breakfast. I am happy to do this. But I also am pleased to meet with business leaders to discuss Kentucky's economy—where we are and where we hope to go and what this Administration has done and what it is trying to do for you and all business in Kentucky.

You hear much these days about taxes, revenues, budgets, debts, and wasteful state spending. And you hear a lot of rumors. I am going to speak bluntly about your state government's fiscal affairs: What we inherited, what we have, and why we have done what we have.

I do not want to bore you with a lot of statistics. But I do want to cover a few important points. This Commonwealth's cash on deposit in the General Fund when this Administration took office was $17.3 million. Warrants issued against that amount totaled $14.4 million leaving a balance of only $2.9 million to meet loans from trust and agency funds that totaled $3 million and no cash reserve left for accounts payable and accrued payrolls.

The General Fund balance sheet, as of January 31, of this year, showed just over $21.5 million with warrants issued against that account totaling over $12.3 million. When the cash in bank was reduced by warrants and accounts payable, there remained only $5.8 million, and $5.8 million was just about half of the monthly payroll due January 31.

Treasury bills and certificates of deposits in several New York and

Chicago banks at this time totaled $243.5 million. But only two of the thirteen special funds, the General Fund, $9.2 million, and the state road fund, $14.8 million—were available for operating the state government and the road program. The other funds were restricted as to their use and in many cases had a built-in factor of creating future obligations on the General Fund.

In January, General Fund tax sources, which provide the money for education, health, welfare, and other services, were not going to produce enough revenue next year even to restore the existing programs to the $397 million level set for the current year. That $397 million was the budget originally planned for the current fiscal year by the 1966 Legislature. And, as you know, Governor Breathitt last November had to order a cut in this of nearly $24 million for the year, because state revenues were falling short of the estimated revenues. Add to this the economic needs of the Commonwealth for the next two years. Competent financial advisors established this figure at $481 million for the next fiscal year and $523 million during fiscal 1969–70 from the General Fund.

If some of you wonder why we had to increase spending, the answer is clear: to give our people a better life and to honor commitments of the previous Administration. Over $104 million of the budget for the next two years will pay for previous commitments of the Commonwealth, commitments for which funding no longer can be delayed. This $104 million is needed just to complete capital construction projects already started, to operate new state facilities already completed, to take care of unavoidable increases in existing programs, and so forth.

A good example of additional money needed for past commitments is educational television, for which $12 million already had been spent for construction of facilities. Lack of funds to operate this system, estimated at $4.5 million, would mean closing the doors of existing facilities and wasting the investment. Then there is the unavoidable caseload growth the next two years in welfare programs. This will cost an additional $17.5 million.

Likewise, additional money necessary for normal growth in elementary and secondary school enrollments the next two years will total over $11 million and additional money necessary for increased enrollment in five state-supported universities and one college will total over $13 million. New vocational schools will cost over $8 million more. Increases in debt service due on highway bonds will total $21 million more. It was not my decision to build the animal disease laboratory at Hopkinsville, the Farm Dormitory at Eddyville, the Jewel Manor Treatment Center for Girls here in Louisville, or the Daniel Boone Boys'

Camp. But they are there, and I think they serve a useful purpose and should be funded and utilized.

We cannot do anything to reduce the number of children who will enter school this fall. We cannot turn away the increasing number of Kentucky high school graduates who want to go to college. We cannot control the number of people who seek, and are eligible for, welfare benefits. And we felt that we had to improve other programs to get Kentucky off the bottom in so many categories.

That's why I recommended long overdue improvements in such programs as rural roads; in the School Foundation program; in mental health and mental retardation programs; including a $9 million construction program for the retarded, public libraries, and the schools for the deaf and for the blind; the TB Hospital; and public health in general.

This Administration has been like the old farmer being interviewed for his first insurance policy. The agent asked the old man if he ever had had an accident.

"Nope," the old man answered. "But a hog bit me once and a cow kicked me."

"My gosh," the agent said. "Don't you consider those accidents?"

"Nope," the old man answered. "They done it on purpose." Your State Government is doing things on purpose, too, on purpose to get us off the bottom of those national rankings. We are also doing some things by necessity, as I have explained.

Business leaders know the value of education at all levels. Indeed, Kentucky's economic and social future depends more heavily on education than on any other single factor. A hard fact, and one we sometimes do not like to admit, is that Kentucky today is not attractive to many fast-growing research and science-oriented industries because of the educational level of our work force. There is an obligation on the part of our educational system to correct this condition and the educational system, of course, must look to state government for its major financing. So that is why more than two out of every three General Fund dollars in the budget are directed to education. We are not only meeting previous commitments; we are also going beyond that in spending a total of nearly $78 million more in the next two years on education. Regulatory agencies pertinent to your work, the agencies which govern utilities, banking and securities, insurance, motor transportation, and so on, likewise are better funded to enable them to operate more efficiently.

As I have pointed out, the State's tax structure at the beginning of this year simply could not produce the revenue necessary to finance the needed public programs and services. There had been no state tax increase for eight years, since the 3 percent sales tax was enacted in 1960. The old tax structure had been squeezed for about all the growth it could produce, and we had reached a financial crossroad. By way of compromise, forty-nine of the fifty states had been forced to enact tax increases since Kentucky's last increase in the form of the 1960 sales tax.

There never is a popular way to raise the tax revenue necessary for state government to provide services the people need. But I insist that there are preferable taxes. And I submit to you that the increase in the sales tax was the best approach under the circumstances. Kentucky taxpayers get help from tourists and interstate travelers on the sales tax—thirteen to fourteen million dollars a year which our people will not have to pay. And with tourism as our fastest growing business, that thirteen to fourteen million dollars will grow and grow and grow.

The increase in the sales tax will not hurt us, whereas an increase in our income tax would have made Kentucky less attractive as a place for doing business. In the heavy competition for new industry, there is no better way to ease the tax burden than by providing more and better jobs. Additional taxes on Kentucky's basic industries, coal, tobacco, and alcohol, would only have depressed our State's economy, putting Kentuckians out of work and creating greater welfare problems.

The sales tax is easy to administer. It cannot be evaded. The sales tax is the only tax which everyone pays. And those who make more and spend more, pay more. And surely it is only fair that all Kentuckians share, to some extent, the cost of their State Government.

Some people have expressed concern that the 5 percent sales tax would result in increased over the border shopping by Kentuckians along our borders. The added expense and inconvenience of such out of state shopping, plus Department of Revenue regulations, will protect our businesses. I see no reason to expect any serious "dollar drain."

What does disturb me is the prospect of the kind of "drain" which this State really cannot afford, the out-migration of our citizens to other states to find opportunity. This State's future certainly will be a bleak one if our young, educated Kentuckians continue leaving for better opportunities. This loss of talented Kentuckians is the one type of drain our state can least afford. And the only way to stop it is to bring about the improvements needed so long in this State.

It is my firm intention to carry out a program which will provide maximum services for every dollar spent. We are streamlining the Department of Commerce to effect a more aggressive program of attracting industry to Kentucky. But we are concerned, too, with the home-based industries which serve so many of our communities so well, and we want to encourage their expansion.

This I pledge to you. This Administration will use the assistance of all levels of government throughout the Commonwealth, and help from private citizens wherever they might be, in carrying out programs designed to move Kentucky ahead.

KENTUCKY EDUCATION ASSOCIATION
Louisville / April 18, 1968

"WHATEVER the public endeavor . . . progress ultimately will be limited by the State's commitment to education. We propose a viable, working partnership in public education at all levels, involving teachers, parents, professional administrators, and the state administration. And we propose that this partnership dedicate itself to one goal only—that of providing quality education at whatever sacrifice it is possible to make."

Some of you may remember those words. They are from the platform I ran on last year. I believe in those words then. And I am living by them today. I *believe* in quality education, at *whatever* sacrifice it is possible to make. So do you believe in it. So do parents and all other citizens who cry for greater opportunity for Kentucky's most cherished resource, the youth of this state.

If you did not believe in it, you would not be here today. You would not have laid down your career in the cause of education. You would not have stuck with it through the lean years, when to be a teacher in Kentucky was to deprive yourself of nearly all of the tangible pleasures of life. You would not be with us even now, as we struggle to keep pace with advancements elsewhere.

I need not remind you that progress has been slow or that we now are trying to accelerate it. You have seen the proof of our determination in the responsiveness of the administration to your requests for greater help. I am proud that most of your requests could be met. And I do not apologize that, in order to do the right thing for Kentucky's children, we had to ask all citizens of the Commonwealth to bear the burden, to sacrifice. It took courage to ask for revenue increases and to vote for them. It could be said even that it took uncommon courage, because we all knew that a cry would go up from the demagogues that we were abusing the poor when, in fact, it is the poor who will be helped most by the new revenue we generated.

There is a question that needs to be asked of the dissenters. How can we best get at poverty except by educating the poor, by providing them with the tools to improve themselves? The budget we offered and, through that, our commitment to education will give them the tools.

The budget will raise the level of education in Kentucky just as certainly as it will give Kentucky new growth, new pride, and a higher level of achievement. We will raise salaries, providing a minimum salary of $5,000 for a degree teacher. We will provide increases per classroom unit of up to $1,400 by the end of the biennium and double the capital outlay for classroom units to $1,200 by the end of the biennium. Neither of these outlays had been increased since they were established in 1960. We will put $4.5 million into educational television in order to make the network's twelve stations operable by next fall.

We authorized more than $170 million for higher education, an increase of $40 million, and we provided funds for the operation of four new community colleges, at Maysville, Hazard, Paducah, and Louisville. We will invest $46 million in vocational education, an increase of $20 million, providing for eighteen new extension centers and increased support of the thirteen area schools. We fully financed the Teachers' Retirement System for the 1968–70 biennium and took care of a million-dollar deficit that was allowed to build up during the current biennium.

Altogether, 66 percent of all anticipated General Fund revenue will go into education. Still, I do not say we did enough. But we did go as far as we could. We did ask the public to make a sacrifice, a sacrifice largely in your name and in the name of opportunity for our children. Time will prove that we did right. I have no fear of that. In all honesty, however, I cannot say that the sacrifice was willingly made. The revenue measure doubtless encountered hostility, but without that increase we could not have done for Kentucky those things which so desperately needed doing.

Again, in all honesty, you must be aware that the public is not all on your side or on the side of education. You must be aware that there are many who feel that teachers have been greedy, that there are too many frills in education today, that we have been overspending, and that many school districts are spoiled and hamstrung by politics. There is no use in pretending that these sentiments do not prevail, because they do prevail, and to an alarming degree. And there is no use in pretending, either, that there is not some basis for these suspicions and distrust. There are politics in many of our school districts and in some cases there is so much of it that the schools themselves suffer from it.

Your public relations have not always been the best, and you have not always been understood. There may be some fat in the education budget, particularly at the top, in administrative services. If there is, it should be got out. Certainly it was my intention, and the intention of your friends in the Legislature, that the bulk of appropriations to education should result in improved instruction, not in a proliferating bureaucracy.

Tomorrow, I am to speak at the dedication of a private research facility in Jefferson County. I plan to reassure the executives who will be assembled there of this State's interest in education and in the development of a technical work force. I say reassure because one of the major considerations of any firm in locating an industrial complex is the quality of a community's schools. Are the teachers paid adequately? Is there much staff turnover? Are facilities adequate? Is there an enlightened school administration? Is there close at hand a modern vocational facility? Does the school system and the community enjoy a pleasant, understanding relationship, or is there constant dissent and unrest?

It is our determination that, if not today, we soon will be able to say yes to each of these questions. Because unless we are able to give the right answers, Kentucky will not long be able to compete with other states for those industries that hire our people and breathe new vigor and vitality into our communities.

I mention this only because it is illustrative of how much of Kentucky's future you and I, and especially you, hold in our hands. I mention it because it illustrates so well that education cannot be isolated and that progress in all of our endeavors will be limited mainly by our commitment to better schools and better education.

More and better jobs, the development of our natural resources, the intelligent use of leisure time, science, and technology, how well we succeed in all of this rests squarely on the shoulders of those who teach our young people. The quality of our education and the strength of the schools spring largely from one source—those who go into the schools and teach. It is your responsibility and there is no escaping it. It is upon you that we all depend. And it is to you that I pledge my unyielding cooperation.

CELANESE COATINGS COMPANY
RESEARCH LABORATORY
DEDICATION
Middletown / April 19, 1968

I BELIEVE that this occasion, the official opening of the Celanese Coatings Company Technical Center, marks one of the most significant steps in the growth of modern Kentucky. It's an honor to participate. We are proud that 1,100 Kentuckians are a part of this organization.

The remarkable growth which you and the chemical industry in general have experienced the last few years is why we attach so much importance to the chemicals industry in Kentucky. We want you to grow still more, especially in our Commonwealth, and we will do what we can to encourage your growth.

I am told that the technical expenditures of the Celanese Coatings Company have tripled in the past twelve years. While this shows an unusual emphasis on advanced technology by the company, it is even more important to Kentucky than you may realize. We know that there is a correlation between the numbers of scientists and technologists in a state and the per capita income of that state. We know that the ratio of scientists, engineers, and technologists to our population in Kentucky is about half of the median for the United States. We know that the high per capita income states of Delaware, Connecticut, Massachusetts, New York, and California, have a high ratio of technical people to the rest of their population. These states have an income of about $1 thousand more per person than does Kentucky. It is our intention to close the gap.

A key factor in attracting technical people into an area is the community's educational program. We are devoting a great deal of attention to our educational system and we are making progress. One way technical men evaluate competitive educational systems is by comparing pupil or teacher expenditures. In the 1966–67 school year, Kentucky ranked forty-fourth in average salary per classroom teacher, and in 1967–68 our ranking rose to thirty-eighth. We now are scheduled to increase this $800 a year for the next two fiscal years which will bring us close to the mean for the country if everyone else stays about the same.

Another important category in education is the money expended for building and current expenses. This is a budget area which had not been increased since 1960, but will be increased in the next two years by an amount greater even than our salary increases. We are fully aware of the importance of technical training, and we are making significant strides in this field, too.

You may prefer to train your own technicians or you may prefer that your technicians receive two years of post high school training in the local vocational schools or the colleges and universities. Whichever way you or other firms go, you are looking to us to meet the vocational needs of this area. In 1965 Kentucky ranked seventeenth in the United States in state and federal expenditures for vocational education. In the budget recently adopted we tripled the State's appropriations, and wished only that we could have done more.

The Kentucky Community College System is undergoing an even more dramatic change. The Jefferson Community College which opened in January, 1968, was scheduled to start with 400 students and had 800. This fall they expect to enroll between 1,600 and 1,800. Celanese's Mr. Francis W. Theis was an original member of the Jefferson Community College Advisory Board.[1] A large new building will be started in the fall of this year to help accommodate this almost explosive demand by this area's young people for higher education.

In the area of higher education, we are very proud of the progress being made at the University of Louisville. State expenditures at the University of Louisville are being increased from $1.012 million in the current fiscal year to $3.1 million next fiscal year, an almost 200 percent increase. In the period between 1963 and 1966 the University of Louisville increased its federal academic science obligations from $2.8 million to $8.4 million and its share of the U.S. total from 0.21 percent to 0.39 percent. This is one of the highest rates of growth of the top 100 universities.

In the state institutions of higher education, the University of Kentucky has already reached a competitive salary position with comparable institutions in the seven adjoining states, and we expect that the other five state institutions will be close to the median of their thirty-two comparable institutions.

We recognize that there must be an increasing emphasis in Kentucky on advanced technology type industry. We must create a condition which will be conducive for industry to increase its numbers of scientific and technological employees in the State.

The Celanese Corporation operates large laboratories in New Jersey, North Carolina, Texas, and Kentucky, so you are in a position to evaluate services provided by local and state government and to examine the cost of operation and performance of employees at four widely separate locations. Your Dr. W. C. Hunt is a member of our Kentucky Science and Technology Advisory Council.[2] We would be interested in learning how we compare with your other locations and what we may do to make Kentucky a still better place for this fine technical center and others like it.

----

1. Francis W. Theis, corporate vice president, Celanese Corporation (1971 –   ); president, Celanese Chemical Company (1967–1971); president, Celanese Coatings Company (1965–1967); and member, Jefferson Community College Board of Trustees (1966–1967). Department of Personnel and Public Relations files, Celanese Coatings Company, September 10, 1971.

2. W. C. Hunt, vice president, Celanese Research Company (1968–   ); vice president, Technical and Manufacturing, Celanese Coatings Company, (1966–1968); and member, Kentucky Science and Technology Advisory Council (1966–1967). Department of Personnel and Public Relations files, Celanese Coatings Company, September 10, 1971.

KEYNOTE ADDRESS
REPUBLICAN STATE
CONVENTION
Louisville / April 20, 1968

SINCE my election last November, I have addressed many groups representing many different interests and concerns. I must say, however, that I have looked forward to coming here today to be with you perhaps more than any other.

You delegates, who so ably represent the party at the grass roots level, along with the party's state, district, and county officials, are here because you have earned the respect and accepted the responsibility that goes with your important position. And I am here today as Governor of the Commonwealth of Kentucky because it was my great privilege to represent you last November. It was you, above all others, who convinced Kentuckians that a Republican administration could lift this State out of the dark hollows of desperation. You convinced Kentuckians that a Republican administration could pull this State up from near the bottom of nearly every category dealing with human services. You convinced Kentuckians that a Republican administration could face the depressing facts of this State's condition and act to correct the situation, not sweep Kentucky's shame under the carpet. And you convinced voters that a Republican administration would operate under a banner committed to progress, not political expediency.

I realize that some of the decisions I have been forced to make since going to Frankfort have left our administration and the party open to attack. Not once, but many times, Republicans who occupy positions of responsibility in the administration and in the party have said that life was not nearly so complicated when we were losing. But we knew it was not an easy job that we were given last November. No one could expect us to clean up in five months a mess created over twenty years. My counsel is patience. The loudest voices of dissent we have heard are those of an irresponsible, self-serving segment, unwilling to listen to reason, unwilling to come to grips with the problems that plague Kentucky.

Instead of the voices of those who would have Kentucky permanently mired near the bottom of the standings among her sister states, let this party and this Commonwealth hear and respond to the voice of a jobless father, forced into unemployment by technology and trapped in a nonproductive life by the bittersweet welfare programs which guarantee subsistence but destroy initiative. And let us hear and respond to the voices of that man's children, the real losers in the giveaway game. These children are crying out only for a chance, a chance to escape the vicious cycle impounding generation after generation after generation in the welfare trap. While Appalachia is our most poignant shame, the same disease can now be seen infecting Kentucky's urban centers and threatening our small towns. Let us as a party and as a people hear and respond to the voices of those living in frustration and misery, powerless to resist either the subtle environmental forces or the easy answers thrust upon them too long by the opposition party.

We saw during the past legislative session an example of how far down the road of deceit some of the members of that party have led us. Giving lip service to the poor, they set out to wreck a program which listens to the voices in Appalachia, the voices of our cities, and the voices of our rural population. They set out to wreck a program which promises better education for our children, better care for our aging and our sick. They set out to wreck a program which not only helps those in need but also lets the needy have a fair share in helping to pay their own way.

The Republican Party has heard the voices of the despairing and has

responded in the tradition of one of our great leaders, Theodore Roosevelt, who told the Republican National Convention in 1912: "We believe that this country will not be a permanently good place for any of
us to live in unless we make it a reasonably good place for all of us to
live in." But let us keep those words and that thinking consistent with
the Republican approach, administering aid with economy and care,
and always mindful that our programs should be directed toward helping our people solve their problems, not learning how to live with them.
Our people do not want a handout; our people want a hand up, so that
they may escape the misery of unemployment and the misery of a nonproductive life which erodes a man's self-respect and lays open his
moral fiber, making him easy prey for the giveaway programs and the
easy answers and the false hopes that have characterized the New
Frontier and the Great Society.

Our victory last fall was a step in the right direction. Our next step
will be taken this November. This party's victory last fall, and the
troubled times we face today, lowered grave responsibilities to our
shoulders, not only here in Kentucky but throughout the nation. Americans are looking to our party for the leadership, the ideas, and the
courage this country needs. They are looking to the Republican Party
to give us new direction and new hope so that we may bind up our
wounds, regroup, and meet the sternest challenge our nation has ever
faced.

I believe that the feeling grows daily among Americans that the National Democrat Party has led us down the road toward a dead end.
It is increasingly clear that the Democrat Party is hopelessly bound to
programs which have not worked, and which have left this nation
hanging on the ropes, not knowing whether the next blow is forthcoming from home or abroad. I am sure you all remember the rallying
call of the Democrat Party in 1960, when it proudly boasted 'We can
do better.' Thank God they did not do worse. I remember, too, how the
Democrats lightly dismissed the peace we enjoyed during the Eisenhower years, citing this as proof that the country had been in mothballs for eight years. Somehow in their amazing philosophy, they
equated peace and prosperity with inactivity, and they dusted off the
old campaign slogan, 'Let's get moving again.' So, by the smallest
majority in the history of modern politics, the government changed
hands, and sure enough, America started moving again. But every
move has been accompanied by the sound of battle, of bullets, and
of burning. Every move has bred turmoil and strife unmatched in this
country's history.[1]

These are the reasons the American people are turning to our party this year. And these are the reasons the Republican Party must respond with its very best effort. We cannot, we must not, be lulled into complacency by the unprecedented success our party has enjoyed in this State since 1952. Our triumphs include delivering Kentucky's electoral votes to the Republican presidential candidate two times out of three, sending to Washington two of this nation's most distinguished senators for two terms each, and electing three Republican congressmen and on the state level, sending a Republican governor to Frankfort and with him forty-three representatives and fourteen senators. Kentucky's two largest cities have Republican mayors and the state's two largest counties have Republican county judges.

But we cannot forget that, despite our successes, we are still the minority. A survey of voter registration early this year revealed that there are more than 1,024,408 registered Democrats in Kentucky as opposed to 476,000 Republicans, better than a two-to-one majority. As you can see, there is no room for complacency or overconfidence in our party. Therefore, let our past victories serve only the intended purpose of all histories, to guide us in our present efforts and remind us of what can be done in the future.

This State Convention and the impending selection of officers by the State Central Committee are all that is left undone in our reorganization process. I am not so naive as to be unaware of the dissention that sometimes accompanies this process, but I choose to believe this is a natural and encouraging sign that we in the Republican Party are concerned with the future of our counties, our State and our nation. I have been told that this has been one of the most actively contested reorganizations in our history, and congratulations are in order for the victors. I hope that you who have been chosen are aware of your most pressing responsibility, which is to welcome and encourage those who were not chosen to join in the battle at your side so that we will not be denied their time and talent in the job ahead. To those who were not chosen as delegates, precinct chairmen or chairwomen, county or district officers, I hope they can put aside the frustration of defeat and come aboard a truly united ship. Our task in the coming months and years is far too vital to be undermined by pettiness and selfish motives on the part of either the winners or losers.

Of overriding concern now is the upcoming primary election, at which time we will decide who shall represent the Republican Party in the race for the Senate Seat vacated by Senator Morton.[2] Regarding the races for Congress, I am very encouraged by the fact that we have Republicans entered for six of the seven congressional contests, and I am hopeful that come November we shall have played a valuable part in capturing a majority in the House of Representatives for our party. We have only to look to the Democrat Party in this State to see clear evidence of the pitfalls of bitter factional politics. We are already too few in number to risk fragmentation in the face of the opportunities which lie ahead.

I call on each candidate to speak out on the issues as he sees them, to clearly prescribe the Republican course and deal with the obstacles which now prevent this country from carrying out the principles of its charter. I call on you and your fellow Republicans back home to unite, to work, and to pay the price demanded by the mission we now undertake. A misguided nation in a troubled world is asking for our help, and we cannot do less than our very best.

---

1. In most of his political speeches Nunn used "Democrat" rather than "Democratic" as an adjective. Assuming that this was a purposeful choice rather than one of grammatical usage, his usage has been retained. This usage may be explained as follows: "In 1955, Leonard Hall, a former Republican National Chairman, began referring to the 'Democrat' rather than the 'Democratic' party, a habit begun by Thomas E. Dewey. Hall dropped the 'ic,' he said, because 'I think their claims that they represent the great mass of the people, and we don't, is just a lot of bunk.' The University of Virginia's Atcheson L. Hench said of this usage in *American Speech*: 'Whether they have meant to imply that the party was no longer democratic, or whether they banked on the harsher sound pattern of the new name; whether they wanted to strengthen the impression that they were speaking for a new Republican party by using a new name for the opposition, or whether they had other reasons, the fact remains that . . . highly influential speakers . . . used the shorter adjective." William Safire, *The New Language of Politics: An Anecdotal Dictionary of Catchwords, Slogans and Political Usage* (New York: Random House, 1971), p. 107.

2. Thruston B. Morton (1907–), Louisville, United States Senator from Kentucky (1956–1968); chairman, Republican National Committee (1959–1961); assistant secretary of state (1953–1956); United States House of Representatives (1946–1953); and numerous other positions. *Congressional Directory, 90th Congress, 2d Session* (Washington, D.C., 1968), p. 64.

CENTRAL KENTUCKY
MENTAL HEALTH
ASSOCIATION
Lexington / May 2, 1968

CERTAINLY, no individual association has done more than the Central Kentucky Mental Health Association to educate its community and to commit its citizens to services. No one knows better than you that the struggle for a modern mental health and retardation program has been all uphill. It's been uphill for me, too, in the brief time I've been in office.

We care for 7,800 persons in our state psychiatric hospitals and schools for the retarded. At Eastern State Hospital, there are patients in a building that is 152 years old. At Western State Hospital in Hopkinsville, patients are in one building constructed during the Civil War. Kentucky State Hospital in Danville is a former military hospital. Most of its buildings were constructed as "temporary" a quarter of a century ago. Central State Hospital near Louisville has twenty-four buildings put up in the 1880's.

And here is what the Legislative Research Commission had to say last year about Frankfort State Hospital and School: "No amount of renovation can change the premises into an acceptable institution for the severely retarded." In hospital after hospital there are leaky roofs, crumbling bricks, walls so far gone that they will not even retain paint. The heating is so bad and the ventilation so poor, that some buildings have 54-degree temperatures in winter, and 105 degrees in summer.

At Frankfort State Hospital this winter, they had to back a truck up to a window, so that a gasoline fired heating unit on that truck could feed heat through the window. The engineer at the Department of Mental Health keeps a check list on his wall. Written beside the names of individual hospitals you will see notes, such as "steam lines liable to explode; smokestack ready to fall, could be very dangerous; water line overloaded, health hazard." I could go on. But still there are those who ask why I asked for a 2 cent sales tax.

I placed in the budget of the Department of Mental Health for the next biennium four million dollars for renovation and maintenance, and nine million dollars for construction, out of which will come a modern hospital and school for our severely retarded children.

There are families in Kentucky who have had their names on waiting lists for 5–10–15 years, while they struggle along under almost unmanageable burdens. But the plans are being drawn, and we will announce soon the beginning of construction for this hospital. We will have a proper place for these helpless children.

We have talked about buildings. But mental health is, above all, a human service, concerned with the whole human being. It is concerned with the development of human beings to their utmost capacities, with the prevention and the treatment of mental illness, and with the habilitation of the retarded.

You have all seen the newspapers this week. I do not need to tell you how we are faring in the area of human services. I do not need to tell you about the pitiful salaries of those who give of themselves—and it must be out of dedication—to care for our psychiatric patients and our retarded children. We have, however, appropriated sufficient funds in the next biennium to raise the salaries of our hospital aides beginning in July to a minimum of $300 a month after training.

The number of clinical staff in our hospitals is below national standards. Those professionals in the hospitals and on the staff of the Department of Mental Health are making a gallant effort to make up in quality what they lack in numbers, but they can only do so much.

The budget cut of last winter has forced a doubling up on duties, a closing of wards, and even buildings. Dr. Farabee tells me that the $300 thousand we gave the Department of Mental Health from our contingency fund before Christmas made it possible to survive.[1] Without it, we would have had to virtually close an entire hospital. But we also know that present funds represent "survival only." The budget we have enacted for 1968–70 will make it possible to raise our level of care, and the two additional cents in the sales tax will help pay for that.

For our hospitals we must have clean, safe, improved buildings. We will replace dangerous steam lines, repair leaky roofs, and remodel buildings. In improved surroundings patients can more easily react to new treatment concepts which we are beginning to implement in all of our hospitals. The limited staffs of the state hospitals are expending every effort, beyond ordinary definitions of duty, to meet accreditation standards in every area from pharmacy to occupational therapy.

The new updated mental health legislation which I signed into law on March 21 will guarantee civil rights for patients, will give them a legal right to treatment rather than custody. New medical bylaws in effect will permit privately practicing physicians to join state hospitals as voluntary staff members, following their own patients into the wards, just as they do in general hospitals. And we will have a competitive decent wage scale for low salaried workers so that we can both keep and attract proficient personnel. All of this is ready to go.

Under the system of Regional Boards, concerned citizens from all of the counties of each region plan, implement, and administer complete systems of mental health care. They are assisted by advisory committees of professionals and government officials. The centers now provide almost complete geographic coverage. The Louisville area has just applied for the first of four centers to be located there. Through utilization of the federal funds, partial state support, and untold hours of dedicated citizen effort, there thus arises a network of services.

The Department of Mental Health offered technical assistance to get these centers underway, but the decisions, the planning, and the administration lies where it should be, in the private sector with the citizens of each region. In this far reaching program lies a promise and a challenge to provide the answers for the mentally ill at a place he most desperately needs them, his home place.

This new approach will enormously lighten the load of the hospitals in the immediate years ahead. But perhaps, the greatest hope of this approach is in the joint effort it brings about with the state hospitals, general hospitals, private physicians, and public and private agencies, each cooperating for the total welfare of the patient. A tiny percentage of our total mental health budget goes to this effort at present, but without state support, it would not have been possible and we are committed to a continuation of this approach. With it we can look forward to comprehensive services for example, for the 100,000 long neglected alcoholics in our Commonwealth. All of our state hospitals now have units for the alcoholic. There are now nine alcoholism coordinators serving around the state in the centers, bringing people and service together. A year ago there was nothing.

Our goal is a day care center for the retarded in every county. We have established twenty-two of these already, with six more being planned. There are nine sheltered workshops, and we plan three more. So we are planning to turn the corner. We know the way, we have accepted the challenge. Let it be known today, the second day of the Mental Health Month, 1968, that this community of citizens before me, and those of us on the platform and in the audience, and those with the state responsibility join together in mutual concern and commitment to mental health.

---

1. Dale H. Farabee, M.D. (1926–   ), Lexington, commissioner, Department of Mental Health (1965–   ); member, President's National Advisory Committee on Alcoholism (1970–   ); chairman, Drug Abuse Task Force, Na-

tional Association of State Mental Health Program Directors (1967–);
president, Kentucky District Branch, American Psychiatric Association
(1967–1968); chief, Psychiatric Section, Student Health Service, University
of Kentucky (1964–1965). Department of Mental Health biographical files.

UNIVERSITY OF LOUISVILLE
LAW SCHOOL HONORS DAY
Louisville / May 15, 1968

I AM very pleased to have the opportunity to come back today to the
Allen Court Room and to this law school which holds so many special
and happy memories for me. To return here as your Governor is one
of the proudest moments of my tenure. And I should like to acknowledge at this time my debt of gratitude to this school and to its faculty
for what it has meant to me. Many times since I graduated from this
University, I have been reminded of what this fine institution symbolizes in the minds and hearts of those of us who were fortunate
enough to share the experience you now enjoy.

As you probably know, the University of Louisville was not forgotten in the budget for the coming biennium. We appropriated $2.2 mil-
lion in support of the medical and dental programs. Another $4 million
was provided so that tuition costs for Kentucky students would be
reduced beginning next semester. I sincerely hope that what we may
accomplish in Frankfort for the people of this state during my term of
office will in some measure reflect credit on this institution, which has
been such a strong force and good influence on Kentucky's progress.

The University of Louisville Law School offers strong proof that the
training and experience of a legal education is a unique preparation for
those who aspire to a career of public service. The life of an attorney
is largely a public life, regardless of whether he chooses to practice the
more traditional course in which he represents conflicting private interests or whether he practices what I shall refer to as public law. In
either practice, there are inherent factors within the profession which
demand of the attorney a commitment to the common good of all society. This, I believe, is necessitated largely by the fact that the lawyer
deals with the sustaining ingredient of orderly living. If we accept that

order is the first principle of a civilized society, then we must also accept the fact that because of their peculiar relationship to orderly structure, attorneys have certain responsibilities in the maintenance of that order within a community.

I would like to briefly discuss today some of the responsibilities which accompany the commitment you should accept after having chosen this profession. First, for those of you who will practice in the traditional areas of law, I believe events of recent years and months should have clearly indicated where you can be of the greatest service. I refer to the crime wave which is sweeping our nation. It has been estimated that crime in the United States is growing six times faster than the population. Add to this the fact that the cost of crime amounts to $27 billion annually and then compound the situation with the most obvious and fearsome problem facing our nation, that of rioting, looting, and burning.

Last year, 107 American cities experienced riots or some form of civil disorder. Now the disease shows signs of engulfing certain college campuses. Suddenly it has become popular to protest in defense of individual freedom by practicing anarchy, intimidation, and mob rule. It is curious that at a time when there has been so much concern for the injustices of society, there has been so little concern for justice.

When I speak of justice, I refer to the idea of due process of law. In the system of free government, due process has traditionally been viewed as a restraint on government, a requirement that if the government must infringe on the private sector of our society, then it must do so by due process of law. Yet while we insist on that concept, some in our society show no willingness to also recognize that the same requirements of due process must be observed by those who seek redress of grievances against the government. I submit to you that we must not sacrifice due process in the name of protest, whether the protest be justified or not.

We who are dedicated to the preservation of legal order must never lose sight of the fact that rioting, civil disorder, and mob rule do not fall within the boundaries of due process. It seems to me that one of the most fearful by-products of all this is the deterioration of our respect for the law. On one hand we have a group which does not hesitate to violate laws in the name of injustice. On the other hand, we have a larger part of the population which steadily loses faith in a system of law which permits these acts to go unpunished.

I know of no more challenging atmosphere into which those who truly are committed to the common good can enter. Here is ample opportunity for those of you whom we honor today to employ your special skill, training, talent, and intelligence. Here is a situation which begs for those of this profession to step in, work with resoluteness and reason toward solving a problem which most Americans recognize as our most serious threat.

From your positions in the mainstream of American life, you must seek ways to restore in this nation a respect for the law. You must promote the idea that only through the traditional legal channels will we tolerate protest. You must discern between those protests and those protesters who rightfully seek justice and improvement and those who would destroy the underpinnings of democracy in protest of the status quo. By your example in private practice and by your efforts as an individual and as a member of a bar association, you can, you must exert the influence of your training. It has been said that "a nation guided by law must be a nation protected by law." And the attorney has a singular responsibility to furnish not only the guidance but also the protection.

And now I turn to that second area of practice which I have called public law. From my vantage point in state government, I have become aware of the strong change which is taking place in the practice of law. More and more, lawyers find themselves out of the traditional channels of criminal law, torts, contracts and title search. In modern practice, we now find ourselves practicing more often before either legislative or regulatory agencies of the government. Where once we were most concerned with court law, wills and title search, practice before the planning and zoning commission or some other regulatory agency now is increasingly frequent.

As government has grown, so has practice of public law. And as government on all levels encroaches on the individual, the scope and importance of public law practice also increases, not only as it affects you as an attorney but also as it touches you as a private citizen. Therefore, it is in this area of the law that your influence can be most keenly felt in the interest of the common good. This is a double-edged sword, for as you grow in the knowledge and workings of public law, and increase your professional ability, so will you also be given the opportunity to make a larger contribution to our society, which, good or bad, has come to depend so heavily on governmental agencies.

The primary lesson of my first six months in Frankfort is very clear. I have seen firsthand just how much state government is at the mercy of the federal branch. As the first order of business nearly every piece of legislation is studied to ensure that it conforms to federal guidelines. Washington's message is simply this: do it our way or do it with your own money.

I recognize the fact that those of us at the state level are partially at fault for encouraging this deplorable situation. For too long, state government failed to move forward and answer some of the needs of its people. It was a simple matter for the federal government to step in and do for us what in some instances we already should have been doing. And, too, states such as ours which have a low per capita income, are particularly susceptible to Washington's not so subtle financing policies. However, I feel that it would be a disservice to the Commonwealth of Kentucky and the people who elected me if I conveniently turn my head and ignore the threat of further Federal encroachment. Rather than this, I am here today to seek your help, your talent, your energy, and your ideas. I want you to consider either a career or at least a tour of duty in state or federal government. With your help and the vast capabilities which you can bring to Frankfort, we will be far better equipped to keep our house in order and not rely on the federal government to do so.

I am particularly proud of the start my administration has made to involve young people in the affairs of state which so vitally affect us all. As proof of our willingness to find a place for you, may I cite some of the programs we have initiated already.

Our Student Legislative Intern program was well received and made a valuable contribution during the 1968 session of the General Assembly. As you may know, although the University of Louisville did not participate, this was a bi-partisan program which gave law students, graduate students, and undergraduate students majoring in pre-law or political science, an opportunity to serve as personal aides to the legislators. Many of the schools which participated also awarded academic credits.

Our budget for the next two years contains money for the second of our youth-involvement programs which we call the Frankfort Semester. Students from Eastern, Western, Murray, Morehead, and Kentucky State spend one semester and the following summer working in the executive branch of various departments and agencies and also take courses in government and public administration at Kentucky State College.

The third program is a demonstration project for those interested in careers in social work. Approximately eighty students will become field workers this summer, handling actual cases. In many instances, the students will also receive academic credits. I believe that law schools soon will recognize the worth of such programs, patterned after the internship plan for doctors, and will join with me in giving Kentucky a backlog of legal talent interested in the practice of public law.

In closing, I invite you to spice your practice, whether it be private or public, with political involvement. I cannot agree, for obvious reason, with Artemus Ward, who said many years ago, "I am not a politician . . . and my other habits are good, also." I don't mean all of you should run for office, we've got plenty of competition already. But both major parties have a lot of room and a great need for new blood and new leadership.

The times in which you as adults will live and raise your families will be even more exciting and more difficult than now. Your leadership will play a large role in maintaining our way of life, our freedom, and our heritage. In the face of the challenge and the opportunity which lies ahead, it would be tragic to have said of you what Queen Victoria said of Lord John Russell, that he was interested in nothing but the Revolution of 1688 and himself.

KENTUCKY BROADCASTERS
ASSOCIATION
Lexington / May 21, 1968

THERE is no question that broadcasting has earned its distinction as an essential channel for public information concerning state government. Certainly, we recognize that broadcasting is the most immediate and direct means of communications available by which government officials may reach their constituency. Therefore, we as public officials and as broadcasters must accept our respective responsibilities to preserve this vital line of communication and keep it free and open.

This will best be accomplished, I believe, if we are able to define the responsibilities encumbent upon each party and recognize the fact that we are on a two-way street. In this atmosphere of give-and-take, of free exchange, of dependence upon each other, it is not hard to understand that our responsibilities are tightly interwoven and interdependent.

This is the way I see it. Our responsibility to the broadcasting industry is to make ourselves available, to invite scrutiny and inquiry, and to operate openly and in full view as much as is possible. The responsibility of the media, then, is to report the news fairly, in its proper perspective, undistorted by sensationalism or selfish, partisan motives.

The new administration is making a sincere effort to carry out its responsibilities and here are some examples. One of our first accomplishments was the establishment of a "message repeater" system, which is being used by many of you each day to keep your audience current to the latest happenings in Frankfort. By dialing our number, you may listen to a three-minute tape recording which describes the latest events in state government. The tape is changed three times each day, and it has opened lines of communication from Frankfort to all corners of the Commonwealth which has never before been available to you.

We have been gratified with your response. You and your colleagues use the message repeater an average of seventy-five to eighty-five times each day and during the legislative session you reached a high of 125 tims each day. What this machine does is give each of you a reporter in Frankfort, a free reporter, I might add, who can supply you with direct quotes from the Governor, top administration officials, and legislators.

Also, in looking for people who would work with the various news media, we were especially pleased to find a man who had an extensive background in radio and television broadcasting. That man is Jim Host,[1] our Commissioner of Public Information. Presently, Kentucky is one of only five states in the nation which assigns one person exclusively to radio and television and I hope you will accept this as proof that we stand ready to help you in any way possible.

Our latest innovation on your behalf is contained in the special announcement I am proud to make at this time. Because this administration believes so strongly in each citizen's right to know what is going on in Frankfort, and because we believe so strongly that radio and television are effective, responsible media, we are instituting next month a half-hour, panel-type news conference in which representatives of this organization will be asked to participate fully. The panel has been set up to include five representatives of the news media. We will ask your association to supply two representatives for each news conference, two more will be invited to participate and represent the Kentucky Press Association, and the Capitol Press Corps will be asked to send one representative.

By holding such news conferences as often as possible and by asking each association to rotate its representatives each time, we hope that every radio and television station and newspaper in Kentucky will have an opportunity to come to Frankfort to participate sometime during the balance of this administration. We plan to meet soon with officers of the three media organizations to finalize details. Tentatively the broadcast will originate from my office where administration officials and I will be available to you for a question and answer session which should interest your listeners. In addition, we will discuss the possibility of a statewide, live network broadcast and we welcome any advice you may be able to offer in this regard.

We plan to beef up our radio-television staff, add new equipment, offer color footage, and supplement our current programs with perhaps a weekly wrap-up of the week's events. As most of you know who recently participated in the poll taken by our Public Information Department, these planned improvements reflect your suggestions and we encourage this dialogue in the future. I hope you will agree that we are making every effort to live by the guidelines which were outlined earlier.

For your part, the responsibility to handle news honestly, fairly, and judiciously has never been more important than now, not only here in Kentucky but throughout the nation and throughout the world. Americans particularly, I believe, are suffering tremendously from a communications gap, a credibility gap, if you will, which has immobilized our efforts to close the gaps of dissension which threaten us today.

Events of the past few years have shaken the nation's faith in itself and in the principles we once accepted without question. Advanced methods of communication have brought into every living room, for all to see or hear, reports documenting the crumbling of law and order and of respect for the educational process—in short, the traditional American way of life. Night after night we watch as mobs defy the law, loot, burn, and even kill. These so-called "protests" in the name of injustice show shamefully little concern for justice. Night after night we watch, in disbelief, as young people mock, threaten, intimidate, and disrupt education. These "protests" in the name of academic freedom show no regard for the freedom of others.

I suggest that this industry honor its responsibility to the silent majority[2] of Americans who build, not destroy, who abide by the law, not violate it, and who practice the American way of life, not prostitute it. The silent majority has been ignored too long, drowned in the clamor and chaos of the minority which distorts our image to the world.

The shame is that the communications industry may be regarded as an inadvertent partner to this tragedy. By its emphasis on those who destroy, the industry has neutralized the silent and forgotten majority. I saw perfect examples of this just last week. It was my privilege to be with the honor students at the University of Louisville Law School last Wednesday. Here was the cream of the crop, the best of a brilliant group, exemplifying those things we as parents hope to see in our children. This group earned only four lines of publicity in the newspaper, very little footage on television, and almost no time on radio.

Yet, that same day, the papers and the television and radio stations found time and space for a group of students who would not permit their teachers to enter the school buildings in Brooklyn. It is time for us all to heed the silent majority, to promote and recall the principles on which this country and this society were founded. This is a challenge worthy of you, of the industry you represent; an industry which can and must fulfill its potential as an instrument for the common good.

My faith in the communications media was reaffirmed last winter during the legislative session and, in fact, throughout my brief administration. When we had decided on the steps which were necessary to correct Kentucky's grave financial situation, we relied heavily on the communications industry to help us explain to the public why a tax was necessary, why it should be a sales tax, and what it would do for the future of this state. And while no tax is popular and no politician is ever happy about raising taxes, I feel that the good job you in the broadcasting media did in handling the budget and revenue measures has gone a long way in helping Kentuckians to understand the situation.

Since you represent such a wide cross section of the state, I would be delighted to know what questions you have concerning state government and my administration. Therefore, I would like to open the floor to any questions you might have.

---

1. W. James Host (1940–   ), unsuccessful Republican candidate for lieutenant governor (1971); commissioner, Department of Parks (1970–1971); Commissioner of Public Information (1968–1970). From Ashland, Host resides in Lexington and is a businessman.

2. This appears to have been the first time in 1968 that the term "silent majority" was used. Governor Nunn elaborated on the "silent majority" in detail on June 20, 1968, in his speech to the Union League of Philadelphia and also used the expression at the Republican National Convention on August 6, 1968.

BLUEGRASS BOYS' STATE
Eastern Kentucky University
Richmond / June 5, 1968

As I look out among you tonight, I see rays of hope shining brightly on this, another dark and ugly day for this nation, when another mark of shame was struck against the reputation of America. For those of you who have shown an eagerness to learn about and participate in state government and have shown that you are determined to make a contribution to the society you are inheriting, the event in Los Angeles has special meaning. Because it will be encumbent on you as leaders of the new generation to attack the causes of this disease, this cancer of lawlessness which threatens us.

I see a warning for the country in the tragedy which struck down Senator Kennedy[1] today, and that warning ironically came from the lips of the would-be assassin.[2] The news media quoted the assassin as saying that he committed his despicable act because he loved his country. Many of you may be too young to remember that this was the same senseless reasoning and the same excuse we heard before, as the Castros, the Hitlers, and others sought to justify their actions.

I ask you to join me in making it clear for all that we will not tolerate or condone in any way the idea that protest can be accompanied by disregard for the law. Help me to make it understood that no person or group will be allowed to operate outside the framework of law and order. Help me to broadcast the idea that the good of the country cannot, by any stretch of the imagination, be promoted by injustice.

It is understandable that this shooting will cause America to retreat temporarily into a state of emotional shock. However, before many days pass and minds recover, I believe there will arise an emotional cry for unrealistic solutions to attempted and successful assassinations by firearms. This approach, however well-meaning it may be, is wrong. This would be attacking one symptom of a serious disease. It would be as misdirected as a doctor placing a bandage over a cancer sore. There probably will be a frantic effort to avenge the shooting of Senator Kennedy with a bandage, that is, a gun registration law. The criminal element of our society will never register its firearms. Therefore, such legislation can never stop the criminal and devious mind from obtaining weapons illegally. It will serve no useful purpose to have only the law-abiding citizen register his guns.

A seriously defective by-product of gun registration is the misuse of such registration lists. In Czechoslovakia and other Iron Curtain countries, the Communists confiscated all privately owned, registered guns. Studies of Communist take-overs show that such coups were made possible because of gun registration laws. Pre-World War II England confiscated all but a few privately owned guns. As a result, the English were extremely fearful of a Nazi invasion. The government pleaded with American sportsmen to send privately owned guns and ammunition to arm the English Home Guard and thanks to American generosity, a possible invasion was forestalled. Gun legislation would be a wrong answer, giving false security.

To find a cure, we must recognize what the disease is! I firmly believe that the moral foundations of this country have been and are being assaulted on a major scale. Respect for proper authority is being challenged from every direction. Belief in God is being questioned. This coincidentally follows on the heels of the U. S. Supreme Court decisions outlawing the Lord's Prayer and Bible reading in our nation's schools.

The very basis of our Republic is being rocked by anarchists and revolutionaries who would destroy our legislative process. They don't want dialogue, they want destruction. They will substitute anarchy for elections and violence for legislation. This pattern has blossomed, as some nationally prominent leaders have said that they would lead a pretty good demonstration. Fuel to the riots was added when another government official used the anarchists' theme song "We Shall Overcome."

The siren song for academic freedom has led to academic license. When Communist revolutionaries are invited to speak on the major college campuses, should we express surprise when students riot? These small but vocal groups of misfits and malcontents reflect the sickening, immoral smog that has developed in America. This same smog enveloped the mind of Senator Kennedy's assassin.

However, for many years, this same smog of moral cancer has blasted forth in the many riots that have touched and tortured this land. Now it belches forth again, darkening America with a staggering increase in criminal activities of all sorts. This is the disease which must be cured, not with a bandage, but with a return to the principles of our founding fathers. We must reaffirm our belief in God and we must reembrace the teachings of the Bible.

I am proud to address my remarks tonight to such an outstanding organization which lives by and promotes the principles of God and country.

1. Robert F. Kennedy (1925–1968), United States Senator from New York.

2. Sirhan Bishara Sirhan assassinated Senator Robert F. Kennedy on June 5, 1968, while he was campaigning for the Democratic presidential nomination in Los Angeles, California.

BURLEY AUCTION WAREHOUSE ASSOCIATION
Lexington / June 10, 1968

IN this, my first opportunity to address any segment of the tobacco industry as Governor, I want to make it clear to you that the new administration in Frankfort stands armed to protect one of the state's most vital economic forces.

Our continuous search for new industries, I believe, sometimes shoves into the background the realization of the importance of tobacco to the economy of Kentucky. This, I am afraid, can only be classified as a penny-wise and pound-foolish operation. To ignore and perhaps impair the tobacco industry would be a serious and even fatal blow to the hopes we all share for this Commonwealth's future expansion. Certainly, your industry must be protected and the heaviest responsibility must be felt on the level of state governments. This is crucial because there has been absolutely no proof or indication that we can rely on help from the federal level except for a few members of the Congress.

From the federal level, we have seen only the increasing and alarming harassment of the tobacco industry, ranging from restrictive legislation based on unproven opinions and theories to allotment shrinkage, price control, and bureaucratic snarl. The industry, I believe, is vulnerable to this stepchild treatment because there are so few states involved in the production and processing of tobacco. This situation prompts and demands that we in tobacco-producing states show a stronger dedication and a stronger commitment to the protection of the industry.

My concern for the industry runs beyond the primary responsibility a governor must feel to protect and promote all sectors which comprise a broadly based economy. I have a personal interest and first-hand knowledge of tobacco. As a boy, I worked in the tobacco fields and I am presently a tobacco grower, and as an attorney, I have represented tobacco interests.

I am aware of the tremendous impact on the state's economy which is created by those engaged in the tobacco industry and I am thankful especially for the employment factor in the various phases of the industry. Over a half-million Kentucky farm people are involved in plowing, planting, cultivating, cutting, curing and finally marketing our annual crop, which amounts to nearly 550 million pounds of tobacco. The fact that you of the Warehouse Association provide much needed seasonal employment is particularly significant and adds greatly to the overall impact.

I want you here to be assured that the new administration in Frankfort is concerned and sensitive where your interests are involved. The record shows that our firmness on this position was tested severely during the last legislative session. I am convinced that we won a victory for the tobacco industry on the issue of increased taxation. But the fight on this particular issue seemingly never ceases. Already, there are those who say the tobacco industry can withstand more taxes. They seem unaware that 49 percent of the price of cigarettes goes for taxes.

I can only say that I will continue to be guided by my conviction that the common good of the Commonwealth was best served by the approach we took during the past legislative session. You may be assured, too, that we do not intend to stand by and do nothing as threat after threat is mounted against this vital part of our economy.

But ultimately, the future growth and vitality of the industry is in your hands. Although we are small in numbers, with only twenty-one states involved in tobacco production, we are strong in economic impact. I urge you as members of this association to join with tobacco-related interests and form a strong, vigilant, vocal protectorate against future threats.

I believe that by mobilizing those forces which stand to profit from your growth, you will be able to ward off further encroachments. For instance, your industry annually generates $260 million for paper manufacturers; $131 million for rail and trucking interests; $50 million for electric power interests; $173 million for chemical-allied manufacturers; $60 million for petroleum interests, and the list could go on and on. By joining the full force of these interests with those primarily involved in actual production, marketing and processing, we can safely predict a bright and expanding future for the tobacco industry.

UNION LEAGUE OF PHILADELPHIA
Philadelphia / June 20, 1968

A NEW America today awaits the various candidates for the presidency of the United States. It is an America shocked into the awareness that perhaps we are losing our way in this brave, new world. It is an America stunned by the violence and prejudice which has tarnished the reputation of the greatest nation in the world. It is an America alarmed by the implications of recent events. Hopefully, however, it is an America ready to rise and face this latest and greatest challenge in the tradition of those who met the challenge of that day of infamy, December 7, 1941; that day of financial chaos in October 1929; and further back, the threat of the Civil War, and the overwhelming odds of the Revolutionary War.

Our new America can and must be brought back together, solidified and set on its course again. And this can only be accomplished when one of America's greatest sources of strength is mobilized. That source of strength is what I shall refer to as America's silent majority. The silent majority is composed of responsible, law-abiding, dedicated citizens who form the heart and conscience of our nation. But for too long, the silent majority has been only a spectator to the tragic spectacle of recent years, content only to go through the motions of participation in a free society. The silent majority has pacified its conscience with token participation, paying lip service to the principles our forefathers set down in this historic city more than 175 years ago.[1]

Now, however, in the wake of the assassination of Senator Robert Kennedy and in the wake of the long, hot, hatred-filled summers of lawlessness and disorder, the silent majority has been awakened to the danger around us. In the coming election, I believe that the presidency of these United States awaits the candidate who can mobilize and give voice to the silent majority. It must be the aim of the major parties to bring forth leadership which can further arouse and activate the silent majority to once more become participants rather than spectators. Then and only then, when this greatest of all our forces for the common good has been fully activated, will America be able to survive this current danger.

This is not a new danger for our country. Indeed, Abraham Lincoln in 1860 sounded a warning which is as appropriate and pregnant with wisdom now as it was then. "Our danger," Lincoln said, "comes not from without our borders, but within." Lincoln said, "If this nation is to fail, it will be because America commits suicide." We have shown strong evidence of doing that very thing.

I am worried that so many extreme philosophies find either acceptance or tolerance in the minds of so many people. It is alarming to see a major candidate for the presidency declaring his support for a guaranteed annual wage. It is also alarming to see most of our leaders acting in a way which I feel is contrary to the Constitution in the matter of gun control legislation. And it is particularly disturbing to see youngsters in high schools and colleges who freely substitute anarchy for orderly protest.

We all have seen some of America's spokesmen promote the philosophy which would have us take from each according to his own means and give to others according to their needs. Is it any wonder indeed that there are those today who have been persuaded that they are no longer morally responsible for their own conduct or financially responsible for their own well-being? Should we wonder that there are those who will not seek employment, but seek unemployment?

America, I believe, needs leaders who are dedicated to the principle on which this country has stood to surpass all others in the world, that we are guaranteed nothing, except the right to compete, the right to overtake our competitors, and the right to produce and earn profit within the framework of a viable free-enterprise system.

That idea, that great freedom, has always had a special meaning for me, perhaps because I am a Kentuckian and because I was fortunate to grow up in a very special section of the Commonwealth. Except for brief periods of time, I have lived my entire life within thirty miles of the birthplace of Abraham Lincoln. There, atop a little hill, stands a magnificent building which enshrines a crude log cabin. And during one of my most recent visits to this national shrine, I tried to think back to the days when that log cabin stood in a clearing of one of Kentucky's virgin forests. That cabin is bare within and it is forbidding without. It speaks of the deepest poverty.

And as I stood there outside that shrine, I could see stretched upon that barren earth floor, a ragged, untaught boy pouring over a borrowed book by the flickering light of the fire. I could see that boy lift his eyes to the burdened form of his pioneer mother, and I could hear him say: "Life is hard. The future seems hopeless, but my forefathers fought in the American Revolution. They gave allegiance to a government not of men but of laws, laws which should be of equal application to all. Their eyes held a constant vision of a nation in which all men should be free to work out their own destinies, to plan their own lives, to possess the fruits of their own labors, and to stand or fall by their own efforts.

"Yes, I am poor, but I have a chance. In my country no doors are barred to me because I am poor. I can work; I can learn. Knowledge will give me power, thank God, I have a chance."

And that ragged boy rose to become the railsplitter, the country storekeeper, the small town lawyer, the advocate of a great cause, the exemplar of individual liberty under the law, the great American President, the emancipator of a race, and the defender and preserver of the American Union. I often wonder what would have happened to Lincoln if one of the poverty workers of the 1960s had gotten hold of him.

And as I think of Lincoln and others before and after him who gave so much to build, nurture, and protect our nation, I cannot help but feel that our generation is not measuring up. By our silence, we have in effect condoned a shameless perversion of the preamble to the Constitution. We have allowed a misguided segment of our society to misinterpret the immortal words, "life, liberty, and the pursuit of happiness." In the dictionary of the anarchists those words are taken as a license to riot, burn, loot, and plunder.

America's situation demands that we choose leaders who will step forward and say unequivocally that our Constitution will never provide a shelter or become an instrument for the use of those who protest against alleged injustices by advocating anarchy and lawlessness. I believe that we must now make it clear that the pursuit of happiness does not mean the guarantee of happiness.

America can no longer afford the luxury of a silent majority. The crisis is far too serious and too advanced to permit us to remain aloof. And certainly, the presidential election year lends itself to the mobilization of the silent majority.

As the silent majority is mobilized to make itself heard, we should be careful not to overlook and ignore the younger segment of our citizenry. We all can become benefactors of the intelligence and concern young Americans bring to the battle to overcome this country's problems. Now is the time, I believe, that we should fully and fairly explore the adoption of nationwide voting rights for eighteen-year-olds. It has become trite, but no less true, to say that if this age group is old enough to fight, bleed and die for America, it is old enough to have a part in deciding who shall lead the country. Even if eighteen-, nineteen-, and twenty-year-olds were not dying this very hour in Viet Nam, I would still hold this opinion. As you may know, Kentucky is one of two states which permits eighteen-year-olds to vote, and I have seen first hand the most commendable way they have accepted this privilege and responsibility since we lowered the age requirement in the mid-1950s.

For young and old alike, 1968 is a year of opportunity, a year in which we can and must reverse the dangerous trends of which I have spoken. And with the full support of the silent majority, we will be able to replace lawlessness with justice, violence with order, burning with building, divisiveness with solidarity, and despair with hope. These are challenges worthy of our best efforts if we are to keep America a beacon of hope in our troubled and confused world.

———————

1. This was Nunn's second and most extensive use of the "silent majority" expression and came before President Nixon's extensive use of the expression in the 1968 presidential campaign. According to Governor Nunn (interview, February 9, 1973) he discussed the use of the expression and its effectiveness with Richard Nixon at the Republican National Convention in August 1968.

TO THE COMMITTEE ON
WAYS AND MEANS
United States House of Representatives
Oil Importation Legislation
Washington, D.C. / July 2, 1968

I APPRECIATE the opportunity to present, for consideration by this committee and the Congress, my feelings with respect to the need to effectively limit the importation of foreign oil. I am convinced that import limits are required if we are to maintain adequate fuel supplies for our growing economy and our nation's security.

Without adequate liquid fuels, readily accessible, the United States could no longer deal with world problems from a position of strength. From whatever means and by whatever government policies required, including import controls, we must see to it that we do not lose our capability to fuel our industrial plants, our vast transportation systems, and our military.

An overextension of our dependence on foreign oil could undeniably thwart our efforts to maintain a strong position as to these basic fuel supplies. I choose to discuss this issue in terms of fuel supplies as opposed to oil, because I am convinced that within a shorter time than any of us suspect, the liquid fuels for our 90 million family automobiles, for our public transportation system, and for our armed forces, will be co-mingled from a number of so-called synthetic sources as well as from conventional petroleum liquids.

We will be fueling the economy, in the not too distant future, with supplementary supplies of liquid fuels from the great shale beds of the Rocky Mountains and from the coal beds of Kentucky and Appalachia. The technology for extraction of such fuels already is in standby. Their development awaits two things—the need and the economic incentive. Both the need and the incentive could be postponed for years, if not decades, should we choose the disastrous course of purposely expanding our use of and dependence upon foreign oil. Should this nation ever find its dependence on a day-by-day basis upon the tenuous oil supply lines which stretch those thousands of miles from the Middle East and North Africa, it will be by design and by choice and by folly. It will not be by necessity.

Beyond our presently adequate but unfortunately declining reserves of conventional oil, the United States has combined sources of liquid fuels adequate to last hundreds of years. The estimation for shale oil alone is 1.8 trillion barrels. The potential for liquid fuels through hydrogenation of coal is virtually inestimable. We need not ever find ourselves short of energy, but just as a search for crude oil is made more expensive, it will take much costly research and highly sophisticated technology to bring to reality the production of synthetic fuels.

As Governor of a state where coal is our primary resource, Mr. Chairman, I am highly concerned with maintaining government policies that will not frustrate the potential of liquid fuel's extraction from coals, with immeasurable benefits to Kentucky and to the nation. And I am convinced that the piece-by-piece growth in imports which has been permitted under the present Mandatory Oil Import Program could frustrate our oil-from-coal hopes not just for a few years but for the foreseeable future.

This fear and this conclusion is based upon simple arithmetic. It happens that the Commonwealth of Kentucky has an oil producing industry of which we are justifiably proud. Synthetic oils cannot yet compete with conventional oil production. And, our conventional oil production cannot compete with foreign oil. The oil producing industry in the Commonwealth of Kentucky is not healthy; it is not expanding. In fact, it is declining.

In the past ten years, the number of producing wells in Kentucky has declined from 17,702 to 16,000; it simply means we are abandoning more wells than we are adding. In this same period, Kentucky's crude oil reserves have declined 32 percent. I am told that this is the disturbing trend for the nation as a whole. We have found, in the United States, less oil than we have produced in four of the last ten years.

As an active and interested member of the Interstate Oil Compact Commission, authorized by the Congress as a forum for the encouragement and sound and proper conservation of our petroleum resources, I find in discussing with officials from other producing states, what is happening to the oil producing industry in Kentucky is not the exception but the rule. Our domestic industry is exploring less, drilling less, and finding less and less oil and gas. Demands for oil and gas, on the other hand, continue to rise sharply. Yet, in this situation, we find the Mandatory Oil Import Program, improvised only for the purpose of maintaining a climate conducive to finding adequate defense fuel supplies, is being systematically dismantled to serve all sorts of purposes which in no way serve that security purpose.

Mr. Chairman, the Commonwealth of Kentucky is but one of thirty-three states which produce petroleum. In the overall scheme of keeping our country supplied with oil, nobody would be particularly impressed with Kentucky oil production except Kentuckians. Our daily production is only about forty thousand barrels. Some 800 to 1,000 individuals and small companies drill the bulk of the wells, find and produce the bulk of the oil in Kentucky.

The small oilmen are not only making important contributions to our economy, but they make important contributions to our state government through state tax payments as well as payments to the counties where oil is produced. In 1968, based on production taxes paid in the first quarter, the Commonwealth of Kentucky will realize approximately $210 thousand from oil production taxes, and county governments will collect directly $416 thousand in production taxes. In addition, the industry is assessed for ad valorem taxes based on the value of oil produced in each county.

The oil producing industry is local in character in Kentucky, Mr. Chairman, because the industry is dominated in our state by small independent producers. They live where they work. The industry employs thousands of workers and they pay taxes. For that reason, the Commonwealth of Kentucky is striving to create a favorable climate for oil exploration and development.

Kentucky, like many other states, has hundreds of millions of barrels of oil that can be recovered only by water flooding or by the more costly fire flooding method of production. Several such projects are now contemplated in the state, and many others are sure to grow if we can maintain a favorable climate including a dependable system of limitations on oil imports.

These secondary recovery projects, just as the eventual and hopeful development of oil from coal and shales, depend upon a system of rational and workable federal policies. With surpluses of oil now existent throughout the free world, an effective oil import program is a vital element in such policies. Without reasonable and stable limits on imports, we are, in my opinion, headed on a serious course toward an American oil famine.

We become aroused about certain "gaps," Mr. Chairman, and I say one "gap" we do not want, and one we could avoid if we are wise, is a fuel "gap." I am pleased that among forty-six sponsors in the House of Representatives who have sponsored or proposed identical bills to prevent further erosion in the oil import program, four are from Kentucky. And the other members of our Congressional delegation are in favor of this legislation. I urge, in conclusion, that this Committee give serious consideration to these bills.

KENTUCKY STATE
REFORMATORY JAYCEES
LaGrange / July 8, 1968

THE progress you have made as individuals and as a club certainly is commendable. More importantly, it reflects your concern for the future, when you are able to return to your role as a private citizen of the Commonwealth. In this area, the future of this state and of its citizens, I assure you that we all share deep concern. That concern has been graphically demonstrated, I believe, in recent months, so that now I hope you know that we are truly dedicated to moving Kentucky ahead and to making this state a better place to live, to get an education, to work, and to raise a family.

I believe that the Kentucky which awaits you will be a better state than you knew before. I am convinced of this because of notable progress we have made recently in two areas of vital concern to those of you here. These are the areas of education and employment. Statistics show that the common denominators of inmates here at the Kentucky State Reformatory are first, poor education, and second, unemployment or underemployment. For instance, of the 1,775 inmates here, only 3.5 percent even attended high school. A total of 1,293 prisoners, making up 72.9 percent of the inmate population here, attained the seventh grade or less.

From the unsteady foundation of a limited education, the next step, the employment problem, was a predictable result.

For instance, 43.7 percent were unskilled laborers and 21.1 percent were semi-skilled. The budget passed in the 1968 session of the General Assembly offers hope for vast improvement in both of these areas which can contribute so much to your future welfare.

In that budget, the Kentucky State Reformatory received an appropriation of $2.4 million and of that total, over a half million dollars will be used for the construction and operation of a vocational training school. If this training school can produce men of skill and talent, men equipped for a productive place in society, the money will be wisely spent. The budget also provides for an increase of 289 vocational education units throughout the Commonwealth, so that we will be able to build an already capable and willing work force into an even greater attraction for industry.

We are particularly proud of the industrial growth in Kentucky already this year, and we are confident that more announcements are forthcoming that companies will either locate in the Commonwealth or expand present facilities. In the first six months of 1968, twenty companies have announced plans to invest $44 million in Kentucky for new plants. This will provide an additional 2,000 jobs, more than enough for every man confined here tonight. In that same period, forty-five firms have announced plans to expand facilities and thus create another 1,900 jobs.

In the field of education, the General Assembly spoke with equal clarity and determination. It said, with the passage of the budget which I recommended, that Kentucky would no longer be satisfied with its low standing among sister states in educational ratings. It said that our children would no longer start one step or two steps or even farther behind other children in other states who will ultimately compete for employment. It said that our teachers would no longer have to leave Kentucky in order to find a suitable wage. And it said that for the first time in eight years, increases in revenue would be made available for classroom construction. It will now be possible to construct $200 million worth of new school facilities in the next two years. In fact, more than 65 percent of the budget for the next two years is directed toward education. It is a commitment which I believe ensures a bright future for all Kentuckians.

By your efforts in the activities of this Jaycees organization, we can only conclude that you are willing to be a part of the effort to help Kentucky grow. Again, I congratulate you on the progress you have made. It is an indication that even greater things are forthcoming.

LIVESTOCK FIELD DAY
Coldstream Farm, Lexington / July 10, 1968

THE opportunity to be with you today was one I did not feel I could afford to miss, because I believe that those of us who are charged with the responsibility of providing leadership for the future of Kentucky must first look to that industry which provides more promise than all the others for the future of our state. Certainly that describes the agriculture industry of Kentucky, and that is an even truer description when applied to the livestock industry of the Commonwealth. For here we find spectacular success, success which has been hard-earned and certainly success worthy of the full protection and encouragement of the public sector as well as every private citizen. I pledge again that this will be the aim of my administration and I welcome your support to that end.

For nearly twenty years now, this Livestock Field Day has been an opportunity for us to look beyond the gratifying accomplishments of the past into the exciting and encouraging future which is so vividly portrayed and embodied in the research projects we see here today. Everywhere we look in the area of livestock production in Kentucky, there are records being broken, previous high marks being surpassed, and previously unthinkable goals being brought within reality. Even the mythical $1 billion gross farm income mark established some years ago by the agriculture leaders of the state is now within range of the advances which are being made and which are being promised by the dramatic research discoveries of our generation. I would hope that the true significance of this is understood and appreciated by all the citizens of Kentucky so that the environment of our state is equally conducive to agricultural progress as is our climate, geographical location, and knowledgeable manpower.

Your pride is easily justified by a quick glance at the impressive records you have rolled up in recent years. For instance, you have put Kentucky first in the nation in beef cattle growth, pushing us from twenty-sixth among the states to thirteenth in just ten years. The next decade, I am confident, will see the Commonwealth well entrenched among the ten top in growth production and income. Presently you rank twelfth in beef cow numbers and in 1966, by way of demonstrating the full impact of this figure, you provided nearly one-third of the increase in beef numbers in the entire United States. The accompanying boom in gross annual income from beef cattle is truly gratifying. In this year, I am told that this part of the livestock industry will contribute nearly $200 million to Kentucky's annual income.

Progress of the swine industry within our borders has defied the national trend, for whereas hog numbers declined by 1 percent last year, Kentucky's figure increased by 6 percent. And where we presently rank thirteenth in the nation in swine production, there are clear indications that we soon will move to ninth or tenth as market hogs increase from the present figure of 2.2 million to a predicted 4 million in the foreseeable future.

Even in the gloom of what I trust is a temporary depression of the sheep industry in Kentucky, there is bright hope. Kentucky led the nation in lambing percentage, averaging better than one lamb per ewe of breeding age. This is significant, I believe, because despite the decline of the sheep industry, it appears that Kentucky is eminently suited for this livestock enterprise. Guided by such notable milestones of progress, we in Kentucky are in a stronger and more viable position to determine the course of future achievement and progress. We do so immeasurably strengthened by the emergence of a strong back-up source of agricultural income for the vital and primary tobacco crop here.

While tobacco continues to lead by a wide margin in producing cash for our farmers, we must recognize that the industry faces grave and increasing threats. I do not want to appear as a prophet of doom, but I am sure you are acutely aware of the danger and uncertainty the tobacco industry has encountered in recent years. And now, with the evidence of the further encroachment into areas of media broadcasting advertisement which was offered only days ago, we should be forewarned. I hope that we are forearmed. This situation played a major part in my decision last winter not to further burden the tobacco industry with excessive and, I believe, unfair taxation. I hope that our decision regarding cigarette taxation defines unmistakably our determination to protect Kentucky's chief cash crop.

I would also hope that the first steps of the new administration into the field of agriculture have been encouraging to the farmers of Kentucky. Certainly all the steps we have taken have not been painless, for you or for me, but I hope that you will accept them as tokens of our sincere effort to correct the situation and the conditions which I inherited on December 12 in Frankfort. It is my honest belief that the future of our state is brighter today because of the courageous manner in which a majority of the Legislature acted.

Our budget enables us to deal with many of the major problems which confront Kentuckians, and I am proud of the progress it guarantees for you of the farming community. After exempting from farm machinery the sales and use tax, including those pieces of equipment used exclusively and directly for tilling the soil, for the production of crops, or in the raising and feeding of livestock, poultry, and for the production of milk, we appropriated $6 million for Department of Agriculture programs.

Of major importance to you who are involved in the livestock industry was the appropriation of funds which make operational the new Animal Diagnostic Center in Hopkinsville. And we were particularly gratified to be able to provide $1 million for the construction of an animal disease diagnostic laboratory which I have gladly committed to be built here in central Kentucky. While final location of the diagnostic laboratory for this area has not been decided, I can assure you that there is one basic and fundamental rule to which the ultimate site must conform. I have instructed our agriculture people that the site must be such that existing facilities and know-how will be fully utilized so that the new laboratory will offer the greatest possible service to those of you in central Kentucky.

In other areas of encouragement to agriculture, our budget makes possible further research which I believe is absolutely vital to the vitality and progress of your industry. Modern technology has confronted agriculture with the threat of competition from farm product substitutes such as soybean steaks and powdered milk, to name just two. Our protection will come as the result of research which is now in progress to determine ways to produce bigger and more tender steaks, healthier animals, better breeding procedures, bigger crops, and better pasture and forage supplements. We commend and congratulate the University of Kentucky College of Agriculture for the notable progress it has made in these areas, and we recognize the valuable contribution you as individual farmers have made in these areas by your concern, participation and support in these efforts.

You have shown the ability to quickly recognize and to effectively attack the common problems shared by the members of the livestock industry, and it is in this spirit that we in state government join you to battle the obstacles of paramount importance. For instance, Kentucky must find ways to more fully utilize its abundance of suitable pasture land. We are currently taking advantage of only 30 percent of pasture land and forage. And we must maintain a vigilant watch against the threat of federal intervention into affairs better left in the hands of state and local authorities.

I am confident we acted in the best interests of our growing meat packing industry by passing our own Wholesome Meat Act during the last session of the Legislature. We are convinced that Kentucky can best police that which is her own. I might also add that during the recent Midwest Governors' Conference, I was able to have unanimously adopted a resolution which asks the federal government to treat those packers who comply with standards at least equal to those required under Title One of Public Law 90–201 in the same manner as if their products bore the United States Department of Agriculture inspection seal. The resolution also asked that foreign meat and meat products imported into this country comply with standards at least equal to those required of American producers under the federal Wholesome Meat Act. This same resolution will be presented later in the month at the National Governors' Conference, at which time I hope to gain broad-based support with which hopefully we can influence federal officials.

Thankfully, the problems which face Kentucky's farmers appear to be surmountable if we will dedicate ourselves wholeheartedly to the task. What we have seen today, I believe, reaffirms the combined dedication of the private and public sectors and in view of this, we must conclude that a grateful Kentucky will benefit handsomely from the progress her farmers are achieving.

INTERSTATE 71
HIGHWAY DEDICATION
Louisville / July 11, 1968

THE official opening of this section of highway brings us another significant step closer to the completion of Interstate 71. Judging from
the volume of mail we have received in Frankfort regarding the opening date of this particular section, I know you are very aware of the
great benefit and convenience this stretch represents to those of you
who live in this immediate area.

Not only does this section complete the loop from the Dixie Highway
to downtown Louisville, but it also puts us within six months of the
completion of this interstate roadway which will stretch from Louisville to the Kenton-Campbell-Boone County urban complex in northern Kentucky. All that is left to be completed is a thirty-four-mile
section beginning here where we stand today and running to Carrollton.
When this work is done our Kentucky Department of Highways will be
able to close its books on a much-needed and long-awaited construction
project which will have cost over $70 million. This figure serves to remind us that highway costs are high and getting higher each year.

We must also be mindful that Kentucky will have poured a huge
amount of funds into the interstate system by the time this particular
program is completed sometime between 1972 and 1975. Sometime
during that period, depending on how much construction costs increase
and how much federal aid will be available, Kentucky hopefully will
finish construction of 730 miles of interstate highways. During this
same period, the national system of interstate construction will have
reached 41,000 miles at an estimated cost of $56 billion.

I submit that this combined expenditure on the part of state and
federal authorities is relatively low in light of the benefits which accrue
to those sections of the country who are now served by this modern
network. We must consider the overall, long-range advantages which
will be ours. For instance, Interstate 71 brings Kentucky's two largest
urban and industrial areas [Louisville and northern Kentucky] closer
by a full hour. Upon completion, the trip from Fourth and Broadway
here in Louisville to downtown Covington will take only two hours.

And all along this seventy-six-mile stretch of I–71, the rich industrial
and agricultural potential of this Ohio Valley section will be exposed
to inevitable expansion. The barriers of sectionalism which divided
Kentucky for so long are being torn down one by one with improve-

ments such as the one we dedicate today, and I am thrilled to have an opportunity to participate in the strong, unified, and successful effort toward progress which Kentucky is making. Together we can confidently look forward to a broadly expanded economy, the benefits of which will fall on all facets of our society.

I solicit and welcome your participation so that we may be assured of many more happy occasions such as this event today, and I hope that you will invite me back in December for the final dedication ceremony of Interstate 71.

KENTUCKY LP-GAS
ASSOCIATION CONVENTION
Louisville / July 16, 1968

FROM the vantage point of the Governor's chair, that which is right and that which is wrong in Kentucky sometimes comes to light more readily and perhaps can be seen more clearly.[1] So tonight, I would like to discuss those two subjects, and I am happy to say that circumstances presently are such that I am forced to dwell more on the former than the latter.

I do not say that all is right in Kentucky, because rose-colored glasses are not and should not be part of a Governor's equipment, and certainly they are not a luxury that the new administration in Frankfort can afford. Rather, since December 12 at least, state government has been in a very serious and penetrating, and I would hope productive, period of introspection.

This has been necessary for two reasons which are tied very closely by our desire and pledge to serve the people of the Commonwealth more efficiently and more economically. First, we have tried to determine and isolate the problems which confront the various segments of our economic and social structure. And I might add here that the response by organizations and associations as well as concerned individual citizens has indeed been gratifying and encouraging to me personally as well as the other members of the administration. The deep and sincere concern you in the private sector have shown for the problems which affect all of us underscores the importance of our investigation of the practices and policies of state government.

We have already undertaken a comprehensive study of the complex and sometimes confusing organization of state government and some spectacular results have been achieved. I am confident that the report of the Efficiency Task Force which is expected soon will offer many other suggestions which we can use to save money and become more efficient in Frankfort.

The purpose of these investigations of state government is not to produce evidence for a massive political purge as some would have you believe. Instead, they have been instigated because we know, and evidently the people of Kentucky know, that waste is the natural product of a political machine in use for twenty years.

This self-analysis and study also has been instigated so that we might bring state government to its best fighting weight, so to speak, and shape it up so that we are ready to join you in the battle to solve the many problems Kentucky faces.

As I said in the beginning, there are many things which are right in Kentucky and which offer promise of greater things to come. I am convinced that as present circumstances proved the necessity of increased budget and revenue measures, history will also prove the wisdom of the action taken in the last session of the General Assembly. For in the pages of the budget which we recommended are written the plans and the necessary financing for a giant step toward a greater Kentucky.

Improved education for our children, expanded health facilities for our sick and aging, and a new school for the mentally retarded are only a few of the progressive changes which are now possible. Kentucky has also substantially improved its position in the vital areas of human services where once we lagged far behind. The climate for industrial and economic growth also has been improved so that we can now take full advantage of our favorable tax structure, expanding road system, trainable manpower, and rich natural resources.

All Kentuckians will benefit from the new road system which was proposed yesterday by the Kentucky Turnpike Authority. The four new roads which were announced run through and across Kentucky's midsection, and I am sure that many of the communities represented here tonight will be directly affected.

The 250 miles of parkways will run from Henderson to Owensboro and on to Bowling Green, then across southern Kentucky to Somerset. Another stretch will link London and Hazard. When these new roads are completed and are joined with others already finished or under construction in the interstate and Appalachian programs, Kentucky will have a complete network of highways equal to those of any state.

And I assure you that they will be our calling card as we search for new industrial citizens. Our proximity to the huge markets of the midwest and of the east is already advantageous when we compete with neighboring states for plant locations. This and the other points I have already mentioned were vital factors in the decision we announced by the Chrysler Corporation to locate its Airtemp plant in Bowling Green near Interstate 65. We have all seen the steady growth of industrial plants springing up along the Mountain Parkway and the Blue Grass Parkway since those two toll roads were completed.

Not only industrial growth, which probably is the most exciting product of the expanded transportation network, but also growth in tourism, agricultural development, and other areas which are vital to Kentucky's economy have followed the improved highway system. Certainly we hope and we expect that the four roads which were approved Monday will produce the same spectacular results and will contribute to your growth as businessmen in the affected areas.

The industrial growth of the past six months has been at a record-breaking pace and is certainly one of the brightest parts of the overall picture. Since December, twenty-one corporations have announced new investments in Kentucky totaling more than $45 million. More important, 3,000 new jobs have been created with the announcement that these new plants will be constructed within our borders. As proof that the companies, which were already here, like the way they are now being treated, forty companies invested more than $67 million for expansion and this added 1,900 job opportunities for Kentuckians. These then are encouraging facts which, joined with the progress we are making in the areas of education and services for our people, add up to a very healthy future.

Certainly your industry is on the threshold of a bright future also. The number of users of liquified petroleum has now reached 400 thousand in Kentucky and new adaptations of your product are being implemented every day. The broad possibilities uncovered by research put your industry in a particularly strong position, and I congratulate you for the way you have adapted to technological change. By using LP gas in standby systems, industrial parks have recognized the importance of your product and your industry. And the use of liquified petroleum as fuel in automobile and truck fleets opens up far-ranging possibilities for those of you who are engaged in this business.

This association has shown its concern for the industry over the years. Many of you here helped to write the regulations which now govern installation and maintenance of bottled gas. We appreciate your help in the past and look forward to your support and suggestions during the remainder of this administration. Together we must promote fair and equitable regulations which protect both the consumer and the dealer. If we are able to do this, the best interests of both will be served and I pledge again that it will be the aim of this administration to see that this is done.

---

1. The Kentucky LP-Gas Association, affiliated with the National LP-Gas Association, is a trade association of liquified petroleum gas dealers, whose purpose is to further the welfare of their industry in Kentucky.

BUSINESS PROMOTION LUNCHEON
Louisville / July 25, 1968

GENTLEMEN, I sincerely hope you enjoyed your lunch and our show.[1] Now, it's time for the closing commercial. Not that it is necessary to sell you on Kentucky; your presence here is indicative enough. I have something else in mind. I want you to sell Kentucky to somebody else. I want you to enlist in a new sales organization and I'll give you a territory the scope of which is bounded only by the four corners of the earth. Your product is the greatest State in the Union and its people, OUR KENTUCKIANS. No one else can make that claim.

Your market is new industry, looking for a fertile place to set down roots and grow a plant. Competition for that new industry is fierce. You might almost call it a war between the states. The forty-nine others have troops on the firing lines from coast to coast and when it comes to landing more jobs for their people, Mexico and Canada cease being quite so friendly. Even Japan shells us once a year, as you saw.

Kentucky, however, has done quite well lately. I point with pride to 151 of the biggest industries in the United States which have planted roots in Kentucky, which provide jobs for Kentuckians and which ship Kentucky-made products the world over. They use Louisville Sluggers in Japan, by the way, and they drive Ford trucks using Ashland Oil and cook on G.E. ranges. Their location here is no accident.

And that includes our latest acquisition just two weeks ago. I refer to the Airtemp Division of Chrysler Corporation and its announcement of the construction of a multi-million dollar plant in Bowling Green.

There are thirty-eight factors which make up the ingredients new site-seekers look for, and the "availability" of trainable manpower is number one. Picture that. Industry's first requirement is Kentucky's prime asset. Can you gentlemen sell that? Can you not say, in all good conscience, that the people who work for you in Kentucky are your greatest asset. I can. I know for a fact that a small plant in my home county outproduces its counterpart in a neighboring state by 25 percent, making the same product, with the same number of people. As for the quality of Kentucky labor, I'll take Dr. Clark's[2] word over that of any sociologist from Washington. The quantity of Kentucky labor is practically untapped. But I will not be a party to any program that would train Kentuckians for jobs elsewhere, unless that is their wish. I have heard no such expression. With the money some have proposed to spend on that scheme, we could build a dozen plants in eastern Kentucky alone.

What is more, we are equipped now to train our people here at home. Put this in your ammunition belt. Kentucky is ranked number one nationally in vocational education by the United States Office of Education, and by the National Chamber of Commerce. Thirteen area vocational schools, twenty-two extension centers, and sixteen high school vocational programs combine for a total of sixty-one different sites of instruction. We will fund seven new centers in the next few months, covering such specialized training programs as aeronautics, health, and mining mechanics. In an age that's getting even more specialized, Kentucky will offer more specialized education to our young people. What they do with that education, without leaving Kentucky, is up to us.

We know that industry likes to locate near vocational schools. Our goal is to put one within commuting distance of every community. Even now, 100 thousand young people are enrolled. These people soon will be ready to take their places in the ranks of Kentucky's booming labor force, 850 thousand of whom were on nonagricultural payrolls in June of this year, an all-time record. Their income, as reported by *Business Week* magazine, was nearly 10 percent higher for the four months of 1968 over the same period in 1967.

If economic factors continue as they are, Kentuckians will enjoy an increase in personal income this year which will bring their total to over eight-and-one-half billion dollars. I might also report that unemployment in Kentucky was down to 4.8 percent in June. We are enjoying record prosperity and record growth, yet our available labor supply is at nearly fifty thousand. If we consider the availability of seasonal employees, the men and women who switch from the farm to the city and back again, that number can swell to two-hundred thousand.

While we're at it, let's look at the record. Since this administration took office, twenty-nine new industries have either broken ground or announced their intentions of doing so, and they will employ nearly thirty-seven hundred people. Plant investment totals roughly fifty million dollars. In addition, existing Kentucky industry has invested another seventy million dollars in plant expansion, providing for another three thousand jobs. Gentlemen, these are the fruits of a climate suitable for growing plants. The business climate in Kentucky, by legislation, by organization, and by the redetermination of the people involved, has been given major credit for the location here of two of our most recent new industries, one on the banks of the Big Sandy and the other in the Northern Kentucky Industrial Foundation Park.

There's nothing the matter with our tax climate, either. Our tax climate is one of the most attractive in the nation. More and more, prospects which later became realities have told us that the Commonwealth's tax structure was vitally important in their decisions to locate here.

There isn't time today nor this week to enumerate all thirty-eight of the prime factors of site selection, and to tell you how Kentucky fills the bill. But we'll put it together for you in a handy compendium and send it to 125,000 *Fortune* readers in December. In the meantime, Kentucky's industrial revolution has already begun and state government is enlisted. We are particularly proud of the highway network which reaches virtually every section and every corner of the Commonwealth. With the announcement two weeks ago of our new toll road system, Kentucky soon will be fully primed to take advantage of its newest asset. Because of its existing network of highways, Kentucky manufacturers are within twenty-four hours of two-thirds of the nation's population by truck. By air, those twenty-four hours shrink to just two.

By water, well, our Department of Commerce has the timetables and the charts. It also has a plan for major industrial developments in the Ohio River Valley and up the nine-foot channel to Paradise, Kentucky, among other places. Kentucky has more miles of navigable streams and rivers than any other state in the Union. But more important in the long run, Kentucky, unique except for two other states in the nation, has a fresh and pure water supply that can be counted on, and planned on by industry and people for years to come. I am grateful that this is one concern we do not have. Other states, unfortunately, do.

This and similar problems in other states were conveyed to me by other governors over the past few weeks at the Midwest, the Southern, and the National Governors' conferences.

Among the duties I assumed at these gatherings was one that I hope will prove particularly fruitful here at home, getting better tax breaks from Washington. At all the Governors' conferences I have attended this year, I have either sponsored or supported resolutions which deal with industrial revenue bonds. As you know, the United States Treasury Department by adopting certain regulations without public hearings, has seriously reduced the effectiveness of industrial bond legislation. I am happy to report that Representative Wilbur Mills now has legislation pending which will reopen this much needed revenue source we need for industrial growth in the future and the governors unanimously support this effort.

My role as a recruiter here today is twofold: I have the feeling that many of you, if not all, believe as I do, that, in Kentucky, private enterprise can succeed where Washington bureaucracy has failed. This means we must work together. We must involve ourselves in the problems that beset other Kentuckians.

Some of the nation's economists predict a business decline and possibly more inflation. It must not happen here, and it would not if we keep up the pace. But that pace now requires a greater effort. To stay above the national average in industrial growth, we have got to work harder. Let me assure you that the Governor's Office is anxious to help. As our advertisement in *Fortune* magazine indicates, I am as close as the telephone, and I hope you will not hesitate to call if I can be of help.

I was delighted to have the opportunity to sit in on early negotiations between the Chrysler Airtemp officials and representatives of Bowling Green, and I will be more than happy to come to your town to personally offer the resources of state government. Together we can sell this great Commonwealth, because we know its potential, because we believe in it, and because we love it.

Let us tell the world about our rolling hills and lush valleys. Our inspiring mountains. Our verdant pastures, our plains. Our Bluegrass and our mineral wealth. Our fishing and hunting, golf, swimming, schools and churches.

Let us tell them about the breath of clean, fresh air that pervades our sweet land. And let us tell them about our people, THE KENTUCKIANS.

We cannot do all of it by word of mouth. So we have selected some important magazines. In the next few months, Kentucky ads are scheduled in such diverse but widely circulated publications as *Busi-*

ness Management, Forbes, Dun's Review, Business Week, U.S. News and World Report, Wall Street Journal, Area Development, Harvard Business Review and, for our major push, *Fortune* magazine. Our story is the Kentucky story and I hope we can tell it together.

As a reminder of this occasion, and of the program on which we are about to embark, I want those of you here today to be among the first, and the few, to wear the small memento which says, "Every Kentuckian Counts." We can make sure that every Kentuckian counts by helping to make him a productive partner, earning his full share of the benefits and opportunities which are available in our beloved Commonwealth.

---

1. The purpose of Governor Nunn's luncheon was to win the support of Kentucky industry for an advertising campaign in *Fortune* magazine to bring new industry to Kentucky. The entire advertising section of *Fortune*, December 1968, was devoted to Kentucky and was financed by existing industry in the state. The *Fortune* issue was the largest in the magazine's history devoted to the promotion of one state.

2. Thomas Clark preceded Governor Nunn with remarks about Kentucky. Thomas D. Clark (1903–), distinguished scholar and American historian; professor, History Department, University of Kentucky (1943–1968); Distinguished Professor of American History, Indiana University (1968–); executive secretary, Organization of American Historians (1968–). *Directory of American Scholars* (New York, 1969), 1:92.

TO THE SUBCOMMITTEE
ON FEDERAL, STATE, AND
LOCAL RELATIONSHIPS
OF THE REPUBLICAN
PLATFORM COMMITTEE
Republican National Convention
Miami Beach, Florida / July 29, 1968

THE relationship of local, state, and national governments to each other embodies perhaps the overriding domestic issue confronting the platform committee, the Republican Party, and the voters of this country.[1]

While the attention of this nation has been focused largely on the dramatic day-to-day crises, we have ignored a far greater problem, the deterioration of the mechanism with which we can effectively deal with these issues. That mechanism is the combined ability, willingness, and resources of the local, state, and federal governments and private sector. The national, state, and local relationship has become less meaningful and less effective because the national government has encroached upon areas which could have been better left in the hands of the government nearest to the problem.

We have arrived at a bleak point in our history where local initiative to deal with issues has been diluted and reduced so that now we are all too willing to dismiss our responsibility by saying "Let Washington do it." The worst effect of this one-dimensional approach, which has been conceived, practiced, and promoted by the Democrat Party since the early 1930s, has been the erosion of grass roots leadership to mobilize and channel the creative talents of Americans toward our problems. Of course, the federal government has important responsibilities it must meet. However, the gravest problems facing our people today are vivid testimony that we have little reason to expect improvement by continuing the "knee-jerk" reaction of the Democrat Party to automatically bring the national government into every problem. For this reason I think the stirring challenge of this committee is to address itself not only to the need to redirect the federal government, but also to focus on and reaffirm a new role for state and local governments and for the private sector.

Let us as a committee, as a party, and as a nation address ourselves to the silent majority of Americans who have been rendered voiceless and are forgotten by a one-sided system of government which attempts to concentrate power, leadership, and creativity on the banks of the Potomac. I know that the Republican Party is worthy of meeting this challenge. I respectfully ask this subcommittee to find ways to make the intergovernmental partnership more effective, to develop a plank which truly reflects our party's dedication to a valuable plan of government—a program which makes fuller use of the best that is available at the local, state, and national level.

---

1. At the 1968 Republican National Convention Governor Nunn was chairman of the Subcommittee on Federal, State, and Local Relationships of the Republican Platform Committee. Nunn was also a member of the Temporary Committee on Resolutions of the Temporary Republican Platform Committee. Interview with Larry Van Hoose, press secretary, July 20, 1971.

REPUBLICAN NATIONAL
CONVENTION
Miami Beach, Florida / August 6, 1968

GOVERNOR Chaffee, let me tell you that not only does the Bluegrass grow but so does the Republican Party, and we will have a tremendous harvest come November.

The Republican Party has taken a long and searching look into the current relationship between government and the American people. Our conclusion is that America's traditional constitutional partnership of federal, state, and local governments is in serious trouble. An increasingly impersonal, centralized, national government has tended to submerge the individual.

Democrat rule has produced "big government and little people." It has created a "silent majority" of Americans, excluded from participation, voiceless, and forgotten. It has made government top-heavy, seeking to concentrate all power and creativity on the banks of the Potomac. The immediate, knee-jerk reaction of the Democrat Party of providing bigger federal programs to meet our pressing problems has proven wholly inadequate.

Because the federal government has become too big, state and local governments have suffered. We are committed to decentralization of power and reorganization of the federal bureaucracy. We will return the government to the people. State and local governments and the private sector anxiously await the opportunity to serve the people. We will provide this opportunity. We propose to share federal revenues and to use block grants to enable states to solve their own problems.

The Republican Party pledges itself to revitalize our traditional American system so that the silent majority of Americans may again find its voice and run its own affairs.

America's youth, the country's great human resource, uniquely qualified and willing to contribute to the society, chafes under the restraints of big government. Ours is a young society in which political unrest reflects the hope of meaningful participation in public affairs. This hope must be satisfied.

Today's youth is endowed with knowledge and maturity entitling them to a constructive part in helping shape the future of the nation. We believe that our youth of eighteen can cast an enlightened vote, as they have during the past twelve years in my native State of Kentucky. For the first time, a national political party now affirms its faith in youth by recommending lowering the voting age for America's youth.

Further, for greater equity and to provide some measure of certainty at a critical time in their young lives, we recommend the revision of current Selective Service policies. We will reduce the number of years during which a young man can be considered for the draft, and we will, as soon as possible, end the draft and establish a voluntary career-type military service for this nation.

Tonight, I ask the youth of America to become a part of our Republican effort, to give new direction and new leadership which this nation so urgently needs and rightfully expects.

The most crucial problem today is crime and violence. For it is the silent majority of innocent, law-abiding citizens, both black and white, who suffer most from such deplorable action. We pledge vigorous, even-handed, fair and firm administration of justice and enforcement of the law. The Republican Party believes that respect for the law is the cornerstone of a free and orderly society. We must, and we will, reestablish the principle that men are accountable for what they do, that criminals are responsible for their crimes, and that while environment may help to explain the act, it is not an excuse for crime.

Ours is a nation of law. In the words of Lincoln: "Let reverence for the laws be breathed by every American mother . . . let it be taught in schools, in seminaries, and in colleges. . . . In short, let it become the *political religion* of the nation; and let the old and young, the rich and the poor, . . . of all sexes and tongues, and colors and conditions, sacrifice unceasingly upon its altars."[1]

Only on the Republican platform, in the Republican candidates, and through the Republican Party will the silent majority be heard. It will speak out eloquently and powerfully in November, telling a troubled world that this nation is back on course and again ready to provide the national leadership so badly needed today.

---

1. Abraham Lincoln, "Address to the Young Men's Lyceum of Springfield," January 27, 1838, *Abraham Lincoln: Selected Speeches, Messages, and Letters*, ed. T. Harry Williams (New York, 1957), p. 10.

NATIONAL LEGISLATIVE CONFERENCE
Miami Beach, Florida / August 21, 1968

IT is indeed gratifying to see the keen awareness and the deep concern for the problem of lawlessness and disorder which is shown here today by you who are charged with the responsibility of making the laws in the statehouses of America.

The most crucial question of our time addresses itself with particular force to the legislators of this nation. That question is: are you willing and able to stop the erosion of law and order in America? The conditions of the nation demand that we give our answer soon. And our answer must come strong and affirmative. Yes, we are willing to face this problem. Yes, we can preserve the law. Yes, we will preserve the law. That must be our answer, because America's course will be determined, for generations to come, by the action we take in this vital matter.

This great nation, which has long been the repository of hope and justice for all the world, anxiously awaits our answer. What will we do to lessen that anxiety and unrest which pervades America? What will we do to crush the tide of violence and crime which poisons our system, immobilizes our people, and inundates our most precious skill—our ability to resolve differences peacefully?

America is asking of her leaders, "Is this still a nation of laws and not of men?" Our people ask, "Are we still guided by the principle that respect for law and order is the cement of our society?" They also ask, "How long must we be afraid to walk in our streets. How long must we stand by, watching helplessly, as our businesses are plundered and burned, our parks shrouded in fear, and our neighborhoods unsafe for women and children? These are America's questions. What are our answers?

Let us say this, that we pledge even-handed, fair and firm administration of justice and vigorous enforcement of the law. That we believe respect for the law is the cornerstone of a free and orderly society. And let us say also that our law will not be sacrificed in the name of protest, whether that protest be justified or not. We must make it clear that rioting and civil disobedience do not fall within the boundaries of due process of the law as we know it. And with our commitment to those ideals, let us reestablish the principle that men are accountable for what they do, and that criminals are responsible for their crimes.

For those who would attempt to justify the acts of lawlessness in the name of social injustice, let us say, once and for all, that while environment may help to explain the act, it is not an excuse for the crime.

Never before has America been so immersed in the throes of emotional overreaction. For example, riots take a deadly toll, and our reaction is to make a study. A leader is murdered and hundreds of thousands of decent, concerned, law-abiding citizens turn in their guns in a senseless, pitiful act of guilt sharing and then cry for firearms registration and control. A city burns and suddenly we are labeled a sick society. These are not the responses America deserves.

We have not come all this way only to surrender to the forces of evil or to be indicted by those who willingly though incorrectly accept blame for the terror and lawlessness which festers in this nation today. We must do more than study lawlessness, we must stop it. We must not act to control the weapons of violence with regulations which are as useless as putting a Band-Aid on a cancer. We must act to control and deter persons who would misuse those weapons. Finally when our cities are in flames, we must fix the blame squarely on those who threw the Molotov cocktails, not on society in general or those who sell gasoline.

Now is the time that we must find answers. Now is the time that we must declare our determination, our purpose and our plan for ending the reign of fear which has seized America. And here, on the outset, let me submit that I do not believe the answers we seek are to be found in the report of the President's National Advisory Commission on Civil Disorders, perhaps better known as the Kerner Report. I am in complete agreement with Governor Ted Agnew of Maryland, when he says that the report reveals more about the mind of our nation than the nature of the violence it purported to study. Governor Agnew was also right, I believe, when he said that the report was self-defeating because of its erroneous first premise, that the American mainstream was responsible for the riots in our cities.

Throughout the report, it is evident that this illogical, masochistic indictment distorts all reason and impartiality which is so vital to the credibility of such a document. Nowhere does the Commission fix the blame on the inflammatory Rap Browns or Stokely Carmichaels and others like them who preach the doctrine of hate and violence. It is they who create in the minds of a segment of the populace, and sadly in the minds of too many of our leaders and responsible citizens as well, the illusion that lawlessness is the inalienable right of the ghetto resident, the poor and the frustrated.

I have no doubt as to the truth of that statement. I have seen the theory in action. Recently a bomb was thrown at my home. Fortunately, little damage was done and my family was not in the house at the time of the explosion. We immediately turned the matter over to local and state police officials and the investigation is continuing.

A week ago a Negro church in Louisville, Kentucky, was dynamited before dawn. No injury or serious property damage occurred. Again local and state officials were called in to investigate. However, that was not enough for the dissident, disillusioned demagogues who saw an opportunity to add fuel to the fire. A meeting was called and quite predictably, violence erupted. Rocks and bottles were thrown, one place of business was looted and fires were started. Evidence established that this was not the act of the members of the church or the responsible Negro citizens of that neighborhood, which is 73 percent black.

Where is the sense in these acts? Where is the justification? Does it lie in the socioeconomic conditions in which these people exist? I do not believe so. We know that two out of three Americans below the poverty level are white. Why don't the impoverished white Americans riot? Could it be that they know their violence will not be met with sympathy, that collective white lawlessness will not be tolerated? This was just one of the disturbing oversights of the Kerner Report. Another point of concern was the vastly underplayed and undefined role of the states in meeting these problems.

I know you will agree that state government sees more clearly, feels more deeply, and can act more effectively in these complex areas than can Washington. With enlightened thinking in Washington toward block grants and other revenue-sharing concepts, these problems could be dealt with effectively by that level of government closest to the problem.

Finally, the tone of the Kerner Report suggests that our main concern must be to correct injustices before we correct lawlessness. I hope you reject that idea, as I do, and I hope you agree that at the very heart of our problem is the crumbling of our traditional respect for the law and the symbols of the law—our police and court systems. On one hand, we have a small group which does not hesitate to violate laws in the name of injustice. On the other hand, we have a large part of the population which is rapidly losing faith in the system of law which permits these acts of crime to go unpunished.

Our people are confused by the logic of a system which permits a mob to break and enter, steal and burn, then casually parade with stolen goods under both arms out of the store, brazenly mocking our policemen as well as a shocked and mystified national television audience. We can logically assume that by this permissiveness we only inspire more crime. We invite the criminal element as well as the disenchanted, desperate American who lives in the grips of poverty to join the fun. In view of this, why should we be puzzled by the spiralling crime rate? How can we extol the virtues and trust the wisdom of a system of law which permits crime by mobs yet punishes that same unlawful act by a lone thief? It should not be at all surprising to see law and order flounder amid the unrest and chaos of America today. It is even less surprising that the symbols of law are objects of criticism, abuse, and disrespect. More would be the surprise if in this climate true justice and respect for the law were to survive.

Facing these sad facts, then, let us begin anew our efforts, first, to stop the violence and lawlessness that threatens our nation and then to sort out the real from the imagined grievances. Let us find and listen to the real victims of injustice and inequality. And let us also find and label, for all to see, those noisy, misguided, selfish parasites who have locked themselves on to the protest movement and have assumed license to riot, to burn, and even to murder in the name of protest against injustice. Let us tell it like it is to our constituencies. We need more policemen, better trained and better paid, and it will take more of their tax dollars. Let us improve our court systems and adjudicate the staggering backlog of cases in our criminal courts. Let us put to rest forever current thinking which pampers criminals and hampers police to a point that crime is skyrocketing into anarchy. And once these vestiges of justice are properly mobilized, then let us say and mean that when instances of violence occur, we will respond quickly, we will use adequate manpower, and we will instruct those men to use whatever force is necessary to put down lawlessness as soon as possible.

These are the teachings of the recent past. If we have learned anything from our experience, it is that we must respond from a position of strength and not weakness. The compelling wisdom of Abraham Lincoln, spoken more than one-hundred years ago, offers direction to this generation. Lincoln said, "Let reverence for the laws be breathed by every American mother to the lisping babe that prattles on her lap; let it be taught in schools, in seminaries, and in colleges; let it be preached from the pulpit, proclaimed in legislative halls, and enforced in courts of justice. . . . In short, let it become the *political religion* of the nation; and let the old and the young—the rich and the poor, the grave and the gay, of all sexes and tongues, and colors and conditions, sacrifice unceasingly upon its altars."[1]

---

1. Abraham Lincoln, "Address to the Young Men's Lyceum of Spring-field," January 27, 1838, *Abraham Lincoln: Selected Speeches, Messages, and Letters*, ed. T. Harry Williams (New York, 1957), p. 10.

WEST VIRGINIA HOUSE
OF DELEGATES RALLY
Charleston, West Virginia / August 24, 1968

In the enthusiasm and concern which prevails here tonight, there is compelling evidence of the dramatic mood that is sweeping through America in this election year.[1] It is a mood which begs for change, for new leadership, and for new direction. Yes, it is a mood that begs for a Republican victory in November. Nowhere is that mood, that feeling, that longing for change more prevalent than right here in West Virginia, regardless of what you may read in the *Charleston Gazette*. This is a Republican year. We are going to win in West Virginia, in Kentucky, and all across this great nation. We will win because in Miami Beach two weeks ago, we nominated a man to seek the presidency who can and will give us the leadership, the creativity, the sensitivity, and the courage Americans are looking for today.

We are going to win this year because in the Republican Platform our party has rekindled the spirit and provided the unity, the hopes, and dreams of America. Our platform is a human document. It clearly reflects the mind and the mood of this land. It reflects the deep concern and the unrest and anxiety which pervades our nation. In that document, our party has spoken clearly and courageously about our problems. Our party has bravely faced these problems and has suggested viable solutions. It deals forcefully with the number one domestic problem in our nation today—law and order. The platform is also decisive about Viet Nam, about our world involvement, about our economic crisis, and about the theory of the present administration which has practiced big government and little people.

The Republican platform has captured the mood of America today because Republicans have shown that they care. They care that our flag is the object of disrespect and scorn, they care that our traditions

are distorted and ignored by the opposition party, and they care that
our principles of law and order, justice, and equality are being trampled
beneath the footsteps of the rioters and the protestors. Our party cares
far too much to settle for the easy answers and the lip service of the
Johnson-Humphrey administration. And because we care, our party
offers the best chance for the silent majority of Americans to speak up
for America and to help us chart a better course for this great nation.

The silent majority embodies our workers, our doers. As Dick Nixon
has said, "They are not racists or sick; they are not guilty of the crime
that plagues the land. They are black and they are white, native born
and foreign born, young and old. They work in America's factories.
They run American businesses. They serve in government. They provide most of the soldiers who died to keep us free. They give drive to
the spirit of America. They give lift to the American dream. They give
steel to the backbone of America. They are good, decent people; they
work, they save, they pay their taxes, they care." It is the silent majority which cries out loudest for Republican leadership.

These Americans remember only too well the battle cry of the Democrats eight years ago. The rallying call then was their boast that "We
can do better!" Sadder but wiser after the years of the Johnson-
Humphrey administration, Americans know that we are now worse off
in any field of comparison. We all remember, too, how the Democrats
lightly dismissed the peace and the economic security which was America's both at home and abroad during the Eisenhower-Nixon years. In
the mystifying logic of the candidate, this peace was offered as proof
that our country had been in mothballs. They equated peace and prosperity with inactivity, so they dusted off the old campaign slogan,
"Let's get moving again!" And by the smallest majority in the history
of modern politics, the government changed hands, and sure enough,
America started moving again.

But every move has been accompanied by the sound of battle, of
bullets in Southeast Asia and of burning in America's streets. Every
move has bred turmoil and strife, unmatched in this country's history.
Now the facts are in. The truth is obvious. The Democrat Party is
hopelessly bound to programs and ideas which have not worked. Instead, the programs of the present administration have broken our
unity, weakened our resolve, and prostituted our purpose. These same
programs have left America hanging on the ropes, not knowing whether
the next blow to our way of life is coming from here at home or from
abroad.

Let us look then at the answers our party offers to Americans who
ask, "Will we stop the tide of violence and crime which poisons our

system?" What will we say when Americans ask, "Is this still a nation of laws and not men?" What will we say when they ask, "How long must we be afraid to walk in our streets?" "How long must we stand by helplessly as our businesses are plundered, and our parks and neighborhoods shrouded in fear?"

Let us say that we pledge even-handed, fair, and firm administration of justice and vigorous enforcement of the law. Let us say also that we believe respect for the law is the cornerstone of a free and orderly society. And let us make it clear that rioting and civil disobedience do not fall within the boundaries of due process of law.

Then, with our commitment to those ideals, let us carry out the declarations of the Republican Platform—that men are accountable for what they do, that criminals are responsible for their crimes. For those who attempt to justify the acts of lawlessness in the name of social injustice, let us say, once and for all, that while environment may help to explain the act, it is no excuse for the crime. The Republican Party is pledged to stop the violence and lawlessness that threatens our nation. We are also pledged to sort out the real from the imagined grievances. Let us find and listen to the real victims of injustice and inequality. And let us also find and label, for all to see, those noisy, misguided parasites who have locked themselves on to the protest movement and have assumed license to riot, to burn, and even to murder in the name of protest against injustice.

The compelling wisdom of Abraham Lincoln offers direction for this generation. He said, "Let reverence for the laws be breathed by every American mother to the lisping babe that prattles on her lap; let it be taught in the schools, in seminaries, in colleges; let it be preached from the pulpits, proclaimed in legislative halls and enforced in courts of justice. . . . In short, let it become the *political religion* of the nation; and let the old and the young, the rich and the poor, the grave and the gay, of all sexes and tongues, and all colors and conditions, sacrifice unceasingly upon its altars."[2] These are the answers we offer to halt the crumbling of law and order in America.

Our next most serious problem is the war in Viet Nam. Here Republicans are united behind the experienced, proven leadership of Richard Nixon. He speaks for America when he says that the record of failure chalked up by the present administration in Washington must be rewarded by a complete housecleaning of those responsible for that failure. Dick Nixon has pledged that while there is hope for an honorable end to the war by negotiations he will say nothing to endanger that hope. But if the war is not ended by November, the new president will have been given a mandate from the people. There must be an honorable end to the war in Viet Nam. And there must be a policy to prevent more Viet Nams. The time has come for other free nations to bear their fair share of the burden of defending freedom around the world. In this respect, our party's proud record bears recalling. Let us never forget, as we compare the records of the presidential candidates, that Richard Nixon was a vital part of the team which ended one war and kept us out of others for eight years. These are the answers America demands of those who seek the presidency, and I am proud of the record and response offered by the Republican candidate and the party platform.

I know, too, that West Virginians everywhere are proud of the response the Republican Party has made to these problems and also to the serious problems which confront the great people of the "Mountaineer State." Republicans throughout the country are excited by the good news that you are making here in West Virginia. Here, as across the country, the Republican tide is coming in and victory is in sight. Victory will be yours because your candidate for governor, Arch Moore,[3] measures up in every respect to the kind of leader this troubled state is looking for. West Virginians have seen this man from Wheeling perform. They have confidence in his ability, in his deep concern, and in his willingness to move this state forward. But above all else, in this state which is shaken and shocked almost daily by the tremor of government scandal, West Virginians find in this man a governor who can restore their confidence and their faith in state government.

While the election of a Republican governor is one of the most important steps West Virginia must take in November, we must always remember that it is only the first step. You must also send to the state house Arch Moore's team, the Republican candidates for the Board of Public Works. And so that West Virginia can have the full advantage of the leadership and new ideas and new approaches of these officials, you must also send to the state capitol a Republican majority in the House of Delegates. West Virginia already has set a shining example for the rest of the nation in this respect. Where there were only nine Republican delegates a few years ago, now there are thirty-five. The magic number of fifty-one is within your grasp; this must be attained if the next Republican administration is to be fully effective.

Let us remind the voters of West Virginia that the lack of progress during the long reign of the opposition party is an indictment of all its elected representatives. All of them must share the blame. None can defend the insensitive, self-serving, political machine which after thirty-two years has still failed to move West Virginia from fiftieth in the nation in education, fiftieth in the nation in economic growth, and dead last among the twelve Appalachian states in highway construction. The Democrat Party has played a game of musical chairs with state government, and it is evident that the people of West Virginia have paid the consequences.

What do you say about this? All of you who want to stop the music say, "Aye!" And all of you who want a Republican majority in the House of Delegates say "Aye!" Now, loud enough so that the *Charleston Gazette* and all the political bosses can hear you! . . . All who want Arch Moore as the next governor of West Virginia say, "Aye!"

That's the spirit! Keep that spirit and that enthusiasm, and you can't lose, no matter how badly outnumbered in registration you might be. I have seen it work in my state. It will work in yours. As you know, Kentucky is perhaps the most Republican of all Southern states. We are one of only four states in America which has a Republican governor and two Republican U. S. Senators. And this November, we are going to elect a Republican majority to send to Congress. These achievements have not been easy, and there is no magic formula. But as Kentucky has been successful, so can you. All the ingredients for victory which we have used in Kentucky are here. You have the candidates, the platform, the concern, and the dedication to solve the problems which hold back your state.

The future of your state for years and generations to come rests on what you do. The children of West Virginia cry out for a better opportunity, for better schools. The fathers of West Virginia cry out, too. They want jobs, not welfare programs. They want a hand up, not a handout. And the mothers of this great state cry out. They cry loudest for your help. They want an environment in which their children can grow up physically straight and morally strong. They cry out for an environment which does not trap their families in despair, in frustration, and in hopelessness. They seek an environment which gives hope and fulfillment to their dreams and ambitions. These are the voices which must guide you in the campaign ahead. These are the voices which must influence every decision, every thought, and every promise of the Republican candidates. And these are the voices which must constantly remind you to make every effort, to leave no voter unaware of your message, to leave no work undone in the great task that lies ahead. These, these are the voices which will shout loudest the news of your great victory in November.

---

1. Governor Nunn spoke throughout the nation in support of the Nixon-Agnew Republican ticket for the 1968 presidential election and for many

other Republican candidates. For another example of a similar speech see Nunn's speech of September 19, 1968.

2. Abraham Lincoln, "Address to the Young Men's Lyceum of Springfield," January 27, 1838, *Abraham Lincoln: Selected Speeches, Messages, and Letters*, ed. T. Harry Williams (New York, 1957), p. 10.

3. Arch Alfred Moore, Jr. (1923–   ), Republican governor of West Virginia (1969–   ); representative, United States House of Representatives (1964–1969); and West Virginia House of Delegates (1953–1955). *Who's Who in America, 1970–71* (Chicago, 1971), 36:1599.

UNIVERSITY OF KENTUCKY COOPERATIVE EXTENSION SERVICE CONFERENCE
Lexington / September 11, 1968

I WANT to compliment and commend this group for the way it has performed during the transition period of the last two years. To keep in step with Kentucky and to help keep Kentucky in step with other states in the nation, you have managed splendidly to adapt to the changing times. No longer is your function limited to rural areas and narrow concentration. In your new role as Area Extension Agents, you have accepted greater responsibilities affecting the well-being of every Kentuckian, and I congratulate you for the way you have responded to this challenge. This change from the County Agents program to the Area Agents concept in extension service reflects a basic change that is under way in Kentucky. We are evolving from a primarily agrarian economy to a broadly based economic foundation. Our economy is rapidly becoming more diversified with industry, agriculture, and commerce equally represented. And those of you who fill the vital roles on the local level are making a valuable contribution toward the achievement of a more aggressive and a more dynamic socio-economic environment in our great state.

We are deeply gratified that you have joined so willingly and are now lending your talents to the total development effort which is changing the face of Kentucky. Frank Groschelle,[1] the state's planning and development officer, has reported that you have taken a leading role in your areas and are making a major contribution to the

Kentucky development team. Working together on the premise that this state's problems demand economic solutions we will achieve a new Kentucky full of hope and opportunity for all our citizens.

Behind this effort, we are mustering the vast people resources at our command in a total development effort which should attract and involve the leadership at every level. We seek the help of dynamic local leadership which accepts its responsibility to initiate and to create viable, self-help programs. To this, we pledge the technical expertise of state government and all its institutions. Together, we must then seek our fair share of the financial resources of the national government. And with this approach, we will strongly discourage the unfortunate present-day trend that federal funds must be accompanied by federal control.

To mobilize this partnership of local, state, and federal forces, we created the Kentucky Program Development Office. This agency is charged with the responsibility of bridging the traditional gap which has separated the three levels of government. And I am pleased to announce that through the efforts and effective coordinating talent of the Program Development Office, we have netted to date benefits of $36 million in facilities and services to strengthen Kentucky communities during the past eight months alone. Through this agency, state government joins the Extension Service within the framework of Kentucky's fifteen multi-county development districts to achieve meaningful economic progress. Our task is to create a sound, attractive environment, an environment which makes feasible the investment of private as well as public capital. That is what total development is about.

Our development concentration is focused in the specific areas of health, education, natural resources, and transportation. We have established a council of twenty-seven private citizens which is already at work producing a comprehensive, statewide health plan. This plan is to advise on the training of medical personnel, location and need for health facilities, and kind and quality of services. In education, for the first time in Kentucky's history we are able to compete with neighboring states in teacher salaries. Our new budget has also paved the way for vast improvements in school facilities. Money was provided for capital construction for the first time in several years and this money will reach every one of the 197 school districts in Kentucky within the next two years.

Water is our greatest natural resource, and we are establishing long-range plans to protect our supply for future generations. Further, our Division of Water is establishing uniform water quality standards for the entire state.

If Kentucky is to compete successfully for its share of the national growth, we must concentrate on transportation facilities. This full development of transportation capabilities is critical because of the advantageous geographical location of Kentucky. We lie strategically between the great northern industrial heartland of America and the emerging industrial South, within a day's drive of 70 percent of the population of this nation and within two hours by air.

With the completion of Kentucky's interstate system and the proposed new toll roads which were announced recently, this state will be eminently prepared for the era of greatness in the seventies. The new toll roads are in reality lifelines extending through the midsection of the state. From Hazard to Henderson, forty counties will be affected directly, that is one-third of all the counties in the state exposed to almost certain progress, industrial and agricultural growth, and expansion of tourism and recreation development. The state's airport system must and will receive our closest attention. We will attempt to establish an airport capable of handling corporate-type aircraft within forty-five minutes' driving time of every community in Kentucky. These are steps in the right direction if we are to provide the climate for new jobs within the framework of a quality environment.

To concentrate our efforts toward achievement of these developmental goals, we must channel the total resources that are available. There are no easy, quick, or sure answers. These are complex matters. But because of this, we are pledged to promote and maintain a people-to-people system of government, effective government, willing and able to deal with the problems of our times.

Again, I congratulate you for your involvement and concern with these problems. We welcome your help and your encouragement. And to all Kentuckians I would say, "Make sure you are involved." It is your privilege and your responsibility.

---

1. Frank J. Groschelle (1932–   ), regional director, United States Department of Health, Education and Welfare, Region number 4 (1971–   ); administrator, Kentucky Program Development Office (1968–1971); and director of planning, State of Ohio (1963–1968). Groschelle is from Somerset. Department of Public Information and Kentucky Program Development Office biographical files.

CHRYSLER AIRTEMP
GROUNDBREAKING
Bowling Green / September 12, 1968

IT is again my distinct honor and privilege to greet officials of Chrysler Airtemp and to join with the people of Bowling Green in celebrating another milestone in this city's industrial history. This is an exciting and gratifying moment for me, a moment we had hoped for from the time we became associated with the Chrysler project and had the opportunity to meet with the company officials and dedicated citizens of Bowling Green in early negotiations.

This is a great day for all of Kentucky as Chrysler Airtemp is officially initiated into the Commonwealth's growing industrial family. And as Kentuckians do when new neighbors come in, we must make them feel at home by exhibiting our special brand of hospitality, helpfulness, and cooperation. With this "good neighbor" policy, Bowling Green and Kentucky can prove the wisdom of the Chrysler decision. I pledge the full partnership of state government in this effort.

Industry does not choose haphazardly, and certainly Chrysler's choice of Bowling Green was not a random selection. This city's phenomenal growth has resulted from a progressive, attractive community and county-wide atmosphere, enhanced by the attributes most sought by industry. And we can never overlook the years of dedicated effort by the local citizens. Without this, no city will win in the highly competitive market for new industry, despite its other advantages. This college community has a rich cultural heritage, heavily influenced by Western Kentucky University, which continues to be a major factor in the area's life and growth. It is because of your efforts that Bowling Green and Warren County, already richly blessed with a solid industrial foundation, has not rested on past laurels. Your efforts to attract new industry are in keeping with the prevailing attitude in this area and throughout Kentucky. Much progress has been made, but there is much left to do.

I have said many times since December that it is our aim to lead Kentucky across the threshold to an era of unmatched greatness. That spirit is catching on across the Commonwealth, and it is truly exemplified here in your community. You have chosen not to be satisfied with improvements of the past. As a result, vocational training facilities here are undergoing expansion. And that alone has played a key role in luring new industry. Transportation facilities are substantial and constantly being improved. We look ahead anxiously to the time when the new toll road through this area will be lined with industrial growth. That time is now closer; that hope nearer to reality. Your labor force is symbolic of the abundant, willing, trainable manpower available throughout Kentucky. These people seek jobs. All these factors make a brighter future for our great state and bring us closer to our goals.

Unequalled progress has been made this year; ninety-eight companies have announced locations or expansions of facilities. The announcement Monday in northern Kentucky by Fess Parker, television's Daniel Boone, of a huge, $13.5-million amusement park swelled total announced investments to over $108 million.[1] New job opportunities created by these announcements have reached a total of more than 7,000. These are the kinds of economic answers Kentucky is finding for its problems. And this is the kind of conducive, stimulating, progressive atmosphere that you of the Chrysler Company will find in the days ahead.

This new plant can also count on the continued support of the team which was so instrumental in bringing Chrysler to this area. . . . The utilities, Louisville & Nashville Railroad, the Tennessee Valley Authority, the Warren County RECC, along with Western Kentucky Gas, the Texas Gas Transmission Corporation, the South Kentucky Industrial Development Association, Kentucky Chamber of Commerce, and our Kentucky Department of Highways, were valuable, reliable members of the team. This is the team which has given Bowling Green and the surrounding area the expertise, the impetus, and the effort which is rewarded here today. They are the foundation on which Chrysler can build and grow.

More than that, you will find a coordinated, effective partnership in Kentucky between local and state levels, a viable partnership symbolized by the united effort which convinced you to locate in Bowling Green, Kentucky. This is a partnership bound by common purpose to fully develop this bountiful state, which is so full of promise.

And now, again we express our appreciation to the Chrysler Corporation for the faith they have shown in our state and our people by making this magnificent contribution to prosperity. Let me take this opportunity to welcome you as our latest industrial citizen to join in our partnership for progress.

---

1. Fess Parker's amusement park, Frontier Worlds, was not constructed in northern Kentucky as originally planned. Department of Commerce, November 2, 1971.

TRADEWATER RIVER AREA
RESOURCE CONSERVATION
AND DEVELOPMENT
PROJECT BANQUET

Pennyrile State Park, Dawson Springs / September 13, 1968

TODAY marks the beginning of the tenth month of this new administration and in the next few minutes, I would like to reflect back over
the first 270 days and also look ahead to what the people of Kentucky
might expect during the next one and a fourth years. Since inauguration day, the theme of this administration primarily has been a movement characterized by economy and efficiency. We have made remarkable progress in this area. We will continue to seek more economical
ways and more efficient ways to serve the state. This progress has
gone hand-in-hand with our concentration on improving and upgrading the services which state government is entrusted to administer.

Our proudest advancements have been made in three areas—
education, highways, and welfare. In each, it is now unmistakably
clear that the new programs and improvements are a direct result of
the budget and revenue legislation adopted by the General Assembly
last spring. Past achievements, however, serve best as guidelines for
the future, and the progress of the past nine months has served as a
special reference for the course which we are charting with tonight's
announcement. From today forward, the vast energy of state government will be mobilized in a concentrated, sincere effort to make "Every
Kentuckian Count."

That is our new theme, "Every Kentuckian Counts," and that will
be the guideline for this administration in the days ahead. However,
let me make it clear from the start that this is more than just a theme.
It is a battle plan against the problems which have held Kentucky
back through the years. In speeches every day this week, I have said
that our problems demand economic solutions—today we appeal to
every Kentuckian to help us find those answers.

This is our message. Every Kentuckian does count, every Kentuckian
is needed, and every Kentuckian must help if we are to find the economic solutions that are demanded. Our goal for Kentucky is greatness,
a decade of unmatched greatness for this state and for its people during
the seventies. And our battle plan is based on the theory that greatness

is not achieved by government, greatness is achieved by people, our people, the Kentuckians.

Nowhere is the spirit and willingness of the private sector more clearly evident than here in the Tradewater River Resource and Development Project. In this six-county area we have seen the unification of local leaders with state and federal levels, all working together to develop this rich and productive area of our state. Together an attack has been launched to solve the problem of the Tradewater River, and I pledge you our full support as we try to eradicate the flooding and pollution which has hindered the communities along the banks of the Tradewater and its tributaries. Mr. McElroy's report was very gratifying, primarily because of the progress that has been made, but also because it reflects the effectiveness of these people-to-people programs. Judging from the report and from the enthusiasm I have seen here, it appears you have already joined our new campaign.

"Every Kentuckian Counts" will be a massive attempt to activate the private sector in a campaign for progress. We seek the help of the silent majority, the decent, industrious, law-abiding citizens who are strangely silent at one of the most crucial periods in our history. Our goal is to mobilize the silent majority, to give it voice, to reawaken its spirit and its concern. Our task is to make the silent majority care again. The effort to make every Kentuckian count will be focused primarily on jobs. This is the quickest route to meaningful progress.

Phase One will deal with involving the private sector in the training and employment of those who are now jobless. Our immediate concern is to train the unskilled and the so-called "hard-core" unemployables for a useful role in this age of mechanization and technology. Then, by attracting more new industry, we will provide job opportunities for those who have been trained. Already this year, employment opportunities have been provided for over 7,000 Kentuckians as a result of new plant locations and expansions of existing facilities. We are very happy to note the industrial progress being made here in the Pennyrile area, reflected by the announcement a few days ago of the $1.25-million Huebsch plant to be located in Madisonville and other significant expansions disclosed earlier this year. We will work toward a greater coordination of our vocational schools and private enterprise, and I am happy to report that one plant in western Kentucky already has asked to participate. We are embarking on a comprehensive plan to solicit the help of others in such programs as Jobs Now.

Phase Two involves a general improvement and self-help program to train and assist the disadvantaged and the handicapped. An intermediate goal is to get these Kentuckians involved in community activities as a way of assuring them that they, too, count. The success of both phases, obviously, is contingent on the theory that the private sector, the silent majority, cares what happens to fellow Kentuckians. We believe that they are the ones who can bring forth the answers to our economic and social problems. Only they can restore confidence in government and respect for the law, which is a requisite for orderly change. A recent nationwide poll offers encouragement. This sampling showed that an extremely high percentage of talented Americans from all professions and trades are willing to spend as much as four hours per week with those who need help.

We will appeal to teachers, honor students, industrialists, doctors, lawyers, and craftsmen—anyone who can and will help. "Every Kentuckian Counts" will have no boundaries, neither geographical, racial, economic nor religious. This is the program we confidently embark on today and we earnestly appeal for the help and cooperation of all Kentuckians. This is an ambitious and massive project, but with the combined talent and energy of our people, we cannot fail to make our dream for a decade of greatness into a reality.

OPENING OF THE KENTUCKY REPUBLICAN CAMPAIGN
London / September 14, 1968

TODAY we begin one of the most crucial campaigns ever undertaken in this state and in this nation. Richard Nixon explained it perfectly in his acceptance speech at Miami Beach when he said, "By our decision in this election, we, all of us, will determine what kind of nation America will be on its 200th birthday and in what kind of world America will live in the year of 2000." That is why we are here today—to echo our concern for America, to rededicate ourselves to America's cause, and to dedicate ourselves to America's victory in November. We gather today as proud Americans, not sick Americans as some have charged. And our candidates gather here today to testify to their concern for the direction our nation will take in the coming years.

I have had an opportunity to talk to all of the candidates who have offered themselves under our party's standard in Kentucky this year. And I can tell you very proudly that all our candidates, the six for Congress, along with our candidate for the Senate, our candidate for the presidency, and vice-presidency—all of these men are running because they believe we must again put America first. One of the reasons we are going to win in November is because the opposition party has failed to put America first.

We have only to look at the three leading issues of this campaign to prove beyond doubt that the Johnson-Humphrey administration has not kept faith with the people of this state and this nation. In its stand on law and order, the Great Society has become the Great Permissive Society. Crime has increased 88 percent. The Federal Bureau of Investigation reports that an American woman is attacked every twelve minutes, a home is burglarized every twenty-seven seconds, and a murder occurs every forty-eight minutes. Yet, when Attorney General Ramsey Clark was asked about the increase in crime last year, he replied that he was "not alarmed." Terror stalks the streets of our cities. Rioting and looting have become the inalienable rights of protestors, and what can we expect of the Democrat candidate for the presidency? Hubert Humphrey said, and I quote, "If I lived in a slum, I think you would have more trouble than you have already, because I've got enough spark left in me to lead a mighty good revolt."

In Vietnam, Americans have watched the fickle, no-win policies of the present administration squander thousands of lives and billions of dollars. And regarding fiscal responsibility, we must only conclude that this is not one of the opposition party's virtues. The cost-of-living index went up 16 percent during the past eight years. At home, today's dollar is under serious attack from the highest rate of inflation in our history. Abroad, the drain on United States gold resources is at an all-time record high.

Still, the Johnson-Humphrey administration continues to overspend and still tries to buy progress with expensive, misdirected, and badly administered programs which have not worked. Those are the issues we must take to the voters. We challenge the opposition to show any instance where it has put America first at home or abroad.

America is looking to our party for strength and leadership in the days ahead, and we can be proud of the contribution that Kentucky has made toward providing that kind of leadership in the past through our two great United States Senators. To continue that kind of leadership, we have nominated a proven leader to carry our banner here in Kentucky. This state and this nation are looking anxiously to see who

Kentucky will send to Washington to try to follow in the giant foot-steps of Thruston Morton. And now it is my pleasure to present that man to you, the next United States Senator from Kentucky, Mar-low W. Cook.[1]

---

1. Marlow W. Cook (1926–), Louisville, United States Senator from Kentucky (1968–); Jefferson County judge (1961–1968); and representa-tive, Kentucky House of Representatives (1958–1960).

NIXON-AGNEW DINNER
Wichita, Kansas / September 19, 1968

As we flew out today I had an opportunity to reminisce about the days I spent here in 1944 as an Air Force Cadet at the [Wichita State] Univer-sity. I remembered all the wonderful people who offered their special, warm Kansas hospitality and made us feel that we were at home. Those were exciting but uncertain times as the war touched the lives of every American and I shall never forget the great feeling of patriotism in Wichita during those days. The people here took a great pride in their participation in the war effort, and it was transferred to the men who were assigned here.[1]

I remember, too, that we took pride in serving our country, in wear-ing the uniform of the armed forces. Those are some of the warm memories I have of Wichita. But there are other, sadder memories, memories of those who served with me and who later were called to make the supreme sacrifice to preserve the American way of life. They gave so that meetings such as this to discuss our nation's affairs could be held.

Tonight, as I stand here in one of America's great cities, I feel a greater sense of uncertainty than I did in 1944 when our country was totally committed, when boys were being taken away from their homes and asked to give their lives to secure this Republic and preserve free-dom around the world. The people in Kansas and throughout America are deeply concerned again tonight, as they were in 1944. Tonight, however, unlike 1944, Americans not only are concerned by a war outside our borders but also by the threat of chaos within our borders. A feeling pervades our people at home that serious, yes, possibly disastrous, trouble lies ahead for this nation here at home.

There is a feeling abroad, promoted by our enemies and perpetuated by our undiscerning friends, that after 192 years as an inspiring example of freedom, justice, and opportunity, America is no longer an example to be followed, but one to be avoided.

The desperation and frustration which grips so many of our people at home and abroad underscores the importance, indeed, the crucial nature of the 1968 campaign. Richard Nixon summed up the impact of this election when he said in Miami Beach: "By our decision in this election, we, all of us, will determine what kind of nation America will be on its 200th birthday and in what kind of world America will live in the year 2000." That is why we need your help.

Americans everywhere are showing a special concern this year because they are dedicated to the principles on which this country was founded and because they share the American dream of peace, opportunity, and prosperity which long ago was a reality in the America we once knew. Because of these things, we confidently await the decision of a concerned citizenry on November fifth.

We are going to win, and it will be a victory not for the Republican Party alone, but a victory for America and all her people. It will be a victory which unites and solidifies our great nation. That victory will be achieved because we have mobilized one of America's greatest sources of strength—the silent majority, a group of responsible, decent, law-abiding, constructive citizens who form the heart and conscience of our nation. For too long the silent majority has been only a spectator to the tragic spectacle of recent years, content to go through the motions of participation in a free society. These forgotten Americans have been rendered voiceless by intimidation and ridicule. Because they once stood up for what they believed, they have been falsely labeled as extremists, racists, scorned as uncompassionate, narrow reactionaries who resist social change because of old prejudices and outdated principles. But finally, however, the silent majority has become aroused. On November fifth, it will break its long silence and join us to tell the nation and the world that it is time for a change. The silent majority agrees with us that America must have new leadership, new direction, and new policies.

In our search for new leadership, however, we must consider a serious and ironic threat. There are some who have become so disgruntled and so disillusioned by the present lack of leadership in Washington that they have turned in desperation to a third candidate, a man who has spoken firmly and passionately on the emotional issues of our time. We commend those who are striving to bring an end to the leadership crisis in Washington, but we must also caution the American people about the danger of this third party movement. The danger, paradoxically, is that a vote for the third candidate in protest of the current administration will only serve to benefit those we seek to replace. The divisive effect of the third party is the only hope left for Hubert Horatio Humphrey. His last chance is to take the decision out of the hands of the people of America and put it in the hands of the politicians in the House of Representatives. Our task, if we are to have new leadership and if we are truly dedicated to purging Washington of those who have carried us off course, is to be sure no American wastes his vote on a third party, splinter candidate. Only by sweeping out the Johnson-Humphrey administration can we halt the spread of their philosophies.

We must and we will change the misguided concepts that we should take from each according to his means and give to each according to his needs and that no one is any longer economically responsible for his own well-being or morally responsible for his own conduct. America can no longer support the theory of big government and little people. A government of charities which feeds the stomach and starves the soul is not the American way. Let us look for better ways.

One of these is to restore the private enterprise system to full effectiveness. Richard Nixon has suggested that the solution to many of our problems will come when private enterprise is encouraged and not discouraged by Washington. Millions of Americans will escape the grips of poverty when private enterprise is encouraged to get into the ghettos, and those who live in the ghettos are encouraged to get off the welfare roles and into private enterprise.

Except for brief periods of time, I have lived my entire life within a few miles of Hodgenville, Kentucky, a small town few of you have even heard about. There, atop a little hill, stands a magnificent building which enshrines a crude log cabin. And throughout the years, I have visited this National Shrine many times with my children. By the use of our imagination, we have returned to the days when this cabin stood in a clearing in one of Kentucky's virgin forests. The cabin is bare within and foreboding without. It speaks of the deepest poverty. And as we looked back into the past, we could see a ragged, untaught boy stretched out upon the barren earth floor, pouring over a borrowed book by the flickering light of the fire. I could see that boy lift his eyes to the burdened form of his pioneer mother, and I could hear him say: "Life is hard. The future seems hopeless, but my forefathers fought in the American Revolution because of their allegiance to a government not of men but of laws, laws which should be of equal application to all. Their eyes held a constant vision of a nation in which all men should be free to work out their own destinies, to plan their own lives, to possess the fruits of their own labor, and to stand and fall by their own efforts. Yes, I am poor, but I have a chance. In my country, no doors are barred to me because I am poor. I can work. I can learn; knowledge will give me power. Thank God, I have a chance."

We all know the story of that ragged boy, Abraham Lincoln, how he became a rail-splitter, a country storekeeper, a lawyer, the advocate of a great cause, the exemplar of individual liberty under the law, the great American president, the emancipator of a race, and the defender and preserver of the American Union. This is the triumph of one man, given equal opportunity under the law. It is the ultimate example of the philosophy of liberty by which America and her people have achieved greatness.

Sadly, however, it is a philosophy which has been lost amid the endless programs of the current administration, a philosophy lost in the flames of Watts, Detroit, and Newark, and a philosophy trampled under the feet of protestors in our streets and on our campuses. But it is this philosophy, equal opportunity with liberty under the law, which demands that America return to greatness and to her place of respect at home and abroad. It is to the preservation of this philosophy that we dedicate our efforts and our victory on election day. We must be so dedicated, because we live amidst a disturbed and a concerned society, but not a sick society as some have said.

Our people are disturbed at the lack of respect for law and order. We are disturbed by permissive leadership which inspires crime in the name of protest, and we are disturbed by permissive courts which pamper criminals and hamper law enforcement while crime and acts of violence breed anarchy. Americans ask, "Is this still a nation of laws and not of men?"

The statistics are frightening. Under the permissive society, the American people have received propaganda, but not performance. The FBI reports that an American woman is attacked every twelve minutes, a house is burglarized every twenty-seven seconds, and someone is murdered every forty-eight minutes. In view of these alarming figures, Americans ask: "How long must we be afraid to walk in our streets? How long must we stand by as our businesses are plundered and burned and our neighborhoods and parks shrouded in fear, unsafe for women and children?" Americans are turning to our candidate and our party, asking what we will do to crush this tide of violence and crime which poisons our system, immobilizes our people, and inundates our precious skills to resolve differences peacefully.

Those are America's questions. What are our answers? First, let us say that we pledge even-handed, fair and firm administration of justice and vigorous enforcement of the law and that we will refute with whatever force is necessary the idea that rioting and civil diso-bedience are the inalienable rights of the disgruntled. Our commitment to those answers is reflected in the Republican Platform of 1968. It says: "Let us reestablish the principle that men are accountable for what they do, that criminals are responsible for their crimes." To those who attempt to justify acts of lawlessness by pointing to social in-justices, we must say that while environment may help to explain the act, it is not an excuse for the crime. For those who cannot see a dime's worth of difference in the two major parties, let us set the record straight. There are differences, differences we are proud of, differences which cannot be obscured by the unclear logic of the third party candidate.

Compare this platform position with events of the recent past: Riots take a deadly toll and our leaders react by making a study. A leader is murdered and hundreds of thousands of innocent, law-abiding citi-zens turn in their firearms in a senseless, pitiful act of guilt-sharing and our leaders cry out for gun registration and control. A city burns, and suddenly we are labeled a sick society. These are not the responses America deserves. We must do more than study lawlessness. We must stop it! We must not act to control the weapons of violence with regu-lations which are as useless as band-aids on cancer. We must control and deter persons who would misuse those weapons. Finally, when our cities are in flames, instead of blaming society we must punish those who kindle the fires.

Let us work together to promote a new, strong respect for the law. The compelling words of Abraham Lincoln, spoken more than 100 years ago, offer wisdom and direction for us today. He said: "Let rev-erence for the laws be breathed by every American mother to the lisp-ing babe that prattles on her lap; let it be taught in the schools, in seminaries, and in colleges; let it be preached from the pulpit, pro-claimed in legislative halls, and enforced in courts of justice. In short, let it become the political religion of the nation; and let the old and the young, the rich and the poor, the grave and the gay of all sexes and tongues and colors and conditions sacrifice unceasingly upon its altars."[2] This is the direction we must take if we are to correct the fail-ures of the past.

While the present leadership has failed at home, it has been even less decisive abroad. Vietnam is an ever-disturbing reminder to our people that new leadership, proven leadership, is called for. Americans are searching for an end to that tragic and costly struggle either through honorable withdrawal or more effective pursuit of victory. We are tired of having the best team and the other team always having the ball. We are tired of forever being on the defensive. Our people are tired of defensive leadership. We want decisive leadership, leadership which acts from a position of strength rather than always reacting.

The record shows plainly that Richard Nixon is a man of decision, of experience, and of courage. He was there in 1953 when the Republican team brought peace to Korea. He was there in the Soviet kitchen, speaking up for America in a face-to-face confrontation with Communism. Dick Nixon was in Washington during the most peaceful and prosperous period in this country's history. He understands what must be done.

Let historians record that in 1968, America, in a time of deep crisis, responded as it has responded before with new ideas, with great traditions, and with the fresh hope that comes from a new unity. Let us do nothing to disturb that unity in the days ahead, for only through unity of purpose and action will we be able to transform the American dream into a reality.

---

1. Governor Nunn gave several speeches on behalf of the national Republican ticket in 1968. This is an example; see also August 24, 1968.

2. Abraham Lincoln, "Address to the Young Men's Lyceum of Springfield," January 27, 1838, *Abraham Lincoln: Selected Speeches, Messages, and Letters*, ed. T. Harry Williams (New York, 1957), p. 10.

INAUGURATION OF
KENTUCKY EDUCATIONAL
TELEVISION NETWORK
Lexington / September 23, 1968

IN the past twenty years, television has had an immeasurable impact upon our society. It has made the world a smaller place, not only by bringing far-off events into your living room, but by bringing them instantaneously as they happen. Through advertising, television has motivated Americans to want more and better things and thereby contributed to a higher standard of living in this country. But the consequent increase of opportunity in our society demands an equally rapid increase in educational opportunity and achievement for every citizen.

One way to answer this need is to use the medium which helped create the opportunity, and to apply the vast potential of television to the support of education at every level, from the child in kindergarten to the adult sitting before his television receiver at home. If educational television, as another teaching tool, can make the classroom instructor's work more effective, and it has proven it can; if it can bring subjects such as foreign language to the elementary level in schools where students could get it no other way, and it can; if it can enrich the teaching of science, history, and geography by taking teachers and students through the tube to the most sophisticated laboratories and to the most distant places; if it can enable sudents to advance faster than students not exposed to it; and if it can do all these things, and it has more than amply demonstrated everywhere in the nation that it can, then I see Kentucky Educational Television as a means of equalizing learning opportunities for all Kentuckians. However, the full potential of this powerful, new tool is in the hands of our teachers. We must never lose sight of the fact that only people teach. Therefore, I challenge each of the thirty thousand teachers in Kentucky to make our aspirations for educational television a reality.

We can proudly boast that while many states now have educational television networks, Kentucky's network is the largest, most complete, most functional, and most flexible in the nation today. Kentucky has been acclaimed first in the nation not only by Kentuckians, but by national educational leaders. This significant achievement has been in the making for fifteen years and gained authorization as long ago as 1960. But while the Kentucky plan was eagerly being adapted and developed by other states, Kentucky dropped to the bottom in the actual implementation because of the absence of state funds. It was not until 1966 that the people of Kentucky saw construction begin. Still, at the beginning of this year, the serious financial crisis confronting the Commonwealth left the system without money to operate the completed facilities. Had not the 1968 Legislature taken action, the ETV antennae would have served only as lightning rods in the sky.

Educational television becomes operative today in Kentucky as a direct result of the money provided by the revenue measures adopted this year in the General Assembly. In addition to providing four and one-half million dollars to put this exciting new educational tool into every classroom in the Commonwealth, sixty-two cents of every tax dollar is devoted to education. The advent of ETV symbolizes our commitment to educational progress in Kentucky, and because we are convinced that any expenditure in education is one of the wisest investments we can make, it is with a real sense of pride and optimism that I now activate the first program for the schools throughout the state.

KENTUCKY ASSOCIATION
OF PUPIL PERSONNEL
WORKERS
Mammoth Cave National Park / September 24, 1968

TOGETHER, we, you and I, are deeply committed to a job which is vital to the growth of Kentucky—namely the promotion of education. The advancement of education is part of our way of developing Kentucky's resources, human and natural. This development, and education's role in it, is an integral part of the theme "Every Kentuckian Counts." Every Kentuckian does count, every Kentuckian is needed, and every Kentuckian must help.

Our goal for Kentucky is greatness and an era of unmatched greatness for this state and for its people as we move toward the seventies. And our battle plan is based on the theory that greatness will not be achieved by government alone; greatness will be achieved by people, our people, Kentuckians. And we must see that every Kentuckian counts in this united effort.

It is unfortunate that a significant segment of our population is unable to stand up and be counted. Last year, this segment numbered nearly 32,000. Who are these Kentuckians? They are the school dropouts. Today's dropout is, in too many cases, the unemployed of tomorrow. And the criminal of tomorrow. He is, too often, a failure in the minds of his relatives, his friends, and his neighbors. And perhaps worst of all and most depressing, he is a failure in his own mind. He has lost hope, and so he has lost motivation. He fails in school. He ends up on welfare, and the welfare system is one that feeds his stomach and starves his soul.

These dropouts are your problem; these dropouts are my problem. We cannot ignore the fact that over 1500 inmates at the Kentucky State Reformatory are school dropouts. We cannot be content with past progress when nearly 73 percent of the prisoners at LaGrange have a seventh grade education or less. A majority of those classified as unemployed in Kentucky have not even completed grade school. Faced with the problem of dropouts, and the disastrous consequences it may have, we can and we must offer possible solutions.

If we investigate the reasons for dropouts, it is abundantly clear that the number one cause is the students' lack of interest. Here we can apply direct methods to alleviate the dropout crisis. We can provide more incentives. We must motivate our students by stressing rewards which accompany a high school education. We must offer more at school. There is no substitute for modern, functional schools, excellent curricula, and enlightened, qualified teachers. We have provided for all three with the new budget and revenue measures passed during the General Assembly this year.

Thousands of Kentucky children will attend new, modern, functional schools because $52 million was provided for construction of buildings and purchase of advanced teaching equipment. That is an increase of $9 million over the budget figure for the previous year and represents the first increase in capital outlay and current expenses since 1960. There were, of course, some who disagreed with us on the revenue measure which was proposed and adopted. There can be no disagreement, however, with the educational progress which is being made as a result of the added funds. For instance, twenty-eight new schools will be under construction before the end of the year. As a direct result of the increased appropriation, construction of new school buildings or major improvements on existing facilities will be possible in each of the 197 school districts in the state. The curriculum in Kentucky schools was dramatically affected by the action of the Legislature in two ways.

First, funds were provided which pushed educational television into a reality. As you know, the first program in educational television was dialed on Monday. Now, more than 700 thousand school children in Kentucky are being exposed to a broadened curriculum, including foreign language at the elementary grade level, by way of this exciting electronic teaching aid. In all, the educational television network will broadcast twenty-two different courses. We felt that the $4.5-million investment to make the network operative was an investment Kentucky could not afford to ignore. We can say without fear of successful contradiction that Kentucky's educational television network is the largest, most complete, most functional, and most flexible in the United States. Our network has been acclaimed number one in America by this nation's foremost educational leaders.

The second major improvement in the curriculum is in the area of vocational education. This is of particular significance in Kentucky because of the wide interest in this course of study. By 1970, we plan to open a chain of eighteen new vocational school extension centers stretching from Harlan and Hazard in the east to Bowling Green and Owensboro in the west. And we will not stop there. Our goal is to locate a vocational school or extension center within 25 miles of every Kentuckian.

The budget also provided more encouragement and incentive to our teachers through substantial salary increases. We have finally raised our teacher salary scale to a competitive level with neighboring states, and hopefully the brain drain of previous years will be ended. Thus, we have attacked directly three crucial causes of the dropout cycle which exist inside our schools.

Now within the broad framework of our "Every Kentuckian Counts" program, we are turning our attention to another source which contributes to the dropout rate, the home. Studies indicate that parents of students who fail in school or quit after reaching sixteen are often themselves dropouts. The latest survey available shows that less than 96 percent of the parents whose children left school did not themselves complete high school. And approximately 49 percent of these parents did not advance beyond the sixth grade.

Unemployment is a recurring fact in the lives of these parents, and it is to this problem that our new program addresses itself with particular force. We are convinced that some of the most serious problems in the lives of Kentuckians must be answered. And so it is that the effort to make every Kentuckian count will be focused primarily on jobs. This is the quickest route to meaningful progress. I am happy to report tonight that our efforts are meeting with record-breaking success. Since January, forty new plants have been located within our borders, sixty-seven plants have been expanded, and together they provide job opportunities for 7,663 Kentuckians. This figure does not include the 1,000 jobs which will be filled when Fess Parker's Frontier Worlds park is developed in northern Kentucky. More than jobs, these achievements pump new capital into Kentucky's economy. Together, these new locations and expansions represent an investment of over $189 million to our economy.

"Every Kentuckian Counts" is, in the simplest terms, a total devel-

I believe there is a void in the lives of our people today which is not being filled by our churches. These people are turning away from the church and substituting instead club work, community service, and social work. They want to be where the action is, and there the church must be also. Then, I believe we will see a favorable shift in the American trend away from today's trend of higher church enrollment but decreasing attendance.

Your challenge is to examine the root causes of crisis and unrest, and with the guidance of the Supreme Authority, attack those causes. We have social workers, economic advisors, medical doctors, and other kinds of specialists, but we need spiritual specialists.

We are living in a period of almost unlimited communication and technical advancement, a period in which more information is available to more people than ever before. And yet, although we are better informed and more concerned for our fellowman, we are more deeply divided than ever. I believe that the division and the unrest of our time primarily result from the failure of each individual to establish moral principles in his own life.

Reaffirming the simple truth that we are all children of God and brothers of our fellowmen, your duty is to lead man back to a place where he can find meaning and sustenance to his life through the teachings of Christ. With the involvement of America's spiritual force, let us put away the inflamed language of the present, let us replace revolution with a united crusade for moral rearmament, and then with your leadership, let us reestablish this nation, under God, as the beacon of hope for mankind.

MIDDLESBORO COMMUNITY MEETING
Middlesboro / September 25, 1968

In the Middlesboro and Cumberland Gap section of Kentucky is where, about 200 years ago, Daniel Boone first passed through the Gap into Kentucky and became an American legend. The Middlesboro of today has very little resemblance to the country known by Daniel Boone. Over thirty-five thousand people now reside in Bell County.

The famous Cumberland Gap is a national park, drawing thousands of tourists to the area.

Middlesboro today is a progressive, growing city. The fact that it has been selected as an "All Kentucky City" by the Kentucky Chamber of Commerce for three straight years attests to its progress, and is, I understand, confidently anticipating a fourth win this year. We are proud of Middlesboro's progress, and your state government wants to help you continue with your fine record of growth.

Highway Commissioner Bill Hazelrigg[1] has talked with you about highway improvements under way or planned for the area. He told you that sixty thousand dollars has been allocated for paving of Cumberland Avenue from Twelfth Street to Twenty-fifth Street and from Twenty-fifth Street to the Nineteenth Street Extension. This work is now complete. He announced awarding of contracts for the first phase of the four-laning of 25E between Middlesboro and Pineville at the Pineville end. That construction is well under way. On 22 November, bids will be let for 2.782 miles of highway from Cumberland Avenue to 1.72 miles south of Yellow Creek. Highway construction and maintenance are essential ingredients in the development of Kentucky communities, and we are not going to fall short in this critical area.

Our Kentucky Department of Public Information, headed by Jim Host, has under way a matching fund program for this district of which Middlesboro is the key attraction. The fiscal year budget for the district is twenty thousand dollars. This is one of the better administered matching fund districts in the state, and has traditionally been so. You have done some fine work with available funds, including your full-color Middlesboro brochure, which we are distributing at travel shows and other tourist information points.

I am glad the Department of Commerce is continuously working with the Middlesboro Chamber of Commerce, the Industrial Commission, and the Industrial Foundation, publishing material on your city's plant location advantages, and attempting to interest industrial prospects in locating plants in this city. We are now preparing a brochure describing these sites, along with sites in Knox County and Williamsburg. The department plans to publish concise facts about each site, including photographs and maps, and go out on the road merchandising them to industry as real assets, as opportunities for industry in southeastern Kentucky. We're promoting this section as an industrial frontierland.

The Kentucky Industrial Development Finance Authority has been able to make three loans to the Middlesboro Industrial Foundation for site purchase and development. They have been gratified to see the foundation's first industrial park become fully occupied with new industries. Vocational training has played a major role in the location of industry in Middlesboro.

Growth of a city or an area can be accomplished in several ways—industrial development, development of tourism, and resource development, depending upon the opportunities and advantages inherent in a particular section. Middlesboro has pursued all three courses.

One locally instigated project which I would heartily endorse for this area is the proposed American Coal Museum and research facility. Coal was an important resource and mining a major factor in Middlesboro's early development. Coal mining in the area has recently undergone a rebirth. Tourism is currently making a significant contribution to the area economy. A venture such as the coal museum and research facility, capitalizing on the historic coal-mining background of the area in a manner which will appeal to tourists appears to be a sound development project. In Kentucky, where coal is one of our major resources, we presently have no coal research projects. Obviously, such a project would draw the attention of the coal industry and major corporations to Kentucky.

About an hour's drive from Middlesboro, at Oak Ridge, Tennessee, the atomic energy museum is attracting thousands of visitors. National museums of nuclear energy and coal, the two major energy sources, within an hour's distance would, I believe, be a definite attraction to vacationers touring the mountain areas of Tennessee and Kentucky. More time would be spent by the tourist in this area, and Middlesboro's overnight tourist trade would be stimulated.

Middlesboro has always been a community of people willing to take innovative steps for self-improvement. I would like particularly to commend the city for its many efforts and actions taken for the betterment of the Middlesboro community. Your community is also presently working with our recently established Program Development Office on improved park facilities within the city. Government has been pleased to participate, at Mayor Wolfe's[2] request, in the southside flood control project in an effort to alleviate some of the suffering of that area's residents throughout the years from the damage to property caused by high water. This project will aid in future development of the section by providing protection to industrial sites in the area which are subject to high water. The conservation of industrial properties in this section of Kentucky is of prime concern to the state, as well as to local citizens.

Middlesboro has been described in many ways, including the picturesque names "Magic City of the Cumberlands," and "Oasis in Appalachia." The descriptions express the writer's wonderment at the existence of an attractive, thriving community in the generally under-developed Appalachian region. Articles have appeared in national publications about this community and its people and their bootstraps efforts—efforts to obtain a national park, which they have seen become a reality, and efforts to locate industry by actually building industrial sites and writing hundreds of letters to industrial prospects. In this area, too, progress has been achieved.

I know you are anxious to achieve even greater progress, and are working toward that goal. I want to assure you that your state government is working along with you, and will cooperate with you on every project designed for the betterment of your community and our state.

---

1. William B. Hazelrigg (1918–   ), commissioner, Department of Highways (1967–1969); chairman, Workmen's Compensation Board (1969–1970); and Commonwealth attorney, Twenty-fourth District (1955–1967); an attorney from Paintsville. Telephone interview with William Hazelrigg, September 8, 1971.

2. Chester H. Wolfe (1921–   ), mayor, Middlesboro (1965–   ); vice president, Kentucky Municipal League (1971–   ); Kentucky Law Enforcement Council (1968–   ); and chairman, Board of Trustees, Cumberland Valley Area Development Council (1968–   ). Office of Mayor Wolfe, September 8, 1971.

NATIONAL INSTITUTE ON NATURAL RESOURCES LAW
Louisville / October 8, 1968

KENTUCKY is proud to host this first National Institute on Natural Resources Law.[1] The professional qualifications and diverse backgrounds of those of you attending indicates the importance and broad implication of the subjects under consideration. Some of the most capable representatives of private industry, professional associations, and state and federal government, are facing one of our most crucial modern problems, that of striking a balance between the preservation and utilization of our natural resources.

Kentucky is blessed and in many ways is unique as a repository of natural wealth. Forty-seven percent of the land area of the Commonwealth is forested and 16,600 square miles contain rich coal deposits. We are the only state, by the way, with two separate and distinct coal-producing fields, one in Appalachian eastern Kentucky and the other in the gently rolling terrain of the western part of the state. Kentucky has more miles of navigable streams than any other state in the union. With the increasing demands of economic growth, much of what nature has stored for us will ultimately be consumed. Yet we cannot allow ourselves to reach the position where our resources are unnecessarily and wantonly depleted.

In seeking an accommodation between industrial growth and the preservation of resources, our laws must recognize both interests. And, if proper conservation practices require the expenditure of money by industry and government, then the people must be made aware that health and production are compatible, yet not free. Advances in technology are demonstrating, however, that cleanliness and conservation are not only desirable but can be profitable and the accommodation less costly to industry and the ultimate consumer. We all appreciate the need to keep our waterways free from pollution. This is a lesson no one knows better than industry.

Over the years there have been abuses caused by the world's most phenomenal production explosion, fed by a world war and unchecked now for more than two decades. In most instances industry has acted responsibly, and now more than ever is seeking to live up to its duties as a national citizen.

Also, the rapid growth of our cities creates the need for disposing of human wastes in quantities unsuited to existing sanitary treatment facilities. If, however, we are faced with the alternative of clean-up or close-up, do we not then, in effect, stop economic growth necessary to solve social and economic problems? I have introduced resolutions at three governors' conferences this year calling upon the federal government to allow the states to meet their own needs. We are fully prepared to adopt control standards deemed necessary by our own experts.

Certainly Kentucky, with the nation's finest state park system, appreciates the benefits of unpolluted lakes and streams. We have embarked upon a campaign to attract new industry which features our water resources, and we will not tolerate pollution. But neither will we impose upon industry unreasonable restrictions where no health danger is shown to exist or is being created.

Kentucky has the toughest strip mine reclamation law in the nation, but, yet, fair enforcement often leaves both the coal operator and the surface owner less than satisfied. Again, this is a question of balance. Our permit system ensures certain precautions during actual mining operations and restoration of the surface thereafter. This is a carefully conducted program which successfully demonstrates cooperation between government and industry. Later this month in western Kentucky we will witness the first cutting anywhere of pulpwood from reclaimed spoil banks, a dramatic illustration of what can be done. New methods, such as aerial seeding, should make mining spoil economically productive. We cannot escape the fact that the trend is toward maximum use planning and away from mere surface stabilization. We must recognize the importance of coal to Kentucky's economy; $400-million worth was mined in the last fiscal year, of which forty-one percent was extracted by strip and auger methods. Aside from our direct efforts and regulatory activities, this year we have made it easier for local soil and water conservation districts to participate in resources preservation through broadened powers and a marked increase in state funds.

This administration is currently engaged in two new conservation projects. Today I have appointed an Advisory Commission on Wild Rivers to help Kentucky preserve some of its streams in their free-flowing state. This is essentially a citizen commission, one which I expect to function vigorously, and to recommend appropriate legislation to implement a workable program.

Secondly, we are exploring means of acquiring Lilley Cornett Woods in Letcher County, a unique stand of virgin timber.

Our balanced efforts to maintain Kentucky's natural wealth and beauty have greatly enhanced our efforts to bring industry to Kentucky. We are enjoying great success in securing new locations and expanded facilities, and our stature in the marketplace has increased very rapidly. Already in 1968 industry has invested nearly $190 million in 40 new plants and 67 expanded facilities which have created jobs for 7,663 Kentuckians. Again I say that this is in part a result of the balance we have achieved, the proper blend of governmental services and free enterprise.

In your discussions here this week you will consider the wide range of natural resources law, from air and water pollution through strip mining and oil and gas production. If you have suggestions or recommendations, we shall be happy to receive them. If there is a service which we can improve or add, we shall be pleased to consider it. All of us, thinking and working together, can find the proper role of government and private activity of resource development and resource utilization.

---

1. The state of Kentucky was the first to call a national conference to deal with the complex problem of interpreting the laws governing natural resources. Information from the Department of Natural Resources, October 13, 1971.

KENTUCKY INDUSTRIAL
DEVELOPMENT COUNCIL
Louisville / October 8, 1968

WE are indeed grateful for this opportunity to personally show and tell you some of the advantages Kentucky offers to industry. We are very much aware that Kentucky has an abundance of land suitable for development and you are going to see some of our finest sites during your visit to the Ohio River area. There is another advantage we are proud of, too. Not only can we offer feasible, suitable sites for industrial development but, every bit as important, we can offer you a climate conducive to profitable industrial operation. Here in Kentucky, profit is the name of the game, and we hope you will recognize the effort that has been made to bring about this climate.

Many of you are already aware of the assets we offer because eleven firms represented here are presently operating plants in Kentucky. In fact, it would be very difficult to assemble any gathering of officials of the leading manufacturing firms in America without including companies with existing operations. This is because today in Kentucky we have branch plants which represent over 70 percent of the country's biggest and best-known firms. We have 351 of the top 500 companies in America here in Kentucky already, and you are witnesses to the fact that we are waging a vigorous campaign to attract the others. And in addition to all these, you represent not only some of the giants of industry, but also creators and producers of products and product names which are part and parcel of our everyday life. You represent products which range from Acrilan and aspirin to Cadillac and Corfam, from Elmer's Glue-All to Teflon, farm tractors to space vehicle components, and axles, saw blades, wire fabrics, hospital beds, Thermopane glass, Lucite, and Reynolds Wrap.

I don't believe it is by accident that you are doing business in Kentucky, or that you are thinking about bringing your business to Kentucky. You're here or you're thinking about coming here because it is good business, because we have something to offer. It is as I told an audience the other day. Fess Parker of Daniel Boone television fame didn't recently decide to invest $13.5 million and locate his Frontier Worlds amusement park in northern Kentucky just because we invited him to dinner at the Governor's Mansion, and gave him a good bed and made sure he had enough blankets so he wouldn't catch cold. And by the same token, you aren't here tonight because the Executive Inn has good food or because you haven't seen a southern Republican governor before. You are here because our great Commonwealth has advantages which spell profit. What are these advantages?

I think you start with geographical location. Consider this: Kentucky is within only one day's drive, 24 hours by truck, of two-thirds of the population of America. By air, we're only two hours away from the nation's biggest marketplaces. And in that connection, let me say that one of the things we will concentrate on during the next session of the Legislature is the improvement of our airport facilities, which are already attracting many new industries to Kentucky. Fess Parker liked our location. His advisors reported to him that in Boone County, Kentucky, where he located Frontier Worlds, the two Interstate Highway Systems under construction and design would bring in more potential visitors than any other site in America which was under consideration.

Another vital asset is Kentucky's abundance of water. This State has more navigable streams than any other state in the nation. And I just came from a meeting of people who are working to see that this advantage is not squandered or ruined by pollution.

We also have a favorable tax climate and we have proof. Since January, 40 new plants have been located in Kentucky, and 67 plants already in operation here have decided to expand existing facilities. All this required an investment of $189 million and it created 7,663 new jobs, so there is a great deal of confidence being shown in our tax structure. During last winter's legislative session, a revenue program was adopted which will finance many state improvements without losing our very competitive tax position.

Kentucky's people are our most unique and valuable resource. You cannot find people anywhere else on earth in such abundance of quality or friendliness. With the resultant increase in our State budget, our educational program already has surpassed seven other states in national rankings. Kentucky education was the chief benefactor of our revenue and budget proposals both from the standpoint of better teachers and increased capital outlay for educational facilities. We now have the best vocational training system of all of the 50 states. We're ranked number one by the National Chamber of Commerce, and we now have the most dynamic educational television system in the country.

Realizing the importance of the Department of Commerce to Kentucky's growth and well-being, we have selected it as the first agency of state government for reorganization and streamlining, a reorganization based upon the recommendation of business leaders, to best serve the business community and the people of this State. We have retained the essential services, while eliminating nonessentials, and have added to the program. Under the new structure we will provide additional community assistance, site development service and specialized research studies.

We are embarking upon an aggressive industrial advertising program in which our existing industries are active participants. An upcoming edition of *Fortune Magazine* will depict Kentucky as a vital, growing State with a mission to tell the world of the opportunities existing here for industry to produce at a profit. We are asking all Kentuckians to help us "sell" Kentucky. We have adopted the slogan, "Every Kentuckian Counts," and indeed every Kentuckian does count.

You see here an excellent example of the interest and participation of all Kentuckians in our industrial development program. Your hosts on this tour are development personnel of utility companies, of railroads, of industrial foundations, banks, and of the chambers of commerce, all of whom have for years been actively promoting Kentucky to industry. This group has worked along with our official state development agency as a team, and the individuals represented have acted as co-sponsors and co-participants in every industry promotion and development project instituted to contact prospective industries outside the state or to bring officials of these firms into Kentucky. We believe when they see for themselves what Kentucky has to offer, these company officials will agree that we have the resources to meet their needs.

Along the route of the tour you will meet other Kentuckians who are delivering the message about the new industrial Kentucky—local citizens, Chamber of Commerce executives, and industrial committee members, who have become a sophisticated group of professional industrial developers. You will see Kentucky communities that have everything that any community can offer in the way of pleasant living conditions, good schools, libraries, churches, recreational and cultural facilities, civic clubs, and country clubs. You have no doubt already heard from your own company management or other Kentucky businessmen that we have here in these communities an excellent supply of dependable workers.

We sincerely hope and trust that you will have an enjoyable visit, and that you will take back with you a picture of a vibrant, growing state and an aggressive, hospitable people. Kentucky is on the move and progress is being made. Our goal for Kentucky and her people is an era of unmatched greatness, prosperity, and peace. We most sincerely invite you to come to Kentucky and be a part of that greatness.

NATIONAL COUNTY AGENTS CONFERENCE
Louisville / October 14, 1968

On behalf of the Commonwealth I am honored to join the University of Kentucky Extension Service in welcoming you to one of the great agricultural states of this country. We are pleased to have you in our State, and we are proud to have this opportunity of displaying Kentucky's rich agricultural resources. I sincerely hope that during your five-day convention you will have an opportunity to see and enjoy our rich farm land and our splendid agribusiness facilities. Your Kentucky hosts will extend to you the fullest measure of southern hospitality. We not only want to make your stay in Kentucky fruitful from a business standpoint, but also to make it pleasant and entertaining. Being an agricultural State, Kentuckians are always honored to be chosen as hosts for agricultural meetings and conventions such as this.

There is no agricultural group which can point to a record of achievement comparable to the record of America's county agents. Through the years you have served all segments of society, both rural and urban. This service has been more than agricultural; your programs have touched many phases of our daily lives. Kentucky and the other forty-nine states are better today because of the dedicated agents gathered here for this national convention. Just as agriculture is changing, so are the roles which each of you play in your specialized field. The fact that your programs have kept pace with the changing needs is a credit to those who plan and direct those programs.

There are many problems to which we must cooperatively apply our energy in the days ahead. The number of farmers is decreasing today, and yet, the average size of the American farm is increasing. This means that while you have a smaller number of farmers with which to work, the agricultural enterprises you serve will be much larger. Larger farms will also demand greater efficiency on the part of the operators. Specialized farming operations will require the services of agents with specialized training. On this score you have prepared yourselves well in moving to the specialist arrangement as compared to the former county agent plan. It is my hope that our farmers continue to have the services of well-trained and highly dedicated extension specialists.

At the same time, I feel that there is a growing need for continued development of our communities. I am speaking about developing those things which raise the standard of living for our rural people and those who live in small towns and cities. Here again, you are to be commended for the foresight which you have put into your training and service programs. Modern methods and conveniences have given Americans more leisure time than ever before. Consequently, we need creative recreational programs in which our people can wisely spend this time. Your organization is already providing specialists to work with recreational program development, and I am pleased to see that this phase of service is placed among those designed to meet other needs of our people.

As we look to the future I hope your association will join those of us in developing programs to meet the needs we will face in the years ahead. Our farmers are faced with growing prices for the supplies and equipment they must buy. But at the same time the prices they are receiving at the marketplace are not keeping pace with the prices they must pay. If our farmers are to survive, we must, and we will, find ways to correct this insecurity.

Many of our rural communities are faced with living conditions which leave much to be desired. Employment opportunities for those who seek either full time or part time employment off the farm are limited. The solution to these problems and many more will not come easily. They will not come at all, however, if your association, if our land grant colleges, and if our governmental agencies do not move to find solutions. This is your challenge. It is the challenge faced by all of us who believe in America and those things which have made America a great country in which to live.

As Governor I am interested in programs aimed at total resource development. To further this goal, we have adopted the theme "Every Kentuckian Counts," because we believe that every Kentuckian is entitled to enjoy the fullest measure of economic, social, and cultural growth our State can provide. Our county agents can help us to make every Kentuckian know that he is being counted. As you go back into your individual states, I am sure that you too will put yourselves to the task of making every citizen count.

Again it is a pleasure to have you in Kentucky. While you are here, enjoy yourselves. Not only do I welcome you today, but I give you a welcome to return any time you can.

HAMILTON MINE DEDICATION, ISLAND CREEK COAL COMPANY
Madisonville / October 18, 1968

I AM pleased to join with you today in the dedication of Island Creek Coal Company's Hamilton Mine. I understand that when it reaches its planned production capacity of five million tons a year, the Hamilton Mine will be one of the largest, if not the largest, underground coal mines in the United States and will provide new jobs for about six hundred people. This will mean much to this immediate area and to Kentucky.

The coal industry makes a substantial contribution to the economy of Kentucky. In fact, in the past two or three years coal has surpassed tobacco as the State's number one single-industry "cash crop." Just a few years ago, Kentucky replaced Pennsylvania as the second largest coal-producing state, and last year, for the first time in history, we mined more than one hundred million tons of coal. The Hamilton Mine and others in the planning and construction stages will materially supplement our production. Perhaps the time is not too far distant when Kentucky will move ahead of West Virginia and become the number one coal state in the nation.

Those of you who know me are aware that I am a strong advocate of the free enterprise system, and that I believe our State's progress can be accelerated through voluntary and sincere cooperation of government, private industry and labor. We in state government have our problems and you in industry have yours. We can solve them faster and more equitably by working together.

I have been Governor of this Commonwealth for almost eleven months. During this short period, it has been gratifying to me to learn that the interests of the coal industry have not been limited to its own problems and well-being, but those of the entire Commonwealth as well. This broad interest in Kentucky has been demonstrated on numerous occasions through the efforts and actions of the Kentucky Coal Association.

Let me cite you a couple of examples. One was a plan to have the business and industrial groups of Kentucky sponsor advertisements in a special issue of *Fortune Magazine* in an effort to bring new industries to Kentucky. I invited business and industrial leaders from all over the State to a luncheon in Louisville to hear a presentation on the project. That group included Frank Thomas and Fred Bullard, chairman and president, respectively, of the Kentucky Coal Association. Following the presentation, Jim Host, my Commissioner of Public Information, asked for comments and, more importantly, commitments of support. Mr. Bullard was among the first to stand up and voice support by committing the Association to a full-page ad. The response has been overwhelming, and when the December *Fortune Magazine* issue is published, Kentucky will have a seventy-two page section, the largest section of this type ever published by *Fortune*. I am glad the coal industry will be represented by the Association's ad.

The second project in which the Kentucky Coal Association was involved was in aiding the financially plagued Spindletop Research. Again, the Kentucky Coal Association accepted the challenge by committing that which they had been asked to do. We have received cash and pledges, and I am confident we will shortly reach or slightly exceed the five-hundred thousand dollars necessary to put Spindletop Research on a sound, businesslike basis. These are but two examples of how the coal industry, through the Kentucky Coal Association, gave tangible evidence of its interest in and concern for the overall progress of the Commonwealth.

I am aware and pleased that Island Creek is a member of this fine organization. As Governor, I know the importance of unity which can provide a spokesman for an industry such as yours in matters concerning legislation and governmental regulation. You have an effective and respected spokesman for the coal industry.

LINCOLN SCHOOL CONVOCATION
Simpsonville / November 14, 1968

YOUR generation is particularly fortunate because it has so many years ahead to live in this exciting era. I think that if I were to choose from human history a time and a place in which to live, I would pick the United States of America in the year 1968. Never before has a nation been so rich with challenge. And never before has any country at any time ever possessed such an abundance of resources and talent that is needed to conquer the challenges which present themselves to our generations. The wealth and vigor and strength of our country today make this the hour for men who dare to dream. Now is the time for us to realize the destiny which awaits the greatest nation and the greatest system of government the world has ever known.

I come to you today as a proud spokesman for my generation and the generations which preceded ours. We take pride in the great progress that has been the symbol of Kentucky and the nation, and we challenge you to continue and improve upon the society you will soon inherit.

The field of education here in Kentucky offers the most dramatic proof of the manner in which our generation is meeting its commitment to the future. One year ago, an independent national study ranked Kentucky forty-eighth among the fifty states in education. One year ago, many of Kentucky's schools were overcrowded, and did not offer adequate facilities. One year ago Kentucky ranked thirty-eighth in teachers' salaries, and we had reached the danger point in the number of emergency instructors. One year ago, educational television in Kentucky was not operative.

Today Kentucky is experiencing educational growth that promises a new world for every Kentuckian. Over ninety million more dollars will be spent in the public school system than was spent last year. To attract qualified teachers, we have provided a minimum starting salary of $5,000. And because of this salary increase, the number of emergency teachers has decreased this year compared to the number needed in the last two years, even though enrollment in the schools has gone up. This year $52 million has been designated for school buildings and equipment, an increase of $9 million over last year. This represents the *first* increase for facilities and equipment *in the last eight years*, a very long time in view of recent inflation.

Kentucky's educational budget has shown concern for all the interests of the students. We will not be satisfied until we are sure that education is geared to the individual and until we are convinced that today's students are being adequately prepared to fill productive roles in society regardless of whether they choose a profession or a trade. That is the reason we have stressed the importance of vocational education. The operation of all existing facilities will continue, and in addition eighteen new extension centers will open during the next two years. Our goal is to have a vocational school or extension center within twenty-five miles of every Kentuckian. Today the nation's finest educational television network is bringing highly skilled instructors, improved teaching methods, and a much wider range of subject to every school in every community throughout the Commonwealth.

In short, our generation has recognized that young Kentuckians cannot, and must not, be sent into today's world without the preparation necessary for fully productive lives. We will either move forward in education or else we fall further behind. And in this area, above all others, there is no economy in retreat. On this point we stand with Thomas Jefferson in his belief that "the most important bill is that for the diffusion of knowledge among the people. No other sure foundation can be devised for the preservation of freedom and happiness."

The Lincoln School is an excellent example of what can and must be done to continue our progress in education.[1] Three years ago there was no Lincoln School. Today the eyes of educators all across America focus on a select group of students and teachers in Simpsonville, Kentucky, who are the pioneers in a great educational experiment. For over fifty years these buildings served as an institute of higher learning for Negroes in Kentucky. When all the educational facilities of this State were opened to every Kentuckian, the Lincoln Institute was left abandoned and purposeless. The Kentucky state government, however, with both foresight and wisdom, I think, restored the Lincoln Institute and gave it a new name and a new purpose. A new dynamic partnership was forged between state government, federal government, and the private sector. A human investment of dedicated, talented individuals was made. And from all of this Lincoln School was founded to help provide the margin of excellence for Kentucky's tomorrow.

Education is basic and crucial to the economic development of a region. Indeed, brain power has become the touchstone of regional growth. Kentucky needs, as never before, leaders in politics, business, religion, education, and other fields, leaders who will dare think in bold and imaginative terms about social problems and the possibilities of improving the quality of community life. And here at Simpsonville, the Lincoln School is an example of what can be done. Kentucky, unaccustomed to acclaim as a leader in education, is pioneering an idea which may set a pattern for the rest of the United States. The existence of this school proves that it is time for Kentucky to stop looking southward for comparison and to dedicate ourselves to the challenge of moving Kentucky toward the top in the nation. But to provide the best education possible is not enough. Books and knowledge are worthless unless the student reinvests his learning in the creative laboratory of life. Education is vain and empty if it rests unused; knowledge benefits mankind only when it is used.

And that is why you are fortunate to be alive in these times. The challenge to America in 1968 is great. We must solve the urban crisis; we must reduce hunger and disease; we must ease the tensions of America; we must give new life to Appalachia. Most important, today we face the challenge of more and better education for everyone. It is imperative that you meet this challenge.

But yours is not only a challenge. It is also a responsibility. It is your responsibility to return to your cities and counties to use the education you receive. It is in our American tradition that to those whom more is given, more is asked. Tomorrow you will be the leaders of our country and on your sholders will rest the burden of our future. The dream that every Kentucky youth can obtain an education as excellent as yours must become your dream, and our dream. I think you will accept this responsibility, for to Americans there is no substitute for challenge. It is our tradition to ever hear the call of distant trumpets. It is in our heritage to seek the farther shore. You are part of this heritage. You are part of the new army, carrying the banner of education, answering to the call of change, a force certain to alter the America of tomorrow. So I urge you to be strong in will, "to strive, to seek, to find, and not to yield."[1]

---

1. The Lincoln School was an experimental school for gifted youth.

2. Tennyson, Alfred Lord, *Ulysses*, ed. Emily Morrison Beck (Boston, 1968).

BUSINESSMEN'S LUNCHEON, CHEMICAL BANK OF NEW YORK
New York City / November 20, 1968

As most of you know, this is my first trip to New York City since being sworn in as Governor of the State of Kentucky last December. I suppose that as businessmen you would like to know from the Governor of the Bluegrass State how the State's economy is faring under the new administration and what is the outlook for the future.

In the first place, let me say in the opinion of most of the industrial development technicians in Kentucky, we have developed one of the best tax climates of any state in the union with the advent of the 5 percent broad-based sales tax. As bankers and businessmen, you can readily see that this creates the kind of business climate that is conducive to capital investments. With the citizens of the State willing to put the State's economy on a pay-as-you-go basis, it no longer becomes necessary for our legislative bodies to engage in the Russian roulette game of selective taxation. The future of any state today will depend, as far as its government is concerned, on such a broad-based tax as we have in Kentucky.

Our own Department of Commerce reports to me that our records in industrial growth and new job opportunities for the past year has been outstanding in comparison to other states of similar economic configuration. Our extensive plan for new toll roads, our water resource development program, our aggressive plans of salesmanship and promotion, our vast labor pool, and our improved business climate is making Kentucky more and more a target for industrial investors.

I do not mean to imply that I am satisfied with the progress we are making in Kentucky. According to our own Department of Commerce, when this administration took over the helm of government, we found ourselves in a tremendous communication gap with scientific and technical experts of the scientific community. Even though we had a Commission on Science and Technology, there seemed to be a great void between these scientific leaders and the practitioners of industrial development. We are endeavoring to close that gap, realizing each day the great importance of gearing our state's future course toward that of scientific achievement and development.

We realize fully that when we build for the future, we are setting a course into the new scientific and technological age. We know that it is of utmost importance that we find our niche in this complex system. A system that is achieving, day by day, important milestones of dramatic growth, with our highly successful ventures into space, and the creation of new scientific and technical resource material that is finding expanded markets throughout the world.

Perhaps you read the other day where the Governor of Illinois announced, intentionally or not, that a major oil company was planning to build a multimillion dollar complex in southern Illinois, which eventually would employ, according to the article, 10,000 persons. According to some news reports this location was selected primarily because of the proximity to mineable coal reserves, with natural gas, petroleum reserves, and surface and underground water as secondary considerations. The research and development aspects of this investment include extensive use of coal-tar derivatives from the South Central Illinois coal mines.

Such a possibility looms ahead for the Bluegrass State, not as a "carrot-on-the-stick" proposition but an actuality. In fact, our state geological survey is now remapping new mineable coal reserves in western Kentucky. As many of you know, we mined over 100,000 tons of coal last year in Kentucky. As many of you know, we have over 1,000 miles of navigable rivers with a twelve-foot channel. As many of you know, we are blessed with natural gas and have an abundance of gas and petroleum transmission facilities within the State. As many of you know, we have one of the best labor potentials of any state in the Ohio Valley. When we are able to put these factors together in a package wrapped in the proper scientific and technological information, we are then prepared for our place in the scientific sun.

When we realize these great dreams as they unfold in the future, we will find a Kentucky with a broad foundation of working people gainfully employed in an above-the-average job to the degree never before thought of in the past decades. We recognize that we must muster our total resources to accomplish these objectives. My Department of Commerce informs me that there are more than a dozen corporations who involve themselves in the total energy concept, and that with the resources we have in our State, our chances of becoming the site of one of these research development and production complexes is very good. We shall work toward that end.

Further, again, my Department of Commerce has estimated there will be approximately twenty-five nuclear power plants in the eastern part of the United States by the 1980's, producing 20,000 megawatts of power. It is our understanding that there will be one, and only one, nuclear fuel plant to supply these electric generating facilities. We have dreams that this will be in our State. Our power needs seem to double every seven years or so, so the nuclear power plants, plus the many steam generating plants should gear us for competitive development as far as electric energy is concerned.

In review, and in perhaps more simple terms, the State of Kentucky is preparing itself for a new age, the age of nuclear energy, the age of total energy, the age of new scientific discovery, and the age of total resource development—the age of new uses and established basic chemicals and for the new technology that must come as we grow.

REPUBLICAN GOVERNORS' CONFERENCE
Palm Springs, California / December 6, 1968

THE hope of America's future rests with the integrity of the judiciary. Congress and state legislatures may meet and enact oppressive or unconstitutional laws, or for that matter, they may enact desirable legislation only to see it flaunted in its administration. In either situation, the place of last resort, the security of the people, rests with our courts. As chief executives within our own states we may extend ourselves beyond the authority provided. Here again the last resort for the citizen is with the judiciary. Consequently, in our American system, the public is concerned with the legislative; they honor the executive, but they find security in the judicial.

I would like to express the hope that the President-elect, the Vice-President-elect, and especially the Attorney General will dedicate themselves to creating a new moral climate in America, a climate in which respect for law can thrive and can replace the permissiveness of the past and a climate in which justice can be more fairly administered.

I would further hope that the emphasis of the new administration would be upon the protection of the law-abiding citizen rather than upon the protection of the law violator. As one judge recently put it, we must consider change in the theory of justice from the three P's to three S's; Probation, Parole and Pardon to Sure, Swift and Severe.

We all realize the challenge and the responsibility which came with the November victory, and certainly nowhere is the challenge greater and the responsibility heavier on the Republican Party, than in the area of justice, law, and order. This is the case in view of the fact that our victory was won in part because in the Republican Platform and through the Republican candidates, we were able to convince the American electorate that we would maintain law and order through justice. So now one of the primary responsibilities of the Party, and a responsibility which must logically fall heavily on this group of Republican governors, is to see that the confidence of the electorate was not misplaced.

We are all agreed, I believe, that law enforcement is and must be first and foremost the duty of local and state officials. It was because of this belief that we were gratified by the passage in Congress of the Omnibus Crime Bill last summer. This legislation was an experiment, or perhaps a trial run in the minds of many Congressmen, to see if the states could indeed make the bloc grant approach work. But as you know, there has been an attempt on the part of the present Attorney General and others in the Department of Justice to accomplish by guidelines what they could not accomplish by legislation, that is the categorical grant approach. It appears that this attempt has been squelched and we can find great comfort in the indication by the President-elect that this will not be a recurring danger in the coming administration.

With this behind us, we stand on the threshold of a tremendous opportunity in the area of law enforcement and justice. In this area, as in so many others, we have inherited with our victory a legacy of complex and challenging problems. More than any other administration in recent history, the new administration must concern itself primarily with problem solving. Thankfully, however, there are many encouraging signs. The President-elect has shown an impressive understanding of the office he will take in January and he has demonstrated by public statements and actions a reassuring desire to strengthen the local-state-federal partnership.

Particularly in the role he has created for Vice-President Agnew has Mr. Nixon given the states reason to hope that finally America's federal system will be revived as conceived. It has also been indicated that in the new administration, the office of the Vice-President will be a forum for prior consultation between state and national governments, a procedure we in state government have advocated for many years. Our experience with the Omnibus Crime Bill and Safe Streets Act has shown the need we have for this opportunity to discuss guidelines and regulations before they become official. It is vital that we put to rest the present situation of always reacting to the mandates of Washington rather than being able to work together from the inception of various programs to forge the rules of the game. In exchange for this opportunity, however, I think we must realize that this will be a two-way street, that we can and must offer something in return.

First, of course, we must show a willingness and a capability to meet our responsibilities. Second, we should mobilize our increasing strength behind the programs of the new administration. In other words, if we are to have a part in creating new programs, then we must also share the responsibility to help sell these same programs to Congress and to the American people.

Another encouraging sign is an attitude on the part of the President-elect which is best expressed in the Republican Platform that for the future, we pledge "an all-out, federal, state, and local crusade against crime, including first, leadership by an attorney general who will restore stature and respect to that office." Second, "continued support of legislation to strengthen state and local law enforcement and preserve the primacy of state responsibility in this area." Third, "a vigorous nationwide drive against trafficking in narcotics and dangerous drugs, including special emphasis on the first steps toward addiction and the use of marijuana and such drugs as LSD."

I believe it is crucial that we on the state level initiate plans and programs to deal with our uniquely individual situations. Some plans which could have the effect of strengthening state leadership as well as causing new policies to be formulated within the Justice Department are—one, a National Law Enforcement Training Center specifically established to provide both basic and advanced training for city, county and state police officers; two, Regional Training Seminars or "Traveling Academies" to assist state and local police in training; three, technical assistance to the states in the fields of law enforcement training and statewide communications networks and computer systems.

LOUISVILLE PERSONNEL ASSOCIATION
Louisville / January 13, 1969

I COMMEND and congratulate each of you for the crucial role that you are playing to build a better community and a better State. The recruitment and sorting out of talented and dedicated personnel for business and industry as well as public service is one of the cornerstones on which private enterprise as well as government rests in America. As an attorney working with local businessmen and corporate enterprise and as Governor over the State's largest single employer, experience has shown me that the intelligent use of human resources is imperative if we are to improve the quality of our society.

I submit to you that our people are without doubt Kentucky's greatest resource, and the use we make of this vast human resource is uniquely your responsibility and your opportunity. Within the scope of your responsibilities as personnel specialists lies the opportunity to directly influence the economic health of the individual companies and organizations you represent and to dramatically affect the economic progress of your cities, of this State, and this nation. How successfully you discover human talent and how well you channel people into their most productive roles within our society are responsibilities which bear heavily on the success of man's effort to improve his quality of living. I would encourage you to continually seek new, improved methods to reduce the costly and wasteful error of misdirected talent.

But technology alone probably will never entirely furnish the answer to whether an applicant for employment will perform successfully. In his book entitled *Excellence,* John W. Gardner, the former Secretary of Health, Education, and Welfare and now director of the Urban Coalition, commented on the relative strength of even the most advanced testing procedures. Mr. Gardner says that even the best tests are far from perfect and any system of identification of talent which assumes them to be perfect will commit grave mistakes. This, of course, long has been realized and accepted by personnel experts in private enterprise.

Unfortunately, state government has failed to keep pace with your progress and your greater understanding of personnel management. For instance, the time has come and gone when private enterprise accepts academic accomplishment as conclusive proof of an applicant's ability to perform. Businessmen and personnel management specialists realize that there must be, at least, one more step. They try by testing, by personal interviews, and by on-the-job observation to determine the human elements necessary for success. They look for the human characteristics—judgment, pride, determination to succeed; in short, they balance aptitude with attitude.

John Gardner says that of all the mistakes made in using tests, perhaps the worst are made in trying to apply the results beyond the strictly academic or intellectual performances for which the tests were designed. And I find little pleasure today in reporting to you that state government has, for the past eight years at least, committed this mistake in every instance of employment. The system of testing which was established at the inception of the Kentucky Merit System is heavily weighted toward determining the applicant's ability to pass a test, not the ability of the prospective employee to perform a service. This is only one problem which threatens our progress toward a goal to which this administration is pledged—the elevation of standards and quality of service by state employees to the people of Kentucky.

There are other obstructions. For instance, we have discovered numerous examples where job qualification standards have been selfishly distorted. The main concern very obviously was not to raise the qualifications of employees and services; the main concern was to wrap a protective cocoon around political allies who were holding the jobs when standards were written. There are examples in which politicians have gone to almost comical lengths to perpetuate a political dynasty. In one extreme case, I recall that the qualifications were so specific as to cite almost course for course the academic background of an applicant. The only thing wrong, as it was later discovered, was that the man who held that position was the only man to possess those exact qualifications. It was not too surprising to also discover that this same man was also the author of the qualifications. Far from promoting better service and better opportunity for advancement of employees, this system guarantees only inbred stagnations of services, as well as ambition and ideas. It breeds only mediocrity.

In 1967 we campaigned on the theme "Time for a Change." And a substantial majority of the electorate, considering the voter registration in Kentucky, agreed with our theme. It was the mood of the State at that time. We have made changes, and we will continue to make changes which will produce better service to the people of the Commonwealth. We have made it clear to state employees that loyalty will be one of the new qualifications. Loyalty not to me or to my political party, but loyalty to the idea that state government has nothing to offer the people of Kentucky except efficient, courteous service.

It is my hope that every change we have made during the past thirteen months in personnel as well as policy has been constructive and that the level of service has been improved. This may not be the case in every instance, but you may be assured that we will continue to demand high work standards of all employees regardless of the fact that they were hired during this administration or during previous terms. We have been attacked repeatedly during the past year because of certain changes which were instituted, and at times we have been hampered by those who for selfish reasons have reason to fear constructive change. We have found that the most vocal obstructionists invariably are persons who have been nurtured by the old political system and who have fed at the public trough during previous administrations. Their fear is not that we will destroy a fair and equitable merit system. Their fear is that we will establish such a system.

Much has already been said about our challenge of the political abuses of the merit system, but not enough has been heard about the disregard of the past for the enactment of sound principles of personnel management. Not until the Efficiency Task Force made an investigation last year of state personnel procedures did this failure come to light. In their report, this group of independent business executives enumerated a point-by-point failure by the Personnel Board and the Personnel Department to keep pace with modern personnel management advances. They urged an employee fringe benefits program, group insurance, educational assistance, awards and incentives, training and quality control, and management development programs—all of which private industry has used successfully for years.

We are going to establish an incentive awards program among state employees. We are contemplating free weekend vacations at Kentucky State Parks to those persons who propose constructive suggestions. We are also studying a proposal for statewide group health insurance. By coordinating coverage we hope to be able to get reduced group rates, which will be paid by employees. We are now investigating the possibility of closer coordination between the Personnel Department, the Department of Commerce, and the Department of Economic Security, in order to provide employment service to Kentuckians who apply for state jobs. Often, a position which is suited to the ability of a qualified applicant is filled. We want to be able to distribute this applicant's name and qualifications to the Kentucky industries which might need him. We don't want to say "No" to any Kentuckian who wants to work and better himself. We are convinced that "Every Kentuckian Counts," and we want to help every Kentuckian to stand up and be counted.

As you can see, the Personnel Department is carefully reviewing and trying the suggestions made by the Efficiency Task Force. It is going a step further. The Efficiency Task Force examined the workings of each department. The Personnel Department is examining each job in order to check its efficiency and effectiveness. Our goal is to encourage the best performance possible from our departments and our employees. We are also continuing the start made by the Efficiency Task Force and hope soon to find a qualified, concerned organization or group of persons to study every phase of the present system. What we seek is an evaluation of the theory and the execution of the system extending from job requirements into testing procedures and enforcement. I believe that if the study group we find is dedicated and resourceful, we will be able to correct and, if necessary, create a system under which qualified personnel can be attracted to positions of responsibility, where they are secure from political involvement, interference, or coercion. I would certainly welcome any suggestions the members of this organization might have in connection with this study.

Certainly you are demonstrating your interest and your united effort and concern and dedication of purpose which could be of considerable help to us in resolving state government's personnel problems. If this problem is to be solved, and if Kentucky is to move ahead into a greater future, we must all develop an understanding and an appreciation for the proper utilization of our manpower potential. And if we are to be successful in our efforts to build foundations for the future of Kentucky, then we must all become aware that the cement of those foundations will be our human resources.

KENTUCKY UTILITIES
Lexington / January 22, 1969

PERHAPS more than any other group, you so closely associated with development know the great strides Kentucky is making today toward the realization of its full economic and social potential. Encouraged by the progress and the accomplishments of the recent past, the people of the Commonwealth today share a new spirit, a new confidence, and a new sense of purpose. And who has been the architect of this new spirit? Certainly it has not been government alone, although government has played a part. The architect of Kentucky's progress and growth has been, and continues today to be, the free enterprise system which you so ably represent throughout this State.

I am not here today to advocate the power and priority of government. I am here today representing more than three million Kentuckians who gratefully acknowledge the contribution which the private enterprise system has made to the welfare of the Commonwealth. As you perhaps know, this is not a new discovery for me, though certainly after a year as Governor, I am more aware and more grateful than ever for the part you play in Kentucky's progress. I have long been an advocate and, whenever possible, a promoter and protector of the free enterprise system. I believe in it, and I consider it one of the basic cornerstones on which this great Republic was founded, and one of the primary reasons America has become the greatest country in the world.

I have just returned from Washington where the inspiring spectacle of orderly government process has again been enacted. Throughout the past year, the inauguration and the national election, America's way of life was on trial before the world jury of nations. The world waited, perhaps as anxiously as any other time in history, to see if this country could remain firm in the face of universal unrest, rebellion, and chaos. Today we are firm, even stronger perhaps, because we have withstood this latest test of our system. America has once again emerged as the model of stability to be admired and imitated throughout the world.

Many of the questions surrounding America's future course were answered during the past year. But the most eloquent and the most important answer that was rendered was in reply to the question of whether America could continue to lead the world in social progress while at the same time refusing to substitute socialism for the free enterprise system. In the coming months, I believe we will see the pendulum swing back toward more traditional American attitudes concerning private enterprise. And with this about-face will come new responsibilities and new demands on private enterprise. The problems facing America today will severely test our theory that each individual must be responsible for his own economic well-being, that each person is accountable for his own moral conduct. It will also test the theory that people, and not government, must determine the course of their lives. In short, as some would say, the time has come when those of us who espouse the free enterprise system must either put up or shut up. There is no problem here because private enterprise has been putting up throughout the history of this country. And certainly here in Kentucky there are vivid examples which illustrate that private enterprise will continue to live up to and surpass its responsibilities.

This group is one of the best examples of dynamic, creative, responsible private enterprise to be found anywhere. For more than twenty years now, Kentucky Utilities has supplied the State with talented, dedicated men and women who channel local initiative into community development and improvement. This is talent that few cities could otherwise afford and yet the results that you have helped to achieve have changed the face of Kentucky. Last year saw over ten thousand new job opportunities created in Kentucky through new plant locations and expansions of plants already operating here. And as we traveled throughout the State last year to meet with prospective industrial citizens, the tremendous impact that you have had on the economic picture of the State became fully apparent.

There have been other examples this year of the willingness of private enterprise to join in Kentucky's quest for greatness. Private enterprise did not hesitate when we asked for top business executives to join our Efficiency Task Force. A conservative estimate of the value of time spent by these businessmen seeking ways to improve the service of state government at a reduced cost would easily exceed two hundred thousand dollars. And when we confronted Spindletop Research last spring with the sad facts of its financial life, it was private industry, and not government, that stepped forward and rolled up its sleeves. That was last May, and now, nine months later, Spindletop Research has just announced that it is operating completely in the black for the first time in its history. Private enterprise raised almost $500 thousand to set Spindletop on solid financial footing, and recent evidence compels us to believe that this is a triumph which could light Kentucky's way into a future which undoubtedly will require our best technical research ability.

We called on private enterprise again last year when we put together a section of advertising in *Fortune Magazine* to tell industry the many assets Kentucky has to offer. Private enterprise again responded, this time to the tune of $300 thousand, and as a result, Kentucky established an advertising milestone with the largest single publication spread in history. Undoubtedly, because of the assets which we were able to advertise and because of the cooperative spirit that was exhibited by private enterprise, new industry will be attracted. These accomplishments and other day-to-day contributions which benefit all of us serve as a reminder that private enterprise is robust and vigorous and willing to exercise its responsibility. And these are all good reasons why we need not be overly concerned that private enterprise is being tested by the new socialistic tendencies which have risen with our heightened concern for social progress.

Now let us move on to discuss how state government can work in concert with private enterprise in the area of our greatest mutual concern, the expanded economic development and improvement of Kentucky's communities. Our interest in economic development is motivated by our efforts to establish the broadest possible revenue base from which to draw the funds which support government service. We are committed to the premise that a broadly based tax structure is the most viable and most equitable solution to the rising expense of continually expanding government service. Our tax burden must be one shared equally according to individual ability to contribute. It must be a responsibility shared by seller as well as consumer, by property owner as well as property user. For too many years already, Kentucky's financial problems have been hidden underneath an expedient plan which taxes selective Peter to pay collective Paul.

The time has now come when Kentucky must turn away from further direct taxation for the revenue which will be necessary if we are to meet the increasing cost of education, of mental health, of corrective rehabilitation, of assistance to the aged, the sick, and the needy. To meet the inevitable financial crisis which awaits Kentucky as we try to answer the public demand for new and expanded services, we must look not to increased taxation but to increased economy at every level of government. And instead of more taxes, we must gather every ounce of talent, of manpower and determination that we possess for an all-out crusade for total development of our resources.

After many conversations with key members of the new national administration, I am confident that economy will be a watchword in Washington during the next four years. Already here in Kentucky, we have been able to put into practice many of the recommendations made by the Efficiency Task Force. As a result, we have already been able to save approximately $7 million. On the local level of government, it is encouraging to see cities and counties unite to trim the cost of services. For instance, Fayette County and Jefferson County have for the past four years entered into joint purchasing agreements which have resulted in substantial savings to taxpayers of both metropolitan counties. These are examples which can be followed elsewhere. These are economies to which all Kentuckians are entitled and should demand at every level of government.

It was unfortunate that the crisis which we faced last year in Frankfort could not be resolved by economizing alone. We were headed for a deficit of $36 million within seven months, and the situation was further aggravated by the State's obligation of nearly $120 million of new money during this biennium for projects already begun, projects such as educational television, Medicare, new state parks, and highway construction. Kentucky must never again allow itself to be undersold and overspent to the extent that increased taxation is the only alternative. And I am firmly convinced that this can be avoided if we will form an alliance dedicated to economic growth through the fullest exploitation of Kentucky's many assets.

Our immediate efforts must continue to be concentrated on two specific goals—industrial growth and expansion of the agricultural economy. In addition, we must begin now to prepare for the rapidly approaching time when the field of technology will offer unlimited opportunity for those who can meet the demands of this new facet of our national achievement.

Our excitement and confidence that these challenges will be met stems largely from the fact that Kentucky's total resources are uniquely suited for this task. For instance, the same factors which induce industry and encourage our agricultural resurgence—our geographical nearness to the nation's largest marketplaces, our abundance of water, our modern network of highways and growing number of airports, our improved educational facilities, our sources of trainable labor—all these things will also give us a head start in making Kentucky a focal point for the scientifically oriented industries which will be an outgrowth of the new technological advances being made today. Exciting new discoveries are being recorded daily, and the most exciting by far are those innovations and new uses being found for our natural resources, coal and gas. Our abundance of both certainly puts Kentucky in the forefront of this unlimited new horizon.

And now, this proud old Commonwealth finds itself in the challenging position of trying to stay ahead instead of trying to catch up. Greatness is ours if we can clutch this vast opportunity. Again I say we will, if private enterprise and public agencies join together, if we will develop our total resources, and if we are willing to take a hard look at our communities, our educational system, our operation of government at every level. Now is the time for introspection and evaluation, and neither pride nor the elation of past accomplishments must keep us from an honest, impartial assessment. Your responsibility on the local level will be to determine if your communities are such that they would be attractive to the highly trained personnel who will accompany the technically oriented industries we hope to bring to Kentucky. Are your schools good enough; are your community leaders progressive; is government responsive to new demands and challenges; are your recreation facilities adequate?

These and many other questions must be answered affirmatively if your communities are to be in the race. These are not new questions because you have asked them before, when you began your efforts to attract new industry to the communities you serve. But these questions are more important now in the face of the opportunity that is ours. You and your community may not be able to answer affirmatively all these questions; very few communities will. I hope then that you will not hesitate to call on us for help as we have called on you in the past.

Our office, along with the Department of Commerce, the newly organized Kentucky Program Development Office, and many other state departments will gladly lend whatever technical assistance is available. From today forward, let Kentucky's opportunity for unmatched greatness bind us together in a new alliance. And joined together in a determination that we will attain new plateaus, let our united efforts lead to a quality environment and a quality of living that will be the destiny of every Kentuckian.

DRUG ABUSE SEMINAR
Louisville / January 27, 1969

THIS occasion is in one sense unfortunate and disquieting; in another sense it is historic and gratifying. It is disquieting because of the very fact of these seminars, because it was even necessary to plan a series of conferences on drug abuse. We have all seen and heard and read of the problem of narcotics use and abuse around us. That is the unfortunate part of this occasion. These seminars, on the other hand, are historic because they mark the first statewide effort to combat this problem through education as well as law enforcement. They are gratifying because they hopefully mark the beginning of a continuing statewide effort in the education of our citizens to the dangers of using narcotics and other drugs.

I am reminded this morning of a story about a young boy who started to school. Soon his teachers noticed a disturbing characteristic about the boy. One day he was given a picture of a dog to color and he colored it green. The next day he was given a horse to color and he colored it green. Eventually he had a collection of pictures of houses, cars, and other animals, all colored green. His teachers became more disturbed when he produced a picture of his mother and father and other people, all of whom were colored green. At this point he was taken to the school nurse, who failed to explain the boy's strange fascination with the one color. He was then taken successively to the school doctor, and the school psychiatrist. Neither had an explanation for the boy's curious tendencies. Becoming alarmed, the school authorities called the boy's mother. So the mother asked the boy why he colored everything green. He replied in an innocent childlike voice that he had lost all of his crayons except the green one. This obviously was a case of making a complicated problem out of a simple one. But the reverse happens also. There is often a tendency to make simple problems out of complicated ones. I think that this is true with the problem of drug abuse.

Some pass off the problem as merely one of fascination with a new toy or youthful desire to experiment, as a passing stage or fad. Others even try to defend the use of marijuana, LSD, and similar drugs as being beneficial, or at least harmless. In many instances the approach is: if we don't talk about the problem, it will go away. But I would remind you that not only has narcotics abuse, as a crime in itself, been rising at an alarming rate, but it has been shown to be the cause of or at least a factor in other social problems: it has caused murder; it is associated with robbery and assault; it has encouraged prostitution and other crimes of morality; it has been definitely linked with many of the riots and civil disturbances which have plagued the nation in the last several years; and it has caused mental disturbances in persons caught in its web. Needless to say, it costs the taxpayers millions of dollars annually for law enforcement and rehabilitation efforts.

The problem is both serious and complicated. It has deep roots. It may have many causes. It cannot be solved by simple solutions and old attitudes. It needs careful attention and new solutions.

One of the most obvious and immediate causes of the growing experimentation with narcotics and drugs is pure ignorance. Drug abuse education is one of the most promising new approaches. It is preventive medicine for the disease. These conferences are part of the medicine. The men who will participate in these seminars are experts. I hope that you will listen to their remarks, and will absorb their wisdom. At the end of the day, you will have an opportunity to comment, to question, to share your wisdom. You can carry back to your respective communities the facts stated, the messages given, the lessons learned. The youth of our Commonwealth, who are most exposed to the dangers of narcotics, will then be better served.

LEXINGTON JAYCEES
OUTSTANDING YOUNG MAN
BANQUET
Lexington / January 28, 1969

TONIGHT, as we join with you and with the city of Lexington to pay tribute to the Outstanding Young Man of 1968, we are particularly aware of what the Jaycees organization has meant not only to this community but to the entire State.

The Jaycees is an action organization with the object and purpose of producing leadership. It doesn't try to build communities; it builds men. But it is these men who build cities and states and nations. The Jaycees is a training ground for young men who want to have a part in shaping the destiny of their communities and their country.

The greatest strength of the Jaycees is that its ideal is far outside itself. Young men are not Jaycees for the sake of being Jaycees. Jayceeism is not an end in itself, but a means to a much larger end. It is only a vehicle to help young men get where they are going, to help them achieve leadership. It doesn't try to hold onto its members, but pushes them out at the age of thirty-six, trained to lead in community affairs without the help of any parent organization. It says good-by to them at the age when they are just beginning to show their greatest values and capabilities. It stays behind while they go on to whatever heights God will lead them. It's an unselfish mother, and it raises good boys.

I have found that the men in the Jaycees make the most valuable employees. I've seen this organization transform the lives of its members. Today a young man may be an obscure clerk; but after a while in the Jaycees, after getting into the bloodstream of the community affairs, he's in a position to hire and fire clerks by the dozen. Today he may be a follower; tomorrow he'll be a leader. But in the meantime, he'll spend time on committees, or running around on cold nights helping on some kind of improvement projects, or standing on the street corner with a loud speaker telling people to give, to vote, and to listen and be concerned. And he'll start getting public recognition and people he doesn't know from Adam will call him by name on the street. He will be on speaking terms with hundreds he never knew before. His boss will begin to realize that all this civic activity inspires the community's confidence and appreciation, and it results in new business so he shouldn't be surprised to find the community looking to his clerk, his salesman, his assistant or his employee for civic leadership.

This leadership doesn't stop at thirty-six. You can spot Jaycees a mile off as they put into practice the things learned in this great organization. They lead in business, the professions, and civic affairs. They know how to get the job done and they don't mind working. Think back, each of you, of the fellows you know, that have gone through this great training vehicle. Many of them are the leaders in your communities today.

What is it about a Jaycee that makes him want to pay the price of leadership? What kind of person is a Jaycee anyway? A Jaycee, some might say, is a naive young man, who gets everything backwards. He thinks personal happiness depends not on how the world treats you, but how you treat the world. He thinks the only thing you can take with you is what you have given to others and the only way that you can rise in the world is to keep your feet on the ground and stay on the level. And a Jaycee has no sense of proportion. There is no job too big for him, and there's no job so small that he thinks he is too big for it. He's also very superstitious, he believes in luck, and the harder he works, the more luck he seems to have. He is so weak and helpless in the face of a really tough problem that he has to call on God for help, and he thinks an ounce of sweat carries more weight with God than a bucket of tears.

I have faith in the Jaycees and faith in their generation. I've seen them roll up their sleeves and get things done that others called impossible. I've seen them wade in and solve a problem with muscle and elbow grease before older and wiser men could even get it outlined at the conference table. I've seen them pump the breath of life into towns that were dead on their feet, and slap the wind out of selfish politicians and private interests that had whole cities in their grip. But more than that, I've seen them turn pipsqueaks to men, pessimists into optimists, and quitters into fighters. That is why my staff and the new administration has so many young men.

I'm sure that as members of the Jaycees, you wonder at times what the public thinks of you as an organization. In every town there are always a few cynics, generally nursing some personal inadequacy, who criticize the Jaycees and everyone else for being eager beavers without the mature judgment of older men. But since I left the Jaycees nine years ago, when I became thirty-six years old, I have discovered that a vast majority of the public likes and respects the Jaycee because of the things he does. To hundreds of underprivileged children at Christmas time he is the Santa Claus they didn't believe in. To thousands of citizens who see him working to build a playground for crippled children, he looks like a pretty decent guy. To millions of people who see him riding on a truck bed in the heat of summer telling people to register and vote, he looks like Uncle Sam in a limp shirt. And to the narrow leaders who creep into governments to pull down the curtain of secrecy over the open doors of public office and who try to lull the people into apathy, he looks like a crusader.

You can be sure that your community respects you as an organization of young men who work together for the common good, and nothing you do with a worthy motive will ever fail or be unappreciated.

But are you everything that your community would like for you to be? Are you everything your town needs? Is it enough to get out the vote, collect the money for a good cause, beautify the city, and sponsor worthy projects, and so on until you're thirty-six? Are you through when the awards are locked in the trophy case and the scrapbook is closed? You're training for leadership in your community. What do people expect a leader to do?

Leadership means doing everything for the good of others, which often means doing it at the sacrifice of personal popularity. Very often it means standing alone in the belief that you are right and the crowd is wrong. Sometimes it means being a busybody, and other times being stubborn—having a strong will and a stronger won't. But sooner or later, the community will follow the man who does what he knows is right, whether the crowd is with him or not, and in spite of the pressures of self-interest and convenience. The city you live in will respect you as long as you respect and follow your own civic conscience. Such a man is never poor, never without friends. There is no cabinet that can hold his trophies, and no scrapbook that can tell his deeds.

There are too many so-called leaders, you know, who are not willing to serve their communities because they are waiting for the call of bigger things. They want an appointment to a big national council, a regional presidency, or a state board and they don't have time to heed the call of the school board or the P.T.A. They want to lead the fight singlehandedly against federal encroachment and preserve the constitution. They want to preserve private enterprise from the effects of creeping socialism. But they don't want to grab the bull by the horns where it will do the most good, down on the local level.

The towns and cities of the United States are begging the Jaycees to produce community leaders who will put courage and spirit and new ideas into local government by serving in office and executing policies consistent with our basic beliefs of integrity, economy, and efficiency. And we need businessmen who will stimulate local enterprise and keep people from being dependent on federal help to develop local resources and finance local improvements. We need bankers who will be quick to give loans to young people just getting started, so they won't have to go to the federal government for the money to build their homes and start their businesses. We need local leaders who are not afraid to start local projects without a guarantee of federal aid, which is also a guarantee of federal control. When leadership on the local level breaks down, the people are forced into the position of having to vote for prosperity instead of working for it.

We seem to have an abundance of able men who want to be leaders, but who want to steer clear of controversial issues. They refuse to get mixed up in politics, or to tell how they stand because they think it will hurt business or antagonize the boss or the union. Show me a man with no identifiable stand on a clear-cut issue, and I'll show you a man with no identifiable character or value to his community. You can try so hard to stay away from the pro and con that you become blind to the right and the wrong.

The question ultimately becomes—can the Jaycees give us this kind of leadership? Can they put men in places of responsibility who will make their own records and stand on them instead of jumping on the other fellow's? We need men who won't get to the top through pull and then stop pulling and who won't let the American way of life die of cold feet because they were afraid to get into hot water. We don't need leaders who can sit on a podium or stand on a platform. We need men and women who can stand on their own two feet and kneel on their own two knees. We need the kind who can be right and still be president.

I feel very strongly that the Jaycees can help to provide that kind of leadership which we need, not only here in Lexington, but throughout Kentucky. As Kentucky begins its third century this year, we find ourselves on the threshold of new and unmatched greatness, if—if we can meet the challenges and if we can overcome the complex problems of our time. And we can only do this if the people, if the private as well as the public sector, if each of you on the local level and each of us on the state level can combine our energies, our concern, and our dedication. Together we can find new approaches and new answers for the moral, the economic, and the social problems of this era. Together, we can shape the direction of the next 100 years of Kentucky's history. And when that history is written, let it be said that this was a time when individual fulfillment matched statewide growth, a time when the destiny of Kentucky was fully realized.

THE TURNPIKE AUTHORITY
OF KENTUCKY
Toll Road Revenue Bonds Series
of January 1969
New York City / February 6, 1969

I SINCERELY appreciate this opportunity to speak to such a distinguished audience about Kentucky. Now, anytime you permit a Kentuckian to talk about Kentucky, you have made yourself liable to a prolonged brainwashing. However, with due regard for your busy schedules, I will attempt to restrain my natural instincts.

Very briefly, I would like to review for you some of Kentucky's more important "vital statistics." Mr. Christen,[1] my Commissioner of Finance and chief financial adviser, tells me that out in our state there are three kinds of liars—a liar, a damn liar, and a statistician. I assure you that you can place complete confidence in the statistics which I will recite here.

Total employment in Kentucky averaged over one million persons in 1968. Of this total, nonagricultural employment accounted for 852 thousand persons, an increase of 46 percent in twenty years. Manufacturing provided 230 thousand jobs, an increase of 36 percent since 1960. In that same period, unemployment decreased from 10 percent to a range of 4 to 5 percent in 1968. Farm employment in 1968 stood at 186 thousand persons, a decline of 112 thousand in the past twenty years. However, farm income was up in the same period from $590 million to $821 million. Personal income rose from a total of $2.8 billion or $990 per capita in 1948 to $8.4 billion or $2,600 per capita in 1968.

Analysis indicates that three programs have been primarily responsible for the continuing economic growth of our state. First, Kentucky is currently experiencing an educational explosion. Unfortunately, we were behind most other states in facilities and educational opportunities. But now we are catching up. Approximately 62 percent of the general fund budget for the current biennium is allocated to education. Within the past year, expenditures per pupil have been increased by 57 percent.

Secondly, Kentucky has an unexcelled state park system which provides the nucleus for a $440 million recreation industry. Our efforts are now concentrated on involving the private sector in recreational development. As you perhaps know, Fess Parker's $13 million Frontier World will be located in Kentucky.

The third program, and perhaps the most important, is an accelerated effort to complete a network of safe, modern, coordinated highways. And this brings us to our main topic, the importance of the proposed toll facilities to our State. Seven hundred and thirty-eight miles of the federal interstate highway system is allocated to Kentucky. The 62 percent of this mileage which has been opened to traffic includes those portions which provide the greatest traffic service. The remaining interstate miles are in varying phases of design or construction. Present federal funding schedules will permit opening the last mile of this system in 1975. The 413 miles included in the Appalachian Developmental Highway System are located totally in the far eastern section of the state. Approximately 334 miles of this system is now being designed with seventy miles open to traffic.

As you will note from the map, all interstate highways have provided for only north-south traffic flow. This situation left a need for an addition to our highway system which would provide for east-west transportation routes thus linking together the diverse geographical regions of the State. In recognition of this need, the Kentucky General Assembly enacted legislation in 1960 which created the Turnpike Authority of Kentucky. Utilizing the provision of this enabling legislation, the Commonwealth has now opened 389 miles of toll roads. Beginning with the Mountain Parkway, which was opened in 1963, we have seen the economic growth which followed the opening of each new facility.

While those facilities now in operation are realizing toll revenues which exceed the traffic engineers' estimates, we do not anticipate that they will become self-sustaining for many years, if at all, during the life of the bonds. However, when economic growth and the resultant tax revenues are considered, the toll facilities must be judged as a productive investment. Reports of manufacturing employment in the counties located within the service corridor of the Mountain Parkway indicate an increase of more than 50 percent between 1962 and 1967, as compared to a gain throughout Kentucky of 36 percent. The increase in this type of employment in counties served by the Western Kentucky Parkway was 67 percent during the four years following its opening compared to an increase the preceding four years of 18 percent.

Again referring to the map, it is apparent that the proposed facilities will complete a transportation grid which will provide safe, high-speed, efficient highway facilities for both north-south and east-west traffic.

Further, the new facilities will open for development the southern section of Kentucky, a region with tremendous potential in terms of natural resources and available labor supply.

By providing these facilities linking the major highway systems, the interstate, the Appalachian, and the existing toll roads, we believe that we have completed the major toll road projects in our state. Certainly we would not presume to commit future administrations, but we can state that insofar as present, long-range planning by the Kentucky Department of Highways is concerned, these projects will complete the toll road system.

And now, let's address ourselves to a most important point, Kentucky's financial condition and fiscal responsibility. The 1968 General Assembly enacted tax legislation which added two cents to the existing three cents sales and use tax and increased passenger car license fees from five dollars to twelve dollars and a half. In addition, the new statutes provide for more effective collection procedures. The increases in revenues have been appropriated primarily to education, much-needed capital construction projects, and to the State Road Fund. The Department of Highways will receive an additional $52.4 million —more than enough to pay principal and interest on the proposed bond issue. The electorate has shown little dissatisfaction with the new tax levies, indicating to us a willingness to pay for these vital needs.

The Kentucky Constitution prohibits the obligation of state funds beyond the biennial appropriations of the General Assembly, in effect, prohibiting the Department of Highways from entering into leases of more than two-year duration. However, the Constitution dedicates revenues from certain tax sources to the exclusive use of the Department of Highways. And this enables the Department to make long-range projections of its available funds, secure in the knowledge that some future legislative body cannot reduce the highway appropriations on political whim. The two constitutional provisions just cited are important to you as prospective bond purchasers. We know that many buyers consider the lease restriction as a weakness in the security of our bonds. But compare, if you will, Kentucky's lease-rental backing of revenue bonds with that of other states.

Many states are able to contract for long-term leases in comparison with our two-year automatically renewable lease. However, these states require agencies to go to the legislature for funds either annually or biennially, whereas Kentucky's source of funds for lease-rental payments is guaranteed by the Constitution. At the risk of oversimplification, it seems to me that there is a far greater risk in relying on a new generation of legislators to appropriate adequate funds to pay bond interest and principal thirty to forty years hence.

Kentucky's record in the lease-rental method of securing revenue bonds must be considered a positive factor in consideration of the investment risk. In almost forty years of financing school construction, as through one-year renewable lease contracts, we have never had a default. In addition, we have had numerous state buildings, and the previously described toll roads financed through the renewable lease contracts, all without loss to the bond holders.

It is totally inconceivable that any future administration would abrogate the toll road leases. To do so would be political and economic suicide. First, such an action would mean instant disaster for the state's credit. It would mean years of high interest rates and inability to issue bonds for desirable capital construction projects, including school facilities. Secondly, toll roads are popular in Kentucky. I found this to be true while campaigning for the office of Governor. To do anything which would hinder or jeopardize the operation of the roads would make the Governor highly unpopular, a condition which politicians avoid if at all possible.

But the most positive security you can have is the attitude of the debtor. The most secure contract in the world will not bind a man or a state which does not recognize the moral obligation inherent in a legal agreement. Kentuckians are a proud people, and I am happy that there remains in our State a strong heritage which requires a man's word to be his bond. We Kentuckians take pride in our long record of good credit—a record of meeting obligations that began long before and extends through the Great Depression of the 1930's. We will not permit this or any other administration to abrogate our legal or moral obligations.

---

1. Albert Christen (1894–   ), commissioner, Department of Finance (1967–1971); accountant, Jefferson County Republican Finance Committee (1962–1967); member, Kentucky State Board of Accountancy (1950–1953); and numerous other positions. Christen, C.P.A., is a partner in the Louisville certified public accounting firm of Christen, Brown, and Rufer. Department of Public Information biographical files.

GLASGOW AREA INDUSTRIAL
GROUP MEETING
Glasgow / March 5, 1969

PERHAPS you have read in the papers recently of our efforts to make Kentucky "The Energy Capital of the World." Earlier today this program was amplified by our Commissioner of Commerce, Paul Grubbs, who enumerated some of the various projects concerning new energy development.[1] These projects will have a far-reaching effect not only in Kentucky, but possibly throughout the civilized world.

We are now preparing resource material for presentation to the various private nuclear contractors who are interested in submitting bids for an atomic fuel facility to be built in Kentucky at a potential cost of $1 billion. This facility will serve some twenty-five atomic power plants in the southeastern part of the United States, and possibly serve some of the remaining seventy-five atomic power plants that are scheduled to be built in the United States by the mid-seventies.

Kentucky is geographically the focal point for existing atomic plants at Oak Ridge, Tennessee, Portsmouth, Ohio, and Paducah, Kentucky. This, plus our many other advantages, could head Kentucky toward a designation as the nuclear energy capital of the world.

In addition to the billion-dollar nuclear fuel plant, the Department of Commerce has generated the momentum necessary to encourage private engineering contractors to bid on a nuclear coal refinery complex also to be located in Kentucky. From this facility will come the development of new fuels and new energy, which already have been patented. Of course, the other ramifications of converting coal to chemicals are vast, not to mention the vast impact this will have on Kentucky as a coal state. We already have issued invitations for bids, and presently six major firms in the United States have indicated they will submit bids for the engineering of this approximately $400 million complex. The coal industry itself will handle in general variations 10,000 to 50,000 tons of coal per day. The new fuel derived from this coal will practically revolutionize the entire business because of its vast advantages over present fuel with a minimum of air pollution.

This whole program was a result of a concept this administration called "total resources development." This program particularly alludes to our natural resources. Other resources will be our man-made resources and our human resources, which in total will give us entirely new plateaus of total development for the benefit of the citizens of Kentucky. Even though these far-reaching projects will probably not come into full development for a period of ten years, it is important that this administration concern itself now with projects that will have a vast benefit for our people in the future. No longer can you plan an economic program to fit the four-year term of a governor or even a president. The thinking and productivity of the scientific and technological community transcends the confines of specific terms in office. Therefore, we in political life must gear ourselves for total, unqualified development for long-range results.

Closer to home the southern Kentucky area of our State is fast becoming the primary target for many of our nation's industries. The federal restrictions on the use of industrial revenue bonds have temporarily redoubled our efforts for industrial locations. Despite the high cost of capital, we are very pleased with our industrial program of new plant locations and particularly in this area of the State. Our response to the great challenge of the development of the State has been to develop the business "climate of confidence among the capital investors of this nation," to fully realizing our scientific potential, to develop the best industrial sites possible, and to create new corridors of opportunity in the form of turnpikes and other major arteries of freight.

Even as we project the future and plan for future generations, we are not bypassing the present; the economic programs this administration is promoting will come to fruition in the near future. Total resource development must include the present and the future. It must serve to build the foundation where we can fully realize the benefits of living and of enjoying life in Kentucky today, and at the same time make plans for our children to do the same in the future.

---

1. Paul W. Grubbs (1918–   ), Louisville, commissioner, Department of Commerce (1967–1971); executive vice-president, Ohio Valley Improvement Association (1967); director, Economic Development, Kentucky Chamber of Commerce (1955–1967); and numerous other positions. Department of Public Information and Department of Commerce biographical files.

KENTUCKY VILLAGE REVISIT
Lexington / March 19, 1969

As you may know, the Fayette County Grand Jury expressed shock and disgust after inspecting Kentucky Village in January of 1964.[1] In subsequent reports through the years, although some improvements were noted, Grand Jury reports generally have had few kind words for this the largest facility for the treatment of children in Kentucky. And I am sure that you also remember that I, too, found conditions both shocking and disgusting after a surprise visit which I made last June 7.

Today, after touring the campus, all of us are aware of the dramatic improvement in conditions at Kentucky Village. Certainly Dr. Perkins, Ken Harper, Evans Tracy, Superintendent Good, and many others are to be commended on the progress that we have seen today.[2] Kentucky Village, although still not ideal for the crucial task that is undertaken here in reshaping young lives, is well on the road to recovery from the alarming state we found last year. But let me say now that this in itself is not enough.

We will not be satisfied and I do not think the people of Kentucky will be satisfied until we can point to Kentucky Village and other facilities and say that Kentucky has the finest facilities for children in America. We must, and we will, remain vigilant. We will maintain the high and very satisfactory level of progress that has been started, and we will continue to strive for improvement here.

One of the most gratifying aspects of the change that has taken place is that not only has there been a drastic physical change, a face-lifting, so to speak, but there has also been a dramatic spiritual change. The attitude of the children and of the supervisory personnel is refreshing and encouraging. It is reflected best by the severe reduction in absenteeism, in vandalism, in littering, and defacing of the facility.

I believe that there is a valuable lesson that we can take from the experience we have shared here. Certainly the opportunity for moral change is more adequate now than before; and we will continue to insist that the children entrusted to the State's care will attend church regularly and participate in regular religious activities. The total of all our efforts—both financial and spiritual—I believe, is the answer to this vital problem of restoring these children for a productive future.

1. Kentucky Village was a state institution for juvenile offenders. It was closed permanently by the state in 1971.

2. George Perkins (1917–   ), Anchorage, commissioner, Department of Child Welfare (1968–1971); president, Kentucky Citizens for Child Welfare (1967–1968); and director, Bellewood [Presbyterian Home for Children] (1958–1968). Kenneth F. Harper (1931–   ), Covington, secretary of state (1971); commissioner, Department of Public Information (1970–1971); assistant commissioner, Department of Child Welfare (1968–1970); representative, Kentucky House of Representatives, Sixty-third District, Kenton County (1964–1968). Evans D. Tracy (1932–   ), Lexington, director, Division of Institutional Services, Department of Child Welfare (1968–1972); chief, Office of Juvenile Probation and Placement (1966–1968); and numerous other positions in the Department of Child Welfare since 1962. Robert Good (1931–   ), Columbus, Ohio, superintendent, Kentucky Village (1968–   ); and superintendent, Lake Cumberland Boys' Camp (1966–1968). Department of Public Information biographical files.

J. U. KEVIL MENTAL HEALTH AND MENTAL RETARDATION CENTER DEDICATION
Mayfield / March 21, 1969

THERE are some days I enjoy being Governor more than others and this day especially is one of them, for it gives me the privilege of helping to dedicate this facility to pay tribute to J. U. Kevil.[1] We also pay tribute today to the wide-ranging and continuing efforts of the foundation's board of directors and to the efforts of a concerned and progressive community. The memorial, of course, is not so much this beautiful and modern building. The memorial is the many thousands of Kentuckians whose reclaimed lives will, through the years, testify to the training, the care, and the treatment they received in this center from a dedicated staff employed through the willing efforts of a far-sighted board.

Nowhere is the motto of state government, "Every Kentuckian Counts," more dramatically exemplified or given more vivid fulfillment than here in Mayfield on this first day of spring. For every Kentuckian, and most especially every mentally disabled Kentuckian, does indeed count in our State today. After generations—after a long winter— of helplessness and hopelessness, the retarded children of Kentucky can now look forward to a long spring and a long summer of useful- ness, of dignity, and of a sense of belonging in a society that cares, a society that disallows mere pity and instead acts effectively on their behalf. Here in this center, not only the retarded but also the emo- tionally disturbed, the anxious, and the mentally ill will be seen and treated and will be helped back to the point that they too can be counted as productive Kentuckians.

The J. U. Kevil Foundation is a literal demonstration of Kentucky's unique and nationally recognized comprehensive service program through which hospitals, community centers, and state and federal governmental agencies are coordinated for a more efficient and econom- ical patient care. Kentucky's program stretches the trained staff for the greatest good, and it couples that with the partnership approach that has been so successful in developing and expanding our resources for the mentally ill and the mentally retarded.

As a result of recent progress, the director of the National Institute of Mental Health has publicly commended Kentucky for setting an example for the nation in mental health services. Briefly, our plan is this: mental health-mental retardation centers, such as this facility we dedicate today, are part of a statewide program of development in Kentucky, tied in with comprehensive health planning, with education, with all programs aimed at development of human resources. In a broader sense, centers such as this are tied in with highways, parks, and industrial development in a package that makes Kentucky a bet- ter place in which to live. For instance, the efforts you are making here to rehabilitate and train the handicapped will help boost the economy of the State. This center produces jobs for staff personnel, who in turn buy homes, cars, and open bank accounts. Those who are entering the State as industrial prospects inquire about our educational system and special services for the retarded and handicapped. And, of course, each person restored to productivity in our mental health and mental re- tardation centers makes a dramatic journey from tax consumer to tax payer; this impact on the State's economic condition is twofold.

The J. U. Kevil Center is the result of a concerted effort to take a vision and shape it into a reality. It is a prototype of coordinated action between concerned citizens and governmental agencies and offers visible proof that community commitment will indeed bloom and flower within the scope of state and nationwide purpose, direction, and need. This merging of public and private concern and resources allows every dollar and every talent to be maximized, and this is the key to success for our program of total resource development. As part of this effort, we are firmly committed to expanded services for the mentally retarded, the mentally ill, and for the alcoholic and his family. We are using every cent within our resources, and every effort within our power to improve, to expand, to plan, and to implement services that will make the Kentucky program for mental health and retardation excel all others in the nation.

I am well aware of the years of planning and working and hoping which brought to fruition the center that we are dedicating today. Like any program that is truly worthwhile, it did not happen overnight; it did not happen in a month or months, but now it has happened. Just as it took time and the dedicated effort of a great many people to bring into being this impressive center, the commitment of state government to improve mental health services will not all be seen within this year. But let me tell you what the results have been thus far. I would like for as many of you as possible to walk into the new Children's Unit for psychologically disturbed children on the grounds of Central State Hospital. With funds allocated in the current budget, the Department of Mental Health has been able to renovate a large section of the Jefferson Building there to move children previously housed in a *drab, cheerless* building into a bright new world of colors and light and space. That is one tangible result that we can show today. We still are not able to provide the funds to expand that unit to care for more than the twenty or so children, but it is a commitment of this administration to find funds in the next biennium to expand service for this previously neglected group. Four million dollars for renovation is providing elevators in hospitals where formerly patients and food had to be carried up three and four flights of stairs. We are providing basics such as new boilers where the old ones were ready to explode, new sewage treatment systems where there was previously danger of pollution. These are tangible results that are visible now. The pay raise we were able to provide the lower-paid employees in our hospitals has leveled off the alarming and costly turnover in personnel of previous years. Improved patient care has resulted.

I know all of you that have worked so hard to meet the problem of retardation here in Mayfield, and in this region, are as delighted as I am to know that a modern, progressive, and beautiful new hospital and school for retarded children is about to be constructed in Somerset. This facility, to be built at a cost of $9 million, will be one of the finest in the nation upon completion, and I intend to dedicate that new facility before I leave office. The J. U. Kevil Center is a first. But your pattern is being emulated throughout the State. In Madisonville many of you may have already seen the new mental health center that has been constructed and dedicated in the past year.

The partnership and the involvement of the community created the force that molds the state efforts and the government funds to bring into your community the kind of services that you need. The bitter experience of the past in the treatment of our mentally retarded and our mentally ill has indelibly marked upon all of us the need for this kind of care. We have shackled and persecuted our mentally ill in the past. We have isolated and ostracized the retarded. We have feared them. We have disdained. Perhaps we have sought to render them invisible. And yet the answer comes back to me, to us, more emphatically with each passing year that we cannot solve our problems in that way. We cannot solve all our problems in any one way. We cannot treat everyone in institutions, and we cannot treat all those that we help without institutions. We cannot solve all your problems with one service in the community, but we can work together, as you are doing in Mayfield, to find common solutions to solve our problems and to meet our needs. It is this total approach that has brought Kentucky to a position of national leadership in the thrust of our program. It is the kind of coordinated action that we have mentioned previously between the community and the regions and the state and federal government, the kind of coordinated action that you see between the nineteen regional citizen boards, such as your Western Kentucky Regional Mental Health-Mental Retardation Board and the Department of Mental Health that has brought our services in Kentucky to a national forefront.

In September 1966 there was established the first and the only Comprehensive Mental Health Center in the State. Three weeks ago, less than two and a half years later, I received word from the federal government that Kentucky has been awarded grants for the nineteenth and twentieth regional mental health centers in the State. These centers today serve 109 counties. Through the utilization of the federal staffing grant assistance, through the technical and financial assistance from the Kentucky Department of Mental Health, and through the untold hours of citizen effort, there is a network of outpatient services, day care services, day care training centers for the retarded, and a comprehensive concern for the total life situation for the mentally retarded and the mentally ill throughout this State.

There lies within these communities and these community services the challenge to provide the answers for the mentally ill and the retarded at the place they most desperately need them—at home. Eighty-one percent of the population previously isolated from services are now receiving for the first time the benefit of the professional training and the community concern that will make it possible for us to bring our mentally disabled back into the ranks of the productive Kentuckians. For we know that the retarded to be served in this center can be taught and trained to be useful and to be happy.

In 1966 there were eight day care training centers for the mentally retarded in this Commonwealth. Today, there are fifty-six day care units, cutting across geography to reach into every section of this State. But we are not finished. We have made really a very small dent in the need because we know that at least 3 percent of our population will need help for retardation problems. We know that 10 percent, in fact one out of every eight, will need the help of a professional person to deal with a psychiatric problem in his lifetime. We have never actually counted the number of alcoholics in this State, but we know from observation and we also know from statistics that the number is astronomical and that services have been almost nonexistent. We are now faced with the growing problem of the drug abuser and the narcotics addict. We know that the problem is not yet as acute in Kentucky as in other states, but mindful of the swiftness with which this has infected other areas, and acknowledging that it is happening here to some extent, we have established a Bureau of Narcotics and Drug Education in the Department of Mental Health so that we can begin to cope with this problem before it becomes overwhelming. It is hoped that the kind of community service that is available now for the mentally retarded and the mentally ill and the alcoholic can be extended to the narcotics addict as well.

Where are we going in the future in mental retardation? We have projected a network of community services for the retarded such as you have here in Mayfield. We seek expansion of our day care training program and expansion of the sheltered workshop program. I hope shortly to make an announcement concerning a new facility for those severely and profoundly retarded who will not be moving to Somerset when the majority of residents at Frankfort State Hospital and School are transferred and which will meet the problem of our distressingly long waiting list of patients in need of service. In addition, there are plans for a new type of service unit for the retarded, a District Service Unit, the first to be completed hopefully in the next two years. Four of these units eventually will span the corners of this State, with the first probably to be built in eastern Kentucky. These units will provide short-term residential care and training for those who will not require the traditional type of residential care to train them for return to the community. These patients can benefit from intensive, twenty-four-hour care on a three-month to two-year basis. A unique plan of these service units will be emergency help for the parents and families of retarded children who need a temporary respite from the loving burden of care.

In short, we are indeed, as the President's Committee on Mental Retardation stated it, on the edge of change. And the key to progress, the leading edge of the change, is the involvement of communities in their own problems. No longer will it be necessary or sufficient, and no longer will enlightened citizens allow families to send their mentally retarded or mentally ill members away to vast, state-operated institutions, putting them out of sight and out of mind. Care and treatment now and in the future is to be carried on wherever possible within the community, close to home and family ties. Here in Mayfield we see the fruits of such enlightened thinking today, and I commend and congratulate you for the example you have set for the rest of the State.

---

1. J. Urey Kevil (1882–1941), Princeton and Mayfield, a businessman involved in tobacco and banking and a cousin of Governor Keen Johnson.

YOUNG AND ADULT FARMER RECOGNITION BANQUET
Hopkinsville / March 21, 1969

LET us today pledge ourselves to the great task of this generation, that of laying foundations for the future of Kentucky.[1] And what does the future hold for Kentucky? Here is one man's opinion based on what he has seen after almost a year in which he has been privileged to see the state from the unique observatory that is the Governor's office.

When all the factors of natural resources, geography, transportation, and education facilities are combined, Kentucky is able to present a strong case when it is in competition for industrial development. But what we must always remember is that the same factors which have paved the way to record-breaking progress in attracting new industry will also underwrite the progress and success we envision in the field of agriculture. Think of it: your grain, your dairy products, your beef, and your pork is only twenty-four hours away from 70 percent of the American population and only one day's drive from the millions of Americans who look gratefully to you for their food. This alone is a challenge which should stimulate agricultural activity and production far beyond the goals which have been prescribed in the past.

In view of your potential, the billion-dollar goal for farm income per year is in truth confining and unrealistic. There is no limit to what you can attain, and it is because of the limitless opportunities you have that together we must lay foundations now which insure that future. To that task, I offer the resources, the talent, and the technical ability of state government. It is my hope that we can form a new, stronger alliance between state government and agriculture, an equal partnership bound by mutual concern for the future of this basic industry and the part it must play if Kentucky is to achieve the greatness it rightfully deserves. The strength of our relationship will largely determine the strength of the foundation we seek to create. Therefore, let this partnership be open and nonpartisan, let it be unencumbered by political history, and let it be instead a meeting ground on which ideas and opinions may be exchanged, discussed, and investigated.

Through various programs, we have tried to demonstrate our awareness of the problems and the opportunities of agriculture. Of primary interest to the farm family is the rural roads program. These roads have been too long regarded merely as a tool for political leverage rather than as the lifeline to our underdeveloped regions. These roads concern the farmers more than the four-lane interstate highways, for these are the roads on which the farmer's children must travel daily to school, and these are the roads on which he and his family must travel for food, for supplies, and for equipment. These are the roads on which crops go to market and on which families travel to church. And so it is with understandable pride that we can say that the rural roads fund was increased to $25 million. In addition to the rural and secondary road program we have embarked upon the most ambitious toll road program in the history of the Commonwealth.

Our program calls for the construction of four parkway systems stretching from Bowling Green to Hazard which will lay open a vast, underdeveloped region to agricultural growth as well as industrial progress. And while we share a deep concern for the economic implications of this project you may be sure that we have given careful consideration to the broader implications of this program. It is our conclusion that the sections touched by these four toll roads can no longer be ignored and shut off from economic progress because of inaccessibility. These roads touch approximately forty counties, fully one-third of the State, and to these counties, they represent an opportunity for fuller participation in a better way of life. Because of this factor alone, construction is not only feasible, it is imperative if we are truly concerned about the foundations of the future.

Another important part in that foundation is the tax climate which has evolved. I am grateful for the response the farm sector has made to our program, and I believe it has been demonstrated that after becoming aware of the facts, a vast majority of Kentuckians agree with the Kentucky Farm Bureau that it is the fairest system available for financing state services. I believe that the State Legislature acted in the interest of fairness by discontinuing the 3 percent sales tax on farm machinery and by excluding it from the new revenue bill. And we were happy to be able to help bring before the voters next year the question of tax assessment on agricultural land. As you know, a constitutional amendment has been proposed to value farm land for tax purposes according to its value for agricultural use. Now we must await the decision of the people next November on this matter of vital importance to the farmers of Kentucky.

These and other areas of concern demand our attention in the days ahead. Confronting agriculture is the continuing crisis of the price-cost squeeze and the scarcity of permanent and seasonable labor. I am looking to the Agricultural Development Council to lay foundations from which we can attack these and other problems. As you know, Barney Tucker[2] of Lexington has consented to head the Council, and we are confident that the best interests of the farmers will be served by this group of concerned and dedicated citizens. I have asked the Council to carefully study and recommend ways to increase net farm income in Kentucky, and I know that the Farm Bureau will be available to offer its assistance and cooperation along with the Vocational Education Department, the Agriculture Department, and other state agencies.

In closing, I want to commend and congratulate each of you for your faithful involvement in the Adult Farmer Program here in Christian County. Your program and your county have long been held as enviable examples of agricultural opportunity realized. The willingness of each of you, your wives, and families to sacrifice the time that has been necessary to the completion of this valuable training program speaks well for your determination to preserve the mantle of respect which all of us share for the farmer in Kentucky and throughout the world. The addition of new skills and new knowledge should produce dramatic results. We look forward to the birth of new farming procedures conceived in the classrooms of the Adult Farmer Program and nurtured on the rich plowed fields and lush pastures of Christian County. And we stand ready to offer all the assistance that is state government's to command in your quest for fair and commensurate profits, comfortable and safer living, and the dignity and respect which the farmers of Kentucky deserve for their involvement in one of man's most noble efforts.

---

1. Governor Nunn opened his speech with remarks on the role of education, natural resources, industrial development, and the transportation system in creating a bright future for Kentucky. This portion of the speech was omitted.

2. Barney Tucker (1915–), temporary executive director, Kentucky Agricultural Development Commission (1969), and a member, Governor's Commission on Agriculture (1968). Tucker is a businessman from London. Interview with Tucker, August 31, 1971.

KENTUCKY SCHOOL BOARDS ASSOCIATION CONVENTION
Louisville / March 25, 1969

TONIGHT we share a continuing dedication to the improvement of education in Kentucky. I believe that it must be our aim and our unyielding concern that in every town no matter how small, in every county no matter how poor, and in every city no matter how troubled, we must offer the children of Kentucky the golden key of education to unlock the unlimited opportunities of the future. Surely we must all realize that a state which is not truly concerned about the quality of its educational system cannot be optimistic about its future. However, as administrators and overseers of the local school systems throughout Kentucky, you better than anyone know that in addition to concern for education, we must also be willing to make whatever reasonable and necessary sacrifices are justified for progress.

I do not propose a blind and unquestioning loyalty to education. Neither do I advocate that we let our interest in education push aside the multitude of other serious challenges we face in our quest to bring greatness to Kentucky. However, I will continue to insist that we bear in mind the fact that Kentucky's future is unalterably linked to the educational attainment of our people. With that in mind, let us work together for balanced growth and development. This can only be achieved in an atmosphere of equality and reason, an atmosphere that is not saturated by unrealistic claims of priority. The willingness of Kentucky's people to support education is unquestioned.[1]

I challenge you to look ahead to the history that will be written in the immediate future, for it is here that education has its greatest stake. And as we go forward into the future, there is one thought which must serve as a guiding star to our efforts. Always in our planning, in our implementation, and in our requests for support from the taxpayers, the children of Kentucky must be foremost in our thoughts. To this primary consideration, we must then add a second factor in the formula which hopefully will produce the quality of education our children need to keep pace with their contemporaries in other states. The second factor is the financial ability of our people. While we must never compromise either factor, I would suggest that at this point in Kentucky's history we must meet on a middle ground if meaningful progress is to be continued.

The need for additional funds is only natural after many years in which the desperate plight of education was never fully realized in Kentucky.

However, the question those charged with public responsibility and those who bear the burden of financial support for education must ask, is simply, "What will be our source of additional support and how much can be committed in view of the ever-increasing demands made of government?" These are the facts that we must face, and these are the realities which must temper our requests made on behalf of educational advancement. Because we can expect that there will be limited funds available during the next session of the General Assembly, a joint effort of all members of the educational family will be required to assure a continuing program.

Let me assure you again that I will do what I believe to be in the best interest of all the people of our State, but the success of the program will depend largely on you. The situation confronting us can and must be met by careful, responsible, and proper evaluation and long-range planning with reasonable offers of solutions. Demands can not dictate our action; our course must be charted to meet needs and not demands. With these views in mind, I now offer you some suggestions for success which I hope will filter down through the educational family in Kentucky, from the school boards to the school administrators and on to the instructional personnel and friends of education.

First, if it is true that the most reliable source of revenue will come from our expected economic growth, it should be abundantly clear that education can make a meaningful contribution to progress by combining every effort to fully develop our total resources. I challenge the educational system to respond to this opportunity. How? Well, first I believe that education should more sharply attune itself to the needs and the realities of modern socio-economic concepts. Education, to be vital and to be deserving, first must be relative to the society it serves, and second, it must be flexible enough to meet the particular needs of each of Kentucky's diverse regions. I see this as the greatest challenge that education faces today. It is the only challenge that need concern our school leaders, for if this confrontation is met, you will have answered the one pervading question that we must ask.

That question is, "What returns are we getting for the millions of dollars we invest each year in our school systems?" Last year, to meet the crisis of education, we found financial answers. I propose a new era of creativity and innovation. These are the answers that are now demanded and the answers you give will serve as a measuring rod with which cost is compared to results. To inspire innovation in our elementary and secondary schools, we recently initiated an award which will be presented for the first time this spring to the Kentucky schools now engaged in the most creative teaching programs. Judging teams have begun to solicit applications from every school in Kentucky so that we might recognize and commend those outstanding private and public systems which are striving to improve the quality of education through sound, innovative programs. While this project is aimed largely toward school administrators and faculty, we have not forgotten the student. We have also established programs to motivate our students to realize that excellence is valued by their society. One of these is the Merit Award presented to every honor student in Kentucky at the high school level.

My second suggestion on how you might serve education's needs relates directly to the current political situation. It is not my purpose to appear before you with partisan intent tonight, and the remarks that follow should not be construed in favor of either major political party. However, the fact remains that the fate of education is decided to a great extent by the members of the State Legislature. I need not tell you that already the political winds are beginning to blow in this election year when all 100 members of the House of Representatives and 19 members of the State Senate will be chosen. And education has a larger stake in the outcome of this election than any other of the services dependent upon state financing.

For that reason, I believe that it is imperative and indeed demanded of those who are truly dedicated to educational advancement that your voices be heard above the din of political oratory that is certain to come. Already there is evidence that some candidates have drawn their political swords and have announced their intentions of slashing the revenue program enacted last year. Educational interests must be made to realize that this is only political doubletalk. When a candidate for the State Legislature declares his intention to reduce the sales tax or to exempt any of the current taxable items, what he is really saying is that he will reduce funds for education, Medicaid payments, mental health, highway construction, social security and welfare benefits and many other critical human services now being offered. I urge you to sound out every candidate, Democrat or Republican, and do it now. Next year, when the next session of the Legislature convenes will be too late. Decide if the candidate in your area will put Kentucky's children above their political ambitions. Send men and women of reason to Frankfort to act in your behalf and this will be the greatest service you can perform for education.

In closing, I urge you as responsible public officials to be leaders and not followers of new thinking. The new challenges we face call for new answers and you are in a position to supply those solutions. The children of Kentucky deserve this much. And we as responsible citizens can settle for no less.

----

1. A portion of Governor Nunn's remarks dealing with the budgetary provisions for education were omitted. See speech of February 13, 1968, pages 21–22, for this section.

"CHALLENGE FROM PRESIDENT NIXON"
Television Seminar
Louisville / March 26, 1969

It is gratifying to be a part of this unique exercise of unity and concern for the challenges we face today in Kentucky and throughout America.[1] The cooperation and coordination that have made this program possible are truly symbolic of the feeling that characterizes the relationship we enjoy today in Kentucky between public agencies and the private sector. Private enterprise has responded in splendid fashion at every opportunity during the past fourteen months. We are indebted for their cooperation on such projects as the preservation of Spindletop Research, the Efficiency Task Force Report, and the advertising section in *Fortune Magazine*. It is this type of cooperation that sows the seeds of progress in a state and in a nation. In addition, we can be tremendously encouraged by the new efforts toward closer coordination of local, state, and national resources.

It is especially gratifying and significant that many of these efforts are being initiated from the federal level to match the willingness of the local and state sectors. I have had an opportunity to know many of the key members of the new national administration, due to the fact that several are former governors. Indeed, three of those on today's program, the Vice-President, the Secretary of Housing and Urban Development, and the Secretary of Transportation, fit in this category.[2] And because we have worked together as governors in trying to find solutions for several of the problems that will be discussed today, I know that each is a man responsive to the need for more meaningful participation by local and state agencies in concert with the national administration.

This is an approach that I warmly endorse, and it is an approach that can produce dramatic results in Kentucky's effort to ease the urban crisis. At this point, however, I would add a personal belief that urban problems are not the exclusive concern of those who live in Kentucky's urban areas. The magnitude of these problems transcends the boundaries of urban living. For if the vitality of Kentucky's emerging cities is weakened, there will be a corresponding disastrous effect on our rural areas. We are fortunate that the trend toward urbanization is still in a manageable phase of development; therefore, we still have the luxury of time in which to plan for orderly growth and transition.

We also realize that Kentucky cannot afford the luxury of inaction and that is why we have established a new state agency, the Kentucky Program Development Office, to coordinate future courses of action and construct clear lines of communication. This agency serves as a bridge to span the traditional gaps between local, state, and national government partnerships, and it also serves as a focal point and meeting ground for the total development efforts we have undertaken. Our development formula is simply to encourage dynamic local leadership and creativity. We will then add the technical expertise that is available at the state level and together we will enlist the financial capability of the national government. Through this coordinated and efficient approach, we seek a positive response from the private sector and the local community. It is through this approach that we can best attack the most crucial problems of urban living, such as gainful employment, adequate housing, abundant recreational areas, improved health services, and the excessive crime rate.

I am firmly convinced that if we are able to find answers to these problems, we must kindle a renewed faith in the local, state, and national alliance that has been the foundation of our past efforts. State government has demonstrated its willingness to cooperate, and abundant federal resources are at your disposal. But these are not enough; these are only the ingredients of challenge for those of you on the local level. It will be the initiative and the creativity of local leadership that will ultimately determine whether our partnership will remain viable and constructive and responsive to change.

Today we must have leaders whose foremost considerations are for the common good of Kentucky and all of America. I urge you as businessmen to make Kentucky's best interests as much a part of your business planning as capital improvements. Then, and only then, I believe that success will be ours. Again I salute your willingness to attack today's problems and to seize tomorrow's opportunities. To this endeavor, I pledge to you the unwavering support of state government.

---

1. The television seminar conducted by the United States Chamber of Commerce dealt with President Nixon's challenge: how to improve the relationship between private enterprise, state government, and national government. Many dignitaries from across the nation and members of President Nixon's cabinet participated in the closed circuit television seminar. Information from the Kentucky Chamber of Commerce.

2. Vice-President Spiro T. Agnew, Secretary of Housing and Urban Development George Romney, and Secretary of Transportation John A. Volpe.

KENTUCKY MEDICAL ASSOCIATION
Lexington / March 26, 1969

THIS opportunity to meet with you tonight and again to pay tribute to a profession so well informed and so deeply concerned for the welfare of mankind is indeed gratifying. You and I are witnesses to a period of tremendous change that is both exciting and challenging. We cannot afford to be spectators. We must be participants. We see each day evidence of great advances in technology, in social concepts, and in human expectations.

Our changing times bring unrest and insecurity, problems and opportunities. To cope with change is a worthy challenge that should summon the best of every individual, but unfortunately, for some, it is a force of suppression, of discontent, and disillusion. And even more tragically, change often is an invitation for added government interference and thus even further repression of personal involvement and initiative. Certainly, your profession and the entire field of health has undergone change, hopefully for the better and toward improved treatment and more effective service. The core of today's change is our health care system. It affects and is affected by all that is transpiring. We are acutely aware that the providence of time has placed this generation in a unique position. For it is within our capability to leave an indelible mark on Kentucky's health programs for the future.

Recent enabling federal legislation clears the way for Kentucky and our individual communities to assume far greater leadership roles in health planning than ever before in the history of our State since the advent of federal intervention. As you may know, the field of health is a crucial laboratory in which, at the insistence of the states, the federal government is testing the bloc grant theory. Within this concept, state and local decision making is all pervasive, including the vital determination as to how the dollars returned to us from Washington will be spent. We are determined to make every effort possible to see that this opportunity will be fully realized. But this will only come about if we are able to formulate viable solutions to the health problems which reportedly plague our crowded cities and allegedly haunt our rural areas. We shall need your help as we begin to plan and to implement a course of action within the realities of what we have now and what we can and must have in the future.

In the context of this challenge I would like to discuss with you tonight three aspects. First is comprehensive health planning and some of its ramifications; my second topic, the Appalachian Health Demonstration Project; and third, the care of our elderly citizens. Government involvement in health, although it remains controversial and sometimes unpopular within some areas of the medical profession, is not new. Its history reaches back to the early days of quarantine and the problems of hospitalization for merchant seamen. I think that we would all agree that as certain problems have arisen, there has been the need for governmental assistance but certainly not so much of it. But as time has gone by, we have added program on top of program until now we have finally reached a point near saturation when there is confusion, apathy, and sometimes abdication of responsibility on the part of states and communities.

To this sobering state of affairs has come some new hope. The Comprehensive Health Planning Law is a breath of fresh air that tends to reverse the dangerous trend of previous years. This legislation returns some of the decision-making responsibility to the more appropriate and responsive levels—the states and local communities. This is a large responsibility, for we must make the new approach work or we may be assured that the Washington bureaucracy will be waiting in the wings to use our money to design and operate our programs. And we have some in state government who would join them.

As you are aware, there are three major requirements of this legislation. First, there must be a single state agency designated to bear the responsibility of state health planning. Last year, by executive order, we established the State Health Planning Commission to serve this role. Second, the law requires that an Advisory Commission be created to assist the single state agency, and in compliance we have established the State Health Planning Council, which is composed of twenty-seven outstanding private citizens and seven ex officio members. Third, federal law requires that area health planning councils be established to complete the planning process. Several of these bodies have already been established. Currently there is considerable activity in all fifteen of the governmental regions organized through the State Planning Office. Doctor Brockman, as chairman of the Kentucky Medical Association's Committee on Comprehensive Health Planning, has worked through your membership to provide invaluable assistance to this effort.[1]

We will look for the leadership necessary for success in health planning. I am of the opinion that on the local level, people know best what is needed. The State can provide technical assistance to help recover tax dollars from Washington, but it has become abundantly clear that we must have local initiative if much is to be accomplished. Our approach to this problem has been through the total development process. In the past, this has not always been the method used and until recently, Kentucky had never established a well-coordinated attempt.

We have seen a wild scramble for federal and state health dollars. There are over twenty state agencies and a similar number of voluntary organizations actively engaged in the health field. All that we know for certain is that the old system resulted in confusion, duplication, and omission which made impossible the proper utilization of Kentucky's scarce fiscal, human, and material resources. In addition, we have also squandered the contributions of the private sector. Our planning should recognize this and develop a system which allows the greatest contribution from nongovernmental resources.

Demands on the new system are mounting each day. For instance, we must improve our systems for administration of Medicare and Medicaid. Recent events have pointed up the fact that perhaps our recipients are not receiving benefits commensurate with per dollar of cost and that some recipients are abusing the program. And at the same time, it has also been revealed that in some instances, you, the provider of these revolutionary new programs, are being buried in red tape. As you undoubtedly know, various agencies of state government are involved now in an investigation of these two programs. There are some disturbing trends which have been uncovered, but none so disturbing as the widespread confusion and misunderstanding of the program on the part of the recipients.

Other problems to be dealt with are air and water pollution, dental care, prenatal services, accident prevention, mental health, and retardation. Above all else, we must begin to strengthen our preventative programs. For too long we have thought in terms of sickness. From today forward, let us think in terms of health.

Unprecedented progress should be the natural result of our improved efforts and more sophisticated planning structure. But this will require the full partnership of the private and public sectors and the equal vigor of local, state, and federal agencies. The Appalachian Health Demonstration Project offers a dynamic example of this partnership.

This effort became a reality last spring after many years of planning. Already it has had significant impact on the eleven southeastern Kentucky counties that are affected. Kentucky was the only state in the Appalachian compact to receive the maximum available amount of federal dollars for this type of project, and certainly this is a tribute to the effectiveness of the Program Development Office. We received $8.2 million, and as a result, a new hospital is under construction in Manchester; there will be a $1 million addition to the Hazard Hospital; a fifty-bed nursing home is planned for Harlan; Corbin will benefit from a fifteen-bed psychiatric unit; and Pineville Hospital plans a $500 thousand addition.

In addition, several new service programs are now in operation. This effort is continuing, as evidenced by the announcement next Tuesday that the Program Development Office will forward to the Appalachian Regional Commission proposals amounting to $17.3 million. These new proposals call for the implementation of an extensive design for emergency care, including communications, treatment facilities, and transportation. Beyond this are proposals for mental health-mental retardation facilities, manpower development, and expanded services. Due to the anticipated new revenue, the present eleven-county area will be expanded to include five other counties. It is all the more gratifying that this program has been carefully designed to dovetail with other important efforts toward total development of this needy area. We anticipate that these activities in the field of health will generate considerable public and private support for other developmental factors not only within this area, but for all of Kentucky.

And finally, we come to one of Kentucky's most critical health problems, the proper care of our elderly citizens. The tremendous growth in this segment of our population is best reflected in a recent survey undertaken by the state. Based on that survey, it is projected that Kentucky will need 31,500 additional personal care beds by 1978. Only eight counties in Kentucky presently have the minimum acceptable number of beds. Twenty-nine counties in Eastern Kentucky have no personal care beds at all.

The dilemma is not one of the senior citizens' inability to afford personal care, because a wide range of government programs are available for this purpose. The dilemma results from the fact that money is not available for construction of the necessary personal care units. It was because of this situation that the Kentucky General Assembly last year enacted legislation for the establishment of the Kentucky Health and Geriatrics Authority. That legislation, which enjoyed wide support from both sides of the political aisle, empowers the Geriatrics Authority to create a unique partnership involving public and private investment. Under provisions of the law, which must yet be tested for legality in Kentucky courts, the state will underwrite loans for construction by private enterprise, which will in turn operate the care facilities under lease agreement until all state funds are returned. Previously, private investment in this area of public need has been marginal to the point that construction has lagged hopelessly behind demand for these facilities. Through this unique new approach, it is hoped that finally this problem will be alleviated.

As we said in the beginning, health planning and implementation have undergone tremendous changes in recent months. New systems, new organizational guidelines, new legislation, and new approaches are being presented. I share with you the prayer that this new thinking will also produce new hope for the sick, the aged, and the afflicted. But this will not become a reality unless there is ample consideration for the human element in our program. That human element is you, the members of the medical profession. We eagerly solicit your ideas, your talent, and your energy to make Kentucky's health program a model for all of America. And we pledge in return that you shall continue to have the maximum effort of state government.

---

1. George F. Brockman, M.D. (1912–   ), Greenville, chairman, Governor's Comprehensive Health Planning Committee for T.B. Hospitals (1969–1970); president, Kentucky Medical Association (1967–1968).

TO THE COMMITTEE
ON PUBLIC WORKS
United States House of Representatives
Extension of the Appalachian
Regional Development Act
Washington, D.C. / March 27, 1969

I AM the Governor of Kentucky and a member of the Appalachian Regional Commission. During my tenure as Governor and as a local offi-

cial I have observed many national programs, and it is my opinion that
the Appalachian program is a departure for the better in our approaches
to governmental procedure. It has represented the beginning of opportunities to deal successfully with the massive problems that confront
us today in the Appalachian Region and in the nation.

We know that we have many problems and that each problem
is severe and massive in itself. However, there is more to it than that.
Our problems today are more complex than they have ever been, and
we must recognize that we cannot and perhaps should not deal with
each special problem in a separate way.

We have gone for too long in the relatively simple approach of attempting to create a special program for each special problem. We have
established programs for unemployment, for distressed areas, for poverty, and for hunger and malnutrition for the cities, for the country,
and for many, many other special categories of problems. In so doing,
we have not only failed to deal adequately and effectively with any of
these problems, but we have created an entirely new problem—that of
proliferation and confusion in our public processes. A most unfortunate
result of this complex confusion is that it tends to take responsibility
away from lower levels and smaller units of governments, and to raise
them to the higher levels and ultimately to the national government
itself. This is not only inefficient, it affects the very moral fiber of our
country, and deprives us of the commitment of the individual citizens
of our country who function most efficiently through the government
that operates directly in their home communities.

The Appalachian program is not a special program. For the first time
it offers a way for the several levels of government, for the many agencies of government, and for the private sector to work together and to
cooperate in a comprehensive approach. Within the Appalachian approach special action is possible, but each special action is taken in the
framework of an overall strategy and there is a practical means by
which various interests involved may work together effectively.

If we are to deal with problems such as poverty, it is no longer effective to establish a so-called "poverty program" which attempts to use
a "Band-Aid" to cope with a major wound. The poverty program has
been operating at a level of about $2 billion a year, and it seems im-
modest to call this a "Band-Aid program." However, it has been Band-
Aid in size compared to its effectiveness against the total problem. We
can deal with the problems of poverty and unemployment and of the
city and of the country properly, only when we begin to find a public
process through which we can mobilize all of our resources properly
to provide the best effect upon the problems.

This kind of "strategic approach" is possible in the Appalachian program. It depends primarily upon supplementation of *regular* programs to do the special kind of job it is best able to do. For instance, in an Appalachian approach, instead of a Head Start Program, which was interesting but less effective than it should have been, a great deal of progress could have been made in the firm establishment of effective preschool programs in our regular education system. Such a preschool program could be designed to have special impact upon the poor youngsters who need its benefits in a special way. But a double premium can be achieved in that not only is the special need of the poor youngsters served but they are served within a regular system, which, in itself, is an investment in the total future of the youth of our country. The same idea can be applied to the manner in which we build our highways, conduct health programs, and carry out our program of community and area development of all kinds. The special goal is far better attained if it is built in as a goal of regular programs.

The Appalachian approach works not only because it is comprehensive in scope and effective in meeting special objectives, but because it allows a responsible action to be taken by those with the greatest capability and, finally, it provides for a natural operation of cooperative management at the most appropriate level for management in our governmental processes.

In the Appalachian program I find the greatest opportunity for state government to take on its full level of responsibility, and I find the opportunity to apply the Appalachian idea to the management and mobilization of programs throughout my State and to the fundamental philosophy by which I have organized my administration of state government.

The Appalachian program particularly enables me to do certain things in state government.

1. It allows me to provide overall management for all of the agencies of state government for many, although not all, of the federal programs which operate in our State.
2. It allows me to establish special goals and an overall strategy against which the effectiveness of our state programs can be measured and for which action can be taken.
3. It allows me to differentiate this strategy to meet the developing problems of Kentucky's major areas from the mountainous east to the level delta of the western part of the State.
4. It allows us in state government to work more effectively not only to assist but to induce the maximum responsible action of the local governments in our State.

5. It has allowed our local governments to work together in multi-county areas in which they are able to enter into effective partnerships, not only with state and federal governments, but with private interests and city organizations of these areas, in a total attack upon the problems of each specific area.

6. It has allowed special action in which our regular program agencies are enlisted and inspired. The special action taken to meet special problems can be tested against regular procedures in such a way that unworkable innovations can be tried and discarded and workable innovations can be tested and built into the regular on-going program.

I emphasize that the Appalachian program is workable. For instance, one of my first actions as Governor was to issue an executive order which established the Kentucky Program Development Office, pulling together all of the planning and program development activities of our state government into one unit attached directly to my office. In this unit, we have been able to provide a practical, working approach to the informational planning, program development, coordination, and technical assistance functions which are so important to all agencies of state government and to local governments. These efforts had previously been scattered throughout government.

As a further step toward making this program effective in Kentucky, I also took action which confirmed the establishment of fifteen multi-county development districts in our State. While the idea of these districts was originally established in the Appalachian program, the philosophy of this program was that such districts should be established *by the State*, and we have moved in Kentucky in this direction. One of the problems again has been that, after the original idea of development districts was established, emulation by a number of other federal programs has retarded rather than accelerated the progress of establishment of these districts. However, in any case, we are working out such problems in the best way that we can and we are moving ahead to make these districts an effective adjunct to local government throughout our entire State. While I may speak well of the progress that has been made in the Appalachian program, let me constantly stress that we need to take further action to expand and improve this program. In my opinion, it is such a major concept in government that its real significance and effectiveness is just beginning to mature. We are just beginning to know how to use it properly.

In Appalachian Kentucky, as is true generally throughout the region, we have established a broad and dual strategy of development. Our twin priorities involve first, the creation of an environment of overall development and the building of opportunity within the region for as many of our people as possible. While this goal will take longer than the second goal, it is the one in which major investments must be made at this time in basic facilities such as highways, water resource development, and others. Secondly, our goal is to provide every social and economic opportunity for each citizen, young or old.

Kentucky's earliest priorities paralleled the investments in the highway system, with a complete system of vocational education facilities to provide training opportunity to every single citizen of the region. Construction of the schools utilize major state investments, plus the available federal aid and the supplementary funds available under the Appalachian program in a joint effort. With construction scheduled over five years, we are now in the fourth year of such construction, with thirty-one schools completed or under construction, and the remainder planned for construction within the scheduled time. Within this general dual strategy of creating opportunity for people and of developing people for opportunity, we have placed a major strategy priority on those investments and program action which would strengthen the urban services of our mountain communities. As you know, this is an area of rather dense population. By providing urban servicing communities within each of the major areas of Kentucky's Appalachian Region, we are creating a keystone to the development of job opportunities through the creation of industry and service activities which must have urban services for viable operation.

In this respect, we are taking a variety of rather exciting approaches. The Midland New Town in northeast Kentucky is a projected new town, made possible because of the prior construction of a Corp of Engineers reservoir and the creation of flood-free land. Actually, it will depend upon the urban services of existing communities, such as Morehead. A second such example is in our plan to create a new residential, commercial, and industrial community at Salyersville in the Licking River Valley, where the process will involve the creation of a water resource project, along with a total complex of development activities, in such a way that the water resource project itself becomes the power trigger and foundation for the entire development.

A somewhat less dramatic, but perhaps more effective, way of developing urban services in this area will involve our plans for clusters of communities such as Prestonsburg, Pikeville, and Paintsville in the Big Sandy Valley, or the Middlesboro to London complex of communities in the Cumberland Valley and the Hazard, Whitesburg, Jackson group of communities in the Kentucky River Valley. Each such action is programmed to develop adequate urban services for these communities on a joint basis. For instance, by a properly planned and activated approach, the three communities of Pikeville, Prestonsburg, and Paintsville could provide the Big Sandy Valley area with virtually one single town of considerable size, with the maximum use of the scarce developable land along the valley between the three communities for industrial, commercial, and residential use.

To this end, and to demonstrate that we are in the action and in the true stage on the coordinated approach, let me cite what is happening. Briefly, in the Big Sandy, with a combination of local initiative in the development district and technical assistance of state government, an overall program of urbanization, housing facilities and institutional construction and job creation is under way. A regional health program and a regional educational program have been organized. Hospitals, health centers, vocational schools, junior colleges, primary and secondary facilities, and new service programs are now being established An airport has been constructed in midvalley and another is being planned in the lower valley. The construction of Pound and Fish Trap reservoirs has freed much of the valley from floods and made possible much of the development I have indicated. Basic to the entire program is the Appalachian development highway corridor of US 23 on which construction is proceeding. A major industrial park has been established in midvalley on one of the new flood-free sites. Pikeville is the nation's smallest "Model City," yet its dramatic program is geared closely to the overall scheme of area development. Finally, new industry service establishments and other activities of private enterprise are beginning to occur in increasing degree in an area where no expansion was occurring prior to recent years. Even the coal industry is enjoying a resurgence, and a major new private power facility established in the valley indicates private enterprise judgment on the value of investment here.

As is obvious from the nature of these activities, they are only in small part funded through the Appalachian program. Federal, state, local and private funds and resources have been utilized. But the effectiveness of all of them together has been geared to accelerate action and priority objectives, by the workable process of the Appalachian Regional program and our own Kentucky program.

I have talked about a broad range of interests in the Appalachian program. However, let me take this opportunity to place strong emphasis upon one major priority problem which still needs our accelerated attention. I refer to the need to keep the developmental highway system which must be the very foundation upon which all of our other developmental efforts must be planned. As you know, for good and sufficient reasons, there has been a difficulty in the full funding of many federal programs in these troubled times. In this light our governors have certainly been understanding of the fact that the Appalachian highway funds have not been available at a sufficient pace to maintain the rapid level of construction set by the states and needed to complete the system. While it may be necessary to extend, to some degree, the time required for adequate appropriation to complete this regional highway system, it is most essential that we do not lose sight of the fact that this continues to be one of the nation's major priority objectives. The full effectiveness of this system cannot be realized until it is completed as a system. I assure you that we are moving ahead with the other programs in such a fashion that the need for this completed system becomes ever more paramount in our developmental consideration for the people of our region.

Finally, let me suggest that the value of the Appalachian program lies fully as much in its concept as in the success of its processes applied against any problem. The Appalachian process is the best I have experienced to enable us to work together effectively in our complex public and private relationship. It provides the best way I know of to define real goals, set priorities, and to mobilize for action.

Obviously, this program gives us an experience with lessons we can and should use in the design of national programs to deal with the problems of both probability and progress of city, town and country, and of the complex of social, economical, and physical problems facing the various great regions and all of the states of our country. I am the one who has concluded, while I face the increasing burden of the office I hold, that we can and should direct our attention to the design and establishment, specifically, of a National Regional Development Program.

While I know that this hearing is concerned with the need to continue the Appalachian program, I want to strengthen my endorsement of that question, emphasizing that not only should the present program be continued, but its concept should be broadened to cover state-federal realization in managing a broader set of programs in Appalachia, and these concepts should be the basis for immediate study of the possibility of applying the approach on a national basis. I have counseled on this matter with members of the Appalachian Commission, and others, and would be willing to discuss the question with you further, at another time, should you desire.

I do urge the continuation and expansion of the Appalachian program. We are having success in our efforts. We want to get on with the job.

TO THE SUBCOMMITTEE ON LABOR
OF THE SENATE COMMITTEE
ON LABOR AND PUBLIC WELFARE
United States Senate
Coal Safety Legislation
Washington, D.C. / April 1, 1969

As the highest elected official of the second largest coal-producing state, I must be mindful of the dual effect of any coal mine health and safety legislation. In the first and most important instance, I am impressed with the need to protect the physical well-being of the more than twenty thousand Kentuckians now actively employed in the extraction of coal. I wholeheartedly support the adoption of any legislative measures that will provide for effective and enforceable safety provisions and health measures based upon proven medical and technical standards.

In evaluating proposed corrective legislation, I must also keep in mind the fact that coal is a $400 million product in Kentucky's economy. Emotions are high and no one can reasonably deny the need for reforms in this area, but I am deeply concerned that caution and careful consideration of all aspects has become unfashionable in our haste to correct present conditions. Since several bills are currently under consideration and are being compared to the existing basic 1952 Federal Coal Mine Safety Act, it is safe to assume that all the provisions of any one bill will not be adopted. Rather, it seems likely that some sort of combined legislation will result. Therefore, these comments will be addressed to general measures as they affect the coal miners and coal mines in Kentucky.

Kentucky's safety record has been good over the past several years, and the last gas explosion in a Kentucky mine occurred on December 6, 1945. Minimizing accidents is the combined responsibility of the federal and state governments, the mine operators and the mine workers; each element has its function. State abdication of its strong role in mine regulation would be to deny its importance in overall regulation. The traditional distinction between gassy and nongassy mines has been based upon the presence of methane gas in the working areas of a coal mine and the distinction bears a direct relationship of a likelihood of an explosion. This distinction has two practical manifestations.

First is the frequency of inspections for gas and the second is a requirement for certain types of equipment and machinery. Ninety-five percent of Kentucky's operating mines are now classified as nongassy and presumably operate under standards now acceptable for mines so classified.

There is no dollar and cents figure available either from the coal mining industry or its critics as to the actual cost of conversion to approved equipment required for the operation of a gassy mine. This represents the small and medium-size mines that would be unjustifiably penalized because of virtually insurmountable logistical and economic difficulties involved in the transition. Kentucky's statistical experience bears out the reasonableness of retaining the distinction and increasing the frequency of inspections of nongassy mines which would provide suitable safeguards against gas, fire and explosion hazards. Penalty provisions are an integral part of any regulatory legislation, yet the punishment should fit the violation. Punishment for willful violations is only reasonable, but additional civil penalties against either the operator or the miner is neither suitable nor desirable.

Health and safety problems in the coal mines are not so new as today's publicity would seem to indicate. This urgency is actually an accumulation of some seventeen years of technological progress unmatched by legislative change. No doubt the Congress expects to build continuity into coal mine regulation by granting the Secretary of the Interior powers to formulate and promulgate standards. I would like to stress that all standards affecting the operation of coal mines be spelled out in the legislation. To do otherwise, even with the inclusion of procedural safeguards, would cloud the legislative authority and lessen dramatically the likelihood of periodic legislative review. Coal workers' pneumoconiosis, its causes and consequences, is the object of the health provisions under your consideration. Your proposed efforts at regulation of conditions in the mines are but a small portion of what is truly needed.

The establishment of specific particulate standards is for the technical experts and I shall leave the numbers game to their judgment. However, there are some statistics readily available and of probative value which indicate that there is not now any fair or reasonably accurate standard which could be adopted. If the Congress seeks a place to start, let it be a standard with a reasonable expectation of enforceability, for it now seems that presently proposed limits are unrealistic.

The Kentucky Department of Mines and Minerals, Kentucky Department of Health, and the United States Public Health Service are currently training Kentucky's mine safety inspectors in the use of air quality testing devices and the evaluation of data. One use to which we hope to put this experience is a survey of exactly what dust conditions prevail. Perhaps this information can be useful on a continuing basis in developing meaningful standards. After making this first step, the Congress should give very careful consideration to the other aspects of pneumoconiosis besides merely prevention. Diagnosis, treatment, compensation, and rehabilitation are other problems to which the state and federal governments must address themselves. Further research is undoubtedly needed and thought should be given to providing federal financial assistance to the states for the conduct of research and implementation of state controlled and operated programs.

Higher mechanization means fewer coal mine jobs. Over the past twenty years coal mine employment in Kentucky has been steadily declining from nearly seventy-seven thousand in 1949 to approximately twenty-three thousand in 1968. A recently completed study by Spindletop Research for the West Virginia Coal Association has pointed out how much is yet to be learned about coal workers' pneumoconiosis from a medical standpoint. Since fewer persons are affected by preventive legislation it becomes obvious where the real human problem lies. Conceding that protection against the inhalation of coal dust seems to be the object of all our efforts, then the point of control might logically be the man and not the mine. What I suggest is the encouragement of the development of useful, efficient, and comfortable respirators, the use of which would then be the responsibility of both the coal mine operator and worker.

On final analysis it is not questioned that meaningful legislation pointed toward the improvement of working conditions for our coal mine workers is now mandatory. Education of all concerned and careful observance and enforcement of laws seem to be the key. I urge the Congress to enact a law which will be observed and which can be enforced equally and fairly, without discrimination between states or individuals. For our part we intend a meaningful evaluation of state laws and introduction of corrective legislation for the next session of the Kentucky General Assembly.

STATE GOVERNMENT AND
HIGHER EDUCATION SEMINAR
Rough River State Park
Falls of Rough / April 19, 1969

LET me welcome you to this seminar and express to you our appreciation for giving your time in being here and sharing with those of us in Government your special talents, training, and skill.[1]

It is ironic that we here in the so-called backwoods of America are meeting today in creative seminars to exchange ideas regarding major problems in Kentucky and in America, while a thousand miles away, one of this nation's greatest universities, a citadel of learning and rationalism since colonial days, has been shaken to its foundation with disorder and violence. The events at Harvard make John Gardner's urgent call for constructive change in American institutions appear most prophetic. In delivering the annual Godkin Lectures recently on that very same Harvard campus, the former Secretary of Health, Education, and Welfare and present chairman of the Urban Coalition, saw the absence of effective problem-solving mechanisms as the cause of our society's current turmoil. However, he strongly rejected any violent or anarchistic response. He argued that only through a framework of law and rationality could progress be made.

John Gardner's analysis of the rupture in American structures included an indictment of both state government and the academic community. With a keen awareness of the imminent threat to our creatively pluralistic society from an all-encompassing and overwhelming federal government, Gardner attacked state governments for operating as if still in the last century. Likewise, he criticized our nation's universities for their inward orientation and "sterile self-preoccupation."

You, not I, are in the best position to judge the validity of his comments concerning our colleges. But I would like to reflect for a moment on his remarks regarding government. Time has proven that the federal government alone cannot solve the problems of metro-America or mid-America. There can be no adequate public response to the complex moral, social, and economic problems that confront us today, without the responsible and dynamic involvement of state and local governments and more important citizens on a local level. What we need now is a dispersal of power, so that there is not just one center of power, but many centers within our representative republican form of government. In this regard, the essential role of the federal government is to return to the states and cities the resources and the creative encouragement that is necessary to meet the challenges we face or better still to leave within the communities the resources to do these things. The talk in Washington about revenue sharing and bloc grants is clear evidence that the national administration will, in fact, promote the revitalization of state government as a key to dealing with our country's needs.

My own experience as Governor convinces me that state government in Kentucky has through the years been allowed to become archaic in some respects. Last year, an Efficiency Task Force of leading representatives of Kentucky industry and education exposed the tremendous disparity between state government and modern business management practices. And soon after inauguration day in 1967 existing financial difficulties coupled with a review of the urgent human needs of our citizens made me fully aware of the inadequacies of the State's then-existing revenue base.

I have also learned that, like most other state governments, one of Kentucky's greatest failures in the past has been the inability to bring enough top talent into state service. However, we have been caught up in the excitement and the challenge of trying to remake state government so that it will work more economically and serve more effectively in these critical days. In this respect, I share the thinking of a well-known Kentuckian, former Supreme Court Justice Louis Brandeis, that the states should be creative laboratories, where the answers to today's and tomorrow's problems are being shaped and molded.

We have begun to streamline Kentucky state government, and Task Force recommendations already are saving millions of dollars and leading to much improved operation.

A bipartisan majority of the last Legislature provided us with the necessary financial foundation on which Kentucky can achieve greatness, if we are willing. For instance, in the field of education, where the determination of a state to achieve new quality and excellence is best measured, Kentucky has taken steps unequalled in its history: $34 million was added to the Minimum Foundation Program. State aid for capital outlay and current operating expenses per classroom unit were increased for the first time in eight years, and teachers received an average salary increase of $500. A new vocational rehabilitation center has been funded for eastern Kentucky, and money has been provided to put vocational education within commuting distance of every Kentuckian in the near future. A 34 percent increase in funds was made available to Kentucky colleges and universities, and our colleges are competitive with the benchmark institutions in neighboring states in attracting and holding talented instructors. A new four-year Northern Kentucky State College will be constructed and four new community colleges began operation. In addition, substantial increase in state support was made to the University of Louisville. This is only one example of Kentucky's quest for progress. We are determined to create an environment of quality.

I am also encouraged by the new wave of able Kentuckians coming into state government service. This new infusion of talent is represented here today, and the next twenty-four hours will show you some of their enthusiasm, competence, and dedication. Yet, I come before you today to say what must be said: More money and more government, in Washington and/or Frankfort, by themselves will never be enough. There is a limit to what government, by itself, can do. I am convinced that one explanation for the inadequacy of state governments throughout the nation has been their failure to mobilize and work with the individual talent of the private sector. So today I am asking you, challenging you, and other concerned persons on campuses in Kentucky to enter into a working partnership with us in Frankfort to build a better Kentucky.

We have already sought to mobilize certain resources in the private sector. For example, the Economy and Efficiency Task Force brought such private talent into play for improvement in government management. Likewise, the Student Advisory Commission is attempting to stimulate greater student volunteer community service.

Today we stand on the threshold of a particularly significant phase of this program. Today Kentucky turns earnestly and openly to its colleges for substantive ideas on new programs and approaches to problem solving. Hopefully, these creative, brainstorming conferences will signal the beginning of a new, deeper relationship between the academic community and state government in Kentucky. We hope to make it possible, as never before, for members of the academic sector to undertake specific efforts to help us meet the challenges. To some extent, members of the academic community have at times taken a special interest and involvement with the federal government; however, there seems to have been a traditional reluctance on the part of these same citizens to become involved on the state and local government level. Both in the classroom and in their personal outside interests, faculty members have been for the most part oriented and inclined toward national and international problems. While students thus may learn about the federal government and about world affairs, only a small number become informed and concerned about state issues, state problems, and state institutions.

Although state and local governments affect the daily lives of our citizens so very much, Kentuckians are too often generally uninformed about how to make the best use of the services we offer. This, I think, is tragic for both student and teacher and carries very severe and undesirable consequences for all of the Commonwealth.

This historic alienation of the academic community is an important reason for the traditional absence of adequate creativity and innovation in state and local government. Just as we need a new, dynamic concept of state government, so we also need a new concept and orientation of concern for state problems among more members of the academic community. And I am convinced that we cannot reshape and revitalize state government as well without the involvement of the great human resources on our Kentucky campuses.

I have asked you to come from across much of Kentucky today to discuss your ideas and suggestions on how we together can build a better Kentucky. Kentuckians, through public and private sources, channel an enormous amount of revenue for higher education and certainly an educated citizenry is well worth this investment. Still it seems to me that we could be getting more for our money. On our campuses are men and women of great training and experience who could be of more service to this Commonwealth, far beyond their primary roles as teachers, researchers, and administrators. Some may be willing to leave the campus for a few years to work full time in government. Others could serve in a part-time capacity as members on state commissions or advisory groups. Even more important, I believe our colleges can be independent think tanks to relay current innovative thinking to state government. Through this new relationship, men and women who remain on campus can communicate fresh ideas to Frankfort and those who care can undertake specific, follow-up efforts on projects of special interest.

The goal of this administration, and one of the primary purposes why we are here today, is to begin the creation of an environment in which *any professor* or college administrator will feel *encouraged* to come directly to appropriate public agencies with ideas for the improvement of our Commonwealth. This seminar is a first for Kentucky and probably for the nation, the beginning of a meaningful exchange of ideas between the academic community and state government. At the outset, I would emphasize again that in no sense should you view your role as that of a representative of a particular college or university. We have invited you as talented, public-spirited citizens, representing the entire academic community. Today there are plenty of people who are blamers or criticizers. But we have too few problem solvers. Kentucky has ranked near the bottom in essential services for too long because too many people have been willing to fix blame, yet too unconcerned to help solve the problems. Believing strongly that you are among our most creative Kentuckians, I ask you to become a part of the growing segment of problem solvers who have stepped forward in Kentucky's behalf.

After this general session, we have asked you to regroup for free and open brainstorming discussions for the remainder of the afternoon and this evening. The suggested topics you have been given identify some of the real problems facing state government today and tomorrow. For example, how can higher education programs be adequately coordinated? What kind of balance should we strike between the demands for education and the financial abilities of our citizens? Other topics are as follows:

1. The development of new crops to bolster Kentucky agriculture.
2. A perspective on industrial health and safety versus the economic burden on industry and society.
3. State action to improve inter- and intra-governmental relationships.
4. The role of a university in community development.
5. Reorganization of state government and the development of an enlightened system of human resource utilization.
6. The coordination of public-private and local-state-federal efforts in human resource development fields.
7. The possible negative results from closer relationships between the academic communities and state government.

I hope you will never allow outside involvement, constructive as it may be, to detract you from your primary mission of teaching youth. Criticize, argue, disagree, but, above all, think. All of you will not agree on specifics or on all that state government is doing or thinking. I am sure I will not agree with all of your suggestions. But we want them; we need them. I believe that conflict between ideas produces a favorable climate for constructive action. In this regard, I agree with Oliver Wendell Holmes that the true test of an idea is its ability to win acceptance in the competition of the marketplace. So, above all, I think we need a dialogue. I would also emphasize that we the academic and governmental representatives think out loud, in opposition if need be, in harmony if possible. This seminar will not lay down official, final, or formal policy, but it should enable us to approach Kentucky's problems and opportunities with greater wisdom and greater effectiveness

—we will be more completely aware of some of the new alternatives.

I close where I began—with John Gardner at Harvard. He said that our salvation will never be handed to us. If we are lucky, we will be given the chance to earn it. We are committed to provide the reformed state government necessary to meet contemporary problems. Today we offer you the chance to share in this exciting but crucial venture. I believe that one of the highest callings of an intellectual is to have his constructive ideas become realities in society. Thus, we offer you this opportunity. Only through such a creative partnership of the public and private sectors can we hope to succeed. We proceed with optimism born of our religious and political convictions that the future *can* be shaped, that man *can* be master of his fate, and that we *can* earn our salvation, but only if we forego the comfortable position of *spectator* and become first-line participants in the arena.

---

1. This seminar was one of several in which officials of state government met with faculty members from Kentucky colleges and universities to improve communication and understanding between state government and higher education. Information from Governor's files.

TO LIGHT A CANDLE FOR DECENCY
Teens for Decency Rally
Cincinnati / April 20, 1969

WHEN tens of thousands meet all across our nation for the rightful cause of decency, then everything is not wrong in America.[1] Today your presence is living testimony to the goodness of your parents, your homes, your churches, and your schools. It is unimpeachable evidence to the greatness of America. When decency and morality inspire such a tremendous and heart-warming display of concern, something is right and good here in Ohio, Kentucky, and Indiana.

This is particularly reassuring at a time when the golden image of youth is being tarnished by the actions of an irresponsible few. It is because of the indecent few that you must carry a heavier responsibility as leaders of your generation. Unfortunately, you are compelled to deal with the outrageous exhibitions of the indecent.

We join today from neighboring states to raise a united voice against the permissiveness that undermines America's moral code and destroys personal self-respect. We meet today concerned that an entire generation could be polluted by obscenity. This shall not happen. We are assembled here to raise our voices and solicit support for decency. We are not here to protest or demonstrate. Those are words of frequent and common usage. Those words do not apply today because this is not a common event. It is an uncommon endeavor, by uncommon people, for an uncommon cause. Surely, then, it is deserving of higher distinction. This is a revival, whose ambition is to lift America's moral dedication to new heights.

Today, together, we light a candle for decency. And this flame can, it must, it shall become a beacon to light America's path in the days ahead. To keep this flame alive will require a moral activism by all of us. Decency must become a commandment by which we not only live but also with which we fight the rising tide of temptation, permissiveness, and resulting indecency. This tide of indecency, of obscenity, and immorality threatens to inundate a whole generation, your generation, our future.

It is so gratifying and rewarding to be here today to see and know the extent of your concern and determination, and to be made more aware that so many young Americans have already tied down the basic fundamental things so essential in their own lives. You, as young people, have recognized this threat and have responded so willingly with this testimonial to decency.

This meeting carries with it a strong and urgent message to those of an older generation. It is not the purpose of this meeting to fix blame, but it should be made abundantly clear that indecency has no age limit. The message you send across the generation gap is clear. Adult America must respond with action rather than self-righteous criticism. Its course of leadership must be along the path of example. Adult America, today, young America has lifted higher the candle of decency and hope. They look to us. Will you join them, pledging your help, affirming your encouragement, and giving evidence of your dedication to meet the greatest challenge of our time.

---

1. The "Teens for Decency Rally" was promoted by Frank Weikel of the *Cincinnati Enquirer* and Bob Braun of WLW-TV and designed basically with an anti-obscenity theme.

DANVILLE ALL-AMERICAN CITY
CELEBRATION
Danville / April 22, 1969

I CAME to say congratulations and to thank you for the example you have set for every city in Kentucky to follow.

How did Danville become an All-American City? Danville is an All-American City today because its people possess an All-American spirit. It is a progressive, concerned, and courageous spirit. You took a hard look and then you did what had to be done. That took courage. You designed a plan and then you followed through with implementation. And that took courage and dedication.

Realizing what you had to offer, you took your product to the marketplace and you sold industry. Danville possessed geographical location, water resources, educational opportunity, and a willing and able labor force. All these are the ingredients of the spirit of Danville.

To win an honor such as this, a city must have pride, not the kind of pride that quenches a city's thirst for improvement, but the kind of pride that won't allow a city to be satisfied with past accomplishments. For some, it would have been enough to have been named an All-Kentucky City and a Model City. But Danville didn't stop there; it started there.

Danville opened the door to success, not by asking government, but by asking its people what they would do. Too often, when there is a job to do, recently the first response has been to ask government's help. In Danville, when a job needs doing, the first response of the people is to roll up their sleeves and start to work. That is local initiative. That is the kind of local leadership that provides the foundation of America's greatness. And if we ever manage to suffocate and snuff out the flame of local initiative and local leadership with layer upon layer of government programs, then there won't be an All-American City Award, because there won't be an America.

Government can't solve your problems as effectively, and certainly not as economically, as those of you on the local level. The handling charges are too high and government's insight into local problems is not as clear. And government too often isn't nearly as excited or in as much of a hurry to get the job done as you are. Government should be a helper, a partner, but not a controller, because government can never supply the vital spark of local initiative that makes the difference

in the kind of community you live in. An All-American spirit, an un-
quenchable pride, and a spark of local initiative, these are the characteristics of a great city. These are the characteristics which have earned
new honors and new distinction for Danville today. And these same
traits which form Danville's civic personality will assure you success
as you seek new worlds to conquer in the future.

Let me assure you of the State's unyielding admiration and cooperation as you strive for more industrial development, better schools and
streets, better housing, improved recreational facilities, and all the
other things which make up a quality environment. And now we salute
you for having been designated Kentucky's leading city, a city which
faced a challenge and seized an opportunity for greatness, truly an
All-American City.

REPUBLICAN GOVERNORS' CONFERENCE
WELCOME ADDRESS
Lexington / May 1, 1969

THE recent success we have enjoyed here, despite being outregistered
by almost three to one, enables us to very proudly say that you are in
Republican country. Kentucky is one of only a handful of states where
the Governor and both United States Senators are Republicans. Three
of our seven United States Representatives are Republicans. The State's
two largest cities and counties, including Lexington and Fayette County, are served by Republican mayors and county judges. And of course
we are very proud that Kentucky was among the first states to register
in the Republican column during last year's presidential election, marking the third time in four national elections that this State gave its
electoral votes to our party.

We're delighted that you were able to come and be with us during
one of the most beautiful times of the year in Kentucky. In the short
time that you are here, I hope the schedule we have planned will allow
you an opportunity to see why we say that the excitement and beauty
of springtime in Kentucky, and especially during Derby Week, is unequalled anywhere.

We're especially pleased that for the first time in twenty-four years, Kentucky can qualify as the site of the Republican Governors' Conference. And certainly the fact that Kentucky was chosen is further proof that the Republican party is alive and vibrant here in the South.

Briefly let me tell you some of the reasons we feel that Kentucky is such an appropriate meeting place for the nation's Republican governors. Naturally we are proud that Kentucky is the birthplace of the founder of our party, Abraham Lincoln. Then, in addition to the political propriety of coming here, I believe that the people of Kentucky will make you especially welcome. The warmth and sincerity of our people and the unique Kentucky hospitality that awaits you in the days ahead will say much more eloquently than I can that we are glad you have come.

REPUBLICAN GOVERNORS' CONFERENCE
ACCEPTANCE OF POOR PEOPLE'S MULE
Lexington / May 1, 1969

THANK you very much, and let me say that here in this State we have twenty-two community action committees.[1] Fifteen of those committees have approved the representation that has been given to them. Some four made no expression either for or against the representation. Those who have honored us here this morning with their presence are those individuals who seek greater representation.

So I am delighted this morning to accept this mule, and I do so with the greatest of humility. I am reminded that it was Mary, the mother of Jesus, who rode an animal such as this into Bethlehem. And we all will recall that tremendous, that greatest occasion of all times when Jesus came to help save the world and to administer to the poor and the downtrodden.

We will also recall that there were those self-serving leaders, those people who went among the populace stirring up hatred and contempt for the one who came to save them and offer them help. He was stoned. He was spat upon, and eventually He was crucified.

So this mule not only is a symbol of hope as it was brought here this morning but it is also a symbol of something else. It is a symbol of the burden that all of us charged with public responsibility have in trying to care for the poor. In our State 82 percent of our budget goes for food stamps, for food, surplus commodities, clothing, drugs, doctors' bills, hospital care, and medicine for the poor. It goes to build better schools to educate the children of the poor, to give them a greater opportunity, to provide better school buses to safely transport their children to the schools, and to give them free lunches when they arrive.

I think that this mule is also symbolic of something else. It is symbolic of the failure of past welfare programs to meet the needs of the people of this country. And consequently, at this very moment the governors are assembled together with the second highest official of this land, the Vice-President of the United States, discussing the failures of these programs and how we can better improve them to help our people.

So when I look into the face of this mule, a somewhat sad, forlorn animal, I shall think of the sadness that dwells upon the faces and in the hearts of the poor of our State. And as I look at the back of this mule I am mindful of the tremendous burden that is placed upon those of us who share this responsibility, the tremendous burden that is upon the taxpayers of this land who are trying to provide the funds to support the poor.

And then as I see the tail of this mule, as he switches it back and forth, I am mindful that he is trying to get off those parasites that have plagued this animal, this beast of burden throughout his history. And then as the mule walks away from me and I look at the rear quarters of this mule, I shall always be mindful of the conduct and the behavior of some of those who made the presentation.

---

1. As host to the Republican Governors' Conference, Nunn gave his guests a Thoroughbred horse. On May 1, the Poor People's Coalition of Kentucky gave Nunn a mule; these were his remarks upon receiving the gift. *Louisville Courier-Journal*, May 2, 1969.

KENTUCKY BROADCASTERS
ASSOCIATION
SPRING CONVENTION
Louisville / May 6, 1969

THERE is a theory, to which I would partially subscribe, that the times make the man. Abraham Lincoln, Winston Churchill, and Dwight D. Eisenhower are notable examples that are used to illustrate the point. Today, however, because of the climate of crisis in which America finds itself, I believe it is appropriate to say that the times also make the media. In the relatively brief history of the electronics media, America has never before faced such a crucial domestic test as it now confronts in the streets and on the campuses. The clamor for change surrounds us. No one can say that some changes are not necessary to keep pace with the problems that have risen out of our plunge into a new technological age.

Our age of technology is also an age of paradox. We live in an era where educational opportunity is more widespread than ever before in the history of the world, and yet, there remain great gaps of knowledge and understanding. We live at a time when the American way of life, embodied in the theory that all men are created equal, has new meaning for more people than ever before, and yet, there is more racial unrest than at any time in our history. We are living at a time when more concern has been expressed and more action taken to feed, to clothe, to house, to employ, and to care for the needy than by any other nation ever created, and still, there is the specter of hunger and poverty. And finally, we live in a nation long revered for its dedication to law and to order at a time when there is more concern expressed for the lawbreakers than the law enforcers. The result is an electric atmosphere, a climate of crisis and confrontation which will test this nation's foundation and purpose.

It is this same emotion-charged time that will test your media's dedication to the idea that it is first and foremost an institution of public service. As disseminators of news, as the eyes and ears of a state and a nation, your responsibility is vastly expanded and more complicated by the multitude of complex problems we face today. Gone are the days of simple answers, if indeed such a time ever existed along the arduous path of this Republic's establishment. I commend you for this extensive search for truth and meaning, because it is an example and a measure of your dedication to meet the crucial responsibility that is yours.

The question now becomes where does your responsibility end? Does it end with the taping and broadcasting of the important events of the day? With reference to your own station, I would ask each of you does your responsibility end after you have presented one side of an issue, or does your search for truth and your exercise of responsibility continue until you have established for your audience both or all sides of the issue? One of the most vital services you must render in these times is to provide the proper perspective by which the listening and viewing audience can judge the day's events.

I believe that the complexity of our problems and our challenges sometimes outstrips the ability of the news media to fully report to their audiences. This is particularly true in regard to the brief one-minute or even five-minute news broadcasts used exclusively by some radio stations. We see evidence of your concern for this inadequacy in the steadily rising number of news specials and in-depth probes, particularly by the television medium. I would again address this question to each of you individually and ask you to examine your own stations to see if you are providing the perspective your audiences need.

There is evidence, judging from at least one recent event, that much needs to be done in this area. I am referring to the incident last week when the so-called Poor People's Coalition garnered widespread coverage with its presentation of a mule to the Governors' Conference in Lexington. Several times during the interval between the time when the plan was first announced and the actual presentation, members of this self-appointed group said in the newspapers, on radio, and television that the poor people of Kentucky are being denied representation on policy-making boards which have been established throughout Kentucky. As far as I have been able to learn, not one reporter has yet bothered to insert in the extensive coverage of this story the fact that several weeks ago this group had an opportunity to present their case and to be heard.

And although it must be common knowledge among the news media, no one has yet told the public that representation of the poor is granted throughout the organizational framework of the Area Development District boards and planning councils. And no one has reported that the Poor People's Coalition, which presumes to represent, by their own modest estimate, "one million poor people in Kentucky," actually represents only a small, self-serving segment that refuses to accept guidelines approved by a majority vote and refuses to abide by the principle of majority rule.

Fifteen of the twenty-two Community Action Program directors in Kentucky have approved the guidelines established by the Kentucky Program Development Office for the Area Development Districts. Of the remaining nine, almost half have expressed no opinion. Thus, less than one-fourth of the state's CAP directors actually are in opposition to the plan. Yet, they are extended wide press coverage and possibly have been magnified completely out of proportion. They have been allowed to overshadow those who are committed to finding answers through established channels to the problems of poverty, unemployment, and hunger. And all because the vital ingredient of perspective was not provided.

Without the ingredient of perspective, it is conceivable that your industry is in danger of becoming a powerful weapon in the arsenal of groups such as the Poor People's Coalition and others who have mastered the technique of harassment, disruption, and protest for the sake of publicity. And this is symptomatic of an even greater threat, the danger that the people's confidence in government and in the representative, republican form of government will be destroyed.

Let me commend and congratulate the Kentucky Broadcasting Association for its efforts in the past year to bring the news of government to the people of this state. Your cooperation with us has led to perhaps the most extensive electronics coverage of state government in the history of Kentucky, and I look forward to the coming months when we shall continue to seek new ways to facilitate the dissemination of news. During the past year, we have initiated the monthly press conference that is carried to every section of Kentucky by your media. This summer we will join in one of the most comprehensive tourist information efforts ever undertaken in the United States. Your members have been invited to Frankfort for a day with top-ranking officials and many of you accepted this opportunity to learn more about the operations of state government. Also during the year, our unique message repeater system reached a new high level of use, and in the coming months, we expect to expand this service significantly. It is our hope that we can establish regular recording sessions several times each week so that direct response from officials in the state government can be provided for your questions. The recording sessions should also be a valuable aid to you in covering next year's session of the General Assembly. This effort is part of our recognition that broadcasting is the most immediate and direct means of communication by which government can be taken to the constituency.

We as public officials and as broadcasters must accept our respective responsibilities to preserve this vital line of communication and keep it free and open. For our part, we must fulfill the responsibility by being available for your questions, to invite inquiry, and facilitate scrutiny of government activity. Your responsibility is to report the news fairly, in proper perspective, undistorted by sensationalism or personal prejudice. I commend you for the manner in which you have met your responsibility in the past and stand ready to help you meet this challenge in the future. For this challenge is worthy of you and the industry you represent, an industry which can and must fulfill its potential as an instrument for the common good if our system of government is to stand. Truly, these are times that can make the media, and I invite you to share this challenge in the days ahead.

UNIVERSITY OF KENTUCKY
FELLOWS RECOGNITION DINNER
Lexington / May 8, 1969

TONIGHT, I appear before you in a dual role as Chairman of the Board of Trustees and as Governor of the Commonwealth.[1] It is within the context of those two roles that I must forthrightly discuss with you some of the past, the present, and the future of the University. In the interest of brevity, I will not burden you with a lengthy attempt to set the stage for my remarks by recounting the recent events to which I address myself.

As concerned citizens and friends, you are aware of the potential crisis situations existing on most every campus in the nation today. There is one recent example, however, which is deserving of your attention. That is the magnificent fashion in which President Kirwan defended the integrity and the purpose of the University.[2] Rarely has such uncommon courage, determination, and wisdom been more timely and more fortunate for a University. A few months ago, many of you were present when the University paid Dr. Kirwan the high honor of dedicating one of the new campus facilities in his name. It was a fitting tribute to a lifetime of service to the University and an appropriate climax to a distinguished career. But now, at a time when for most the race would have been run, the challenge met, and victory gained,

Dr. Kirwan has again brought honor to his good name and distinction to his University. To you, sir, on behalf of the Board and the people of Kentucky for whom I have been authorized to speak, I extend our eternal appreciation. I hope that your example of fortitude and good judgment will be an inspiration for others on the campuses of America.

Certainly, it is because of men such as Dr. Kirwan and friends such as you who have demonstrated so generously your faith in the University of Kentucky that I feel such a special obligation and responsibility to do my duty as I understand it. As Chairman of the Board and as Governor of the Commonwealth, I pledge that as long as I am privileged to serve, this University shall have whatever assistance I command so that it may be preserved as one of the best repositories of Kentucky's intellectual future.

Speaking now as Governor, I would further assure you that I recognize a responsibility not to preempt the first authority of those in charge of the campus. But I would here emphasize for you the words of Father Theodore Hesburgh, the President of Notre Dame University, who said, "I truly believe that we are about to witness a revulsion on the part of legislatures, state and national, benefactors, parents, alumni, and the general public for much that is happening in higher education today. If I read the signs of the times correctly, this may well lead to a suppression of the liberty and autonomy that are the lifeblood of a university community. It may well lead to a rebirth of fascism, unless we ourselves are ready to take a stand for that which is right for us. We rule ourselves or others rule us, in a way that destroys the university as we have known and loved it."

It was demonstrated so well a few days ago that this is our first line of defense against those who, intentionally or not, would destroy the University. I pray that we shall always have men and women in leadership, not only in the administration, but also among the faculty and student body, who are capable and who are willing to meet this grave responsibility. If we do not, I shall not hesitate to meet force with superior force if it is necessary to save this University and her sister schools across the Commonwealth from illegal or violent action.

I trust that the situation on our campuses will not deteriorate to that point, but recent events here and elsewhere illustrate the necessity and the wisdom of planning. It was in this regard that a committee of the Board of Trustees will soon begin deliberations on the code for students entering the University next semester. I would point out that faculty, students, and administrators have been involved in the development of the Student Code and the proposed amendments now before the Board of Trustees. The governing Board intends to make the necessary decisions soon, but only after full deliberation which will include giving campus representatives an opportunity to be heard. I have asked that the rules, responsibilities, and rights of those on campus be clearly established and presented to prospective University students and their parents. In the future, there should be no misunderstanding as to what is expected. Let me assure you that I shall stand with the University in both of my capacities, as Chairman of the Board and as Governor of the Commonwealth.

There are those who have expressed some concern as to the urgency of naming a new president. It is my considered opinion that it is far better to have a good president than just to have a president. I appointed a search committee, which I believe to be representative of the University. They have, with careful and thoughtful deliberation, sought a president to meet the needs of this University. Let me say that the search committee has had full authority. I feel that the president of the University should not come by virtue of any influence that I might exert—that he should be the University's president, not the Governor's president, nor the Board's president. There is no place for political manipulation within the University. As evidence of this, I would only call to your attention that for the first time within many, many years, the Board is now constituted as required by law—that is, an equal number from each of the two major political parties.

Now turning to the financial aspects. As Governor, I must maintain a balance between that which is desired, that to which we all aspire, and that which we all can afford. We cannot create an educational system, either secondary or in higher education, that the economy of the state cannot support. Last year, the University of Kentucky, as did all universities and all school districts, received the greatest single increase in appropriations in the history of the Commonwealth. Recently, our Commissioner of Finance, the State Budget Director, University administrators, and the Board of Trustees came together for a session to analyze the financial status of the University. We have determined that $17 million will be required from the state appropriations for the next year, if the University is to merely *maintain* its present status.

The matter of adequate financing of the University and education in this state soon must stand a critical test. Already the political drumbeats are being heard by self-aspiring politicians who clamor for a reduction in revenue. These same candidates who ask for a tax reduction are failing to tell the people which programs will suffer. As private citizens, as community leaders, and as enlightened participants, you have an opportunity and a responsibility in this matter. You will help determine the makeup of the next General Assembly. To those who are asking for a reduction in the current revenue needs, I would suggest that you pose the following question. Ask if these candidates also advocate a reduction of the University's appropriations, and if not, where will the money come from to maintain the necessary level of support?

I know that you share my determination that the strides this University has taken toward greatness shall not be lost in retreat. Your faith in the theory that the University has a destiny of greatness undoubtedly has been the inspiration of your generosity in the past. And because you believe, and because you have demonstrated your faith, the mission of the University and the expectations of those who attend it have been elevated to a higher plane. For the first time, Kentuckians now view excellence as a reasonable and attainable goal. And because of this, because of you, a state is richer and its future more secure. Undoubtedly, your continuing support will inspire others to join in this private effort to help the University attain excellence.

Tonight, however, I would ask your support to also inspire adequate public financing. I would ask that you continue to inspire public confidence that the University is deserving of public support. The very future of this University will be decided this year and we must have the strong, concerned, informed support that you can give. We appreciate your past support, your friendship, your loyalty, your encouragement and your understanding. They are the vital ingredients which form the cement of this great institution. Let us all work together to insure that they may always be deserved.

---

1. University of Kentucky Fellows are those who have made major financial contributions to the University's development fund.

2. Albert D. Kirwan (1904–1971), interim president, University of Kentucky (1968–1969); distinguished scholar and American historian; professor, Department of History, University of Kentucky (1954–1971); and Fulbright lecturer, University of Vienna (1966–1967). Kirwan was also a member of the Advisory Commission on Public Documents (1971). *Directory of American Scholars* (New York, 1969), 1:277. The incident to which Nunn referred was student opposition to the University's suspension of six students following their arrest on drug charges by the Lexington police. Kirwan refused to accept student demands for the removal of the suspension of the six students; ultimately changes in the Student Code were adopted. *Louisville Courier-Journal*, April 29, 1969.

KENTUCKY EDUCATIONAL TELEVISION
DEDICATION
Lexington / May 9, 1969

THIS ceremony, in reality, is a benchmark of Kentucky's quest for excellence in education. Today, I ask each of you to join me in a commitment to that aspiration for excellence. Today is a time to recognize the vast potential that this space-age communications device holds for the betterment of our people.

Educational television, although scarcely one school term old, is making a desirable difference in Kentucky. There is evidence that it is helping to make the work of the classroom teacher more effective and meaningful. It is bringing new material to the elementary student in schools that could not otherwise receive it.

Educational television also has enriched the teaching of subjects vital to the new technical age in which we are living. Today, Kentucky students are privileged to look into the world's most sophisticated laboratories with the help of this network. As a result of these factors, educational attainment is reaching new, higher levels throughout our state.

As we dedicate this network, let us also dedicate ourselves to the task of equalizing and expanding learning opportunities for every student in Kentucky. Because this new instrument of learning is available to us, we can also provide greater opportunity for adult Kentuckians to better equip themselves in the television classroom of their own homes for a more productive role. To some, who have not kept abreast of the new Kentucky, it may come as a surprise that the people of this state are now served by the nation's finest educational television system.

For those who may doubt that Kentucky will achieve greatness, I trust that the facility we dedicate today will serve as additional, convincing evidence of our determination. Let it also stand as a monument to the people of Kentucky, to whom this challenge of greatness most directly addresses itself. The Kentucky Educational Television Network is but one of many symbols of the willingness with which the people of this Commonwealth are meeting that challenge. To those people, their hopes and aspirations, and to the youth of Kentucky, for whom we have hope and aspirations, let this facility be dedicated.

GOVERNOR'S INNOVATIVE EDUCATION AWARDS DINNER
Frankfort / May 21, 1969

TONIGHT, as the accomplishments of these ten unique and progressive schools are recounted, the people of Kentucky are offered proof that progress is being made in education.[1] The taxpayers can see evidence that their revenue is being invested properly and wisely. More significantly, however, we are seeing innovative educational techniques originated and practiced on a wider scale. Innovation not only has made a major contribution to the betterment of the educational process, but it has also become one of the best hopes for future progress.

This is particularly true as we enter an important stage of educational development here in the Commonwealth. After years in which the needs of education were not adequately met, the people of this State have set an impressive record of support in recent years. Since the creation of the Minimum Foundation Program, more and more of our revenue has been invested to provide better education for our young people of Kentucky. In 1968 we reached the highest plateau of financial support for education in the history of the State. Shortly after Inauguration Day in December 1967, we found that Minimum Foundation payments to the 195 school districts were two and one-half months in arrears, or approximately $30 million behind. That situation was corrected due to the revenue program passed by a bipartisan, responsible majority in the Legislature last session.

And recently, when extraordinary growth of enrollment caused a deficit of $1.7 million, funds were available to meet the crisis. In addition to erasing the shortage of educational funds, we were also able to provide an increase of $34 million to the Minimum Foundation Fund over the allocation of the previous biennium. And beyond that, revenue was made available which will permit construction or renovation in every one of Kentucky's school districts. Teacher salaries were raised across the board, with starting salaries increased to $5,000, and experienced teachers rewarded for their continuing devotion and dedication to education. So it is only natural that there would be a feeling among the taxpayers that, at least for the present, education should not expect new taxation to underwrite the continued progress we all desire.

Let me say that funds should and will be made available to meet the predictable year-to-year growth of education's needs in the immediate future as Kentucky's economy expands. And because of the favorable business climate that has been inspired by the new revenue structure created in 1968, certainly we can look forward to accelerated economic growth in the days ahead. But instead of asking for new taxes and additional revenue, now is the time for education to implement new methods by which current revenue may be better utilized. To this goal, we should expect innovative education to be of significant value. This is precisely one of the foremost reasons why we have initiated this program which encourages and honors those who show true concern for Kentucky's youth.

The concept of innovation offers education new latitude for meeting growing demands, new alternatives for growth and, of equal importance, new incentives for public support. It embodies not frivolous experimentation, but the responsible, comprehensive search for new and better ways to transmit learning. The concept of innovation, as we envision it, also embodies an objective, challenging evaluation of present educational techniques. There must be a sorting out of old, unworkable, nonproductive teaching methods. At the same time, there must also be an incorporation of the viable, tested, and proven practices that have pushed man to the edge of his environment and to new depths of technology. In our demands for improvement and change, we must not forget that education has made possible Apollo 10, transplantation of vital human organs, the conquering of age-old diseases, and unmatched economic and social progress. Innovation will lead to the challenge of new as well as old theories and techniques. For what we seek, our ultimate goal, is to infuse education with a new, creative sense of excitement and learning.

One of education's failings has been the traditional absence of excitement in the learning process. Perhaps this is one of the fundamental reasons for some of the student unrest in America's high schools and colleges. Opinion and comment is widespread among educators and students alike that education lacks relativity to our society, that it is outdated, stereotyped, and inflexible. Quality education comes as the result of human effort, commitment, and involvement of administrators, faculty members, PTA organizations, students, and community leaders. There must be a spirit and a desire to serve and to improve the educational process. These are factors that cannot be instilled simply by expending more revenue.

As many of you know, already we are devoting 62 percent of the General Fund to education in an all-out effort to maintain progress and keep abreast of the growing needs of Kentucky's young people.

Knowing of the desperate struggle to provide adequate revenue, I am sure you share my concern for the political talk that we hear today. As the primary election approaches, some candidates and elected officials have committed themselves to either reducing the present revenue or repealing the program enacted last year. If you allow this to occur, you must realize that education will have to bear its share of the reduction of funds that will inevitably follow. I urge each of you to challenge those candidates who have no regard for the future of education. Ask them where they will cut the current education program. Will they halt the construction of new classrooms? Will they force us to postpone the purchase of new, safe school buses? Will they reduce the instructional tools available to our classroom teachers? Or will they reduce instructional and administrative salaries and push Kentucky still lower in this category of the national rankings?

Now is the time for all of us to stand by education, not desert it. We stand on the threshold of unimaginable human progress and change. We turn to education to provide the knowledge and the skills to meet this challenge. With the help of adequate resources, through concerned and spirited leadership, and by developing new, innovative methods of teaching, I am confident that we shall meet that challenge.

---

1. The schools were L.B.J. Elementary School, Breathitt County; Woodford County High School; Lansdowne Elementary, Lexington; McNeil Elementary, Bowling Green; Horace B. Slaughter, Louisville; Cairo Elementary, Henderson County; Danville High School; Hopkinsville High School; Durrett High School, Louisville; Fleming County High School. *State Journal*, May 22, 1969.

INTERSTATE 65 DEDICATION
Park City / May 21, 1969

TODAY's ceremony has been described as a milestone event for Kentucky. And certainly, as we look at the newly published, official state maps, there is dramatic evidence that Kentucky has reached a new plateau of achievement in transportation. The maps give evidence that, one by one, the barriers of inaccessibility and isolation which have hampered the Commonwealth's progress for so long are being overcome by our new highway network.

In trying to persuade industrialists to come to our State, I frequently point out that we are only twenty-four hours by highway from two-thirds of the population of the United States. Corporate leaders never fail to be impressed by the fact.

This is a significant factor in our favor as we strive for new industrial growth. This information refutes the traditional image which many persons outside our borders have of Kentucky. They think of Kentucky as rural, remote, perhaps backward.

Today, with the help of the people, several programs have been started to erase that unfortunate and erroneous image. For instance, last year revenue was provided by a responsible majority that prevailed in the State Legislature to bail education out of a desperate financial situation. And as a result, at every level from grade school through college, funds were made available to insure Kentucky's youth of better educational opportunities.

In the area of mental health, a program was begun to do something about past neglect and talk of care for the long suffering. We decided to replace the oldest mental retardation facility of its kind in the United States, the 107-year-old Frankfort School and Training Home, with a new $9 million treatment center. We took steps to polish Kentucky's image in several other areas, and I am pleased to report today that the effort is showing progressive results.

No field of endeavor illustrates more clearly the remarkable progress we are making than in the field of highway development. Again I turn to the map. There are now approximately 500 miles of Interstate highways open to the motoring public. More than sixty-four million state dollars have been used, along with almost five hundred million federal dollars, in this effort. And in no part of the State is the highway development program of greater significance than here in south central Kentucky.

As a native son, I must admit a feeling of regional pride and loyalty today in helping to dedicate the first Interstate route to be opened all the way across the State. Interstate 65 is many things to the people of this area. To the businessmen along its 150-mile path, it represents the hope for strong industrial growth. To industry, it represents a shorter, more economical route along which raw materials can come in and finished products can go out. To hundreds of thousands of tourists, it represents a new path into a section rich in history and heritage, an area dotted with recreational facilities and natural grandeur. The economic impact of I-65 undoubtedly will be tremendous. Today we can confidently say that this can be the beginning of a new era of progress and prosperity for south central Kentucky.

Yet there is another factor of equal importance and concern to the people of this section. For years we have traveled perhaps one of the most dangerous and accident-marred highways in the nation. With the opening of this twelve-mile section, undoubtedly many lives will be saved.

So now, as we dedicate this modern, safe, vital link and officially open I-65 to travel, we look ahead to new priorities and needs. We turn our attention now to completion of a vast new toll system that will stretch from Henderson to Hazard. Fed by traffic from I-65 and other Interstates, this new toll system will carry the world to vast, undeveloped, and underdeveloped areas of our State, regions bursting with natural resources and manpower. Therefore, today let us dedicate I-65 not as a milestone, but as a stepping-stone dedicated to development in a State deserving of progress.

MURRAY STATE UNIVERSITY COMMENCEMENT
Murray / June 2, 1969

Two hundred years ago tonight, a small band of adventurers gathered around a campfire just east of Cumberland Gap in Virginia. They had come searching, exploring, and seeking a new land later to be called Kentucky. They were met by a rugged green wilderness inhabited by untamed savages. As they gathered that night long ago on the eve of their great adventure, no doubt many emotions filled their hearts.

These were men of vision and courage who dared accept a challenge because they sought something better. And I am sure that they, like you tonight, felt a surge of excitement and pride, perhaps some anxiety or even fear for the unknown that lay ahead, certainly some happiness in the prospect of new discovery, and a bit of sadness as their thoughts stretched back to loved ones left behind. And so it is with you tonight, a new generation of pioneers who gather here on the eve of your highest adventure, your voyage into life. Certainly your emotions must be much like those of the frontiersmen who blazed the trail into our State.

I would add that the emotions of this moment are also shared in the hearts of your parents. We see in your faces the pride that comes from solid achievement and we, your parents, share in that pride. As we stand by at this moment of recognition and look back to other times, this moment of triumph recalls for us the steady flow of accomplishments and milestones that have marked your lives. Yes, we, too, are proud.

Along with your pride, it is understandable that there is also a touch of anxiety as you, like the frontiersmen, face the uncertainty of the future. This is also a time of happiness. The unspoiled and joyous confidence of youth is an inspiring spectacle for all of us. And, too, this is in some respects a time for sadness as you say goodbye, perhaps for the last time, to classmates and teachers. But more than farewell and finish, graduation should be a beginning, the first step toward a full and productive life. The journey toward that aspiration begins in earnest tonight. From this point, the world will no longer view you as children, but as active participants, charged with the responsibility of improving the lot of mankind.

To this new role and to this larger responsibility, an older generation challenges you to bring a new spirit of adventure, of courage, of understanding, and of appreciation. We challenge you to properly fan the flames of individualism, for it has been this almost forgotten virtue that has kindled America's greatness. When the star of genius fell from the heavens, it was not a group, a crowd, and certainly not a mob that picked it up. Individuals picked it up, individuals such as Mozart, Einstein, Edison, and Washington, those who have shaped the course of history.

Not even in the days when this country was in its infancy was there a greater need than today for a revival of the spirit of individuality. This was a time when conformity was seen, at least by youth, as the exclusive sin of adult America. Today, with certain gratifying exceptions, those positions appear to be reversed.

Since this nation entered the age of crisis and confrontation, of turmoil and unrest, young America has often been a joiner, or at least a silent partner of the crowd, rather than a generation of leaders. You can change this trend by lifting your head above the crowd. First, you must agree that living aggressively changes the whole complexion of life. So many today have fallen prey to fear, fear of losing a job, fear of failure, and fear of public opinion. Remember that courage is not the *absence* of fear, it is the *conquest* of fear. Not until you dare to attack will you master fears. Why should you dare? Because unless you dare, you cannot experience the taste of victory.

Deep down in every heart is the desire to be somebody, to get somewhere. So often we sit waiting for the opportunity, but American history is full of evidence that opportunities do not come to those who wait. They are captured by those who attack! The opportunity for individual success has never been greater than today. I invite you and I urge you to seize this chance as you stand facing the best years of your lives.

In addition to lighting the flame of individualism, I hope you will carry the torch of spiritual living to illuminate your path. But more than that, I hope your life will be a spiritual adventure to be shared with others. One of the highest tributes ever paid is on a tablet to the memory of General Charles Gordon in St. Paul's Cathedral, London. It reads: "Who at all times and everywhere gave his strength to the weak, his substance to the poor, his sympathy to the suffering, and his heart to God." Religion only becomes an adventure when we use it in every phase of our lives—building the physical, developing the mental, and inspiring the social.

And finally, in the journey you are about to undertake, we challenge you to share of yourself, your talent, your energy, and your concern. Many of you have read the novel *Magnificent Obsession*, the story of an aimless young man who was saved from drowning at the cost of a world-famous brain surgeon's life. From that time on, the young man's magnificent obsession was to give back to the world what he had caused the world to lose. We can only hope that it will not take a tragic event to put a magnificent obsession in your life.

All that we have, all that we are, has been made possible through the sacrifice of others: the pioneers at Cumberland Gap, the Minutemen at Concord, the patriots at Philadelphia, the Marines at Iwo Jima, and the fallen heroes in Viet Nam. All of these inspiring Americans now challenge you to be worthy of the sacrifices that have been made in your behalf.

Tonight you reach the full age of responsibility. From this point you are held accountable to your heritage, a heritage and a tradition of individualism, of spiritual living, and of sharing which has made America and its people worthy of greatness.

KENTUCKY MOUNTAIN CLUB
Lexington / June 17, 1969

Just a few days ago, we observed the passing of the second century since Daniel Boone walked through the mountains and down into the meadows of Kentucky. The magnificence of the mountains, the green, untouched beauty of this new land, and its abundance of fish and game all were part of the legend Daniel Boone took back to North Carolina. Because of that legend, others followed Boone's trail through the Cumberland Gap and carved civilization out of the wilderness. And from that auspicious beginning, the mountains of Kentucky and the people of this unique region have played an important part in the creation of our Commonwealth.

It is ironic that while the majesty of our mountains is widely known and appreciated by natives and tourists alike, this is often the most maligned and misunderstood region of Kentucky. Recently, Joe Creason of the Louisville *Courier-Journal* made this a subject of his daily column. He was in Chicago at a meeting of University of Kentucky alumni. People who have lived in Kentucky and should know better startled him with their questions. They asked about all the one-room, one-teacher schools, and the rural slums. On closer examination, Creason found that the image of our mountains is largely the product of television documentaries, news clips, and magazine articles that are being produced with more concern for commercial value than for fact.

I understand that there is a new television documentary on eastern Kentucky that is so one-sided that it should be banned from the screen. With material such as this being circulated and shown, it is not hard to understand why people think of our mountains as they do. And it is not difficult to understand why industrialists are reluctant to go to eastern Kentucky in search of new plant sites.

The tone of this latest documentary is so negative and so insulting that we are now preparing a rebuttal to correct the false impressions that have been left. In the film, it is said that our mountain people are drenched in ignorance, filth, and disease, that they are an invisible and forgotten people living in a panorama of ugliness. They imply that there is no hope, that a once noble people, once a special breed with resolute character and proud traditions have allowed welfare to become a preferable way of life. Point-by-point exaggeration, I want to refute this picture of our mountain region. And I want your help.

This is still a noble, resolute breed of people, people of great strength of character and great energy. They bear their heritage proudly. The mountains are full of men who suffer the indignity of unemployment and who undoubtedly are smothered by a system of welfare which sometimes causes rather than cures problems. But these men do not prefer welfare to work. What they want is a hand up not a handout.

We recognize the fact that there are problems in eastern Kentucky. We realize that the educational level in Kentucky is not yet as high as we would like it to be. But these people have unusual dexterity and natural skills. They are trainable and once trained, they are loyal and industrious employees. What they need is not more depressing criticism that snuffs out their pride and their chances. What they need is opportunity. And that is where you and I come in. That is where the efforts of the public sector and the private sector must be concentrated.

I can say without fear of successful contradiction tonight that there is progress and hope for eastern Kentucky. Tomorrow morning officials of one of America's most highly respected companies will have breakfast with me in Frankfort. They have an exciting announcement to make regarding the location of a new plant in eastern Kentucky. We regard this announcement as another example of the breakthrough we are making in bringing industry to the mountains. Earlier this year, Paintsville landed its first industry, a plant that will employ 400 people. Within the next few weeks we hope to have another announcement of a new industry to be located in far southeastern Kentucky.

In addition to new industry, eastern Kentucky can see other signs of progress. Hopefully, within the next two and one-half years we will dedicate and open for travel the most ambitious and exciting highway system ever undertaken by Kentucky state government. We are rapidly approaching the time when our new tollway system from Hazard to Henderson will move from the drawing board into the construction phase. This is more than a highway network. This is a tremendous corridor of opportunity that will stretch through the middle of a long-neglected area.

There are other encouraging signs. The demand for coal continues to increase. Technology is on the threshold of new discoveries which will further enhance the value of this, the most abundant of our mountain resources. We have slowed down the destruction of the natural beauty of the mountains with strict but fair laws which have won the support and cooperation of our coal operators.

With desperately needed new revenue, we have been able to underwrite a new, important page in the history of education in eastern

Kentucky. By the end of the next fiscal year, new school construction or major renovation will be possible in every school district in Kentucky. A $9 million mental retardation treatment center will be constructed in Somerset. A $3 million rehabilitation center will be built in Johnson County. New vocational training schools are being constructed throughout the region. Tourism and recreation continue to grow in economic importance. This is progress that cannot be denied and cannot be obscured by erroneous magazine articles or one-sided film productions.

Although progress is being made and although the future is brighter, we now need your help more than ever. We need organizations such as the Kentucky Mountain Club to constantly remind the people of our own state and those outside our borders that the mountains are alive, that our proud traditions are alive, and that our people want a chance—a chance to work, to educate their children, to own their homes, and live in harmony with the world.

All Kentuckians are saddened by thoughts of the many native-born sons and daughters who have been forced to go outside our state for a better life. They have gone from the mountains to Detroit, to Chicago, to Cleveland, and to Cincinnati but, like those of you who did not stray so far, their hearts remain in the hills and valleys of eastern Kentucky. Their melancholy is described in a verse from "Cry of the Hillborn" which says: "I am homesick for my mountains, my heroic mother hills, And the longing that is on me, no solace ever stills."[1] It is my hope that through a united and intense effort, we can end the homesickness and the melancholy. This can only be accomplished if we open wide the corridors of opportunity.

---

1. Bliss Corman, "Cry of the Hillborn," in *The Nature Lover's Knapsack*, ed. Edwin Osgood Groves (New York, 1927), pp. 119–20.

COLLEGE REPUBLICANS
NATIONAL COMMITTEE
Biennial Awards Banquet
Chicago / July 8, 1969

You have honored me with this invitation to address what must be considered one of the most significant organizations in the changing American political strata. In 1967, I became the twenty-sixth Republican Governor in the United States. This is the first time in modern political history that our party has had control of a majority of the statehouses. College Republicans in Kentucky earned much of the credit for that victory. The extensive use of young people in that campaign has been well documented by the College Republican National Committee in its booklet entitled "The New Student Politics."

But in the hope that the Kentucky experience might inspire each of you to a greater effort in the campaigns to which you will return in your home communities and states, let me describe how much the participation and involvement of youth can mean to a candidate. Since eighteen-year-olds have voting privileges in Kentucky, it could be assumed that we are perhaps more receptive to youth participation in politics than other states. But while both parties have actively sought the votes of young people, the Republican campaign in 1967 was the first in which the impact of student voting and participation was fully realized. The young people in our state brought tremendous enthusiasm and idealism into that campaign. They injected new life and new excitement into the effort and more importantly, because the great majority of today's youth is unfettered by skepticism and unafraid to accept a challenge regardless of the odds, they helped inject the winning spirit that is absolutely crucial to every campaign.

One of the main goals of our campaign, perhaps the main goal, was to create a winning psychology. In the 1963 Governor's race, we came within 13,000 votes of victory out of 900,000 votes cast, and we lost that election because our own people never really believed we could win. And in July of 1967, the Kentucky Republican campaign was bogged down for the same reason. I think that this holds true for our party nationally and in the various individual states where we are a minority party in official registration.

A major campaign problem is to convince Republicans that we can win. Only then can we be assured that our own people will give maximum effort. In 1967, because of the untiring efforts of our volunteer youth organizations on the campus, we carried every major mock election. And it seemed that invariably these victories came just when the overall campaign needed a boost. Each of those campus victories was significant to the winning image we were creating. And in the late stages of the campaign, the mock election returns gave a snowballing effect that helped put us over.

Since that time, we have made a sincere effort to build on this foundation in forming a partnership with youth. Just as we asked during the campaign that young Kentuckians vote for a change in government, we have now asked young Kentuckians to help govern the direction of our future. I would illustrate this by pointing out that we probably have the youngest staff and the youngest cabinet of any state in the nation. In addition to the young people who have accepted positions in the administration, we also have included a student representative on the governing board of each state college and university. I believe that we have the distinction of being the first state in the nation to take this step and the low incidence of unrest on Kentucky's college campuses may be one result.

Student government leaders from Kentucky's public and private universities also were asked to join our Student Advisory Council so that they might "tell it like it is" and like they think it should be. Progress to date is extremely encouraging. Lines of communication are uncluttered and a useful dialogue is being established. The result has been that the mistrust and cynicism which may exist elsewhere between students and government is not evident in Kentucky. One of the most gratifying by-products of the association between students and government is the new insight and understanding on the part of both parties.

It is indeed encouraging to note that the College Republicans have seen first-hand one of the basic truths that is interwoven between the lines of the American Constitution, that politics is a healthy and necessary catalyst to our form of government. To put it bluntly, you are learning very early in life that politics is not a dirty word or a backroom sport for the greedy and corrupt. This is an important lesson and one that will serve you well as you shoulder the responsibilities of student leadership in the days ahead.

Tonight, I challenge you as College Republicans to grasp the opportunity that is uniquely yours. Nowhere is the opportunity for political progress greater than on the American college campuses. I am convinced that this is where the new majority in American politics can be achieved by our party. A recent survey made this unmistakably clear.

Forty-two percent of the students on America's college campuses label themselves independents in the political spectrum. Think of these figures in terms of the magnificent opportunity they present to those of us who are dedicated to the principles and goals of the Republican party. Almost half of an entire new generation of America's best young minds are uncommitted politically. Perhaps never before in American political history has there been a greater opportunity or a greater challenge for the two major parties. Without question, the balance of power and the role of leadership awaits whichever party can attract the majority of this undecided generation.

And what must we as Republicans do in order to achieve the "New Majority"? I would offer these suggestions. Ours must be the politics of concern for the new problems that have shaken America's faith in itself. Ours must also be the politics of commitment to the basic principles on which this country has grown to its present position of leadership in the world community. In his address on the challenge of revolutionaries on the campus, the President said that at first glance there is something homely and unexciting about traditional American values, but that they can be like sleeping giants: slow to rouse, but magnificent in their strength.

And what are some of those values which are so familiar now, and yet once so revolutionary? The President eloquently described them in this manner: Liberty, recognizing that liberties can only exist in balance, with the liberty of each stopping at that point at which it would infringe the liberty of another. Freedom of conscience, meaning that each person has the freedom of his own conscience and therefore none has the right to dictate the conscience of his neighbor. Justice, recognizing that true justice is impartial and that no man can be judge in his own cause. Human dignity, a dignity that inspires pride, is rooted in self-reliance and provides the satisfaction of being a useful and respected member of the community. Concern for the disadvantaged and dispossessed, but a concern that neither panders nor patronizes. The *right* to participate in public decisions which carries with it the *duty* to abide by those decisions when reached. Human fulfillment in the sense not of unlimited license but of maximum opportunity. And finally, the right to grow, to reach upward, to be all that we can become in a system that rewards enterprise, encourages innovation, and honors excellence.

Ours must be the politics of allegiance to a system of government that offers every man an opportunity both to create and to criticize. Let me make one point perfectly clear. We must, and I am confident that we shall, offer today's youth a viable alternative to the destructive politics of the so-called New Left. As members of the university generation you can make no greater contribution than to preempt the disruptive, misguided, self-styled, and self-appointed apostles of revolution who are at work on the campuses. To their angry demands for change and to their unreasonable militancy and lust for violence, we must answer that change is best brought about by constructive, responsible political action. This is at the heart of the entire matter of campus violence. For too long, the disruptive, noisy minority has been the only voice heard on the campus. We should not be surprised that the seeds of discontent are now being harvested across America. These seeds have fallen on ground fertilized by our silence and by our reluctance to speak out in defense of the established mechanisms for change.

The business of making a better world and answering the problems that have been thrust on our generation is tough, grinding, unglamourous, and never-ending work. Clearly, this is not a task for the immature. It cannot be accomplished by those who foolishly demonstrate at every opportunity. It is one thing to rebel against injustice, but quite another thing to be willing to carry out the ofttimes thankless work which precedes any significant change.

Our responsibility as dedicated partisans does not end with narrow party involvement. Our responsibility extends to the task of rising in defense of the system that has made America great. Only then shall the undecided campus majority have an alternative to the SDS, the New Left, and the others.

I see among youth today another challenge that demands response from the College Republicans. There is growing evidence that your generation is attracted far more by the glamour of national politics than by local and statewide efforts. I submit that if we on the grassroots level can find answers to legitimate human needs and problems, our national dilemma will be greatly lessened. So I urge you to direct your energy and your talent toward local projects and toward courthouse and statehouse contests.

The recent success of our party in electing a national administration, thirty Republican governors, and a host of city and county officials is almost unparalleled. But the same can be said of the responsibilities that now rest on us. To answer this challenge and to meet the new responsibilities entrusted to the Republican Party, we must have the concern and the commitment of your generation. If this is forthcoming, as I am sure that it will be, I think there is no question that our party will be able to piece together the New Majority of American political life.

FIFTY-FIRST ANNUAL
AMERICAN LEGION CONVENTION
Owensboro / July 11, 1969

THANK you very much. You know, as of late I am extremely pleased to get an introduction and for the audience to be told who I am, after what happened the other day.

You know, I've been living in Frankfort now for about eighteen months, and there at the mansion we have some trustees from the reformatory at LaGrange who frequently drive the automobiles back and forth to be serviced for gasoline and so on. And as the usual thing, I have a trooper that drives me.

Well, the other afternoon I had about an hour, and I thought that I might go out to the golf course and get a little exercise by hitting a few golf balls, so I decided that I would drive myself. And I put on a tee shirt and got into the car and started across the bridge.

And a little boy ran out in front of me and he said, "Hey, Buddy, how about a ride?"

I said, "Well sure, get in."

And we started up the hill. He looked over at me and he said, "You haven't been around here too long, have you?"

I said, "No, not too long."

And he said, "I know most of the boys over there. You have to be pretty tough to drive this car, don't you?"

I said, "Well, reasonably so I guess."

"Yes," he said, "I understand most of you are over there for shooting someone."

I said, "Well that, or something worse."

He said, "How much time did you get?"

I said, "Four years."

He said, "You don't think you'll get into trouble for letting me ride, do you?"

I said, "Well, I hope not."

He said, "Police watch this car all the time."

I said, "That's good."

He said, "Let me out right up here."

I pulled off the road. The little fellow got out. He said, "If you do get into trouble, you let me know. I'll be glad to talk to the Governor for you."

And then a few days ago, Dr. Dale Farabee and I—he is Commissioner of Mental Health—were over at one of your institutions visiting, and several of the patients gathered in the room, and Dr. Farabee suggested that maybe I should speak to them. He thought that would be good therapy for them.

I commenced to speak, and in a little while one of the patients stood up in the back of the room and said, "That's the worst speech I ever heard."

I looked over at Dr. Farabee, and he indicated I should go ahead. And I did.

And in a few minutes the fellow stood up again and said, "That's the worst speech I ever heard."

I said, "Dr. Farabee, I'm not going to go ahead."

Dr. Farabee said, "You go ahead, Governor. That's the first sensible thing that man has said in three years."

As the Commander said, you usually invite the Governor, and I certainly want this opportunity and every opportunity that I have to be with members of the Legion, and with other veterans who have demonstrated their courage and their concern, and their dedication to the American way of life.

You know, it was almost 200 years ago that a child was born. It was bathed in the waters of freedom. It was clothed in the garments of liberty. And it was fed upon the succulent food of opportunity. It was named the American Republic. It was sired by conscientious, dedicated men who pledged their lives, their fortunes, and their sacred honor. And during the life-span of the American Republic the wisdom and the words of many men have documented and have been documented by the history that has been written.

One of those men who helped to write the history of the Republic, one of the men who helped in the founding of it, said, "The generation which commences a revolution rarely completes it." That man was Thomas Jefferson. Almost 200 years have passed since Jefferson's statement was first uttered, and today we are surrounded by evidence that the greatest revolution the world has ever known, the American Revolution, has never really ended. There have been lulls in the fight. The battlefronts have changed. And today a new generation of soldiers are pledging their lives, their fortunes, and their sacred honor on the altar of freedom.

The men of the American Legion once offered themselves so that freedom might be preserved in America, and for the entire world. And truly, those men can appreciate the sacrifices that are being made in Vietnam today. And perhaps it is only natural that we continue to be a proud and strong advocate of the military. The daily flow of news stories tells us of the heroism and of the personal sacrifices on the part of countless American soldiers that are doing battle for us in Vietnam. And we can now realize that our own efforts in the past conflicts were not in vain. But unfortunately, sadly, we cannot share that feeling when our attention is sometimes focused on shaggy, bearded, gutless, cowardly individuals back home who would, if they had their way, plunge America into its darkest hour by burning their draft cards. This is not what men fought and died for at Concord, in Germany, at Iwo Jima, in Korea, and now in Vietnam.

The single most tragic spectacle in my memory is the disgusting sight of a mob of war protesters trying to conceal their cowardice behind an antiwar placard. They serve only to remind all of us that indeed the American Revolution still must be waged, not only on the battlefields of Vietnam, or within the dark shadows of the Berlin Wall and the Iron Curtain, but also in the streets and on the college campuses of America.

Today two great battlefields still exist. The first is in Vietnam, where we're meeting a test of America's dedication to freedom, just as we have met and successfully passed with honors that test in days gone by.

The second battlefield is in the minds of men, where we are experiencing a test of America's basic principles. Some of the finest young men America has ever produced are answering the call to duty in Southeast Asia. They are justifying our confidence in the overwhelming majority of America's young people today. We must remember that just as on the campuses the protesters and the demonstrators, the self-styled, self-appointed apostles of disorder and intimidation are vastly outnumbered by the good, decent, young people who make up the new generation.

I want to say that I commend the Legion for what they have done. One of the most moving moments that I have had as Governor of the Commonwealth was when I attended Boys' State at Eastern Kentucky University, and I saw there a room larger than this, filled with good, clean-cut, young Kentuckians. And when I spoke of our proud heritage and when I spoke of the good things in the American life, they came to their feet, and they applauded, and they expressed not only with their hands and their voices but in their eyes their appreciation for what you and other veterans have done to give them the opportunity to assemble, to know, to appreciate, and to love America and the things that have made it great.

I believe that it is vital that our point of view should not be distorted by the news media's constant overplay of the destructive forces now at work within our society. Our attitudes must be inspired by those who are paying the high cost of freedom in Vietnam, by those who want an education, and by those who seek to participate with us in the continuing American Revolution. It is they who will help keep the flame of Americanism alive.

Hardly a day goes by that I do not receive a letter from a Kentucky soldier in Vietnam, and without exception these messages are filled with sincere expressions of patriotism, of dedication, and of courage. These letters come as eloquent and refreshing proof that regardless of what our critics would say, things are right in America. The words and the actions of our fighting men clearly demonstrate that they richly deserve our wholehearted support.

I remember last year that Mrs. Nunn and I thought we would send Christmas greetings to all of the boys in Vietnam. And we received so many letters expressing their appreciation for the fact that we thought of them and took time to send a Christmas card. But the amazing thing was how many of them wrote back and asked for the flag of our Commonwealth, and we have spent several dollars buying Kentucky flags to send to those boys in Vietnam. And I was proud to do so because throughout the history of America the men of Kentucky, and their forefathers, those who settled Kentucky, have gone forward into battle to defend and protect liberty and freedom and justice and opportunity. And even though I regret very much their necessity to be there, I was proud that our Commonwealth would be represented by men who had appreciation not only for America but for their native land of Kentucky.

You know, there are some citizens upon whom this patriotism and courage that is being demonstrated there, and in other places, is sometimes wasted. Mistrust and suspicion of the military prevails in the minds of some fuzzy-thinking people, and as the President pointed out recently, it has become open season on the Armed Forces. Military programs are ridiculed as needless if not deliberate waste. The military profession is derided in some of the best circles. Patriotism is considered by some to be a backward, unfashionable fetish of the uneducated and unsophisticated. If for no other reason than to repudiate this mess, I hope, I sincerely hope, that the American Legion will remain strong and vocal in the days ahead.

For us the Revolution has moved to a different, somewhat quieter battlefield than that on which our sons are fighting, and that on which many of you have engaged in combat. Our battle must be for the minds of men, and I submit that we must show the same determination, the same commitment, and the same courage on the home front as on the battlefront.

And that is why I come today to commend the Legion for its unyielding commitment to America, and to encourage you to continue your support of the ongoing Revolution to preserve our most cherished principles.

We live in a country which has given real meaning to the ideals of freedom, justice, order, and to the right of self-determination. Yet there still remain the small, vocal, and sometimes destructive groups who are disenthralled, discouraged, and distrustful of the American way of life. Of this group the most dangerous and those who most severely challenge America's sanity are those who would prostitute individual freedom. It is time that we declare unequivocally that the privilege of freedom in America does not carry unlimited license to trample on the rights of others. In some parts of the country there has been a reluctance on the part of public officials to take appropriate action when lawlessness has accompanied the protest of alleged social injustice. We have learned, finally, that this is only an invitation to further lawbreaking and ultimate violence. We have learned that when reason fails, mob force must be met and controlled by a greater force.

Certainly we must not infringe on the rights of any citizen to dissent, or to protest orderly, but we must recognize that there is a misguided new breed who lock on to legitimate emotional issues in order that they may have a platform from which they can spew their contempt for law and for the things that we love and appreciate. These parasites must be separated and held accountable for their unlawful acts, and we must make it clear that society can adequately express its concern only after those who bear legitimate grievances have dismissed the advocates of violence and have silenced these prophets of intimidation.

I believe that there is one other course of action fundamental to the defense of our national principles. In order to reach a new pinnacle of trust for the American way of life, our people must be made aware that the American dream can become a reality in their lives.

Just a few days ago I had a group of people who called upon me, allegedly representing the poor of our Commonwealth. Certainly we have done all that the taxpayers of the Commonwealth can afford to do. Certainly we have done all that the laws of the Commonwealth and of the United States would permit us to do in order to try to care for those who cannot, for reasons of their own, care for themselves. But among this group was one individual who said to me she wanted her boy to have a chance. And I asked this lady if she had a television in her home. And she said she did. I asked her if they had a refrigerator in their home and she said, "Yes." They owned an automobile, and I asked her if the school bus passed her door each day to take her son to school, if he received a free lunch when he did get to school, and if she did not receive a monthly check to buy his clothes? She said she had all of those things. She wanted her boy to have a chance. And I said to that lady: "Your boy has a chance, because when I was his age we didn't have any of those things, and today I am able to sit here."

Any boy, any girl, has a chance. That's the way it has to be. As long as we have dedicated people such as you who have rendered your services and who today sit here in the interest of those who have rendered their services in the interest of America, they will always have that opportunity.

But I submit to you today that it's not fair that you should make the sacrifices in the defense of the country that you have made. It is not fair that there are those who have made the supreme, the last, sacrifice, and many of you have observed them fall beside you, and yet come home to see the country that you have protected destroyed, because there are those among us who are so spineless that they will not for political reasons, for business reasons, or for social reasons stand up and be counted and say and do that which must be done in a time of crisis.

No! The boys that went in at Normandy, and I flew over that beach just a few days ago, and those who stood on Corregidor, and I am going down to Florida in a few days to speak to the survivors of Corregidor and the Bataan Death March, they didn't do those things because somebody had a bayonet to their back. They did it because they believed, because they had conviction, and because America had been good to them. And America will be good to all of us if we'll just be good to America. But it won't be done unless we have people of the same courage and the same conviction that have brought us to where we are.

Certainly there are things in this country that maybe are not as we would like for them to be, but they will only be better if we go about the remedial job in an orderly, dedicated, and conscientious American way. There are those who would try to throw aside that which we have, but get them to tell you what they would substitute therefor.

No, there is an opportunity; and we must help those who lag behind, who have been deprived, not through reasons of their own. But even if they have, we must help them. We must teach them that initiative is the father of opportunity. Although easily said, these answers cannot be achieved by words alone, because words are easier than deeds. They cannot be achieved by idealism, because that is more convenient than effort.

The time has come when we shall either reaffirm our aspirations to greatness, or we will lay aside the mantle of leadership and forfeit the American Revolution. It is not the history of our country; it is not the tradition of our people to lay aside the mantle of leadership, or to forfeit that for which so many have given so much. Yet we all pray and we all hope that soon the hand-to-hand combat may end upon the battlefields, because so many know the tragedy thereof.

But let us never for a moment cease to be aware of the battle that exists in the minds of men, because it is here that the final page of the history of the American Revolution will be written.

OPENING OF THE
KENTUCKY STATE FAIR
Louisville / August 15, 1969

THE space-age theme selected for your 1969 Kentucky State Fair and Exposition reflects the great advances that inborn ingenuity and human resolve have made possible in the field of technology. There are those among us today who can remember when receiving erratic voice transmission from a few miles away by a quartz crystal represented a major scientific achievement. Today we watch a fellow American step into immortality at the touch of a button.

While the eyes of the world are lifted unto the heavens, it is particularly fitting that we should look around us here today at the fruits of this same inborn ingenuity and human resolve. Surrounding you are displays of agricultural products that represent the greatest output per acre in the history of mankind. Spread before you are examples of the animal husbandry that has made Kentucky the fastest growing center for beef cattle production in the nation and has enabled our swine industry to defy national trends.

Everywhere you look, you will also see indications of Kentucky's mineral wealth and industrial might. Mineral wealth made more valuable today because of prudent conservation practices; industrial might made stronger by more than 120 new companies that have located here in the last eighteen months. What you will *really* see here, though, are the products of Kentucky's greatest resource—people at work, people who are using God-given capabilities in service to their fellowman.

While the eyes of the world are lifted unto the heavens, it is particularly fitting, too, that we should look beneath our feet, because technology of the soil is the foundation for the exploration of space. The same wizardry that intensifies production per acre develops the energy to launch mankind into another millennium. On the other hand, lessons learned in space exploration may well be applied to increasing further the output of a verdant soil necessary to sustain a growing earthbound population.

There are those today who question the investment that we have made in the voyage of Apollo 11. They follow in the footsteps of those who scoffed at the queen for underwriting the voyage of the Niña, the Pinta, and the Santa María. Who among us can predict the advances in soil chemistry made possible by analysis of the moon's surface? How many millions now starving may one day be fed and sustained because of new discoveries in soil technology made in a world once reserved for poets, lovers, and dreamers?

It is not surprising that their first act on the moon was to collect soil samples, even to the point of gathering a "contingency" sample so that they might return to earth with this if nothing else. Nor is it surprising that these explorers of the unknown are largely representatives of rural America, men of the soil as well as the sky. Wherever they go, they take with them values that are eternal ones; values nurtured by a nearness to the soil that provides sustenance for the body and inspiration for the mind and tranquility for the spirit.

Kentucky has its own astronauts, those young men and women possessed of those same values who explore new pathways of service to the Commonwealth in pursuit of excellence for their fellowman. The fruits of their labors you see around you today. They should assure all of us that the potential of this great state is unlimited and that the future for Kentucky knows no bounds.

STUDENT SEMINAR
Frankfort / August 24, 1969

TODAY we pause in the midst of a seminar on state government in order that we might demonstrate an awareness of the importance of a strong spiritual foundation. It is not accidental that those who have made the greatest contributions to mankind, those who have made a difference in our world, were of strong religious conviction and spiritual substance.

During the devotional program, I was struck by the similarity of the goals and the problems which both the church and the state now face. Certainly, communication is both a goal and a problem for the church and for government. That is why so much of our effort with students has been directed to rebuilding and keeping open lines of communication. That was the basic purpose of our legislative intern program. The same reason motivated me to appoint a student advisory council and to ask for legislation which enables student representatives to sit on the boards of our state colleges and universities.

The seminar you are attending this weekend, and especially this hour of meditation and discussion, is a continuation of our effort to communicate with you and those you represent. We feel that it is crucial that the most concerned and the best educated generation in the history of this country and perhaps the world is allowed an opportunity to contribute its talent and its energy. Your generation is the one resource we can least afford to disregard, to squander, or to misuse, because to do so is to forsake the future of this state and nation.

By holding this three-day seminar we hope to impress on each of you the absolute necessity for your generation to become attuned to state government. It is an institution and a force that affects virtually every facet of your lives—the dormitories you live in, the quality of education you receive, the roads on which you travel, the job that you will seek, and the laws by which you are expected to live.

There is another reason that our attention has been focused on the youth and particularly the student leaders in Kentucky. It is because we have the greatest concern for the future of the American federal system of government. We have seen the development of an overbalance of power in Washington, most often at the expense of state and local government. Now, however, I am pleased that we have begun to move in another direction with plans for revenue sharing and bloc grants to the individual states. It appears that in the near future those of us on the state and local levels will be allowed to shoulder more of the responsibilities of government. To meet this challenge we must have the best brains, the best talent that is available.

We have begun to plan now so that we may be prepared to meet the future opportunities that are implied in the latest efforts to decentralize the national government. And that is why we have encouraged a fuller participation by the private sector and particularly the academic community, including student leadership, as well as administrative and instructional leadership. We are determined that there not be a gap of despair and distrust between the students and government here in Kentucky. And it is this determination that causes us to invite you here to meet with the leaders of government in a spirit of understanding so that we may openly and frankly discuss the needs of your generation and mine. We want you to know we have been listening as well as talking to Kentucky students.

As I said in my initial charge to the Student Advisory Council, we want you to tell it like it is, but we also want to hear how you think it should be. We want you also to know that state government, perhaps best of all, knows that communication is a two-way street. We did not invite you to come to Frankfort merely to listen but to talk freely and frankly to the leadership of state government. In that way we will both learn. We have already learned in our contacts with students this year of the great informational gap that exists between students and government. While this is disturbing and distressing, we are deeply gratified by the sincere interest on the part of the students to know more about and be a part of government.

As a direct result, this summer we conducted one of the most extensive student intern programs in Kentucky's history. We have tried to show through programs such as this that government must serve as a source of strength and direction in the advancement of human idealism. We have tried to convey the message that the only legitimate purpose of government is service and relevance to the needs of all the people. And more importantly we have tried to make it very clear that you are the government. Therefore, if government is allowed to falter or to fail, then a look within ourselves is at least as relevant as a look around us.

In my personal view, government is an effort to cope with human conditions, to master those factors which control our lives and our destinies. If our tolerance for governmental inadequacies is reduced by our sense of idealism, then I am convinced that we owe it to ourselves to lift up our institutions rather than lower our ideals. This is a challenge that must provoke individual response, individual commitment, and individual concern. I hope that you will take this message back to your respective campuses this fall.

We live in a State anxious for change, for progress, for economic growth, and for human betterment—a State that has repeatedly shown its confidence in young people. But with the faith that has been bestowed on your generation comes a commitment to responsible action and behavior. I believe that your generation also has a deep commitment to speak up for the basic institutions on which this country has obtained its position of respect and honor in the world.

I close with these words from the Bible, which in my opinion apply particularly well to your generation. St. Luke wrote: "Everyone to whom much is given, of him will much be required." [Luke 12:48] And of him to whom men commit much, they will demand more.

EULOGY OF CHIEF JUSTICE
MORRIS C. MONTGOMERY
Lawrenceburg / September 5, 1969

LAST Saturday, Morris[1] and Frances stood at the base of Pikes Peak as they affectionately and fondly reminisced of their days together there during World War II, while he served, as he did during all his years on the Court, in the cause of freedom.

Throughout his life, he did not hesitate to serve those things in which he believed. He has gone forth from Liberty, a place he always loved, a word he always cherished.

His opinions reflect uncompromising dedication and deep respect for the American system of justice. His years of honorable and distinguished service to his beloved country and to his fellowman stand to him today as Pikes Peak stands as a towering monument to God's handicraft.

Upon their leaving Saturday, he said, "We must go on." Today, those parting words take on special meaning. His efforts, his many contributions, his concern and his high ideals will go on. Respect and admiration in the minds and hearts of all those privileged to know him will be but a small part of his legacy.

The final summons has been served. The evidence is in—freedom, liberty, justice, honor, dedication, respect, concern. Daily, he has written life's judgment. His final admonition undoubtedly will be "Sustain my Country in all of these things."

---

1. Morris Carpenter Montgomery (1907–1969), chief justice, Kentucky Court of Appeals (1959–1960, 1968–1969), and judge, Kentucky Court of Appeals (1954–1969); Kentucky commonwealth attorney (1951–1952); born in Hustonville, Kentucky, and resided at Lawrenceburg, Kentucky. *Who's Who in the South and Southwest, 1969–70*, 10th ed. (Chicago, 1969), p. 710.

TO THE FINANCE COMMITTEE, UNITED STATES SENATE
Legislation on the Horse Industry
Washington, D.C. / September 22, 1969

My purpose for appearing before this distinguished Committee is to present facts and statistics on proposed legislation which would materially and adversely affect the economy of my own State and that of twenty-six additional states that are involved in horse racing or breeding. In addition to the twenty-seven states to which I refer, others who will make presentations to this Committee no doubt will give further information as to how this proposed legislation would affect them. Realizing the importance and the significance of the proposed legislation and the limited time resulting from the tremendous workload of this Committee, my remarks shall be brief and to the point.

Kentucky has achieved a position of worldwide preeminence in Thoroughbred, Standardbred, saddlebred, and quarter-horse breeding and racing. While these endeavors are most drastically affected by the legislation that you must now consider, they are not the only areas about which we have the greatest concern.

Other testimony no doubt will dwell on the detrimental effect that H.R. 13270[1] will have on the cattle industry and other phases of the suffering farm economy. But in passing, I would only relate that my State ranks tenth in the nation in the production of cattle and dairy products. Therefore, my interest is not directed toward a single purpose. Indeed, even though I shall make frequent reference to my own State, this legislation is of such wide geographical and economic concern that I am sure any number of governors could appear before you, and many of them stand ready to do so if your time permits.

Let me make it abundantly clear to you that I am not here today to ask for special favors for Kentucky or for special treatment for the Kentucky horse industry. My purpose is to outline the importance of the horse industry in the United States and to help the members of this Committee to weigh carefully the consequences of the various tax changes that have been proposed.

My statement is not mere conjecture or verbiage. It is based on statistics developed by Spindletop Research, Incorporated, a nonprofit, independent research institute established to stimulate the economic and industrial development of Kentucky and its region. Spindletop has engaged in many projects that relate to Kentucky's most important industries, as well as having done work for the federal government and many private enterprises. The study entitled "Economic Importance of the Horse Industry in the United States" was performed as a special public service in hope of clarifying some of the questions and misconceptions surrounding the horse industry. Attached to this statement and to be filed herewith is the complete text of the Spindletop Research report.[2]

When viewing the horse industry from a national standpoint, it is necessary to consider not only its economic importance, but also its recreational and educational significance. Directly affected are those who engage in the commercial activity of the horse industry. This includes breeding, training, racing, and showing, since people in these activities make their living directly from working on or with horses. In other words, horses are the tools of their trade. Indirect commercial activities are conducted by the manufacturers and suppliers who furnish products and by professional people who furnish services for either commercial or recreational horses. Therefore, the total horse population can be considered applicable to indirect commercial activity.

Furthermore, in some areas of the country, especially in Kentucky, the tourist industry is considerably strengthened by substantial numbers of visitors to our famous horse farms. Last year alone, the tourist industry resulted in $43 million in direct taxes being paid into our State's economy. The horse industry was responsible, either directly or indirectly, for attracting more than 50 percent of this amount.

The most difficult factor to measure in terms of the recreational aspects of horses is the tourist potential for horse farms, horse shows, racing, and rodeos. There are certainly many secondary factors that merit consideration, such as the extra time that families spend in an area because of these attractions, the extra distance traveled to view or participate in these activities, and the promotional value of the image created by the horse recreation activities.

In 1968, the total horse population of the United States was estimated to be in excess of six million. Of this total, 1.2 million horses were known to be registered. Of the registered horses, 832 thousand were listed as recreational and over 428 thousand were listed for commercial purposes. The labor utilized for commercial horses alone in the category of breeding, training, racing, and showing amounts to more than 125 thousand full-time jobs. In addition, there are between 25 thousand and 33 thousand full-time jobs in the supportive services and supply industries for all horses, bringing the total employment to more than 150 thousand full-time jobs, with many more persons employed throughout the year on a part-time basis. Much of this employment is in the agricultural sector. The known total annual wages for this labor amounted to more than $727 million. Wages paid by service vendors and suppliers were approximately $250 million. Thus, this proposed legislation would adversely affect total annual wages of $1 billion.

Total capital investment in breeding facilities and equipment is $543 million. An additional $79 million is invested in training, and $602 million is invested in race tracks. The value of the commercial horse is $1.12 billion. This adds up to a total capital investment of $2.34 billion. Although substantial, this figure must be considered only a very conservative estimate, in as much as there are many items of equipment, such as horse trailers, which could not be estimated with any degree of precision.

Land devoted to commercial horse uses in 1968 amounted to more than 1.9 million acres having a total value of $1.26 billion. I would remind you that these values apply only to those portions of farms that are devoted to commercial horses. The statistics make it abundantly clear that this extensive industry employs a large number of workers in agricultural jobs and further, that the capital investment in facilities, equipment, and land represents a major generator of economic activity. Gentlemen, these statistics are particularly significant when those of us charged with public responsibility face the multitude of contemporary problems with which we are expected to deal. The horse industry provides jobs at a time when we are seeking solutions to unemployment.

The horse industry generates substantial revenue directly to the states at a time when you are being asked to provide federal revenue to the states. Last week at the Southern Governors' Conference, I said that the states must commence to solve their own problems rather than look to the United States Congress. The states cannot solve their problems without revenue any more than the federal government can solve the problems for the states without revenue. In 1968, the total pari-mutuel revenue to all states amounted to $426.9 million. This combined with the $18.9 million in other taxes paid by race tracks brings the total tax from tracks and pari-mutuel betting to $445.8 million.

Proponents of this legislation might argue that you are indirectly subsidizing this sector of the farm economy. If that argument be true, I would only say in response that subsidizing employment, encouraging industry, and supporting a viable revenue-producing source, certainly is far more preferable than subsidizing unemployment and nonproductivity. I would also add that migration from the rural to the urban areas is considered a major problem in this country. This proposed legislation conceivably compounds the problem.

In this period of urban sprawl and urban blight, it is gratifying to note that a substantial amount of land, much of it within easy commuting distance of our cities, has been set aside for horse industry activities. Land used for horses is generally well cared for, with good cover and a minimum of erosion. In some parts of the country, such land represents the only open space and "green belts" in what would otherwise be an endless sea of houses. It is clear to me, coming as I do from a state having an unparalleled richness in scenic attractions, that the conservational and aesthetic aspects of the horse industry have great intangible value. It is my sincere hope that changes in the tax structure will not result in fragmenting these farms, or in drastically altering existing land-use patterns.

Many federal dollars are being invested in recreation. It is therefore highly significant that the number of horses used in recreation has increased considerably in the last decade. Horseback riding is a major outdoor recreational activity and even without being federally subsidized has contributed to the health and vitality of our citizens. Furthermore, Future Farmers of America, 4-H Clubs, and other farm-oriented youth organizations are becoming increasingly engaged in horse projects. Thus, it is clear that the success of many of these projects depends strongly on the availability of horses at reasonable prices.

To further demonstrate the recreational aspects of this industry, in 1967 the attendance at horse racing events alone exceeded the attendance at all other professional or amateur spectator sports. There were 63.4 million spectators at horse races in America while only 43.4 million attended professional and college football games and 24.2 million attended all major league baseball games.

In summary, I urge you to carefully reflect on the dimensions of this important industry that I have outlined briefly today. I respectfully ask that you also consider the many other factors which either have not been measured or are by nature intangible. Still, these factors, too, substantially increase the economic impact and other contributions of the horse industry to America. I salute each of you for your diligent efforts to find equitable means for sharing the burden of taxation. At the same time, however, I would urge you to take care that you do not throw out the baby with the wash water.

---

1. H.R. 13270 was an act to reform the income tax laws and could adversely affect the horse industry and farming in Kentucky. Public Law 91–172, H.R. 13270, December 30, 1969, Title II, Section 211–16, *United States Statutes* (Washington, D.C., 1970).

2. *The Economic Importance of the Horse Industry in the United States* (Lexington, Ky., 1969).

EULOGY OF JUDGE E. P. SAWYER
Louisville / September 25, 1969

TODAY we come to pay tribute to a man of quiet strength.[1] But for all his strength, his was a soft, calm voice, a voice of reason and understanding in a time of discord and confusion; a voice that never once faltered in the defense of the convictions and the principles that he so tenaciously cherished.

He came from a proud, resolute family of pioneer ancestry and in his rural upbringing learned early in life the basic virtues that great men possess. From childhood, he found nourishment in the sweet fruits of religious conviction, patriotism, and family devotion.

The essence of this man was his self-reliance, his courage, and his high principles. And these characteristics made him a relentless advocate of truth, integrity, and stability in both public and private endeavors.

His life has been devoted largely to the common good of his fellow-man. As a soldier, as an attorney, and as a trusted public official, he demonstrated unflinching dedication to freedom, justice, and service to others.

---

1. E. P. Sawyer (1915–1969), Jefferson County judge (1968–1969); Jefferson County attorney (1962–1968); assistant commonwealth attorney, Jefferson County (1947–1952); born in Beaumont and resided in Louisville. *Who's Who in American Politics, 1969–70,* 2d ed. (New York, 1969), p. 1013.

BOONE COUNTY REPUBLICAN
EXECUTIVE COMMITTEE DINNER
Burlington / September 26, 1969

TONIGHT, we meet in a cooperative venture, united in the firm belief that the candidates we have chosen to support are committed to better government. Naturally, my most immediate concern is with the candidates that have been nominated to serve you in the State House of Representatives. Without any reservations, I endorse them for election, confident that they will continue to put the interests of Kentucky above any personal or political considerations, and confident, also, that they will continue to aggressively and capably represent this great section of our State. Certainly, my interest in their races does not overshadow the importance of total effort and victory for your county candidates. Experience has proven that it is here, on the local level, that the enduring strength of our system of government as well as our party rests.

Tonight, let the battle begin in earnest here in Boone County. And let me make it very clear that I wouldn't be here if I did not think that each of you is totally dedicated to victory. I am here because I believe that we can win, that we shall win, and that we deserve to win in November. You have all the ingredients that are necessary—you have good candidates, you have strong issues, and you have desire and enthusiasm.

Tonight, I would like to set out what I believe to be the main issues of concern here. First and foremost, I believe that your people are concerned about the attitude of state government toward northern Kentucky. They are concerned, and rightly so, that this section no longer be regarded and treated as a stepchild. For as long as I can remember, politicians have called northern Kentucky this State's "Promised Land," and they promised it almost to death.

Now the time has come for a look at performance, not promises. Performance is the best reflection of this administration's attitude toward northern Kentucky. So let's get to specifics, and let me say on the start that I will match the performance of this administration, despite the fact that it is only in its twenty-second month, against that of any other administration you would care to name.

The engineers have said that the C. & O. Bridge, the single most vital and heavily traveled bridge in northern Kentucky, was allowed to steadily deteriorate during the twenty long years prior to our administration. Not only have previous Governors neglected Ohio's generous offer of one hundred thousand dollars a year for maintenance of the four bridges that connect our states here in northern Kentucky, they also callously turned their backs and their consciences on an engineer's report in the early 1960's that major repairs were then needed.

We inspected the C. & O. Bridge as one of the first official acts after Inauguration Day. But by then it was too late. Twenty years of neglect had taken their toll. We decided that inconvenience is really a small price to pay for the safety of a father traveling to work, or a mother out on a shopping trip, or certainly, a busload of children out for their first visit to the Cincinnati Zoo. And let me assure you that as long as I am privileged to serve as Governor, I shall gladly welcome the abuse and political criticism that have come from closing the C. & O. Bridge if it will save just one life.

I am pleased that we recently have had a breakthrough in our negotiations with the United States Bureau of Public Roads. Our plans have been approved and our engineers already have begun design work. We are also making substantial progress on an agreement on the final cost distribution for the project. We offer progress toward the construction of a new bridge and concern for the safety of the people of northern Kentucky. We proudly compare this record of performance against the proven record of neglect and discrimination of past administrations.

Public hearings were held on the Interstate–275 project eight years ago, and every year since the promise of I–275 was dangled before the people at election time. As you know, those promises were no good. But that isn't too surprising, because neither were the plans for I–275 that were made by previous administrations. They were disapproved in Washington. Plans have been approved, design is nearly complete and $5 million in construction contracts will be awarded next year. That is only half of what is being planned. We will also award $5.1 million of contracts for improvements on Kentucky highways 18, 20, 237 and 1334 here in Boone County so that first-class connector routes will be available to I–275 from the Greater Cincinnati Airport and other areas.

The fact is that political promises and faulty planning have been replaced by definite progress. And even more importantly, we did not confine our progress only to the Interstate system, we also planned ahead to meet the increasing traffic demands of the connector roads. I would only mention in passing that when the first two years of this administration are completed, we will have invested $766 thousand in the construction and improvement of the rural roads in Kenton, Campbell, and Boone counties. And that is $160 thousand more than the total spent in the two years previous to our election.

Nowhere is the change in attitude toward northern Kentucky more apparent than in the establishment of Northern Kentucky State College. In 1964, the administration in Frankfort apparently decided that this area would never amount to much, and they seemed determined that it would not. Instead of recognizing the real potential of your area, they established a Community College that was condemned by its location on extremely limited acreage to be dwarfed by its sister institutions in other sections of the State.

When we look to northern Kentucky's educational needs today, we think big, as big, we hope, as the potential that is here waiting to be exploited. Instead of a two-year college, we're going to build a full, four-year state college. The site has been chosen, academic and physical requirements are being studied, administrative personnel are already being interviewed, a bonding capacity of several million dollars has been created, and an operating budget of $160 thousand has been made available. In addition to that, we are conducting an intensive search for private financial support that could significantly clear the final hurdle that stands between the realization of a dream that has long been cherished by the people of northern Kentucky. Particularly in the field of public higher education, nearsightedness, although preferable to being completely overlooked, is nevertheless a bitter pill for the second largest population center of the Commonwealth. We have offered a better prescription.

In 1960, the State reluctantly accepted the deed for Big Bone Lick State Park. That was the last we heard from it until 1965, when the people of this area were led to believe that their vote for a $176 million bond issue would be the first step toward the development of this historically valuable tourist facility. The bond issue passed, and it finally appeared that the park would be developed. But again, the distance in thinking between Frankfort and northern Kentucky was clearly illustrated. Instead of the magnificent park that had been painted at election time in the minds of the people here, Frankfort had other ideas. Their idea of a park for northern Kentucky was an open-air shelter and acres of weeds and thorns.

In the past twenty-one months, we have completed the most extensive construction program in the history of the park. Camping facilities and utilities are now being developed at a cost of $201 thousand. And we are exploring with complete success a sizable federal grant to further enhance this long neglected stepchild of a parks system that knows no equal in the country. By the end of this administration, Big Bone Lick State Park will have become the Cinderella of the Kentucky Parks System.

I could go on and on with other examples, such as the Daniel Boone Boys' Center for very young juvenile offenders. Here was a facility that, if properly equipped and administered, could be a powerful instrument for reshaping the lives of scores of misguided children. Immediately after it was opened, conveniently at election time in November of 1967, construction flaws became apparent, the water lines burst, sewage backed up, and the fire alarm was faulty. I recall very well that this was one of the first items that Leo Lawson[1] brought to our attention. He demanded that we either make it safe and clean and useful or close it down. If any of you has been out to the Daniel Boone home recently, you know what our answer was. The repairs have been made, the staff has been increased, and today we are carrying out one of the most unique juvenile care operations in the country.

There are other accomplishments, such as the Banklick Creek study that is now under way, the $5,363,000 increase in education for the tri-county elementary, secondary, and vocational schools, a children's reception center that we are going to build here in northern Kentucky, and many other projects that we are proud to have a part in. But, as

I said before, all these things reflect the really significant difference in attitude. This is the thread that runs through every action that has been taken. And certainly, I cannot overemphasize the part that your Representatives and Senators had in the formation of this new attitude.

Where once this area and its people were only tolerated, now they are welcomed. Where once there was negligence and a lack of concern, now there is genuine interest in the growth and prosperity of your region. Where once you had only promises, now you have been given performance. And more importantly, where once state government thought in small terms when it thought of you at all, we have recognized the vast potential of northern Kentucky, and we have eagerly joined in meeting the challenge that for too long you have faced alone.

---

1. Leo Lawson (1905–   ), Republican, representative, Kentucky House of Representatives, Sixtieth District, Boone and Gallatin counties (1968), and unsuccessful candidate (1969); a businessman from Boone County. Telephone interview, Republican State Central Committee, Louisville, September 7, 1971.

KENTUCKY COUNCIL ON
CRIME AND DELINQUENCY
Louisville / September 29, 1969

THANK you for the opportunity you have provided for me to talk with those who must design and carry out the State's adult correction and juvenile treatment programs. Just recently, I was able to address two other concerned groups about the problems of crime and delinquency in Kentucky—the Juvenile Judges' Conference and the Conference of Regional Crime Councils.

The problem of crime is receiving widespread attention throughout the nation today. And Kentucky, recognizing the urgency of the problem, is making extensive plans to examine the extent of crime within our borders, to combat it through every resource available, and to provide adequate rehabilitation programs for those offenders committed to the State. During my talk with the juvenile judges, I complimented them on the theme of their conference, which was "United Efforts Pay Big Dividends." It follows well the philosophy of this administration to promote greater harmony and a spirit of cooperation among state agencies, local governments, and public and private agencies, so that the citizens of this Commonwealth may be better served.

Certainly, we are encouraged by the effective cooperation that exists between the Department of Child Welfare and juvenile judges. The judges have been assured that the executive branch of state government stands ready to assist in upgrading the corrective role of juvenile courts in Kentucky. Together, we must develop broad community support and genuine citizen involvement if we hope to reduce the rising incidence of delinquency. The Kentucky Crime Commission is designed to assist us in just such an effort. And, through the Commission, we have a real opportunity to develop new and expanded juvenile delinquency prevention and control services on the local level.

There is another factor that must also be considered. That is the manner in which we conduct our courts. I know from my experience as judge of Barren County that this makes a profound and lasting impression on youngsters. The same applies to adults coming before the courts. This will have a measurable effect on the offender's ultimate respect, or lack of it, for law, authority, and the administration of justice. The judges are on the "front-line," so to speak, and they may be able, through that healing touch of concern and attention, to chart a new, productive, and happy course for an offender in trouble.

While addressing the problem of adult and juvenile crime and the maintenance of law in an orderly society at a meeting of all the Regional Crime Councils recently, I cited three strong personal beliefs that I would reemphasize here today. First, no other problem that we face addresses itself so clearly and so forcefully to each of our local communities. Secondly, human resources, not financial resources, can supply the lasting answers we seek. Thirdly, the time has come when we must divert much more of our human and financial resources from the apprehension, adjudication, and imprisonment of criminals to the actual prevention of crime.

Certainly, we are all aware of the strident demands that law and order be maintained. Every day we read polls that reflect broad citizen unrest with the growing incidence of violence and lawlessness. But to do anything about it we must be willing to take a hard introspective look at our local communities and do what must be done. This is where the participation of the Regional Crime Councils comes in, and I believe that they must launch a two-dimensional approach. First, they must work toward the establishment of strong, effective deterrents to crime and obtain unflinching community support for their efforts. Secondly, they must focus on the root causes of crime and design the programs necessary to correct them. I hope that they, and certainly each of us, will add an extra dimension to our efforts—that is the improvement of our basic institutions. We must strengthen the family unit. We must seek added relevance of our educational system to the problems of today. And we must lend ourselves to a greater effort on the part of our churches to reach out and touch the lives of those most desperately needing spiritual guidance. After all, moral problems, such as crime and violence, require more than economic and legislative solutions.

Today, we turn our attention to those who have failed in society, who have committed overt acts which have caused their removal from society and imprisonment at a State adult correctional institution or one of our juvenile treatment centers. Some will be in our institutions for most of their lives; others, for a few years or a few months. For those who will be returning to society, we must make an effort to help them to change attitudes and upgrade their lives so they may become useful, productive citizens. On one hand, you face an often hostile individual who generally has a poor concept of his own personal worth. On the other, you face a public which has little understanding of our task or the methods used in the treatment of that person.

We should also note that treatment resources have been limited. The number and type of treatment facilities available are too few to provide the diversity in treatment programs necessary. A number of State facilities need extensive renovation and repair because of the pressures of overcrowding and the lack of attention to proper maintenance and care in past years. Of course, the recruitment and retention of professional personnel in the fields of adult corrections and juvenile counseling is a problem that continually plagues our efforts to provide adequate programs. But I want to assure you that this administration is prepared to make an all-out attack on crime and delinquency and to provide adequate rehabilitation programs. We have begun by structuring the forty-eight member Kentucky Crime Commission to serve the major areas of crime and delinquency control and prevention—the courts, corrections, juvenile delinquency, and police.

The Commission is fulfilling well its responsibility of assessing the extent of crime in Kentucky, planning for a statewide attack on the problem, and developing comprehensive state projects in close cooperation with the various departments of state government. But its major contribution, in my judgment, has been to focus attention on local community action through Regional Crime Councils. I have long felt that, by focusing attention on Kentucky's children and youth, we can make great strides toward the prevention of crime and delinquency and the successful rehabilitation of youthful offenders. That is why almost 25 percent of the funds made available to us through the Federal Safe Streets Act was earmarked for this purpose.

As some of you may know, I have made a firsthand examination of some Kentucky juvenile treatment facilities, and I have seen the deficiencies, the need for repairs, and new construction. We are, naturally, elated that we were able to provide additional resources to the Department of Child Welfare through a sizeable budget increase for operations. Funds have been provided for major renovation and maintenance, in addition to budgeted monies. Capital construction funds were in the executive budget to provide new facilities and diversified treatment programs at Frenchburg, here at Ridgewood in Jefferson County, the Green River Boys' Camp, and two reception and diagnostic centers, which will be announced soon.

I would just like to take this opportunity to commend the Department of Child Welfare for taking the initiative in planning and action projects to move Kentucky forward in services to children and the rehabilitation of delinquent youth. Its officials have used vision in their plans for future needs and approaches to serving Kentucky's children. They are not satisfied with just operating from one crisis to another or from budget to budget. Their efforts have brought Kentucky national recognition as a model for the delivery of services.

In years past, far too little attention was paid to the area of adult corrections. However, this administration has now taken a hard look at our system in this area—its facilities, its probation and its parole programs. We have determined the necessity for providing more than just "human warehouses." We need diversified facilities, innovative work training programs, and better programs to assist the inmate in his effort to return to the community from the structured environment of institutional life.

The Department of Corrections has taken a number of steps in new directions in adult treatment, rehabilitation programs, and internal administrative processes. I would only say that much care and attention went into the selection of the new Commissioner, and he was chosen because of his demonstrated administrative ability, his leadership qualities, and because his approach to adult corrections emerges from hard-nosed experiences and not just theoretical concepts.[1] The internal changes have been highlighted by better utilization of professional staff, more effective administration, cost reduction, and improved farm management.

The forward-looking approach in treatment of the adult offender is a result of highly individualized, accelerated treatment programs, a philosophy that encourages rehabilitation so that offenders may return to the community as useful, productive, and law-abiding citizens. It is a philosophy that recognizes that the problem is within the community and that, therefore, prevention and rehabilitation programs are in a large part the responsibility of the local community and that changes are needed in community attitudes about the treatment and training of adult offenders. After all, confinement alone will not improve the person, but the satisfaction of accomplishment gained from work and training programs while in the institution will go a long way toward helping the offender to accept the responsibilities of good citizenship.

Following this approach, the Department is setting up a new treatment facility for selected first offenders at Frenchburg. The Department has expanded its prison industries to provide a wider variety of relevant work and training programs, such as the establishment of the data processing units at LaGrange and Eddyville. This operation provided an opportunity for 125 inmates to be trained for future employment, a prime example of how the talents and time of inmates can be better used. State government agencies benefited also by saving $115 thousand for these services since the inception of the program in January 1968.

And what of the future? We are planning now for a more comprehensive and effective program of correctional services. These plans include, first, a new medium security institution for relatively short-term offenders. This facility would accomplish three objectives. First, it would reduce overcrowding in the present institutions through removal of selected offenders who show the greatest rehabilitation potential. For example, it would allow us to reduce the population at LaGrange to twelve hundred from its present level of over seventeen hundred. Secondly, it would permit implementation of sound treatment and classification programs and separation of tractable offenders from those more sophisticated in crime. Thirdly, the medium security institution would provide preparatory treatment just prior to the release of offenders through community correctional centers as part of the gradual orientation process.

The need for an institution of this kind has long been recognized. It was recommended in a comprehensive survey of Kentucky's Department of Corrections made by the National Council on Crime and

Delinquency in 1963. It also was recommended in the Governor's Task Force Report on Corrections the same year.

Our plans for the future also include the establishment of community release and work centers, or half-way houses as they have been called, to act as a "decompression chamber" for those who are about to return to the community, and the establishment of a furniture repair industry, which incidentally will not compete with private enterprise. Plans call for continued personnel upgrading and a determination of the need for a maximum security hospital for the mentally disturbed offender.

The past twenty months in state government have been eventful, and many positive changes have been made marked by reexaminations, reappraisal, and a reordering of priorities. We hope that one of the hallmarks of this administration has been the effective cooperation between departments of state government, such as exists between the Department of Corrections and the Department of Child Welfare. The newly established Human Resources Coordinating Commission will give great assistance and leadership to our efforts and eliminate wasteful duplication.

In closing, I commend and thank each of you and the departments and agencies that you represent for your vision, energy, and leadership. I am proud to be associated with you in our cooperative venture to maximize, conserve, and employ Kentucky's greatest asset, its human resources, to the best use of the Commonwealth.

---

1. John C. Taylor (1909–   ), Casey County, commissioner, Department of Corrections (1969–1972); career officer, Federal Bureau of Prisons (1933–1967); and special consultant, corrections systems of New York, Indiana, and Oregon (1967–1969). Department of Public Information biographical files.

KENTUCKY ASSOCIATION OF
SOIL AND WATER CONSERVATION
Gilbertsville / October 1, 1969

In a few months, we will enter a new decade, the decade of the seventies. History has a way of putting labels on those ten-year spans. All of us have heard of the Gay Nineties and the Roaring Twenties, although few of us remember much about them. The question confronting us is what they will call the seventies. Of course, only time will tell.

But I can tell you that this will be an era that will require the most prudent use and conservation of our natural resources. Soil and water districts will be called on to provide new levels of leadership in tempering unlimited demands on limited resources. During this decade, we will have to launch a twenty-year program to double our supply of drinking water and our sewer treatment facilities. We will have to find a way to dispose of 30 million pounds of garbage every year. Just to stay even, we will have to duplicate 40 percent of our highway system and produce 60,000 new housing units. In view of the magnitude of the task, we must start during the decade ahead. We cannot, we must not, wait until crisis overtakes us.

How shall we meet demands such as these and still conserve our God-given and irreplaceable resources? Much of that answer is up to you.

Fortunately, our soil and water conservation districts have a history of taking on the difficult jobs and coming up with the right answers. They were formed by concerned citizens in local communities more than twenty-five years ago to develop local programs with local leadership to eradicate erosion and silting of streams. Your success dramatically and forcefully refutes the theory that leadership and initiative can be found only in a Washington think tank.

Kentucky today is blessed with reforested timberlands, good pastures, and prudent conservation practices, many of which are based on decisions that soil and water conservation districts have made over the last quarter century. More recently, you have been called on to solve problems that cross county boundaries, problems that have required county leadership to lower the banner of provincial desire and raise the standard of the common good in its place. You have made major contributions to programs of flood prevention, recreation, municipal and industrial water distribution, and other projects under the Small Watershed Act. Accomplishments at the Mud River Watershed and the new $150 thousand program we announced in Russellville last Saturday offer evidence that your concepts of local and regional development really work.

It is to this kind of leadership that state government must and does pledge its support in order to ensure that our mutual objectives are achieved. Recognizing this, we have added $250 thousand to the Equipment Revolving Fund, bringing to more than $1 million the amount available for the purchase of machinery. To strengthen the Direct Aid Program, $75 thousand has been added to provide a realistic total of $225 thousand for equal distribution to your 121 districts. But now we must look to the future, to the seventies.

I came to urge you to extend your spheres of influence and concern in two areas that are becoming more crucial every day to the environmental quality of our lives. The first of these is in the field of conservation. I am well aware of the intensive education and information programs, the radio broadcasts and the appearances at schools and civic clubs in which you already participate. But I hope and trust that there will be an even greater concentration of effort toward conservation in the future. We have tried to demonstrate, through increased appropriations to the work in which you are engaged and through projects such as the preservation of Lilley's Woods and the Red River Gorge, that there are no lost causes in the endeavor to conserve our natural resources. It is our hope that these two projects will inspire each of you to believe, as we do, that lack of concern in the past, that lack of proper planning in the past, and that lack of adequate funding in the past should not and will not determine the extent of our concern, our planning, and our financial support in the future.

The second area in which you should seek a larger role is in the effort of total resource development. By far the most abundant demonstration of concern for the efforts that you are making was the addition of $600 thousand to the Small Lakes Program. I share wholeheartedly your conviction that we must continue to fully develop and make usable our vast water resources. And certainly, I share your enthusiasm for the multipurpose projects that grow out of the Small Lakes Program, those projects that provide new water supplies, flood protection, and recreational opportunities in one package. These projects are the epitome of the total resource development concept. They symbolize the underlying principle of your role in public life, that natural and human resources are unalterably bound to and dependent upon each other. The Mud River Watershed Project that I referred to is a good example of man conserving his natural resources in such a way that our human resources are enhanced. Not only did this project provide for the conservation of water resources, but it also increased both agricultural and industrial opportunities. This is total resource development in its finest form.

On behalf of all your fellow Kentuckians, let me again thank you for your contribution to the quality of our lives. The fruits of your labors are abundantly clear. You have helped Kentucky maintain its green forests, its rich meadows, and its abundance of pure water and unpolluted air. We recognize that it is up to all of us to defend our natural heritage and to use it wisely. And in this effort, your record of achievement shall serve as a beacon toward which all of us may turn as we further plan for the orderly growth of this Commonwealth.

PRAYER BREAKFAST
Frankfort / October 10, 1969

WE join today in a common cause and in a unified purpose, consolidating the electronic force of man's technical genius with the spiritual force of his Christian heritage so that we might lift a united voice of prayer unto our Lord.[1]

Above all other things, our prayer today is for divine guidance through the narrow straits of the time in which we live. Ours is a time in which man often is set against his fellowman—on ideological grounds; on military battlefields; on racial issues; and even on religious convictions. It is a time in which the young people of our State and our nation desperately, and sometimes destructively, search for an identity and a purpose in what some of them say is a less-than-perfect society that has been shaped for them by past generations.

Now is also a time in which an older generation looks with mixed emotions to the younger, anxiously awaiting the inevitable moment when the gap between them is closed, and the reins of leadership can be handed down with some assurance that there will be mature, responsible acceptance of that burdensome challenge. It is a time when the sanctity of our basic institutions—the church, the family unit, and the law—has been challenged and violated. Yes, these are times of conflict, of misunderstanding, of anxiety, and confusion.

More importantly, these also are times of unmistakable opportunity. We live in a period ripe with hope and promise for the future. Why opportunity, why hope, and why promise? Of this we are convinced, that out of our belief in God has come the civilization of mankind. And from the adherence to that belief in God and from the practice of His teachings comes the strength of civilization, strength adequate to meet the turbulence and the tension of today; strength to light the flame of human understanding; strength to resist the erosion that gnaws away at human dignity in a world that moves too fast at times for human kindness; and strength, also, to turn back the daily assault of the modern world on the moral fiber of mankind.

Realizing the imperfections of man, we can more fully understand how essential, how vital, it has been that laws be established and basic institutions created to guide and shape our relationships with one another. We should be mindful that the laws of man, as well as our basic institutions, find their foundation in the teachings of God. Thus, we cannot hope for a resurgence of respect for laws, for the church, or for the family concept unless we first return to the religious beliefs and principles on which they were founded.

A great American left Springfield, Illinois, in 1861 to assume the office of the Presidency of the United States at one of the most crucial junctures in our history. As he began his journey to Washington and to the White House, he said to his friends who had gathered: "Without the assistance of that Divine Being, I cannot succeed. With that assistance, I cannot fail. Trusting in Him, who can go with me, and remain with you and be everywhere for good, let us confidently hope that all will yet be well."[2]

We unite today in prayer across his native Commonwealth and ask the blessings of divine guidance in our search for the path of truth, light, and opportunity.

---

1. This speech was given to the Business and Professional Women's Clubs of Kentucky and was televised statewide from the Governor's Mansion. Telephone interview with Larry Van Hoose, Governor Nunn's press secretary, October 2, 1971.

2. Abraham Lincoln, "Farewell Address at Springfield, Illinois," February 11, 1861, *Abraham Lincoln: Selected Speeches, Messages, and Letters*, ed. T. Harry Williams (New York, 1957), pp. 135–36.

LOUISVILLE SUBURBAN ASSOCIATION
OF LIFE UNDERWRITERS
Louisville / October 16, 1969

EARNING your livelihood in the manner that you do, I thought it appropriate that I talk with you today about salesmanship, and more specifically, some of the sales pitches that are being used toward the end of the current political campaign. I think that it is becoming apparent to the thinking people of our State that some of the candidates, particularly those who seek membership in the General Assembly, are guilty of what those of you in the insurance business would call "overselling." Certainly, it is clear that they are overcommitting themselves. And in many instances, they do so with complete disregard and disdain for the facts and conditions that exist.

This is a dangerous trap, and I can speak from first-hand experience because Henry Ward and I were dropped into it in 1967. We said that we could operate the State under the existing revenue structure. What I didn't know, what the people of Kentucky didn't know, and what the people in Frankfort wouldn't reveal during the gubernatorial campaign was that we were headed for a $36 million deficit in finances as compared to appropriations. Education, highways, mental health and mental retardation facilities, and all the other services and assistance that state government provides were seriously threatened. As a state, we were forced either to retreat or move ahead, to turn our backs to the future or find the necessary revenue to support this State's development.

Happily, fortunately, a majority of the legislators were willing to put party labels and selfish interests aside. A responsible majority that cut across party lines decided that we would offer our children the opportunity that only quality education ensures, that we would take care of the elderly, the sick, and the needy, and that we would expand our highway system and our airport network. And thanks to them, we have been able to do all these things and more. We have restored fiscal solidarity.

We have restored the confidence of the people in the ability of this State to respond to real needs and deserving programs. For instance, last year when enrollment in the public schools rose well above estimates, we were able to dip into the State's reserve fund and provide $1.7 million to alleviate the situation. But so much for the past.

Just as in your business, it is not the policy you sold yesterday or what you did last year, but what you are going to do today and tomorrow that really counts. And that is what the election this November is all about. That is also why I am concerned and disturbed about some of the sales pitches that are going around. Of course I understand what motivates the candidates; they want to be elected. But I feel compelled to do all that I can to keep the facts before the candidates so that they will not let today's campaign oratory or political expediency box them in when they begin next January to decide the future of the Commonwealth. Neither I nor the people of Kentucky want them to come to Frankfort in January so hamstrung by campaign commitments that they cannot face up to the needs of those they represent.

You have a good example of what I am concerned about right here in Louisville and Jefferson County. Some of the candidates say they will lower the tuition at the University of Louisville. Some favor the merger between the University of Louisville and the University of Kentucky. Some indicate that they would favor financial relief for the parochial schools. Some want more state funds paid directly to the city of Louisville. All of the candidates say they will lower taxes. We all know that for every pitch, there is also a catch. And the catch here is that the proposition is simply impossible. A quart pitcher holds only a quart of water, and a state can spend only as much money as its tax structure provides.

There is another facet of this situation that must also be considered. That is the matter of tax relief. I have offered a plan that would eliminate the sales tax on medicine; eliminate the use tax on automobiles transferred within a family; give extra tax credits to the elderly and the sightless; and significantly raise the standard deduction allowances and tax filing requirements for the low income group. This plan is budgetarily responsible and acceptable. Certainly, it offers tax relief where the pinch of inflation and high living costs are felt more severely.

Whether tax relief is granted or denied is a matter that the Legislature must decide. But ultimately it boils down to a question of priorities. In the last session they had to decide whether to cut back services or expand them to meet the state's needs. This session, the members of the General Assembly will be called on to decide between tax relief and new demands for state revenue. I hope all of you will be listening during the final weeks of the campaign when each of the candidates addresses his sales pitch to this crucial problem.

KENTUCKY COAL ASSOCIATION
Lexington / October 17, 1969

I STAND before you today realizing full-well the contribution that your industry has made to the energy of this great nation in times of war and in times of peace. I also realize the significance of the coal industry as it directly affects the economic well-being of the Commonwealth of Kentucky. Speaking for the citizens of this state, we commend you for your record production of over 100 million tons last year. We are grateful that your efforts accounted for an addition of $400 million to the economy of Kentucky. We are well aware of the fact that in the process, you created twenty-one thousand jobs in direct mine employment and nearly fourteen thousand more jobs in related services for an annual payroll of some $230 million. Although coal is mined in thirty-seven counties in both eastern and western Kentucky, it is of special importance that your industry has been and today remains the economic backbone of an otherwise underdeveloped region that has come to symbolize poverty in America.

In view of these laudable contributions, you must be disturbed and perplexed that you now appear to be under attack from all sides—from candidates and conservationists, and from the communications media and concerned citizens. You must wonder about the future of an industry so beset by doubt and uncertainty, despite the fact that within a couple of years you will produce more than 125 million tons of coal from fields that hold documented reserves of 66 billion tons. Thus, it is particularly significant that the theme of this conference is directed toward the future.

Before I go further, let me make it very clear that I am not here today as an advocate of special interests. I did not come offering to fight your battles. But of this you, and every other Kentucky enterprise that contributes to the growth and development of the state, may be assured that I stand ready to go into battle for you as long as your cause is right, and I stand ready to do battle with you when your cause is wrong. As long as I am privileged to serve as Governor, the laws and regulations of this Commonwealth shall be of equal application to all. And as we have demonstrated during the past twenty-two months, these rules and regulations shall be applied fairly and firmly.

When I came into office, my position was made abundantly clear to all concerned, including the coal operators as well as officials of the state departments who regulate your industry. I said then we would assume that the members of the coal industry knew the laws and regulations in effect. We assumed as much of those in the various departments who regulate your industry. Of both the industry and the regulatory agencies, we expected, in fact we demanded, full respect and adherence to the existing laws. I am not aware of a single incident or instance during the past twenty-two months that would cause the industry, the governmental agencies, the conservationists, the news media, or the other citizens of the state to believe that there has been a change in that position.

Reflecting back over the past twenty-two months, that basic policy and mutual understanding has remained intact. Evidence was presented during the tours I made this summer to surface mining locations that the industry has shown a willingness to comply of their own volition, at least at the places to which I was exposed. This, I believe, has been the necessary spark that has kindled a new spirit of cooperation which has marked our relationship. And that is the spirit in which I come today to look with you at the future of the coal industry.

If we are to be realistic, we must first admit that several serious problems cloud your future on both the national and local horizons. The first of these could be termed legislative problems. In Congress recently, new laws are being debated that are considered detrimental and discriminatory to coal interests by many knowledgeable persons both in and out of the industry. Here in Kentucky, the voices who for years have screamed "Severance Tax" appear to have increased their volume and added to their forces.

Recently, a sizeable group of candidates for the Kentucky Legislature who reside, interestingly enough, in a metropolitan, noncoal-producing county, joined together to proclaim that a tax on coal was a cure-all for Kentucky's financial problems. These candidates decided that they will, if elected, replace state revenue in the approximate amount of $85 million by placing a severance tax on coal, oil, gravel, and perhaps other minerals. Of course, even they realized that if this were accomplished, we would be forced to cut back needed services and programs. So they proposed to replace the $85 million by imposing a severance tax.

What they apparently do not realize is that this would require a tax of approximately forty cents per ton on Kentucky coal. As all of you know, that is totally unrealistic and irresponsible. In the first instance, I am reliably advised it would put Kentucky coal at a distinct competitive disadvantage in the marketplace. Sales would suffer and less revenue would be collected. Employees would be laid off the job at the mines and more of the taxpayers' dollars would have to be spent for welfare. The end result is a net loss in revenue to the State and a reduction of services to the people. *This is a lesson we should have learned already—that discriminatory taxes ultimately discriminate not against those on whom they are imposed but against those for whom they were intended to benefit.*

There are other matters of concern affecting your industry about which the next Legislature will deliberate. These problems must be alleviated by men who offer rational answers that are backed up by solid facts and documented evidence and not charged up by emotionalism. I commend you for your assistance in sponsoring the recent Conference on Coal Workers' Pneumoconiosis at Spindletop Research. I am personally convinced that this was a wise investment in reason that eventually will pay dividends for both the industry and the employees.

Looking to other problem areas, we can foresee a time when stricter pollution laws will be both demanded and desirable. More demanding air pollution controls to guide the burning of your product and more restrictive water pollution controls over the actual mining operations have gained the sympathy of a concerned citizenry that is suddenly worried about its deteriorating environment. Properly handled by reasonable men among the coal operators and the conservationists, these problems can and must be met. Briefly, these are some of the problems that tend to obscure the future of the coal industry, as I see the situation.

However, there is a better side. I have never believed in dwelling only on problems. Opportunities should occupy an equal part of our concern and our energy. Fortunately, your opportunities deserve equal billing alongside your challenges in the future of the coal industry. The advance of the technical and nuclear age has assured this. The demand for coal is at an all-time high in recent years. New uses for coal are being discovered almost daily. New equipment to recover coal is being designed and perfected. Shorter, more economical avenues of transportation are being opened for the shipment of your product.

What does the future hold for your industry? Clearly, great problems lie ahead, problems that will test man's ingenuity and determination. But great opportunities await you also, opportunities that will require perhaps an even greater degree of ingenuity and determination if you are to seize them.

I would offer two keys, which combined can unlock the doors to your future. The first is the key of reason—harder, perhaps, to acquire in this age of emotionalism but infinitely more useful in its application. The second is the key of communication—truly invaluable in the hands of an industry long misunderstood, sometimes rightfully maligned, and often wrongfully condemned.

In this regard, I would compliment you in your choice of Fred Luigart to carry on for our friend, the late Fred Bullard.[1] I knew Fred Bullard as a gentleman, a dedicated representative of your industry and a good citizen of our Commonwealth. I also know Fred Luigart. He is an honorable man of good conscience and passionate concern for his state and its people. In his hands and in yours, the keys of reason and communication can lead toward a brighter future for you and all of Kentucky.

---

1. Fred W. Luigart, Jr., Lexington, president, Kentucky Coal Association (1969–1973); vice president and member, Kentucky Coal Association (1969); and industrial-management representative, Kentucky Water Pollution Control Commission (1969–1973). Telephone interview with Luigart, September 20, 1971.

Fred B. Bullard (1913–1969), Lexington, president, Kentucky Coal Association (1961–1969); secretary, Technical Advisory Committee, Kentucky Reclamation Commission (1968–1969); executive director, Kentucky Coal Association (1957–1961). At the time of his death, Bullard was a member of the Kentucky Water Pollution Control Commission; director, Spindletop Research, Inc.; and director and chairman of the board, Bank of Lexington. *Lexington Herald*, August 28, 30, 1969.

NEW CIRCLE ROAD DEDICATION
Lexington / November 24, 1969

YESTERDAY, the *Lexington Leader* described the opening of this last section of the New Circle Road as a "major milestone" in the growth of Lexington and Fayette County. Certainly, even in this age of dissent, there must be unanimous agreement on that conclusion.

I am sure that the thousands of Lexingtonians who have had to battle heavy traffic every day for the last fifteen years on their way to work at the industrial plants located on New Circle Road would agree that this is, indeed, a very significant occasion. But pride in this accomplishment must be tempered somewhat by disappointment in the fact that it took such a long time to complete this project. That it required nearly a quarter century to build New Circle Road is, of course, inexcusable by any standard. It has also been costly, not only in added tax dollars that have been required because of rising construction costs, but even more costly to the citizens of this community and the entire Bluegrass region, because of the opportunities for growth and progress that may have been missed.

Happily, Lexington has been able to grow as few other cities in America during the last two decades. This fact in itself is testimony to the tremendous potential of this city and this section of Kentucky. But, as your city officials know, the growth that Lexington and Fayette County have experienced was not without pain. Rapid urban growth such as yours rarely is painless. And certainly traffic and transportation problems have been among the most agonizing and persistent ailments with which you have contended.

Now, however, through the cooperation of the city, the county, and the State, several of these problems have been solved. Certainly, with the completion of work on Tates Creek Road and the opening today of this last gap in New Circle Road, two of the most severe traffic problems of this community have been solved. Let me assure you that this in no way means that we will be contented to rest on these accomplishments. Lexington did not grow into Kentucky's second largest city by living in the past. Historically, the prominence of this community has been based on its potential for greatness as a cultural, educational, and economic center for the State.

Lexington's potential has never been greater than today. And this fact alone should guide all our efforts and our plans for the future. The new East-West Expressway to be built soon into downtown Lexington is proof of our realization in state government that there is much to be done here. Completion of I–64 to span the gap between Frankfort and Lexington is another item of high priority for the Highway Department.

So in view of the many projects that lie ahead, perhaps we should take this opportunity to add a footnote to the *Lexington Leader*'s observation that this is a "major milestone." Let us today dedicate ourselves to the proposition that the completion of New Circle Road will be *both a milestone and a stepping-stone* toward the greatness that has always been Lexington's destiny.

COUNCIL OF STATE
GOVERNMENTS DINNER
Lexington / November 24, 1969

IF you are taken aback at the prospect of being addressed by one of those "administrative anachronisms" that some call today's governors, imagine how I feel before a group representing units of government said to be "indecisive," "antiquated," "timid," "ineffective," "not willing to face problems," "not responsive," and "not interested." No less a light than Chet Huntley commented flatly that states "should be solving problems at their own levels, but they can't do it. They're just not equipped for it." David Brinkley suggests that "states are pretty much disappearing as a political force." He adds: "The states are almost through. I think in another generation they will be just about insignificant." One United States Senator once predicted that "the only people interested in state boundaries will be Rand-McNally." Historian James Bryce writing in *The American Commonwealth* in 1888 said, "Fault with state government is not an exercise limited to our time. The real blemishes in the system of state government are inferiority in knowledge, skill, and sometimes conscience improvidence in matters of finance and want of proper methods for dealing with local and special bills."

And more than a hundred years before that, when the United States Constitution was being drafted, most participants believed the states should be subordinated to the national government. Some favored drastic subordination. James Madison of Virginia felt it imperative that Congress have the right to invalidate the acts of state legislatures. Charles Pinckney of South Carolina would have had all state laws approved by Congress before they could become effective. Sometimes I wonder if we should not implement his program, turned around, of course, so that state legislatures could pass on the acts of Congress. And Alexander Hamilton, after losing earlier battles to abolish states altogether, was in favor of having state governors appointed by the federal government.

For almost two centuries, the states have been losing ground to the national government. For sometime they have been increasingly by-passed and increasingly ignored by national officials who deliberately write states out of federal programs or place punitive restrictions against states not acquiescing in the plan. The states are sometimes victims of alliances between local officialdom and national agencies that can only subvert the system of federalism—the same system that nurtured the orderly realization of freedom and justice this country has enjoyed. In spite of these ominous warnings, both past and present, I believe we are here tonight because we refuse to accept the end of state government. If we did, I think we would have joined forces with Ethan Allen, whose challenge is inscribed on the walls of the capitol of Vermont. It reads: "I am as determined to preserve the Independence of Vermont as Congress is that of the Union and rather than fail, I will retire with my hardy Green Mountain boys into the caverns of the mountains and make war on all mankind." Happily, I do not think such drastic steps will be necessary.

To paraphrase novelist William Faulkner, I believe that state government will not merely endure; it will prevail. Why? For three good and quite substantial reasons. First, it provides a political base for national leadership. Second, it is constitutionally secure. Third, it is responsive and has served the people well.

Politically, the states have been, are now, and will continue to be the focal points in our party system of selecting national leadership. Congressmen and senators are products of state and not national political systems. Many have seen service in state government. Most are usually responsive to state party leadership.

More important to the preservation of our federal system of government, however, is the fact that the states have occupied, still do occupy, and will continue to occupy, a strong constitutional position in the nation. The states created the Constitution, if not the Union, and retain constitutional rights which make them far more than administrative subdivisions of the national government. Let me state, too, that only the national government has its seat in Washington. The federal government is based in every town hall, every county courthouse, and every state capitol across this great land of ours. The states form the backbone of the federal system. They are the only governments with a basis in the United States Constitution. They are not creatures of the Congress. Nor do they serve at the whim and convenience of the national government. They exist and thrive by the fundamental authority of the land. State government is at least as constitutionally secure as the national government. Both are political units within a federal system. Both the parts and the whole rest on the same documented foundation. We would all agree, I believe, that the demise of one would lead to the destruction of the other and of the federal system of government as well.

Political logistics and constitutional security are but preambles, though, to the third reason that state government is destined to prevail. The duties of state government are to develop services and delivery systems for diverse constituencies, to cooperate with the national government in achieving national goals, and to assist and coordinate the strengthening of local government. Critics to the contrary, state government is discharging these responsibilities and discharging them well. Charges of ineptitude, indifference, and inefficiency could accurately be leveled at almost any agency, commission, board or department of national government at some given time. The truth is that state government has pioneered in the development of individual opportunity.

The very existence of the Council of State Governments testifies to the unanimous dedication of all fifty state governments to the welfare of the people they serve. For fifty years, its research, its counsel, and its recommendations have helped individual states and joint ventures that cross state boundaries to analyze problems, formulate solutions, and implement programs. Under the early guidance of Henry Toll and Frank Bane, and now with the continued leadership of Brevard Crihfield, the Council has remained a dynamic symbol of state concern and eagerness to respond.[1] The decision of the Council to locate its headquarters in Kentucky is, of course, proof of its wisdom.

Contrary to popular belief, it is creative statecraft, rather than Washington witchcraft, that provides what one former Governor called the "laboratory for democracy." It is this creative statecraft that has encouraged experimentation, innovation, change, and local leadership. And all the while in highway construction and maintenance, the national government's share of total costs has been slightly less than a third while the states provided well over half. Its programs assist the region in meeting its special problems in promoting its economic development and in providing a framework within which joint national and state efforts can be most effective. The major burden, for planning, for policy-making, for decision-making, and for administration, rests solidly with the states and their elected officials. Because of this fact, each state approaches each program a little differently, submitting new alternatives as it capitalizes on existing ones and contributing its own experience to the diversity that is the underlying strength of the regional concept. The Appalachian Regional Commission, the multitude of interstate ventures, and the pioneering of individual states are proof enough that there is no single wellspring of ultimate wisdom and devotion to duty in the affairs of government.

It is not my intention here to do battle in a futile attempt to weaken the national system, but rather to accept a challenge to strengthen the federal system and to seek intelligent, responsible ways to keep our power plural. For virtually every important function of government, there is a shared responsibility in our federal system. We're all in the same boat, tossed about by the same waves and equally dependent on the paddle-power each of us brings to bear. When anyone fails to row, we all move more slowly. When anyone breaks the rhythm of stroke, the waves take on added peril for us all. The answer is a new thrust in intergovernmental relationships, a rising tide that lifts all boats, one that encourages states to move in new directions, to attempt "other" solutions, and even to make mistakes.

There is a price for such freedom. Laggard state governments must overcome the inertia and inaction that have drawn national government into fields where state supremacy was once unassailable. State governments must have the courage to exercise the taxing powers reserved to them, and them alone, before asking for an unrestricted tithe from the national collection plate. Custodial state governments must give up short-range responses to statutory obligations for a new boldness in seeking out the legitimate needs of their citizens. If we are not willing to pay this price, and if we cannot change where renovation is called for, we should prepare now for the orderly transfer of our remaining responsibilities to the federal government.

Simply "holding" the office of Governor is a singular honor, but an empty one. It has been my own ambition to function actively and effectively as the Chief Executive of one of this nation's great Commonwealths and to be instrumental in expanding and developing opportunity for each of its citizens while protecting his liberty and freedom of action. For this is what government is all about—the citizen, his responsibility, his freedom, and his opportunity. How foolish it is, then, to draw battle lines between national government and state government. The citizen constitutes both and must control both. The question is not whether national government will triumph, or state government will triumph. There is but one question: Will the citizen they were created to serve triumph?

---

1. Henry Toll, founder and executive director, Council of State Governments (1924–1938); honorary president and member, Executive Commission, Council of State Governments (1938–   ); National Commission on Uniform State Laws (1931–   ); senator, State of Colorado (1923–1931). *Who's Who in America, 1970–71* (Chicago, 1971), 36:2289. Frank Bane (1893–   ), executive director, Council of State Governments (1938–1958); chairman, Advisory Commission on Inter-government Relations (1959–   ); director, American

Public Welfare Association (1932–1935). *Who's Who in America, 1970–71* (Chicago, 1971), 36:103. Brevard Crihfield (1916–   ), executive director, Council of State Governments (1958–   ); secretary-treasurer, National Governors' Conference (1958–   ); and numerous other positions with the Council of State Governments since 1944; Board of Directors, Governmental Affairs Institute (1969–   ). Council of State Governments biographical files.

PRELEGISLATIVE CONFERENCE
Kentucky Dam Village
Gilbertsville / December 1, 1969

WE come here tonight representing two of our three branches of government. Every section of our state is represented. Although we are of different religions, different races, varied educational, social, and economic backgrounds, and of different political parties, we have an unalterable obligation and an unusual opportunity to serve the people, all the people, of this Commonwealth. Our obligation and the people's opportunity for service cannot be fulfilled if personal ambitions, sectionalism, partisanship, or any other divisive force is permitted to overshadow the primary objective for which each of us has been elected. That objective is to serve in the most honorable way the people of the Commonwealth through representative self-government.

Throughout the world, these are tumultuous times. Problems are many, complex, and commanding. They demand the best in each of us —our diligence, honesty, intellect, sacrifice, dedication, convictions, and courage. To solve the multitude of problems and seize the equally great opportunities that await this session of the General Assembly also will require cooperation, which I pledge to and seek from each of you. This is the beginning of the third century since Daniel Boone first came to Kentucky. We will be entering a new decade. What you do or fail to do during this legislative session will as surely mark the future of Kentucky as the past acts of others have written its history.

Kentuckians look to us for enlightened leadership. The probing eye of television, the attentive ear of radio, and the discerning interest of the press will carry to every citizen in every corner of this Commonwealth daily reports on our every action. I welcome the news media

and encourage you to afford them every accommodation, because we
are engaged in the public's business, and we and our acts should be
held up to wide public scrutiny. The people are entitled to know
whether our acts are responsible, constructive, and dedicated, or
whether we are merely being loud, belligerent, and partisan.

Two years ago the budget, which will be of prime concern to all in
this session, was approved by all except one member of both houses.
The budget which is now being prepared is for all practical purposes
a continuation budget. It will be submitted to you in adequate time
for you to make a thorough study and analysis of its contents, and to
act upon it so that services you approved two years ago may be continued to the people we represent. Each department head, and I trust
each constitutional officer, stands ready to answer any questions you
may have relating to its contents.

Prior to your election, I made known to you and the public certain
areas for tax reductions. Our budget is being prepared upon the assumption that some tax relief will be granted. However, you should
be aware that the request for funds for deserving and worthwhile projects far exceeds the anticipated revenue even before any tax reduction
is considered. This is not unusual. Two years ago when the budget
request had been prepared by Governor Breathitt's cabinet members,
the requests for funds were $462 million in excess of the anticipated
revenue. I would only point out to you that these requests by his administration indicated to them what must be apparent to all of us, that
there are not adequate state funds to meet the growing needs of an
expanding and demanding population. However, your responsibility
goes beyond merely appropriating funds.

Your attention must also be focused on several very complex legislative problems that involve the economic, social, and moral future of
our State. I trust that you will deal with these problems forthrightly in
the time allotted to you. The decisions that you have been elected to
make will not be easy decisions. A high degree of political courage will
be required if you are to face up to such issues as aid to parochial
schools, the Sunday Closing Law, Daylight Savings Time, and property
evaluation as it relates to the constitutional amendment that was approved last month, professional negotiations in the school systems,
local property tax roll back laws, and many more. In addition to these
very serious and compelling issues, it is my understanding that nearly
300 pieces of legislation have been or are being processed out of your
own interim committee system. As a result of the legislation you have
prepared already and in consideration of the many other new financial
issues confronting you, it appears that there is sufficient and important

work awaiting your attention from the first to the last day of the session. No doubt, as a result of the work of your interim committees, there will be no delays at the beginning of the session and the traditional log-jam of legislation at the final hour will no longer be necessary. Let me hasten to say, these are your problems and prerogatives, not mine.

Yours is one of three separate and distinct branches of government. I firmly believe that the strength and the protection of our system of government resides in the theory of separatism and the checks and balances that it offers. The interests, rights, and privileges of the public are best safeguarded when the legislative, executive and judicial branches are strong enough, wise enough, and courageous enough to stand separate, yet bound solidly together in common concern for those they serve. The legislative branch should, and insofar as I am concerned it shall, enjoy the same independence that the judiciary now experiences from the executive and the same independence that the executive branch has a right to expect from the judicial and legislative.

FRANKLIN COUNTY
EXTENSION CENTER DEDICATION
Frankfort / December 6, 1969

WE have come to realize an important truth about education. Education is more than the teaching of history or English literature or mathematics or science. Education must involve the development of the whole person. The fulfillment of each student's particular interests and talents must be of prime concern. Sometimes this means a student should pursue college preparatory courses. That is why the financial support to local school districts was increased last year by $80 million. With this foundation a student can go on to college and graduate school.

Often, however, a student cannot nor does not wish to go to college. His life needs a different direction. His talents lie elsewhere. Just as a lawyer would be lost without a legal education, so would this person be stymied without proper training. Kentucky is providing this training in the nation's best system of vocational schools and centers. This comprehensive network includes fifty-one schools already in operation and eight more that are now under construction. Our dedication to each, the student who chooses vocational or technical training, must be of equal intensity and application. In Kentucky, not only the student just out of high school but also the older person who has been subjected to the unstable world of the unskilled labor market can learn a rewarding and profitable skill through vocational and technical education. He will be better equipped to work and earn, to discharge his civic responsibilities, and to enjoy a healthy and happy life. The contribution made by this person extends beyond his own family into his community.

Our society is complex and changing. Its needs are diversified. Today is an age of technology and specialization. The contractor needs the carpenter and the bricklayer to build a house. The engineer needs the welder and the mechanic to raise the skyscraper. The businessman needs the clerk and the typist to run his office. The doctor needs the lab technician and the nurse to treat his patients. Which is more important—the contractor or the carpenter, the engineer or the welder, the businessman or the typist, the doctor or the lab technician? There should be no quarrel here because without one, the other could not function.

They all are part of a team of individual specialists with separate talents. Together they build our subdivisions, develop our cities, run our businesses, and care for our people. They contribute to their communities and further the progress of the State as a whole. Industrialists and businessmen appreciate this winning combination, a fact proven by their willingness to invest more than $600 million in Kentucky's economy the past two years. They are attracted to a state or a region where they can find the brains and the skilled manpower to run their plants and businesses. In turn, new jobs and business opportunities are opened to more and more Kentuckians and an economic cycle of progress and prosperity begins and grows.

Kentucky's attraction to industry is obvious. In the past two years, 367 new or expanded industries announced their intentions to locate in the Commonwealth. As a result, 23,243 new jobs will be made available. These industries have located or expanded in Kentucky for many reasons. Our natural resources are the richest in the nation. Our geographic position puts us in ready access to America's marketplaces. Our highway system can compete with any other state's. Over half of Kentucky's parkways, 352.7 miles, and over two-thirds of the interstates have been completed. Four new toll roads, approved last year, will open up over forty counties to industrial, commercial, and tourist development. Our recreational facilities and state parks are the finest in the country and bring millions of tourist dollars into the state each year. And we have the manpower, an industrious people who are being educated in our schools and trained in our vocational centers.

The future of Kentucky's vocational education is currently under discussion. The question is whether the administration of the extension centers should be transferred to the local school boards. We must consider this question seriously and hear all sides in the debate. Our vocational schools are too important to the economic development of the entire state for us to make a hasty decision. If by our actions, Kentucky's system of vocational and technical training is impaired, then all of us will suffer.

The Extension Center we are dedicating today is the most recent member of this system. We dedicate it with the recognition of its importance to the economy of Franklin County and surrounding counties and to the Commonwealth of Kentucky.

RUBELLA CONFERENCE
Frankfort / December 16, 1969

IN 1964, an epidemic of German measles or rubella swept through Kentucky and across the United States with devastating effects on thousands of mothers-to-be. It left in its wake a legacy of heartbreak and anguish. Thousands of children were stillborn; thousands more were maimed for life with the crosses of congenital deafness, blindness, and mental retardation. The economic toll of such a plague is also devastating. In Kentucky alone, the cost of treatment, special education, and institutional care for the afflicted runs to more than $3.6 million a year. Lost economic potential of the stricken has been estimated at an additional $30 million.

Medical experts are now forecasting another epidemic of rubella for Kentucky and the nation. This time we will be ready. We will not be caught off guard and defenseless as we were in 1964. You have been invited here today to join with state government in making sure that the next cycle of rubella shall not again victimize our people. You, and the organizations you represent, exemplify the concern of aroused men and women for the welfare of their fellow citizens. The brotherhood of man is nowhere better fostered than in the ranks of volunteer agencies. Your personal concern is evident in the distances many of you have traveled to be with us today. I also recognize the sacrifices you have made in time and energy, commodities always in short supply and especially limited during the rush of the holiday season. As Governor, I commend you for your interest and concern. I thank you for coming.

As you will learn in the next few minutes, the goal we have set is a monumental one. Elimination of this blight will require the immunization of 823 thousand children between the ages of one and twelve, those most likely to expose childbearing women to this dread disease. The cost of the vaccine alone for this program will amount to more than $1.2 million and total immunization must be accomplished now. Tomorrow may well be too late. The urgency of this impending epidemic requires that priorities for immunization be established so that prime carriers are inoculated first. The Department of Health has identified these prime carriers as preschool children and those in kindergarten and the first and second grades, 166 thousand in all, aged four through eight. I am today directing that $50 thousand be appropriated from the Executive Contingency Fund for the immediate purchase and administration of rubella vaccine with parental consent to members of this primary group. Obviously it is not enough.

It is the gentle legion of voluntary support you represent that must shoulder a major share of the responsibility for making this program, so desperately needed, a successful one. Volunteers are needed to work with local health departments to secure community support, volunteers are needed to help secure additional funds to purchase needed vaccine, and volunteers are needed to assist in the process of community education. Coordinating the activities of volunteer groups and state agencies in our attack on rubella is a task of great proportions. I have asked Mrs. Jewel B. Hamilton, former president of the Kentucky Federation of Women's Clubs and now my personal aide for human resources development, to assume this responsibility.[1] Many of you already know her and her tremendous capacity for getting things done. I would hope that those of you who do not know her will join the ranks of her admirers and co-workers. With her services as coordinator of this vital program, all of you, individually, and as members of local support groups that have already contributed so much in other fields, can act now to protect the well-being of our children yet unborn.

1. Mrs. Jewel B. Hamilton, Bardstown, administrative assistant to Governor Louie B. Nunn (1969–1971); unsuccessful Republican candidate, superintendent of public instruction (1971); chairman, 1970 White House Conference on Children and Youth (1968–1971); president, Kentucky Federation of Women's Clubs (1964–1966); dean of students, Nazareth College. Jewel Manor, a treatment center for delinquent girls, was initiated by and named for Mrs. Hamilton. Information from Mrs. Hamilton, October 16, 1971.

EULOGY OF SENATOR GEORGE M. PLUMMER
Vanceburg / January 20, 1970

TODAY we gather amid the hills and among the people George Plummer loved.[1] We come to pay a final tribute to one who gladly lived his life rendering service to others. Throughout his days, he carefully guarded the friendship and the trust placed in him. To touch the heart of his life, we found in him one thought, the thought of duty, of owing something to God, to his neighbor, to himself. This was the foundation of his success.

Few fields of endeavor are more demanding than public trust. Yet, he always equalled the challenge. He endured the rigors of public life with unyielding compassion and concern for others. Because he cared for others, others cared for him. Let it be said: "Life's race well run, life's work well done, life's victory won, now cometh rest" to a good and faithful friend.[2]

---

1. This speech was delivered at State Senator George M. Plummer's funeral. George M. Plummer (1912–1970), Vanceburg, Republican state senator, Eighteenth District (1970); county clerk, Lewis County (1942–1969); chairman, Lewis County Republican Executive Committee (1948–1964). *Kentucky General Assembly, 1970* (Frankfort, Ky., n.d.), p. 6; telephone interview with Senator Luther Plummer, brother of George M. Plummer, Vanceburg, September 6, 1971; telephone interview with Mrs. Shirley Hinton, county clerk of Lewis County, Vanceburg, September 8, 1971.

2. Quoted material is from "Funeral Ode on James A. Garfield" by Edward Hazen Parker (1823–1896). John Bartlett, *Familiar Quotations*, 12th ed. rev. (Boston, 1951), pp. 555–56.

ELFUN SOCIETY
Louisville / April 6, 1970

IT is gratifying to see the interest that you as individual citizens and as members of our largest corporate family have expressed in the outcome of the 1970 session of the General Assembly.[1] I believe this is a positive indication of the state of our civic health. Certainly it is an encouraging comment on the future. Tonight I would like to present a brief overview of the legislative session just ended and then open the floor to any questions you may have regarding the General Assembly.

Persons more familiar with the Legislature than I have said it was an unusual session in many respects. It was perhaps better organized and better prepared to do the people's business than ever before. Over three hundred pieces of legislation were ready for introduction on the first day of the session. From what I have been able to gather the sessions were orderly and the committees functioned with exceptional diligence and regularity.

The leaders asked for independence from the executive branch and independence was given. In fact, many observers have said that the 1970 Legislature had more independence than any other in the modern history of our State. I believe it is the first time that the Governor has refrained from making any public statements on legislation pending before the two houses. But tonight as we look back on the events and the statements and the production record of the past session, the thought clearly emerges that independence was a painful experience for the Legislature.

Let me make it perfectly clear that the noninterference policy I adopted was not for the purpose of self-preservation, but for the preservation of the integrity and the intent of our system of government. It was my hope that this policy would breathe new life into our constitutional concept of separation of powers and responsibilities within the three branches of our government. It was a policy that reflected sincere respect for the frequently expressed desire, but the seldom exercised right, of the legislative branch for independence. The response to this policy offers a clear indication that the sanctity of our form of government, and of more importance, the sanctity of the Legislature's right to be free of interference, has greatly diminished during the many years of one-party domination over the past two decades.

A review of the 1970 session can only evoke the overpowering realization that independence without courage is useless and independence without a commitment to the common good is meaningless. In the legislation that finally was delivered for action by the executive branch, there was, in my opinion, an appalling lack of either courage or commitment. And these were the most frequent reasons why I was forced to exercise the power of veto last week. I realize that perhaps some of you have disagreed with some of the judgments that were made in vetoing, signing, or allowing various bills to become law without signature. As an answer, but certainly not as an apology, I would only say that these decisions were not hasty reactions to political pressure or selfish interest. They were based on what I deeply believed to be the best course for Kentucky.

Some of the legislation was needed and well intentioned. The goals they strived to reach were worthy and certainly desirable. But on closer examination and more careful analysis, some of these same pieces of legislation were found to carry serious and detrimental consequences. On some good bills, bad amendments had been attached. For instance, I am sure all of you were interested in the bill that would have brought the University of Louisville into the state system of public higher education. As a graduate of that university, I have always felt a personal obligation to see that it continues to serve this community and this State. We felt fully justified in raising state support by 300 percent in the last two budgets. Entry into the state system, while not the unanimous sentiment, was favored by a substantial majority of the school officials and, I believe, the local community. Senate Bill 117 would have brought the university into the system. That was the clear intent. But the bill fell into political hands along the way. There were some who sought to extract their pound of political flesh even at the expense of the university and the people of Jefferson County. An amendment was added which completely negated the purpose for the bill, blocked entry into the system and threatened the $13 million appropriation as well as the school's bonding capability. Fortunately, we were able to remove the most objectional amendments before the bill was passed.

Other legislation did not fare so well. The Legislature passed numerous bills that committed the State to worthwhile programs, but failed to include the financial resources that were necessary for implementation. Transportation of children to school certainly is a deserving cause. House Bill 209 would have made it mandatory to transport all children who lived more than one mile from the school. But for all the oratorical attention this bill received, not one of its supporters was willing to propose a means of raising the required $7.7 million.

An even better example was legislation appropriating $500,000 to the chronic dialysis kidney center at the University of Louisville. This is a life and death proposition for nearly one hundred persons who require periodic treatment to stay alive. Yet no funds were made available. In the revised budget, proposed and passed by the majority party, no provisions for surplus are made for projects such as this. It would have been easy to sign this bill. That would have been the popular decision, but any satisfaction would have been temporary, to say the least, because next July patients could no longer look to the federal government for help, but would be forced to depend on this legislation for continued treatment. And then the cruel reality of the situation would have been realized, perhaps at the expense of human life.

Kentucky has been through that kind of situation once before in recent years. The previous administration wrote a $24 million cold check to the teachers of this state in 1966 and then asked the sick, the aged, the needy, the mentally ill, and the dependent children of Kentucky to bear the consequence. That was where we stood when the present administration went to Frankfort two years ago. Fortunately, we had men such as Vern McGinty of your company and many others who put the interests of Kentucky above narrow personal interests.[2] As a result the teachers were paid, the sick were treated, and young and old alike received the care they needed.

This Legislature could have achieved as much, but unfortunately, it appears that more attention was given to politics than to the people. There was a lack of leadership. Timidity exceeded courage. Studies were proposed where action was required. If there is one good thing that can be said for this session it may be this: the people of Kentucky are fortunate that the legislative acts for the most part were sins of omission rather than sins of commission. The real tragedy of the 1970 session was that we lost opportunities to push Kentucky across the threshold into a new era of greatness.

What we do about our opportunities is now the question, and that is up to each of us. Your Vice-President, Mr. Gauss, offered some very constructive thoughts on the subject last Thursday at the Industry Appreciation luncheon.[3] Certainly, businessmen must take an active interest in education, labor law, and politics, as Mr. Gauss said. The entire State and industry in particular must be concerned with the quality of education offered in Kentucky. The subject of labor law is becoming more critical each day as it is put to the test in public enterprise as well as private enterprise. But what is even more disturbing than the threat of labor disruptions is the apathy of business and industry toward legislation traditionally regarded as harmful to their best interests.

I am deeply concerned that on several occasions during the last session of the Kentucky Legislature, the voice of industry was not heard. There were two reasons for this. First, industry's voice could have been drowned out by its opposition. Labor has recognized the importance of political involvement throughout its history and has been far more active than industry in electing those sympathetic to its viewpoint. Secondly, on several vital issues industry apparently chose to sit in silence, perhaps on the assumption that to speak out would be futile. All of this underscores the truth in Mr. Gauss's remarks the other day about politics. Politics is not a spectator sport, particularly in this age of citizen involvement and social concern. We should be aware that political apathy on the part of business and industry does a serious disservice to the free enterprise system. Now is not the time for those who have developed and been a part of the world's greatest economic system to withdraw from the contest.

In closing, once again I would like to congratulate your organization for its continuing interest in public affairs and commend your corporate leadership for its enlightened involvement in the effort to preserve the free enterprise system and bring progress to Kentucky, the nation, and the world.

---

1. The Elfun Society is an organization of General Electric Company Management personnel.

2. Vernon Charles McGinty (1915–   ), state senator, Thirty-eighth District (1962–1968); Republican caucus chairman, Kentucky Senate (1966–1968). McGinty is financial manager for the General Electric Company (1941–   ) and a resident of Louisville. *Who's Who in American Politics*, *1969–70*, 2d ed. (New York, 1969), p. 726; *Kentucky General Assembly*, *1968* (Frankfort, n.d.), p. 11; telephone interview with McGinty, Louisville, September 13, 1971.

3. Joseph H. Gauss (1915–   ), vice-president and general manager, Air Conditioning Products Division, Major Appliance Business Group, General Electric Company (1968–   ); born in St. Louis, Missouri, resides in Louisville. Office of Joseph H. Gauss, Louisville, September 15, 1971.

ADDRESS CONCERNING
UNIVERSITY OF KENTUCKY
CAMPUS DISORDER
Lexington / May 6, 1970 / Afternoon

THE unprovoked, premeditated, senseless action which has occurred on the University of Kentucky campus will not be tolerated and has necessitated the action I now must take.[1]

I have determined that a state of emergency exists on the campus at the University of Kentucky. There exists a clear and present danger to the lives of students and to University property.

Therefore, as Governor of the Commonwealth of Kentucky, and as Chairman of the Board of Trustees, I am directing that a curfew be imposed upon the UK campus from 7:00 P.M. tonight, Wednesday, May 6, until 6:30 A.M., Thursday, May 7, and pursuant to requests from the Mayor of Lexington[2] and under the authority of KRS 38.030, I hereby authorize and direct the Adjutant General[3] of Kentucky to issue appropriate state active duty orders for the necessary number of officers and men of the Kentucky Army National Guard to assist the various police agencies of Lexington and Fayette County, Kentucky, in maintaining law and order.

I am further requesting that all students remain in their rooms and that all people stay off and away from the campus during these hours.

The Kentucky State Police and an adequate number of National Guardsmen with mounted bayonets and live ammunition are being moved onto the campus to protect the students and University property. These officers are under orders to use such force as is necessary to perform their mission of protection. Anyone attempting to defy them does so at his own peril.

Please comply for your own safety and safety of others.[4]

---

1. On April 30, 1970, President Nixon enlarged the theater of the war in Southeast Asia by ordering American troops and air power into Cambodia. Following this action student strikes and demonstrations occurred on a number of college campuses throughout the country. On May 4 at Kent State University in Kent, Ohio, four students were killed by National Guard troops. This event prompted further campus demonstrations including those at the

University of Kentucky, where, on the night of May 5, the ROTC Annex building burned. The address included here was Governor Nunn's response to the events at the University of Kentucky. *Louisville Courier-Journal,* May 1, 4–7, 1970. The first handwritten draft of the address was delivered over television from Lexington. The address was later issued as Executive Order 70–453. Interview with Larry Van Hoose, Governor Nunn's press secretary, September 10, 1971.

2. Charles Wylie (1907–), mayor of Lexington (1968–1971); Lexington mayor pro-tem (1966–1967); Fayette County attorney (1952–1958); state representative, Forty-seventh District (1936–1937). Office of Mayor Charles Wylie, September 9, 1971; Legislative Research Commission, September 22, 1971.

3. Major General Larry C. Dawson (1912–), Louisville, adjutant general (1968–); various other ranks with the Kentucky National Guard (1930–1967, 1968–). Office of General Dawson, September 10, 1971.

4. At 2:30 A.M. on May 6, 1970, immediately following the burning of the ROTC building, Governor Nunn issued the following statement:

The unprovoked, premeditated, senseless action which has occurred on the University of Kentucky campus within the last few hours *will not be tolerated.* Lives of students were endangered and public property was destroyed without any reason or provocation.

I have ordered a full investigation of these criminal acts and those responsible for the wanton destruction of property and other violations of the law will be prosecuted.

In addition, I have assured University officials that the Kentucky State Police, the National Guard, and such other authorities as may be required have been placed on alert and are at their disposal if necessary.

So that there will be no doubt whatever as to the response that will be made to violence and disruption on Kentucky's campuses, I am hereby reiterating my position.

When governing officials at the University of Kentucky or any other state university request assistance, then assistance will be given *in sufficient numbers and under direct orders to use such force as is necessary to put down violence and stop disruption as quickly as possible. The amount of force that will be used will be determined by those who provoke the violence.*

On the morning of May 7, 1970, Governor Nunn's office released this statement:

Following discussions with the President of the University [Dr. Otis A. Singletary] the Kentucky State Police, and the State Adjutant General, I have determined that a clear and present danger to lives and property and a general state of emergency continue to exist on the University of Kentucky campus at Lexington. Therefore, I am committing a sufficient number of National Guardsmen and Kentucky State Police to remain on the campus for as long as this situation prevails.

To guarantee that lives and property are protected, to be sure that students at the University are allowed to complete their year's work without disturbance, and to ensure that order is maintained, the National Guard and the Kentucky State Police shall remain under the same orders to use such force as is necessary to perform their mission of protection.

Now I would like to address some personal remarks of commendation and praise to the overwhelming majority of dedicated, responsible members of the University community who have once again shown their appreciation for the difference between rational, lawful dissent and reckless violence. With those honestly concerned for the preservation of the University I share a deep sense of regret that curfew and other security measures were necessary to protect lives and property and keep alive the opportunity for a college education in Kentucky. Yet, I am deeply gratified and proud that your positive response and support has again clearly shown you believe that temporary inconvenience is a very small price to pay to keep the campus out of the hands of that small group who promote violence and destruction.

Tuesday evening's violence, with the use of firebombs and other instances of arson, was followed on Wednesday by several bomb threats and evidence of further plans of destruction and presence of dangerous outside agitators, and finally the willful disregard of President Singletary's policy made one thing perfectly clear: The security measures taken were the only way to ensure that there would be no tragedy on the University campus last night. We can all be thankful that the course of action chosen successfully eliminated violence and danger last night and permitted a continuation of the University schedule today.

Working together, we can preserve and strengthen a University which has meant so much to you, to me, and to this State and its three million citizens.

On the afternoon of May 7, 1970, Governor Nunn issued Executive Order 70–456:

By the authority vested in me as Governor of the Commonwealth of Kentucky and as Chairman of the University of Kentucky Board of Trustees, I, Louie B. Nunn, hereby direct a curfew be imposed upon the University of Kentucky campus from 7:00 P.M. tonight, Thursday, May 7, 1970, until 6:30 A.M., Friday, May 8.

On the morning of May 8, 1970, Governor Nunn released this statement:

As the father of a college student, as chairman of a university board of trustees, and as a citizen and Governor of Kentucky, I am extremely proud of the responsible leadership Dr. Otis A. Singletary has again shown this morning as President of the University of Kentucky. Dr. Singletary's courageous decision to keep the University open exemplifies the determination of this great institution and the people of Kentucky to guarantee educational opportunity to those who seek it.

Encouraged by that decision, I again pledge whatever assistance is necessary to keep the Lexington campus out of the hands of a small, disruptive group whose aim is the denial of academic freedom and educational opportunity. Kentucky State Troopers and National Guardsmen shall remain on the UK campus as staunch and untiring allies of those students whose lives may be endangered—intentionally or unintentionally—by the persistent recklessness of this group of agitators. The safety of students and the protection of property are of immediate, compelling concern, as is the continued guarantee of rational and lawful dissent. Provision for each of these objectives shall continue to be made here.

Turning to another part of Dr. Singletary's statement issued this morning, it is to his eternal credit that he has emphatically decided not to permit a noisy few to cancel commencement exercises at the University. Graduation from college is the inspiring culmination of years of hard work and academic growth toward self-improvement. I strongly concur in this and shall actively support the observance of graduation exercises at the University of Kentucky, so that we may honor the thousands of mothers and fathers whose love, inspiration, and sacrifice have encouraged their sons and daughters toward this significant plateau of achievement.

Issues of unprecedented gravity have been confronted and difficult, agonizing decisions have been forged this week in Kentucky. The proudest facet of these decisions lies in the sure knowledge that they reflect concern for present as well as future generations of students, parents, and citizens alike. At the same time, the dangerous precedents of accepting irresponsible concession, expedient compromise, and temporary alternatives have been studiously avoided in order that more and worse campus disorder can be averted in the future.

These decisions come at a crucial turning point in American history. The time has come for this nation to decide whether our educational institutions shall survive as free, rational communities, or whether they shall succumb to the paralyzing effects of violence, intimidation, and anarchy. Because reason and responsibility prevail among the overwhelming majority of students here, Kentucky has resisted the tide of campus violence which has been swelling in this land. We proudly offer this as an example to the nation.

At a press conference on the afternoon of May 8, 1970, Governor Nunn made the following statement:

After talking with President Singletary, the State Adjutant General, and the commanding officer of the Kentucky State Police [Colonel C. B. Crutchfield], it has been concluded that the extent of danger to lives and property has been considerably lessened. The demonstrating group has dispersed and is behaving in respect of campus rules. Therefore, the National Guard and the Kentucky State Police have been instructed to begin withdrawing in proportionate dimensions to the improving situation.

For additional information on the UK disturbance, see the United States District Court Case, *American Association of University Professors, University of Kentucky Chapter et al.* vs. *Louie B. Nunn et al.*, Lexington Civil Action File Number 2139, May 7, 1970. Regarding this case, Governor Nunn released the following statement on May 14, 1970:

I believed at all times during the crisis on the University of Kentucky campus that I was not only acting within my rights but also performing my duties. Having so acted, I felt secure in the courts. The opinion of the court, coupled with the action taken, should give comfort to the people of this State and this nation that peace and tranquility can be maintained everywhere.

PRESENTATION OF
J. GRAHAM BROWN PORTRAIT
Capitol
Frankfort / May 21, 1970

J. GRAHAM BROWN never sought publicity, but he was deserving of public praise throughout his life.[1] His private acts of kindness touched the lives of those closely associated with him as well as those he never met personally. He was a quiet man whose genius was equaled only by his determination, his initiative, his appreciation of life and opportunity, and his generosity. He respected knowledge and he helped to build and sustain the college that educated him.[2] He appreciated the arts and patronized them faithfully. He loved animals and helped to build a zoo for his adopted city. He believed in sportsmanship, and in that spirit he participated in the sport of horse racing.

He was not a native Kentuckian, a government official, or politician. But his portrait deserves to hang here among the portraits and statues of Kentucky's most famous sons, government leaders, and political figures, because this man believed in Kentucky, he was dedicated to our form of government, and he helped to maintain our political process.

I am pleased to unveil this portrait so that it may hang here as a constant reminder of one whose appreciation and generosity is unparalleled in the history of our Commonwealth. It is being permanently affixed at the Capitol today in the hope that others may follow Mr. Brown's example of concern for Kentucky and its people.

---

1. James Graham Brown (1881–1969) was a Louisville businessman with hotel, lumber, and creosote interests. In his will Mr. Brown left approximately $80 million to the James Graham Brown Foundation, Inc., for philanthropic purposes in Kentucky.
2. Hanover College, Hanover, Indiana.

DEDICATION OF LAKE BARKLEY
STATE PARK LODGE
Cadiz / May 25, 1970

AMID such natural splendor as we see here today, there can be no question in my mind, nor in the minds of those people who designed and created it, nor in the minds of those of you who have seen to it that this magnificent edifice is the crowning jewel for Kentucky's state park system, a system which has already been recognized as the finest and most progressive in the nation. The distinguished architect, Edward Durell Stone, who designed Lake Barkley Lodge, said last week that only at Yellowstone National Park is there a building that compares with this one, that this is the largest and most unusual wooden structure to be built in the United States during the past forty years.

But my coming here today is not merely to dedicate a building, be it wood or stone or mortar. Let us instead rededicate ourselves to the conservation, preservation, and development of Kentucky. The opening of Lake Barkley Lodge is another step in our commitment to this purpose. Barkley and its 3,600 acres of fresh, pure, air and water brings to thirty-seven the number of jewels in Kentucky's unmatched system of parks, resorts, and shrines. Even now, we have under construction lodges at both Barren River and Greenbo Lake. The overnight lodging capacity of our park system will have been increased by 50 percent at the close of this administration. The Army Corps of Engineers and the Tennessee Valley Authority have proposed to us that we assume responsibility for thousands of more acres of land. This land will be developed by us and forever committed by us to the generations of Kentuckians to follow. It will be our purpose to acquire these lands and to develop them for recreation as quickly as possible.

But let us examine that word *recreation*. Let us, for example, break it into two parts, *re-creation*. Here we find the true purpose of Kentucky's park system; unparalleled lands of splendor provided for nature, protected by man, so that man today and mankind to come can always find in Kentucky an unspoiled place of beauty to re-create himself in mind, in body, and in spirit.

In his state of the union message of January 22, 1970, President Nixon asked the great question of the seventies: "Shall we surrender to our surroundings or shall we make our peace with nature and begin to make reparations for the damage we have done to our air, to our

land, and to our water?" In answer let me say that we have not surrendered nor do we intend to do so. We can and will meet this challenge and at the same time attract to Kentucky the new industry that
will provide opportunity for our people. Creation of employment opportunities is genuinely compatible with the preservation and conservation of our environment. Surrender to pollution? Never. Surrender
to the ravaging of the land? Never.

We must never cease in our efforts to bring work to those who
need it to replace the dole with dignity for every Kentuckian. Recreation is a major factor if we are to accomplish this. Here in western
Kentucky, for example, between our parks at Barkley, Kentucky Dam
Village, and Kenlake we are providing jobs for nearly 600 people and
pour into the economy of the area many millions of dollars every year.
We know for a fact that the Land Between the Lakes and all the land
surrounding it will become America's prime tourist attraction, sur-
passing in sheer number of visitors the great national parks of the
western states and the historic attractions of the east. As we continue
to nurture this system, to complete a championship eighteen-hole golf
course, to lay out our riding and hiking trails, to lay out our campgrounds, to build a multipurpose meeting room, Barkley gets even
bigger. But, as I have said before, Barkley and all other Kentucky
state parks should be looked at as seeding for what is well on its way
to becoming Kentucky's major industry—travel and recreation. Last
year alone this industry contributed $510 million to the economy of
Kentucky and $38 million in direct tax revenues.

The price Kentuckians are paying for this installation in no way
detracts from its splendor, but it does give ominous warning for the
future. This building alone cost more than $6 million, nearly 50 percent
of all capital construction funds available to the State Parks System
for the past two years. This lodge represents an investment of nearly
fifty thousand dollars a unit. It is the most elaborate and expensive
of all our overnight park facilities. Its counterpart at Jenny Wiley State
Park, for example, cost less than twenty-five thousand dollars a unit.

We have honored this inherited commitment, but it should be apparent that state government cannot continue to underwrite such an
elaborate travel and recreation effort at the expense of other needed
facilities. It is not our intention to do so. The State has led the way,
and we shall continue to help, but time has come for the private sector
to get more deeply involved in making Kentucky the recreational
heartland of midwest America. There are thousands of acres of lake
front available, and thousands of acres in the woods and streams off
our highways and parkways. Developing these lands with resorts and

campgrounds is just as much "industry" as bringing in new factories.

I want to see Kentuckians have the first opportunity at these developments. Don't let them slip by. Situated as we are at the center of the nation's population, a family population that is increasingly on the move to re-create itself, our Commonwealth can indeed become the land's end, the haven, for which these people search. We can help, and we want to. You can help. We can all work together for benefits that will accrue not only for today, but for the generations that will follow us, the generations that will inherit the greatest possible legacy we can bestow: pure streams, lakes, fresh air, woodlands, and recreational areas which will culminate in a cleaner, more prosperous Kentucky to enjoy.

FRANKFORT HIGH SCHOOL
COMMENCEMENT
Frankfort / May 28, 1970

TONIGHT I speak to my son, to your son and to your daughter, to 45,000 high school seniors, their parents, and their fellow citizens.[1] I speak to you as the proud father of a high school senior, and as the Governor of a great Commonwealth.

Events of the past few weeks make obsolete the usual recitation of timeworn platitudes so dear to the hearts of commencement speakers. For there is today a gathering in the air of something that hates humanity. Our public scene is full to overflowing with irrational love groups and hate groups, irrational peace groups and war groups. Each seems equally zealous, arrogantly certain of its righteousness, and violently insecure in the face of opposing arguments and ideas. Their spokesmen are intolerant of traditional procedures with which they cannot cope. They appear impatient to take matters into their own hands, either to retreat from, or to destroy the institutions of society. Nowhere is this behavior more prevalent than on certain college campuses. It is the unfortunate irony of our time that violence has struck frequently and most tragically at those institutions established by our society for the pursuit of intellectual excellence limited only by the gentle rule of reason. It is into this world, one tainted with turmoil by a treacherous few, that we send tonight some of Kentucky's finest young people.

To you high school seniors we say: You have been loved since the day you were born. We have watched and nurtured your development from birth through grade school and now through high school. You have been given more tangible assets than any other generation in the history of our country. You have lived your life in a period of more comforts and more opportunities than any other graduating class. You have been called the most intelligent, the most enlightened, and the most concerned generation in history. Because of these advantages, no generation has had so much to live up to. Now you face your first step outside the protection of your home. From this day forth, wherever you go, whatever you do, you will cast a reflection on the homes and the parents from which you come. No one will ever love you more or give you better advice than those who have directed you through your early life. However, the training in your home and the teachings of your church can be but the foundation of your emerging maturity. For now you are, or soon will be, legally adults and you shall be fully accountable for your own actions.

Speaking for all parents, guardians, teachers, and friends, we are proud of you. We extend to you our sincerest and warmest congratulations. Now let us look at your future. While the future is bright, there is more need today for common sense, love of God, and love of country than ever before. It is time that those with something to offer are heard. It is not the time for rebellion. It is not the time to listen to those bent on destroying our republic.

As we honor you this evening, so must we honor those whose sacrifices over two centuries have brought us to this place at this time. For this land of ours did not just rise up out of the Atlantic to greet Columbus. It was sought as a refuge from tyrants, conquered at great sacrifice, and nurtured into national maturity by the patriotic appreciation of those ideals that America symbolizes to the world.

In Kentucky and throughout America the sacrifices of the past are prologue to the opportunities of the future. This is particularly true when applied to our educational system. The people of Kentucky have paid unselfishly for the costly privilege of applauding you tonight. Over the years they have shared more and more of their substance with you, so that today almost sixty-eight cents of every general fund tax dollar is allocated to education in our State. By investing millions of tax dollars, a place has been prepared for you in a progressive system of state colleges and universities that has significantly improved Kentucky's educational image.

This system of colleges and universities belongs not just to the professional educational community, and certainly not to a radical student minority; it belongs to all of us. Therefore, if decisions within that system of higher education begin to represent a retreat from reality and tend to reflect the will of a misguided few, then all of us have an interest at stake. All of us have a right to be heard and a duty to speak. This is the duty I discharge tonight.

Events of the past weeks in Kentucky and throughout the nation have focused both scorn and consternation on American colleges. Tonight, as Governor, I want to make clear the policy that government in this State shall pursue relative to our public colleges and universities and to those who use them. These policies should not be misconstrued as a warning to youth. They should be accepted as a pledge to youth. Kentucky shall continue to meet the danger of campus violence. And we shall meet the positive challenge that lies at the heart of student unrest.

These policies were formulated with the understanding that campus disorder and student unrest are not one and the same. It is even more important to understand that those responsible for campus disorder and those caught up in student unrest are not one and the same group. These policies are intended to separate each by his acts and treat him accordingly. Random reaction will not solve specific problems. Only a very small number of students have resorted to violent behavior. The fact that this tiny group is responsible for the chaotic atmosphere that shrouds some of this nation's colleges is testimony to the lack of courage of those who permit it.

On the other hand, student unrest affects a much larger segment. These are students caught between youth and maturity and torn between difficult positions of responsibility. There are other differences. Campus violence is a quirk, peculiar to a small portion of your generation of college students. It is to be abhorred. It can and must be ended. Student unrest is the more natural outgrowth of an idealistic, concerned, and impatient age. It should and must be channeled toward constructive action, not stifled and not shoved toward revolution.

The challenge to find a solution to these two diverse and complex problems now confronts nearly every college administrator and governor in America. Within the past two years Kentucky has addressed itself to the problem and has set an example for the nation by effectively meeting violence while developing innovative outlets for student unrest. These carefully constructed solutions reflect concern for present as well as future generations. Expedient over-reactions have been rejected. Irresponsible concessions and meaningless compromises have been avoided so that effective permanent solutions might be found.

For the violent and unlawful, Kentucky's response has been and will continue to be, one of unyielding firmness. Violence and disruption will not be tolerated. It will not go unpunished. Our answer to this situation is deeply rooted in the belief that the first task of government is the preservation of civil order. To honor that commitment we shall not hesitate to use whatever strength is necessary to put down dangerous and illegal interruptions as soon as possible. Our foremost obligation is to safeguard the purposes for which our public colleges and universities were created.

Clearly, our allegiance must remain with those students, faculty members, and university administrators who want to pursue legitimate educational goals. It is for their benefit that discipline must be maintained. Legal tools must be sharpened and used against professors who advocate anarchy and students who practice disruption. Rules of reason and law dictate that such professors should be fired and such students should be expelled immediately before their sickness spreads. The power to expel has been the legitimate recourse of universities for over 750 years. It must never be denied to Kentucky's system of public higher education.

To meet the recent disturbance at the University of Kentucky, I concluded that a massive show of strength was necessary to make it clear that we would not permit civil authority in Kentucky to be overwhelmed on the campus or elsewhere. Prompt, sufficient response by law enforcement agencies prevented the loss of life and kept the university open. However, damage to property has run well over a quarter of a million dollars. If all available means are not exhausted to recover these damages from those who were responsible, it will be a slap in the face of every Kentucky taxpayer. I urge and encourage university officials to institute civil suit, if necessary, to recover full damages.

These firm methods of dealing with disruption are in the public interest, as well as in the interest of university students. The public and the academic community are not insensitive to the circumstances. They recognize and applaud the action that is needed. Safeguarding the sanctity of life and property has met with overwhelming support. But it also has drawn predictable criticism from the radicals, their allies and sympathizers, and the uninformed. These groups have claimed repression. They have charged that constitutional rights of assembly and speech have been violated. They have dared to claim justification for their senseless destruction because of the presence of the police. The courts have found these claims unjustified in Kentucky.

These criticisms must be answered not because of their validity—they are not valid—but because some would like to sweep them toward credibility by creating a tide of national hysteria. To these critics, let us say that the strong hand of our society must be maintained not only to help those who are unable to help themselves, but it must also be used without hesitation to restrain those who would destroy our society. Too much sympathy already has been wasted on a few in freakish garb who pause between obscenities to advocate freedom of speech and then shout down those who dare to speak out against them. Too many academic buildings have been burned or occupied by mobs waving nonnegotiable demands and mocking society with their indecent language. It is a national disgrace that some of our heretofore respected educators and high elected officials have shown more concern for the mobs than for their victims. If my generation continues to abdicate its responsibilities, your generation will inherit a lawless society in which the might of muscle has replaced the right of reason.

The disrupters may regard these remarks as inflammatory. If so, let it be regarded as an admission of their guilt, and not an excuse for their actions. What is truly inflammatory, particularly to those who support education with their taxes and to the many responsible students and faculty members, is the reckless threat to life and the senseless destruction of property.

For instance, during the ten years from 1960 to 1970, when disrespect for those over thirty became fashionable and disruption came into vogue among the radicals, Kentucky taxpayers, 80 percent of whom are over thirty, paid over $500 million to support this State's system of higher education. These same working citizens paid the bill when Kentucky's program to provide higher education for all its young people created staggering demands on all of our colleges and universities. College enrollment in this State increased by 122 percent during the last decade, and Kentucky responded by adding to its system the most modern and fully equipped facilities to be found in the nation. Yet, tuition at our public universities remains one of the best educational bargains offered anywhere. It is time we remember for what and for whom these sacrifices were made.

As long as certain opinion leaders and some members of the journalism fraternity persist in their determination to equate bad news with big news they perpetuate the injustice of allowing the loudest and most radical to speak for your generation. Society defeats its purpose by lavishing publicity on those who have no useful solutions.

And what of those among the young who are concerned for the preservation of our basic institutions, who diligently pursue legitimate academic goals, who appreciate the opportunities their parents and their government have provided, who quietly go about their business and find no gratification in mob acceptance, no intellectual value in a disorderly appearance, and no advantage in establishing a police record. It is in this category that all but a handful of this year's graduating seniors will be numbered. They deserve our support; they justify our confidence; they encourage us to plan for the future. They have rights, too: the right to study, to attend class, to take examinations, and to be honored at commencement without fear of arson, intimidation, or interruption. It is because of them that we must never allow the forces of civil order to be outnumbered or overcome. It was they who inspired Kentucky's innovative response to their desire and their need to be heard.

Kentucky has set the pace for the nation in opening channels of communication and participation to young people. Eighteen-year-olds have voted for almost fifteen years. Kentucky was the first state in the nation to welcome student leaders to membership on the boards of all public colleges and universities. State government in the Commonwealth has established a productive relationship with the young. A number of America's most able young leaders hold major positions of responsibility in the present state administration. A student Advisory Council to the Governor was formed eighteen months ago and includes elected student leaders from public and private colleges. Some of our most intellectually gifted students brought new and constructive ideas to state government during the weekend brainstorming sessions. And students have gained firsthand knowledge of government through Kentucky's unique student Legislative Intern program and its accelerated summer employment effort.

Tonight I am pleased to announce that another opportunity for participation will soon be invested in our young people. Because it is the young who will inherit our land, and because the duty to protect the quality of our environment will reach life or death dimensions during their adulthood, young people deserve a meaningful role in the design of public policies dealing with pollution control. Therefore, I shall appoint qualified students to serve on the State Air Pollution Control Commission. They will have full rights and responsibilities of membership. With this latest vote of confidence in the ability and the stability of a huge majority of our young people, let us again disprove the claim that our system of government is closed.

To say that these programs were solely responsible for the tranquility that has characterized Kentucky the past two years would be unfair. But it would be fair to say that they have helped. Their success was assured because virtually all young Kentuckians have shown a mature sense of responsibility, a deep respect for the law, and a strong faith in an established system of government of, by, and for the people.

These same principles have been supported with equal vigor on our state campuses. It is up to you and your generation to ensure that they shall endure. The maintenance of order is in everyone's interest. Those who would risk anarchy to achieve their ends are a threat to legitimate dissent. People can rally and speak and express opinions and seek changes without disrupting academic activities, throwing stones, or burning buildings. As long as our Republic remains free, the end can never justify unlawful means.

If our universities are to survive, it is not the state police and National Guard but the students themselves by their own responsible conduct who must form the first line of defense. It is imperative that students and faculty totally repudiate those who bring unlawful disruption to the campus and take every possible step to separate themselves from such individuals and groups. It is important that students help the universities survive because of the key role these institutions play in human society.

Higher education must seek both to stimulate man toward individual excellence and inspire him to appreciate his responsibilities to other men. If this is the true purpose of the university—and I believe it is—then some of the political and social demands being made on it today must be rejected as incompatible.

As any educational institution becomes fragmented into warring parties, the creative potential for that institution is drastically reduced and valuable resources of time and energy are dissipated in waging war. Neither you nor the society from which you have sprung can afford this cruel waste, for the problems of tomorrow, like those of today, will require solutions that can only be provided by trained leadership. There is but one source of this leadership: young people like yourselves standing on the threshold of maturity, daily making decisions that will shape your destinies and those of the world around you. These decisions must be made in a time of great social turmoil and in an atmosphere hostile to clear thinking. I believe you are capable of meeting this challenge. I have confidence in your ability to choose wisely.

The manner in which you go forth tonight into a vocational, professional, or academic world will live with you forever. Some will attempt to use you. But it is our expectation that you will rise above their level and speak out for America.

Remember, no one gets something for nothing. Change is brought about by informed leadership. It requires sustained, dedicated effort. Be yourself. Use your power of reasoning. Use your intelligence to gain a sound education and a strong conviction of what is right and what is wrong. Speak softly and with purpose. Be at peace with God, whatever you conceive Him to be. Whatever your labors and aspirations in the noisy confusion of life, keep peace with your soul. You are a child of the universe. Respect the counsel of previous generations. Gracefully surrender the things of youth. And then, my son, you will be a man.[2]

---

1. Stephen Roberts Nunn, the Governor's son, was among the graduating seniors at the commencement. Larry Van Hoose, Governor Nunn's press secretary, September 15, 1971.

2. The lines "Be at peace with God, whatever you conceive Him to be," "You are a child of the universe," and "Gracefully surrender[ing] the things of youth" are from the "Desiderata," by Max Ehrmann in *The Poems of Max Ehrmann*, ed. Bertha K. Ehrmann (Boston, 1948), p. 83. The "Desiderata" has been widely circulated with the citation "Found in old St. Paul's Church —Baltimore, dated 1692," which is in error.

KENTUCKY FEDERATION OF REPUBLICAN WOMEN
Cumberland Falls State Park
Corbin / June 11, 1970

MORE than two decades of Kentucky politics have proven that you ladies can bring a special kind of excitement into the political arena. This isn't anything new. Throughout history, all the way from Cleopatra to Martha Mitchell, women have added another dimension to what has often been misconstrued as a man's world.[1] Politics needs the woman's touch, and women truly concerned about their world need politics. Concerned, committed ladies such as you have given politics a new measure of respect, and I commend especially this organization for the constructive force it has been in shaping a new political majority in our State.

Tonight I ask for your help again. Not for myself—I ask in the interest of good government and a better Kentucky. I ask for your dedication in preserving the gains that two-party government has made in our State. I ask your continued support for the ideals on which our party was founded, a party that believes in the rights and the wisdom of the people, one that continues to cherish and embrace this great Republic in which we live, and one that protects the representative form of government as the best yet devised.

Along with these requests for your help, I suggest tonight a plan that can effectively, realistically carry us from tonight's theme "Together We Did" to tomorrow's challenge "Together We Shall." This plan is not new and its simplicity may account for the fact that it has never been used to full effectiveness. Consider first the fact that until 1967, the Republicans had not held the governor's office for twenty years. We were out of office so long that the biggest problem we had was convincing our own party members we could win. And during that time, it became fashionable to rationalize our defeats by reciting the registration figures. It is true we are outnumbered approximately two-to-one, but the time has come when we must do something more about it than use the figures to console ourselves in defeat. We don't have to be outnumbered two-to-one. The people of Kentucky are no longer slaves to a party label. They saw right here in their own Commonwealth the results of one-party domination over a number of years. I believe we have shown a better way to run government for the people the past two years.

Let me recite some other interesting figures: Of Kentucky's 3.2 million people, about half, or 1.5 million, are registered to vote. And approximately 400,000 citizens who are eligible to vote are not registered. Now how do these figures relate to elections past and future? I can speak from experience on this point, if I may be personal for a moment. Remember the 1963 governor's race, when we needed only 13,000 votes to win, when victory was in our grasp, but slipped through our fingers? Just four unregistered voters in each precinct would have made the difference between victory and defeat.

There are some other important statistics that your organization should consider in planning for 1971. Since 1935 our party has failed to win in only one statewide gubernatorial election when we have received as much as 80 percent of the Republican vote. The only exception came in 1963. Four hundred thousand unregistered voters and 80 percent of our party's vote—translating into political reality these figures clearly underscores the lost opportunities of the past twenty years. That part of our past can be the prologue to the future of our party only if it serves to warn us of the pitfalls that lie ahead. The victories that were won during those same years offer hope and indicate a direction for the future. And it is the future that we must concern ourselves with tonight.

I trust that a minimum of our effort will be expended needlessly in the selecting of the candidate for 1971. And by the same token I trust that a maximum effort will go toward preparing our party for victory in 1971.[2] The depth of Republican leadership on local, state, and national levels affords our party an opportunity to present to the voters one of the most complete, the most dynamic, and the most talented selections in our history. The choice of individual candidates for specific positions on the Republican ticket in 1971 is not the task of one man alone. These are decisions in which all of us can and must participate. *But we have an obligation to our unparalleled chance for success in 1971 to make the selection process a constructive rather than a destructive one.* The senior senator from Kentucky shares my optimism for 1971.[3] On numerous occasions it has been said, and I firmly believe, that not only could Senator Cooper be elected governor in 1971, but other Republican candidates can be elected governor as well.

I trust that whoever carries the Republican banner in 1971 will find comfort and inspiration in the support of Kentucky's Republican women. They will need your special talents, your deep concern, and your sensitivity to the problems and the issues that confront the people of our State. Only one who has experienced your support, your trust, and your understanding, as I have during countless campaigns and especially during the last two and one-half years, can fully appreciate all that you are capable of giving. Recalling the sacrifices and contributions that you have so generously made to the success of the Republican Party in the past, I have no doubt about the future.

---

1. Martha Mitchell, wife of John N. Mitchell, attorney general of the United States, 1969–1973.

2. A deletion was made at this point. The omitted section consisted of a review of administrative accomplishments, a call for an ambitious voter registration campaign, and an expression of confidence in the election of a Republican governor in 1971.

3. Senator John Sherman Cooper (1901–　), Somerset, United States Senator (1946–1948, 1952–1954, 1956–1972); United States delegate, General Assembly, United Nations (1949, 1950, 1951, 1968); United States Ambassador to India and Nepal (1955–1956). *Who's Who in American Politics, 1969–1970,* p. 242.

REDEDICATION OF
CHANDLER ISLAND
Burnside State Park

Somerset / June 16, 1970

MANY men have served as Governor of our Commonwealth, each in his own way leaving his mark, each making his contribution, some great, some small. The one we honor today was held in such high esteem that not once—but twice—his fellow citizens chose him to serve as their governor.[1] I cannot say today that I have agreed with all he has done in his long career as a public servant. We have disagreed before and probably will disagree again in the future. But I recognize, as do many others of our Commonwealth, that this man has made notable contributions to the progress of our people and our purposes of representative government. And the fact that we are of different political faiths, the fact that we have vigorously engaged in public affairs from different, sometimes diametrically opposing viewpoints, does not change the fact that here is a man who has accomplished much good in his lifetime.

Our differences will not permit me to deny him the public acknowledgment he deserves. Because I now hold the office from which he made his most significant contributions, I fully appreciate the trying circumstances under which many of the decisions of a governor must be made, even when the most noble and generous purposes are truly desired. And certainly it would not be fitting for me, or for any other man who is chosen governor, to desecrate the dignity of that office by tearing down the accomplishments and abolishing the symbols of gratitude that the people might bestow on preceding governors. If I or any man were to choose this course, it could only be evidence of envy, prejudice, and even hatred. There is no place in Kentucky or in America, particularly in public life, for those who would demonstrate these most undesirable characteristics. Vindictiveness and intolerance such as that must be taken as a sign of the smallness of those who display it in their decisions.

When this beautiful lake was constructed, Governor Chandler was serving his State. His appreciation for the opportunities this development held for the surrounding area, and his desire to create a place of recreation and relaxation in which man and nature could be at peace one with another, won the appreciation of members of both parties serving at that time, not only at the local, but at the state and national levels. And even though he urged that this island be named for another man, the people caused his name to be placed here in tribute to his assistance and concern.

Years later his enemies uprooted the very plaques commemorating his contribution and threw them into the waters of the lake he helped to make possible. They acted as though the waters of Lake Cumberland might somehow wash away the memory of his good works.

Today we return to General Burnside State Park to memorialize one who demonstrated his deep concern for the welfare of our people; to restore to its proper place this plaque, placed here by his fellow Kentuckians, and telling of his devotion for them; and hopefully to write a proper ending to a bitter chapter in the old politics that darkened Kentucky's future for so long.

---

1. Albert B. Chandler (1898–   ), governor of Kentucky (1935–1939, 1955–1959), candidate for governor (1935, 1955, 1963, 1967, 1971); United States Senator (1939–1945); lieutenant governor (1931–1935). Governor Chandler was commissioner of American baseball (1945–1951), is from Versailles, and is presently a member of the Commonwealth party (formerly a Democrat). Department of Public Information biographical files.

CHESAPEAKE AND OHIO BRIDGE DEMOLITION
Covington / June 18, 1970

DURING the past two and one-half years there have been many bridge and highway dedications in which I have been pleased to participate. They are constructive, inspiring events which help the people measure Kentucky's progress in providing safe, modern transportation facilities. And these events serve also to rededicate us to the belief that government has a solemn responsibility to make good and prudent use of public funds, a responsibility not only to build, but to maintain the public properties. It is a sad and tragic journey from the dedication to the deterioration of a bridge. Unfortunately, it is a journey Kentuckians have learned all too well, one we have been forced by disgraceful circumstances to acknowledge too many times during the past two and one-half years. Upon taking office, this administration uncovered 171 bridges in need of emergency repairs. Some, like this one, were found beyond repair, doomed to destruction because for nearly a decade the only attention they received was a promise and sometimes a coat of paint.

The C & O Bridge suffered for years in silence; to my knowledge no one in northern Kentucky, and certainly no one in Frankfort, raised his voice in defense of this once fine and useful servant of the traveling public. Because it was permitted to suffer in silence, because the cancer of neglect and disrepair was permitted to spread for years, inspectors found that the C & O Bridge was too near collapse to be treated. So today it falls our lot to conduct a requiem for this graceful landmark, a bridge that died from the fatal disease of neglect.

It is neglect that forces us here today. It is neglect that causes us to spend millions of dollars to replace a bridge that, by all rights, should have been in service for years to come. I regret that this occasion is necessary. I regret that all the architectural genius, the engineering skill, the public concern, and the taxpayers' money that went into the construction of this bridge were not properly respected by persons in responsible positions previous to this administration. I sincerely regret the frustrating inconvenience that motorists have endured in recent months. And I regret that lives were endangered by the neglect of the past. Fortunately, the danger was detected and ended before the loss of life occurred. And I am here to assure you today that the inconvenience you have suffered will be ended as soon as possible and a new bridge will be erected here as quickly and as judiciously as possible.

Choosing an appropriate name for the new bridge was a special challenge because of the special nature of this project. Hopefully, the new bridge will stand for ages as a daily reminder that we have closed the ancient gap between northern Kentucky and Frankfort. Hopefully, this bridge will truthfully represent the faith, the confidence, and the understanding we have in this section of the Commonwealth. And finally, this bridge must stand as a durable adversary of governmental neglect. The man for whom we have decided to name this bridge has worked for thirty-three years to close the communications gap between your section and Frankfort. He represents a durable and considerate friend of the truth, and a persistent foe of governmental inefficiency and neglect. With a unique talent for fairness and a deep loyalty to the truth, Clay Wade Bailey has probed amid the public affairs of our

Commonwealth for more than four decades as a respected newsman and concerned citizen.[1] Therefore, we deem it highly appropriate that the new bridge be named in his honor.

It has been said that bridges, unlike other public facilities, assume an individual character with age and use. I trust this bridge will assume the character of the man for whom it is being named; if it can leave such an honorable and indelible mark on our memory as Clay Wade Bailey has, the people of northern Kentucky need never fear that the new bridge will fall victim to neglect.

---

1. Clay Wade Bailey (1905–1974), Frankfort, capitol reporter for the Covington-based *Kentucky Post & Times Star* (1938–1974) and for the *Louisville Courier-Journal* (1928–1938). Interview with Bailey, Frankfort, August 30, 1971.

TENNESSEE-TOMBIGBEE
WATERWAY AUTHORITY
Fort Walton Beach, Florida / July 13, 1970

HOPEFULLY, today's meeting signals the end to what surely will be the most arduous phase in the development of the Tennessee-Tombigbee Waterway. Because it is our hope and our full expectation that, by this time next year, we finally will have moved this vital project from the fertile minds of our forefathers to actual construction.

Needless to say, it has been a long and difficult journey from the time, more than a century ago, when the Tennessee-Tombigbee Waterway was first envisioned to next spring when construction is expected to begin. And today, as we pause at this important juncture in the life of the project, it may be well for each of us to reassess and reevaluate our stake in the waterway, to justify our respective states' participation, and to consider a new proposal for enlightened, planned utilization of America's rivers and streams in the future.

Kentucky's stake in this effort is the same as that of each member. That stake is progress, progress toward the economic and cultural and environmental goals to which our section of the country is moving with unparalleled speed today. Kentucky joined the other member states of the Authority because we share wholeheartedly their confidence and their conviction that the Tennessee-Tombigbee Waterway is vital to the development of the entire southeastern section of America.

Being a crossroads state between the North and the South has made Kentuckians well aware of the importance and the significance of total transportation facilities. Like many of you, we are eagerly and successfully competing for industrial growth, most of it from the North. And we have come to realize that one of the most crucial portions of our portfolio when we are talking to industrial prospects is transportation.

Manufacturers want to know where they can get the necessary raw materials for their products. They want to know how long it will take to get raw materials. And certainly they want to know how much it will cost. If we can give the right answers to these questions, and we will be better able to when the Tennessee-Tombigbee Waterway is completed, then we can turn the proposition around by 180 degrees and apply the questions of where, how long, and how much to the more profitable aspects of industrialization, the shipment of their finished products.

Kentucky is fortunate that it can usually answer these particular questions to industry's complete satisfaction. You will excuse a bit of provincial pride if I remind you that Kentucky has more miles of natural navigable waterway than any other state in the nation. And, in addition, we are within twenty-four hours by highway of two-thirds of the country's population, and only two hours away from 70 percent of the nation's population by air.

Certainly, these facts have given dramatic impetus to our drive for new corporate citizens. In flying over the Ohio River (which, incidentally, Kentucky owns) one is seldom out of sight of barge traffic. It is a reassuring sign of emerging prominence in the field of industrial development. But, like each of you, we are not content to live in the past or to think only of past accomplishments or present efforts. We, too, are planning for the future. This future includes the need to develop a more comprehensive grasp of river environment and a more complete knowledge of our rivers, a need that naturally encourages us to turn to our colleges and universities for help.

In 1835, the Congress became concerned with the lack of broad understanding of another enormous resource, our land. Out of this congressional concern came a proposal which President Lincoln signed into law authorizing land-grant colleges. As you know, this legislation provided financial assistance to colleges devoted to the study of the land, particularly as an agricultural resource. The knowledge generated by land-grant colleges has made American soil the richest agricultural resource in the world and has enabled us to share generously the fruits of our land with the people of the world.

In 1966 Congress turned its attention to another of our natural resources and passed a law establishing the sea-grant college. This concept has provided for comprehensive academic examination and exploration of our oceans within existing colleges and universities. Much of the applied concentration of the land-grant college approach has spilled over into the sea-grant concept.

Today there is a new need and a new concern, the preservation and enhancement of America's rivers. To meet this new need I propose that we carry the land-grant and sea-grant concepts a dramatic step further by establishing river-grant colleges. River-grant colleges can eradicate the lopsided use of our navigable streams as merely avenues for travel and can provide entry to many of the opportunities our rivers offer a growing nation. Just as scholars in the land-grant college developed a passion for the land, a river-grant college can instill a new and crucial passion for our flowing waterways.

This focus on our rivers and streams can be instrumental not only in developing new systems of transportation—such as the Tennessee-Tombigbee Waterway—but also in finding ways to preserve flowing water. We can reverse the current role of our universities of merely calling attention to the pollution of our rivers and streams, and pointing an academic finger at those who are responsible. We can provide our universities a system whereby students can study and seek real solutions to this plague of modern society.

Our rivers today figure prominently in recreation, urban planning, open space conservation, and water resource planning—they are no longer merely avenues of transportation. A broad understanding of our rivers can coordinate wasteful single-use projects into more economical multi-use projects.

The river-grant system can also explore and bring forth carefully studied methods of environment protection which encourage productivity without pollution. By approaching rivers as an environment we can begin to meet the ultimate challenge: governing their anxious and ambitious exploiters with reason and balance. Let us be mindful always of the fact that by failure to utilize our rivers productively, we squander this great resource just as surely as when we pollute our streams. The river-grant college which I envision could add meaningfully to the crucial task of striking a balance between productivity and preservation of our streams.

Such balance is particularly crucial to Kentucky, as well as the other members of this organization, because the Tennessee-Tombigbee Waterway represents yet another outlet for the abundant natural resources and mineral wealth of our part of America. Those in the western Kentucky coalfields have anxiously followed the slow but improving pace at which this project has begun to move.

All of us are aware that an acute power shortage is developing throughout the nation and in this section particularly, as industrial growth in the South begins to outpace our ability to provide the necessary ancillary services. This is, in itself, perhaps one of the most viable reasons that coal production in Kentucky has undergone such a dramatic rise in the past few years. Only last year, we produced 101 million tons, the highest total in our history, and we are now second in production in the United States. There is little doubt that events and circumstances already are conspiring to make Kentucky the number one coal-producing state. I refer, of course, to our abundant supply of coal; to the increasing demand for coal that has been brought by the industrialization of our own State, as well as our neighbors to the south; and perhaps more importantly, our proximity and accessibility to that demand.

Then, too, agriculture in our State and in all the states represented here is following the national trend toward selectivity and specialization, thus creating a far greater demand than ever before for export facilities. The value of our grain, pasture crops, and livestock, as well as coal, would be greatly enhanced with the completion of the Tennessee-Tombigbee Waterway.

Frankly, what I am saying to you is this: when the industrial North and the industrial South grow to the point that their borders, and perhaps their barriers, are crossed, then Kentucky fully intends to seize its unique opportunity to become the meeting ground and the focal point of this important economic merger.

But what I have said of the Kentucky economy can be applied to our several states. We all have our respective contributions to make to the economic well-being of our citizens and to the gross national product.

We realize that this will only happen if we continue to expand and develop our image and our role as "The Crossroads State of Eastern America." That is why we have joined this effort to open a new avenue of transportation and that is why we share your excitement for the fact that the Tennessee-Tombigbee Waterway stands today on the brink of reality.

Last year I said I looked forward to participating in the groundbreaking ceremonies for this project during my term as Chairman of the Authority. And now, more than ever before, I believe that I will. Because finally, our visits to Washington have been rewarded in the most positive way. President Nixon has heard the story of the Tennessee-Tombigbee Waterway. And he has responded to our request for assistance by including $1 million in his budget in order that construction may begin. Now that the United States House of Representatives has approved the President's allocation of funds, the only hurdle that remains is concurrence by the Senate. While we are optimistic about Senate approval, certainly we must continue to work faithfully in support of the project until final action is completed.

Speaking for those who have preceded me as Chairman and for those who have and are working to make the Tennessee-Tombigbee Waterway a reality, in closing let me thank you for your support and your concern. Together we can all anticipate the start of construction next year with pride in the knowledge that the future of our respective states, the progress of our South, and the strength of our nation will have been measurably assisted by the efforts that have been made.

MIDWESTERN GOVERNORS'
CONFERENCE
Columbus, Ohio / July 21, 1970

In our State we have a slogan for development—"Every Kentuckian Counts." Our emphasis is on total development, and to this end, we welcome the efforts of the Office of Economic Opportunity and their implementing agencies—the State Economic Opportunity Offices and the Community Action Agencies. Through the efforts of these agencies some good has been accomplished in such areas as Project Head Start, job training, and health services. But in the past there has been a missing link in OEO efforts which may have prevented any final and complete success. There has been little or no permanence in breaking the cycle of poverty. Although the conditions of some poor have improved, too few have actually graduated from poverty.

Opportunity for the poor cannot be provided by OEO programs which are isolated from the balance of community life. It must be provided by other public and private development within a state, development which does not always seem and actually is not always directly pointed at helping the poor. For example, health programs cannot just work for better health for the poor; they must work for better health for the whole community. Thus, the poor benefit as members of the community and not as "the poor" in the community. When programs created to help the poor tend instead to isolate the poor, the opportunity to escape the cycle of poverty is tragically limited. Predictably, isolation leads to degradation. The invaluable assets of dignity and self-worth are lost, and polarization of the poor from a society seeking only to help is perpetuated. Under such circumstances as these, we should not be surprised when the poor begin to march to the beat of another drum, the drum of the misguided, and sometimes militant, using the cause of the poor for their own selfish or political reasons.

In the past, OEO has had many enemies on both sides of the poverty barrier. The loudest voices are from those dissatisfied with the lack of permanency in breaking the poverty cycle. The President has expressed a willingness, no later than last week in Louisville, to do something about this problem. In recent actions he has made it clear that the emphasis of OEO should be less on continued services and more on developmental enterprises, specifically those affecting both the jobless and the working poor.

It is becoming more obvious each day that the old approach to poverty, a sort of Band-Aid treatment of the problem, only deals with symptoms. It does not deal effectively with causes. In recent months, however, there has been evidence of a shift in approaches. For example, in March the Office of Economic Opportunity issued a new policy instruction to expand and improve the participation of state governments in agency programs. I have been assured this is only one of a series of steps being taken to strengthen state and local participation in poverty programs.

As governors, certainly we must recognize that this new policy throws the gauntlet of responsible partnership action directly at the feet of the states. The new policy appears to take into consideration the unique role of states when it says: "The State Economic Opportunity Office shall give priority to the mobilization and coordination of antipoverty resources, particularly at the state level. This requires effective inter-agency mechanisms to assure good communication between state agencies and offices whose activities affect the poor." To me this means the State Economic Opportunity Office should not be viewed as a federal agency acting as an outsider in the State. It should act as a state agency whose programs are to be coordinated with other state agencies. As such, each State Economic Opportunity Office will participate in annual Community Action Agency *previews* and state operational funding plans for grantees within their states.

I believe the national administration realizes that total development is necessary to bring progress out of poverty. That is how I interpret the June 1970 statement prescribing a general direction for Community Action Agencies. This statement points out that the Community Action Agencies shouldn't attempt to solve all the problems of the poor or expect to become the master planner and coordinator of all social programs in the community. Rather, it says that their programs "must serve the larger purpose of stimulating broader community effort." I interpret this to mean that the Community Action Agencies must be aware of and work within the total development concept. They must emphasize full utilization of all resources—state, local, and private—for the betterment of all. And above all else, they must help stimulate the willingness and the ability of the poor to be involved in determining their own destiny. The programs we formulate to help the poor must never disregard the human elements involved—the deep sense of individuality and pride that characterizes the people of midwest America. Our people don't want a handout, they want a hand up.

All of this points to a greater realization of the advantages and the opportunities of a federal-state-local and private partnership for development. Not one of these can operate at top efficiency in isolation. During the course of remarks to State Economic Opportunity Office Directors in 1969, Director Rumsfeld said, "Words like 'coordination,' 'cooperation,' and 'participation' can easily become lip-service phrases surrounding a policy of inactivity. But I intend to see that these words mean what they say in relationship to the Office of Economic Opportunity and to the states. This new posture is consistent with the overall administration policy of giving states a greater share of the responsibility for the operation of government programs in our federally structured system."

I am pleased Mr. Rumsfeld is determined to follow the mandate of our federally structured system. At the same time, I agree with his statement that "There is no question about the past record of local governments—including state governments—not performing well in certain areas. That's why many programs ended up with the federal government."[1] In the past the states may have earned that reputation, but in the last several years, we have witnessed the emergence of a greater capacity on the part of the states to enhance development through comprehensive planning and coordination.

What we are trying to say to Washington and to OEO, Mr. Rumsfeld, is that the government closest to the people offers the best opportunity to serve the people. And what we are also trying to say, particularly as it affects the success of the effort to help those deserving of help, is that we shall not fail to accept our responsibility and our right to be involved on an equal basis in solving our problems and in seizing our opportunities to advance our respective states and their people.

---

1. Donald Rumsfeld (1932–   ), director of the United States Office of Economic Opportunity (1969–1970); appointed director of the United States Cost of Living Council in 1971. Files of the Kentucky State Office of Economic Opportunity; and Donald Rumsfeld, "How Controls Will Be Enforced," *U.S. News and World Report* 13 (December 1971): 42–43.

GROUNDBREAKING FOR CENTRAL KENTUCKY ANIMAL DISEASE DIAGNOSTIC LABORATORY
Lexington / July 30, 1970

THIS year, of course, marks the beginning of a new decade. But more than that, it marks the start of a new century for Kentucky. This is a convenient intersection in human events, an interlude to take stock of our progress and our problems, and a proper time to set new courses of action. But because these are tumultuous and uncertain times in our nation and around the world, reflection too easily and too often turns to remorse. It is easier to talk about problems than to solve them. And it suits some purposes to speak constantly about what is wrong rather than what is right.

In our own State for too many years there have been those who have talked so much about failure that we have forgotten about success. This is particularly true of those who frequently discuss Kentucky's agriculture. While we are at this intersection of history, and while we have come together to break ground for such a positive cause, let us talk about the positive aspects of our State and particularly of our agricultural community. Let's talk about the tremendous productivity of our farmers. And above all, let's talk about the boundless opportunities that are in store for every Kentucky farmer.

We should not face the future with remorse, but with realism. We must not succumb to the epidemic of doom some would promote throughout this nation. We realize that vital economic problems are facing America, and they must concern each of us. But we can look to recent events within our own borders for hope and reassurance. For instance, in eastern Kentucky, coal production and coal prices are up dramatically. Together with the industrial breakthrough experienced during the past two years, these developments signal the return of economic vitality to that region. In western Kentucky, a $175 million industrial investment has just been announced. Anaconda Aluminum's decision to locate here is evidence that our march toward a new industrial age is continuing, despite somewhat unfavorable national economic circumstances.

These advances are all the more important because they come at a time when the state's agricultural economy has achieved an all-time record. For the first time in history, Kentucky's gross farm income reached and surpassed the billion dollar mark in 1969. The message in these accomplishments is that a new, balanced economic foundation is emerging here, a foundation based on the equally dynamic growth of agriculture and industry. If balanced growth can be maintained and if the economic foundation now under construction can be permanently secured, there is no question of Kentucky's future. What we are seeing today is the embryonic stage in the life of a new national leader in agricultural and industrial development. The key word in Kentucky's progress must continue to be "balance," and the key question for the farm community today is, "How will it respond to this challenge?"

If agriculture is to keep pace and hold its own as an economic factor, we must immediately resolve several crucial issues. One is the population shift which has been tentatively documented by the 1970 census. The loss of farm population exceeded perhaps even the most pessimistic estimates, decreasing by nearly a quarter million persons or 45 percent in only ten years. Among these are the young persons who have been forced or have chosen to look elsewhere for their livelihoods. This loss clearly presents the most persistent challenge in the decade ahead. But in addition to the absence of strong, vigorous, well-trained young farmers, agricultural interests apparently must now face perhaps a significant loss in legislative representation. If legislative reapportionment is necessitated by the reported shift in population, all Kentuckians must be aware of and must studiously avoid a destructive battle between urban and rural interests. Such a fight can only weaken the cause of each and can leave needless obstacles in the path of progress. This need not occur if we remember that this State will not be a good place for any of us to live in if it is not a reasonably good place for all of us to live.

In the days ahead I am hopeful that the out-migration of farm families will be ended. A partial solution to this problem may be a provision that is included in the statewide bond issue to be voted upon in November. One of the basic causes for a drop in farm population is the difficulty of many farmers to obtain the capital that is necessary to purchase or improve farm property. I believe very strongly that we can and we must give encouragement to the ownership and operation of small-acreage farms. By guaranteeing all or a portion of farm loans, many of our farmers will be able to continue operation and many young Kentuckians will be able to purchase farms of their own. The General Obligation Bond Issue now before the voters of this State provides $400,000 to stand as a guarantee for such loans under the Farm Development Authority Act passed last spring by the Legislature.[1] It has been estimated that this fund will be multiplied by private lenders to more than $10 million and will provide a significant incentive for agricultural growth.

In addition to the dwindling farm population, the development of Kentucky's farm economy also hinges on another issue, the protection of our tobacco industry as this State's major cash crop. Recent emotional attacks, restrictive governmental controls, and a growing insistence on discriminating taxation threaten the future of this vital crop. We now have two clear alternatives: First, we can and we must try to protect tobacco, through research, through technology, and through careful legislative action. Secondly, we must continue to develop the livestock industry to stand as a viable contributor to our farm economy. In 1969 the livestock industry demonstrated its potential as the touchstone of Kentucky's agricultural growth in the future. And despite the record-breaking accomplishments of last year, experts all agree that we have barely scratched the surface of our capability. Good pasture land, a stable forage supply, suitable climate, and dedicated farm manpower are available in abundant supply to guarantee Kentucky's place among the nation's leading livestock states. In addition, we are blessed with the geographical proximity and modern transportation facilities necessary for marketing success.

Today, in hopes that the future of the livestock industry will be enriched, we begin construction of a second animal diagnostic laboratory.

When this facility is completed, Kentucky will be unmatched in the technical support it provides for the livestock industry. One million dollars has been committed for the completion of this facility. And for this investment we shall expect full service, rendered at no cost, to the farmers of central and eastern Kentucky, no matter how large or how small their operations. In the years to come, it is my hope that this and other technical resources available to our farmers will serve as a daily reminder of our determination that Kentucky's farm families are not forgotten. And let it also stand as one of the milestones in Kentucky's march toward a balanced prosperity in which all our citizens can share according to their efforts.

---

1. For further information concerning the General Obligation Bond Issue and the Farm Development Authority Act, see the March 2, 1970, legislative message on the bond issue.

THIRD KENTUCKY CONFERENCE ON VOCATIONAL EDUCATION
Louisville / August 12, 1970

WE all have seen a growing trend in parental thinking that education is the answer to their children's happiness and success. And I think it only natural that they carry this line of thinking one step further and conclude that the more education the better, regardless of the aptitude and interests of their children. All of us have to believe that education is the strongest single determining factor in the lives of a free people. And I trust this country shall always be reminded that education is the strongest and best guarantee we have that America shall remain free. That is the reason why government at all levels today spends most of its available revenue for education. That is why Kentucky taxpayers have consented to the allocation of sixty-eight cents of every state General Fund tax dollar for education.

But I believe it is time more parents consider what kind of education best suits the needs and desires of their children. And I believe it is past the time those of you in education and those of us in government look and respond positively to those needs. I am concerned very deeply, just as you are, that in the minds of too many people today, education is translated to mean a college degree. Well-intentioned legislators and educators have contributed to that misconception by declaring that the only requirement for entrance into Kentucky's system of higher education is a diploma from an accredited state high school.

Let there be no misunderstanding: I believe in and I have worked very hard to provide the opportunity for a college education to every Kentuckian. Record appropriations have been made during this administration to enlarge and develop our colleges and universities. We have fought successfully to keep tuition within the reach of most parents and working students. And we have taken and we shall continue to take whatever measures are necessary to keep our colleges free from a relative handful of radicals who would destroy the academic freedom of the majority of Kentucky students who seek an education, not a confrontation, and not a demonstration.

Every Kentuckian deserves the opportunity to go to college. That is not the question. The question is: Should every Kentuckian go to college? Most parents seem absolutely obsessed with the necessity of a college education for their children. I am concerned that this desire is prompted more out of a yearning to "keep up with the Joneses" than to satisfy the realistic educational needs of their children. And I deplore the trend to view a college degree as a status symbol of an affluent age, rather than the true symbol of solid intellectual achievement and capacity.

No one can blame a mother and father for wanting their children to have more advantages and opportunities, more comforts and more security than they might have had. But I detest and condemn those intellectual snobs sequestered away from reality in academic ivory towers who lead parents to believe that their children will become society's outcasts without a college degree. Too many people are swallowing that philosophy already. And as a result, we see today a young generation convinced that a college degree is the only passport to dignity and success in our society. Parents aren't the only ones so believing. Government officials, high school principals, guidance counselors, classroom teachers, and curriculum experts have gone along, too.

We hear the results every day. You live with the results. It happens at the start of every school year. A high school freshman is faced with the decision to take a foreign language. It is assumed that this boy wants to go to college, or that he should want to go to college, and most universities require an entrant to have had two years of foreign language. So the boy sees his guidance counselor, and the counselor suggests that he take Spanish. The boy says he doesn't want to go to Spain. To which the counselor answers: "You may want to go to South America in the next twenty-five years, and you'll want to be a part of it." But the boy says: "I don't want to go to South America. All I want to do is become a computer operator. Computers fascinate me. The pay is good. I'm not out to change the world. Don't you have any courses that will teach me to run a computer?" All the counselor can say is, "No, you will have to get those courses after you get out of high school." Right then the boy becomes discouraged. He realizes that his high school like so many others is oriented for those who will be going to college. The effect this penalization will have upon his attitude, his motivation to learn, and his scholastic achievement during the next four years is anyone's guess, now that he has found out what too many others have discovered in our technical age: Our high school education system, for the most part, is not in step with the 60 percent who will never go to college.

Still, Kentuckians are more fortunate than most, because we have the number one system of vocational education in the nation. Approximately 125,000 students took advantage of that program last year in 13 area vocational-technical schools, 38 extension centers, 11 community colleges, one university, and 325 high schools.

I believe in vocational education, because I believe in the world of work. And I believe that somewhere among the 124 different vocational-technical courses you teach, from agriculture to welding, some Kentucky boy or girl, man or woman, can gain the knowledge that will transform his or her life and make our world a better place. Not only do I believe in vocational education, but I believe in you, the people charged with carrying out this program, strongly enough that during my term of office, the budget for vocational education has more than doubled, from $30 million to $62.4 million. But I also happen to believe that money doesn't solve all our problems. So, in addition to doubling the budget for vocational education, the Kentucky Advisory Council for Vocational Education has been established.

This council of twenty-one outstanding lay leaders currently is evaluating selected areas of our program and examining how well we are meeting the needs of business and industry and how well vocational education is relating to the people and their needs. It is my hope and my expectation that when the council reports its findings in October of this year, several useful suggestions will be made toward a more effective program. Already, the council has uncovered several new trends which are expected to alter the traditional vocational-technical education concept. For instance, emphasis has shifted from serving occupational areas to serving people; it has shifted from services to needs. There is increasing awareness and concern for serving the handicapped and disadvantaged. Innovation is creeping into virtually every phase of vocational education. One of the immediate results of the shift from services to human needs is the greater demand for strong teacher preparation programs and in-service training.

We are spending tremendous amounts of the tax dollar for vocational education, and naturally, thankfully, this has prompted both concern and attention from the American public. We hear the term "accountability" more often. The public is holding the spenders of public funds accountable for the use of their tax dollars. They are demanding positive results. They deserve a dollar's worth of service for a dollar spent, and I know of no other program that can fulfill this demand as well as vocational education. But more can be done, not only to justify the confidence and expenditures vocational education has received in the past, but also to build more support for vocational education in the future. And that is why we must begin immediately a cooperative effort to institute the necessary changes, make the necessary improvements, and develop the new techniques demanded by the technical world in which we live.

Toward the achievement of those goals, I have these specific suggestions:

1. We must develop more flexibility in curriculum and in teaching methods, in order to prepare to fill the trained manpower needs of our free enterprise system.

2. The structure of vocational and technical education must be more pliable, if we are to adapt promptly to rapidly changing needs.

3. Our system of vocational and technical education must become more relative to the changing economy of the Commonwealth and more sensitive to the challenges of our emerging as a national leader in agriculture as well as industrial development. It is important to remember that we reached the billion dollar mark in gross farm income for the first time in Kentucky's history. And at the same time, we also attracted eighty-six new industries to Kentucky, the highest number in our history. Such balanced growth and progress must be reflected in the preparation of our students.

4. The concept and the worth of vocational-technical training must be introduced earlier in the development of the student, on the intermediate and even primary grade levels. There is no logical explanation for waiting until students reach high school before

they are made aware of the opportunities available through vocational training.

5. We need a more comprehensive and better coordinated program
of job placement for vocational students.

6. We need more guidance counselors who understand the complexities and the unique features of our vocational-technical training
program.

7. We must redirect our colleges and universities toward the training of greater numbers of vocational-technical instructors.

In regard to this point, may I say that certainly we recognize that
the key to success in any classroom situation rests with the person in
whose care the people of this state have entrusted their children's education and that is you, the teachers. It is in your hands, those of you
who teach vocational education, that we place the burden of guiding
our system as we explore the new paths and experiment with new
methods to enrich the lives of Kentuckians, young and old alike.

There are serious hurdles ahead, such as attracting more dedicated
teachers and administrators, providing a comprehensive guidance service, and improving the unfortunate stigma that has plagued the development of vocational and technical training.

Throughout Kentucky there are thousands of boys and girls, men
and women, looking for help from their educational system. They
don't want to live on welfare, as some of their parents may have in the
past. They don't want to depend on a monthly check from the government or empty training programs by the government. They don't want
society's pity, and they don't deserve society's scorn. They don't want
to drop out of school; they shouldn't be pushed out of school by an
insensitive, outmoded, irrelevant educational system.

Today's youngsters aren't that much different from their predecessors. Perhaps they are more sophisticated and certainly they have been
exposed to more information. But all they want from their schools and
their government is a chance—a chance to learn, a chance to be trained
to use their hands as well as their minds in carving out a place of dignity and achievement in this American Republic. And after all, isn't
that what America is all about?

CHICAGO 500 LUNCHEON
Chicago / August 28, 1970

My remarks will be brief today, because I am aware that, as business-men, as members of the so-called "establishment," you are very busy.[1] You probably are in a hurry to return to your desks and again take up the battle to earn more for your company, for your families, and earn enough to pay your taxes.

It is unfortunate that those of you in business and industry and those of us in government don't have more time to spend together. But it appears to me that the same vicious cycle that prevents us from meeting more often is of our own making.

Perhaps if more time had been shared in the past, the stark economic realities of keeping a business alive today might have been avoided to some degree. Perhaps if private enterprise had been heard at the beginning of the last decade as well as it was heard in the closing days of the decade, we would not be faced with the distressing conditions of high interest, high taxes, high inflation, high unemployment, and greater welfare rolls which confront us now. And perhaps if there were more meetings such as this, at which representatives of private enterprise and public service could come together to discuss affairs of mutual concern, more of the productivity of your businesses could be devoted to your own benefit rather than for the benefit of the government and those who have become wards of the government.

What we need to remember, what we need to repeat to labor, to management, to government, to those among the young who cry out against the establishment, is that America is great today because individual men have been given the incentive to create, to produce, to invest, and to save.

America offers its elderly citizens more health care, offers its disabled more assistance, offers its young better education, offers its workers more opportunities because, up to this point, our country practiced the principle that individual men should be rewarded with an equitable share of the goods they produce.

Incentive is the essence of free enterprise. But there are those in America today who have drifted away from that idea. We see industry castigated as a polluter, as an exploiter. And as a result we see selective taxation levied against business and industry each time the government fails to live within its budget.

Just a few days ago, forty-four of the nation's governors met in

Missouri. Without exception every state is in the midst of a financial crisis, brought on partly because the federal government has prempted most sources of revenue and created a chaotic maze of social programs requiring state participation. We find ourselves caught in a squeeze between dwindling revenue sources and systematic withdrawal of federal funds from programs originated and regulated and legislated in Washington. Medicaid, for example, started six years ago at $3 million. Next year it will cost more than $60 million, and federal support has been reduced from 81 percent to 75 percent.

The question the states are trying to answer is: where is the money going to come from? That should concern each of you. It should concern every businessman in America, because there is a rising tendency on the part of too many politicians today to try to answer their revenue problems by taxing selective Peter to pay collective Paul. That is why you need to be involved in the political process. I submit to you that if businessmen don't begin to take a larger part in government, then government is going to take a larger part in business, and of business. Take an interest in those who are seeking public office. Show a greater concern for the manner in which they are spending your taxes.

The headlines in a recent newspaper illustrate why I am concerned and why you, as revenue providers, should be concerned. Some of you may have read the story about the bombing at the University of Wisconsin. The headline read: "Family Tragedy: Happy birthday, Christopher, Daddy's been killed by a bomb." We've read about the Charles Manson case. The latest outrage was the murder of a federal judge and kidnapping of witnesses. We read of banks being bombed and planes hijacked.

We all know and I trust we all support the massive efforts by local, state, and federal governments to combat the rising crime rate. Billions of tax dollars are being spent to apprehend, to convict, and to punish those who choose to live outside the law. Yet, on the other hand, we have a group of bleeding hearts and social activists who say that we should also use your tax dollars to hire an attorney for the criminal and build him a better prison if he is unfortunate enough to be convicted.

In the same newspaper which carried stories about the Wisconsin bombing, the Manson murder trial, an attempted airplane bombing and the burning of a bank, there was a headline which read: "Public Defender Pay Issue Is Pressed." It just seems to me that the time has come for us to decide whether we want our criminals *in* prison or *out*. And speaking of prisons, recently I heard a jurist describe his distressing visits to some of our penal institutions. He was concerned that two criminals were forced to share the same cell. His outpouring of concern for the criminals caused me to wonder if he shouldn't stop by the cemetery on the way home and show some concern for their victims.

This same sense of misplaced concern is evidenced for the radicals who have turned America's campuses into lightning rods and powder kegs. At the University of Kentucky, 15,000 students are dedicated to receiving an education, while 150 radicals, or 1 percent, are dedicated to disruption. Let's stop fooling ourselves about these misfits. They aren't all the young generation. They aren't dedicated to finding answers. They aren't students. Many of them are criminals. And criminals belong in reformatories, not dormitories.

During the last ten years in Kentucky, we spent $500 million on public higher education to keep up with the population explosion. That is a tremendous investment, not only in terms of tax dollars, but in terms of the future of our State and our nation. We need people in public life who will protect that investment. We need to decide on whose side we are going to be. I'm aware that one of the new words these days is polarization, and certainly we witnessed enough division in this country in the sixties. But if we must make a choice between polarization of a relative handful of radicals and submission of the principles on which America grew into the greatest society in the world, I trust that we shall choose the former and not the latter.

This is not a time to be silent. This is not a time for those who offer something constructive to stand idly by. All of us, whether we are engaged in a profession, whether we are in business or in government, have a right to be heard. More importantly, all of us now have a duty to speak.

---

1. The Chicago 500 organization is a group of Chicago industrialists and businessmen.

SOUTHERN GOVERNORS' CONFERENCE
Biloxi, Mississippi / September 22, 1970

KENTUCKY has tried to set an example for the nation in the confidence it has shown in its young people. Eighteen-year-olds have voted in Kentucky for more than fifteen years. Kentucky became the first state in the nation to appoint students to the governing boards of public colleges and universities soon after this administration took office.

Several other new efforts have been initiated to communicate with and listen to young Kentuckians. These include: an extensive summer student intern employment program; a Student Advisory Commission composed of the elected college student government presidents from all public and private colleges; brainstorming sessions at which government officials and student leaders meet to exchange ideas and discuss current state problems; and the appointment of two college students to serve as full voting members on the Kentucky Air and Water Pollution Control Commission.

Our most successful attempt at actually involving young people in the political process has been the Legislative Intern Program. The program is unique in that it offers undergraduates an opportunity to participate actively in a state legislative session and at the same time earn a semester's academic credit. Basically, what we do is select twenty undergraduates from participating colleges and universities in Kentucky. These students are selected on the basis of their academic record, extra-curricular involvement, and interest in a career involving public service. They are then assigned to either a legislator or a legislative committee for work during the session. When the legislative session is completed, the students return to the classroom for several months of intensive seminars relating to state government and the legislative process.

More important, however, than the experience of observing and studying state government is the opportunity of actually participating in the political process. The interns are involved in researching legislation, in drafting bills, in writing speeches, in preparing committee reports, and most of the other diverse activities in which legislators are involved. As I observed these young interns during the last two sessions, I was encouraged to see them develop a deeper faith in the usefulness of the machinery of government. I saw them arrive at the conclusion that the two political parties can work together, that city and farm can talk together, and most importantly, that a young person who takes the time and expends the energy can learn the ropes of government and then possesses an unlimited ability for constructive change. Additionally, this legislative intern program provides the legislators with access to the ideas and beliefs of our idealistic and talented young people in an atmosphere where progress and constructive change are possible within the framework of established law.

This program was not a concession to the young. It was a challenge for the young, a challenge for responsible participation, for intelligent action, a challenge to work within the orderly and established process of representative government for the betterment of our society and the world in which we live.

GRAYSON RESERVOIR
STATE PARK ANNOUNCEMENT
Grayson Reservoir State Park
Carter County / October 7, 1970

WE are here today to announce much more than the master plan for the development of Grayson Reservoir State Park, although this particular plan in itself is of such bold and creative design that it sets your park in a league by itself in Kentucky's recreational future. We are here today to announce and to begin a new total concept in recreational development in Kentucky. Just as Kentucky led the nation in the rush toward resort facilities in the last decade, today we embark on a venture that will regain the national recreational initiative for our Commonwealth during the seventies.

The needs of recreation-minded Americans have been altered drastically in recent years. Concern for our environment, a new awareness and appreciation for the outdoor greatness of our land, and low-cost recreation equipment are part of the shifting emphasis. Certainly, we are encouraged that greater emphasis is being placed on family recreation, on recreational activities that bring families together instead of separating them.

The master plan which we unveil today embodies Kentucky's total concept. It exemplifies the new thinking of our parks department. Total recreation refers not only to parks, but to people. From today forward, not only will we strive to attain maximum use of the natural resources and man-made improvements within our park grounds, but we will also strive to provide recreational opportunities for all the people of our State. This new approach offers a pleasant paradox for those Kentuckians who provide the revenue for our parks development, as well as the many other programs administered by state government. Instead of costing more, which would seem to be a logical consequence for a program as ambitious as this, it costs less.

Perhaps the economics of this new approach can best be explained by example. Earlier this year, we opened Barkley Lake State Resort Park in far western Kentucky, a beautiful, luxurious, yes, even lavish facility, an architectural and aesthetic success, but a very doubtful economic success. Construction of the lodge at Lake Barkley cost $5.8 million. It contains 120 rooms, which, according to generous estimates, may serve perhaps 360 persons per day. On the other hand, if we go the recreational route, as we are planning to do here at Grayson Reservoir, rather than the resort route, as we did at Lake Barkley, the results are very significant. We would have to invest perhaps only a third of the initial amount to establish a facility which would accommodate, at a bare minimum, at least 100 times as many people per day.

What we're saying is this: Kentucky has the most sophisticated resort parks system in the world. Now, let's move toward the establishment of that same kind of record in recreational facilities for the masses of Kentuckians who seek a place in the sun. Proceeding on that philosophy, we are pleased and gratified to reveal now the development plans that have been created for Grayson Reservoir. This plan underscores the beauty of your area. It maximizes the scenic effect of Grayson's palisades, its crystal-clear waters, its wildlife, and its secluded waterfall.

Our plan shows ten specific areas of development. The first to be developed will probably be the Bruin area, which is envisioned as the most water-oriented of the ten areas because we want to take advantage of its peninsular nature. Plans call for a sizable marina, a restaurant, and a picnic area. Two complexes will be developed at the area we now call Rolling Hills. In the east section a swimming pool and bath house, restaurant, fishing dock, picnic area, and boat dock provide the components of what we call a concentrated play area. In the remaining portion of Rolling Hills we plan a vast camping complex with room for 700 improved campsites, 120 modular cottages, playgrounds, a swimming pool, riding stables, stores, an amphitheatre, boat docks and launching ramps, and residence cottages and offices for parks personnel. This will be a destination campground, not a pass-through point, but an area where vacationers will stay for an extended visit.

Here in the Rosedale area our present beach and boat ramp will be improved; a pool and bath house, picnic areas, and restaurant will be added. This will become the embarking point for new hiking paths. To the west, on the north bank of the reservoir, is one of the most beautiful waterfalls in our State, Lick Falls. We don't want it to be a secret any longer. And it won't be a secret when we establish a boat landing and picnic area nearby and provide a trail to the top of the ridge where a scenic overlook is to be constructed.

These plans, along with the plans for Clifty Creek, Walker's Point, and other areas, must now be reviewed for feasibility, cost, and timing of development. On October 20 we have an appointment with officials of the United States Bureau of Outdoor Recreation to whom we are applying for the federal share of funds for the first phase of this new development. And I am confident that Kentucky's new total concept will be readily accepted and ground can be broken here at Grayson Reservoir next year.

In the past six days we have announced plans for two new state parks in Louisville and in Paintsville, and development of this park. Tomorrow in Pikeville, another announcement of this general nature is planned. And some more of the same exciting and creative plans for Kentucky's recreational development are on the drawing boards in Frankfort. That is why I am confident today that Kentucky will not surrender its position of national leadership in recreation in the seventies. Rather, I believe that our margin will be increased and that our State will be ensured a permanent position as number one in the development of a parks system dedicated to the total recreation concept.

RALLY FOR SENATOR
RALPH TYLER SMITH
Mount Vernon, Illinois / October 13, 1970

I WANT to commend and congratulate you for the deep concern and the contagious enthusiasm you are showing in this campaign to send

Ralph Smith back to the United States Senate and elect these state and local officials.

Here in Illinois we see the mood of America. It is a mood which begs for courageous leadership, not indecision; for unswerving allegiance to the principles that built America up, not permissive tolerance of those who want to tear America down. Yes, it is a mood which begs for a Republican victory in November, and we are going to have that victory in Illinois and all across America.

The people of America are particularly concerned this year, and for very good reason. They have seen a positive change in the course of our Republic since the election of 1968. In Vietnam we see American boys coming home from war instead of leaving home to wage war. Around the world we see confidence being restored in America; we see an American president cheered by millions; we see the American flag respected instead of trampled.

And here at home we see this same positive influence being felt. We see a new determination to halt crime replacing the former permissiveness which encouraged crime. We see tough anticrime legislation proposed to ensure that the wave of crime will not be the wave of the future in America. We see courageous fiscal management; we see basic reforms in the way government serves the people; we see government administered on top of the table instead of under the table. We see the end of irresponsible economic policies, because we have an administration in Washington which has rejected the theory that America's problems can be solved by deficit spending. These are the issues which are transforming America and have so drastically changed the mood of the nation. And these are some of the reasons that our party today has captured the mood of America.

What we seek is a victory not for the Republican Party, but for America and all her people. And we are going to have that victory. We are going to win, because in our candidates and in our platform we are giving voice and hope to the responsible, decent, law-abiding, constructive citizens who form the heart and conscience of our nation.

We must and we will change the misguided philosophies which found new life in the last decade, when there were some who advocated taking from each according to his means and giving to each according to his needs. There are those now who advocate that no one is any longer economically responsible for his own well-being, or morally responsible for his own conduct. Americans are getting sick and tired and will no longer trust or support policies designed to feed the stomach and starve the soul. Nor will they any longer tolerate the theory of big government and little people.

Our people are disturbed by the lack of respect for law and order, by permissive policies which inspire crime in the name of protest, by permissive politicians who pamper criminals and hamper the police while crime and acts of violence breed anarchy. America needs those who support even-handed, fair, but firm administration of justice and vigorous enforcement of the law, and not those who would say that rioting and civil disobedience are the inalienable rights of the disgruntled. Let us reestablish the principle that men are accountable for what they do, that criminals are responsible for their crimes. Let us turn back those politicians who show more concern for the perpetrators of violence than the victims of violence. And let us deny the responsibility of public service to those who would prosecute the police rather than the criminals.

Let us work together to promote a new, strong, living respect for the law, such as that advocated by Abraham Lincoln more than 100 years ago. Lincoln said: "Let reverence for the laws be breathed by every American mother to the lisping babe that prattles on her lap; let it be taught in schools, in seminaries, and in colleges; let it be preached from the pulpit, proclaimed in legislative halls, and enforced in courts of justice. . . . In short, let it become the political religion of the nation; and let the old and the young, the rich and the poor, the grave and the gay of all sexes and tongues and colors and conditions sacrifice unceasingly upon its altars."[1]

Many times in the past Illinois has rendered to America men of great integrity and principle. And America is asking again that you choose one with the commitment, the strength, and the sense of history to lead us to a renewal of our national spirit.

Two years ago I was honored to serve on the Temporary Platform Committee at the Republican National Convention in Miami. To have this opportunity to contribute in even a small way to the philosophical direction of our Party was in itself gratifying. What was even more gratifying was to observe firsthand the eloquent tenacity with which your favorite son, the late Senator Everett Dirksen, grasped the essence of America in his authorship of our platform. It was he who recalled Lincoln's challenge to America 108 years ago when he wrote to Congress: "The dogmas of the quiet past are inadequate to the stormy present. The occasion is piled high with difficulty, and we must rise with the occasion."[2] And it was Senator Dirksen who inserted into the 1968 platform this challenge: "In this, our stormy present, let us rededicate ourselves to Lincoln's thesis. Let the people know our commitment to provide the dynamic leadership which they rightly expect of this party, the party not of empty promises, but of performance; the party not of wastefulness, but of responsibility; the party not of war, but the party whose administrations have been characterized by peace."

With this challenge let us look forward to November 3 and to the election of those candidates who are pledged to keep America on its present course of progress, both at home and abroad.

---

1. Abraham Lincoln, "Address to the Young Men's Lyceum of Springfield," January 27, 1838, *Abraham Lincoln: Selected Speeches, Messages, and Letters*, ed. T. Harry Williams (New York, 1957), p. 10.

2. Abraham Lincoln, "Annual Message to Congress," December 1, 1862, ibid., p. 207.

REGION SIX HIGH SCHOOL
TRAFFIC SAFETY CONFERENCE
University of Kentucky
Lexington / October 20, 1970

LAST year almost 4,000 drivers involved in fatal automobile accidents in the United States were under the age of eighteen. In the same year 20,000 drivers between the ages of eighteen and twenty-four were involved in fatal traffic accidents. In other words approximately one-third of this nation's fatal automobile accidents involved drivers under twenty-four years of age. Statistics for nonfatal accidents are equally alarming: 293,000 drivers involved in nonfatal accidents last year were under the age of eighteen. The eighteen-to-twenty-four age group was involved in 1,354,000 property-damage accidents. Again approximately one-third of the accidents of this nature involved drivers under twenty-four years of age. Here are some other grim statistics: Traffic accidents are the number one cause of death among Americans between the ages of fifteen and thirty-five. Among male teenagers highway accidents claim more lives than all diseases combined.

It is ironic that while we have been able to make notable progress toward finding cures and developing preventative medicine for man's most dreaded diseases, we have not been as successful in reducing the accident and death tolls on our highways. And unless we take some positive, concerted, direct action now, I am of the opinion that the number of persons killed or maimed on our highways will become even greater in the future. That is why I am here today. You are here today because the statistics clearly point the finger of responsibility toward your age group, and I know you want to do something about that. If we are to achieve any notable progress in this area, it must begin with you.

Today we kick off a series of seven regional conferences involving representatives of every school in Kentucky. As leaders in your respective schools, as class presidents, student body presidents, and school newspaper editors, you represent the more than 700,000 young people enrolled in Kentucky's public, private, and parochial schools. To our knowledge this is the most comprehensive effort to involve young people in traffic safety that any state has ever undertaken.

During the next seven weeks meetings such as this one will be held at Jenny Wiley State Park, Rough River and Cumberland Falls State Parks, Kentucky Dam Village, and in Louisville and northern Kentucky. What we're interested in during this first round of meetings is establishing effective lines of communication between those of you who are most directly involved and affected by this problem and those of us who are charged with a public responsibility for action. Let me make one thing clear at the outset: We are not here to lecture, but to listen. We hope this will be a learning experience for everyone who is involved.

It is encouraging to note that this series of meetings already has experienced the fullest cooperation and commitment of both the private and the public sectors. Nor will we be satisfied to let this spirit of cooperation and concern be a temporary thing. We are interested in permanent answers, not temporary solutions. The young people of Kentucky must be a vital part of the solutions we seek. That is why today, for the third time during this administration, I am pleased to announce an unprecedented effort to provide a public forum for those young Kentuckians who have something constructive to say about the policies that affect them.

As you know, in 1968 we asked for and received legislative approval of our plan to include student representatives on the governing boards of all state-supported universities. Ours was the first state in the nation to take this step. And just two months ago Kentucky became the first state in the nation to have student members appointed to the air and water pollution control commissions with full membership privileges.

Today we are pleased to cast another vote of confidence for the young people of our state by appointing seven high school students to serve on the Kentucky Traffic Safety Coordinating Committee. This is the statutory agency established in 1969 to help create, coordinate, and implement a comprehensive traffic safety plan for the Commonwealth of Kentucky. This committee is composed of representatives from various state agencies, including the Departments of Highways and Public Safety, the Traffic Safety Institute at Eastern Kentucky University, and interested citizen groups.

Today, following this general session, you will be divided into five workshop groups. We have asked each workshop moderator to nominate one person in his group and from this list of five names will come the student representative on the Traffic Safety Coordinating Committee from this region. This procedure will be followed in each of the seven regions where conferences such as this one will be held. In addition to these nominations, I look forward to receiving a summary report of your discussions today in the various workshops. Let me assure you that these reports will be read and I encourage you to participate fully in the discussions. Hopefully, you will be able to present ideas that can be translated into life-saving solutions to the growing problem of traffic accidents.

In yet another effort to hear the solutions and the opinions you may have to offer, we are also pleased today to announce a contest among your high school newspapers. Hopefully, this contest will encourage the student media to become active participants in the effort to convince students of the real need for traffic safety. A one hundred dollar savings bond will be awarded to the newspaper submitting the best material to the Traffic Safety Coordinating Committee with prizes of seventy-five dollars and fifty dollars going to the next highest finishers.

Today, in the individual sessions, you will get down to the specifics of traffic safety. Discussion will center around such topics as the effectiveness of traffic citations, the impact of alcohol on driving, the growing problem of drug abuse among teenage drivers, Kentucky's point system, and the current high school driver education program. Experience as a judge, as a prosecuting attorney, as a defense attorney, and now as governor has made me realize the importance of these topics. Individually and collectively they are vital components of the solution to traffic safety. But, as the father of two teenage drivers and as a member of the motoring public, I feel that the key to solving this problem lies in the driving attitude of every individual who uses our highways.

Effective law enforcement will help reduce the mounting toll of traffic fatalities. Safe, sensibly engineered automobiles will eliminate the causes of some accidents. Well-designed highways will aid us in preventing needless deaths and injuries. But in the end, there is no substitute for the conscientious, careful, knowledgeable citizen who drives with respect for the lives, the property, and the rights of his fellow motorists and himself.

Your generation has professed an admirable respect for human life. You have been called the most concerned, the best educated, the most enlightened generation in history. You have been given more tangible assets, you have lived your lives in a period of more comforts and more opportunities than any other generation. Because of these advantages, no generation has ever had so much to live up to. But because of these same advantages, if any generation has a chance to effectively confront the problem of death and destruction on our highways, it is yours.

We challenge you to develop within your generation an attitude of respect for the laws of our society and a concern for the life and well-being of your fellowman. Because ultimately, the success or failure of this effort to make our highways safer will rest with you.

JOINT CONFERENCE OF THE
KENTUCKY COUNCIL ON
CRIME AND DELINQUENCY AND THE
KENTUCKY WELFARE ASSOCIATION
Louisville / October 30, 1970

DURING the thirty-four months of this administration we have tried to establish two major policies with regard to Kentucky's people programs.[1] The first of these principles is that people programs will take precedence. This policy recognizes the fact that people are Kentucky's most important asset, that every Kentuckian does count, and that theories and plans and programs must include full consideration of the human element if they are to have a chance for successful application.

The second of these principles is that full cooperation between agencies of this administration is not only desirable; it is mandatory. I recognize that there are limitations on the ability of the executive branch to enforce this principle, no matter how sincerely and strongly we may try. Cooperation cannot be enforced; it must be inspired. And while it is not my prerogative to enforce, certainly it is my sincere desire to inspire a spirit of cooperation that will pervade all the helping agencies and professions, regardless of whether they are private or public, or on the federal, state, or local level.

We share your dedication to the idea that what we need is to work in concert and reaffirm our ultimate goal to serve the greatest number of needful Kentuckians to the greatest extent possible with the resources that we have available. It was for these reasons that the Human Resources Coordinating Commission was established by Executive Order in July of last year.[2] This Commission represents one of the first efforts in the country to view the separate people programs as part of a total system and to approach people problems with total solutions. It is unique in that it includes the heads of all related departments concerned with serving the human needs of the people of our Commonwealth.

This Commission has special significance for the two groups you represent here today, the Kentucky Council on Crime and Delinquency and the Kentucky Welfare Association. The concept that inspired formation of the Human Resources Coordinating Commission reflects a particular sensitivity to the thrust and concerns of your two groups. When they are viewed in a total and coordinated context, we realize that the problems of violence and crime, about which we are all so concerned, are not unrelated to the problems of education and even preschool programs. If we are to ever have the answer to overcrowding at the Eddyville Penitentiary, we must view this problem with one eye while the other is on the problems of delinquency, dependency, childhood development, emotional disturbance, and malnutrition.

Two of the prime current projects of the Commission are the Interagency Committee for the Kentucky Infant and Preschool Program Planning Project in sixteen eastern Kentucky counties, and the county case conferences which you have activated in seventy-five of our counties.

We must learn to do coordinated planning, instead of each agency pursuing its own goals independent of the responsibilities and resources of others. Your profession, as well as many of us charged with public responsibility, has rightfully emphasized the individual case work approach. But there is a need for social workers also to become more involved in developing overall plans for a community, including jobs for clients. You must enlist the services of everyone in the local communities to share this burden, if the proper goals are to be achieved. The job should not and cannot be done by one agency, one profession, or even all professions and professional agencies combined. You must increasingly call on lay citizens to recognize and help meet the needs of their neighbors.

Legislation sponsored by this administration and passed by the 1970 General Assembly has finally provided a method for the sharing of records and information between the departments of the State and with other appropriate agencies.[3] This will do much to ensure better cooperation and coordination of services to people. This legislation gives responsibility to the agency to share that information which is relevant to the problem being discussed with those assisting in its solution. Obviously, the rights and dignity of clients must be protected. The profession's concern with the confidentiality of relationships with clients has often been carried to extremes, however, including withholding information from other interested agencies. Such extremes do not lend themselves to a better cooperation and coordination of agency attack upon the problem. Nor does it further public understanding or good relationships with the news media. We can no longer afford this counterproductive perversion of your service and talent. In many instances these unrealistic rules actually have hampered steps which could lead to improvements for the clients they were meant to help.

There comes a time when those of us who deal with the lives of other people must ask ourselves some questions: Do I cooperate fully with other agencies when their resources might be just what is needed? Can cooperation between social agencies really be accomplished, or is peaceful coexistence impossible even among those dedicating their lives to helping others? Would there be a benefit by sharing information and pooling knowledge and energy? Is there duplication or lack of cooperation which causes confusion to the frequent detriment of clients?

I need not remind you of the tragic starvation death of Robert Ellis[4] a year ago here in Louisville. This youngster seemed to be everyone's child, yet no one's responsibility, least of all his parents'. A very serious effort is being made in Frankfort to weld the humanities departments into a team and to ensure that the tragedy of a neglected child, ill-clothed, unfed, and unloved, will not be repeated. But no army is stronger than its foot soldiers; unless those of you who are on the front lines and do the work decide we are one dedicated group working together, no amount of Frankfort or Washington planning will change the picture to a very great extent.

The Human Resources Coordinating Commission is the single state agency for the human resource planning function of the Commonwealth. Its responsibilities are to improve quality of services, promote comprehensive planning, provide uniformity for program plans at a state and regional level, and determine that available resources are utilized to produce maximum benefits. Each of the agencies represented here today will also be represented on its committees and task forces.

The Human Resources Coordinating Council was created by the same Executive Order that created the Commission. It is chaired by a citizen well known to most of you by voice and TV image, if not in person: Bill Gladden, Program Director of WAVE.[5] The Council is composed of twenty-one citizens representing a wide cross section of backgrounds, interests, vocations, and stations in life. It is responsible for advising the Commission in the planning for human resource development, including: 1) The inventory of existing human resource services, facilities, and needs; 2) The determination of service facilities and manpower to meet those needs; 3) The determination of priorities in granting approval of programs; 4) The establishment of guidelines for regional human resource planning and development; 5) The designation of minimum standards for maintenance and operational service programs; 6) The evaluation of operating programs.

We have entrusted this Council with a great responsibility, and we have great expectations that it will fulfill that responsibility. This is an unusual opportunity to make the ideal of citizen participation in social planning a working reality that will ensure citizen input into this vital area of state government.

An example of the increased coordinated planning of the human resource agencies brought about through the mechanism of the Commission is the Kentucky Infant and Preschool Planning Project. It is designed to expand and develop comprehensive services for infants, children, and their families in sixteen southeastern Kentucky counties by strengthening and expanding the services of the existing agencies: Child Welfare, Corrections, Economic Security, Education, Health, and Mental Health. I am also vitally concerned that your county case conferences, which bring together representatives of the private and public agencies in each county, continue and increase their effectiveness in delivering better services to people in need.

I wish to commend you for the outstanding conference programs you have had over the years. You have had an active and involved membership. I invite your further participation in the new approach to citizen involvement and to closer cooperation in the administration of our services.

---

1. The Kentucky Council on Crime and Delinquency is a private, non-profit organization of professionals (primarily in the fields of law enforce-

ment and adult and juvenile corrections work) and lay citizens concerned with the criminal justice system in Kentucky. The Kentucky Welfare Association is a private, nonprofit organization of professionals and lay citizens concerned with social problems in Kentucky.

2. See Executive Order 69–534 (July 30, 1969).

3. An act "relating to the sharing of case information by state and local governmental agencies" providing for the sharing of information concerning individual clients, applicants, or patients by any state or local governmental agency with any other state or local governmental agency, or with any private or quasi-private agency agreeing to maintain the confidentiality of such information. A "direct, tangible, legitimate interest in the individual concerned or his immediate family" was required on the part of the agency receiving the information. The act was signed by Governor Nunn on March 30, 1970. *Acts of the General Assembly of the Commonwealth of Kentucky, 1970*, Chapter 269 (H.B. 544), p. 929.

4. Robert Drew Ellis (1960–1969), a nine-year-old Louisville boy, died on Thanksgiving eve 1969 of malnutrition. His five sisters were subsequently treated for the same condition. *Louisville Courier-Journal and Times*, November 27, 1969; *Louisville Courier-Journal*, January 9, 1970.

5. William Gladden (1917–), Louisville, director, Public Relations and Advertising, Greater Louisville First Federal Savings and Loan Association (1971–); director, Public Relations (1965–1971), and member of Program Staff (1947–1965), WAVE Radio and Television (Louisville). Telephone interview with Gladden, Louisville, September 27, 1971.

AGNEW APPRECIATION BANQUET
Washington, D.C. / November 12, 1970

DEAR EDITOR:

I had not intended to discuss this controversial subject at this particular time.[1] However, I want you to know that I do not shun a controversy. On the contrary, I will take a stand on any issue at any time, regardless of how fraught with controversy it may be.

You have asked me how I feel about whiskey. Well, brother, here is how I stand on that question. If, when you say whiskey, you mean the devil's brew, the poison scourge, the bloody monster that defies innocence, dethrones reason, creates misery and poverty, yea, literally takes the bread out of mouths of babes; if you mean the evil drink that topples the Christian man and woman from pinnacles of righteous, gracious living into the bottomless pit of despair, degradation, shame, helplessness, and hopelessness—then certainly I am against it with all my power. .

But if, when you say whiskey, you mean the mint and the oil of conversation, the philosophic wine and ale that is consumed when good fellows get together, that poses a song in their hearts, laughter on their lips and the warm glow of contentment in their eyes; if you mean Christmas cheer, if you mean that sterling drink that puts the spring in an old man's step on a frosty morning; if you mean that drink that enables man to magnify his joy and happiness and to forget, if only for a moment, life's greatest tragedies, heartbreak and sorrows; if you mean that drink, the sale of which pours into our treasury untotalled millions of dollars, which are used to provide tender care for our little crippled children, our blind, our deaf, our dumb, our pitifully aged and infirmed, and to build our highways, hospitals and schools—then, brother, I am for it.

That is my stand. I will not retreat from it, I will not compromise.

---

1. Following the congressional election campaign of 1970, Governor Nunn was invited to be one of the speakers at a dinner honoring Vice-President Spiro T. Agnew. Governor Nunn presented the vice-president with a collector's bottle from the Beam Distillery and read from what was identified as a letter by a "now-forgotten Senator from Kentucky to a constituent whose views on bourbon whiskey were unknown to the writer." The recitation of the letter comprised Nunn's total remarks. Larry Van Hoose, Governor Nunn's press secretary, September 10, 1971.

KENTUCKY FARM BUREAU
Louisville / November 17, 1970

HAVING been a member of the Kentucky Farm Bureau, and having worked with your officers and directors, I know of your dedication and your concern not only for Kentucky's farming interests, but also for the growth, development, and prosperity of every facet of our society in the Commonwealth. The objectives of your organization encompass not only the hopes and the plans of rural Kentuckians, but of all Kentuckians.

I remember very well the opportunity that you afforded me as a candidate for Governor in 1967 to review the objectives of the Farm Bureau and to declare my position on the legislative goals your organization had adopted at that time. Among the major issues that concerned your organization on that occasion were: formulation of a more equitable farmland assessment method, construction and improvement of our farm-to-market rural roads, protection and promotion of our livestock and dairy industries, conservation and control of strip-mining, completion of the Agricultural Science Center at the University of Kentucky, staffing and operation of the Animal Diagnostic Laboratory in western Kentucky, construction of a lab for central and eastern Kentucky, and continued improvement of our public school system.

Needless to say, I am proud and you must be pleased with the record of achievement thus far. First, Kentucky farmers today benefit from a more equitable assessment method of their land. A constitutional amendment providing equitable assessment on agricultural value was passed in 1969.[1] This more realistic method of assessment has now been implemented by legislation which we supported in the 1970 General Assembly.[2]

Secondly, in response to the Farm Bureau's concern for safe, dependable, hard-surfaced rural roads, we pledged a rural road fund of not less than $25 million. We also pledged to build roads on the basis of need. In the first biennium of this administration, the County Road Aid Program was increased to $25 million; during the current biennium we are investing $26 million. In addition, the Rural Secondary Road Fund has been increased by $23.2 million during the first three years of the present administration.

Thirdly, you asked for support to staff and operate the Animal Diagnostic Laboratory in western Kentucky and to construct laboratories to serve central and eastern Kentucky, as well as completion of the Agricultural Science Center at UK. Approximately $1.25 million has been and is being invested in the operation of the Hopkinsville laboratory. We have broken ground and construction is well under way on the million dollar diagnostic lab in Lexington which, because of its convenient location near major highway systems, will serve the needs of central and eastern Kentucky. Earlier this year we broke ground for the $4.5 million Agricultural Sciences Building at the University.

In the field of conservation we have established a more adequate level of funding to support and revitalize the state's 121 soil conservation districts. For example, the equipment revolving fund has been increased to $1 million. Recently developed regulations in the Division of Strip-Mining and Reclamation give the Soil Conservation Service a key role in the concerted effort we are making to preserve Kentucky's streams. Surface mine operators must now have approval of sediment control structures from the Soil Conservation Service before a mining permit can be issued. In addition to strict, fair enforcement of the laws regarding surface mining, we have sought new alternatives to current practices in both mining and reclamation. This effort has attracted a grant of one-half million dollars from federal sources for an extensive research and development project which will begin soon. This is the only such project in the nation. Preservation of the Red River Gorge and purchase of Lilly's Woods in Letcher County are further examples of the concern we share with you for Kentucky's rich natural heritage.

Finally, in the field of education we offer the following achievements as a tribute to the people of Kentucky for their unwavering efforts to bring quality to our public school system:

1. State support for elementary and secondary education has been increased by 53 percent during this administration. The people have provided a 48.1 percent increase in support for each young Kentuckian in average daily attendance in our schools.

2. The average salary of classroom instructors has been raised by $1,512, permitting Kentucky to maintain its distinction as first in the nation in the percentage of pay increase for its teachers.

3. Capital outlay for classroom construction has been doubled—the first increase in eight years. This increase in state support has provided every local school district in Kentucky with additional financial capability to meet its construction needs. Since July 1968, construction has begun or final plans have been approved for the addition of 1,713 new classrooms, costing more than $94 million.

4. The number of classroom units has increased by 61.4 percent for handicapped children and 36 percent for vocational education.

5. Today Kentuckians invest in each pupil an amount equal to more than 23 percent of our average per capita income.

In this area we now rank twenty-third among the fifty states and fifth among the fifteen states in the southern area. This effort on behalf of better education surpasses the records of six of the seven states that touch Kentucky's borders.

That is the record in the five specific areas about which the Kentucky Farm Bureau Federation expressed the greatest concern in 1967. It is a record of which all can be proud, and it is our way of saying again and proving that our farming families will not be forgotten in Kentucky. I did not come here today to serve any partisan causes or to take undue credit for these several accomplishments in which the farming industry has shared so generously. In bringing about this progressive record during the past two legislative sessions, we have been able to forge a nonpartisan majority among the people's representatives. This majority was composed of men and women who were willing to put aside party labels and concentrate on the task at hand. They deserve your appreciation not only for the progressive farm legislation that has been enacted, but also for ridding the Commonwealth once and for all of the myth that a Governor of one party and a Legislature predominately of another party could not carry on the business of this State.

Last year, for the first time in the history of this State, gross farm income surpassed the billion-dollar mark. Despite unfavorable conditions affecting our major cash crop, and despite the continuing migration from the farms to the cities, the attainment of this record plateau offers assurance that agriculture will continue to be a vital and dynamic part of our economy. At the same time that we attained the billion-dollar gross farm income, and despite the adversities of high interest rates, inflation, and tight money, we were also able to report that new and expanding industries have invested over a billion dollars during this administration. In addition, we are also pleased to note that for the third consecutive year we will pass the 100-million-ton mark in coal production in 1970, and for the first time in history the coal economy will exceed the billion-dollar level of return to its producers. This balanced growth has moved Kentucky another step closer to a vigorous agri-industrial economy which promises a better life for all our people. Particularly at a time when many farm families are searching for supplemental income, at a time when tobacco has come under attack from many quarters, this economic progress comes as a hopeful sign for the future.

Let me make it clear that until the current economic situation affecting the tobacco farmers in our State has stabilized, and until the very serious contentions regarding the effects of smoking on health have been proven beyond doubt, we should avoid any action which might be misconstrued as jeopardizing the tobacco industry. I have always supported the tobacco industry, and I will continue to oppose any project that might prove detrimental to this vital part of our economy.

Today, the economy of this State is sound. Financial solidarity has been achieved. As much as any group or organization in this Commonwealth, your federation deserves to be commended for the progress of the past three years. It is gratifying that your interest has not been confined to agricultural issues alone. Hopefully, the example you have established will lead us out of a generation during which too little concern was shown for the principles that made America the greatest nation in the world.

America became great because its unique system of government emphasized individual responsibility to live and to work in a lawful society. It should not be surprising, however, that respect for our laws and respect for an honest day's work have diminished in America. For years we have seen a growing number who advocate that we should not be held accountable for our moral conduct, nor should we be held responsible for our own economic well-being. Until we make it clear that men will be held fully accountable for their moral conduct, whether it is in our streets, on the college campus, or in positions of public responsibility, we will continue to have a crisis of lawlessness and disorder in America. So long as I assume any responsible position in government you can rest assured that I will perform my duties to maintain lawful communities, and the college campuses will not become sanctuaries for the dissenters. Until we make it clear that men will be held responsible for their own economic well-being, until we have the courage to give public assistance to the *can-nots* and stop rewarding the *will-nots*, I believe that the world of work may become only a dim memory for future generations of Americans.

These two problems strike not only at two of the most cherished principles of America, but more importantly, more unfortunately, they strike hardest at the spirit of America. And today there is a new and even more dangerous threat to the American spirit—the growing problem of drug abuse which has swept across this country. This problem recognizes no boundaries. It jeopardizes rural America as well as urban America. It respects no age group, no religious sect, no creed, no color. For years we have watched this terrible epidemic develop in various parts of the country. And we have told ourselves that it cannot happen here in Kentucky. The time has come for us to recognize that the problem is happening here. And it is happening now at this very moment: not just in a few communities, but in many communities; not just in a few schools, but in many of our schools; not just in hundreds of homes, but in thousands of homes in every corner of this State.

For years the Kentucky Farm Bureau Federation has proudly stood on the side of law and order. For years you have deplored the permissive trend toward pampering criminals and hampering the police. For years you have condemned the unnecessary dependency on welfare instead of work. Today we look again to you for support as we prepare to meet the challenge of drug abuse. On Thursday, December 3, at the Convention Center here in Louisville, we will attempt to coordinate and mobilize every segment of our society against the illegal use of drugs and narcotics in Kentucky. We have asked every community in the State to be represented here by a broad cross section of its citizens. Many school systems are providing busses to transport interested citizens, public officials, ministers, law enforcement officers, students, civic leaders, and business and agricultural leaders to this meeting. I hope and I trust that you will be here and that you will urge other local farm leaders to be aboard those busses and to become a part of this massive effort to prevent and correct drug abuse in our State.

In the past I have called upon you for your support, your guidance, and your prayers, and we have worked together to build a foundation for the future of Kentucky. Together, we have faced many threats from within and from outside this State and nation. We have been confronted with world wars and smaller military conflicts in many parts of the earth, and we have been equal to the challenge. We have known the tragedy of fires and floods and other natural disasters, and we have survived. We have suffered horrible epidemics of disease, and we have developed cures. We have lived through times of great economic crisis, and we have bounced back. In every instance America rallied its forces and came back to know peace and safety, good health and prosperity, because the spirit of this nation and its people remained strong. But the terrible menace of drug abuse, and the most dangerous aspect of narcotics addiction, is that they sap the energy, dull the intelligence, and douse the spirit of their victims.

If the mental and physical strength of this nation is taken, if the spirit of America is drowned out by the wave of drugs that today floods our country, then America will relinquish the mantle of leadership, and the brightest beacon of hope for liberty and justice that the world has ever known will be lost. Today I ask again for your help, so that together we can fight and together we can turn back the greatest threat to its future that Kentucky has even known.

---

1. See Section 172 A of the Constitution of Kentucky.

2. An act "relating to revenue and taxation" provided that land used for agricultural and horticultural purposes be assessed for taxation at a value based on its use rather than on its cash value. The act was signed by Governor Nunn on March 30, 1970. *Acts of the General Assembly of the Commonwealth of Kentucky, 1970*, Chapter 249 (H.B. 442), pp. 868–74.

AMERICAN STANDARD PLANT
DEDICATION
Paintsville / November 18, 1970

PARTICULARLY here in eastern Kentucky, where much of the effort to develop our natural and human resources has been concentrated during the past three years, the results have been most gratifying. Our confidence in this area has been upheld in a measure I would not have dared to forecast at the beginning of this administration. During this past thirty-three months, forty-three new industries have come to eastern Kentucky. These companies have invested almost $50 million in their future and in your future. More importantly, because of their confidence in you and in your section of the State, five thousand new job opportunities have been created.

With this encouraging start we can now realistically look forward to a new era of progress in eastern Kentucky: an era in which the payrolls of eastern Kentucky will grow, and the public assistance rolls can become smaller and less burdensome on the producers of our society; an era when mountain families will come back to their native land to work, instead of leaving in search of work; and finally, an era in which this section will shrug off the yoke of poverty, seize the opportunities, and fulfill the legacy that is yours.

I am deeply honored that you have invited me to share with you this moment of such significance and satisfaction. I am well aware of the tremendous effort, the years of frustration, and the moments of keen disappointment you have endured in order that we might be here today. In my memory and, I trust, in the memory of future generations of eastern Kentuckians who will have a better opportunity to realize their full potential because of what you have done, this plant will always stand as a monument and a reminder of your endurance, your concern, and your dedication to the betterment of this section of our State and its people.

As we look back over the history of this part of Kentucky, we can truthfully say that adversity has been both a companion and a foe of the progress that has been made. Natural disasters, periodic flooding, governmental neglect, isolation, rugged topography—all of these barriers had to be broken down before the bright ray of economic hope which this plant has brought here could become a reality.

We are proud that during our time of service we have seen positive changes which have led us to a dramatic breakthrough in the effort to bring industry to eastern Kentucky. The annual threat of spring flooding has been reduced. No longer will homeowners here be forced to endure the agony and the heartbreak of these disasters. And no longer should industrialists be discouraged from settling here because of the threat of high water. In addition to flood control, the updating of our highway systems, and particularly U.S. 23, has encouraged businessmen to make a reappraisal of the opportunities you offer for profitable operation. With a greater emphasis on vocational education, including a 99 percent increase in the budget and additions to the Mayo School, training centers will soon be located within twenty-five miles of every Kentuckian who wants to become a skilled participant in today's technical age.

The most significant effect of these and other improvements we are making has been that the unfortunate image of eastern Kentucky has been corrected. The dedication of this plant is symbolic proof that there are those outside the hills of Kentucky who know the real story of this area and its proud and industrious people.

To those officials of American Standard who may be here for the first time today, let me join those in the company who have been here since the start of this project in commending to you the people of this area. Every day the industrial expansion of eastern Kentucky is producing further testimony of the willingness, the skill, and the loyalty of the people of this section as employees.

With equal confidence and pride I would commend this dynamic, progressive company to the people of Johnson County and the surrounding counties. Here and elsewhere in Kentucky they have demonstrated that they will be good neighbors, good citizens, and willing supporters of civic betterment. In Louisville recently the American Standard Company voluntarily established a million-dollar pollution control system which not only met the standards of that city's emission standards, but was four times more effective than the regulations required.

Much has been written and spoken about the location of American Standard in eastern Kentucky. It has been described as an experiment, a trial of the people's willingness to work, and a pivotal test upon which the future development of this region may be decided. Understandably, some of you who have lived here and know the character of the people of this area may have taken offense at these statements. But local pride notwithstanding, what we must understand is that the only picture many of this nation's industrialists have seen of this region is the misleading picture that has been painted by the sensationalists of the national news media. So, in a sense, perhaps the eyes of the nation, or at least the eyes of industrial America, are on Paintsville and American Standard.

All of us, but particularly those of you who live here and work here at American Standard, have an obligation to the future of this area to make this venture a success. The only way to do this is through loyal dedicated effort to American Standard. They have offered the opportunity of employment; they have made the investment; their success will be your success.

Working together in our respective roles as employers, employees, public officials and private citizens, I am confident that we will justify the confidence that has been shown here. We will paint a positive picture of this great section of America. And we will, by the success of this effort, greatly assist the industrialization and the progress of this area. To these worthy goals, let us dedicate ourselves today.

ASHLAND COMMUNITY COLLEGE
DEDICATION
Ashland / November 18, 1970

TODAY, as we dedicate this beautiful campus, we and all Kentuckians can be exceptionally proud of the progress this State has made in every phase of education. But our pride today is directed toward the tremendous support and confidence our citizens have demonstrated toward higher education. The dedication and sacrifice of these people have been rewarded by an unparalleled growth during the past decade. Within the last ten years the number of full-time students enrolled in State-supported colleges and universities in Kentucky has increased from 19,000 to approximately 65,000 students. During this time the total State appropriation for higher education has risen 549 percent to a total of $120 million this fiscal year.

Ten years ago the Commonwealth spent $436,000 to support five extension centers, the predecessors of our present community colleges. These five centers had a total enrollment of about one thousand students. Today Kentucky has a vital system of fourteen community colleges, which has made higher education more readily accessible to every Kentucky student. This fiscal year the taxpayers of Kentucky will provide almost $3.7 million to a community college system which is now educating more than 8,000 young Kentuckians. Ashland Community College is an excellent example of this phenomenal growth. Ten years ago 305 students attended class in a refurbished Sunday school building. Today nearly three times as many students are enrolled in Ashland Community College, and we are here to dedicate the first of eleven buildings on this new forty-seven-acre campus.

But let us refrain from the tendency of praising our past deeds and accomplishments. Rather let us turn to the more important task of examining the future and determining the proper path of higher education in the 1970s. As we design the course of higher education for this and future decades, let us keep in mind those to whom we owe a great debt of gratitude for the support they have given in the past. The people of this State have generously supported higher education during one of the most difficult periods of its history.

During the last decade there were moments of disillusion and despair as we witnessed the irreverent attempts of a radical few to destroy the very fabric of academic freedom. The most discouraging and the most puzzling moments of all came when it appeared to many Americans that members of the faculty and some of the college administrators had joined these few who seemed bent on destroying all that we had known and loved of our institutions of higher learning.

The confidence of those who support particularly public higher education has been engendered by the respect that we have traditionally accorded those in the teaching profession and those who guide our colleges and universities. We should not expect that same confidence to prevail in the future if there are those in the academic community whose perverse philosophy of academic freedom allows them to condone and to comfort the violent, the obscene, and the unreasonable element on and around some of our American campuses today. In those to whom we have entrusted the minds of young America rests an almost overwhelming challenge. If they are unwilling or unfit to meet this challenge, they should not be allowed to hide behind a shield of tenure or the sacred cloak of academic freedom. They do not deserve anything more than outright expulsion from their position of trust and respect. Failure on the part of college administrators and public officials to do so only encourages the tragic possibility that the confidence of those who support higher education will be irretrievably lost.

This must be one of the priorities of any plan which presumes to guide higher education into America's second century as a nation.

There are other priorities that must also be set. The 1960s witnessed an astounding increase in the number of college students. As Americans grew increasingly aware of the importance of higher education, and as low-cost public higher education became more accessible, enrollment at our State schools multiplied dramatically. In Kentucky, college administrators, taxpayers, and elected officials were hard pressed just to provide essential educational facilities. The decade of the sixties was marked by a frantic effort to construct classroom buildings, laboratories, libraries, cafeterias, and dormitories to accommodate such a rapid increase.

Kentucky is meeting this challenge. The present physical plants at our State colleges and universities encourage us to believe that the frantic capital improvement program which was necessary in the 1960s will not confront us again in the foreseeable future. But Kentucky now faces an even more formidable and decisive challenge. Bricks and mortar compose merely the shell of a university; the learning which takes place inside is what the university is all about. The communication of knowledge is the essence and vital spirit of the university. The quality of our system of higher education will be determined by the degree of academic excellence which we are able to achieve, and not by the architectural excellence of our buildings.

The progress of the last decade should prove beyond question that excellence in academic quality is within the reach of the people of Kentucky, and we should not be satisfied with anything less. The responsibility rests with those people in positions of educational and public leadership to focus their energies and skills and commitments toward achieving this standard of excellence. Kentucky is meeting the physical needs of higher education in spite of limited financial resources; with the help of better planning and coordination we can also meet the academic needs of our colleges and universities despite the limited resources we have available.

The Council on Public Higher Education is charged by law with the responsibility for efficiently and economically coordinating public higher education within the Commonwealth. In the future it will be essential that the Council assume a more aggressive role in the execution of these duties of planning and coordination. If excellence is to be ours, it is necessary that the Council exert its leadership to ensure that we avoid lavish or senseless duplication of programs among our state schools. The Council must protect the citizens of this State from a random, ad hoc development of higher education which, because of its inefficiency, will be too expensive for the State to afford and too ineffective to meet the needs of Kentucky students.

The Council must serve as a catalyst to the separate academic institutions in order that each may develop its own unique potential and personality. A quality system of higher education is dependent upon the diverse contributions of each of the individual institutions. For too long, growing enrollment figures and massive construction programs have been used by some within our colleges and some outside the academic community as a yardstick for measuring the quality of an institution. In a few instances costly competition has produced a duplication of programs without proper regard for the needs of higher education. Competition among our academic institutions is necessary and healthy, but the competition must be limited to the pursuit of excellence rather than the pursuit of new programs and new buildings.

The financing of higher education is another area which demands constant public vigilance and concern. Higher education is indeed a bargain for Kentucky students. This is only right, for their parents have supported with their tax money the building, development, and operation of these institutions. But higher education is an even greater bargain for students from other states. In many instances it is more economical for out-of-state students to attend one of our State universities than to attend school in their own State. This is unfair to Kentucky taxpayers as well as Kentucky students. While we realize that a diverse student body is part of the college experience, there should be a reassessment of our out-of-state tuition policies. One suggestion worth considering is the possibility of raising out-of-state tuition to a level equal to the taxpayers' cost of educating a student at one of Kentucky's public colleges and universities. At the same time perhaps this tuition rate would serve to limit the number of out-of-state students.

Another important financial question is the allocation of money between higher education and elementary and secondary levels. We are all cognizant that each is an integral element in a system of quality education. However, there are those who are trying to drive a wedge between those two levels. The proper allocation of our resources is a difficult and complex task which can be determined only after much thoughtful study and consideration. Emotionalism and fiery partisanship will only serve to impair the future of education in general and could deny the young people of this State the opportunities which we have pledged to them.

If the decade of the seventies is to be characterized by any single effort, let us hope it will be characterized by our quest for excellence. And to achieve this goal both our institutions of higher learning and their supporters must practice self-restraint. They must be dedicated to performing their existing functions well before they seek new academic areas to conquer. The money directly expended on thin and mediocre courses is but a small fraction of the costs involved. A fearful price is exacted of the student who leaves the institution ill-equipped for the heavy responsibilities which he will face. Today we are here to dedicate a building, but more importantly, we are here to dedicate ourselves to academic excellence in Kentucky's system of public higher education.

LEXINGTON JAYCEES AND CHAMBER OF COMMERCE
Lexington / November 24, 1970

MEETINGS such as this are significant because they provide men of different backgrounds and ages, different religious and political loyalties, an opportunity to come together and to discuss the things that will make a difference in our society. I trust that despite these differences, we are truly united in our endeavors to *preserve* America, to *protect* the private enterprise system, and to *promote* progress in this community which has been such an important part of Kentucky's educational, cultural, and economic development.

I commend and congratulate you for your willingness to accept these goals and work toward their realization. Certainly, we share your concern, and we are proud that we have been able to work with the people of Lexington and Fayette County in bringing about some positive changes during the past three years. For example, there have been several favorable developments in the highway system in the Lexington-Fayette County area. These include the completion of New Circle Road, the widening of Tates Creek Pike, and the progress being made on Interstate-64 from Frankfort to Lexington.

Also, during the past three years Spindletop Research has been revitalized and redirected into an important planning resource for local, state, and national agencies, as well as an asset in attracting new industrial and technical concerns. The Inter-American Institute of Business Administration being developed at Transylvania University is a functional monument to the American system of private enterprise, and an ally to those in Central America who would resist the spread of socialism, an example of which we saw the past weekend with the nationalization in Chile of two more American-owned industries.

There has also been progress in the recreational field, and in the preservation of historical monuments. Plans for Thoroughbred State Park are completed and site acquisition is under consideration. We are endeavoring to obtain the designation of a thirty-five county area as a National Recreational Area. Work on the purchase of the Mary Todd Lincoln home[1] is proceeding satisfactorily, and I am pleased to announce that White Hall, the home of Cassius Clay,[2] will be opened to the public next year.

One of the reasons I am especially pleased to be with you tonight is to deliver some good news to those of you who are interested in the development of recreational facilities in Fayette County. It is my privilege to present a check for $133,590 which will be used to purchase the land on which Kirklevington Park will soon be established. The park will be located on thirty-six acres of land between Lansdowne Drive and Tates Creek Pike near the Camelot and Lansdowne subdivisions in southern Fayette County.

When Kirklevington Park is open for use, it will represent the end result of a cooperative effort not only between governing agencies at the county, state, and federal levels, but also between government and the private sector. Half of the land for the park was donated to Fayette County by private citizens who, incidentally, live outside Kentucky. To purchase the remaining land that was needed, the Fayette County Fiscal Court and our Kentucky Program Development Office teamed up to win from the Bureau of Outdoor Recreation in Washington the grant that I am able to present tonight. During the past thirty-five months, this team has produced over a half million dollars to purchase and develop five parks that encompass 360 acres in Fayette County.

Still, there is much to be done. We shouldn't allow achievements of the past to blind us to the needs of the future. The simple truth is that in the past ten years Lexington has not gotten a proportionate share of the industrial growth experienced by other sections of Kentucky. It is encouraging that your Chamber is concerned and is doing something about this. The "Forward Lexington" plan which you announced last week is, I trust, an indication that the business community here is aware of the need for action and the need to become involved in directing this city's future.

I am not a citizen of your community, and therefore, it is not my prerogative to comment favorably or unfavorably on the specifics of the "Forward Lexington" program. I can only say it is gratifying that the designers of your plan share a belief I have held for some time that we can't truly help a community find permanent solutions to its problems by developing a maze of programs that promise a cure for the eternal ills of society.

Too frequently in recent years we have had separate programs established for each particular group in America. We have separate programs for the young and other programs for the elderly, different programs for the poor, and still other programs for minorities. What we need are coordinated programs that benefit the whole community. Then, all the different groups would be helped, probably at a considerable saving of our human and financial resources.

"Forward Lexington," from what I have been able to learn, seems to recognize the need for comprehensive approaches and long-range planning toward progress. I hope you will become involved in making it such a program, and the various agencies of state government look forward to assisting you in any way we can to help make the program a success. I am encouraged to believe that it will be a success, that it will build the pride of this community, and that it will lead to a new unity of purpose among all who are interested in Lexington's progress.[3]

---

1. Mary Todd Lincoln (1818–1882), wife of Abraham Lincoln, was born in Lexington. *Dictionary of American Biography*, s. v. "Lincoln, Mary Todd."

2. Cassius Marcellus Clay (1810–1903), abolitionist, diplomat, and Kentucky state representative. Clay was United States Minister to Russia (1861–1862, 1863–1869); and state representative, Fayette County (1840), and Madison County (1835, 1837). *Dictionary of American Biography*, s. v. "Clay, Cassius Marcellus."

3. A deletion was made here in which the need for businessmen to become involved in government was stressed. For an almost verbatim text of the omitted material see the August 28, 1970, speech to the Chicago 500 organization.

SPECIAL SESSION ON DRUG ABUSE
Louisville / December 3, 1970

OPENING REMARKS: Ladies and gentlemen, today, unfortunately, I must say to you that we have an undeniable, serious, widespread, and growing problem involving the illegal possession, use, addiction, and sale of dangerous drugs and narcotics.[1] This tragic epidemic of drug abuse has spread to Kentucky, and it can be documented by the following statistics: The Department of Public Safety reports that in the first six months of this year alone, the number of drug-related arrests increased by 600 percent. The Federal Bureau of Narcotics and Dangerous Drugs has now disclosed that the number of arrests for violation of federal drug laws has doubled in Kentucky in only two years.

This problem neither recognizes nor respects any boundaries. It is not confined, as some would have us believe, to the young. But the most alarming and most disturbing truth of the matter is that drug abuse seems to be most prevalent among college, high school, and even junior high school age groups. The number of persons under eighteen years of age arrested for drug violations has increased by 2,500 percent during the last ten years. This fact offers only a small glimpse at the tragic dimensions of the problem. These figures in many cases represent only the tip of the iceberg. Experts now suspect that as many as one of every three students completing four years of college has smoked marijuana at least once.

While Kentucky appears to be below that national average, investigations by law enforcement agencies have established beyond doubt that the illegal use of drugs and narcotics is taking place in an overwhelming majority, if not all, of the colleges and universities in this State. That same statement has now been documented and can be said of our high schools and junior high schools in Kentucky. What we are faced with is not just a problem of experimentation, but also the problem of addiction and its resulting effects. In only five years the reported number of fifteen-year-olds addicted to heroin has increased by 1,000 percent. We must repeat, however, that this is not a problem of the young alone. The use of illegal drugs and narcotics also has risen dramatically among older age groups. The number of adults arrested on these charges has risen 500 percent in ten years.

And just as it is not a respecter of age, the problem of drug abuse is not limited by geographical boundaries or population figures. No community regardless of how large or how small is safe from this problem. Federal authorities estimate that in Kentucky's most metropolitan area there are as many as three thousand heroin addicts. Law enforcement officials here in Louisville recently arrested forty-six persons on drug charges in one series of raids. In eastern Kentucky frequent arrests have been made within the past three months. Throughout central Kentucky in rural communities as small as 250 persons as well as cities of several thousand, police activity has uncovered widespread use and the illegal sale of marijuana and drugs. In south central Kentucky on the outskirts of a community of 1,500 persons police recently seized approximately $15 thousand worth of drugs. Recent studies indicate that this problem actually is spreading faster in proportion to the population in the rural areas of the nation than the urban areas.

These unsettling facts offer little comfort for any of us. They reflect the critical phase and almost staggering proportions drug abuse and narcotics addiction have reached throughout the nation. It is not a pleasant task to stand before you today and recite these ugly realities. But it is a necessary task if we are to meet the challenge that is evidenced by the facts and figures you have just heard. This is not the time for wringing our hands and surrendering to despair as we view the magnitude of this problem. This information must not be hidden under a veil of hopelessness. Your presence here signifies there is hope for Kentucky, there is hope that we can and we will confront this problem successfully. It is to that goal that we dedicate this Special Session on Drug Abuse.

This meeting has three principal purposes that can best be summarized as awareness, education, and action. First, we hope to replace apathy with awareness and concern for the dimensions and dangers of drug abuse. Secondly, we are here to provide answers to the basic questions that surround this problem. And finally, this meeting was called in the hope that out of it would come inspiration for the formulation of a coordinated plan of action to protect every community in our State from the crippling effects of drug abuse.

Perhaps never before in the history of Kentucky at a meeting such as this have the leaders of so many public and private organizations representing such a comprehensive geographical and social cross section so dramatically come together, pledging their time, their talent, and their energy to a common cause. And if we will enlarge upon this beginning, if we will coordinate our resources and our efforts, if we will take this campaign into every home, into every church and school, before every governmental body and civic organization in Kentucky, in the future it can be said that we were able to save not only the future of our State and its people, but our nation as well.

Closing Remarks: There is a proverb which says that even the longest journey must begin with a single step. Kentucky already has taken that crucial first step. And today perhaps we have taken another significant step toward preventing the spread of drug abuse and correcting the horrible chaos and tragedy it has brought to the lives of many of our fellow citizens. But this Special Session on Drug Abuse will not have been successful unless each of us leaves here today personally committed to making sure that this will not be the last step in our effort.

The drug problem in Kentucky will not be solved at conferences such as this, but these sessions are helpful in providing an opportunity for learning. Nor will this problem be solved by the efforts of government alone. But government must, and I pledge to you that government will, do its part in Kentucky. And drug abuse will not disappear at the sight of more and more of your tax dollars being spent. But a carefully planned expenditure now to combat this problem may prove to be one of the best investments the people of Kentucky could ever make. Drug abuse cannot be legislated out of our lives, but constant review must be made of our drug laws and constant search must be made for more effective legal remedies. We must not rely on a campaign of fear and sermons of exaggeration, because the physical and moral reality of drug abuse and addiction is frightening enough. Education, governmental leadership and spending, legislation, sermons, and all the other approaches are not in themselves the final answer that we seek. What we must take back to our homes and to our communities today is the realization that each of us has a personal responsibility to work toward the solution of this problem.

Already in Kentucky we are beginning to see a dramatic response on the part of many segments of our society. And given the impetus of today's meeting each community should begin immediately to formulate its own comprehensive response to this problem. To assist local communities in their efforts we are pleased today to announce a six-point follow-up program which is being implemented through the Governor's office. As the first step $100,000 is being made available through the State Crime Commission for the establishment of a special Narcotics Division within the Kentucky State Police. This unit of agents will concentrate on apprehending and arresting drug pushers and those who traffick in illegal drugs and narcotics.

There is mounting evidence to suggest that Kentucky, because of its geographical proximity to large population areas in both the north and south, is in danger of becoming a major center for the illegal trafficking of drugs and narcotics. The primary goal of the new Narcotics Division will be to make sure that this does not happen here.

Secondly, we are gratified to announce that Kentucky has been awarded $50,000 by the United States Department of Justice to begin establishing an Organized Crime Division within the State Police. The involvement of organized crime syndicates in illegal drugs already is well established. Therefore, these two new intelligence units within the State Police have been designed to dovetail as an effective deterrent to drug trafficking and abuse.

Thirdly, with a contribution from the Governor's Contingency Fund we will establish a special fund within the State Bureau of Narcotics and Drug Education to purchase additional drug abuse films and informational materials. This fund will be used to match local contributions from civic clubs, governmental agencies, schools, churches, and other organizations and institutions who are willing to join the effort to bring drug awareness to every Kentuckian.

Fourthly, we will ask the Narcotics Committee of the State Crime Commission to study the feasibility of an immunity law for drug abusers who are willing to share information about pushers and other users as well as to ensure needed treatment for themselves.

Next we will purchase a series of specially prepared television films on drug abuse which will be offered to every station in the State within the next month.

Finally, we are now making personal appeals to our many volunteer organizations and to the state's legal, medical, and spiritual institutions for a concerted response to the menace of drug abuse. We are pleased to report that all have assured us of their full cooperation. For example, as a fitting climax to Drug Abuse Week in Kentucky, many of our clergymen throughout the State have prepared special sermons to be delivered this weekend.

We offer this program, not as an answer to drug abuse in Kentucky, but as a plan of assistance for those of you in the local communities with whom the final responsibility for action must rest.

Every generation has its special set of problems and opportunities. Perhaps ours could be called the "Generation of Crisis." A depression, a world war, two agonizing conflicts in Southeast Asia, and unparalleled domestic strife have left their mark on the past four decades of American history and undoubtedly on those who have lived through all or part of these events.

Today we frequently speak of the environmental crisis. We are concerned, as we should be, about the pollution of our streams, the air we breathe, our natural resources, and the earth on which we live. I do not suggest that we lessen our efforts to prevent pollution in the future and to correct the transgressions of the past. I do ask that we intensify our efforts to prevent also the pollution of our human resources—the minds, the bodies, and the spirit of our people.

The primary crisis of our time has now become that of the human mind and spirit. It will not be solved until we have joined together to build bridges of understanding, communication, and education to stem the rising tide of drug abuse in America.

---

1. For background information on this Special Session on Drug Abuse, see Governor Nunn's address to the Kentucky Farm Bureau, November 17, 1970.

THIRD ANNIVERSARY PARTY OF THE INAUGURATION OF GOVERNOR LOUIE B. NUNN
Louisville / December 12, 1970

THREE years ago today, because of the efforts of you and others, it was my privilege to ride up Capitol Avenue and to be listed among less than half a hundred men who had been chosen by the people to help guide the destiny of this great Commonwealth. On that day pride and humility were strangely intermixed. The elation of political victory was tempered by the certain knowledge of a great public responsibility. Before me were the faces of our ill and aged, who looked to the State for health and life itself. I could see the faces of our mentally ill and retarded, longing for the gift of hope, incapable of knowing the immediate crisis we confronted in merely keeping open the State's mental facilities where they were. Before us on that day paraded proud young Kentuckians who depended upon our administration for improved education and opportunity, perhaps unaware that at that very moment the State was delinquent by $20 million in its payments to local school districts through the Minimum Foundation Program. The responsibility to all the State's citizens, from the richest and most self-sufficient to the poorest and most helpless, was ever present.

The stalwart column of my predecessors, likewise, passed in review, and I recognized that the contributions or the failures of the past would have an imprint upon the achievements to which we aspired. With equal clarity on this occasion you see those who will follow. They are your judges. You know, likewise, they will inherit your successes and failures, your achievements and errors.

What lay ahead was distressing. The political overbalance was alarming. The deficit looked insurmountable. If we were to accomplish for the people what deserved to be done, we would have to depend upon a Legislature, the majority of which was made up of members of an opposing party. Approximately half of the constitutional officers were of the opposition party, and we could expect nothing more than minimal cooperation, if any. The situation was further complicated by the fact that a few saboteurs had been hidden in strategic positions and cloaked with the security of a corrupted Merit System to spy, obstruct, and delay the efforts of this administration.

Other difficulties lay ahead. Kentuckians will never forget that between Election Day and Inauguration Day the people were told for the first time what a select few in and close to the previous administration had concealed throughout the campaign months, that a serious financial deficit was being carried by the state. Neither shall I forget that day Beula, Jennie, Steve, and I were in Hawaii when that unexpected and shocking message came.

At the fear of being immodest can I say here that whatever accomplishments I may have shared in, my family deserves much credit. They have been understanding, loyal, devoted, and interested. Beula loves working for conservation, preservation, and restoration of our historical shrines and homes.

Kentucky had been overspent and overcommitted. We were faced with an impending shortage of $36 million. All of these factors conspired to form a set of circumstances which had never before confronted a governor in the annals of Kentucky history. The bleak clouds of Inauguration Day served as a nagging reminder of the distressing financial situation that was ours to solve. Not only was there a shortage for the present year, the shortages would be carried forward and other commitments had been extended into future years without any financial provisions to meet those commitments. The physical property of the State, its buildings and facilities, had deteriorated from years of governmental neglect and political excesses.

On that day there was agonizing distress about our mental health facilities. They were in desperate need of repairs and renovation—yes, even food. Some were about to be closed. They were unsafe, inhumane, and deteriorated to the point that they could no longer qualify as hospitals. They were mere warehouses of human suffering. The coldness of the inauguration hour sadly reminded me that young delinquents were shivering through the winter in drafty, dirty, dilapidated buildings at Kentucky Village near Lexington, an installation condemned by grand jury investigators for more than a decade. There was also the frustration shared by teachers and parents alike as they watched their children, their students, denied for eight years adequate funds for new schools.

These were but a few of the almost overwhelming emotions and problems which imprinted forever the memory of Inauguration Day 1967 in my mind. But tonight, thirty-six months later, there is evidence that positive changes have taken place in our State. I will not tell you that we have been able to solve in three years problems that had been in the making over many years. But I can tell you that we have made a significant start. We have laid a foundation for progress and change on which others can build better in years ahead.

When we took office, the machinery of State government appeared powerless, hopelessly bound in red tape, and bogged down in mismanagement, confusion, and political expediency. To correct that situation the Kentucky Efficiency Task Force was appointed. This team of 157 specialists from private enterprise, public and professional service, was directed to document the waste, the flaws, and failures of management. Out of their independent investigation have come 380 specific recommendations of ways to improve and revitalize state government and save millions of dollars for the people of Kentucky. A majority of these recommendations already have been implemented. Others may require years to be completed. But they have begun to produce more efficient service in less time at less cost and with fewer employees.

What we are striving toward is a sound management system, better coordination of programs, prevention of waste and duplication, and creation of a planned approach to progress. Kentucky's electronic data processing system offers a perfect example. Without regard for the future, previous administrations had committed your funds to an extravagant, fragmented, and sometimes overlapping computer program. The Task Force noted that, for the most part, "the departments and agencies have built data systems with an eye to accommodating only their own needs."[1]

Today, at the suggestion of the Task Force, we are developing a consolidated computer system, which is predicted to save over $4 million over the next few years. Not only will we be able to reduce the cost of the computer operation, but we will also be able to use the new system to deal more effectively with the complexities of modern government.

Also in the area of improved management and coordinated planning, the Kentucky Program Development Office has made a sizeable contribution. By designating this as the single state planning agency, and making it the specific liaison agency to the federal government, we have been able to generate well in excess of $335 million in federal grants and matching funds, and we expect this figure to exceed one half billion dollars during this administration.

Through better management of these funds, through creative innovations in the use of available revenues, and with the assistance and growing confidence of the people of Kentucky, we are able to report to you tonight a series of related developments and accomplishments which have changed our Commonwealth during the past thirty-six months. To recite this record in many specific details would be unnecessary, because the changes already are apparent in daily lives. Your children perhaps attend one of the new or remodeled schools being built in every one of Kentucky's 193 education districts. Their teachers are better paid by approximately fifteen hundred dollars than when we took office. Their learning materials and tools have been improved and expanded by the first increase in classroom operating funds in eight years.

Your children travel to school, and you go about your business safer, quicker, and more conveniently today because our administration has engaged in the most massive highway construction program in the history of the State. The rural road program has been increased by 77 percent over the previous administration. The County Road Aid Fund has been increased by 78.4 percent. More than three thousand miles of new, blacktopped roads have been constructed in thirty-six months. A 254–mile parkway system now under construction will provide a "corridor of opportunity" from Henderson in western Kentucky to Hazard in eastern Kentucky. With the addition of 310 new miles of Interstate highways Kentucky has become the "crossroads of America."

Both agriculture and industry have responded dramatically to the stimulation of this new and growing system of safe modern highways. Until now a billion-dollar gross farm income had been only a topic of conversation. In 1969 that goal was reached for the first time in Kentucky's history. At the same time that our agricultural industry was breaking records, industrial expansion began to set new standards. Over one billion dollars of industrial investment capital has been attracted to Kentucky in less time than required by previous administrations, despite the fact that we have been hampered by the loss of industrial bond financing privileges, rising inflation, high interest rates, and scarcity of capital.

Over 35,000 new job opportunities have been created. Over 115,000 persons are being trained each year in our expanded system of vocational schools. A positive plan of welfare reform is also being implemented to help Kentuckians escape from the relief rolls and get on payrolls. During the last session of the General Assembly we passed a plan which will provide welfare to those who can't work and deny welfare to those who won't work.

There are other changes which have helped improve the quality of life enjoyed by our citizens. Our natural and human resources are being protected better than at any time in modern history. The air we breathe, the water we drink, the scenic beauty that surrounds us here in Kentucky is being guarded by an enforced policy of protection and correction. The strict but reasonable application of pollution and surface mining regulations has fostered a new spirit of cooperation between those who guard the land and those who use the land.

In addition, our State has been firmly established as the recreational heartland of mid-America. The state parks system has been expanded by 50 percent. At the same time, we have embarked upon a comprehensive community recreational plan. We are concentrating on family recreational needs with the addition of camping facilities at the state parks and the establishment of sixty-two new community parks, many of which are located near the urban areas too long neglected in the past.

These are but a few of the changes through which we have endeavored to restore a feeling of confidence and trust in state government. Through these new programs we have tried to say that government in Kentucky is capable of achievement and is courageous enough to fulfill its responsibilities and obligations. We have tried to discern between political expediency and public service. We have tried to do not just those things which would guarantee the most personal satisfaction or win the most partisan approval, but those things we felt to be in the greatest public interest.

The complexities and perplexities of our time call for cooperation of government with the people, not alienation of government from the people. If during the past three years we have been able to implant a cornerstone of trust and respect, then the foundations we have tried to establish will endure, and many of the fondest dreams of this administration will be transformed into reality.

No one can predict exactly what the political harvest of 1971 will bring to the people of Kentucky or to our party. But with the knowledge that we have done the best we can, that we have taken the course we believed right, that we have fought for and not surrendered those things in which we believed, and that our efforts have not been blemished by scandal, we eagerly await the judgment of the people. We look forward with confidence to the political challenges of the next ten months, encouraged that within our party there are several young men of undisputed integrity, principle, courage, and concern, willing to accept the responsibility of public service. Never before has our party won two successive terms in Frankfort. I am convinced that we can and we will establish political history next year by electing another Republican Governor of Kentucky.

Next Inauguration Day I shall again ride up Capitol Avenue, again with pride and humility strangely intermixed; I shall be humbled by the experience of serving this great Commonwealth and its people, but proud that on that day there will be no need for apprehension about the financial security of the State. There will be no impending deficits to face, and there will be no agonizing distress or doubts about the ability of the State to care for those who cannot care for themselves. The crowning glory of that day will come when we are able to pass to our successor the mantle of leadership in a Commonwealth so secure, its financial strength so completely rejuvenated, and its human programs on such a progressive course, that all of us can look to the future with confidence and pride.

---

1. Kentucky Efficiency Task Force, *Kentucky Efficiency Task Force Report and Recommendations, 1968* (n.p., 1968), p. 20.

CONGREGATION OF THE
FIRST CHRISTIAN CHURCH
FELLOWSHIP DINNER
Louisville / January 10, 1971

A FAMOUS Kentuckian said that this is a government of, by, and for the people. When we understand that, then there can be no misunderstanding between government and the people, because the people are the government. The misunderstanding arises when the role of government is distorted, and when the function of government becomes something other than that for which it was created. A famous Kentuckian said, "Government should do only that which the people cannot do for themselves." We don't need to strengthen government. That isn't the problem. What we need to do is to strengthen the people's understanding and knowledge and empathy, so that they may have confidence in their government. For the house, it could be the start of a dramatic change in what has become an outmoded and generally discredited institution.

Like you, I am concerned that the people's confidence in their government appears to be slipping. We might go even further than that. We might also say that the people's confidence in some of the most cherished institutions that are basic to American life also is slipping. The church, the home, the family unit, the education system—all these institutions have been and are being subjected to some harsh realities.

Why? Well, perhaps this is one result of the turbulence of the decade from which we have just emerged in America. Regardless of the reasons, people are questioning these institutions. We're living in a time of deep stress. We see shifting values. Emphasis is changing. The role of the individual is clouded. The function of the church seems to be confused in the minds of some. The legitimate task of government at times appears to be defined by whim rather than by constitution. We are confronted by painful social and economic transition. Events and circumstances have conspired to produce a time when the problems that affect us all alike are greater than the problems that affect us as individuals.

There is a great deal of confusion, ironically, at a time when man has more information at his disposal than ever before in history. This may result from the failure to tie down basic fundamentals of life. This is also a time of greater material comfort and worldly satisfaction than ever before, but, at the same time, it is a period of greater frustration than ever before.

Now let us relate these circumstances to government, and to our topic, increasing understanding between people and government. We find ourselves in a period when more is expected, and often demanded, of public officials and the government than ever before. But it is also a time when people are becoming more and more unwilling to demonstrate their confidence and tolerance for those who hold positions of public responsibility. What we have are the ingredients of instability affecting both government and politics.

In the recent elections in this nation we can easily discern a current of deep frustration. Raw emotions are beginning to surface. And they are beginning to intensify, rather than fade away into the political subconscious of this nation. I have a feeling that the agony, yes, agony of officeholders at all levels may be coming to a head. The next few years are crucial. The next elections are vital if we are able to prove that our system can withstand the economic and social challenges that have shaken the confidence of some and have led to misunderstandings among others.

Government is being swept up in one of the great voter conflicts of our generation, the race between a new, militant, economic individualism and the deeply rooted fear that our society is breaking down. Of these, by far the most crucial is the latter. Recent polls have detected a strong sense of frustration and even fear among parents who feel they are losing the ability to bring up their children. I recently heard a famous political and social analyst describe a remarkable change he had noticed while conducting polls across the nation. He said that husbands in the past tended to do the political talking in most families. However, during the past campaign more women interrupted his questions and then began arguing with their husbands about the issues that were important in a particular campaign. These arguments almost always took place in families with young and teenage children, seldom among couples who had no children. Always the debate centered around how to bring up children, and what kind of society we would have in which families would be raising their children. He told of a couple in Houston. The husband, a businessman, was explaining how smart it would be to elect a Democrat Senator since Texas already had a Republican Senator. His wife, though, talked of how "so many of my friends are having their children leave home."

Whatever the issue—drug addiction, campus unrest, the war, school busing, violence—we are coming to realize that there is one overriding concern on the minds of the American voters today, that is, what will help me to hold my family together? And the problem is that there are too many people today who have begun to think that government can provide the answer. We may have strayed so far from the intentions and the guidelines laid down by our constitutional forefathers that we simply won't accept that any more. And perhaps that is why there is a crisis of confidence today as people look at their government.

How can we increase understanding of the people about their government? Perhaps the first thing we need to do is retrace some steps back into history and try to find the course of representative government from which we seem to have strayed. We need to remember the legitimate area of service into which government was intended to extend itself. A lot of the problem began when people started believing they were no longer economically accountable for their own well-being or morally responsible for their behavior. This philosophy has led some of our people to allow government to absorb some of or even most of the responsibilities that rightfully are theirs as Christian individuals. They stopped looking to the churches and to God for help and they began looking to the government and to the men in government.

The imperfection of that logic has now begun to surface, because we're beginning to see the imperfections of man showing through. But the danger is that this is being misconstrued. The imperfections and the evils of man are being seen as imperfections in our system of government. That's a part of the essence of the credibility gap and the confidence lag we are experiencing today. We have to realize that ours is a government of laws, not a government of men. We can't make government function at the whim and fancy of man any more than we can allow religion to conform to the congregation rather than vice versa.

Let's take a key word very prevalent in America today. That word is equality. There isn't a word in our beloved Declaration of Independence, there isn't a word in our immortal Constitution, that guarantees equality. What we are guaranteed in America is equality of opportunity. That's the difference. No group as a group is guaranteed anything at all. America is based upon the sovereignty of the individual. And the fact that you belong to a particular group entitles you to nothing whatsoever.

Our Declaration of Independence says we believe all men are born free and equal. We believe they are endowed by their Creator with certain inalienable rights, among them life and liberty; and it does not say happiness. The government cannot guarantee individual happiness. It says the pursuit of happiness.

Now look up that word pursuit in a sizeable dictionary where you have nice shadings of meanings, and it means this: to pursue means to follow with hope of overtaking. Technically speaking, if you are following with no hope of overtaking, that is not pursuit. Thomas Jefferson used the word perfectly when he wrote the Declaration of Independence. What then is the promise of America to the individual? Not to a group but to the individual there is promise that he shall have the opportunity to follow happiness with hope. That's all. That's it. That's all there is. No promise of any results. But we have literally millions of Americans today who don't understand it. We have millions who don't want to understand it. We have millions who never knew it. And we have millions who knew it, and have conveniently and profitably forgotten it. But it won't work. And that is one of the reasons for the confusion and the lack of confidence we are feeling today.

This is a wonderful opportunity and a tremendously appropriate place to recall some of the basics of our system of government. America introduced an entirely new concept to the world. Our forefathers started from the premise that the ultimate source of individual freedom under the American system was FAITH IN GOD. They understood that all men are born free and equal, that they are endowed, not by any earthly power or by any mortal government, but by their creator, with certain inalienable rights. They understood that man inherits his rights and his freedoms directly from the Heavenly Father, just as the son inherits from his father. That was a wonderful beginning, a wonderful legacy that we as Americans have inherited. But, unfortunately, we seem to be squandering that legacy today.

I'm deeply disturbed, and I hope you are. I hope these meetings and especially this series of discussions are indicative of the fact that you are disturbed by the fact that right now, right here, where that wonderful concept of faith and freedom was conceived and fostered, this is the only country in all of Christendom where voluntary prayer is not allowed in the public schools. We should be disturbed.

What is the answer to it all? I believe we are on the right track here in this place, here in the house of the Lord. His example, His words, His ways are the way back for America; and His people—all of us—must become bridge builders to span the chasm that separates us from our basic institutions.

If you will recall, Jesus of Nazareth spent a good deal of time making speeches in what we today would refer to as slums. In looking back over those speeches as they are recounted in the Bible, I have tried to find one on slum clearance. We hear a lot about that today. That is one of the knee-jerk answers of some today when the subject of poverty or urban crisis is explored. Well, as far as I know, Jesus never did make a speech on slum clearance. There is not a single illustration where Jesus gathered the multitudes around him and said, "You folks are getting a bad deal here. We ought to take from each according to his means and give to each according to his needs." He never said anything like that to anybody in all his life.

But time after time, he did say: "I am the LIGHT. I am the LIFE. I am the WAY. I am the OPEN DOOR. I am the OPPORTUNITY." He did not say to anyone, "If you do not take advantage of it, that will be all right. Society will take care of you." He did not say, "If you call the shots wrong, do not worry about it, because government will see that you get the proper results." He said, "You, and you alone, must make the decision, regardless of your circumstances. Society cannot do it for you. Government cannot do it for you. And it does make a difference how you decide. It makes a difference for all of eternity."

That is Christian charity. And we need to remember it today. We forget sometimes. It is a lesson those in government have forgotten after three decades of "pocketbook voting" and centralization and expansion. We have forgotten that it is not the Christian way when we do things for people that weaken them in the process, because they should be doing those things for themselves. Today we are subjected to all sorts of criticism for daring to suggest a hand-up instead of a handout. When it is said that we should take welfare away from the "will nots" and give it to the "cannots" who need it, that is labeled callous and selfish. And it has become politically dangerous. The critics seem to have forgotten that it is God's work when we help people to help themselves. You see, Jesus never tried to rebuild the slums. He tried to get the slums out of people, because He knew when He did that, the people could help themselves.

Our predicament today in government is somewhat like that which you have faced as parents when your children bring home their school work. All of us have experienced it. The children get confused because we will not do their homework. We can do the problems faster. We can get the answers right more often. They do not understand why we will not do it. Sometimes they get so annoyed and so vexed they say, "You don't love me!" And it is sometimes terribly difficult to make the child understand that the reason we do not do his homework is because we do love him. That is the way it is with government today. Issues are stirred up by this individual or group. Irrational demands are made. Partisan politics are injected. And you have an emotional confrontation. Logic is forgotten. Laws are conveniently reconciled. And there is a great demand for government to go along. When government doesn't, then government is the villain, unresponsive, insensitive, unrepresentative.

What can we do to increase understanding between people and their government? How can we span the tides of frustration and intolerance? One way is the way you have chosen. We can have meetings such as this. We can work toward a revival of the basic philosophies and the Christian faith that inspired our forefathers to establish the greatest form of government the world has ever known. Each one can teach one. They, in turn, can build bridges of understanding to others. Then, Americans can once again understand this magnificent thing that we have, and they will be ready to go out again and fight and die for it, if they have to, because they honestly understand it, because they honestly appreciate it, because they feel an obligation to the legacy of freedom that is theirs from a generation past, and because they feel a responsibility to build the bridge to future generations. As others have been bridge builders, so must we. Not just government officials, and not just ministers.

AMERICAN AUTOMOBILE ASSOCIATION
TRAFFIC SAFETY MEETING
Ashland / January 25, 1971

TONIGHT's meeting is the last of a very encouraging statewide series sponsored by the Louisville Triple A Club.[1] Out of these meetings with local enforcement officers from Paducah to Ashland has come a new awareness and a new sense of urgency about traffic safety.

To supplement these meetings the State has conducted a rewarding campaign against drunk drivers, and a coordinated effort to involve young Kentuckians in a traffic safety movement more comprehensive than any ever initiated in America. It is impossible for us to know exactly what part the campaign against drunk drivers last year played in reducing Kentucky's death toll. But we do know that 50 percent of the traffic fatalities in Kentucky involve drunk or drinking drivers. And during the campaign, which lasted through the period from Memorial Day to the Fourth of July, 2,361 drunk drivers were taken off the roads; they were fined a minimum of $236,100; and convictions for drunk driving increased 35.8 percent over a comparable period the previous year. The results were gratifying, particularly when we note that the number of traffic deaths in Kentucky were lower in 1970 than 1969, despite the fact that traffic on our highways increased by almost one billion miles.

With the help of last year's campaign Kentucky established a new all-time record in the number of citations and convictions of drunk drivers. Over 8,000 citations were issued by the Kentucky State Police alone, an increase of 20.4 percent over the previous year. Most encouraging, however, was the dramatic jump in convictions. In 1968 there were 5,395 convictions. In 1969 the total rose to 6,919, or a 28.2 percent increase. Last year, 9,129 persons were convicted, representing a jump of 32.1 percent over 1969.

So we are getting results. Our efforts are paying dividends in safer highways, less accidents, and less traffic fatalities. I want to publicly commend and congratulate those of you who are making this possible: the arresting officers, the judges, and certainly the news media. Their responses to the campaign were tremendous: page after page of free advertising, stories about drunk driving, and editorials—all of these have helped to promote a new awareness of this problem.

We haven't solved the problem, but we've met the problem. And the statistics indicate that we have begun to *win* the battle. But government has a way of forgetting too easily, and the public sometimes becomes contented too quickly. If we are going to achieve lasting results, what we need is a *continuing, never-ending, day-in* and *day-out campaign* to rid our highways of those who show no regard for their fellowman. We need to get rid of those who disregard the laws of traffic safety as well as public decency.

Unfortunately, one of the major stumbling blocks continues to be an inadequate response to duty on the part of *some* judges. Drunk driving campaigns won't succeed, the point system won't work, and additional funds to hire more state troopers won't do any good until the county judges convict the drunk drivers, send abstracts of the court records to Frankfort, and show more concern for the arresting officers. We still have three judges, all in eastern Kentucky counties, who completely ignore sending court abstracts to the Department of Public Safety. In one county 323 state police abstracts or citations were issued. Of these, 205 were filed away, six dismissed, and the Driver Licensing Division received only one court conviction. In another county 957 state police abstracts or citations were issued. Of these, 348 were filed away, eighty-one dismissed, and the Driver Licensing Division reported receiving only 430 court convictions. In another county 977 state police abstracts or citations were issued. Of these, 556 were filed away, four dismissed, and the Driver Licensing Division reported receiving only 269 convictions.

A newsman recently reported that almost 87 percent of the traffic tickets issued by Louisville police last year which went to court were filed away or otherwise voided or dismissed. In August the Driver Licensing Division received only eighteen abstracts of court convictions, one in September, and none in November. The situations are worse where drunk driving is concerned, especially when defendants have a jury or appeal a conviction to circuit court. In one recent set of fifty-eight such convictions appealed to a circuit court, *not one* was sustained, while fifty-four were amended to reckless driving, two were dismissed, one was continued, and one was lost.

One circuit judge was recently asked why he would amend a DWI conviction to reckless driving when the driver had registered .27 percent on a Breathalyzer. His reply—on the recommendation of the city prosecuting attorney. What kind of respect for our laws can we expect when our laws are so abused? And what kind of respect can we expect for our courts when they fail so dismally to uphold the sacred trust that has been entrusted to them? This is indicative of the growing trend among some people in America today who are showing more concern for the criminal and for the law violator than they are willing to show for their victims. Instead of being concerned for the drunk driver, we ought to be more concerned that someone is killed on our highways every eight hours and that someone is injured in a traffic accident every few minutes of every day. And we ought to remember that more Kentuckians lose their lives every year on the highways than have been killed in the last eight years combined in Vietnam.

Reluctance of some city and county prosecutors and failure of some judges to uphold the law or report those who violate the law has become so common in some instances that the Department of Public Safety is now drafting new, get-tough regulations in an effort to correct the situation.

The State Police have estimated that between 50,000 and 100,000 arrests are made for drunk driving each year. But the conviction rate, despite the records that have been set in the past two years, is still shamefully lagging behind. We shouldn't wonder why drinking drivers continue to cause 50 percent of our problems. They have little or no fear of facing the consequence.

The new regulation now under discussion in the Department of Public Safety would impose a nine-point penalty on the driver when the court amends or reduces any traffic charge which would cause a mandatory revocation of license upon conviction. This proposal would not prevent the court from hearing the case, then dismissing or filing away the charge. It would offer an alternative to the judge who sees the need for more latitude than offered now under the law.

There is a very good reason why nine points has been suggested as the penalty in these cases. Presently, drivers accumulating eight points now only receive a letter from the department. If he accumulates nine or more points, he is required to meet with a Driver Improvement Officer and is offered an opportunity to attend the ten-hour Driver Improvement Clinic.

Drunk drivers and chronic traffic law violators need more than a letter. They need more than fear of the law. They need help, help such as is now being provided by the driver clinics. The Driver Licensing Division of the Department of Public Safety could be classified as a doctor for problem drivers. In this department traffic court convictions and points are assessed to licenses, or they are suspended. When these court convictions aren't received in Frankfort, the driver is the one who will lose or an innocent victim. During 1970 this department, through their Driver Improvement Clinics, enrolled 8,005 drivers who have gotten into trouble through the point system. Of the drivers completing the course, 98 percent never experienced difficulty with this again.

There is growing concern about the effectiveness of the present law which suspends traffic violators for six to twelve months. During one week in August 102 persons were convicted for driving while their licenses were suspended or revoked. This would project over 5,000 such cases each year. A newspaper editor in south central Kentucky pointed out the other day that the teeth of the law seem blunt indeed when we note in one column that three persons lost their licenses as a result of drunk driving, while in another column we read that fourteen persons were being charged with driving without a license. The Traffic Safety Coordinating Committee recently conducted an analysis of the traffic fatalities which occurred on one weekend. They found that over 50 percent of those persons involved were either driving without a license or had lengthy records of traffic violations. These figures clearly indicate that it is time for stricter enforcement of the law, and it is perhaps time also to develop a more workable method of protecting the traveling public.

The problems of traffic safety among young drivers, or drunk drivers, or those who drive without a license cannot be solved by government alone. The State Police, local law enforcement officers, the courts, concerned private citizens, and the news media all must have a part. As we face these problems, each from the standpoint of our individual responsibility, we should be encouraged by the success of the drunk driving campaign that we *can* find the answers to highway safety in Kentucky.

---

1. Similar speeches in the AAA traffic safety series were delivered at Somerset (October 2, 1969), Lexington (December 4, 1969), Louisville (May 13, 1970), Bowling Green (September 8, 1970), and Paducah (December 2, 1970). Governor Nunn spoke in person at all these meetings except those at

Somerset and Paducah. William O. Newman, commissioner of public safety, spoke on these two occasions. Telephone interview with Arthur E. Beard, executive director, Traffic Safety Coordinating Committee, September 8, 1971; and telephone interview with Newman, September 15, 1971.

CONFERENCE OF
APPALACHIAN GOVERNORS
White Sulphur Springs, West Virginia
February 5, 1971

NUMEROUS welfare programs have been designed and enacted to help eliminate poverty, reduce unemployment, and improve the quality of life in the nation. The eastern section of Kentucky, Appalachia, has been considered an area of prime need. Millions upon millions of federal and state dollars, through these numerous welfare programs, have been spent in that area of our State. Unfortunately, some of these programs have resulted in complex confusion, taken responsibility away from local government, produced no permanent improvements within the area, encouraged the breaking down of the family unit, condoned illegitimacy, and encouraged idleness.

Some programs have served their intended purpose and rendered assistance where aid was needed. The most effective program for eastern Kentucky—Appalachia—is not a poverty program. It is a program for economic growth. It serves the basic needs of the entire community. Thirty-four governors and previous governors have acclaimed the Appalachian Regional Commission as the most effective tool of meeting the needs of the area it encompasses.

The Appalachian program is a workable program, workable within all frameworks of government. It has allowed our local governments to work together in effective partnerships in multicounty units, and not only to work among themselves, but also to work with the state and federal governments, as well as with private enterprise and civic organizations, in a total attack upon the special problems of each specific area. This program provides services to help people develop for themselves opportunities, and it provides facilities and services for the full development of the opportunities created.

We can specifically point with pride to the accomplishments of the Appalachian Program as compared to the expenditures of public dollars in other programs. As examples, in the past five years in Kentucky $95 million has been invested in 38 new vocational educational facilities and equipment; educational television; library, college, and science buildings; housing; and hospital and medical facilities. In the same period $213 million has been invested in highway development and $36 million has been invested in health demonstration projects.

From these investments, we must ask the ultimate question, what has Appalachia accomplished? As one measure of success, while the unemployment rate has increased across the nation, Appalachian Kentucky has decreased since 1967 by a full 2 percent. Appalachia has contributed more, either directly or indirectly, to this reduction of unemployment than any other single factor.

In his Inaugural and recent State of the Union Message, the President said, "The time has come to reverse the flow of power to Washington and start power and resources flowing back to the states." The Appalachian Regional Commission is serving that stated purpose. The Appalachian concept is an example of a tried, tested, and proven vehicle for reversing that flow, and it is an established vehicle for revenue sharing. The Congress would do well to adopt this highly successful method of revenue sharing, which can be applied equally well to urban as to rural areas, and which would not be constrained by geographical limitations.

I urge support for the Cooper-Randolph bill continuing the existence of the Appalachian Regional Commission and must be opposed to any plan or program that would prevent the finishing of the programs originally designed by Congress to serve the objectives accomplished by the Appalachian Regional Commission.[1] These projects are the basic elements of a well-balanced, growing, viable community. They are programs that meet the needs of all the people within a community. They are essential and importantly lasting and enduring.

---

1. For more information on the Cooper-Randolph bill, see U.S. Senate Bill 575 on the "Public Works and Economic Development Act Amendments and Appalachian Regional Development Act Amendments of 1971," *United States Code*, 92d Cong., 1st sess., no. 7 (September 5, 1971), pp. 1745–46.

TO THE COMMITTEE
ON PUBLIC WORKS
United States Senate
Extension of the Appalachian
Regional Development Act
Washington, D.C. / February 9, 1971

I AM the Governor of Kentucky. The eastern section of Kentucky is part of a region which for decades has been regarded as a symbol of backwardness—Appalachia. I represent this region and its sincere desire for development as one of thirteen members of the Appalachian Regional Commission.

The region represented by this commission, although it still lags behind, has actually shown more rapid improvement in average income and rate of unemployment during the last few years than the rest of the nation. It is my opinion that the Appalachian Program, for the most part, is responsible for the tremendous improvements. The Appalachian Program is an original. Never before has a regional program incorporating such a large number of states been undertaken. Never before has a government program so successfully exemplified the working partnerships of local, state, and federal government. The cause is a good one; the need for development is genuine.

The Appalachian Program is not a poverty program. It is a program for economic growth. In Appalachian Kentucky, as is true generally throughout the region, we have established a broad and dual strategy of development. Our twin priority involves, first, providing services to help people develop themselves for opportunity wherever it exists. Secondly, it involves providing facilities and services to develop opportunities with each significantly sized area. While providing opportunities will take longer than developing the people to meet opportunity, it is the one in which major investments must be made. Basic facilities such as highways, water resource development, etc., must be developed.

Guided by our belief in the twin objectives, Kentucky's earliest priorities paralleled investments in the highway system with a complete system of vocational education facilities to provide training opportunity to every single citizen of the region. The total Appalachian Highway System for Kentucky is presently about 585 miles, of which construction is required on approximately 420 miles. As of December

31, 1970, 103 miles of the system requiring construction have been completed and are open to traffic. Work on the remaining miles is at various levels of completion, with forty-four miles under construction.

The developmental highway system is the very foundation upon which all of our other developmental efforts must be planned. We have experienced delay in our highway construction schedule due to the reduced federal funding level, new safety standards which have required design changes, and changes in basic design standards. Kentucky's projected share of the total allocated funds for the Appalachian system is $213,672,000. To finish the system Kentucky will need an additional $104 million. While it may be necessary to extend the time required for adequate appropriation to complete this regional highway system, it is most essential that we do not lose sight of the fact that the full effectiveness of this system cannot be realized until it is completed as a system. Much has already been accomplished. For example, it is now possible to commute from Hazard, Kentucky, a mountain community with an excess labor supply, to Lexington, where jobs are available. Before 1968, the trip took three and a half hours. Now it takes an hour and a half.

Construction of the schools utilized major state investments, plus available federal aid and the supplementary funds available under the Appalachian Program in a joint effort. Through this combination we in Kentucky have funded thirty-eight new vocational education facilities in the Appalachian region in the past five years. As of today twenty-three of these facilities are open. More than 7,000 persons, both young and old, in need of training are enrolled in these facilities.

Funds have been sufficient through this year to maintain the two-shift high school program during the day; however, it has not been possible to use the facilities throughout the Appalachian area during the evening hours. Funds are not sufficient to operate all schools on a two-shift basis and to provide additional training to out-of-school youth and adults. The problem will become more severe during fiscal year 1972. New facilities will be open this fall in Kentucky, both in and outside the Appalachian region.

If any programs are to be offered for out-of-school youth and adults, there will need to be a substantial increase in funds. Congress has not increased vocational funds to the level of authorization, and the Kentucky Legislature will not meet until next January. It seems realistic that some of the funds available through the Appalachian Program should be used to supplement funds to operate the facilities in the Appalachian region.

In pursuit of our goal to create opportunity for people and develop people for opportunity, we also have placed a major strategy priority on investments and programs which will strengthen the urban services of our mountain communities. A major problem in Appalachia is the lack of urban centers large enough to provide a service base for industry already there. Urban service industries help recirculate payrolls and multiply the economic benefits. We also want to make it easier for people to live in the country and work in the city. We are accomplishing this in two ways: creating new towns and renovating and expanding existing urban communities.[1]

As is obvious from the nature of these activities, they are only in small part funded through the Appalachian Program. Federal, state, local, and private funds and resources have been utilized. More specifically, in the past five years $95 million has been spent on vocational education facilities and equipment, educational television, land stabilization, libraries, college science buildings, housing, and hospital and medical facilities. Included in that figure is $61 million in federal funds. I think the point here is that the effectiveness of all of them together has been geared to accelerated action by the workable process of the Appalachian Regional Program and our own Kentucky program.

I would like to give just one more example of the potential power in the boost the Appalachian Program gives. In the past three years $36 million has been spent in Kentucky's sixteen-county Health Demonstration Project. That is perhaps not an alarming figure to you. The significance is that a little over a third of the amount has been non-federal monies (local and state). Once given the initiative and a boost, the local areas made providing basic health services in a hard-core problem area of Appalachia a top priority. The cooperation factor is not to be overlooked. It constitutes a potent factor of long-range effect in advancing the overall development and progress of the area.

Cooperation and federal and local monies have brought a regional solid waste system to the Kentucky River Area Development District (eight counties). A similar system is planned for the five-county Big Sandy Area Development District. It has brought a regional communication system for crime to three area development districts (Kentucky River, Big Sandy, and Fivco). Others are in the planning process. Because of a regional emergency ambulance and medical care communications system in the Kentucky River and Cumberland Valley Area Development District, fifteen ambulances were at the site of the recent mine explosion in Hyden within two hours of the explosion.[2]

In both his Inaugural and State of the Union Message, President Nixon said, "The time has come to reverse the flow of power to Washington, and start power and resources flowing back to the states." As

Governor of Kentucky, I say the best way to do this is through the cooperation of the states. The Appalachian Program is demonstrating an effective way to initiate revenue sharing. Through this program the federal government shares revenue with states and communities based upon effective plans developed jointly by state and local levels of government.

The Appalachian Regional Commission provides a bloc grant for the State to use in health and education. The basic intent of the Appalachian Program is to create a balanced growth for local, regional, and national development. This is to be accomplished at three levels: (1) The idea of ARC improves the federal delivery system, (2) it improves state government's role in decision-making management and planning functions, and (3) improves local government's planning through regional cooperation and programs, sharing of facilities, etc.

The Appalachian Regional Commission does not directly implement programs which can be implemented by existing agencies, but provides supplemental authority, funds, and technical assistance to such agencies (state, federal or local) for programs which they implement. The Commission decisions require a negotiated agreement of the Federal Co-chairman, a majority of the states, and the governor of any state thereby affected. The success of the Commission's program has been obtained through this decision process.

Through the commingling of authority and funds of the Commission with the funds and policies of the operating agencies, a great deal of flexibility is obtained. In effect, this Commission procedural requirement has brought about one of the most important benefits of the Appalachian Program approach in that the Commission has become a "broker" in coordinating and combining elements of various individual fundamental programs to meet problems of broader scope or unique situation.

My belief in this program is so strong that I feel that it should be expanded to include environmental programs, health planning, and human resources. The area should be expanded in its coverage either to cover entire Development Districts, or an alternate method would be to expand coverage for the three regions of New York, Philadelphia and Atlanta.

Finally, let me suggest that the value of the Appalachian Program lies fully as much in its concept as in the success of its processes applied against any problem. The Appalachian process is the best I have experienced to enable us to work together effectively in our complex public and private relationship. It provides the best way I know of to define real goals, set priorities, and to mobilize for action.

I respectfully urge the continuation and expansion of the Appalachian Program. We are having success in our efforts. We want to get on with the job.

---

1. Examples of the creation of new towns and the improvement of existing urban communities was deleted because it is included in the March 27, 1969, address to the United States House Committee on Public Works.
2. A lengthy description of the Appalachian Program and its advantages, which is omitted here, can be found in the March 27, 1969, speech.

MIDWINTER MEETING
OF THE NATIONAL
GOVERNORS' CONFERENCE
Washington, D.C. / February 24, 1971

WITH any federal program the major consideration at the state level must be the implementation of the will of Congress. While those of you in the Congress are considering and debating the merits of the President's revenue-sharing plan, those of us in the states and on the local levels must be devising ways to implement the program, or we will be lost in the shuffle when the plan becomes a reality.

I chose to take a positive view of the response that the Congress will make to the proposal of revenue sharing and to the serious financial plight of the states and cities. Perhaps revenue sharing will not be totally accepted during this session, but I am convinced that it is an idea whose time has come. It is an idea consistent with the goals of the American federal system. It is a concept that can more clearly translate the will of the Congress into meaningful service for the people. Therefore, we in Kentucky, and in many of the other states represented here, have begun preparation. The Appalachian governors, in particular, have a long headstart in this respect, because for five years the Appalachian Program has represented an effective, productive, successful experiment in revenue sharing to a thirteen-state region.

In Kentucky we have gone a step further in refining the concept of regional revenue sharing by creating a Program Development Office as the single state planning agency within the executive branch. The necessity for this approach was dramatically and forcefully shown one day last September when my office received a voluminous document entitled *Federal Catalog of Domestic Assistance Programs*. It enumerates some 1,019 different programs created by the Congress over past years. Each of these programs to some degree demands administering, planning, or partial financing by the states. We found that valuable time was being lost by our department heads in simply trying to keep pace with existing programs and familiarizing themselves with funding opportunities, requirements, and guidelines of the proliferation of new programs. In large part this accounted for the nearsighted approaches that have marked the efforts of government in the past. What we sought and what we feel we have created with the Kentucky Program Development Office is a longer, broader view toward planning, toward implementation of programs, and toward attacking the persistent domestic problems of our time.

Under the Kentucky plan the State has been divided into fifteen distinct regions within which there are cities and counties with contiguous economic and social patterns. The identification of needs and priorities is the responsibility of the local communities. Once this initiative has been seized on the local level, then and only then, can the State through its technical and financial assistance, and the federal government through legislative and revenue sharing, make an enduring contribution to the betterment of those communities.

I recite the Kentucky plan simply as an illustration of a willingness that is shared by every governor here to find more direct and effective methods of translating the intentions and the will of the national Congress. It is through plans such as this and others that have been devised by the various states that government on all levels can come together on a plateau of service and share a common vantage point from which to survey the long range needs, problems, and opportunities of those we have been elected to represent.

We have not grasped the concept of revenue sharing as a way of circumventing the Congress. Rather, we endorse this concept because it demands that the integrity of the Congress, the sovereignty of the states, and the initiative of the local communities are preserved in the light of present day reality. It is through this concept that we can achieve the closer coordination and accountability which is sometimes lacking today between those of you who enact legislative programs and those of us who are charged with the responsibility of administering them. And it is through the prompt enactment and judicious administration of the concept of revenue sharing that together we can preserve the political morality of our system of representative government.

GOVERNOR'S CONFERENCE ON EXCEPTIONAL CHILDREN
Frankfort / March 17, 1971

I SALUTE you, all of you who have worked so long wthout recognition, without personal reward, but never without love and hope, for Kentucky's exceptional children. This is your day; it is dedicated in your honor, those of you here any many who were unable to be here—all who have given so gladly and cared so much. You are the real heroes, the catalysts, who have made this day possible, this day when Kentuckians from every corner of our State and from every walk of life dedicate themselves to making it possible for every exceptional child in the Commonwealth to attain his full potential for achievement.

The words "exceptional child" mean something different to each of you, I am sure; but who is the exceptional child? Perhaps he is the child who has trouble coordinating what he sees with what he tries to tell an anxious mother who desperately looks for a flicker of hope in his eyes. It is the impish little boy with a hidden learning disability who is sent to the blackboard and forgets why he is sent, or trips on the way, or drops the chalk. It is the emotionally disturbed child, a fragile little girl with sunshine hair who cowers in the corner, staring at the drapes, and spins like a top when you try to test her. Or it may be the retarded child, one who has grown so tall but learned so little that he is unable even to ask for our love. It may be the husky, clear-eyed young man, so brilliantly gifted that normal schooling techniques can lead to academic and social trouble he may never overcome. The exceptional child may be a brave little girl, physically handicapped, who faces the same challenges, and clings to the same desires for appreciation and success as other children but without vision, or hearing, or intact limbs. It could be the appealing little redhead who has a smile for every freckle on his face. He doesn't understand what we say, or say what he means, or say it so we can understand, yet his I.Q.

says he can do better. These are but a few of the exceptional children to whom we pledge ourselves, our energy, our ability, and our love today.

We must never forget that these children also are a part of the human plan. The plan is there for you to see each day in the home, in the classroom, in church, in business, in your community. Watch these exceptional children and see how much or how little they offer now. And then let your determination soar so that they, too, will be able to offer all their potential through the united, cohesive effort to which we together commit ourselves today.

State government cannot take care of all the children in our Commonwealth. But we can, and today with your help we are beginning to make sure that all of Kentucky's children are being taken care of in a much better manner. Through coordination of state resources, through the continued involvement of individual parents and citizens such as you, and through the various associations and groups who have struggled for years in their lonely crusade to solve single exceptionalities, we can help Kentucky's exceptional children find the assistance they need, rather than the hopelessness they now feel.

Until now your efforts, although they were directed toward the same broad, general goal, were bound together only by your love and mutual concern. Those efforts were loosely knit, tied only by the common thread of anxiety and compassion and sometimes grief. But today the lonely struggles you have waged so courageously are united into one single, comprehensive crusade. Today let us have your support, your ideas, and your prayers as we emerge from the legislative phase of this program to the survey of exceptional children, the documentation of existing services, and the development of a plan that will meet their compelling needs.

I must leave now to go with the President to the final rites for an exceptional Kentuckian, Whitney Young, Jr.[1] But I would like to leave with you a letter I received on Monday, one of many which eloquently focuses attention on the urgency of our meeting today. Although this letter relates to only one handicap, it shows very clearly the burden and the endless seeking of help for that child who doesn't fit the mold.

To this crusade, to this child, and to the tens of thousands like him across our State, I ask each of us to make our own personal commitment today, a commitment that the exceptional child of today will not become the forgotten adult of tomorrow, a commitment that Kentucky will extend to its exceptional children and their families a full generation of hope in the days ahead.[2]

1. Dr. Whitney M. Young, Jr. (1921–1971), Lincoln Ridge, black social work administrator, civil rights leader, educator, and author; executive director, National Urban League (1961–1971); dean, School of Social Work, Atlanta University (1954–1960). *Who's Who in America, 1970–1971* (Chicago, 1971), 36:2525.

2. The following letter was read by Mrs. Jewel Hamilton, Governor Nunn's administrative assistant. Mrs. Jewel Hamilton, September 10, 1971.

> Route 1
> Falmouth, Kentucky 41040
> March 10, 1971

Gov. Louie B. Nunn
Frankfort, Kentucky 40601

Dear Sir:

I am sorry my husband and I will be unable to attend the Conference on Exceptional Children on Wednesday, March 17th. My husband will be at work, and I must be at home by 12:00 noon each day. We are the parents of an exceptional child, and I am only free for three hours each morning while he is in class.

Our youngest son, David, age 11, is a brain damaged child. He began having epileptic seizures when he was five years old. Since that time we have had many tests made and seen numerous doctors. They say he suffered brain damage at some time, but cannot determine when, how, or why. As a result of this he has epileptic seizures, is very hyper-active, his coordination is poor, his perception is damaged, and he is emotionally immature. However, when we first took him to the University of Kentucky Medical Center for tests, they told us his intelligence was not damaged, but that he would need a special type of education to be able to learn, because of the brain damage. Now David is eleven years old—we have failed to find the special education he needs, so he cannot read or write. As a result of not being able to learn in a regular classroom, he is now classed as mentally retarded.

When we first were told of David's problems, we were told it would be extremely important for him to begin special education at the earliest age possible.

We immediately started to look for a special school for him. We failed to find anything. We found Kentucky has no boarding-type school for brain damaged children. We did locate several schools of this type in other states, but we could not afford the $6000.00 tuition. Incidentally, they were all full and had a waiting list, so someone must have a lot of money.

David has large medical expenses, and we also have three other children, so anything very expensive is out of the question, financially.

The closest day schools for brain damaged children are in Covington or Lexington. This is too far to travel each day with a handicapped child.

Our county has a retarded class and David attended this class for a short while, even though the doctors advised against placing him in a class of this type unless nothing else could be found.

The Comprehensive Care Center in Covington has opened a Day Care Center here in Falmouth, which has been in operation for several years now. David has been attending this class since its beginning. He has done quite well in this type of class, but has now outgrown it. The people from Comprehensive Care say he doesn't belong in this class because he is much too advanced for the type of work they do. The retarded classes in the county are full and they say David wouldn't fit in there either, which is true. He needs to be worked with individually, and with 18 children in the class, all with various learning problems, it is impossible.

So, due to lack of special education of the type David needs, we have a basically intelligent child who is unable to learn because we don't have the special type of education he so desperately needs.

Whenever discussing this problem with educators, it always comes back to the fact that there isn't enough money available to provide all the different kinds of special education needed by all of the various handicapped children of our state, and only some of them receive what is needed.

I can't see why people cannot realize how much better it would be to spend the money to train and educate these children so they will be able to find gainful employment when grown and support themselves and their families, rather than let them remain untrained and uneducated and put them on welfare.

I do hope your conference will be a success and sometime in the future, all children can be educated to their highest potential, not just those who fit a certain mold. I am afraid it will come too late for David, but the need for special types of education will be with us not just now, but always.

Being the parent of an exceptional child makes it impossible for me to participate in many activities, but if there is anything that I can do from here that would be of help, please let me know.

Sincerely,
Mrs. Robert W. Aulick

CRUSADE VERSUS CRIME LUNCHEON
Louisville / March 29, 1971

DURING the past several years we have seen an unprecedented clamor on the part of the American public for law and order.[1] Some politicians have preached for it; and other politicians at times have appeared to be preaching against it. We have all heard the strident demands that law and order be maintained. National polls have reflected a growing dissatisfaction and frustration among the American people as violence and lawlessness become more and more frequent.

In all of this we have established the fact that most Americans are outraged by our spiraling crime rate. What we must now establish is how far our people are willing to commit themselves to the preservation of order and the reduction of lawlessness. Well, certainly, those of you associated with the Crusade Versus Crime organization in Louisville are providing us an eloquent answer to that question. I commend and congratulate each of you for being willing to stand up and be counted on the side of law and order. That isn't as easy as it once was here in America. Today someone always seems anxious to criticize and find fault, or attach labels to those who are concerned enough and who have courage enough to speak up for America and its system of justice and order and opportunity.

We need more organizations like this. We need a concerned effort in every city and in every town in Kentucky. As a judge, a prosecutor, a public defender, a practicing attorney, and now as Governor, I have been privileged to observe the struggle of law-abiding citizens against the criminal element from several unique vantage points. And each of these experiences has proven to me that no governor, regardless of how concerned he may be about crime; no judge, regardless of how determined he may be to have law and order respected; indeed, no public official is going to be any more effective than the individual citizen in helping to reduce the rate of crime in a particular community or county or state.

During my term as Governor over eight million dollars will be channelled through the Kentucky Crime Commission to fight lawlessness. We've provided for more than one hundred additional state troopers, raised their salaries, improved their training methods, and made available better equipment. A new instant crime information network is being established. The Kentucky Bureau of Investigation has been created. Regional Crime Commissions have been formed throughout the State. A four-week training course at Eastern Kentucky University for local law enforcement officers will soon be expanded to six weeks. A mobile training classroom for rural officers has been provided. Eight group homes for juvenile offenders have been started, as Dr. [George C.] Perkins will probably tell you later this afternoon. Kentucky's broad-scale plan to replace its large institutions with smaller, more personal, and more community and family-oriented facilities has won national praise and recognition.

Today I am pleased to announce plans to significantly expand the newly created Organized Crime Division within the Kentucky State Police. We have just received a Department of Justice grant for this project and I certainly want to thank our special guest, Mr. Danzinger, for his help in expediting our application.[2] These funds will enable us to put eleven highly trained special agents into the field, and to back them up with four intelligence officers and a systems analyst, as well as sophisticated laboratory and technical assistance. This unit will concentrate its enforcement activities against illegal gambling operations, burglary, auto theft rings, and organized fencing of stolen property.

So we are making progress, and we've taken some useful steps toward an effective confrontation with crime in Kentucky. But the fact still remains that crime isn't a national problem, and it isn't a state problem. It's a local problem, and no amount of national or state effort is ever going to be as effective as the type of intelligent, systematic, courageous local crusade that you are a part of here in this community. No other problem we face today addresses itself so clearly and so forcefully to the local community; and in no other problem is it so abundantly clear that human resources, not financial resources, can supply the lasting and enduring answers we seek.

Ladies and gentlemen, we have been through a period when some of our people began preaching the idea that individuals were no longer economically accountable for their own well-being or morally responsible for their own behavior. And there have been those who believed that philosophy, or at least they adopted it in order to further their own special goals and ambitions. So it isn't surprising that today we are being confronted by those who want to change the laws and weaken punishment for criminals. It is said that they want to make the laws more meaningful to modern society. They want the law to bend a little so it will accommodate the present-day mode of living. I just think it is time we stood up and said that rather than making laws to fit our conduct, we're going to make our conduct fit the laws. And when we do that, we can put an end to the age of permissiveness we have witnessed here in America during the last decade.

But it is going to take your support; it is going to demand your involvement and your dedicated commitment. It is going to take effective organizations throughout our State who will support their local law enforcement officials, who will watch over our courts, who will encourage their elected officials' support, and who will help our schools and churches to reach out and touch the lives of those who have failed or strayed.

I want to especially commend you for your efforts to preserve our judicial system. Of our three branches of government, none is nearly as important, yet nearly as fragile, as the judicial. There is much talk today about judicial reform, and I certainly would agree that some administrative support is needed, among other reforms that could be helpful. But let us never stray from the basic truth that the major imperfections lie not in the American system of justice, but in those within the system.

It wasn't the judicial system that was responsible for the fact that last year in one Kentucky county, a judge filed away 205 of the 323 state police citations for drunk driving. It wasn't the system that was responsible for 87 percent of the traffic tickets issued by Louisville police last year being filed away, voided, or dismissed outright, as a newsman reported. But the system is being blamed, and if it continues to be blamed, and if there are those who continue to lose confidence in the judicial process, America stands to lose the most useful tool she ever had in shaping the way of life that has made her the world's greatest country.

So I urge you to keep watching your courts, keep looking over the shoulder of your elected officials, and perhaps it might help if you insisted that the news media join you and fulfill their responsibility. It must be clear that until we are willing to insist on strict law enforcement, until we are willing to make it politically expedient to convict the criminal rather than dismiss the criminal, our case is hopelessly lost.

Ever since Henry Clay said he would rather be right than president, the American people have believed that their public officials couldn't be both. It's up to you to prove the fallacy of that logic. It's up to you, and the unknown hundreds that you may have inspired, to prove that our system does work, that our public officials can enforce the laws and still be elected. And it is up to you to continue your efforts in such a way that a grass roots crusade against crime will be waged in every part of our State and in every phase of our system in order that once again, in the words of Lincoln, "Reverence for the laws [will] be breathed by every American mother to the . . . babe that prattles on her lap; [it will] be taught in schools, in seminaries, and in colleges; [it will] be preached from the pulpit, proclaimed in legislative halls, and enforced in courts of justice . . . . In short, [it will] become the political religion of the nation; and . . . the old and the young, the rich and the poor, the grave and the gay of all sexes and tongues and colors and conditions [will] sacrifice unceasingly upon its altars."[3]

1. The Crusade versus Crime organization is a private, nonprofit, anti-crime group based in Louisville. Office of Charles L. Owen, executive director, Kentucky Crime Commission, September 27, 1971.

2. Martin Danzinger (1931–   ) was the chief of the Organized Crime Section, Law Enforcement Assistance Administration, United States Department of Justice (1969–1971).

3. Abraham Lincoln, "Address to the Young Men's Lyceum of Springfield," January 27, 1838, *Abraham Lincoln: Selected Speeches, Messages, and Letters,* ed. T. Harry Williams (New York, 1957), p. 10.

GROUNDBREAKING FOR NORTHERN KENTUCKY STATE COLLEGE
Covington / March 31, 1971

FOR those of us who were privileged to be present in 1968 and have a part in the legislative creation of Northern Kentucky College, today shall always be a very special and a very significant occasion. Not entirely unlike proud parents, we have come here today for the birth of a very special child, a child whose prodigious mission will be fully as demanding as it is unique in the educational history of our Commonwealth. I have always envisioned this child, this college, as a great deal more than simply a much-needed addition to Kentucky's system of public higher education. And I fully realize that it is of little consolation to you that this is the first public, four-year college to be constructed in Kentucky in half a century. That is understandable, because so many of you have waited so long, too long, through too many barren years of unfulfilled hope for the privilege of educating your children at a state college in your own community as other parents in every other section of the Commonwealth have been privileged to do.

And so, because of you, Northern Kentucky College must be more than an institution, more than bricks and mortar, more than a center for continuing education. For the people of this region, for the problems you face, and for the limitless potential that is yours to seize, Northern Kentucky College must be, and with the care and consideration of its administrators, its faculty, and its students, and with the unflinching support of the total community it will be the welding force through which the high aspirations and hopes of this area shall be attained. I envision this school as the unifying element, the cohesive nucleus, for a brighter tomorrow for northern Kentucky. It is my sincere hope that this child of opportunity and enlightenment will finally replace the stepchild complex of the past.

Today culminates a long, sometimes frustrating, and always strenuous battle for those who dreamed and planned and worked to establish a full-fledged public college here. But this should not be considered an ending. It should be considered, as it truly is, a beginning, a commencement of unity so strong it will stimulate the kind of public progress Kentucky's second largest urban area so eagerly awaits and so richly deserves.

We have come through the political, legislative, economic, and educational barriers to this groundbreaking ceremony as one—one region, one state, one nation, and one people. And the questions of where we go from here, how well this school fulfills our expectations, and how much it will mean to this regional community, will in large measure be answered by the manner in which we depart. Northern Kentucky State College can be a magnet for progress. It can attain its potential as a center of culture. It can help attract new economic development. It can instill in young and old alike the sense of community that has been missing for too long. It can do all these things, it can be all these things, if a spark of unity can be kindled into an enduring flame.

I recall very clearly that there were some protesting voices three years ago when a measure was before the Legislature that would provide funds for your college. At that time their noisy discord almost blew out the spark of hope for this school. Today those voices are silent. But this is not a time for silence. This is a time for support. And I urge them to join the chorus of support we hear so plainly today and let their voices now help to fan the flame of hope we are endeavoring to light for this area.

Now I should like to turn from the community mission of the college and discuss briefly the crucial educational mission that lies ahead. There are no paths to guide you on this mission because Northern Kentucky State College is blazing an original trail for public higher education here. But that does not necessarily mean you are at a disadvantage, for paths sometimes become ruts, tradition can stifle as well as inspire, and habits can be destructive as well as efficient.

Mark this trail with care, those of you on the administrative level and on the faculty, because in the days ahead some young man or young lady will come this way. Their eyes may be so filled with the future or so clouded by inexperience that they can observe only the most vivid of guideposts. Their parents, their communities, and their State deliver them into your hands. Teach them well, give them information, but more than that, give them knowledge at this formative juncture in their lives. Provide them with training that is relative to the needs of today and consistent with the lessons of yesterday. Instill in them the creativity with which they might apply their knowledge toward a better world. Teach them to be solvent. Show them the difference beween financial solvency and moral, spiritual, and intellectual bankruptcy. Anchor their valuable lives with the basic fundamentals for happy, productive, serene existence.

To the students now enrolled and to those who are privileged to follow them through this new institution falls a special responsibility. Because of the advantages you have and because of the opportunities being provided to you, no group has ever had so much to live up to. Kentuckians are proud of their young people and they have proven it by their unselfish support of education. Since 1968 support for elementary and secondary education has increased by 53 percent. And support for higher education increased more than 35 percent. We look to the students of today and tomorrow to honor the generous commitment that has been made on their behalf by the taxpayers of this Commonwealth. We look to you, and not to the local law enforcement officials or the state police or the national guard, to form the first line of defense against those who would defile this place of learning and destroy the confidence we have placed in your generation. We look to you as maturing young adults to establish a wholesome pattern of respect for those who are here to guide you and for those whose sacrifices made this facility possible.And we look to you with confidence that you will set standards of excellence in all that is undertaken here at Northern Kentucky State College.

There is a third segment that can help this institution to fulfill its educational mission. I am speaking of the individual citizen in each of the communities served by this college. The success of this school is dependent upon the active support of each person within its sphere of influence. Nurture this child with understanding, protect it with your interest, stimulate its growth with your concern, and guide its path through your example.

If Northern Kentucky State College is properly guided by its administrators, if its faculty meets the challenging needs of the students, if its students live up to their responsibilities and seize the opportunities that have been provided, and if it continues to be showered with community support, we can all look forward to that day when it shall deserve and receive full university status. In its recent report the Kentucky Council on Public Higher Education expressed my fervent desire that this college some day join the University of Kentucky, Louisville, Western, Murray, Eastern, and Morehead on equal footing. Let it be your goal to become a university not in name alone but a university in the truest sense of quality and excellence.

As I said at the beginning, you have a prodigious and demanding mission, within both the academic and total communities. This is not the time for those of you here or those of us in government to become satisfied with past efforts and abandon the future. For our part, we shall continue to look for innovative ways to assist you through this very difficult early stage of development. I would underscore that pledge with the following announcements of action now being taken to speed up the process of evolution to a four-year college: First, I have asked the State Department of Finance to transfer immediately both the language laboratory equipment and the highly specialized science laboratory equipment from the discontinued Lincoln School to Northern Kentucky State College.

Secondly, some two weeks ago, we began inquiries into the possibility of immediate construction of additional campus buildings. This series of inquiries and investigations was prompted by our sincere desire that this school become the civic rallying point for your region. And so it is with a great deal of pride and expectation that I announce that arrangements have been finalized and confirmed, an architect has been named, and design work has already begun on an auditorium-civic center here on the campus of Northern Kentucky College. Preliminary drawings have been made and the initial blueprints of this latest addition to the campus will be on display tonight at the dinner being sponsored by the Chamber of Commerce.

Ladies and gentlemen, we could not have come this far nor gotten this institution off to such a fast start without the spirit of unity that has prevailed, and the courage and dedication that has persisted. All who shared in this effort can be proud, and this occasion is dedicated to them.

In closing, I would remind you that as large as our colleges or universities may grow, as great as we desire them to be, as exalted as they become, let us never forget that it was the citizen who conceived them and gave them the power of creation. And therein, with the free and informed citizen, lies the hope of our State and our nation. It is in this spirit that we break ground today for Northern Kentucky College.

KENTUCKY PUBLIC HEALTH ASSOCIATION
Louisville / April 6, 1971

To accept the privilege of serving as Governor of our Commonwealth also is to accept the commitment of serving the needs of all its people. Nowhere is this commitment and this obligation more personally compelling than in the field of health. We can take a great deal of pride in the progress that has been made in fulfilling that commitment in the nearly forty months of this administration, and in a few moments I would like to share a brief progress report with you. But despite the instances of achievement and notable progress, this is and I am sure will continue to be a bitter-sweet experience, because the battle to ease human suffering is perhaps destined to be a never-ending one. And as long as one of us suffers from illness or disease, all of us must share in alleviating that suffering. There have been moments of success during these three and one-half years. But there is the nagging frustration of delay and inadequacy as well. Having felt this mixed result, I can appreciate even more than ever the magnitude of your contribution during the twenty-three years of this organization, and I commend and congratulate each of you for the part you have played in this vital work.

Many compliments have been given the efforts for educational progress that have been made during the past forty months. Certainly, we are proud that aid to elementary and secondary schools increased by 53 percent, state aid to our public colleges and universities increased by more than 35 percent, and the budget for vocational education increased by 99 percent. Our road-building program has received favorable local attention as well as national recognition. Industrial growth reached the billion-dollar mark in capital investment and gross farm income went over a billion dollars in both 1969 and 1970 for the first and second times in our history.

But these achievements are small indeed when compared to the fact that more Kentuckians now have a better opportunity to enjoy a higher quality of health services than ever before. And we can go a step further to say that the health of Kentuckians should improve even more rapidly in the future as the full impact of many significant changes recently made in our health planning and delivery system are fully implemented. This has been made possible through a comprehensive program that might best be divided into three distinct parts. They are: coordination of planning, reorganization, and concerted action.

One of the major failings of state government in previous years was the absence of planning. We never got beyond the crisis stage. We spent our time and our resources putting out brush fires. We practiced corrective medicine, rather than preventative medicine, so to speak. This had a particularly distressing effect on our health care programs, where it was complicated by the fact that, as you know, we had inadequate health manpower and resources. To make matters worse, the resources we had were being dissipated by duplication, waste, and fragmentation.

Believing that Kentucky is blessed with talented and dedicated citizens, we turned to concerned members of the private sector for help and asked them to serve without remuneration on the Comprehensive Health Planning Council. This group has served with distinction in putting this State far ahead of others in this effort. We are now better able to utilize available resources and deliver health services more efficiently to those in need of help.

The second step was coordination of the various departments of state government which dealt with human resources. These included the commissioners of Health, Mental Health, Child Welfare, Economic Security, Education, Corrections, and Finance in a group called the Human Resources Coordinating Commission. I personally credit much of the success we have realized to this group of commissioners who were willing to put departmental prejudice aside and attack their mutual problems on a very creative and innovative plane. From this successful experiment has come the cooperative and creative leadership so essential to human programming.

In addition to these two basic efforts toward better coordination, we have experienced an ever-widening circle of reorganization in the Health Department. Many of the changes made came as a result of recommendations from the Kentucky Efficiency Task Force. For instance, the Deputy Commissioner for Administration has been appointed. Management practices have been upgraded. Personnel activities have been separated from other administrative functions to increase efficiency. Significant changes also have been made in the structure of our environmental control section and more authority has been granted. Reorganization of our environmental control personnel has significantly strengthened this crucial effort.

Composition of the State Board of Health has changed greatly in the past three years. The most recent changes include the appointments of a nationally prominent leader in American medicine, Dr. Robert Long of Louisville, and Dr. Guy Cunningham of Ashland, an extremely gifted clinician. I am pleased to announce today the appointment of Dr. John Trevey, of Lexington, a public-spirited physician and possibly the youngest member ever appointed to the State Board of Health.[1] Dr. Trevey is the managing physician for the IBM Corporation in Lexington and brings with him experience in public health and industrial medicine.

These changes in the state board and the administration of the department quite naturally bring a new look to the Kentucky health program. Dr. McElwain has spoken of the reorganization and the change in philosophy of the delivery of service by the department.[2] The philosophy of administration that charges the local health departments with the main responsibility for the delivery of service has broad and far-reaching implications. This increase in responsibility will necessitate an increase in productivity if we are to be successful. We believe that local health department employees will respond with dedication and commitment. This increase in responsibility should be adequately compensated, and to this end, we have revised upward by about 10 percent the salaries of local employees. The importance of our local health departments and their responsibility in the delivery of health services to our citizens cannot be overemphasized.

What are the effects of these steps in coordination and reorganization? Not only are we now more efficient and not only are we able to make better uses of our resources, but we are now moving more confidently into several important areas of public health. Now I would like to review briefly some of the accomplishments in a few of the more crucial areas.

As you perhaps know, one of my concerns in recent months has been the growing problem of drug abuse. This problem is no longer confined to far-off places such as New York or San Francisco. It is now found in many of our smaller towns and cities here in Kentucky. To prevent this terrible blight from spreading, we have formed a volunteer front-line of defense on the community level. With your support, with the assistance and direction of those of you from the local health departments, and the continued surveillance of state and federal experts, Kentucky can be spared the tragic epidemic that has been experienced elsewhere.

In 1964 an epidemic of rubella swept through Kentucky and across the nation with devastating effects. Because we were unprepared that time, it left a legacy of heartbreak and anguish. In Kentucky alone, an estimated 285 infants were stillborn. At least 360 more were maimed for life with the crosses of congenital deafness, blindness, heart disease, and mental retardation. The cost for treatment and special education and institutional care for these children today totals more than $3.6 million per year, and their loss in economic potential has been estimated at an additional $30 million. With a prediction of another epidemic in the early 1970's, a national drive to develop a vaccine was instituted, and in June 1969, the first proven vaccine against rubella was licensed. Shortly thereafter, a modest federal grant for the purchase of a limited supply of vaccine was awarded the State Health Department. Kentucky immediately became one of the first states in the nation to begin a rubella eradication program.

In December 1969, at a Conference on Rubella in Frankfort, we asked the hundreds of representatives of voluntary agencies and service organizations in attendance to join with the state government in making sure that the next cycle of rubella would not again victimize our people. To further this effort, I made an appropriation of $50 thousand from the Executive Contingency Fund for the immediate purchase and administration of urgently needed vaccine. As a result of that conference, more than thirty-five voluntary and professional organizations and their affiliates contributed unselfishly of their time and money to Kentucky's "Stop Rubella Campaign." Since that time, additional federal grants have been received and a half million dollars in state funds has been appropriated to carry this vital program through to completion. To date, through the efforts of official health agencies, private physicians, and the gentle legion of voluntary support, *387,917 Kentucky children have been inoculated against rubella*. I commend you for your efforts to protect the well-being of our children yet unborn. We must all recognize, however, that the job is far from completed, and must pledge our continuing efforts to totally eradicate this costly and tragic disease.

The last session of the General Assembly enacted the State Tuberculosis Act of 1970. This law created within the State Department of Health a Division of Tuberculosis Control with authority to relate to all aspects of tuberculosis control in the Commonwealth. The development of chemotherapeutic agents for the treatment of tuberculosis, along with the development and refinement of the art of tuberculosis control, has resulted in a marked change in our situation during the past twenty years. There is a change in emphasis from the treatment of the patient with advanced disease to detection and treatment prior to symptoms. This necessitates a redirection of the use of our resources. One of the reasons for the merger of the Tuberculosis Hospital Commission with the State Department of Health was to bring our resources to bear on our tuberculosis problem for the best possible result. The combining of the resources of the Tuberculosis Hospital Commission with those of the State Department of Health and our 120 local health departments should result in significant accomplishments in the control of this dreaded disease in the very near future.

In step with the change in treatment procedure, the Hazelwood Sanitorium in Louisville will be converted from its use for tuberculosis patients to a facility for the treatment of the mentally retarded on July 1, 1971. Full provisions have been made for the adequate care of those in state governmental Region VI who will require inpatient care.

This is being accomplished through a contract for hospitalization of these patients in the Louisville Memorial Hospital. The contract has already been signed by Louisville's governing authorities. This represents another example of the cooperative efforts that state and local government can make in the solution of common problems. We have every reason to believe that there have been improvements in the tuberculosis program in this district while at the same time an economy of approximately a million dollars has been effected. This savings can be used to extend other needed health services.

One of our significant environmental problems is that of the safe handling and disposal of solid waste. Kentucky has recognized and committed itself to an early solution of this complex and rapidly expanding problem. In 1968 we successfully recommended passage of the Kentucky Solid Waste Disposal Act, which charges the State Department of Health with the development of an adequate program and also to secure the benefits of the Federal Solid Waste Disposal Act for our Commonwealth. A comprehensive solid waste management program for Kentucky was published in June 1970. *Kentucky became the first state in the southeast to have its plan approved and one of the first in the nation to accomplish this task.* The Resource Recovery Act of 1970 made provision for funding assistance to communities, counties, and regions for long-range planning for solid waste management in those states with an approved state plan. Now, because of the prompt response to this opportunity, local communities in Kentucky are eligible for funding from the federal government. I urge each of you to encourage your local communities to take advantage of these federal grants for the preparation and implementation of plans to solve the solid waste problems.

Occupational health and safety has not gone unnoticed. Only a healthy, productive work force can maintain the quality of life. The Ninety-First Congress passed the Occupational Safety and Health Act of 1970. The purpose of this act is to assure, so far as possible, every working man and woman in the nation safe and healthful working conditions and the preservation of our human resources. This act provides federal grants to assist states in the identification of the needs and responsibilities in the area of occupational safety and health and the development of state plans to meet these needs. I have designated the Department of Health as the single state agency for the receipt of these grants and the development of our State's plan to fulfill our responsibilities toward our working people. The Division of Occupational Environment in the State Department of Health is now engaged in the development of this plan.

Air pollution control efforts throughout the Commonwealth have accelerated dramatically during the past year. Eleven regulations have been adopted by the Air Pollution Control Commission and nine air quality control regions covering the entire State have been designated for planning purposes. A new permit program has been successful in preventing air pollution from new industrial growth while also proving equally effective in abating air pollution from other sources. In this regard, since March 14, 1969, voluntary compliance programs have been initiated with fourteen Kentucky industries. These will produce an estimated reduction in particulate emission of about 4,700 tons per year. Monitoring of pollutant levels is currently being conducted in fifty-five communities located in twenty-three counties. Open burning at public and private dumps has been attacked in eighty-five communities. All but fifteen of these have been abated and the remaining are in various stages of resolution. Industry-wide abatement programs have been initiated with asphalt plant operators, quarry operators, and electrical utilities. Process industries such as steel making, petroleum refining, and chemical production are being handled on a case-by-case basis.

To assure more effective enforcement, and to encourage and assist compliance, we are now in the process of opening field offices throughout the State. The first of these was announced for Ashland in February and is expected to be operational by late spring. Others are scheduled for Paducah and the Newport-Covington area. Future emphasis will be placed on development of special inspection programs for motor vehicles including private autos, trucks, and buses to check their pollution emissions.

The Kentucky Medical Assistance Program has been successful in making available to many citizens of the Commonwealth the personal and health services that they need but cannot afford. The Kentucky Medical Assistance Program has been able to broaden its coverage to include laboratory, X rays, mental health center services, expanded dental payments and certain other hospital costs. The cost of this program is now in the vicinity of $65 million a year and represents a significant expenditure of the funds of the Commonwealth.

It became apparent some time ago that the rising expenditures were approaching a level which the State would be unable to bear. Consequently, I requested the Medical Advisory Council for the Kentucky Medical Assistance Program to review the program and recommend ways in which the use of funds might be improved. The Council responded by designing a system of peer review to systematically survey the program and assure proper utilization of services—with adequate standards of care—while maintaining compliance with participation agreements and program regulations. Preliminary reports indicate that this procedure is proving very helpful in reducing unnecessary expenditures and controlling abuse in order that we may serve those in need of medical attention. This program will be modified and expanded in the near future.

One of the major problems facing medicine and the public health and welfare is the lack of trained individuals, available facilities, and research equipment for the discovery, evaluation, diagnosis, treatment and prevention of kidney disease. The development of a comprehensive program to combat kidney disease will require the combined and correlated efforts of state and local governments, medicine, universities, nonprofit organizations, and individuals. In order to bring to bear and coordinate all possible resources of the State in this vital matter, I supported and signed into law last year a bill establishing the Kentucky Kidney Disease Institute. The Department of Finance and representatives of our two medical schools are already involved in attacking the immediate crisis for those presently suffering from kidney disease by assuring the availability of care for these citizens. But on this occasion, I would like to dwell on the important long-range aspects of the kidney disease problem.

The State Health Department is involved in the documentation of the extent of our problem. They will proceed with an intensive survey of current needs and progressively implement programs for prevention, early detection, and adequate care in the future. This is extremely necessary to avoid crises in the future. Consultation to the State Department of Health is being furnished by Dr. Robert R. Siegel, a distinguished renalogist currently on the University of Kentucky Medical Center staff.[3]

Also in this regard, the legislation which established the Kidney Disease Institute provided for the appointment of an advisory council. I am pleased to take this opportunity to tell you that these appointments will be completed tomorrow. These distinguished individuals share my deep concern for this problem and bring to our effort the considerable expertise and personal experience that can lead us to a solution. I shall follow this program with a great deal of personal interest, and without hesitation pledge my continuing support to those who seek to solve the complex problems of diagnosis, treatment, and prevention of diseases of the kidney. Already I have pledged $50 thousand from the Governor's Contingency Fund to help implement a workable plan and to see that these individuals who cannot afford needed treatment do not go without proper and adequate care.

The Maternal and Child Health Program of the State Department of Health represents a very important investment to the citizens of this Commonwealth. Over 1,000 children with neurological problems including cerebral palsy, epilepsy, mental retardation, and learning disabilities have been examined, evaluated, and treated at special pediatric clinics in thirty-four counties. Significant progress has been achieved in maternal and infant care. Maternal mortality has been reduced from 3.6 deaths per thousand births to a low of 1.9 per thousand. Infant deaths have been reduced from 24.1 to 20.5 per thousand live births. Through the regional pediatric clinic program, 8,705 medically indigent children have for the first time been given comprehensive medical care and rehabilitation services. Dental services have also recently been added to this program. Most of the maternal and child health programs are dedicated to the maintenance of the health of the mother and to the development of a normal, healthy infant. This is a very significant part of preventing mental retardation and other disabilities that affect our children. In view of the recently initiated effort to develop a program for the adequate care of exceptional children in the State, these endeavors can produce dividends far in excess of their cost.

Sound government programs deserve adequate financing. And yet many well-planned programs have been underfinanced in the past, not because they were unworthy, but simply because the money was not available. The present upturn in state revenue collections, then, is more than just an encouraging economic sign—it is a means of extending services. Agencies which have documented their goals and demonstrated their competence will now have appropriations more nearly commensurate with their needs. The Department of Health is one such agency. I am happy to announce that additional funds in the amount of $137 thousand are being channeled into health's budget. A substantial part of these funds will be used to give a long-deserved salary increment to local health department employees. We will also be able to provide additional services in Tuberculosis Control, including the Outpatient Drug Program. We can assist with the Water Quality Control program, as well as provide equipment to identify and measure the highly toxic substances in pesticides that are intended to replace the banned DDT.

No one thinks or claims that these actions will solve all the problems facing either the State Department of Health or local health departments. Nor should anyone believe that these funds and efforts represent the limit of this administration's concern. All of us in state government feel as you do that the protection of the health of our fellow Kentuckians is a responsibility to be cherished and an opportunity for service that can be exercised only by the dedicated. Let me assure you of our profound gratitude and our continuing support.

---

1. Robert C. Long (1916–   ), Louisville, member, Kentucky State Board of Health (1971–   ); member, Advisory Committee on International Health, Agency for International Development, United States Department of State (1966–   ); and trustee, American Medical Association (1963–1970). He has also served as chairman, Physicians for Nixon, Commonwealth of Kentucky (1968); and is a member, Jefferson County Republican Executive Committee (1966–   ). Office of Dr. Robert C. Long, September 8, 1971.

Guy Cunningham (1921–   ), Ashland, member, Kentucky State Board of Health (1971–   ); clinical professor of pediatrics, University of Kentucky School of Medicine (1971–   ); chairman, Board of Advisors, Ashland Community College (1970–   ); state chairman, Kentucky Chapter of the American Academy of Pediatrics (1969–   ); and member, Board of Directors, Kentucky Blue Shield (1969–   ). Telephone interview with Cunningham, Ashland, September 8, 1971.

John Edwin Trevey (1933–   ), Lexington, member, Kentucky State Board of Health (1971–   ); member, Fayette County Republican Executive Committee (1971–   ); Republican campaign chairman, Fayette County (1971); managing physician for IBM Corporation. Telephone interview with Trevey, Lexington, September 7, 1971.

2. William Paul McElwain (1933–   ), Lexington, commissioner (1970–   ), and deputy commissioner (1970), Kentucky Department of Health; associate director, Lexington-Fayette County Health Department (1968–1969). Office of Dr. William Paul McElwain, Health Department, September 9, 1971.

3. Robert R. Siegel (1930–   ), Lexington, associate professor of medicine, Renal Division, University of Kentucky School of Medicine (1970–   ). Telephone interview with Siegel, Lexington, February 7, 1972.

BOURBON COUNTY SOIL AND
WATER CONSERVATION DISTRICT
COOPERATORS' DINNER
Paris / April 8, 1971

FOR a few moments tonight I would like to talk to you about the future use of your land and other related resources and, as I see it, the role your district will play in the use of this land. In the nineteen years since this Soil and Water Conservation District was organized, all of you have seen many changes in the local landscape. These changes were made by people like yourselves, voluntarily working with the Soil and Water Conservation District in an effort to do a better job of farming, and at the same time, not only conserving what you have, but improving your farms as well.

Today what we hope and believe are constructive changes still are taking place, and let me take this opportunity to commend and congratulate your present Board of Supervisors for the outstanding conservation program it has developed and implemented to meet the demands of today. Mr. Kearns and Mr. Galloway deserve particular mention, since they were on the original Board of Supervisors; I would certainly like to commend them for the long years of service they have rendered.[1]

Back in 1952 Soil and Water Conservation Districts were yet to prove themselves. Their primary task at that time was erosion control. Then, as you recall, they began thinking in terms of land capabilities and soil improvement. They began to advocate using the land according to its natural capabilities and also improving the land while it was being used. Today we are concentrating on another goal—total resource development. The winds of change are still blowing. I believe we should proceed carefully and take every precaution to see that the seeds of progress that you have sown over the years are not scattered and wasted. Change is necessary, but all changes are not necessarily good. Methods of doing things should change, but time should not change our principles or ideals.

You all are aware of the much discussed population explosion and the demand for increased production of food and fibers. Here are a few points to consider: The population of the United States will double by the year 2000. A 36 percent increase is forecast in the demand for farm products by 1980, despite the fact that we will have 50 million fewer crop land acres than we had in 1960. A 120 percent increase in demand is expected by the turn of the century. The demand for certain types of foods will increase, and the requirements for others will decrease. This often shifts the locale of food production, too, not only because of population concentrations, but also because of the soil and water requirements related to changing food trends.

I have complete confidence in the American farmer, and he can meet these demands if given the opportunity. It's the opportunity that concerns me, because without good land, he doesn't have this opportunity. Let me explain what I mean. Besides the agricultural demands, here are the nonagricultural demands that we will have to meet by the year 2000, less than thirty years from now:

Land for recreation—up 300 percent over today's level.
Land for homes, schools, factories—up 215 percent.
Land for transportation—up 125 percent.
Land for wildlife refuges—up 133 percent.
Land for reservoirs—up 180 percent.

We shall have to make a piece of land serve more than one purpose at the same time. We shall have to explore and refine and perfect the multiple-use concept.

Demand for forest products will double in 30 years; 300 million more acres will have to be added to the existing 484 million acres of commercial forest lands. Land needs by the year 2000 will mount up to a total of far more than our full land area. But who will determine what land will be used for these various uses? Will our best agricultural land go to the top bidder, be it for agriculture, highways, homes, factories, or what have you? Will the farmer twenty years from now be farming the leftovers after our best land is covered with blacktop, brick, or concrete?

Let's go a step beyond who will make this decision. Let's also be sure to find out what their philosophy is. A lot of people claim to be conservationists. A lot of people talk about conservation. I feel it has become one of the most misused words in the English language. When it comes to our natural resources there seem to be three philosophies. One is exploitation; the second is preservation; and the third is conservation.

First let's take exploitation. This philosophy may be described as man working against nature. According to this line of thinking, man is not a part of nature. He is superior to it. He attempts to conquer or tame nature. Proponents of this philosophy feel that man should eventually domesticate his entire environment. They feel that this is a desirable goal. The philosophy argues that resources need minimum regulation of use because we shall find substitutes as our present resources become depleted. Full use of resources is necessary if we are to have progress. The "cut-out and get-out" era of the lumber industry in the past exemplifies the exploitation philosophy. We also see it in the present concept that man need not worry about limited land resources because he is on the verge of farming the ocean bottoms. The idea of complete climate control by man in the future is another manifestation of this philosophy. Exploitation is a philosophy of "mining" resources. Summed up, it might be described as an optimistic philosophy of unrestricted and irresponsible resource use.

Next let's take the philosophy of preservation. It is at the opposite pole from exploitation. It says that man should not tamper with nature because he cannot improve upon it. Man's use of natural resources, especially renewable resources, should be primarily aesthetic and intellectual rather than physical. These resources should be seen and felt, but not physically used. In its purest form the preservation philosophy does not recognize man as an integral part of nature, but merely as a visitor or intruder in nature. Like the exploiter, the preservationist wants man to rely on substitutes—but right now, instead of later—so that certain resources can be kept inviolate. Preservationist philosophy says, for example, that it is wrong to cut trees and wrong to kill wild animals. As soon as man uses a resource, he ruins it. Man is a polluter and a destroyer, and can be no better. Summed up, it is a pessimistic philosophy of nonuse.

Now let's take conservation. This philosophy is the middle ground between the previous two. It says that man should work with nature, not against it. Man is an integral part of nature and can't consider himself superior to it, or an intruder upon it. It is an ecological approach to resource problems. It is a philosophy often expressed as "wise use." It is permeated with the idea of responsible cropping of resource while maintaining their productivity over an indefinite period of time. It believes that the physical, aesthetic, and intellectual use of natural resources can be made compatible through planning. It is a philosophy of harvesting crops while preventing erosion, of tree farming, of sustaining yields of fish and game, and of using water without destroying water values. Proponents of this philosophy say that man will never be free from his dependence upon natural resources. Therefore, we must constantly renew such resources as soil, water, trees, fish, and game. Summed up, it is a cautious philosophy of use, but not misuse, of natural resources.

I believe this is the philosophy of your Soil and Water Conservation District and the men who govern it. You have done well in developing programs with this in mind. Here let me commend you and mention briefly some of these programs. Today environment and ecology are household words because your district and others throughout the Commonwealth have worked to have conservation education in the schools for years. Your district didn't wait for the State Department of Education to get our schools started on this important issue. Instead, you worked with your local school district and local schools and, as I understand it, have one of the outstanding programs in the State. This includes some outdoor laboratories and a grant to develop such laboratories. This is a result of work of your board of supervisors.

To do a good job in carrying out conservation programs takes money. Your district has secured funds for these purposes. During the past three years more than $31 hundred has been granted from the Direct Aid program of the Division of Soil and Water Conservation to your district. Since part of this is a matching fund this has permitted your district to raise some ten thousand dollars in local funds during the same three years. The results of these funds are most rewarding.

These are some of the more prominent programs. There are many more. I only used these to point out your supervisors are sound conservationists. They develop programs and plans to meet the demands of the day and serve the future.

In closing, it has been said that conservation is what you eat, and what you wear, and where you live; and if you don't, you won't.

---

1. Herman Kearns (1909–), chairman, Bourbon County Soil and Water Conservation District, a retired farm manager from Bourbon County. Telephone interview with Mrs. Herman Kearns, Bourbon County, September 27, 1971.

Roy Galloway (1892–), secretary, Bourbon County Soil and Water Conservation District, a retired farmer from Bourbon County. Telephone interview with Mrs. Roy Galloway, Bourbon County, September 28, 1971.

INTRODUCTION OF PRESIDENT
RICHARD M. NIXON
Republican Governors' Conference
Williamsburg, Virginia / April 19, 1971

MR. PRESIDENT, I want to welcome you here on behalf of all the Republican governors. Your presence is further proof that you recognize the vital role governors play in making federalism work. We recognize that if problems are to be solved, it will require a concerted and a cooperative effort on the part of the local, state, and federal governments. I am sure that all of us have been encouraged by your leadership, by your grasp of not only what America and the free world need, but also what the state and local governments must have: an equitable share of the public revenue to be responsible and responsive to the needs of our people.

We are all aware that the first half of your administration dealt with inherited problems. A war had been escalated to the point that a half million American soldiers were involved, and there was no plan to bring them home. Seeds of inflation already had been sown and fertilized by irresponsible spending policies. Years of neglect showed upon our environment. An overgrown bureaucracy had made government big but not strong. There were programs in need of reform: welfare, the draft, and education, to mention a few.

We commend you for your courageous leadership at a time when many felt they had been misled; for your tolerance in an age marked by intolerance; for your reason in an age spoiled by irrational behavior. We are grateful for your positive attitudes, for your positive programs, and we thank you for coming.

Ladies and gentlemen, the President of the United States.

SPINDLETOP RESEARCH
APPRECIATION LUNCHEON HONORING
PRINCIPAL CONTRIBUTORS AND
GOVERNOR AND MRS. LOUIE B. NUNN
Lexington / April 23, 1971

ONLY three years ago, in May 1968, I came over to meet with Spindle-top's Board of Directors. I asked at that meeting that we determine whether this organization could be saved and, if it could, whether it was worth the effort. Some of you may recall that at that time Spindle-top had mortgaged not only its present but its future. The building, the land, laboratory equipment, furniture, and even the accounts re-ceivable had been committed. Furthermore, Spindletop had overdrawn its account of good will. Its public image had been tarnished badly.

On that occasion in 1968 pride motivated me to say that I did not want to be a part of any failure. And I would not be involved in a project whose sure destiny was more of the same failure and frustra-tion Spindletop had experienced before my term of office. In my re-marks to the Board of Directors three years ago, I said that there were certain things I was willing to do as governor to assist in rejuvenating this organization if, and only if, the Board itself would shoulder its share of the responsibility for solving Spindletop Research's many problems.

First of all, it seemed to me that the Board itself was too large and unwieldly to accomplish much. A feeling had been allowed to spread that the Board served mainly in an honorary capacity. It was my view then, as it is now, that it is no honor to serve on any board unless we make it an honor. I was particularly pleased and encouraged when Spindletop's Board reacted positively to that challenge. The self-im-posed reform process included a reduction in the number of directors from seventy-four to twenty-five. The Executive Committee was trimmed from fifteen to nine. And the term of office for directors was reduced from ten years to one year so that only those vitally interested in this organization would remain active Board members.

At the same time, the Board adopted certain policies and procedures to be implemented by Spindletop's operating management. A direct and almost immediate result of these suggestions was a dramatic about-face of the flow of red ink that had marked the previous months of operation. Operating losses were trimmed sharply. Operating profits began to pump new life into the nearly exhausted veins of this organization and the nearly exhausted patience of those who supported it. We owe a considerable debt of gratitude to the Board and to the operating management here for taking the necessary steps to put Spindletop on a firm, businesslike basis.

And at the same time operations were being firmed up, we also launched a very ambitious fund-raising campaign to raise a half million dollars. This much was needed: first, to retire the debts that had been built up over the years; and second, to provide something Spindletop had never had since its inception, working capital that would permit it to function while it was being healed.

I am extremely gratified by the magnificent and public-spirited response business and industrial leaders in Kentucky demonstrated when we called for assistance. Certainly, I would like to commend and publicly thank those of you here today and the few contributors who cannot be with us for picking up the gauntlet and responding with generous pledges that helped to save Spindletop Research.

Those pledges were fully redeemed, and because of that, because of you, the progress of the past three years has been possible. That is why I am especially pleased to report to you and to the people of Kentucky that Spindletop Research is completely out of debt. Over and above that, the stability of this vital technical resource is underscored by the fact that it has been operating in the black for more than two and one-half of the past three years since its transformation. And the bright future so many have predicted for Spindletop for so long is now strengthened by the actual fact of a current backlog of projects that have been commissioned.

These projects, already under contract, represent not only a half year's research work, but far more importantly, these projects also reflect a very healthy mixture of private and public clients, as well as work from several other states in addition to Kentucky.

The quality of Spindletop's work for the past three years encourages us to look to this facility for new insight into the problems unique to our generation. I am personally familiar with several of the significant projects Spindletop Research has performed during this period because of the positive effects they have on the most crucial issues of our time. Spindletop has made a meaningful contribution to the agricultural industry of Kentucky and the nation. Through several projects relating to the economic importance of the horse industry, crippling damage from proposed legislation was averted, and this vital sector of Kentucky's diversified economy and an important part of our heritage was preserved.

Spindletop Research has gained worldwide recognition for the important research work performed here in the area of coal workers' pneumoconiosis. It is significant that this work was completed during a time when there was more heat than light being applied to this subject, particularly in the coal-producing regions of the world. With Spindletop's assistance, Kentucky has the best state park system in the country; we have the best system for comprehensive statewide water planning; we are the third state in the nation to have an approved statewide solid waste management plan; and this fall we will have the most advanced statewide plan for development of our airport system. These are but a few of the more than 175 projects performed for 16 departments and 14 agencies and commissions of state government during my administration.

From personal experience I can attest to the fact that Spindletop's staff is producing high-quality work, work that is useful and practical in solving many of the complex problems of our time. This is further borne out by the fact that in the same period of time Spindletop has worked for twelve other state governments in providing many of the same types of services. An encouraging omen for the future is the fact that work for other states represents the fastest growing segment of Spindletop's business.

It is my hope that Kentucky's next governor will find ways, as I have tried to do, to make good use of the wide range of services that is available here. I would place special emphasis on the word service, because neither Spindletop nor the people of this State should ever again accept an expensive doling out of make-work assignments whose results in many instances were never fully implemented.

It is now clear that this organization has had a remarkable recovery, and a firm foundation has been laid for service to the Commonwealth and its people. For those reasons and many more, I know you will agree that the investments of time and money made by all of you and by the Commonwealth of Kentucky during the past three and one-half years already have paid handsome dividends, and will continue to do so in the years ahead if we continue on the same businesslike, nonpartisan basis.

Certainly, I look upon the recovery of Spindletop Research as one of the most significant accomplishments during my term of office, and for that, I extend most sincere thanks to all of you, and also for the courage you have shown and the faith you have demonstrated in preserving Spindletop. Throughout my experience and involvement with this organization I have tried to do what I believed to be in the best interest of all Kentuckians, because I believe that the inherent benefits of Spindletop can, should, and now will accrue not only to state government, but to all of the people of this State.

The future of our Commonwealth and its people is brighter today because we have this strong and viable resources facility to perform needed applied research and planning projects. To those who resurrected this organization; to those who applied so well to this organization the same principles and practices that made them successful in their own enterprises; and to those whose contributions breathed new life into Spindletop and gave it a fighting chance to survive successfully, we gratefully dedicate this, the proudest day of Spindletop's troubled history.

Now if Bill Young will join me, I would like to formally retire the mortgage on Spindletop Research.[1] In the days when the environment was not of concern to many, it was customary to burn the mortgage. But we now know that there are better ways, ecologically speaking, to handle such matters. Therefore, we will shred the mortgage and dispose of it in a model sanitary landfill which Spindletop is developing with the assistance and approval of the Kentucky Department of Health.

---

1. William T. Young (1918–   ), Lexington, chairman, Board of Directors, Spindletop Research, Inc. (1970–   ); director, Heublein, Inc. (1971–   ); director, Kentucky Fried Chicken, Inc. (1969–1971); chairman, Board of Directors, Royal Crown Cola Company (1966–   ); chairman, Board of Directors, W. T. Young Storage, Inc., Lexington (1966–   ).

SOUTHEASTERN ASSOCIATION
OF RAILROAD AND UTILITIES
COMMISSIONERS
Louisville / May 13, 1971

I REALLY don't know why I agreed to talk with men of your expertise and special knowledge in a field in which I am not nearly as well versed; but I am delighted that I did, because in preparing to do so I have come to realize the tremendous responsibility that is yours, the significance of what you do, the problems confronting you, the opportunity you have to direct our country, and the services you can render to the people.

It is disturbing to me, and I think it should be distressing to everyone, that in the last several years, whenever we read a story about America's railroads, it almost certainly will fall into two categories. The story will either relate that the rail company has filed for bankruptcy or has discontinued certain routes in order to avoid bankruptcy. And the problem is that too many Americans are saying, "So what?" The individual is not directly in need of or aware of the service being rendered.

What we need to realize is that today in America the problems that affect us all alike are greater than the problems that affect us as individuals. And certainly all of us are affected when an industry as vital and as meaningful and as instrumental in shaping the history of this country as the rail industry has been is threatened with economic chaos.

About the only spokesman for the railroads these past few years has been Johnny Cash. Now I enjoy his songs about the railroads, but I'm worried that the right people aren't getting their contemporary message. The message is simply this: The railroads are in trouble, serious, complex, deep trouble, and we can't expect them to live on nostalgia and romance any longer. They need our concern. They need help, and they need it now, before it is too late for the companies to help themselves.

What they don't need, and what they can't afford—what we can't afford to accept—is federalization of this nation's railroads. First of all, the basic monetary cost of a takeover of the railroads by the federal government would be $60 billion and that should be reason enough to reject the proposal.

If we need another reason, perhaps we should look at the philosophical aspects of this proposal. Very frankly, gentlemen, I believe we ought to be concerned that federalization isn't just socialism under the guise of public service. We ought to be concerned that it isn't just more of the same old philosophy of big government and little people. And we ought to be concerned about some deeper and far-reaching implications of such a move as federalization. I don't believe it is in America's best interest for us to conclude that private enterprise failed in such an important task as basic transportation of people and goods. Because, if we do admit failure, how are we going to advocate private enterprise as an alternative to socialism and communism in the other free countries around the world?

There is a story about the various "isms" in the world. Under socialism, you have two cows and give one to your neighbor. Under communism, you have two cows; the government takes both and gives
you the milk. Under fascism, you have two cows; the government
takes both and sells you the milk. Under Nazism, you have two cows;
the government takes both of them and shoots you. Under New Deal-
ism, you have two cows; the government takes both, shoots one, milks
one, and throws away the milk. Under capitalism, you have two cows,
sell one, and buy a bull.

We have to have faith in the free enterprise system. We have to
have faith in the genius of individual men. Today there are those who
seriously and constantly question the ability of our system of free enterprise to meet the demands of a growing industrial economy. There
are those doomsday prophets who insist that we are ill-equipped to
provide enough energy to meet the needs of this nation. Certainly, we
all realize that we face a difficult assignment, even when this problem
is limited only to the availability of energy. Today's projections call
for a doubling of the generating capacity in your service areas from
68,000 megawatts today to 165,000 megawatts nine years from now.

I have full confidence that we will meet those requirements, if certain
conditions are met. And I know that Kentucky will continue to play
a major role in providing the energy on which the southeast United
States will emerge as the developmental center of the nation. Despite the
optimistic predictions about developments in nuclear energy, the fact
remains that today's needs, as well as those of the foreseeable future,
will rely more and more on energy that is generated by fossil fuels.
And, as you know, Kentucky is blessed with coal reserves in two major
fields. Utilities presently use the West Kentucky field for most of their
coal supply, about 16 million tons a year. And in eastern Kentucky,
we have an estimated 9.5-billion-ton reserve of recoverable fuel. That
is why I believe we are going to meet the growth demands of the immediate future.

As I indicated previously, however, there are conditions to this
confidence, and that is where you come in. At one time the role of the
regulator may have been limited to setting rates of income based on
complex formulas of outgo. But current events make it abundantly
clear that this role must be expanded, because today both the environment which energy produces, and the environment that produces
energy, are being questioned in great detail. Again, this is an example
that the problems that affect us all alike are indeed greater than those
affecting us as individuals. And nowhere is this phenomenon more
apparent than in the field of fossil fuels on which all of us will rely so

heavily in the years ahead. And so, it will come as no surprise to you that we in Kentucky are particularly concerned.

Circumstances have conspired to place all of us in government, but especially those of you on the utility commissions, squarely in the middle of a collision course between some very diverse schools of thought. You will not satisfy everyone; you cannot satisfy some, so prepare for criticism.

On the one hand, you are being involved in the philosophical struggle between those who, for the sake of classification, might be said to advocate either conservation, preservation, or exploitation. The exploitation philosophy is advocated by those who see man not as a part of nature, but superior to nature. This philosophy argues that resources need minimum regulation of use for the sake of progress, because when present resources are depleted, substitutes will be found. Summed up, it might be described as an optimistic philosophy of unrestricted and irresponsible use of our resources.

Preservation is at the opposite end of the philosophical pole. Advocates of this school of thought say man should not tamper with nature because he can't improve upon it. They see man not as an integral part of nature, but merely as a visitor or an intruder upon nature. The preservationist wants man to rely on substitutes—but right now—not when our resources are depleted. In some instances they indicate no substitute, but show a lack of willingness to do without. Summed up, preservation could be defined as a pessimistic philosophy of nonuse.

Conservation is somewhere between these somewhat extreme poles of thought. This philosophy says man should work with nature, not against nature; that man is an integral part of nature and neither superior to it nor an intruder upon it. The conservationist believes in the wise use of our resources, because he realizes that man will never be free from his dependence upon nature. Therefore, he must constantly renew the soil, water, trees, fish, and game. We might sum it up by saying this is a philosophy of use, but not misuse.

While sorting out these philosophies is difficult and demanding, it doesn't stop there for those of us who are elected and those of you who are appointed to the utility commissions. That struggle relates primarily to the extraction of our resources. There is another, ever widening struggle over the pollution from the use of these resources by the industries you regulate. Regardless of whether it is extraction or use that we are concerned about, there is but one course toward the solution of either argument. That course is balance.

We cannot question the fact that present-day productivity does present a severe challenge to our environment. But on the other hand, we are a nation dedicated to productivity, to private enterprise, to personal initiative, and to progress. This is not the time to blame America's producers. This is not the time to fault those who advocate conservation. This is the time to fuse them together in order that we can design realistic, balanced, equitable goals that serve our needs for both productivity and conservation.

This responsibility falls very heavily upon you. It is our hope, and our expectation, that you will lead the cooperative effort to find practical, enduring solutions which will assure America of the utilities and the environment it must have if we are to continue to light the path of freedom for the world.

GOVERNOR'S ENVIRONMENTAL CONFERENCE
Natural Bridge State Park
Slade / May 27, 1971

THIS may well prove to be one of the most significant meetings in the course of my four years as Governor of the Commonwealth. I say that for several reasons. First, we all recognize that the kind of natural environment we have determines what kind of human environment we create. Secondly, because no other issue has generated so much heat and shed so little light as the question of environmental use and protection. Thirdly, because Kentucky's natural abundance, despite countless abuse and years and years of unconcern, still is such that we have a chance to save it from the chaos we see in many of the states of this nation.

As this conference begins let us remember that all of our problems will not be resolved here today and that all of the environmental opportunities in Kentucky will not be seized by what we do here. This issue can be resolved in the best interest of all Kentuckians, and because we play such a vital role as an energy center for the nation it can be resolved in the best interest of America only if we take a studied, thoughtful, enlightened course. The course I advocate, the course I truly believe will lead us to the solutions that are in the best interest of Kentucky and America, and the course so eloquently advocated by nature itself, is one of effective balance. Let me elaborate.

I know that to some of you who are our most passionate and dedicated conservationists, the course of balance is often misinterpreted. It is sometimes misunderstood. It has been labeled as a concession to those who exploit, plunder, and abuse the environment. I want to make it perfectly clear that we cannot and we must not concede our natural heritage. We must not vacillate. We cannot equivocate on this issue. It has to be faced squarely. It should be faced openly in meetings such as this. It must be faced with complete disregard for political advantage or disadvantage, and it must be faced truthfully.

One of the many meaningful passages of the Bible that has compelling significance for me has always been I Corinthians 14:8: "For if the trumpet give an uncertain sound, who shall prepare for battle?" By proposing that we blaze a balanced path in the field of environmental protection and use, we cannot be uncertain. Our message cannot be unclear. Nor can the voices of concern for this issue be so loud and so impassioned and so irrational, even if the cause is justified, that our message falls on deaf ears.

The cause of environmental protection is not served by a government so unrealistic that its demands and requirements and regulations cannot be met. Nor is it served by those in private enterprise whose alienation and greed promote a callous disregard for our land, our water, and our air. This cause also suffers at the hands of those at the other end of the spectrum, the radical conservationists and preservationists whose bitter rhetoric and litany of overstatement and doomsday prophecy attack the integrity and insult the intelligence of their fellow citizens. Instead, government must determine realistic goals. We must establish standards which are reasonable in implementation as well as effect. Government must enact fair and equitable laws and regulations to accomplish these goals. And finally, government must act firmly and courageously to enforce these laws.

Law and order cannot be confined to human acts of violence against another person. To desecrate God's handicraft by wanton mutilation is a crime against both God and man. Private enterprise has a very plain responsibility. This nation has long honored the principle and concept of private enterprise. It is one of the cornerstones of our country. The policy of this administration has been not one of alienation but of cooperation in encouraging industry to conform to the strengthened environmental regulations we have designed. If private enterprise is to continue to be entrusted with our faith and our support, then it must voluntarily assume the responsibility not only to maintain the present quality of our environment, but also to rectify previous transgressions wherever possible.

We need also to ask what we as individuals, as private citizens, and as conservationists can do not just to criticize and repeatedly point the finger of blame, but to show a sense of direction both in knowing the problem and in giving answers. First, if we are truly concerned about this problem, we must also be dedicated to the proposition that the environment is everyone's responsibility. Governmental action is futile and corporate cooperation is meaningless if private citizens continue to exercise the individual irresponsibility characterized by the driver pointing the finger of blame at industrial smokestacks while his family throws trash out the window of the car.

During the length of this conference, I hope that you will judge for yourselves how this administration and private enterprise and you as an individual have met the responsibilities I have just outlined. But it is more important to determine how we can better meet the challenge and seize the opportunity to do a better job, to appraise, to assess and reassess, to evaluate, and to try to formulate proper solutions.

One of the primary purposes of the meeting is to report to the people of Kentucky, through those of you who have so much concern and interest in our environment, some of the major steps we have taken during the last three and one-half years to guard the natural resources and the beauty of our Commonwealth. It would seem appropriate to mention first that the scenic beauty of Red River Gorge finally has been preserved. In addition: the pristine majesty of Lilley Cornett Woods is now safe; there has been a major expansion of our reclamation regulations to include all minerals; we have established the Environmental Resources Coordinating Commission; a memorandum of understanding with Kentucky's 121 soil conservation districts has, in essence, tripled our manpower at the local level to guard against unmanageable strip-mining operation; new regulations to upgrade the standard of all streams in the Commonwealth are in final stages of adoption; new regulations have been written and new standards set to control air pollution; and finally, Kentucky is the first state in this region and among the first in the nation to have an approved solid waste management plan.

These are some of the most dramatic demonstrations that we are attacking Kentucky's environmental problems and that we are developing mechanisms through which effective, equitable solutions can be found. In addition to reporting our efforts, as well as many of the very complex problems we have encountered, we have also come here to solicit your ideas, your constructive comments, and your support for the protection and proper utilization of Kentucky's land, water, and air. We have made a special effort to build into the schedule of this meeting opportunities to hear what you have to say. I urge you to take this unique opportunity and make use of this forum on behalf of Kentucky's environment.

Julien Hyer once wrote: "On the plains of Hesitation lie the bones of those who chose to die by standing still, or when accused of fault or wrong would not defend their convictions to the end. Their thinking was not positive. They had no arguments to give. By inaction they paid the cost, for he who hesitates is lost."[1] It is in this spirit of positive thinking that we open this first annual Environmental Protection Conference.

---

1. From "The Shepherd," a poem by Julien C. Hyer (1894–   ). The poem was originally published as a syndicated newspaper verse about 1950. Hyer is a Dallas attorney and the author of The Shepherd (1955), a collection of syndicated verse. Telephone interview with Hyer, Dallas, Texas, October 13, 1971; Who's Who in America, 1970–1971 (Chicago, 1971), 36:1116.

UNIVERSITY OF LOUISVILLE
MEDICAL SCHOOL COMMENCEMENT
Louisville / June 6, 1971

FOR those of you most directly involved in this commencement exercise, the graduates, parents, families, faculty, and administrators, I can well appreciate the feelings of pride and accomplishment and responsibility you must be experiencing at this moment. Savor this rich and significant moment, relish the special attention we focus upon you today, and take from this ceremony a memory of our appreciation and gratitude for the fact that you have chosen one of mankind's noblest professions.

We truly recognize the difficulty of the path that brought you here today, and we know the demands and the complexity of the path that lies before you. Both have been and will be cluttered with a special kind of sacrifice the medical profession asks, indeed demands, of its practitioners. Along with the sacrifices you and your families and many others have made, you also have made a sizable investment. That investment has been much more than dollars and cents. You have invested important years of your life, time that cannot be retrieved, time for which you cannot be compensated adequately, except by the satisfaction you gain in easing and preventing human suffering.

What more worthy goal is there for man to achieve? And what more enduring reward is offered in our society than the unique satisfaction that comes to those in your profession? Certainly, you are entitled to be adequately compensated for the long hours of study and preparation and sacrifice that have culminated in the attainment of the high academic plateau on which you stand today, and you are fully entitled to be rewarded in proportion to the valuable work you will perform. That is the essence of our American system. That is the spirit of our way of life. But you and I also know that the greatest reward awaiting you will not come in monetary terms, but in terms of personal satisfaction gained from rendering comfort and restoring health to those who will turn to you for help: that mother, whose anxiety about her newborn child you alone can calm; that father, on whose health and strength the security of his family rests; and that young person, to whom we look for the vitality and the energy to carry forward the ideals of liberty and justice for all the world.

Your reward may be at the end of a rat-infested alleyway in the inner-city ghetto; or at the end of a lonely, dirt road in rural America; or in the modern and well-equipped medical centers that stand as monuments to the compassion and the concern of our people, one for another. Whichever path you choose is filled today with new and complex hurdles that seriously complicate the practice of medicine and compound the problems of health care delivery.

You enter a profession that faces an era of unprecedented challenge. You take your oath at a time of severe social and economic crisis at a time when health care costs spiral upward to a point where the financial ability of many families to meet these costs is seriously overburdened; at a time when increased insurance benefits as well as new discoveries of cures and development of new treatment procedures outpace the medical manpower of the world; in a day when we hear much about the alienation of doctors and patients; in an era of disturbing abuse of health care, ranging from drug addiction to overutilization of medical assistance; and in an age of consumerism when greater demands, some reasonable and some irrational, are being made of our medical manpower, facilities, and government programs.

To further complicate the difficulty of this situation, the epidemic of emotionalism apparently is spreading among the self-appointed guardians and critics of America's health care system, a system they would tell us has run amuck. These emotional parasites are first to point the finger of blame at your profession. They have no compunction whatever in ascribing selfish motives on your part as the root of the problem, despite the abundant proof that yours has been one of the most unselfish and humanitarian professions throughout the history of mankind.

Instead of the constant critics who forever seem to be pointing the finger of blame, what we need are more who are willing and able to point the way to a solution of the serious problems surrounding health care today. The problem of rising costs is a direct reflection of the crucial supply and demand situation that affects both our health manpower and facilities. This conclusion is borne out by the fact that we spend $70 billion each year in America on the health industry, yet there is still only one physician for 650 persons. Further, there is an immediate need in America today for 50,000 more doctors, yet you are among only 8,000 medical students graduating each year. We should also consider the effect of the trend toward specialization, which is perhaps more prevalent in medicine today than in any other profession. Eighty percent of the 8,000 annual medical school graduates become specialists. On an average, this leaves one family practitioner to provide the bulk of primary health care to 1,750 persons.

Here in the Commonwealth of Kentucky, we are faced with an even more painful shortage. Ten of our 120 counties have reached a critical point in terms of their physician-population ratio. In each of these ten counties there is only one physician to serve at least 6,000 potential patients. In some of these counties physicians sixty years of age or older minister to more than 9,000 persons. Here, as well as in the rest of the nation, there is a serious imbalance between urban and rural medical service. Two counties, Jefferson and Fayette, have a majority of Kentucky's physicians.

How many of you, more specifically, how many of the fifty-six native Kentuckians in this graduating class, plan to practice in the hollows and hard-to-reach corners of the Commonwealth? I would urge each of you to investigate the possibilities of a career in rural Kentucky. Nowhere is there greater potential for humanitarian service and professional as well as personal growth. Nowhere is the status of the physician more revered, his influence in civic and social affairs more welcomed and more widely felt, and certainly nowhere are his services more desperately needed. I believe you might be surprised by the dramatic progress we have made in these areas in recent years.

For instance, modern, safe, convenient highways, including the 254-mile "Corridor of Opportunity Parkway" which touches forty-one counties from Henderson to Hazard, will soon permanently dissolve the isolationism and parochialism that limited our horizons for so long.

Wherever you may choose to practice in Kentucky, you will be near the center of things, not only within our State, but in America as well. Kentucky is becoming more and more a growth center of the United States, and there are many reasons for this, including our natural resources, our trainable and hospitable people, and certainly our geographical location. We are within twenty-four hours by highway of two-thirds of America's population and within only two hours by airplane of 70 percent of the people of this country.

Improved educational opportunities at every level reflect the generous support the people of this State have given during the past decade. There is a new or renovated school in all of our 192 elementary and secondary school districts. We have finished thirteen area vocational-technical schools, completed fourteen community colleges, and established a new, four-year, public college. Tomorrow, as an example of the progress that is being made, we will dedicate a Health Occupations Center at the Madisonville Area Vocational School. It can become a model for the nation in meeting the demands of more trained medical personnel.

We invite you, and we urge you, to consider this State very carefully. Evaluate the advantages of living and rearing your family and practicing your profession in an environment of concern not only for the natural beauty that God so generously bestowed upon us, but also where there is a deep concern for the human values that led this nation out of the wilderness to world leadership.

Wherever you go, take as your constant companion the high aspirations that have led you to this very significant point in your life. And also take the sense of deep responsibility that is inseparable from your profession. Throughout your careers guard constantly against the temptation to become so immersed in your profession that you develop a one-dimensional outlook toward life. Be involved. Live your life that, when it is finished, it will have mattered to the struggle of freedom and justice and the effort to end human suffering. Take time from the practice of your profession to protect your profession against those who would repress and restrict your individual latitude and reduce the practice of medicine to an impersonal and uncaring bureaucracy. Do all these things, and you will have added honor to a most honorable human undertaking.

KENTUCKY FEDERATION OF REPUBLICAN WOMEN
Lake Barkley State Park
Cadiz / June 9, 1971

WE meet tonight as partisans to a cause not only of our party, but also of our State and nation. We need to view the issues that affect us all not just as Republicans, but as Kentuckians, Americans, and as free people. During the past three days you have had a concentrated course in the nuts and bolts of political involvement.

The story is told of three bricklayers who were approached on a construction site one day and asked what they were doing. The first bricklayer paused long enough to reply: "Why, I'm just doing my job. I'm laying bricks." The second explained that he was building a wall. But the third man stood, lifted his eyes to an imaginary spire, and said proudly, "Who me? Why, I'm building a cathedral."

Like the bricklayers you are the craftsmen who must lay the strong and durable foundations of partisan progress, but like the third man you must never lose sight of the ultimate aim of your efforts. In our dedication to the things for which our party and our candidates stand, and in our desire to further those causes and those candidates, we should never forget the ultimate goals to which we aspire: to build and maintain those magnificent cathedrals of freedom and justice and opportunity.

Let our partisanship not become an end in itself. We need to pause at times to reassess and to evaluate our involvement. We need to ask "Why are we involved? What do we stand for? What do we hope to accomplish?" Certainly, our goals reach far beyond personal and partisan horizons. What we are concerned with is more than just another victory at the polls, or the continuation of a strong two-party system.

What we have to be concerned with is the preservation of responsible and responsive government. We have to be concerned with the continuation of vital human programs that have been started or redirected or revitalized. To sum it up, our goal should be to enhance the spirit of Kentucky today: the spirit of confidence, not despair; of progress, not retreat; of concern, not neglect; of courage and willingness to build from past efforts and sacrifices and achievements, so that an even brighter and more secure future for every Kentuckian may be continued.

During the past forty-two months, we have visited practically every county in Kentucky. And of course delegations from almost every community have come to Frankfort at one time or another. From these contacts we have detected a common thread running through the thoughts of the people of this State. There is a sense of urgency and expectation, a resurgence of pride, a feeling that we are on the threshold of an era of greatness, that we've taken some long, hard steps toward fulfilling the promise and realizing the potential this State holds for our people. There is another feeling, a feeling of concern that comes from acceptance of the fact that we face several important challenges during the next few years.

There is no denial of the fact that we face some big problems in Kentucky today, complex problems, difficult, demanding problems that affect us all alike to a greater extent than as individual citizens. Three great issues—the economy, the environment, and education—place Kentucky at one of the most crucial junctures in our history. Which way we go and who we choose to lead us and the quality of leadership that is shown during the next four years will determine to a large extent the quality of life enjoyed by the people of this State many years beyond the term of the next governor.

Whether we continue on the confident and progressive course of the present, or whether we retreat to the desperate patterns of the past is the real question we are going to answer this year. What we are really deciding is whether we will forfeit the bold advances that have been made in recent years, or whether we will seize this unique time in our history and this unusual and unique opportunity to keep Kentucky's rendezvous with greatness.

And before we set the course for the future, perhaps we first should look back and analyze the reasons we now have this unprecedented opportunity. Kentucky did not arrive at this moment through partisanship, but through partnership. The footstones of progress were put into place not by government alone, but by a government of, by, for, and with the people. It was private and public enterprise, not political enterprise, that gave us this chance for a brighter future. And it is in that spirit, the spirit of partnership between the people and their government, that we must look to the challenges of this election year and beyond that to the opportunity for service in the next four years.

I spoke a moment ago of three specific issues. One of the meaningful lessons of the past three and one-half years has been that every issue, regardless of how minute or how unrelated or isolated it might appear, has a bearing on the quality of life in our State. And the common thread running through all these issues, whether we are talking about the economy or the environment or education or drugs or highways or health, is the effect they have on the family unit. During the campaign it is imperative that we address ourselves to the things that matter to the families of Kentucky. That is really the most important issue with which we need to be concerned, because, in my opinion, the major concern today, not just among Kentuckians, but among the American people, is how to keep the family together.

At the Republican Governors' Conference in Sun Valley, Idaho, last December, a well-known and respected public opinion analyst confirmed the significance of this issue. His nationwide surveys during the 1970 election detected a great anxiety among parents, because they felt they were losing the ability to bring up their children. It was a new feeling, one that had never surfaced to such a widespread extent before. The speaker said that it unfolded in a strange way. In previous surveys he had found that husbands tended to do the political talking in most families; but during the last campaign more women interrupted the questions and volunteered their impressions about the issues and the effects they were having. They would ask, "Why don't you ask me something? Is this private? Don't I have anything to say?" This seemed always to take place in families with young and teenage children, seldom among couples who had no children. And always the focal point was on how to bring up their children and what kind of society we would have, or should have, in which families would be raising their children.

This expression of concern showed up in every part of the country and at varied income levels. Whatever the issue—drug addiction, campus unrest, the war, school busing, violence, economics, the environment, or whatever—people today are viewing this campaign with one primary thought: "What will help me hold my family together, or under whose leadership will this opportunity best be presented?"

And look at how all the most frequently mentioned issues fit into this overriding issue. Take the economy, for example. What do we mean when we use the term "economy"? The head of a family doesn't see it in terms of Wall Street, or the Dow-Jones averages, or inflation, or balance of payments. He defines the economy in terms that apply to the standard of living he is able to achieve for his family. And to him it isn't nearly so important that he understand why we have high prices and why home mortgage interest rates are so high, and why it costs so much more to educate his children or who is responsible. What he wants to know is what can be done about it so that his family can be properly fed and clothed and live in a comfortable home and get a good education and still have something left for retirement when his family is grown.

We can be proud that the Kentucky economy today presents a picture of balanced optimism. Because of the diversification of our economy, we are not subjected to the peaks and the valleys that some other states must endure. We are very proud of the fact that during this administration we reached the billion-dollar mark in capital investment by new and expanding industry in less time than in any previous administration. This was achieved in spite of inflation and higher interest rates. It was achieved without industrial bonds and at a time when President Nixon was winding down the war he inherited. This meant job opportunities for more than 35,000 Kentuckians in all parts of the State. There has been a breakthrough in Appalachia to the extent that unemployment there has been reduced by a full 2 percent. And these facts translate into something more important. Young Kentuckians are not forced to leave home to seek opportunity.

Agriculture continues to be the cornerstone of our economy. And of course there is a great encouragement here, because in 1969 and 1970, for the first time in the history of Kentucky, our farm families surpassed the billion-dollar mark in gross income. Again, this farm income is a hopeful sign that the migration of young people from our farms to the urban areas can be slowed down, and we can continue to be a major producer of agricultural commodities.

The people of Kentucky also care about the environment in which their families live. And during this administration we have responded to that concern with strict new regulations and more effective enforcement of the laws that guard Kentucky's land, water, and air. For instance, we are the first state in the southeast and among the first five in the United States to establish an approved solid waste management plan. Within the next few days water quality standards for every stream in Kentucky will be adopted for the first time in our history. Air pollution control regulations have now been adopted where none existed before, and we are seeing dramatic evidence that Kentucky has acted in time to avoid environmental chaos.

In the area of education, we could point to the unstinting generosity of the people of Kentucky in supporting our schools at every level. We are sixteenth in the nation in support of education as compared to per capita income. We are eleventh in the nation in terms of support granted at the state level. And we have valid indications that the people of this State will do even more, if—if they are convinced that our school administrators and faculties are meeting their full responsibilities and fulfilling the sacred trust of their profession to guide the lives and impart the wisdom and knowledge that is basic to a productive and happy life.

Education is too important to the security of our families as well as the security of our State and nation to be vilified and misused and abused by a campaign of innuendo and spite. The youth of Kentucky cannot be crucified on a cross of political expediency. What we need is a candid, rational discussion about our schools, not an expedient campaign of fear that could permanently impair education's long effort to light this State's path with knowledge and open the doors of opportunity for the young people of Kentucky.

But most of all during this campaign, what we need to keep sight of is the relationship of this and the other issues to the well-being of the family. Perhaps it was the affluence, but more than that, it was the permissiveness of the last decade that contributed to the deterioration of the family. But here in Kentucky important foundations have been shaped in recent years on which we can reconstruct and strengthen our family ties. And it is on these foundations that we can replace the cornerstones of a better life and a better future through our efforts in the coming months.

ECONOMIC DEVELOPMENT
ADMINISTRATION
Shakertown
Pleasant Hill / June 15, 1971

THE restoration of this village [Shakertown] is a benchmark of our recent progress to preserve for future generations the historical and cultural values of our heritage. This project is an outstanding example of the cooperation of the Economic Development Administration with a nonprofit organization of private citizens dedicated to the preservation of a unique chapter in Kentucky's history.

When the Shakers settled here in 1805, only thirteen years after Kentucky became a state, they were seeking a new and better quality of life in the midst of ferment and turmoil, much as we are today. To see this village and hear the story of the Shakers is in reality a walk into the past when people were dedicated to work and a high degree of excellence and pride in all things they did. Their agricultural produce and livestock were recognized as the hallmark of quality in the marketplace. The soundness of their architecture and its functional simplicity has attracted designers and artists from all over the country. In the early days this community must have been the experiment station of Kentucky because on the floor of the Kentucky Senate in 1831, Robert Wickliffe made the remark: "Let a stranger visit your country and inquire for your best specimens of agriculture, mechanics, and architecture, and, Sir, he is directed to visit the Society of Shakers at Pleasant Hill."[1]

This restoration is the fourth attempt in the past thirty years to preserve not just this historic community, but also its message for future generations. This effort might also have failed had the Economic Development Administration and its predecessor not made a loan for the first phase of its preservation.

In 1961, when the present nonprofit organization was formed, this was a sleepy little village consisting of a country store and a filling station at the crossroads. A few farm hands lived in the back of some of the large buildings, one family ran a small dining room, and a rural Baptist church used one building. Other buildings were used to store farm equipment and supplies, and for a junk automobile repair shop. Busses and trucks sped through the middle of the village on U.S. 68, but all they were able to see was a tangle of overhead wires and posts with road signs. Within a few miles of the village were dozens of people without jobs and many women who could take a second job in the family if there was one. High school senior and college students had few chances to work during their summer vacations.

The Department of Commerce listed Mercer County as an area eligible for development loans which would increase employment and improve the economy. For two years the Shakertown organization struggled to raise about $250 thousand to start acquiring some of the village property. It was then that the Shakertown officials approached Mr. William E. Davis, a Kentucky attorney for your predecessor, the Area Redevelopment Administration, for advice and counsel.[2] The Area Redevelopment Administration convinced him that the preservation of this historic landmark was truly a sound community project. With the cooperation of Mr. Davis, the application for a $2 million loan was approved in 1964. Then followed three years of master planning and restoration construction.

The initial approval of the loan established the credibility of the project in the minds of hundreds of people and a number of foundations. As a result, Kentuckians, together with certain individuals and foundations in Indiana, Maryland, Pennsylvania, Illinois, Georgia, Ohio, New Jersey, and New York, have contributed sufficient additional funds to bring the project to where it is today.

Since the partially restored village was opened to the public three years ago in April 1968, there has been a dramatic influx of interested visitors. Each year tourists have registered at the reception center from all fifty states of the union. In the three years and two months to date 185,600 tourists have come to see the restored village and 250,900 people have been served delightful Kentucky food at the inn, for a total of 436,500 guests of Shakertown. So far in 1971, the overall volume in the village is running about 25 percent more than the same period last year.

It takes a lot of people to manage this operation and take care of all these visitors. Of the present staff of 130, all but three live in the town or on the farms within a ten-mile radius of the village. A wide variety of job opportunities has been created including museum hostesses, kitchen and dining room personnel, maids, vegetable gardeners, furniture craftsmen, carpenters, masons, sewer plant operators, maintenance personnel, clerks, accountants, secretaries, and supervisors. The surrounding countryside was acquired for the protection of the village against undesirable roadside commercial stands. On these lands farm hands look after more than 900 head of cattle and raise 140 acres of corn and share farmers raise 100,000 pounds of tobacco. In 1971 the total Shakertown payroll will be over $500 thousand.

In addition, the gift shop in the village buys thousands of dollars of merchandise from the handcraft shops and potteries of southern and eastern Kentucky. Food purchases for the dining room will exceed $100 thousand this year. One farmer alone in central Kentucky has been selling about $10 thousand of old hams each year to the village dining room. From your dinner tonight you can see what it takes to feed 100,000 guests expected to be served this year.

This village is attracting a new type of tourist to Kentucky, the middle aged and older, who appreciate the serenity of this place and the cultural values which have been recaptured in this authentic restoration. While a good deal of the attendance in the past three years has been through word-of-mouth publicity, the Department of Public Information has brought many of the nation's top travel editors to Shakertown, and their stories have caused many others to come. Mrs. Nunn has spread the word to thirty states by entertaining the wives of the governors who were attending a conference in Lexington two years ago. Feature stories have appeared in many magazines of national circulation and in the travel section of a dozen or more of the nation's largest metropolitan newspapers.

This village after all is the most notable historic restoration this side of colonial Williamsburg. It has been an inspiration for many Kentucky communities to look at the values of their historic buildings and attempt to save them from the ball and hammer.

Early in my term as Governor, and with my full support, Mrs. Nunn began to revitalize interest in preserving our historic buildings and has led the movement which has saved and restored the Madison County home of Cassius Clay, one of the most interesting personalities of Kentucky's past. She likewise has done yeoman service to save the home of Mary Todd Lincoln in Lexington, and she has not given up yet. The Historic Heritage Commission has named her Honorary Chairman, and as such she has presented to several hundred owners of old buildings over the State the Heritage Commission Certificate of the historical and architectural significance of their buildings, with the view that this recognition will deter the bulldozer. The Heritage Commission, with the assistance of local committees in all 120 counties and Spindletop Research, has published a volume on more than 2,000 buildings and sites of historical significance in Kentucky, an edition much sought after today in view of its limited printing.

You might be interested to know that I have had the Program Development Office sponsor a plan for historic preservation in the State and have appointed a Historic Preservation Review Board to nominate outstanding buildings and sites for the National Register of Historic Sites, all with the view that Kentucky would be prepared to participate in the use of any federal funds which might be available for restoration in the future.

It is all very fitting here at this historic village that I point to the commitment of my administration to the preservation of our historic heritage and commend the officials of the Economic Development Administration for their foresight and wisdom seven years ago, not only in making possible this monument to historic preservation in Kentucky, but in so doing making it possible for so many fine people who work here to greet thousands of visitors from other states with the kind of courtesy and hospitality for which our great Commonwealth is famous far and wide.

In the course of a Governor's term, there are many opportunities to meet distinguished visitors to our State. We are especially honored that you have chosen Kentucky as the site of your conference, but more importantly, that you have come in the same spirit in which we have worked together during the course of my administration. And I want you to know how sincerely appreciative I am, and how grateful many communities throughout Kentucky are, for your cooperation and assistance.

I have said repeatedly that the primary goal of my administration, indeed, the primary function of government in a representative society, is to build foundations for the future. I know of course that those of you in the Economic Development Administration share that goal, and I trust that a mutual feeling of confidence has been inspired by the manner in which those who represent the Commonwealth have joined with you these last three and one-half years to achieve the progress we seek.

I believe very strongly that Kentucky's future lies in the strength and the vitality and the pride of its individual communities and individual citizens, not in the strength of its government or the number of dollars that come down from Washington to be funneled into programs that offer temporary, but not enduring, solutions. Perhaps more than any single agency of the federal government, the Economic Development Administration has realized that the legitimate object of government is to do those things which the people cannot do for themselves. I see nothing in the guidelines of your many programs and nothing in your performance to indicate that you have accepted the modern adaptation of Lincoln's philosophy. As you know, there are those today who advocate that government should do all that the people are unwilling to do for themselves.

Basic to the success of any effort is the concern and the willingness of those involved to plan, to prepare, and to work for the development and the progress they seek. Believe this: it has been our intention in designing a basic developmental course for Kentucky that the initiative for local progress and development must come from the local level. This local input is the key to a three-step formula for economic development that we have tried to implement through the Kentucky Program Development Office.

As many of you know by working with this agency in recent years, the Kentucky Program Development Office was established during this administration as the single State planning agency. By encouraging local initiative and local planning, this new agency has provided technical planning assistance to countless communities who have then qualified for financial assistance from the federal government. The effectiveness of this formula and the regional planning concept now being implemented by the Kentucky Program Development Office is dramatically emphasized by the fact that nearly $400 million has been invested in community service projects during the last three and one-half years.

We trust that you are complimented by the fact that our concept of fifteen area development districts follows very closely the principles of development pioneered by the Economic Development Administration. Surely, this sameness in principle and our kinship with mutual goals is responsible for the success of our cooperative efforts. I believe that our shared commitment to these mutual goals and principles is the underlying reason that Kentucky is benefiting today from $7 million in public works grants and loans from the Economic Development Administration. The projects have improved the quality of life from one end of our State to another. You touch upon the basic requirements of development and progress. Kentucky has a distinguished and enviable reputation as the recreational heartland of mid-America.

---

1. Robert Wickliffe (1775–1859), state senator, Fayette County (1825–1833); and state representative, Fayette County (1819, 1823–1824). Lewis Collins, *Historical Sketches of Kentucky, History of Kentucky*, 2d ed. rev. (1874; reprint ed., Frankfort, 1966), 2:170, 199–200.

2. William E. Davis (1919–), special assistant for field operations, United States Economic Development Administration (1970–); director, Mideastern Office, United States Economic Development Administration (1966–1970); resident of Kentucky from 1962 to 1970. Office of William E. Davis, Economic Development Administration, Washington, D.C., September 20, 1971.

KENTUCKY WHITE HOUSE CONFERENCE ON AGING
Lexington / June 22, 1971

WE convene the Kentucky White House Conference on Aging today as a salute to those whose lifetime of useful service in field, factory, office, or home entitles them to our respect and continuing concern. In a culture that puts a premium on newness, on youth, and on so-called change for the sake of progress, we should never fail to show proper respect for those who have helped to build this nation.

In a society grown so mobile and so busy, there are more and more who equate "old" with being outmoded, outdated, useless. There is the tendency to dismiss as old-fashioned the wisdom and valuable experience of those who have climbed the hill before us. And just as some dismiss the wisdom of the elderly, they also dismiss their special problems and overlook their special and unique values in making a continued, productive contribution to mankind.

We meet here to confront those problems: to listen, learn, dissect, and discuss for the next two days the vital needs voiced by the elderly themselves. Then, through specific policy proposals, our goal is to fulfill the promise of a full life for all aging Kentuckians:

The opportunity for financial security, not dependency, in one's later years.

The opportunity to retire, if financially able or if necessary, without suddenly becoming poor.

The opportunity to enjoy a sufficient income to provide a decent diet, a warm house, a bus token, and refilled prescriptions.

The opportunity, if sought, to find employment based on ability rather than some arbitrary chronological age.

The opportunity to be free from the sixty-five age limit on productivity.

The opportunity for consistent and competent medical care.

The opportunity for accessible transportation.

The opportunity for companionship.

The opportunity to serve others, to be useful, to be needed, and counted.

The opportunity for serenity.

In the earliest days of this administration, we pledged to increase the opportunities for our aging citizens to live out their lives in usefulness and comfort. For the past three and one-half years, we have worked to make good on that pledge, to forge strong foundations on which we now can build:

To provide personal care facilities for the aged, the Health and Geriatrics Authority was activated in 1969.

To ease the financial burden on an age group often faced with illness requiring medication and special aids, we proposed a measure to remove the sales tax from prescription drugs and prosthetic devices.

To improve the service of Kentucky's personal care homes, standards of need and the payments given to all recipients of aid to the aged, blind, and disabled who reside in those facilities were raised by $30 a month.

To further improve their care, two additional increases in payments to the aged, blind, and disabled were granted in April and June of this year.

For older citizens requiring nursing home care, effective July 1, we will extend Medicaid benefits from full payment for six months to full payment for an entire year.

To give aging Kentuckians the best possible benefit from recent Social Security increases, Kentucky was among several states to adopt an optional "federal income disregard" for computing Public Assistance grants to those receiving Social Security as well.

To assist clients who need outpatient mental health services, we added community mental health center visits to the Commonwealth's Medicaid program.

To curb glaucoma which plagues the sight of many older Kentuckians, ophthalmic drops have been added to our Medical Assistance Generic Drug list.

To improve health care for the elderly, a separate physician-insurance policy was purchased for 65,000 of our aged grant recipients.

In addition, we have enthusiastically supported the work of Kentucky's Commission on Aging. The Commission and its twenty senior citizens' centers throughout the State receive nearly 7,500 calls for assistance from older Kentuckians every week. They call to request legal services, eye care, and food stamps. Other calls echo the basic need for human companionship.

Older Kentuckians need transportation, proper nutrition and housing, and we are responding. We are responding with programs where persons over fifty-five on a fixed income can earn wages working on public projects which beautify the landscape and raise the spirit. We are responding with meaningful projects, not make-work programs.

The day is past when all the elderly could expect was bingo games and cut rates at the bowling alley. The brighter day of the Foster Grandparents program is here. As Foster Grandparents, seventy-one older Kentuckians are giving love and attention to emotionally deprived youngsters in two state mental hospitals, and are being paid for their work. The brighter day of "Telephone Reassurance" is here. A daily phone call from one of the State's senior citizens' centers helps erase loneliness for people like the aged Kentucky widow who goes to bed every evening fully clothed. She fears dying alone with no one to care, no one to know.

The foundations we have laid to guarantee the rights of the elderly are the legacy we leave. These are the foundations on which you can now build. I challenge you to develop ideas that are truly worthy of our senior citizens, not programs that condescend and demean their pride and destroy their dignity. We will not have helped, indeed, we will have hindered and performed a grave disservice to the elderly, if all that is accomplished here is a program of dependency on government.

The Kentucky White House Conference on Aging represents a unique approach in tackling and solving the needs of the elderly. For the first time older Kentuckians have composed the agenda. For the first time they have told us what their problems are. In 139 community forums held across the State during the past year, they told their story. In fifteen regional conferences providers of services to the elderly had their say. And now the task of formulating specific policy proposals in the areas of need voiced by the elderly and agencies themselves is yours.

To ensure that our momentum is not lost, to guarantee that your efforts come to meaningful fruition, we announce today one further step toward reaching our goal of a full life and continuing opportunity for all aging Kentuckians. To advise me and the next governor on means of implementing the recommendations of the Kentucky White House Conference on Aging, we have by Executive Order established a Special Committee on Aging, with members to be taken from the leadership of this Conference.[1] In addition to advising on implementation of the Conference proposals, the Special Committee on Aging will advise the Commission on Aging, which is the single state agency for administering the purposes of the Older Americans Act of 1965. With the Special Committee working on your proposals, and the Commission on Aging administering federal programs for the aging, we can strengthen our efforts on behalf of those who have climbed the hill before us.

For those who have topped the crest of the hill and who find now that the shadows fall behind them, who have earned the right to be useful and serene, we pledge ourselves to making beautiful the last of life for which the first was made.

---

1. See Executive Order 71–652 (June 15, 1971).

PINE MOUNTAIN BOYS CAMP
DEDICATION
Harlan County / June 30, 1971

WE meet today on this beautiful ridge, which ranges through Harlan County, with high hopes for the young lives to whom we dedicate Pine Mountain Boys Camp. It is our hope, our prayer, our goal that this facility will be a place where young Kentuckians will be renewed, refreshed, and rechanneled to useful and proper purposes. Today we dedicate much more than a facility, far more than buildings and land. We dedicate ourselves, both as individuals and as a Commonwealth, to more thoughtful juvenile care, human care which truly reflects our belief in the potential for good that is in every young Kentuckian.

It has been said that the destiny of any nation rests in the hearts and minds of its youth. Kentucky has done more than give lip service to the idea that today's youth determine tomorrow's greatness. During the last three and one-half years the people have given to public education a priority never before witnessed in the Commonwealth. We have invested in elementary, secondary, and higher education with a generosity unparalleled in the state's history. But at the same time, we have also refused to look away from the harder problems of youth. We have refused to ignore the shame of a rising national crime rate and the realization that every hardened criminal was once young.

The past three and one-half years have seen Kentucky emerge from obscurity and shame to a place of national prominence and leadership in yet another vital human service. In the field of child care, three and one-half years ago there was not enough money, despite the generous support of the private sector, to open a desperately needed juvenile care center for young delinquent girls. Today that facility, Jewel Manor, near Louisville, is in operation and making a constructive impact on the lives of its inhabitants.

Similarly, three and one-half years ago young delinquents shivered through the winters in drafty, dirty, dilapidated buildings at Kentucky Village near Lexington, an installation once condemned by grand juries, but now praised for the professionalism of its staff and the work they are accomplishing. The dramatic turnabout at Kentucky Village was achieved despite the difficult physical conditions of an antiquated facility, and by July 1 of next year, we will have closed the doors at Kentucky Village altogether as a juvenile center.

A new home for culturally and academically deprived delinquents has been established at Frenchburg, and renovation is nearly completed on the Lynwood Girls Center for older delinquent girls in Louisville. A treatment facility similar to Pine Mountain is being constructed in Butler County. A new reception center will soon be under construction in northern Kentucky, and we will have an announcement soon regarding plans for leasing yet another facility in eastern Kentucky.

Since 1967 the number of additional children experiencing a happy and more complete home life in foster homes throughout the Commonwealth has more than doubled, with the promise of an even greater increase as a result of the contract our State Department of Economic Security has signed with Child Welfare to allow federal funds to pay the costs of foster care.

These achievements have led the National Council on Crime and Delinquency to identify Kentucky as among the nation's top three states in juvenile care and delinquency prevention. And today marks yet another step in our determination to continue until we are number one. In dedicating the Pine Mountain Boys Camp, we open the Department of Child Welfare's eighth specialized treatment facility. These facilities represent the proudest achievement of our reform in juvenile care in the Commonwealth—a shift in emphasis and a change in image that has gained national attention, while providing the close, personal, helpful attention to those who are on the threshold of either a life of crime or a life of worthwhile endeavor.

Kentucky has brought its philosophy of child welfare from the dark ages of punitive institutionalism in large, impersonal complexes, to this brighter and more promising day: to the day of Pine Mountain Boys Camp and other smaller, more specialized facilities like it; to the day when young Kentuckians are adequately cared for in facilities designed to house no more than forty youths, facilities with corrective programs geared to specific age groups, their interests, and the seriousness of their offenses against society.

Gone is the day when a first-offender juvenile was thrown into the same crowded dormitory with more experienced law-breakers. Here, surrounded by the beauty of God's handiwork, boys from sixteen to eighteen will benefit from a treatment program of spiritual and recreational rejuvenation and a realistic preparation for the world of work. With the Division of Forestry, Pine Mountain residents will make up maintenance and improvement crews. They will aid in fire fighting and constructive work projects designed to benefit the general community. They will participate in remedial and vocational education, and in group therapy sessions. On a year-round basis, young Kentuckians will find here the discipline and direction too long lacking in their lives.

We are grateful to a number of people who have made this day of promise possible: to the Commissioners of Corrections, Natural Resources, and Child Welfare who have collectively worked out arrangements for Pine Mountain to be used by Child Welfare;[1] to those who will staff this camp, a total of twenty dedicated citizens to be found largely in the local community; and to the community of Harlan, whose compassionate welcome ensures the success of the Pine Mountain effort.

---

1. John C. Taylor (1906–), Frankfort, commissioner, Kentucky Department of Corrections (1969–1972), assistant director, Federal Bureau of Prisons, United States Department of Justice (1965–1966), and other offices within the Federal Prison Service (1933–1966).

James S. Shropshire (1906–), Lexington, deputy commissioner (1968), and commissioner (1968–1971), Kentucky Department of Natural Resources.

George C. Perkins, commissioner, Kentucky Department of Child Welfare. See footnote 2, page 239, for more information.

POKE SALLET FESTIVAL
Harlan / June 30, 1971

Your homecoming celebration has a very special and very significant meaning for me. Four years ago, when I came to Harlan County during the campaign for governor, one of the commitments I made to the people of this county and the other counties of southeastern Kentucky was to develop programs that would encourage families to come back to these hills rather than to leave in search of jobs. I made that commitment mindful of the love the people of this area have for Kentucky, and mindful, too, of the special feeling you have for preserving the sanctity and security of your homes and your families. I was confident that if the government was redirected, if it was truly committed to working for and with the people, if we coordinated our efforts and cut out the waste and duplication and red tape and found better and more effective ways to deliver services to the people, then we would see the people of this section of our State coming back home instead of leaving their homes.

The confidence we had in this area and in you has been justified in a measure beyond even our most optimistic hopes in the last three and one-half years. So I am especially grateful today for this opportunity to take part in your homecoming celebration. I am proud that because of some of the things that have been accomplished these last few years, homecoming is no longer a one-day, annual event; it is happening every day throughout Harlan County and eastern Kentucky.

One of the reasons it is happening is because there has been a breakthrough in industrial development here in the mountains. During the past three and one-half years, forty-six new industries have come into eastern Kentucky. They came because they shared our confidence. They shared our belief in the people here. They shared our conviction that the way to help eastern Kentucky was not through hand-out programs, or make-work programs, or other government programs that filled the stomach but starved the spirit and the pride of the people here. And because these companies believed, they have invested more than $50 million in their future and in your future. In addition to the forty-six new industries, sixty-seven companies like your own National Electric Coil here in Harlan have expanded their operations in eastern Kentucky. These companies have invested $87 million because they knew from first-hand experience that this was a good place to grow, to make a profit, and to live in peace and security with their families.

These new and expanding industries have created almost 9,000 job opportunities, and that is why we have seen the change from out-migration here in eastern Kentucky. While the rest of the nation has experienced rising unemployment, here in eastern Kentucky unemployment is down by 2 percent, and that's a record we can all be proud of, because that is the kind of enduring progress we need here in the mountains.

We don't need temporary government programs. We need permanent programs, programs that uplift the entire community, not just for one year or for one governor's term, but for an entire generation. And that is the kind of program we have invested in here and throughout the Commonwealth these last three and one-half years. Throughout the years isolation has been one of the primary obstacles to progress here, isolation not only from surrounding counties and other sections of Kentucky and America, but isolation of neighbor-

hoods within the county. We have invested over $20 million to cor-
rect that problem. For instance, $11 million has gone into the Harlan
by-pass project. Here was a project that the people of Harlan County
have been promoting for the last fifteen years. Two years ago we made
you a commitment to build that by-pass, and since that time, all the
design work has been completed. The money has been appropriated,
and half the right-of-way has been purchased. We've done in two
years a job that ordinarily takes four years to complete. This is one
of the top priority projects known to the Department of Highways,
and we're working to see that it's completed during the next administration.

As long as I can remember, there has been construction work on
the road from Harlan to Pineville. This was an off-and-on project for
the last seventeen years. Let me tell you today that the project is on
again, and it has been on full-time the past three and one-half years
because we have been able to complete fifteen miles. In addition, U.S.
421 from Harlan to Hyden has been completely blacktopped, and
funds from the Rural Roads-County Road Aid Program have been
increased approximately 30 percent in the last four years.

In education, $11,256,000 has been appropriated to the elementary
and high schools of Harlan County in the past three years. That represents an increase of $105 thousand. The new area vocational school
is completed. For the community college $1 million has been appro-
priated, an increase of $361 thousand. I understand that the grade
school and high school in Harlan may need replacing sometime in the
future, and I want to assure you that funds were made available in
the first budget we wrote in 1968 for that purpose. Because capital
construction funds were included in that budget and continued in the
1970 budget, construction of new schools was made possible in every
one of Kentucky's 192 school districts.

Natural disasters aren't uncommon to the people of the mountains.
Over the years floods and fires and landslides have been a familiar
part of the struggle for progress here. I am particularly pleased that
we have been able to help whenever called during these periods when
lives and property were threatened by elements over which neither
you nor I had any control. One such example is at the Green Hill
School across Pine Mountain. As you know, a $1 million school had
just been completed there when a slide threatened to erase in one night
a project that had taken years of planning and effort to become a reality.
The only financial resources the school had were in funds that had
been set aside to equip the school and give the children who would
attend classes there an equal opportunity to learn. Rather than see

that opportunity denied, we have committed the State to remove the slide and prevent a reoccurrence. Here are the plans. They're being completed now in the Department of Highways, so that next fall the Green Hill School will be in operation, and the children will have a safe, modern, new facility in which to shape their lives.

Recreation and tourism have become almost the largest industry in Kentucky during the past three and one-half years. And there is a great opportunity for eastern Kentucky in this field. The beauty of the mountains and the hospitality of the people of this area can attract millions of visitors each year. That is why we have worked to expand and improve Kingdom Come State Park. In the last three years nearly a half million people have visited there, and if the work we have begun is continued, that figure can be doubled during the next five years.

Recreation has been a concern of Harlan Countians for many years now. The development of recreational facilities is not a new concern for Harlan Countians. In fact, very few Kentucky communities have so dramatically expressed that concern as you did a few years ago when you mortgaged your courthouse in order to have a recreation lake at Cranks Creek. But because of bad engineering design work and a lack of proper planning, about all the people of Harlan County had to show for their money two years ago was one of the largest mud-holes in America. I recall very well coming here to the Poke Sallet Festival three years ago and seeing youngsters carrying signs urging us to put water in Cranks Creek Lake. We have responded to those pleas by committing $250 thousand to a modification program and reconstruction of the lake. Today, the necessary studies, the careful planning, and the expensive repairs have been completed. And following this ceremony we are going to Cranks Creek to close the valve and officially begin putting water into the lake.

This project, and the others I mention today, contain an important message for all of us. They prove that we can meet the transportation and education and recreation needs of this area, that we can overcome natural disasters, and that we can construct facilities to protect the people of this area from floods and from isolation and out-migration and unemployment. We can do all these things, if we continue to care, to listen, to cooperate, and to build on the solid foundations for progress that have been established.

REPLY TO "ONE MAN'S OPINION"
Louisville / July 7, 1971

EVERY person is entitled to his or her opinion, together with the right to express it. However, not all of us have monopolistic news media through which we can impose that opinion upon others.[1]

Regardless of whether we are in a position of public trust or possess unusual power to disseminate the information upon which others form opinions, there is a responsibility to be fair and factual. An opinion based on distorted facts and half truth is more deceitful than a deliberate misrepresentation, and because it is seen on television, read in the newspaper, or heard on radio doesn't make it true.

The bias, prejudice, and political bigotry of the management of this monopolistic press and those writers, broadcasters, and others they are able to control shows through almost daily if not hourly. "One Man's Opinion" of June 29 fits their usual pattern of neglecting all the facts and the whole truth about Kentucky's water quality standards. There were innuendoes, accusations, and charges that conservationists were sabotaged, industrialists benefited, that deceit was practiced under federal pretext, that members were strong-armed, and that Kentucky was without satisfactory water standards. The truth is that it was essential for us to have acceptable water quality standards adopted by July 1, that the standards first offered would not have been acceptable to federal authorities, that this could have resulted in Kentucky's losing $15 million in available funds, that the plans finally adopted had already been approved by the federal government for interstate streams, that those standards meet the federal requirements in every aspect as they relate to the health, safety, and well-being of our people and the wildlife within our State.

The truth is that Kentucky now has federally acceptable water quality standards for the first time in its history, standards comparable or superior, standards that require the best technology available, standards that were studied, written, and examined by both federal and state officials who have special qualifications and expertise in the field of water quality.

Now who should we depend upon: those who have special training in water pollution, or those trained by the *Courier-Journal* to pollute the minds of men? We recognize that the earth is the Lord's and the fullness thereof. But I have not yet become convinced that Bob Schulman and the *Courier-Journal* are the Lord's sole guardians of the earth and its environment. And that, I am sure, is not just one man's opinion.

---

1. This speech was broadcast on the WHAS (Louisville) radio and television show "One Man's Opinion," in answer to news commentator Bob Schulman's criticism of the water quality standards drawn up by the Kentucky Water Pollution Control Commission on June 21, 1971. In speaking, Governor Nunn availed himself of the show's standard offer to reply. The comment on the "monopolistic news media" referred to the joint ownership of WHAS and of the *Louisville Courier-Journal*. Telephone interview with Bob Schulman of WHAS, Louisville, September 1, 1971; interview with Charles Zimmerman, Jr., administrative assistant to the Governor, September 1, 1971.

WHITNEY M. YOUNG, JR., RESIDENTIAL MANPOWER CENTER DEDICATION
Simpsonville / July 16, 1971

As we come here today, my thoughts are guided by two emotions. First, I feel a deep sense of humility as I recall the efforts which have guided this institution and the history which pervades it. Second, a great deal of pride evolves from the knowledge that we are able to revive and continue the fine tradition so long associated with the campus here at Lincoln Ridge.

Recalling some of the history of this campus takes one back to the turn of the century, when the atmosphere of the times demanded that a special institution be created where all men could improve their minds and thereby improve their opportunity for a better and happier life. Although the circumstances which mandated that such an institution exist are regrettable, I cannot help but feel that all men benefited by the lessons taught at Lincoln. I speak not just of the knowledge imparted to those who passed through these buildings. It is more—for the history of the Lincoln Institute has been a microcosm of the larger society.

However, the advent of integration did not destroy the aura of accomplishment long associated with the institution. Rather, Lincoln became a center specializing in educational opportunities for the enlightened, but socially and economically deprived, young people of the Commonwealth. We enthusiastically sought and obtained funds which would allow a program of national acclaim to operate here in the first two years of my administration. I recommended comparable support in the following budget presentation. However, the 1970 Legislature felt the goals sought at Lincoln were unworthy of further financial backing, and they saw fit to order the doors closed on the Lincoln School, without regard to the consequences forced upon those enrolled here at the time. That action necessitated a contingency appropriation which allowed thirty-five students to finish one more year in an accelerated summer session. Most of that group are presently attending college, and it is our hope and our most fervent wish that their conduct and achievement and constructive contribution will justify the trust and confidence shown in them by the people of Kentucky.

It has been nearly a year since the doors of Lincoln closed. This period has found us burdened with expenses of over $3 thousand per month as we sought to protect the premises from vandalism and unwarranted depreciation. But, it was not the costs of maintaining the facility which were most troublesome; it was the thought that an institution so perfectly suited to serve Kentuckians was standing vacant—an ironic and tragic fate to befall a campus which had so capably served us in the past. That is why we were not idle during this past year. We began constantly looking for the *right* program which would once again regain the spirit of Lincoln. Eventually, it was decided that a program designed to help people help themselves would be a most appropriate use for this facility.

Realizing that any program would be severely limited by present state budgetary restraints, aid was sought from the federal government. Concurrently, the Louisville Board of Education indicated a strong interest in administering a residential vocational school, thereby utilizing their elaborate city facilities for actual job-training. After lengthy consideration, it was realized that only through the combined efforts of all three levels of government would our objectives be obtained. The State would supply the land, the federal government would supply the funds, and the Louisville Board of Education would plan and operate the program. Ultimately, the Commonwealth was awarded a grant of approximately $1.8 million by the United States Department of Labor to fund a "Residential Manpower Center" at the Lincoln Ridge site. That is why we are here today. We feel the

Louisville School System is extremely qualified to operate the program. Justifying our confidence is the fact that a request to the Department of Labor that they be designated as sole contracting agent for the program now has been approved.

The lease I am about to sign will transfer this campus to the Louisville School System to be utilized by them as a Residential Manpower Center. Contract negotiations will be completed in the immediate future, and a viable program will be under way by early fall. The approach will be to place approximately 200 youths between the ages of sixteen and twenty-one on campus as residents. Here they will receive educational and social orientation courses. Each day they will be transported to the Louisville School System facilities for vocational training with 100 nonresident students. The rationale behind the "in-residence" philosophy is that too often the streets and home environment undo all that is accomplished in the classroom.

Our goals are simple: to offer to as many individuals as possible the chance to achieve self-reliance and respectability through the attainment of those skills necessary to assume a position in the ever-expanding job market which we have sought to encourage and stimulate through policy actions in other areas.

This is no ordinary program we embark on today. As I have previously indicated, the degree of intergovernmental cooperation has been exemplary. Additionally, the encouragement and advice offered by the Lincoln Foundation have been of the highest caliber and most helpful. Our program is unique in yet another aspect. We do not intend to train and educate individuals for jobs which will not exist. This only adds fuel to the fires of frustration. Rather, we envision a close alliance with industry and other job centers for continually determining needs of these sectors and training participants in the program accordingly. Furthermore, we will maintain a placement and counseling service which will continue to serve the participant even after his departure from the program.

Finally, our program is unique in that it is dedicated to the memory of an outstanding citizen. I refer now to the late Dr. Whitney M. Young, Jr., a graduate of the Lincoln Institute who was born in a house within sight of where you now sit. Perhaps no tribute to a great man can be more meaningful than for those left behind to actively continue striving toward the primary goal which that individual sought. Let this institution serve as a living memorial to Dr. Young, created out of respect for his deeds, and dedicated to the fulfillment of his basic tenet that social equality is best obtained through economic equality. [For Dr. Young, see note 1, page 448.]

In closing, I would like to announce that members of my staff met with Dr. Young, Sr., this week to explore the possibilities of memorializing the house in which his son was born. I have offered my support to his plan, and will encourage the Kentucky Historical Society to declare the Young house a historic Kentucky site. Hopefully, Dr. Young will see fit to place the writings and works of his son on display here at the Whitney M. Young, Jr., Residential Manpower Center, so that all who enter upon these grounds can gain a keener insight into the Kentuckian admired and respected by all who made contact with him or his work.

MIDWESTERN GOVERNORS' CONFERENCE
Sioux City, Iowa / July 20, 1971

ABE MARTIN, an old armchair philosopher, once observed that when a man says "It's not the money; it's the principle," it's usually the money.[1] But I hope, and I want to believe, that isn't the way the governors of the United States are approaching the acute fiscal problems that confront us all today. Because I earnestly believe that had there been more concern for the *principle* shown on the federal level in years past, we would not find the states at such a severe fiscal disadvantage now.

The fiscal crunch we are feeling today didn't come just as a result of the federal government's preempting state and local revenue sources. It came partly as a result of the federal government's preempting the state and local communities in the area of planning and administration of various services needed by the people. And by the same token, if we are going to alleviate the fiscal crunch, we're going to have to revive the basic tenets of federalism. We're going to have to have much more to say about where federal funds are being spent. We're going to have to make a greater input to the planning of programs. And we're going to have to be involved to a greater extent in determining how the various programs are administered.

Our whole fiscal outlook is dominated by programs such as Medicaid, which were originated in Washington, legislated in Washington, and administratively controlled in Washington. And now, as the clamor for medical aid for the aging and poor temporarily subsides and is replaced by other programs hastily conceived to meet other crises, we find the states being left holding the bag. Under that kind of system, the states are nothing more than addicts to the federal treasury. We've become mainliners. We get hooked on matching programs. The people get hooked. And we can't break the habit, no matter how much it costs, or how little we can afford it.

Presently, in most states, the growth rate of available revenue lags from 40 to 50 percent behind the growth rate of state and local expenditures. While state taxes of all types have increased, the cost of services has far outweighed these increases. For example, while the states' general revenue was rising by 13 percent, the cost of vital human services also climbed dramatically: the cost of financing education rose 15 percent; public welfare, up 23 percent; health and hospital care, up 13 percent; and housing and urban renewal, up 17 percent.

So there remains an imbalance, just as there remains a marked imbalance between the fiscal postures of the state and federal levels of government. By having a graduating income tax, the federal government has been able to increase its revenue as the economy has expanded. In fact, the federal government has been able to provide five tax cuts since the Korean War. But on the other hand, the states have been compressed between spiralling service expenditures required to meet the population growth, while states revenue sources have been considerably lower than the gross national product.

These facts, and others equally compelling, can lead us to only one logical conclusion: federal revenue sharing is an idea whose time has come. But to stop there, to simply turn toward the Potomac with outstretched hands, cerainly is not enough. Revenue sharing is not and must not become an end in itself. It is only a mechanism, a means to end the fiscal squeeze that has so tragically reduced the influence of the states in the establishment of balanced national goals and priorities.

While some members of Congress delay and dodge the inevitable and circumvent the will of the majority, we at the state level have a clear duty to assume. It seems to me that the states would be well advised to spend this time working to perfect our planning capabilities. It is time for us as governors to put up or shut up about this matter of who is best able to govern. It isn't good enough for us to convene here and pound our chests and claim that the states are best suited to deal with the problems confronting government just because we in the governor's chair are closer to the problem. What we need to be able to say is that the states are best able to deal with the problems because, through proper planning, we have found viable solutions.

We have found in Kentucky that planning is best accomplished if it is consolidated within one single planning agency. Like many of the states represented here, Kentucky has been divided into multi-county planning regions, regions defined not only by geographical boundaries, but also by trade characteristics and social and cultural compatibility. Within each of these regions we have tried to establish a healthy mix of representatives from both the public and the private sectors. We believe very strongly that successful, balanced planning must have local input. Therefore, we have stressed the importance of local initiative, in order that solutions can be developed that will benefit not just one county or one city within that county, but solutions that will benefit an entire region.

Based on the Kentucky experience, one of the most dramatic and enduring methods of alleviating the fiscal crunch of the states is to adopt a regional approach to the problems within the respective states. Not only does the federal government recognize and encourage this concept by allowing more favorable matching fund ratios, but the regional approach also allows maximum utilization of available local and state resources, both fiscal and human.

Today at every juncture there is a new program with a new name, providing an additional executive director and an advisory committee to make another study. It is time we perfected the art of problem solving, as opposed to problem studying. And if we are able to do that, if we plan well, if we search out the permanent solutions and forsake the temporary, if we maximize our existing resources, and if revenue sharing becomes a reality, we not only will have solved the current fiscal crisis, but we also will have revitalized and reaffirmed the greatest system of government the world has ever known.

---

1. "Abe Martin," pseudonym for Frank McKinney Hubbard (1868–1930), caricaturist and paragrapher for the *Indianapolis News*; and author of *Abe Martin's Sayings and Sketches* (1915) and *Hoss Sense and Nonsense* (1926). John Bartlett, *Familiar Quotations*, 13th ed. rev. (Boston, 1956), p. 841; *Who Was Who in America, 1897–1942* (Chicago, 1943), 1:600.

BARREN RIVER STATE PARK DEDICATION

Barren River State Park

Lucas / August 4, 1971

WE have all had the experience of being away from the places and people we love for a while, and returning home to be amazed at how rapidly younger members of the family have grown.[1] So it is as we return to Barren County today to dedicate the Commonwealth's fifteenth resort park. We are happy and deeply gratified at how quickly and how beautifully the youngest member in Kentucky's family of state parks has grown up.

Barren River Lake State Resort Park came of age July 20, when she officially opened her doors to the public. But long before the handsome new lodge began to accept guests, swimmers and sunbathers flocked to the beach in such numbers that we already are now considering further expansion of the beach facilities here. Five hundred thousand people visited Barren's Park last year, and over a million fishermen and sunbathers enjoyed the lake. Clearly, Barren River Lake promises to be one of the most popular parks.

Barren is uniquely equipped to help accommodate millions of visitors who will pour into Kentucky for the state's bicentennial celebration in 1974. Bass, blue gill, and croppie abound in the lake to such an extent that we've never had to stock Barren River Reservoir. The result is a growing reputation for some of the best fishing in the south. Fifty-one lodge rooms and twelve deluxe vacation cottages offer modern comfort in rustic settings. And because the park is here for all Kentuckians, seventeen rooms on the lobby level of the lodge have been carefully designed for the comfort of the handicapped persons we hope will visit Barren often. Equipped with extra-wide doors, strategically placed rails, water temperature controls that can be dialed with one hand, and light switches within easy reach, the lodge rooms open onto the entire first floor so that all major lodge facilities are easily accessible by wheelchair.

It is unfortunate that modern-day advertising has nearly worn out the claim of "something for everyone," for Barren does indeed have something for every member of every Kentucky family. A nine-hole golf course and new putting green, scenic trails for hiking and riding, a ninety-slip marina, picnic grounds, tennis courts, and one hundred full-service campsites make Barren Lake one of the most complete resort parks in the Commonwealth. And that is an accomplishment in a family of state parks widely recognized as the finest anywhere in the nation.

At Lake Barkley State Resort Park, where earlier today we dedicated an eighteen-hole championship golf course and other additions to the facilities there, we spoke of the key role our state parks play in attracting tourist dollars to Kentucky. We spoke of the $28.5 million invested in park improvements since 1967—a figure that by the end of this year will have reached $35 million. And we spoke of the fruits we are reaping from that investment. More than 25 million visitors enjoyed our parks in 1970. Last year tourists spent $542 million in Kentucky, the highest rate of travel spending in the State's history. Ten percent of all retail business is generated by travel, and a third of every traveler's dollar finds its way into the personal income of Kentucky citizens. Travel provides jobs for more than 28,000 workers, and since 1967 state taxes collected directly from travel and tourism have increased $50 million.

These are the economic facts of life for Kentucky parks and tourism we cited at Lake Barkley. Then we flew from Trigg County to Henderson for the dedication of sixty-eight additional acres of land to serve as a protective buffer between beautiful Audubon State Park and nearby industry. On the way the view from the air gave dramatic evidence of another major factor in the phenomenal growth of Kentucky state parks. We looked down to see shining ribbons of interstate and parkway completed as part of the largest highway development program the Commonwealth has ever undertaken: the completion of 585 miles of interstate highways and the opening of final links of I-71, I-75 and nearby I-65; the approval for 683 additional miles of parkways, with 411 miles now open and the remainder either under contract or well under construction, including the parkway from Owensboro to Bowling Green and from Bowling Green to Somerset; and now in the design stage, the improvement of U.S. 31-E through Allen County to the Tennessee line. There can be no doubt that the dramatic growth of our state parks has directly paralleled the completion of modern expressways and parkways to bring travelers quickly and safely from every corner of the Commonwealth.

There is a greater need, however, for more Kentuckians to come and enjoy their magnificent park facilities, to reap the benefits of the investment they have made, and then to go back home and sell Kentucky to more Kentuckians. For despite the fact that this administration soon will have invested $35 million in park improvements, despite the fact that we have expanded our lodge facilities by 50 percent, despite the fact that Kentucky now boasts thirty-nine state parks and shrines, one within an hour's drive of every Kentucky home, only 22 percent of the visitors to the state parks last year were Kentuckians. It hardly seems necessary to repeat these facts to our friends in this region. After waiting over a decade, Barren finally has a state park we can be proud of, and I have no doubt that our families will use it and promote it proudly to all Kentuckians.

During the time I've been privileged to serve as Governor, information has come to my office touching on the vast panorama of problems besetting our State and nation today. I am convinced that the single most crucial problem, the issue of vital concern to most Americans, rests in the question: "What will help me to hold my family together?" Find the answer to that, and all other concerns from student unrest to rising crime rates, to the urgent crisis of drug abuse, will begin to heal. All else pales beside the need to preserve the American family; to restore the mutual respect of parent and child; to provide security and stability in a world grown too crowded and impersonal; to instill a love for responsibility, honest work, and ultimate self-reliance; in short, to keep the family together. And this, far more than the pursuit of tourist dollars or handsome lodges, has guided our determination to provide campgrounds, playgrounds, shining water and shimmering sand where Kentucky families can be together. This has led us to expand the scope of Kentucky's parks beyond large facilities like Barren Lake to include smaller local expanses of green and fresh air closer to where people live. With matching funds from state government and the federal Bureau of Outdoor Recreation, seventy-three family parks are now being built in local communities throughout the Commonwealth. And we are taking the story of the great Kentucky outdoors to families this summer in a "Re-Discover Kentucky Caravan."

Kentucky poet Jesse Stuart, after leaving his native Greenup County to see the world, returned home and wrote these words: When

> . . . I went for the first time into other states
> . . . I knew my Kentucky was different.
> As I observed the closeness of the tombstones
> In the eastern cemeteries
> This gave me a feeling that land was scarce.
> . . . .
> [I saw cities so large they frightened me,
> Cliff dwellings as high as mountains.]
> . . . .
> And while it interested me
> To see how fellow Americans lived,

> I longed for Kentucky sunlight, sights, and sounds
> And for logshacks and . . . lonesome waters.
> I was homesick for the land of the fox
> And spring's tender bud, bloom, and leaf,
> For white sails of the dogwood, and the crabapple
> And . . . flame of redbud in the sunset.
> I knew my Kentucky was different
> And something there called me home.[2]

Like Jesse Stuart, we know our Kentucky is different. Kentucky has the spaces and places for wholesome outdoor recreation at such a premium today. She has miles of unspoiled beauty where families can refresh and reflect. And she is well on the way to becoming the cultural and recreational heartland of all America. For us, it is enough that Kentucky is our land:

> . . . a place beneath the wind and sun
> In the very heart of America.
> . . . neither southern, northern, eastern, or western,
> It is the core of America.
> If these United States can be called a body,
> Kentucky can be called its heart.[3]

As we dedicate Barren River Lake State Resort Park to Kentucky families everywhere, we return to where our hearts have remained. AND IT'S GOOD TO BE BACK HOME.

---

1. Lucas is located approximately ten miles from Glasgow, Governor Nunn's former place of residence.

2. Jesse Stuart, "Kentucky Is My Land," *Kentucky Is My Land* (New York, 1952), pp. 14–15. Jesse Hilton Stuart (1907–   ), educator and author of *Man with a Bull-Tongue Plow* (poems), 1934; *Head O' W-Hollow* (stories), 1936; and *Kentucky Is My Land* (poems), 1952. Stuart was born at W-Hollow, near Riverton and resides in Greenup. *Who's Who in America, 1970–1971* (Chicago, 1971), 36:2219. On July 14, 1971, Governor Nunn dedicated Jesse Stuart Lodge at Greenbo Lake State Park, Greenup.

3. Stuart, "Kentucky Is My Land," p. 9.

THE JOCKEY CLUB
Saratoga Springs, New York / August 15, 1971

MOST Kentuckians come to appreciate the horse very early in life, but perhaps very few come to fully understand how truly significant the horse industry is to the progress of our Commonwealth and to the nation.[1] It was as a high school and college student with a summer job as a guide in the caves region of Kentucky that I first experienced the wide impact of the racing industry. Tourist after tourist explained that they were attracted to our state primarily by the beautiful horses and Bluegrass farms. That lesson takes on added significance today for the Governor of a state which receives almost $50 million annually in direct tax revenue from the tourism industry, a great part of which still depends on the matchless beauty of the immaculate horse farms, the racing classics and traditions being carried on by our horsemen.

Kentuckians, like others who share their appreciation for the horse, may have assumed too much throughout the years by assuming that their appreciation was universally shared. And perhaps that is how to explain the fact that not enough has been done on a nationwide basis and in an organized, concentrated manner to promote and protect the industry. This is somewhat like the situation elsewhere in the country today. There are those willing to assume that if a person is born in America, he will automatically become a good American. We learned during the last decade that this wasn't true. Certain basics have to be taught; they have to be advertised and they have to be practiced. It is some of those basics I would like to discuss today, some fundamentals that have been recognized in Kentucky and elsewhere in order that this important industry might be allowed to grow and remain a significant part of our state's economic and cultural tradition.

Let me preface my remarks with the observation that when we have meetings such as your Round Table, the subjects under discussion naturally are specialized and tightly focused around one particular subject. I think it would be harmful and unwise, however, if the focus of this great industry ever was allowed to become narrow to the point of exclusion. We should not neglect the fact that the horse industry has a great many unsolicited supporters, both in the private and the public sector. Literally thousands and perhaps hundreds of thousands of people share our admiration for the Thoroughbred, and there is no reason to doubt that if properly motivated, they would also share our enthusiasm for protecting and advancing the racing industry. It seems to me that what we need to do is mobilize this support. This isn't the time for anyone to be waiting in the wings.

As you know, the present-day quirk of one particular American life-style is an almost fanatic obsession to attack the so-called "establishment." Unfortunately, there are those even in positions of public leadership today who appear more responsive to this movement than to the country's well-being. And for them, racing is too often the natural target. As the "sport of kings," it is a ready-made scapegoat for those who want to change the American system, who despise success, who constantly complain about free enterprise when they've never tried it, and who find something very sinister and despicable about the word profit.

What we need is a scorecard comparing what some of these critics have contributed and what the so-called "establishment" has accomplished. The horse industry is a good example. From its inception, this endeavor has been nurtured and directed and protected by those who represent and personify the establishment in America. Based on the tangible results of those efforts, even the critics must admit that you have not only served the industry well, but you have also served the nation well.

But regardless of this, regardless of the beauty and splendor of this sport, regardless of the positive contribution it has made and continues to make today, the horse industry is not immune from unfair criticism, unjust legislation, and unreasonable economic threat. That was the lesson we learned in 1969 when ill-conceived legislation was proposed that would place this vital segment of American agriculture and recreation in jeopardy.[2] We also learned during that time just how ill-equipped the industry was to defend itself. Supporters of the industry were somewhat unorganized; factual information on which a defense could be based was either fragmented or nonexistent. To put it bluntly, we were unprepared.

That is not the case today. A great deal has been accomplished because a coordinated and concentrated effort has been made to assimilate the necessary information and to organize a nucleus around which the positive defense of this industry can be made in the future. In anticipation of the impending legislative battle and the possibility that testimony before Congress in defense of the industry might be necessary, as you know Spindletop Research in Lexington was asked to make a special analysis of the economic impact of the horse industry on the United States. Using the information uncovered by that study, we were able to testify not for special favors for Kentucky breeders or for special treatment of the horse industry, but to testify positively to the economic, recreational, and educational importance of the industry throughout America.

What obviously had been overlooked by those who drafted the proposed tax changes was the large number of persons involved. They preferred instead to concentrate their attack on a very small group. Little concern had been shown for the thousands of persons employed by the industry who earned a total of $727 million each year and who were making their individual tax contributions. And obviously there had been little concern for the fact that $543 million had been invested in breeding facilities and equipment; that, as you know, an additional $79 million is invested in training; that $602 million is invested in the construction and operation of race tracks; and that the value of the commercial horse is $1.12 billion. What was being overlooked was the fact that tax revenues derived from horses amounted to nearly $450 million annually.

With the aid of the Spindletop findings, we were able to refute the charge that the Congress was indirectly subsidizing this sector of the farm economy. We were able to say: if that argument were true, what they really were subsidizing was employment, that they were encouraging industry, that they were promoting recreation and tourism, and that they were supporting a viable revenue producing source, rather than subsidizing unemployment and nonproductivity. The facts were indisputable; we were on safe, solid ground from which to attack. And I have been encouraged by remarks following the Congressional hearing that facts made the difference.

I look forward to the day when those who legislate and regulate this industry come to understand that in many ways this is a business proposition. And it deserves to be treated like a business. For instance, the breeding of horses is to racing what the manufacturing of steel is to the automobile industry. If, through discriminatory legislation or regulation, breeding interests are damaged, if it becomes economically impossible to continue efforts to preserve and improve the American bloodlines, then racing will suffer and the related fields of recreation and agriculture will suffer. All of us should have learned a great deal from the experience we shared in 1969. I know that we in Kentucky did.

Even before the legislative battle Kentucky was looking for ways to attract new investors into the industry. Shortly after I became Governor we placed an advertisement in the *Wall Street Journal* which stressed the investment opportunities of breeding Thoroughbreds in Kentucky. From that ad we received over 400 inquiries, not from curiosity seekers, but from people who could afford to invest. This experiment led to a partnership being formed between Kentucky state government and the Thoroughbred breeders of Kentucky in which the cost of advertising and promotion campaigns within certain limits is now shared equally.

We are concerned not simply with maintaining Kentucky's prominence in the sport. We also are concerned with properly fulfilling our responsibility to demonstrate leadership. Having learned almost too late during the Metcalf crisis of the almost complete lack of data about the horse industry, we have enthusiastically supported ensuing efforts to collect usable information.[3] With the technical assistance of Spindletop Research, real progress can be reported today.

Following the 1969 study, which had so conclusively proven the importance of hard economic data in talking to legislative committees, we authorized the initiation of a statewide data collection project for the race horse industry in Kentucky. To complete this work, Spindletop had excellent guidance from the National Association of State Racing Commissioners and when finished gave Kentucky for the first time a complete set of data for all aspects of the race horse industry. From this information came the very concise and impressive publication entitled "The Race Horse Industry in Kentucky," which has been distributed widely to those who have an interest in or should develop a greater interest in and understanding of the subject.[4] This included horsemen, media representatives, legislators, and regulatory agencies.

We believe the industry will benefit when those who support it, those who write about it, and those who regulate it know, for instance, that horse racing in Kentucky provides nearly $8 million in tax revenues annually; that over 12,000 persons are employed and earn nearly $19 million each year; that the state economy is stimulated by a turnover of nearly $25 million in purchases each year by the horse industry; that valuable greenbelts of open land are not only preserved but enhanced; and that a quarter of a million tourists visited the horse farms in 1970.

Presently, Spindletop Research has been retained by the National Association of State Racing Commissioners and is performing an extensive analysis of the economic considerations of off-track betting. The thrust of this effort is to provide reliable information to states considering legislation in this field. A procedure for each state to follow in debating the pros and cons of this question has been prepared. The continuity of all these studies now remains to be ensured and this is being accomplished by a planning grant for the design of an annual program of analysis of the horse industry.

In addition, Kentucky is embarking upon two completely unique projects through which both the horse industry and the state's economy will benefit and again prove the dynamic connection between the two. The first is preparation of a statewide system of horse trails which will link together areas having the proper combination of horses and travelers. Naturally, Kentucky's nationally respected system of state parks, most of which have stable facilities and existing trails, will figure prominently in our plans. Perhaps the most exciting plan to promote the horse industry, however, is encompassed in our effort to create a Thoroughbred State Park in central Kentucky. Plans call for developing themes for all breeds, with special emphasis given to this country's major breeds. The major purposes of the park will be to provide both an educational and a recreational experience for its visitors. The initial development would include a model horse farm complex, a training track, museum, tourist center, picnic area, theater, and food service facilities. We already have received assurances that retired racing champions could be acquired for exhibition, as an example of the spirit of enthusiasm and cooperation with which Kentucky horsemen have greeted plans for the new park. A survey indicates that between 1.4 million and 2 million visitors can be expected if the park is opened in 1972, and this figure could be expected to grow to 3 million by 1980. We do not intend this park as a memorial to racing's past. We are creating this facility to be more than a token of our appreciation for what your industry has meant to our state and to America. Kentucky's Thoroughbred State Park will be dedicated to the future, a future that is filled with a number of very crucial challenges and opportunities.

In closing, I trust that my remarks today and the suggestions I am about to leave with you are not interpreted in the narrow context of what is good for the racing industry in Kentucky, but what is good for the nation's horsemen. It is in this spirit that I would recommend the following methods by which we might avoid the repetition of unjustified attacks on this industry or successfully repel them if they are attempted:

1. The effort begun in Kentucky to gather significant and complete data concerning the industry should be repeated on a nationwide basis. The promotion and the protection of this industry depends on availability of such data.

2. The absolute necessity for intensified, unified equine medical research is proven by the recent outbreak of VEE. Every breed, every level of government, every state must be involved.

3. Continue to strive for a more realistic image. As long as this industry is viewed as a tax haven for the wealthy, it will continue

to be the target of unfair and discriminatory legislation, ill-conceived tax schemes, and lethargic public support. At this point I would especially commend the leadership of the American Horse Council for its renewed efforts to involve pleasure horse groups and 4-H groups. Certainly, this is a wise step toward a much broader base of support for all the horse industry and one that will pay large dividends in the future.

4. Continue to concentrate on the battles at the state level. Don't take your state legislatures for granted. That is where the fiscal squeeze is felt most intensely and the states are continually shopping for new revenue sources to replace those preempted by the federal government.

5. Continue to speak with the strong, united voice that was forged by the threat of 1969. Use that united voice not just in times of crisis and threat, but also on those more frequent occasions when the good of the industry must have priority over personal goals or regional pride.

6. And finally, continue to attract and hold men of high character and unselfish motives who will propagate your zest for sportsmanship and horsemanship in the best traditions of this great industry.

---

1. The Jockey Club is a private, national organization of persons "with proven interest in the Thoroughbred" and the central registering agency for Thoroughbreds in the United States. The Jockey Club, New York, New York, October 7, 1971.

2. See Governor Nunn's remarks to the United States Senate Finance Committee (September 22, 1969).

3. On September 19, 1968, Senator Lee Metcalf (Democrat, Montana) introduced Senate Bill 4059, "to limit the amount of deductions attributable to the business of farming which may be used to offset nonfarm income." Similar legislation was proposed in 1969. For further information see U.S., Congress, *Senate Journal* (September 19, 1968), p. 801; and U.S., Congress, *Congressional Record* (September 19, 1968), 114:27, 558–64.

4. "The Race Horse Industry in Kentucky" (Lexington, n.d.) is a brochure summarizing the impact of racing on the economy of Kentucky.

ANNOUNCEMENT OF EXPANSION OF FLORIDA TILE INDUSTRIES, INC.

Lawrenceburg / August 18, 1971

EARLIER this week I said the President's new economic proposals and initiatives were good news for all Kentuckians and all Americans.[1] Today we can be more specific. By the good faith again being demonstrated here today by Florida Tile, the people of Lawrenceburg and Anderson County and the surrounding counties have a concrete example of the revival of economic confidence that is spreading across America. Florida Tile's decision to expand their Lawrenceburg plant clearly reflects the changing economic mood of the country. It also reflects the giant strides of the Kentucky industrial movement in recent years. And more significantly, this company's fifth major expansion since coming to the Commonwealth thirty-nine months ago is an accurate forecast of what is in store for Kentucky in the years to come.

Together, Florida and Kentucky have grown in equally dramatic fashion over the past three and one-half years. Through the efforts of those of you who work here and who have made the Lawrenceburg plant such a successful experience, this company has grown to become one of the three largest producers in the tile industry. Its growth, like Kentucky's, has defied adversity. In a year in which the carpet industry reported its first decline in over two decades, Florida Tile was achieving an industry-wide record for first year sales.

Kentucky's efforts to bring new industry and new job opportunities also has grown out of adversity. Despite the uncertain national economic conditions of the past few years as America has begun the transition from a wartime to peacetime economy, despite high interest rates, inflation, and high cost of investment capital, and despite the withdrawal of industrial bonding privileges which helped attract so much of the industrial expansion we experienced in the sixties, Kentucky has set new records in its march toward a balanced agri-industrial economy since 1967. Since 1967, 270 new industries have located in Kentucky. But listen to the next statistic. During that same period, 371 companies expanded their Kentucky operations, and that says something about the confidence of the business community in Kentucky's working men and women, in the economic climate of the Commonwealth, and in the attitude of government here. One additional fact further illustrates industry's growing confidence. These new and expanded companies have invested $1,278,600,000 in Kentucky these past forty-four months, which is an all-time record for any four-year period in the history of the Commonwealth.

These new and expanding industries, and we should mention that Florida Tile can be counted in both categories, have provided nearly 40,000 new job opportunities; opportunities for those who were unemployed, but who wanted to work; opportunities for those who were underemployed; opportunities for those who wanted to remain on Kentucky's farms but needed supplemental income; and opportunities for our young people, who were born and educated here, who wanted to live here and raise their families and make their contributions here toward a better Kentucky. Stimulated by this industrial growth, we will achieve a goal established in 1967, 223,000 more jobs by 1977. Employment in Kentucky has increased from 1,090,000 in 1967 to 1,178,000 today. Eighty-eight thousand more jobs have been filled. That is an average growth of 22,000 jobs each year, which is precisely in line with the goal that was set. Today, however, I believe we can confidently adjust that goal upward. In view of the progress made despite adverse conditions and in light of the dramatic impetus of the President's action Sunday evening, I am encouraged to believe that Kentucky now stands on the threshold of the greatest era of economic development in its history.

Certainly we should acknowledge that the next ninety days will be difficult. Transition so drastic as this naturally will not immediately conform to the plans and hopes and budgets of all families. But I believe Americans understand this. They understand that the President's prescription is a strong one. And I think they agree that for too long we've treated the world as our patient and even paid for the medicine while America was left sitting in the waiting room. And I think the American people will respond in the proper manner.

The President's appeal for voluntary support of the program that has been proposed is not an appeal to our pocketbooks, but to our patriotism. And if we meet that appeal, if we put America first, then we can meet the needs of the people at home: the working man and woman, the farmer, the teacher, the businessman. We can revitalize America's economic resources. And we can renew this nation's generous commitment to freedom, opportunity, and peace throughout the world.

---

1. Governor Nunn was referring to President Nixon's actions (announced on August 15, 1971) regarding the nation's economy. Among the presidential

initiatives were a ninety-day price-wage freeze; the imposition of a 10 percent surcharge on all imports not subject to quotas; and the termination by the United States of the use of gold in international payments and of the purchase of gold at $35 per ounce.

OPENING OF THE
KENTUCKY STATE FAIR
Louisville / August 19, 1971

SHORTLY after the State Fair closed last year, I received a letter from a Kentucky father who had been here with his family. He wrote to say how much they had enjoyed themselves, to compliment all the improvements that had been made, and to say his family appreciated what we had done to help with the Fair. But he was concerned and puzzled about one thing: he wanted to know how we could afford to operate the Fair when he, his wife, and eight children could come here, stay for twelve hours, and spend only one dollar and seventy-five cents. His question underscores an important fact about the Kentucky State Fair. This is one event where the emphasis is on the family, on clean, wholesome, and inexpensive entertainment, an event where families can review and revel together in the progress that is being made in their State.

This year the theme of the Fair is "Kentucky's World of Progress," and nowhere do we see our State's progress more vividly illustrated than right here at the Fairgrounds. During the past four years, $920 thousand has been invested to make improvements like the paving and expansion of the 4,800-car parking lot, widening of the Crittenden Drive gate to eliminate traffic congestion, and doubling the electrical capacity of the West Wing to attract more trade shows. And the investment has paid off. In 1967, before improvements were begun, the Fairground's total operating profit for a full year was $1,041. Last year our improved facilities made $242,285. And though the auditors have not completed their review of the books for 1970–71, figures through the end of May indicate that this year operating profit has reached the half-million-dollar mark.

We have come this far because Kentucky's commitment to her farm families has been 100 percent. During State Fair time, it is traditional for Kentuckians to pause and reflect on the vast contributions that have been made to the well-being of us all by the farm families of our State and nation. It is a special pleasure to note again this year that the farmers of Kentucky have reached new plateaus of production and income. For the second year in a row, and for the second time in history, Kentucky's gross farm income surpassed the billion-dollar mark in 1970. But more significantly, we can also report that real progress has been made to guarantee that our farmers will bring home from the marketplace a greater share of their productivity. The dramatic growth of farm income is largely due to the ingenuity and hard work of the farmer. But I would like to think that the cooperation of state government and the concern of all the people of the Commonwealth for the well-being of our farm families also have been contributing factors. Today, the farmer benefits from a more equitable method of property tax assessment, one which received the overwhelming support of both rural and urban Kentuckians. Since 1968, farm machinery has been exempted from the state sales and use tax. We are now completing the largest farm-to-market road improvement program in the history of Kentucky. And the State has worked closely with its universities to improve the quality of agriculture.

The growth of our livestock and dairy industry is a good example of how Kentucky agriculture has flourished with government's cooperation. Kentucky now ranks eleventh in the nation in the number of milk cows. Annual milk production per cow hit a record high last year. And we now stand second in all of America in production of evaporated milk, and second in the nation in manufacture of natural cheddar cheese. Only weeks ago the first cheese to bear a Kentucky label went on the market. We are looking forward to sampling some of it today.

Farmers throughout the Commonwealth, including those whose dairy industry has produced this fine cheese, stand today alongside workers in our cities and towns as full partners in the progress of Kentucky. It is fitting that they all can meet at the Kentucky State Fair and share in the world of progress they have worked to establish. The Kentucky State Fair reminds us each year that while there are differences, while there are divisions, the things that unite us in Kentucky and in America are far greater than the things that would divide us. We all share the same goals, whether we live on a farm or in the largest city in the State. We all want a secure life for our families, a sound education for our children, and progress for our communities. And the State Fair also reminds us that by working together we shall achieve these goals.

As we observe today the official opening of the 1971 Kentucky State Fair, we rededicate ourselves to the continued strength and vitality of our farmers, to the enhancement of rural life in our State, to the encouragement of a balanced agri-industrial economy—in short, to enduring progress. For as it has been said, we should so live and labor in our time that what came to us as seed may go to the next generation as blossom, and what came to us as blossom may go to them as fruit. That is what we mean by progress.

DEDICATION OF BUILDINGS
AT KENTUCKY STATE COLLEGE
Frankfort / August 24, 1971

AT 4:30 a. m. today when the Governor realized it would be physically impossible to be with you today, he wrote a special preface to his remarks and asked that I read it to you.[1] The Governor wanted to say to the faculty and student body and administrators that Kentucky State was not the usual or ordinary college. Its creation was a ray of hope to a people that had been denied opportunity, that it was uncommon in its creation, and that he hoped it would never become the usual or ordinary or common college.

It is the Governor's hope that Kentucky State will be a beacon of opportunity for those who come here. And on this special occasion, the Governor asked me to reiterate his conviction that the bricks and mortar of the buildings we dedicate today are not enough to make this institution all that we hope it will become. It is the spirit of the faculty and student body and administrators and their desire and drive for excellence that will develop this college to its fullest potential. And that is the challenge he sends to you this morning.

During recent years we have witnessed tremendous growth in higher education in Kentucky. Within the past decade the number of full-time students enrolled in state-supported colleges and universities in Kentucky has increased from 24,000 to more than 62,000 students. During the eight years of Dr. Hill's presidency, the student body has increased here at Kentucky State College from 868 to 1,754, an increase of 102 percent.[2]

To keep pace with such growth, the total state appropriation for higher education has risen from $18.5 million in 1960 to $120 million last fiscal year. Out of necessity much of this investment has been in physical plant expansion at our state institutions. That building program is now virtually completed, and we have facilities at the established colleges and universities of this Commonwealth which will equal any in the country. Certainly we as Kentuckians take pride in these modern facilities that will enable our children and their children to pursue higher education to benefit them and the State.

The fact that today we dedicate thirteen buildings on this campus indicates that Kentucky State College has not been overlooked in Kentucky's massive program of physical plant growth. Here, as all over the Commonwealth, present physical plants at our state colleges and universities encourage us to believe that the frantic capital improvement program which was necessary in the 1960s will not confront us again in the foreseeable future. The dedication ceremonies today by no means bring to a close the development of this school. But the Commonwealth of Kentucky, and Kentucky State College, now face an even more formidable and decisive challenge. Bricks and mortar compose merely the shell of a university; the learning which takes place inside is what the university is all about. Future development must look toward the improvement of programs offered here. This is what we want for Kentucky State College and for all institutions of higher learning in the Commonwealth.

For years this institution was required to serve the function of educating black students only. But today's laws now relegate that mission obsolete. No longer is race a determining factor in the acceptance of an individual to this college or any other college in the Commonwealth. The factor that once made Kentucky State unique has now been dissipated by the rules of rational thought and human decency. Even though the original mission which necessitated the operation of Kentucky State College has passed, the college can continue to take pride in having served a vital function for the education of black students and can continue building on that tradition. But now it is time to seek a new role in Kentucky's system of higher education, a role every bit as unique and as useful as that which Kentucky State College has played in the past. Let the dead past bury its dead. But let the spirit of service that characterized this institution's past live today and tomorrow and always.

In a recent report the Council of Public Higher Education urged university status for this institution. As you await this new status, it seems an appropriate time for reflection: for remembering all that Kentucky State College has been, all it has meant to Kentucky, and what it can be in the days ahead. Use this time to chart a useful course. Use this time to prepare for the journey into a whole new era in the life of this institution.

Serving the identical roles for graduate education now provided in our other colleges and universities can become needless, wasteful duplication. Initiating programs which emulate exactly those of your sister schools can, in my opinion, only jeopardize the future of this institution. The course of duplication leads only to the port of inefficiency. And inefficiency is the corroding element that eats away at the foundation of public education. That foundation is the public confidence, and if it is destroyed by neglect, by overt or covert acts, then the temple of public education that has been erected in Kentucky will also fall. Instead, I suggest strongly to you, President Hill, members of the Board of Regents, faculty representatives, and students, that this is the time to seize fully on the primary uniqueness of Kentucky State College today, its proximity to the state Capitol, the center of government in Kentucky.

If you look to the future, what could be more appropriate than for this institution to concentrate heavily on those concerns most closely associated with this region, particularly state government. I suggest for future program development you turn your attention to this area of government. Three studies since 1960 all suggest that government-oriented courses at Kentucky State College are needed and would be beneficial to both the students, to the state government, and thus to all the people of our Commonwealth.

This college's cooperation with the Frankfort Administrative Intern Program is illustrative of the major role that Kentucky State College can fill. Dr. Hill was among the founding fathers of the Frankfort Semester Program before this administration began. We recognized the value of providing undergraduate students the opportunity for first-hand participation in state government and moved quickly to provide funds in the 1970 Executive Budget for the program's continuation and expansion. But there were those in positions of leadership in the Legislature, who either for political or prejudicial motives, saw fit to amend the Executive Budget to end all funding for the vital work begun by Dr. Hill and other men of vision. What those short-sighted individuals failed to reckon with was the power of a good idea. The seeds of success had been planted; the interest of all state agencies had been whetted. So it was not difficult for us to go directly to the individual agencies and secure their pledge to continue the program by absorbing the costs in their own budgets. The entire cost of the Frankfort Administrative Intern Program is now borne by interested state agencies who pay the full stipend to the student. Coupled with the Legislative Intern Program, which this administration initiated and which now has the full support of twenty-one colleges throughout the Commonwealth, Kentucky's two undergraduate programs for students in government are the only fully accredited programs of their type in the nation.

The State Department of Personnel shares our faith in cooperative programs of this nature and has been fortunate enough to secure the services of Dr. Robert Sexton as full-time Director of Student and Academic Programs.[3] With the apparatus for coordination and administration of government training programs, Kentucky state government stands ready today to respond to this institution's new call to excellence.

I do not propose that Kentucky State College vacate its role as a liberal arts institution. Today we need men broadly trained for positions of leadership in government. We need minds with the solid background in the physical and biological sciences offered at Kentucky State College. Your fine science program here can become an integral part of the new direction. Kentucky State College can provide manpower resources to grapple with environmental problems that are sure to be with us in the future, and a necessary input at the highest levels of state government where a commitment to preventive and corrective action must begin.

I do not suggest that you merely expand or offer master's degree programs in political science or public administration. Rather I suggest a more innovative approach where you utilize the resources of the various social sciences, physical sciences, and business disciplines in a core curriculum that will train young Kentuckians for public service both at the state and local level. Perhaps through a governmental institute utilizing the resources and personnel of state government, as well as your sister institutions, and, of course, your own institution, you can offer the greatest support role for good government that I can conceive in the State today. The governmental institute could offer not only degree programs at the undergraduate and graduate level, but short-term training courses for virtually every agency of the state government. This effort will be an absolute necessity as the State is to continue to tackle the varied, tremendously complicated problems of the future.

Because Kentucky State College has actively sought and successfully obtained more than $560 thousand in federal funds under the Developing Institutions Act, you are aware that resources are available for planning, developing, and implementing cooperative arrangements which show promise for strengthening developing institutions like Kentucky State. Internships, education programs with alternate periods of academic study and public employment, and teaching fellowships are among the programs encouraged by the Developing Institutions Act. Its purpose seems tailor-made to what you may decide to be the purpose of Kentucky State College.

So I challenge you to embark on a unique path. Do not let this school fall into the trap which the Carnegie Commission on Higher Education has labeled the "homogeneous institution." Pick your niche and make yourselves the best in that field. Let Kentucky State College become the prime institution for all of those who seek involvement in state government. The decision would seem to be yours. The pattern selected by the other state institutions is largely the result of their geographic uniqueness, but for Kentucky State College with its close proximity to two major state institutions, selection of a similar path would be an invitation to mediocrity. Rather, you should encourage a new, creative, but utilitarian pathway that will lead this institution to greatness through service to the state government and consequently to all the people of Kentucky.

---

1. Finance Commissioner Albert Christen read this speech for Governor Nunn.

2. Carl M. Hill (1907–   ), black educator, college administrator, and author. Positions held by Hill include president and professor of chemistry, Kentucky State College (1962–   ); dean of the faculty and dean, School of Arts and Sciences (1958–1962), head, Department of Chemistry (1944–1951), Tennessee Agricultural and Industrial State University. *Who's Who in the South and Southwest, 1971–1972.* 12th ed. (Chicago, 1971), p. 284.

3. Robert F. Sexton (1942–   ), Lexington, director, Office for Experiential Education, University of Kentucky (1973–   ); director of student and academic programs, Kentucky Department of Personnel (1971–1973); chairman, Board of Directors, National Center for Public Service Internship Programs (1971–1973).

KENTUCKY-TENNESSEE
KIWANIS CLUBS
Lexington / August 30, 1971

WE are beginning to realize at meetings such as your district convention that we live in a time when the things that affect us all alike are greater than the things that affect us as individuals. And for a few moments this morning, I would like to talk to you about some of the things that affect Kentuckians and Tennesseans and all Americans alike much more than the things that affect us as individuals. But first I want to preface my remarks with a philosophical frame of reference, a philosophy that would seem to be in keeping with that of your organization, an organization of individual men joined together in dedicated service to their communities and their fellowman.

Before discussing the role of government in either domestic or foreign affairs, I want you to know that I believe that the best government is the least government. And like another Kentuckian, I believe the only legitimate object of government is to do for the people that which they cannot do for themselves. After four years as a county judge and after three years and nine months as Governor, I can tell you very frankly that there are very few things government can do as well as those it tries to serve. But with the help of the people, with the concern of the individual citizen, with the mobilized energy of service-oriented organizations such as yours, there is nothing we cannot do for those who are willing to try to help themselves.

Government is asked to deal with many complex situations. That is why we cannot be satisfied with short-term solutions or short-term planning any longer. Real progress, the kind of progress the people of Kentucky, the people of Tennessee, and all Americans deserve, cannot be achieved with patchwork programs. I trust that this conviction will be evident as I share with you some details of Kentucky's answer to one of the most critical problems of our time, a problem which should concern all of us. It is the tragedy of drug abuse, addiction, and wasted lives. The fact that Kiwanis International for the first time in its history elected last year to have not many but one major emphasis program, and the fact that in 1970 and again this year you have emphasized Operation Drug Alert, shows that you are well aware of the magnitude of the problem. More important, it shows that you care enough to do something about it.

Kentuckians share your concern. And because Kentuckians cared, eight to ten thousand came to Louisville last December for a statewide Drug Awareness Conference. They heard the tragic facts of an epidemic that had spread to every corner of our Commonwealth. In Kentucky alone, the number of drug-related arrests increased 600 percent during the first six months of 1970. Arrests for violation of federal drug laws have doubled here in only two years. The number of Kentuckians under eighteen arrested for drug violations has increased 2,500 percent during the last ten years. During the same time the number of adults arrested on these charges has risen 500 percent.

The facts they heard left no time for wringing hands or surrendering to despair. The information they heard was not hidden under a veil of hopelessness. We pledged then to take drug education into the home of literally every Kentuckian. And in the six months since the conference, in three distinct areas of accomplishment, we have done that and more. Kentuckians have united in an unprecedented effort to combat drug abuse through education, treatment, and law enforcement.

First, our progress in education. The Drug Conference generated such an awareness that today 120 citizen committees for drug education, one in every county in Kentucky, have been organized. Assisted by professional drug coordinators appointed by the Department of Mental Health, these citizens groups have held thirteen regional workshops and rallies attended by more than 4,000 Kentuckians. They have aided local drug education in a variety of innovative ways.

In Calloway County, as an example, every parent has received literature describing symptoms to watch for in drug abuse. The young people of Murray pooled their talent in a benefit performance netting hundreds of dollars to purchase drug films and other educational materials. In Union County a speakers bureau has been organized to supply speeches on the drug crisis for church, school, and civic groups. The bureau enlisted the help of a former marine addicted while in service. He is now remarkably effective in speaking to high school students throughout the county. One high school girl voluntarily told the county drug chairman that she made the decision to quit smoking marijuana after hearing him. In Greenup County, living room discussions led to a committee-sponsored hot line called "We Care." Volunteers now man the answering service, with a major portion of the calls drug related. In Madison County 800 students have marshalled forces in a massive "Teens against Drugs" effort.

Following our Drug Conference, the Kentucky Educational Television network broadcast what is probably the most comprehensive series on drugs in the history of broadcasting. It was called "The

Turned-On Crisis." The Kentucky Department of Public Information has distributed TV spots to stations throughout Kentucky and neighboring states providing vivid information on the danger of drugs. Twenty-five drive-in movies have shown a short film entitled "The Seekers" all summer long. Seventy-three thousand Kentuckians have seen drug films made available by the Department of Mental Health.

Over two thousand dollars from the Governor's Contingency Fund have gone to local drug education efforts on a two-to-one local-state matching basis, and many more grant applications are being reviewed now. A team of fifteen state troopers have been trained as information officers and dispatched throughout the Commonwealth to conduct drug abuse programs for schools and local civic groups. Nearly 33,000 teachers and school administrators have been involved in making drug education a part of the regular curriculum.

Education is one of the surest tools in preventing drug abuse, and we are deeply proud of the progress Kentucky has made in this phase of the three-pronged attack. But there are those for whom drug education comes too late. For them, the hundreds, perhaps thousands, of Kentuckians who need professional help to escape from addiction, Kentucky offers real hope through a nationally recognized program of rehabilitation. Last month Kentucky received the second largest drug services grant ever awarded by the federal government. That $5 million will enable us to expand drug and alcohol treatment services dramatically throughout the Commonwealth. In addition, our four state psychiatric hospitals have geared up to offer treatment and withdrawal help. Their staffs are now professionally equipped to cope with the complexities of drug emergencies.

Kiwanians from Tennessee probably realize that Kentucky was the first state in the nation to pass legislation creating a Drug Offender Program. And you can be proud that your state now has a similar program. The program's aim is salvaging lives. No longer is a person who has been convicted for a first-time drug offense sent to prison, where he might learn more about drugs from experienced offenders than he knew before. Instead, we require that first-time dangerous-drug offenders "serve their time" in weekly education and rehabilitation sessions, rather than behind bars.

But no amount of rehabilitation or education will ever change one fact: as long as illicit drugs are available, someone is going to experiment with them. There is only one sure way to eliminate the problem: apprehension, conviction, and imprisonment of those who traffic in drugs. To help the user, we must stop the pusher. This is a job for law enforcement. The scope of our state troopers has been expanded from highway traffic to drug traffic. A new Criminal Investigation Command with two special sections, a Narcotic and Dangerous Drug Unit and an Organized Crime Unit, has been created. During the first five months after the Drug Conference, state police arrested 68 percent more drug offenders than in the same period in 1970, 42 percent more than were arrested in the entire twelve months of 1969. Most of these arrests involved not drug users, but persons caught in the act of selling or transporting drugs and narcotics.

Undercover intelligence work is penetrating drug circles with encouraging success. This aspect of the effort will be increased soon. Since late last year investigators of the new state police drug unit have concentrated on pinpointing high drug action areas, identifying pushers and transporters, and tracing intrastate routes over which much of Kentucky's illicit drugs are supplied. This information is being shared with our neighboring states. Security reasons prevent any detailing of their findings, but I can report to you that more than a dozen key sources, both within and outside Kentucky, have been uncovered, some as far away as Mexico and California.

We are catching on to some of the pushers' trade. Armed with the right information at the right time, law enforcement officials at both the state and local level are taking the pushers off Kentucky streets for good. Information developed by our state police units has led to other investigations and arrests by federal agents and local police, sometimes in neighboring states.

It is appropriate that Kentucky-Tennessee District of Kiwanis International share in Operation Drug Alert, for the drug problem is no respecter of boundaries and jurisdictions. We all share the burden. We all share a mutual concern, as you have demonstrated so effectively through your drug awareness program.

This, then, is what Kentucky has done. The task is not completed, by any means. But the start we have made in combatting drug abuse shows what can be done. The agencies of Kentucky state government have supported the effort. The Governor's office has helped dramatize the effort. But the people of Kentucky are getting the job done, people like you—concerned, dedicated, service-oriented people—who realize that there is much more to be done.

In the weeks ahead I will announce a new package of major programs to continue the fight we have begun. These programs will touch all three areas I have mentioned today: education, treatment, and enforcement. We know pushers come into Kentucky from all over America with maps showing the location of fields where hemp, or marijuana, grows wild. They bring with them harder drugs and trade for the marijuana. And we will have an announcement within a few weeks aimed at stopping that. We know our state police are understaffed and overworked. We want to free some of their more seasoned troopers to do undercover work in drug traffic.

These are the areas we will be hitting hardest as we announce the next chapter in Kentucky's continuing commitment to end the threat of drug abuse. I thank you for what you are doing as Kiwanians, as Tennesseans, and Kentuckians to help. But these programs, like others that have preceded them, are only as effective as you, the private citizen, demand that they be. I trust you will continue to care, to activate your concern, to support the education, treatment, and enforcement phases of your state's attack on one of the most serious challenges of our time.

TESTIMONY CONCERNING THE FEDERAL COAL MINE HEALTH AND SAFETY ACT OF 1969
Lexington / September 16, 1971

I AM Louie B. Nunn, Governor of the Commonwealth of Kentucky. First allow me to thank you for this opportunity to testify in regard to the Federal Coal Mine Health and Safety Act of 1969.[1] I would not appear here today as an expert witness or attempt to offer any degree of personal expertise. But as chief executive I feel a responsibility to an industry which comprises a major portion of our economy and affects the safety and well-being of many of the citizens of this Commonwealth. More importantly, however, there is a sense of personal responsibility and a sincere desire to aid and assist in the safety and security of our fellowmen.

It is this concern for physical safety, economic well-being, and environmental protection that compels me to say that the Federal Coal Mine Health and Safety Act of 1969 has failed to achieve the good intentions of those in Congress who supported its passage. The Kentucky experience in the twenty-one months since this law became effective has shown that instead of helping to solve a serious problem it has helped to compound the problem. The law has become an administrative nightmare as well as an exercise in contradiction, confusion, and futility. There have been instances (and no doubt testimony will be offered later today to prove) in which this legislation has seriously and unfairly jeopardized lives instead of saving lives. It has jeopardized the economic stability of a segment of the mining industry. And it has jeopardized the ecological grandeur of our state.

What appears to be the most glaring mistake of the law is the removal of the distinction between gassy and nongaseous mines. This portion of the Act has hit hardest and most inequitably at the small mines, particularly in eastern Kentucky. The new and highly expensive permissible machinery required by the new law simply is out of the financial reach of many small operators. And this requirement is even further beyond the understanding of these operators. No one, either at the federal, state, or local level, has yet been able to explain to these operators why they should have to sink huge sums of capital into equipment to be used in gassy mines when their mines contain no gas. Many of the small mines in Appalachia have been forced to close because of inability to comply with the Act. Many others have closed before being inspected out of fear of the high penalties provided by the new law.

It is ironic and most unfortunate that while we have finally realized an industrial breakthrough in eastern Kentucky (a period when nearly fifty new industries were locating in that part of our State) many able-bodied men have been denied an opportunity to work because of a discriminatory law. In 1970, 969 underground mines were in operation in eastern Kentucky, employing 17,321 men. Today the number of mines has dropped to 820 and nearly one thousand fewer men are employed. It is tragic that many of those employed at these mines may have no other recourse than to leave payrolls and join the welfare rolls. Surely, this was not the intention of the authors of the law.

The burden is not limited to small mines only. Many large mines are suffering from a supervisory shortage brought about by the wholesale employing of federal mine inspectors. Those supervisory personnel who are left spend much of their time accompanying inspectors on the mine property and are otherwise deskbound by volumes and volumes of paper work. Unless there is a reversal of the present trend, we may reach a point when there will be almost as many federal inspectors as there are coal mines to inspect.

Almost two years have passed since the law became effective and the most knowledgeable people in the Bureau of Mines and the industry are still trying to determine its full meaning. Interpretations are still being attempted, but seemingly with little success. It must be evident that if those responsible for implementing the law cannot agree, the coal operators could hardly be expected to understand how they are to comply.

In looking at Kentucky's mine safety record it shows that the Commonwealth covered a period of almost twenty-five years without a major disaster. The year before the Act went into effect (1969) the Commonwealth enjoyed its best year from a coal mine fatality standpoint. Thirty-three miners lost their lives in 1969 as compared to thirty-seven to this date in 1971. This in itself shows that the Act is not working.

Almost as distressing as the adverse effect the new law has had on the safety of the coal miner is the devastating setback it has dealt to Kentucky's environment. As more and more small mine operators have been forced to close, more and more strip mine operations have been started. In 1968 there were 189 surface mining operations in Kentucky. Today, that number has increased more than three times. Now there are 556 strip mine operations. Production figures reflect the same disturbing trend. In 1969 underground mines produced 64 million tons of coal in Kentucky, while surface mining operations yielded 44 million tons. Last year, however, underground mines produced only 63 million tons, while the figure for surface operations skyrocketed to 62 million.

These statistics in human, economic, and environmental damage vividly underscore the need for immediate remedial action by the Congress. It should be obvious to all that if the Kentucky coal industry is to remain sound, and is to provide safer, more rewarding employment for our people, and is to flourish in compatibility with our environment, the Congress must take another look at the 1969 Act.

To show further why such action is needed, I have asked a team of five experts from Kentucky's nationally respected Department of Mines and Minerals to appear with me here today. Together these men represent almost a century and a half of mining experience. They have experienced first hand the frustrations inherent in the Coal Mine Health and Safety Act. They are: Commissioner Kirkpatrick; Assistant to the Commissioner J. H. Mosgrove; Cecil Sherman of the Martin District; Everett Bartlett of the Hazard District; and James Thorp of the Western Kentucky District.[2]

Mr. Kirkpatrick is from a mining family whose entire working career has been associated with underground coal mines in Muhlenberg County of western Kentucky. Mr. Kirkpatrick has always had an interest in mine safety, having worked with several safety organizations during his career. Mr. Mosgrove has been associated with the mining industry of Kentucky over forty years, having started as a miner at a very young age in Letcher County. His career has included working as a mine laborer, and supervisor, and he has been directly engaged in safety work for over twenty-five years.

Mr. Sherman started his career in 1931 as a mine laborer. He has advanced from that position to the job he now holds as District Supervisor with the Department. Many years of Mr. Sherman's background have been directly connected with safety promotion. Mr. Bartlett has been associated with mining in Kentucky for over forty years. His work experience ranges from mine laborer to mine superintendent. He has served with the Department of Mines and Minerals almost seventeen years. Mr. Thorp, supervisor of the Western Kentucky District, has worked in the western Kentucky coalfields for a number of years. He was very active in safety team work and has served as a mine laborer and supervisor.

All these men are well qualified by their experience as laborers, supervisors, and safety inspectors and administrators. They are here to help, not to hinder. They are here to offer constructive criticism, not to obscure the facts. We do not ask that changes be made at the expense of lives, because we fully realize that productivity must be judged in human terms. But neither shall we be silent as unjustifiable and illogical obstacles are placed before productivity. We ask only that necessary revisions be made in order that we might have legislation that can be readily understood both by those charged with its implementation and by those who are required to comply—legislation that will effectively assist us in attaining a new high in the safety, economic, and environmental standards of the coal industry.

---

1. Delivered at a public hearing held by the United States Bureau of Mines to determine what changes, if any, to recommend for the Coal Mine Safety Act of 1969. For additional information see "An Act to provide for the protection of the health and safety of persons working in the coal mining industry of the United States, and for other purposes," Public Law 91–173, in U.S., *Statutes at Large*, Vol. 83.

2. Harreld N. Kirkpatrick (1919–), commissioner, Kentucky Department of Mines and Minerals (1968–); J. H. Mosgrove (1913–), assistant to the commissioner, Kentucky Department of Mines and Minerals (1962–); Cecil Sherman (1913–), district supervisor for the Martin District, Kentucky Department of Mines and Minerals (1969–); Everett Bartlett (1911 –), district supervisor for the Hazard District (1959–), Kentucky Depart-

ment of Mines and Minerals; James Thorp (1923–   ), district supervisor for the Western Kentucky District (1968–   ), and mine inspector for the Western Kentucky District (1968), Kentucky Department of Mines and Minerals.

WHITE HALL DEDICATION
Richmond / September 16, 1971

KENTUCKY pays homage today to a remarkable statesman who lived his years in such a forceful manner that the course of human history was forever altered and improved. Such were his contributions to freedom and justice that the long shadow he cast upon events of his time was extended across the pages of history into our time. And today we are here to ensure that the heroic shadow of that man, the Lion of White Hall, Cassius Marcellus Clay, will also fall upon the future.

In dedicating this Commonwealth's forty-second shrine, we are reminded most vividly that this thing we call history is in reality only an unrolled scroll of prophecy. And as we and the thousands of visitors who come here examine the tangible legacy of Cassius Clay—the dueling pistols, Bowie knives, and other authentic artifacts of a life crowded by conflict and courage—let us all be reminded that history not only teaches but it also sounds a warning to those of future generations who bother to listen. In human relations, in warfare, in domestic and international diplomacy, and in politics, Cassius Marcellus Clay personified in his time the foresight, courage, and tenacity that we need in our time to alter and shape history.

Cassius Clay was unawed by opinion, he was unseduced by flattery, and he was undismayed by disaster. He withstood the privation of adverse public sentiment and stood undaunted in support of the principles on which he felt America had achieved her greatness. He never sought the safety of popular opinion, nor did he indulge in the comforts of compromise and consensus politics. He was a man about whom facts and fiction swirled in equally swift currents. For like all strong men, he aroused the deepest passions of both friends and enemies. He provoked one fight in his life. Yet, his reputation as a fighter stalked him throughout his adult years. He abhorred violence. But his life was filled with the most violent of events. He sought peace, and saw constitutional and legislative processes as the best way to achieve that peace. But he was denied the avenues of peace, and thus was relegated to the paths of war. He was born to a life of ease, but spent his energy and fortune in defense of man's right to pursue the immense promise of America unshackled by oppression and indignity.

As an editor, orator, emancipationist, ambassador, and respected advisor to his fellow Kentuckian Abraham Lincoln, he made personal sacrifices of such magnitude that the course of human events was forever altered. He withstood the public disfavor and loneliness reflected in memoirs written at the end of a long and useful life. "At night, I am left all the more alone. I often open the shutters that the bats should enter . . . and their fluttering—life—is a pleasure to me."[1] Here lived a man so wedded to his convictions, so dedicated to his ideals, that to a great extent he sacrificed his family, his friends, and himself. Yet his sacrifice helped change a world.

With his abolitionist newspaper, *The True American*, he waged one of the earliest fights for freedom of the press. His generosity and interest in education founded Berea College, where the honest labor of young Kentuckians still sustains a rich cultural heritage of mountain crafts. His influence at the Republican Convention of 1860 helped Lincoln win his party's nomination for president. The views they shared on the evils of human bondage shaped Lincoln's Emancipation Proclamation. And as Lincoln's Minister to Russia, Clay's rapport with Czar Alexander was instrumental in America's purchase of Alaska.

To the memory of a courageous Kentuckian, we dedicate his beloved White Hall as a state shrine today. And as we do, let us also rededicate ourselves to those things which characterized the good acts of its master: an abiding commitment to our convictions; willingness to take a position; and readiness, if necessary, to weather popular opinion to defend it. For, in the final analysis, as the Lion of White Hall liked to say: "Every man should be estimated, not by his personal success—the trappings and honors of office—but by the triumph of those principles which add to human happiness."[2]

Cassius Marcellus Clay was a man not for a day but for all time. Yet largely it has been his enemies who have written the history of the man. By repairing, by restoring White Hall to its original splendor, our goal is to resurrect more than just a home. Our hope is that we shall have helped to restore the magnificent spirit born here, a spirit which never really died, but still touches the lives of free men everywhere.

1. Quoted in the *Louisville Courier-Journal and Times*, April 9, 1967.
2. Cassius Marcellus Clay, *The Life of Cassius Marcellus Clay* (Cincinnati, 1886; reprint ed., 1968), p. iv.

REPUBLICAN RALLY
Levi Jackson State Park
London / September 18, 1971

FELLOW Americans, good Kentuckians:

It's great to be in the Fifth District and to share with you the beauty of God's handicraft; to see here such abundant concern for the future of our State; to feel among you the strong, patriotic spirit of a people who believe in America, and who are willing to stand up and defend its principles and, yes, even die for them. I come here today to speak in support of a native son of the Fifth District and to support the finest team of candidates ever to seek state office in Kentucky's history. From top to bottom these are the kind of men and women Kentuckians need. These are the kind of public officials Kentuckians deserve. And these are the candidates that Kentuckians are going to elect on November 2. And this time they're going to elect a team for Kentucky. They're tired of bickering and nit-picking. They're tired of officeholders who constantly stand in the way of progress.

During the past four years the people of this State have seen what can be done in spite of public officials who constantly complain and obstruct just for the sake of their own political ambitions. Now they want to see what can be done when their public officials are united in a common cause, the cause of a good government for everyone. Look at what has been accomplished over the past four years. And think what might have been done if we could have had a Lieutenant Governor who was willing to do his part, who would have put the future of our State above his own political future. Think what might have been accomplished if the Lieutenant Governor [Wendell H. Ford] had been as interested in finding jobs for his fellow Kentuckians as he was in finding a job for himself the next four years. Think what might have been achieved if the Lieutenant Governor had spent his time fighting the problems that confront Kentucky, instead of spending all his time fighting the people who are trying to solve the problems that confront Kentucky. Think what might have been done if the Lieutenant Governor had devoted any of his time helping us seize the great opportunities that lie within Kentucky's grasp, instead of spending all his time chasing his own political opportunities.

Ladies and gentlemen, for three years, nine months, and seven days, I have concentrated on carrying out the mandate the people of this State gave me in November of 1967. And I had hoped that the opposition's campaign would be conducted on a respectable and responsible and truthful level that would allow this administration to devote every waking hour of the eighty-two days that remain to projects that can mean a better life for the people of the State. But the opposition has made it perfectly clear in the last few weeks that he will resort to the same irresponsible, deceptive, and irrelevant tactics he used in the primary election. It might have worked for him in May, but it won't work in November.

If anyone except the Lieutenant Governor were to make some of the wild statements he has made these past weeks and months, we could only conclude that he was being deliberately untruthful. But after watching his actions over the past four years, we have to conclude that he just doesn't know any better. For instance, the other day, August 6 to be exact, he was in Ashland. He promised that if he were elected, he would complete the Interstate to that city. The truth is: contracts were let last spring, May 5th, and the last section of that Interstate system will be open to traffic this fall. Well, that wasn't so bad. After all, we can't expect the constant candidate to keep up with everything. But then he went too far. If you've followed his campaign, you know that he seems to have a gift for spreading gloom and doom. At that same August 6 meeting he bemoaned the fact that Ashland was losing its status as a divisional center for the C & O Railroad. Of course if that were true, it would be a reason for concern. But, as an official from the railroad pointed out in the paper the next day, "That has absolutely no basis in fact."[1]

In his hometown newspaper last year, August 10th, 1970, to be exact, he was taking credit for rewriting the executive budget during the previous legislative session.[2] But he's changed his tune now. Because now he's saying that I am the only person who has the ability and the information that is necessary to revise the state budget. I'll agree that he doesn't have the ability, because we let him try it in 1970, and he's still choking on watermelon seeds. But the truth is: budget information is a matter of public record in the Finance Department, and revenue estimates are available from the Department of

Revenue anytime he wants to get them and try to undo the mess he made of the 1970 budget.

Two weeks ago the Lieutenant Governor said that if he were elected, he would try to work out a plan to employ the veterans President Nixon is bringing home from Viet Nam. That's a good idea, but he's a little late because, through the program already in effect here in the State, more than ten thousand veterans came home to jobs last year. And then a day or two later at Alice Lloyd College he announced that he had a plan for a coordinated attack on drug abuse and alcoholism. He thought we should have a separate division to handle that. Well, that's another good idea. And two months ago, we established the Division of Alcoholism and Drug Abuse in the Department of Mental Health. The truth is: He was nowhere to be seen last December when nearly 10,000 citizens from all over Kentucky came to Louisville to help us launch the most comprehensive and the most coordinated attack on drug abuse in America. The truth is: He was nowhere to be found when drug education committees were formed earlier this year in every county in Kentucky. The truth is: He was not even aware that the federal government was so impressed by the Kentucky plan that we were awarded $4.7 million last month, the second largest grant ever given any state for this purpose in the history of the Department of Health, Education, and Welfare.

The truth is: He has been out of his office politicking at your expense, on your time, constantly criticizing those who were trying to find answers to many complex situations that we face in Kentucky today. The truth is: He's been so busy campaigning for the last three years, nine months and seven days, trying to find something negative to talk about that he hasn't taken the time to find out what is being done about these things. The truth is: In all the time he has squandered as Lieutenant Governor, he's never initiated a single program, he's never presented anything positive, he's never pointed the way. He's just always pointed the finger of blame.

He's been grooming himself the past ten years in one position or another in government at your expense. But what is his record? What has he done? The only vote he has cast in his term as Lieutenant Governor forced Daylight Savings Time on the people of Kentucky from April to October. He had a chance to rewrite the executive budget, but he thought it was a watermelon, and he turned an $18 million surplus into a tax increase. And he still had to raise interest rates, he still had to rob the teachers' retirement fund, and he still had to destroy the Lincoln School for underprivileged children.

He had a chance to show what he was capable of during the Special

Legislative Session on redistricting last spring. He had complete control of the General Assembly. There were ninety-five members of his party and only forty-three members of our party. He drew his own redistricting plan and pushed it through and then took credit for it. And do you know what the courts did? They ruled it illegal and unconstitutional. So it's all going to have to be done over next year.[3]

Ladies and gentlemen, with a record like this you can see why he says now that he is trying to break with the past. Here's a man who has had his chance to serve the people of Kentucky. He was an assistant to the Governor in 1961. He was a State Senator. He was Lieutenant Governor the past four years. But what do the people of Kentucky have to show for all the years they have paid the high cost of his political ambitions?

The truth is: This fellow's time to serve has come and gone. He had his chance to help his State and serve his fellow Kentuckians, but he tried to serve himself instead. He had his chance to earn the people's gratitude and trust, but he ignored it. He had his chance to lead, but he chose instead to follow. He had his chance to inspire confidence, but he chose instead to try to destroy confidence. It's time to turn away from this doomsday politician who thinks his political success depends on Kentucky's failure. It's time to turn away from this man who thinks the only way he can climb up is to pull someone else down.

Now is the time to turn to a man who has the educational qualifications, the understanding of what Kentucky needs and the plan to meet Kentucky's opportunities. Now is the time to elect a man who understands that it is more important to develop than to destroy. Now is the time to elect a man who supported the effort that has brought seventy-seven new or expanded industries into the twenty-four counties of the Fifth District and helped bring 6,000 more jobs to the men and women of eastern Kentucky who want to be on payrolls, not welfare rolls. Now is the time to elect a governor who supported the effort that has increased state aid to the elementary and secondary schools of the Fifth District by more than $30 million in the past four years. Now is the time to choose a man who helped the building of ten new vocational training centers here in the Fifth District over the past four years. Now is the time to elect a native son who had seen the people of the Fifth District send their children to school and take their farm products to market through mud and dust for twenty years while the State looked the other way.

It's time to decide whether you want to go back to the years of neglect and political discrimination and poor roads or elect the team that will continue to see that the Fifth District is treated fairly, that the Fifth District, like every other district, like every other district in the State, regardless of its political tradition, shares in the progress that has marked Kentucky's recent years. It's time to elect a man who will see in the foundations that have been established these past four years an opportunity to build a better and a stronger Kentucky. That man is Tom Emberton and that team is the Emberton-Host team. In their hands, Kentucky's future will be secure.

---

1. The newspaper referred to is the *Ashland Daily Independent*. Interview with Governor Nunn's press secretary, Larry Van Hoose, January 20, 1972.

2. The newspaper referred to is the *Owensboro Messenger and Inquirer;* ibid.

3. The court case referred to is Hensley v. Wood, 329 F. Supp. 787 (1971).

BURLEY AND DARK LEAF
EXPORTERS ASSOCIATION
Louisville / September 28, 1971

As Governor of a state where over half a million workers are employed to bring 500 million pounds of tobacco from farm to market each year, I welcome this opportunity to thank you collectively for the dedication and expertise you bring to the exportation of Kentucky tobacco. Burley and dark leaf tobacco exports last year contributed $37.2 million to Kentucky's economy. It also helped boost the Commonwealth's gross farm income past the billion-dollar mark for the second successive year and for only the second time in our history.

As we look at the export situation we find a somewhat contradictory picture. As you know, in the first seven months of this year's market, burley exports had fallen slightly short of last year; however, improved market patterns and several other encouraging factors point to increased exports in the months ahead. First, the quality of American burley tobacco is unequalled anywhere in the world, and our margin is being increased constantly through the dedicated efforts of growers and scientists alike. Therefore, as nations all over the world increase cigarette use, the demand for our fine burley tobacco clearly must increase. Secondly, international cigarette output last year was the greatest in a decade—3,177 billion, a 127 billion increase over 1969, and the biggest production increase on record. Japan alone increased her cigarette output by 30 billion. Thirdly, President Nixon's economic policies have made American products more competitive in all world markets, especially in Japan where the *yen* has been revalued by 10 percent. The floating dollar will enable the emerging Japanese market, and 95 percent of the world markets where cigarette output has increased, to buy more American tobacco. In addition, import surtax gives us leverage to get into new markets.

But let us turn briefly from the export picture to the industry on which your business depends. I would like to take this occasion publicly to express my gratitude and the gratitude of the entire Commonwealth for what you have done in recent years to save an industry so vital to our economy and our people. Together, the leaders of the tobacco industry, representatives of the people, and government officials have met challenges to the industry. We hope a stronger industry has emerged. But there are other crucial issues yet unresolved. One is the grower's perennial problem—the shortage of labor—which continues to pose a serious threat. The 1970 census documented the population shift that has in recent years come to mean too few hands to do too much work.

The most crucial problem is the effect of tobacco on health. It must be answered. Until it is we cannot chart a realistic course. Kentucky is facing this problem. And because we have faced this harsh fact of life, in 1970 Kentucky became the first state in the nation to earmark a portion of the revenues from a tax on the product for health research. So once again, as has historically been true, tobacco is paying its own way, answering its own hard questions through the newly created Tobacco and Health Research Institute.

The Institute receives $2.6 million annually from the tax, and coupled with $1.5 million in federal funds appropriated each year by the Agricultural Research Service, this funding has made Kentucky's tobacco and health research the largest effort of its kind anywhere in the world. Coordinating a number of research programs within the University of Kentucky's various departments, in less than two years the Institute is already making important headway. The progress we are making in research, the realistic poundage marketing controls now in effect, and the upturn reported just last week by the United States Department of Agriculture in per capita cigarette consumption—all these factors point to good years ahead for the tobacco industry and its exporters.

Once more let me reiterate my thanks for all you have done and for your continuing efforts to help us build a balanced agri-industrial economy that will mean a better life for families throughout our region.

INTERSTATE MINING
COMPACT COMMISSION
Lexington / October 21, 1971

THE Chinese seem to have assumed a new significance in recent days, and so it might be appropriate to our purposes today to note that in the Chinese language, the word for crisis is composed of two characters. One is danger; the other is opportunity. Clearly these are days of crises for the mining industry in the states represented by the Interstate Mining Compact.[1] There is the so-called energy crisis. There is an economic crisis. There is our environmental crisis. There is a regulatory crisis. Certainly each of these poses both an element of danger and an atmosphere of opportunity. The industry is being challenged as never before to meet increasing demands for energy. But at the same time it must also fulfill its obligation to protect and ensure a livable environment.

As you know, it is projected that by 1980 the total United States energy consumption will be one and one-half times greater than in 1965. And by the year 2000 it will be about two and one-half times greater. To meet this growing demand for electrical energy some say that the electrical generating capacity of the states will double by 1980 and then double again by 1990. So if at present only 2 percent of the country's generating capacity is being met by nuclear power, and only a small portion is met by hydroelectric power, the heaviest burden for meeting the energy needs of our country must continue to be carried by those in the fossil fuel industry. What this means is that the mining of minerals is and will continue to be the nation's major source of power, and that we should judge the emotional and sometimes irrational attacks made against the mining industry in that context.

Given the technical and physical factors with which we must work to meet the energy needs of today, it seems inescapable that surface mining could replace other mining methods as the principal means of extraction. This type of mining has proven to be faster, safer, and more economical. That much is undeniable. But there are other considerations that cannot be forgotten. Some inherent and compelling problems still plague the surface mining industry. The technique is not perfected to the point that economic and environmental considerations are compatible. But we—and I specifically want to include not only those in government, but also those in the industry— we are working toward that goal.

Kentucky has put forth a concerted effort to solve these problems, just as other members of this Compact have. Between 1954 and 1966 we experimented with and developed methods of maximum recovery of coal with the least environmental impact. The 1966 Legislature passed what has been hailed as the most comprehensive law in the nation. Even at that early date the Kentucky General Assembly was aware of the nation's increasing demands for energy and that a percentage of these needs could be met with Kentucky's natural resources. Their accurate projection can be shown by a 90 percent increase in electrical power production within the state between 1966 and 1970. Further, in 1970, 15 million more acres were surface mined and 25 million more tons were produced than in 1966.

These figures add up to the fact that 49 percent of the State's total coal production in 1970 was by strip mining. However, research and cooperation are increasingly needed to keep abreast of new reclamation techniques. In this field Kentucky has qualified for and received $550 thousand from the Appalachian Regional Commission to conduct research and demonstration projects on problem areas. These include revegetation, sediment control, water quality, slope stability, design of surface mining systems, and demonstration of mining techniques.

Kentucky also received $460 thousand from the Environmental Protection Agency to demonstrate the technique of reusing treated active surface mining drainage for revegetation. In the near future we hope to receive approximately $800 thousand from the Federal Bureau of Mines for further experimentation and research into the problems associated with surface mining. The results of these research and demonstration projects will be of great benefit to Kentucky and other states when additional mining legislation is discussed or regulations necessitated.

Like Kentucky, various states are gradually becoming storehouses of knowledge and experience in devising and implementing effective legislation for the surface mining industry, and in creating a better balance between the demand for energy and the need for a livable environment. The Interstate Mining Compact can serve as a forum where the ideas and experiences of these states can be pooled and shared in order to best guide and further develop the mining industry, both surface and underground. And that is the real basis for our enthusiastic involvement in the Compact. However, I would like to propose today that we dramatically expand this concept of sharing information and expertise.

Nothing I have observed during my term as Governor has convinced me that government has all the answers to the many complex and technical situations in which we have become involved. The bigness of government in most instances has no relationship to the actual strength of government. State agencies, despite some progress, still are severely limited by outdated salary schedules that will not permit us to compete for the technical expertise that is needed today. And unfortunately, I have found that in too many instances, government tends to operate more comfortably in a world of theory than in a world of realism.

For all these reasons, if we in government are going to confront the dangers and seize the opportunities that abound in the energy crisis, the environmental crisis, the regulatory crisis, and the economic crisis surrounding the mining industry, we are going to need a great deal of help. I'm not talking about the kind of help we spend most of our time seeking: financial help from the federal government. Instead of turning to Washington with outstretched palms, what we need to do is turn to the industries we must regulate. What we need is the practical, realistic, first-hand expertise of men who live every day with the problems that confront us in the mining industry. And I sincerely hope that this interstate concept can be expanded to permit the industry to share its knowledge, its experience, its research information.

Of course, there are some who might criticize this suggestion. That is to be expected when there are those who have become so misguided that they see government regulations as a way of strangling private enterprise rather than assisting private enterprise. But let us remember that with the help of government, private enterprise has taken us from that lonely wilderness beach in Virginia all the way to the moon in less than 200 years. And if it can do that, then the same cooperative formula can succeed again in solving the problems and seizing the opportunities we have come here to discuss. I do not visualize this Commission's purpose as another regulatory agency. I visualize the interstate body as an assisting agency, assisting both government and industry.

One of the things that can materially add to our capability in meeting that goal, in my opinion, is a centrally located and accessible permanent headquarters. And so I am pleased to recommend Lexington, Kentucky, as such a location. We have been assured that sufficient space is available at Spindletop Research Center which is adjacent to the Council of State Governments headquarters. I hope you will seriously consider Kentucky and Lexington as the home of the Interstate Mining Commission, and that in the years ahead government and industry will forge an even stronger partnership and develop more effective methods of sharing information about the problems that affect us all alike in today's world.

---

1. The Interstate Mining Compact Commission is a public organization overseen by the governors of Kentucky, North Carolina, Oklahoma, and Pennsylvania. The commission serves as an information exchange and an advisory board to state governments in furthering the interests of the mining industry and the protection and restoration of land and water resources.

DEDICATION OF SOMERSET
COMPREHENSIVE TRAINING CENTER
Somerset / October 22, 1971

It is written in the Scriptures: "Now abideth faith, hope, love, these three; but the greatest of these is love" [1 Cor. 13:13]. The words of the apostle Paul, written to the Corinthians over two thousand years ago, assume new significance today as we dedicate the Somerset Comprehensive Training Center. There are those who say the age of miracles is past, that it died with the apostles and their good works. But as we see here at Somerset, faith, hope, and love have worked a miracle in Kentucky. And we are here today to celebrate that miracle and dedicate it.

This day, for which so many have waited so long, is filled with many human emotions. We can look upon this facility with a great deal of pride, because Kentucky now is the envy of the forty-nine other states in this nation. We are filled with a sense of anticipation as we eagerly await results of the improved care and treatment this modern facility allows us to provide the children who will live here. But perhaps the strongest emotion of this day is that of gratitude. Truly, this is a day of thanksgiving, a time to identify the components of this remarkable achievement.

Today marks the beginning not only of a new day, but a whole new era in treatment and care for Kentucky's mentally retarded. The miracle is that this complete transformation has required less than forty-eight months. Miracles don't just happen, as those of you who have furthered the cause of mental retardation through so many lonely years well know. This miracle was conceived in tragedy. It was born of necessity. It found comfort and warmth amid the pages of the human document that was the Executive Budget of 1968. And it was protected by a courageous majority in the 1968 Legislature which had the fortitude and the foresight to nurture this fragile miracle into the strong, enduring facility that has now grown out of this once barren hillside.

I especially want to commend those legislators who stood their ground, who resisted strong currents of personal or partisan consideration in order that this facility could be built and other deserving programs advanced for the people of Kentucky. Their legacy of compassion and concern will endure throughout the years, and ours will be a better place in which to live because of the enlightened service they have rendered. They did not stand alone, however. The cause of mental retardation has traditionally attracted a legion of dedicated citizens from every section and every walk of Kentucky life. In a very special way, this day belongs to you.

Several agencies of government at both the state and federal levels are deserving of our recognition and gratitude, also. Foremost, however, is the Kentucky Department of Mental Health. In less than four years this dynamic, creative, caring agency has lifted Kentucky out of the disgrace of mediocrity and carried it to a position of honor and national leadership. In the pages of the *Congressional Record*, in testimony before committees of the Congress, and on the floor of the United States Senate, Kentucky's mental health care has been praised by experts as the finest in the country and a model for the nation. What we have forged in Kentucky is a circle of services encompassing hospitals at Hazelwood and Dawson Springs, ninety-two day-care treatment centers, twenty-three regional centers, twenty-six adult activity centers, and fourteen sheltered workshops.

This facility which we dedicate today will provide a vital link in the circle of care constructed by the Department of Mental Health in recent years. But without the groundwork which has been laid, without the wide range of services added through the State to meet the varied needs of the mentally retarded, the special and exciting programs that will unfold on this hill would not be possible. Clearly our faith in a responsive state government has been amply justified. But the most inspiring faith has been that of the Somerset community, apparently because you believe that miracles do still happen, and because you want them to happen here.

Not many years ago it was unthinkable that the mentally handicapped could be trained to be self-sufficient members of a normal society. But within the model programs already under way in Kentucky and the new innovative techniques to be employed here, we are confident that miracles *will* be performed. Unlike the outdated institution it replaces, the Somerset Comprehensive Training Center is not the end of the road. It is the beginning of hope: hope because individuals will learn to care for themselves, acquire job skills at the finest work training center anywhere, and acquire social skills in the family atmosphere to be promoted here; hope because innate curiosity and freedom will be encouraged in a program geared to individual needs; hope because the whole idea of the Somerset Center rests in the security, warmth, and fun of family life; and above all, hope because the aim of that family life is to prepare the retardate for his ultimate return to his home community.

Through countless acts of faith and hope, we have traveled to this point in the development of the Somerset Comprehensive Training Center. But it will be through the love that is shown for those who are treated here that the real contribution of this facility will be made. And it is this feeling of love for those children who will soon be brought here that will never again permit us to settle for the dilapidated, antiquated buildings whose ceilings crumble, whose pipes freeze, and whose atmosphere—despite some of the most innovative programs in the country—stifles the spirit and smothers the soul.

Ladies and gentlemen, the long night of custodial care for the mentally retarded is near an end. The days of institutionalization are clearly numbered. Because today we dedicate a facility that has been designed primarily to teach children how to live at home, not how to live in an institution. Today we dedicate a beautiful, modern, functional treatment center for the mentally retarded. With the opening of the Somerset Training Center, we open a new, progressive chapter in Kentucky's ongoing effort to improve the quality of life for each of our citizens.

It is appropriate that this facility has been constructed at the close of the second century since the first pioneer settlers came to this land. Because in a very real sense, as we prepare for the end of one century and the beginning of another, Somerset Training Center is both an end and a beginning. It is an honorable ending for two hundred years of human endeavor that have seen a great state emerge from an uncharted wilderness. But more importantly, it is an inspiring beginning, the encouraging start of a time in which Kentucky surely is destined to cross the threshold of greatness.

CLOSING OF KENTUCKY VILLAGE
Lexington / October 28, 1971

In less than one week in Kentucky "two centuries" have come to an end. First, the long night of custodial care for the mentally retarded gave way to the new era which dawned last Friday with the dedication of an innovative treatment center in Somerset. And today we close the doors of disgrace on a detention center whose chains and bars have shackled the spirit of young Kentuckians for a hundred bleak years.

It is no secret that a surprise inspection of Kentucky Village in June 1968 held surprises for the visitors as well as the visited. It is no secret that when we returned to Kentucky Village half a year later, conditions had improved so dramatically that grand juries which once condemned this facility praised the improved physical surroundings, the professionalism of the staff, and the bold new programs they were pioneering here.[1] Yet all that has been achieved in recent years at Kentucky Village has been accomplished despite enormous odds, the difficult physical conditions of an antiquated facility, and even worse, the depressing atmosphere of an institution founded a century ago to serve as a warehouse for the undesirables, the unloved, the unwanted —young misfits for whom society had no other answer.

Today we close the doors on that human warehouse forever, confident that the foundations we have laid can ensure that the next hundred years of child care in Kentucky will be more enlightened ones. We are proud that the National Council on Crime and Delinquency has identified our Commonwealth as among the top three states in all America in delinquency prevention and thoughtful juvenile care. For in preparing to close the doors at Kentucky Village, we have lifted our sights, shifted our emphasis, and changed the image of child care in the Commonwealth.

Kentucky has brought its philosophy from the dark ages of punitive institutionalization in large, impersonal complexes to the day when young Kentuckians can be adequately cared for in facilities designed to house no more than fifty youths, facilities with corrective programs geared to specific age groups, their interests, and the seriousness of their offenses against society; to the day when ten of these smaller, specialized treatment facilities now provide the close, helpful attention for young Kentuckians on the threshold of either wasted lives or years of worthwhile endeavor.

More than half of these specialized centers have opened in the past four years, and just last month we broke ground for a new diagnostic center in northern Kentucky which will enable us to diagnose a child's educational, emotional, physical, and medical needs twice as quickly as one reception center could before. This will hasten a child's commitment into the care of the most appropriate Child Welfare residence for his continued treatment and rehabilitation: perhaps in Jewel Manor near Louisville, or at Lynwood, or at the Morehead Girls' Center, where individualized programs are already making a constructive impact on the lives of young girls; perhaps in intensive group therapy at the Barkley Boys' Camp, Lake Cumberland Boys' Camp, or at Woodsbend, where a population of fifty boys and seventeen staff members create a scene that is much closer to the ideal of rehabilitation than to punishment; perhaps at the Daniel Boone Center for younger boys, or at the Pine Mountain Boys Camp high atop a beautiful ridge in Harlan County; or perhaps at Frenchburg, where the young residents have already left a legacy of clean streets, refurbished houses, and a newly built picnic area outside town in return for the community's gift of compassion, respect, and love.

So great has been the success of the Frenchburg effort that the Morehead Girls' Center in Rowan County is designing a similar program for low achievers. Remedial academic programs at Morehead will carry the weight of high school credit when the residents return to their hometown schools. A modern kitchen, bedroom, and sewing rooms are labs for classes in the homemaking arts. Other courses are offered in the business professions and to train nurses' aides. And all these lessons will come to life through the community program which will match a Morehead resident with a senior citizen who needs the young girls' skills and services.

Closing the doors on a hundred years is easy to do when it means opening the way for opportunities like these. Closing the doors on a hundred years is easy when it means not only a physical change but a dramatic spiritual change already evident in the attitudes of the children, staff, and especially the communities to which they must one day return. Closing the doors on a hundred years of disgrace, today we begin a new era of care for Kentucky's children who need us most.

----

1. For Governor Nunn's earlier visit to Kentucky Village see the address delivered there on March 19, 1969.

SOUTHERN GOVERNORS' CONFERENCE
Atlanta / November 9, 1971

It has become fashionable for those in public life to pinpoint our age as a time of trial and testing. Surely the responsibilities facing today's governors make that description appropriate to every day of our lives. Major decisions ranging from highways to welfare, from sound fiscal management to industrial growth, from agricultural programs to the needs of our cities are made every day. Yet these same responsibilities may cause us to forget that the states themselves are on trial. Our performance in that trial can chart the course of government for decades to come.

I refer, of course, to the Omnibus Crime Control and Safe Streets Act, which was enacted by the Congress in 1968. Quite simply, as you know, the act seeks to improve all phases of the criminal justice system in our respective states. Our mutual success in administering this act could make it one of the most important legislative actions of our time. For this act places the power and the funds to do a job squarely in the hands of the individual states. With this power comes accountability. We will be judged by our stewardship of this program. If we succeed, the people will demand similar state control for other programs. If we fail, those who oppose the right of the states to control their own destinies will have new ammunition with which to shoot down our hopes. Strong words? I think not, for we are charged with administering a fast-growing program. It was as recently as fiscal 1969 that the first Safe Streets appropriation was made. It totaled $69 million. An appropriation of some $700 million is expected for fiscal 1972. The growth is rapid and the responsibility is fixed, fixed upon each of us in our respective states. For the bulk of these funds are coming to the states in bloc grants. We, in turn, are charged with the task of planning for the use of these monies and seeing that they are disbursed properly. And, as the program matures, we have the additional vital responsibility to guarantee that the money has been used wisely and frugally. We must go back to monitor and assess our criminal justice programs. And we must, as surely as we can, demonstrate that our methods have brought results.

I have avoided the use of labels here today. Yet you have certainly sensed that I am talking about a trial of a program that could be the pioneer effort in revenue sharing. Or, speaking frankly, it could be the program that marks the end of that idea before it is truly tested. That is one reason why our progress in implementing the Safe Streets Act is a major test. But it is not the only reason. We may live in a cynical age, but there are millions of citizens in our respective states who believe fervently in the right to live in peace and safety, and in the right to be assured fair, swift, and equal treatment in our courts. Thus we have a practical cause that will result directly in a more secure life for all of the people. It is a cause worthy of vigorous defense.

How should we embark on this defense? I suggest to you that we should and must guarantee that our respective criminal justice programs are staffed by the best qualified people we can find. I suggest to you that we must forget party labels and be certain that criminal justice efforts in each of our states are completely nonpartisan. This is an effort that transcends individual parties. It exemplifies the very purpose of government itself. It will determine the confidence or lack thereof by the populace. I also suggest to you that the program is worthy of your close personal attention. Safe Streets funds may not be a major part of your state's budget, but it is a major part of your state's future.

Perhaps we should take stock. How are we, individually and collectively, carrying out our duties in this area? No doubt there has been criticism. There have been some errors of judgment. This would be true of any new program. In some cases these lapses have been trumpeted by the sensationalists within the news media. What has sometimes been overlooked is the clear, crisp, and effective reaction by those states whose programs have been found in need of improvement. Since good news is all too often judged to be no news at all, the success of the criminal justice program in the overwhelming majority of our states has been taken for granted or ignored.

I am not here to defend your state or mine, for no defense is needed. We have a relatively new program. We have an exciting program, one that can bring untold benefits to all of our citizens, both in the improved performance of criminal justice and in the future improvement of other programs that can best be administered at the state level by those persons closest to the needs of the people. And finally, we have a program that is indeed a trial and a test that we should face gladly and enthusiastically. For our collective performance well may be recorded as the turning point in the process that returned rightful authority and adequate financing to every sovereign state.

SALUTE TO THE PRESIDENT
DINNER
Washington, D.C. / November 9, 1971

SOMEONE once said that Washington was a town full of politicians and newsmen. There may be nothing wrong with that, but the trouble with Washington these days is that too many of the would-be Democratic politicians are spending all their time trying to get in the news, and too many of the newsmen are trying to get into politics.

But seriously, ladies and gentlemen, it is sad to see that some of our political opponents have reached the point where it appears they would rather see the President's programs fail than to see America succeed. And after all that America endured in the 1960's, we just don't need a crowd of doomsday politicians whose only message is criticism and whose only hope for election rests upon the alleged mistakes of others. We don't need candidates who measure their political opportunities by how badly the country is doing. We don't need candidates who have to take a poll before they can decide where they stand. That isn't what the people of this country will settle for, either from the Democrats or from our party.

Exactly one year from tonight the American people will choose the national leadership to guide us into this country's third century. Their choice is very clear. I am confident they will again endorse one who has proven he has the capacity and the courage to point the way for America; one who has taken this country and the world from the brink of war to the brink of international peace; one who has reversed the tide of war that carried American men away from their homes and loved ones, and who is now bringing those men back to their families; one who has reduced the toll of American casualties to the lowest point since 1965; and one who on the domestic front has taken the courageous action that was required to ease the pressure of inflation and stimulate investment opportunities that will, in turn, provide employment opportunities for our people.

We can all recall a time in the 1960's before Richard Nixon became President when America was virtually paralyzed with despair and frustration, when serious doubts were being expressed as to whether America could even survive the steady dissipation of an unpopular and costly war in Vietnam and the rising incidence of crime and violence here at home. At that time our international policy was dangerously broad, unclear, and defensive. Militarily and economically, the whole world became our patient. We became the world's watchdog, fireman, and policeman, as well as its financier. Our foreign aid policy became a sort of international Medicaid, and Washington became a haven for handouts. There were those who became as generous with the lives of Americans as they were with American dollars. And here at home, nearly a decade of permissiveness began with nonviolent acts of civil disobedience, and ended with the eerie spectacle of the nation's capital on fire, college campuses turned into battlegrounds, and entire cities terrorized by hateful and irrational forces within our society. But despite all these clear mandates for effective response, those in positions of leadership moved uncertainly, patronizing here, coddling there, still trying vainly to hold onto a political majority at the expense of the country.

The administration of vital human programs suffered the same fate. The need for reform went unnoticed. The demand for creative government was unheard. For instance, the welfare system over a thirty-year period had become an unworkable, unmanageable web of complexities and contradictions. It confused and angered the taxpayer who financed it. It frustrated and discouraged the needy whom it was designed to serve. There was almost unanimous agreement that the welfare system was at cross purposes with the intent of its originators. It encouraged illegitimacy; it promoted dependency. It fed the stomach of its recipients, but it starved the soul and crushed the spirit. Yet no attempt at reform was introduced. Instead, more tax money was poured in, confusion spread, and frustration deepened.

At the same time the governors and city and county officials pleaded with the Democratic administration to help restore some semblance of balance to the federal system of government. State and local revenue sources were almost totally preempted. The Congress continued to pass legislation and create programs requiring matching funds on the part of state and local governments. And the steady rise of inflation placed us in the middle of a taxpayers' revolt. During that time every governor in America recommended and even pleaded for revenue sharing. But the national administration at that time, and some of today's candidates for office who were in the Congress at that time, refused to act.

It was no wonder that in 1968 the American people were fed up. They couldn't understand why if Americans had the best team, we never seemed to be able to score. Then it dawned on us that both at home and abroad the reason we couldn't score was because the other team always seemed to have the ball. That is why they demanded new leadership in 1968.

You know what has taken place since then. All the problems that were inherited have not been solved, but real initiative and creativity in meeting those problems has been exercised. And under President Nixon America has the ball again. We're winning again. And we've got what the American people have wanted and needed all along, a leader who leads, who points the way. That is one of the reasons we salute him tonight. That is why we are proud to be working for his reelection as President. And that is why a year from tonight America will be assured of four more years of sound, courageous leadership by Richard M. Nixon.

LEXINGTON ROTARY CLUB
Lexington / November 11, 1971

FOR a few minutes today I would like to give you my personal assessment of where we stand in Kentucky and perhaps a glimpse of what lies ahead. Of course, I can speak more factually about the past than the present. The future depends largely on the action or lack of action by the next Governor.[1] And let me say that I certainly am not here today in any partisan capacity. I particularly want there to be no misunderstanding about any remarks I might make concerning the next administration in Frankfort. Let me make it clear where I stand on that. I hope, I sincerely hope, that the next four years are even more productive for Kentucky than the last four years. The important consideration now isn't WHO the Governor is. It's what he does for Kentucky that counts. All of us have an interest in that.

As I have said on previous occasions, I plan always to be a resident of Kentucky. I hope my children will live in Kentucky and rear their children here, because this is a great State. We have so much to be proud of. And we have so much to look forward to. The opportunities are great, and I want Kentucky to continue to meet its responsibilities in a way that will allow every Kentuckian to seize the opportunities we are afforded. You don't serve as Governor for four years and live with the burdens and the joys and sometimes the agony and the criticism that goes with this office and then walk away from it when your term of office is concluded. I will always feel a special obligation to the people of Kentucky for placing their confidence in me and giving me the opportunity and the privilege to serve them as Governor.

I hope we all share a vital interest in the future of our State. I am tremendously excited about Kentucky's future because I have seen what has been done in the past, and I know what can be done in the days ahead. The events of the past four years should inspire and encourage us to set high goals for future generations of Kentuckians.

It was almost four years ago to the day that my predecessor announced for the first time the critical financial condition of the State. By ordering a drastic cutback in state services, he revealed that Kentucky was headed toward a budgetary deficit of some $24 million. And it was under that completely unexpected burden that our administration began. But it was the unfunded future commitments that really put us in a tailspin. On December 12, 1967, State funds were nearly exhausted. The State was delinquent by $27.5 million in funds for education. We faced a $3.5 million cutback in medical assistance for the aged and needy. Needed immediately was $300 thousand just to keep open our mental hospitals. Interstate and Appalachian highways could not be completed. Projects already under way stacked approximately $100 million on top of the existing deficit. Kentucky had been overspent and overcommitted. When it came time to pay the bills there was no money in the state purse.

The fact that this challenge has been resolved, financial soundness restored, and a $25 million construction program authorized from current revenues, is in itself a tribute to the courage and the dedication of the 1968 Legislature and to the people of Kentucky. Today, as our term of office nears an end, we can truthfully say to our successor that he will inherit a surplus, not a deficit; he will find adequate funds to continue the plans and programs of each agency, instead of being forced to cut back those services. The Governor-elect will find funds already set aside for commitments that have been made, not unfunded commitments. He will find in the Governor's office a new resource, the Kentucky Program Development Office, which has helped to attract some $400 million in federal funds these past four years, funds which not only ease the burden of the Kentucky taxpayer, but enable us to provide new and vital human services as well.

These have been four good years and the next four can be even better. First, the next Governor will have a strong, solid financial base from which to build. Second, economists and revenue experts are now forecasting a steady if not dramatic growth in state revenues for the balance of this decade. And finally, as the President continues to ease the pressure of inflation, more and more of these new revenues can be used to keep Kentucky ahead instead of catching Kentucky up. The economic outlook for state government is bright, but there are even stronger indications that good years of progress and prosperity await the families of Kentucky.

This is not to say that all the problems that confront us in Kentucky have been solved. Four years have proven to be too short a period in which to complete several of the projects that were originated during this administration. And then, too, we must recognize the fact that each new governor faces a different set of circumstances and problems, some of his own making as a result of the programs and the priorities he outlined during the course of his campaign.

I am sure the people of Lexington and Fayette County are pleased that they can expect financial assistance from the state revenue sharing program which the Lieutenant Governor has announced. Of course, this is a desirable program, one the cities and counties have long sought. They deserve assistance. Obviously, our urban centers are caught up in a financial bind in trying to meet the requirements of growth which they are now experiencing. But the problem, at least during the past four years, is that the State is caught up in a fiscal crunch of its own. This is a result of the preemption of revenue sources by the federal government and the proliferation of matching funds programs by the Congress.

I would hope that Lieutenant Governor Ford's plan is substantive. By that, I mean a plan that offers the cities and counties the kind of relief they need, not a plan which simply permits them to extend their indebtedness and postpone their obligations. Lieutenant Governor Ford's revenue sharing plan takes on added significance now that the Homestead Amendment has passed.[2] The Governor-elect supported the amendment and did so, of course, with the knowledge that it would cost local school districts and some governmental agencies some $10 to $15 million a year in revenue they now collect. And for that reason, there is an even greater need for revenue sharing than before.

In addition to making up the lost revenue for local school districts, the new Governor and the members of his cabinet also have endorsed a comprehensive program for education. And certainly, I trust we all would agree that this is an area in which we cannot afford to stand still. Kentucky children deserve the advantage of good schools and good teachers. And our educational personnel are entitled to compensation in keeping with the vital role they play in shaping the lives of young Kentuckians and, in fact, the very future of our State. During the course of the campaign, the Lieutenant Governor committed himself to an education program which, according to the budget specialists, would cost at least $100 million a year in new money over and above that which is now being invested in our school system.

Mr. Ford has said he can save $30 million a year through reorganization and I assume this would be applied to the cost of his education plan. I would just mention two things in connection with this reorganization plan. First, while I would hope his reorganization will be successful, quite naturally I am disappointed that he has waited this long to share it with us. Efficiency and economy have been two major goals of this administration, and we feel that real progress has been made in these areas. But we would have welcomed his plan—particularly if it would have meant a savings of $30 million a year. Second, I would express a word of caution. Traditionally in Frankfort, reorganization has been a much abused device employed not so much for the sake of economy as for political purge. I trust this will not be the case in this instance because, inevitably, it will result in more cost instead of more savings for the people of Kentucky. Of special interest to those of you here in Lexington is the future of higher education. Looking ahead to the next four years, we can see new demands for additional revenue in this area. We face a great challenge here, because it is absolutely essential that we preserve the quality of our institutions of higher learning. I know you in the Lexington community will continue to be vigilant and will work to insure that the University of Kentucky receives its fair share of State funds. Of course, competition for these funds has increased with the addition of the University of Louisville and Northern Kentucky State College to the state system. These two new institutions are expected to request between $25 and $50 million in growth funds for the next biennium.

According to last evening's *Lexington Leader*, Governor-elect Ford is committed to seeing that each State university and college receives growth funds. In addition to these increases, the next governor will have to budget for approximately $15 million in additional funds to keep pace with the built-in requirements of federal matching programs. He will also need to keep an eye on legislation now pending before the Congress which would increase the minimum hourly wage to $2. This will drastically affect state government because, in effect, it wipes out the first three pay grades, all of which are under $2 per hour.

Speaking from a budgetary point of view, there is another cost item which must be considered. That is the removal of the sales tax from food, which was an unequivocal promise made by both candidates for governor. This will cost the State approximately $60 million each year, of which approximately $15 million is from food stamps. To partially offset this, the Governor-elect has promised a severance tax on coal, which is expected to produce approximately $25 million although no specifics have yet been announced.

I personally regret that Kentucky is taking this route because of several inherent dangers that should be recognized. Under our present tax system, the coal industry has helped to stimulate the economy in some of the State's hardest pressed sections. You may have noticed an announcement we made last week that Kentucky is now the number one coal-producing state in the nation.[8] The effects of this are evident in eastern and western Kentucky today. Unemployment is down. Wages are up. Welfare costs are being reduced. If the imposition of a severance tax has the effect of placing this state at a competitive disadvantage with the other coal-producing states, this trend would be reversed: unemployment could increase, welfare costs would increase, and any revenue gains from the severance tax could be wiped out.

I might also mention that there is speculation today that the next governor is considering elimination of the federal exemption from Kentucky individual and corporate income taxes to help offset the revenue loss expected from the removal of the food tax. In my opinion, this would be a devastating mistake. Four years ago, when we were faced with the task of making up the deficit and meeting the obligations to which the State had been committed, we carefully analyzed Kentucky's revenue picture. It was our feeling and our desire to establish a tax system that would be adequate for long-range needs without requiring new taxes by every succeeding governor. That is why we recommended a broad-based tax structure. Under the present plan, industrial development and economic growth are encouraged. This builds in a steady increase of revenue for the State, but in a way that does not require new taxes. However, it appears now that this system may be partially dismantled. The Governor-elect has made that commitment; he has received a mandate from the people of Kentucky; and he should honor that obligation. But I would caution in the strongest possible terms against resorting to any revenue plan that would adversely affect industrial growth and economic expansion in Kentucky. Our present tax structure is attractive to both business and industry; yet, it makes no unfair concessions. And judging from the strong fiscal position of state government today, the fact that we are ending this administration with a healthy surplus, revenue receipts are exceeding our estimates, and a very substantial growth is being forecast for the coming biennium, the present tax system has successfully met our intended goals.

What we have been discussing affects only the general fund portion of the state budget. The next Governor is also faced with some important decisions in connection with the road fund. Since he is a member of the Turnpike Authority and a chairman of the Legislative Research Commission, he is aware of the fact that the General Obligation Bonds voted by the people in 1965 have now been exhausted. The basic decision is whether or not to continue the road-building program at its present level. This would seem unlikely in the face of the Governor-elect's campaign promise of no new taxes.

As I said at the outset, each new governor faces a different set of circumstances, responsibilities, problems, and opportunities. Whichever way he proceeds, all of us should wish him Godspeed, because the next four years are crucial to our State's future. We have an opportunity, perhaps for the first time in several decades, to guarantee that Kentucky will no longer be a follower, but will be a leader in the vital efforts that determine the quality of life of our people. It is to this opportunity that all of us owe our support, our efforts, and our prayers.

---

1. On November 2, 1971, Lieutenant Governor Wendell H. Ford was elected the fiftieth Governor of Kentucky. The official returns were: Wendell Ford (Democrat), 470,720; Thomas Emberton (Republican), 412,653; Albert Chandler (Commonwealth), 39,493; and William Smith (American), 7,924. *Louisville Courier-Journal*, November 3, 1971; and election certification records, Office of the Secretary of State.

2. On November 2, 1971, the Homestead Amendment to the Constitution of Kentucky was ratified by the electorate by a margin of 252,333 to 79,044. Section 170 of the Constitution was amended to "include as property exempt from taxation, a homestead, which is a single-unit residential property maintained by the owner, who is sixty-five years of age or older, as his personal residence, up to the assessed valuation of sixty-five hundred dollars on said residence and contiguous real property, except that such property shall not be exempt from assessment for special benefits." Election certification records, Office of the Secretary of State.

3. Governor Nunn's information concerning Kentucky's primacy in coal production was supplied by Fred Luigart, president, Kentucky Coal Association. Luigart based his conclusions on United States Bureau of Mines weekly production figures. Telephone interview with Fred Luigart, Kentucky Coal Association, Lexington, December 17, 1971.

REPUBLICAN GOVERNORS' CONFERENCE
French Lick, Indiana / November 17, 1971

WE convene this winter meeting of the Republican Governors' Conference under drastically changed and far more encouraging circumstances than at any time in the past four years. The change that has come over America since 1968 is clearly reflected in the agenda you see before you. It is an agenda more concerned with opportunities than problems. The program for this conference is not one of despair for worsening problems. Ours is a program of hope for enduring solutions. And for that, let us give full credit where it is so clearly deserved. The positive change we see in America today is a direct result of strong, courageous, precise, and creative leadership by the President of these United States.

Consider a few of the facts: In 1967 and 1968 we conducted this conference under the dark cloud of a war fanned by Democrat ineptness and escalated by Democrat miscalculation, a war which appeared to be without end. Today the end of that war is in sight. Today we can realistically anticipate the end of six years of "Black Thursdays," the days on which American war casualties are reported.

Here at home we can point to a spreading spirit of domestic unity. Compare that with the stifling atmosphere of distrust and polarization and disunity in 1968, when, we all recall, riots and threatening demonstrations threatened even our chances of meeting. Security was of major concern. This was the undeniable legacy of Democrat administrations that promised so much and delivered so little to the American people.

Today, in the place of a Democrat administration which stood wringing its hands in despair because of an endangered environment, a Republican administration is busy implementing effective, long-range plans to conserve and protect our environment. This subject will be discussed in greater detail this morning.

Throughout the first eight years of the 1960's, governors not only at this conference but at every governors' conference made repeated pleas to Washington for welfare reform, for an end to the politically expedient cradle-to-grave handout programs that not only encouraged illegitimacy and idleness, but also drained the states of their financial resources and promoted higher and higher state taxes. Those pleas were unanswered and ignored until a Republican president occupied the White House and offered the most comprehensive plan of welfare revision ever undertaken in the United States. But a Democrat-dominated Congress still continues to deny needed changes to an American people sick and tired of a system that asks more and more of the taxpayer and offers less and less real hope for its recipients. The subject of welfare reform and the creative, successful efforts of Republican governors to meet this challenge is on the agenda this afternoon. Tomorrow's discussion will focus on the economy, and particularly on the efforts of a Republican administration to bail this nation out of a Democrat-produced flood of inflation that has inundated American families under the burden of high unemployment and high living costs.

Let me assure you that the agenda for this conference was not accidental. The subjects under discussion these next two days were not random selections. They were carefully chosen because they encompass the issues of most direct concern to the well-being and security of American families, and because they provide a dramatic opportunity for comparison between the quality of leadership offered by administrations past and administrations present.

No one can seriously question the fact that the condition and the mood of America is improved today. And no one, except the doomsday chorus of Democrat presidential candidates and their monotonous national chairman, denies the fact that Richard Nixon has been a stabilizing force for the country the past three years. Recent surveys indicate very clearly that a majority of the American people agree with and support the strong initiative of the President, both on the foreign and domestic fronts. Because of this—because of the fact that the President has reversed the tide of war, because he has harnessed runaway inflation, because he has proposed meaningful reform of old policies and revolutionary new programs to make government work better—we confidently face the challenge of the 1972 presidential campaign.

For three years the efforts of our party have been directed toward disposing of the sad legacy of war, inflation, and ineptness bestowed upon this country by the leaders and would-be leaders of the opposition party. And throughout those three years we have had to contend with an array of political parasites who have tried to feed their presidential ambitions on this country's problems, problems which were all too often of their own making. Where were Senators Muskie, Humphrey, Kennedy, and Bayh when America was pointed down the path of war? Where were they when the seeds of inflation were being sown? What plan did they offer to curb inflation? In fact, when was the last time they pointed the way instead of pointing the finger of blame?

The states represented here reach from the Atlantic to the Pacific and from the most northern to the mid-southern states. The problems that affect us all alike are greater than those that affect us as individual states. We are here as governors of our respective states to discuss the ways to improve the quality of life for the people we represent. But the time has come for us to do more. Gentlemen, the time has come and the circumstances demand that we become not defenders of the President, but more effective advocates of the President and the programs that have done so much to put America back on course. The time has come to launch a counterattack on the doomsday politicians whose only message is one of criticism and whose only hope for election lies in their relentless efforts to find fault with America. It is difficult to get America up when would-be leaders try to knock her down. Let us begin this conference with a determination to pursue the positive course, to find lasting solutions to the problems that confront us, and to seize the opportunities that are ours to perpetuate the constructive leadership offered by our President and our party.

VALEDICTORY ADDRESS

VALEDICTORY ADDRESS
Frankfort / December 7, 1971

As history is recorded today, we should not allow it to pass without thoughtful appreciation of its full magnificence.[1] This is a day of triumph, for one chosen to lead our Commonwealth. But greater than personal triumph, this is a day of victory for our representative form of government. The choice has been made by free Kentuckians, free Americans, made by advocates and defenders of the greatest form of government yet devised by man. In a government of free people periodic change in leadership is both essential and desirable so long as the interest of all the people is kept paramount.

Though we may be of different social and economic backgrounds, of different opinions and persuasions, there are common touchstones which require an orderly transfer of constitutional authority when ordained by the people. It is around the common touchstones of service and responsibility we gather today to transfer the reins of leadership and the cloak of responsibility to a new Governor. He and his administration need and deserve the support of every citizen in the cause of good government. To that objective I pledge my support. The responsibilities and obligations they assume are exceeded only by the vast potential for a better Kentucky.

During the past four years I have endeavored without fear of favor or affection to so perform my duties that the efforts of my successors might be even more productive for the people we are chosen to serve. Much has been accomplished. Much remains to be done. This could have been said by most who preceded me. It will be appropriate for those who follow, because the people's business is an unfinished and never-ending responsibility. Our stewardship is recorded in a legacy of significant gains in areas of vital human concern. God's handicraft of natural resources has been better preserved to serve His intended purpose. Encouragement of our human resources has found expression in new programs for education, health, and care so bold and innovative that Kentucky has risen from national disgrace to national respect. The economic development of our Commonwealth is proceeding with rapid and unusual success. Yet potential still far exceeds accomplishment.

For two consecutive years—and 1971 soon will be added to the record—our farmers have experienced for the first time in Kentucky history the one-billion-dollar gross farm income. The largest highway construction and improvement program both in miles and dollars invested has brought us more safely and closer together. A strengthened government, improved management, and more creative programs have made it possible now to give tax relief to the people of the State without imposing any additional taxes. As the mantle of responsibility is transferred, a surplus in excess of five million dollars exists in the General Fund. We leave a surplus in excess of one million dollars in the Capital Construction Account. More than half the Executive Contingency Fund awaits the new Governor.

Governor Ford, you are assured that in every department adequate funds are available to continue the operation of government at its present level of progress. You can find comfort in the fact that no unfunded future commitments will stand in the way of any commitment you have made to the people of Kentucky. The nine constitutional officers elected to serve the next four years are experienced in the operation of state government. By virtue of their past, all have had an opportunity to know the challenges and opportunities as well as the present condition of the government. All have publicly committed themselves to serve in the best interests of all the people of the Commonwealth. To each of you, I wish the very best in that endeavor. You will find in this government men and women of concern, dedication, and creativity to assist you in your efforts.

To all who have assisted during my administration, to the people of this city and this State who have extended friendship, courtesy, and respect to me and my family, we are most appreciative. We have labored these past four years to ensure that what came to us as seed would go to our successor as blossom, and what came to us as blossom would go to future generations as fruit. Now, our assigned labors are completed. The time of service is at hand for others.

---

1. This speech was delivered at the inauguration of Governor Wendell H. Ford and Lieutenant Governor Julian M. Carroll.

APPENDIXES

APPENDIX 1
The Nunn Administration

At the request of the editors, the following analysis of the Nunn administration was prepared by Larry Van Hoose, press secretary and director of public information, 1967–1971.

Since only a few of Governor Nunn's speeches can be included in this volume and since limited editorial comments are employed, this brief background should bring better understanding by showing the circumstances and conditions existing during Governor Nunn's term of office.

A severe fiscal crisis, unexpectedly announced near the end of his predecessor's administration, dominated the attention of the Nunn administration during its first two years. Resolving that situation successfully and establishing what the seventh Republican governor in Kentucky history often later termed "foundations for the future" were among the achievements Louie B. Nunn judged to be the most satisfying of his term.

On November 14, 1967, only a few days after the Glasgow attorney had been elected, Governor Edward T. Breathitt made public the first disclosure of Kentucky's financial plight. The *Louisville Courier-Journal* reported that revenue receipts had fallen short of biennial revenue estimates by $24.1 million. The 1966 fiscal year had ended with revenue receipts trailing expectations by $9 million; $15 million less revenue had been received in the first four months of fiscal 1967 than had been estimated. To compensate, Governor Breathitt ordered a $24 million budget reduction and directed each state agency to reduce its budget in order that the constitutional requirement of a balanced budget be met by the end of the fiscal year, June 30, 1968.

Governor Nunn painted a more vivid picture of the situation on January 2, 1968, in a State of the Commonwealth Address to the Kentucky General Assembly. "I wish I could say, as many governors before me have said, that the present is secure, the future bright, the economy vigorous, our financial structure sound, and that we have no worry. I cannot do this. . . . The cold hard facts are distressing, . . . unpleasant, bitter," Governor Nunn said. The announced deficit was only part of the story; recurring budget costs had not been reduced. Much of Governor Breathitt's budget cut was only a postponement of expenditures, the governor said.

Citing pressing needs in human service agencies such as Mental Health, Economic Security, and Child Welfare, the governor said, "They look to us, these unfortunates, and for my part, I cannot look away. It would serve no useful purpose to take you further into depressing detail at this time." He promised to deal with all these problems, point by point, department by department, in his executive budget to be presented to the legislature the following month.

While the legislature disposed of other matters, Governor Nunn began around-the-clock sessions with the state's fiscal experts, budget analysts, and the Kentucky Efficiency Task Force, composed of leading citizens from business, industry, finance, and education, in an effort to solve the crisis. "It soon became apparent that there were only two alternatives," the governor said later. "We could either recommend that the Legislature approve a tax increase and go forward with a realistic budget, or we could preside four years as a referee over a bankrupt, stagnating Commonwealth."

On February 13, 1968, before a joint session of the General Assembly, the governor delivered his budget address. In one terse statement, "There is no economy in retreat," he made clear the course he had chosen. The governor described the budget as "a human document." "In this budget, you will find the human faces of Kentucky. In its pages are the faces of children who depend upon it for their education; the faces of young men and women who depend upon this budget for their university and college education; the faces of our ill and aged who depend upon this budget for the hopes of health and life itself; the faces of those who tremble in fear of those who hold our laws in contempt; the faces of our mentally ill and retarded who find in this budget the gift of hope. From the richest and most self-sufficient to the poorest and most helpless—each and every Kentuckian has a stake in this human document."

To underwrite the budget and alleviate the deficit fiscal position of the Commonwealth, Governor Nunn recommended that the legislature increase the existing 3 percent sales tax by 2 percent and increase from $5 to $12.50 the cost of motor vehicle licenses. "These are my recommendations to you. I have now drained the bitter cup. The burden passes from me to you," the governor told the legislators. "I have done what the time, circumstances and conditions demand I do. To do otherwise, I would not be worthy of the office I hold."

The governor's budget sailed through both chambers of the opposition-dominated legislature with only one dissenting vote, that cast by a Democrat House member who voted against the bill and changed his decision the next day. Nunn's revenue recommendations faced a stiffer challenge but passed through the House and Senate intact, even though the Democrats held a 57–43 majority in the lower chamber and had a 24–14 advantage in the upper chamber.

The tone and substance of Governor Nunn's 1970 State of the Commonwealth Address reflected the success with which his 1968 fiscal policies had met. "For the first time in the history of our Commonwealth, the Governor can stand before you and say that a tax reduction for all the people of Kentucky can be given without shifting the tax burden to other shoulders and without reducing the existing level of services to the people. Of this, I am proud, not because I am the first, but because the state of our Commonwealth is so secure, its financial strength so completely rejuvenated, its most crucial programs on such a progressive course, that you have an option to give the people needed tax relief or to provide new programs or to expand existing programs that are desirable and worthwhile."

The governor's four-point, $18 million tax relief plan for 1970 was outlined in his budget address. It included elimination of the sales tax on prescription medicine; elimination of the use tax on automobiles transferred within a family; reduction of the personal income tax on low-income families; and extra tax credits for the blind and elderly. To fund the tax relief proposals, Governor Nunn's budget provided an uncommitted reserve of $18 million. The governor's proposal to remove the tax on medicine and family automobile transfers became law. His recommendations for income tax relief were disregarded by the legislature. In addition, the legislature made selective minor shifts in funds, raised the tax on whiskey and used the remainder of the uncommitted reserve to increase appropriations for environmental protection, teacher salaries, law enforcement, and higher education. The Nunn budgets offered broad-range improvements, particularly in the field of education, mental health, child care, road building, and capital construction.

In addition to major increases in funding for education at all levels during the Nunn administration, the state's vocational education budget was doubled, a statewide educational television network was completed and became operative, special education plans were formulated for exceptional children, and teachers received an unprecedented increase in salary. These four years also saw Kentucky's system of state-supported institutions of higher learning grow. Northern Kentucky State College, the state's first new four-year college in nearly fifty years, was established, and the University of Louisville was brought into the public system.

The 106-year-old Frankfort Training Home for mentally retarded children, the oldest institution of its kind still in use in America, was replaced by an $11 million facility in Somerset. In addition, all Kentucky's mental hospitals became accredited for the first time in history. A departure from large, coeducational, institutionalized surroundings for juvenile offenders, the placement of the youngsters in smaller, family-atmosphere cottages won national acclaim for Kentucky's child welfare program. A coordinated health planning program was established, rubella and sickle cell anemia programs were initiated, and an extensive campaign against drug abuse was launched.

In the field of natural resources and protection of the environment, Kentucky's most extensive effort was made to create air, water, and solid waste pollution regulations. The United States Soil Conservation Service was enlisted to help state officials control the flow of siltation from surface mines into streams. Kentucky's surface coal mining regulations were broadened to include all minerals. The unique beauty of Red River Gorge in the eastern Kentucky foothills was saved from inundation by a proposed dam site when Governor Nunn personally intervened. Likewise, executive action preserved Kentucky's last known tract of virgin timber, Lilley's Woods in Letcher County.

Kentucky's nationally respected system of state parks was expanded by the addition of a record number of overnight lodging and outdoor camping facilities. Barkley Lake, Greenbo, Grayson Reservoir, and Barren River resort parks were constructed and opened and parks were proposed, planning was begun, and funding was committed for parks on Nolin River Reservoir, Dale Hollow Lake, and Paintsville Reservoir.

The Nunn administration invested heavily in construction of farm-to-market roads and multilane parkways vital to industry, commerce, and tourism. Over 3,000 miles of rural roads were built, a record for any four-year period. Additionally, a 254-mile parkway system was begun, stretching from Henderson through Owensboro in western Kentucky, to Bowling Green and Glasgow in the south, and on to Somerset, London, and Hazard in the east. The new highway touched forty-three counties along its route and represented what the governor said was "a corridor of opportunity" for sections of Kentucky virtually without modern east-west travel arteries heretofore.

Gross farm income grew past the billion-dollar plateau for the first time in 1969 and again in each of the subsequent Nunn years. Kentucky farmers also benefited from substantial tax reform. At the governor's recommendation, the state sales tax imposed in 1966 was removed from farm machinery by the legislature and voters approved a more favorable system of tax assessment for farm property.

At the same time, industrial growth also set records with over $1.3

billion invested by new and expanding corporate concerns. To encourage industrial growth Governor Nunn recommended and the legislature approved reduction of the Kentucky intangible property tax to the lowest rate possible under the state constitution.

Significant changes in government operating procedures were made. The Kentucky Program Development Office was established within the Governor's Office, its task to provide technical expertise and assistance to local and state agencies seeking federal funds. Substantial progress was realized by coordinating efforts of the government agencies involved in development of human and natural resources.

In the area of legislative relations, Governor Nunn emerged practically unscathed, contrary to the dire early predictions by seasoned political observers that the Republican chief executive would be hindered by a General Assembly overwhelmingly populated by members of the opposition party. Governor Nunn did not hesitate to challenge the legislature by exercising executive veto power, which he used perhaps more than any governor in Kentucky history. Not one of the governor's vetoes was overturned by the General Assembly in the four years.

Governor Nunn called the legislators into Extraordinary Session only once, February 25, 1971, for the purpose of redistricting Kentucky's legislative districts for population equity. A plan was enacted and sent to the executive branch for approval, but Governor Nunn refused to sign the measure, contending that it was constitutionally unfit. Months later, a federal court upheld the governor's judgment and ordered the politically sensitive task of redistricting done again.

Kentucky experienced only two violent demonstrations of the type which plagued many American cities and states during this period. In both instances, Governor Nunn promptly ordered the Kentucky National Guard into action, order was regained immediately, and further injury or property damage were averted. Troops were sent to Louisville in May 1968, when a civil rights demonstration erupted into disorder. Two years later, in May 1970, the Guard was dispatched to the Lexington campus of the University of Kentucky when anti-war protests culminated in the burning of a small frame building used by the Reserve Officers Training Corps. The University of Kentucky disorder prompted a special address broadcast on statewide television and radio networks in which the governor, speaking from remarks prepared for delivery to his son's graduating high school class, outlined state policy and personal philosophy in dealing with campus unrest and violence.

Youth involvement in Kentucky government was vigorously extended between 1967 and 1971 through student legislative and administrative intern programs, inclusion of students on the governing boards of public colleges and universities, and voting membership of young persons appointed by Governor Nunn to state pollution regulatory panels.

The governor's wife also was active as First Lady of the Commonwealth. Mrs. Nunn's interest in restoration and preservation of historic and public facilities led to major redecoration of the Executive Mansion in Frankfort and complete restoration of White Hall, the home of noted abolitionist and United States Ambassador Cassius M. Clay near Richmond.

On December 7, 1971, the Nunn governorship ended. In his farewell address at the inauguration of his successor, Governor Nunn noted the early fiscal crisis and deficit situation he had inherited four years earlier and then reported the improved condition of the government whose reins of authority he was relinquishing:

> A strengthened government, improved management, and more creative programs have made it possible now to give tax relief to the people of the State without imposing any additional taxes. As the mantle of responsibility is transferred, a surplus in excess of five million dollars exists in the General Fund. We leave a surplus in excess of one million dollars in the Capital Construction Account. More than half the Executive Contingency Fund awaits the new governor. . . . in every department adequate funds are available to continue the operation of government at its present level of progress. . . . We have labored these past four years to ensure that what came to us as seed would go to our successor as blossom, and what came to us as blossom would go to future generations as fruit. Now, our assigned labors are completed. The time of service is at hand for others.

How did Louie B. Nunn view his tenure as governor of Kentucky? His sentiments were expressed in a news interview during the final days of the administration when he told reporters: "Generally, I am well pleased with the progress that was made. But history will be the final judge. Twenty years from today, if knowledgeable, impartial observers can look back on these four years and say the State and its people were better for our efforts, I will be satisfied."

APPENDIX 2
Speeches of Governor Nunn

INAUGURAL ADDRESS, Frankfort, December 12, 1967*

LEGISLATIVE CONFERENCE, Kentucky Dam Village, Gilbertsville, December 18, 1967*

LIGHTING OF KENTUCKY CHRISTMAS TREE, Frankfort, December 20, 1967

STATE OF THE COMMONWEALTH ADDRESS, Kentucky General Assembly, Frankfort, January 2, 1968*

AGRICULTURAL COOPERATIVE CONFERENCE, Lexington, January 11, 1968

KENTUCKY PRESS ASSOCIATION, Lexington, January 19, 1968

BOWLING GREEN-WARREN COUNTY CHAMBER OF COMMERCE, Bowling Green, January 26, 1968

ASSOCIATION OF SOUTHERN AGRICULTURAL WORKERS, Louisville, February 5, 1968

GOVERNOR'S CONFERENCE ON TRAVEL AND TOURISM, Louisville, February 6, 1968*

BUDGET MESSAGE, Frankfort, February 13, 1968*

CONSERVATION RALLY, JEFFERSON COUNTY SPORTSMEN'S CLUB AND LEAGUE OF KENTUCKY SPORTSMEN, Louisville, February 13, 1968

ANNUAL COMMUNITY AWARDS LUNCHEON, KENTUCKY CHAMBER OF COMMERCE, Lexington, February 14, 1968[1]

FARM-CITY COMMITTEE AND THE KENTUCKY DEVELOPMENT COMMITTEE, Lexington, February 15, 1968*

KENTUCKY JAYCEES OUTSTANDING YOUNG MEN BANQUET, Louisville, February 17, 1968[1]

GOVERNOR'S CONFERENCE ON FORESTRY, Lexington, February 27, 1968*

EASTERN KENTUCKY UNIVERSITY, Richmond, March 21, 1968

HISTORIC HOMES FOUNDATION (delivered by Ken Hart), Louisville, April 3, 1968

MOTOR VEHICLE INSPECTORS MEETING, Frankfort, April 3, 1968

* Address is included in this volume.
1. Address has not been located.

Consumers Association of Kentucky, Louisville, April 5, 1968*

Louisiana Young Republican Convention, New Orleans, Louisiana, April 6, 1968

Kentucky Chamber of Commerce, Louisville, April 10, 1968*

Kentucky Education Association, Louisville, April 18, 1968*

Celanese Coatings Company Research Laboratory Dedication, Middletown, April 19, 1968*

Elkhorn Coal Operators Association, Lexington, April 19, 1968

Keynote Address, Republican State Convention, Louisville, April 20, 1968*

Kentucky State Sunday Service, Washington Memorial Chapel, Valley Forge, Pennsylvania, April 21, 1968

International Nickel Company Expansion Dedication (delivered by Tom Emberton), Ashland, April 23, 1968

Industry Appreciation Luncheon, Louisville, April 24, 1968

Kentucky's Role in Physical Education and Recreation, Bowling Green, April 26, 1968[1]

Republican Fund-Raising Dinner, Tell City, Indiana, April 27, 1968[1]

Bellarmine Medal Award Dinner, Louisville, May 1, 1968[1]

Central Kentucky Mental Health Association, Lexington, May 2, 1968*

To the Subcommittee on Appropriations of the Public Works Committee, United States Senate and House of Representatives, Water Resources Development Projects in Kentucky (delivered by Jewell Graham), Washington, D.C., May 7, 1968

Industrial Development Retreat, Lexington, May 9, 1968

"Why Kentucky Went Republican—The Candidate's Story," Public Relations Seminar, Chicago, Illinois, May 10, 1968

University of Louisville Law School Honors Day, Louisville, May 15, 1968*

Morehead University Honors Day, Morehead, May 16, 1968

Spindletop Research Board of Directors Meeting, Lexington, May 20, 1968

Florida Tile Industries Groundbreaking, Lawrenceburg, May 20, 1968

Kentucky Broadcasters Association, Lexington, May 21, 1968*

OHIO VALLEY TRADE CONFERENCE, Cincinnati, Ohio, May 22, 1968

SIGNODE CORPORATION GROUNDBREAKING, Florence, May 22, 1968

HISEVILLE HIGH SCHOOL COMMENCEMENT, Hiseville, May 22, 1968

FAYETTE COUNTY EDUCATION ASSOCIATION, Lexington, May 23, 1968

SIXTH JUDICIAL CONFERENCE, Lexington, May 23, 1968

BOONE COUNTY HIGH SCHOOL COMMENCEMENT, Florence, May 27, 1968

BLUEGRASS BOYS' STATE, EASTERN KENTUCKY UNIVERSITY, Richmond, June 5, 1968*

GLASGOW ROTARY CLUB DINNER, Glasgow, June 6, 1968[1]

LEAGUE OF KENTUCKY SPORTSMEN, Jenny Wiley State Park, Prestonsburg, June 7, 1968

BURLEY AUCTION WAREHOUSE ASSOCIATION, Lexington, June 10, 1968*

INTERSTATE OIL COMPACT COMMISSION, Mobile, Alabama, June 11, 1968

REPUBLICAN GOVERNORS' CONFERENCE, Enid, Oklahoma, June 13, 1968[1]

UNION LEAGUE OF PHILADELPHIA, Philadelphia, Pennsylvania, June 20, 1968*

GIRLS' STATE, Frankfort, June 21, 1968

YOUNG REPUBLICANS' CONVENTION, Owensboro, June 22, 1968

TRAVELERS PROTECTIVE ASSOCIATION, Louisville, June 24, 1968

LOUISVILLE BAR ASSOCIATION, Louisville, June 26, 1968

POKE SALLET FESTIVAL, Harlan, June 26, 1968[1]

TO THE COMMITTEE ON WAYS AND MEANS, UNITED STATES HOUSE OF REPRESENTATIVES, OIL IMPORTATION LEGISLATION, Washington, D.C., July 2, 1968*

KENTUCKY STATE REFORMATORY JAYCEES, LaGrange, July 8, 1968*

LIVESTOCK FIELD DAY, Coldstream Farm, Lexington, July 10, 1968*[2]

INTERSTATE 71 HIGHWAY DEDICATION, Louisville, July 11, 1968*

KENTUCKY LP-GAS ASSOCIATION CONVENTION, Louisville, July 16, 1968*

WEIGHTS AND MEASURES LABORATORY DEDICATION, Frankfort, July 19, 1968

JEWEL MANOR DEDICATION, Louisville, July 21, 1968

BUSINESS PROMOTION LUNCHEON, Louisville, July 25, 1968*

2. Press copy of address is the only available copy.

To the Subcommittee on Federal, State, and Local Relationships of the Republican Platform Committee, Republican National Convention, Miami Beach, Florida, July 29, 1968*²

Republican National Convention, Miami, Florida, August 6, 1968*

Student Summer Seminar, Frankfort, August 14, 1968

Opening, Kentucky State Fair, Louisville, August 15, 1968

National Legislative Conference, Miami, Florida, August 21, 1968*

West Virginia House of Delegates Rally, Charleston, West Virginia, August 24, 1968*

Ohio Young Republicans' Convention, Cleveland, Ohio, August 24, 1968

Republican Rally in Support of John Grisso, Aiken, South Carolina, August 27, 1968

International Banana Festival, Fulton, September 6, 1968¹

Location of Frontier Worlds, Greater Cincinnati Airport, Covington, September 9, 1968

Rotary Club, Honoring the Governor, Falmouth, September 10, 1968

Kentucky Bankers Association, Louisville, September 10, 1968

University of Kentucky Cooperative Extension Service Conference, Lexington, September 11, 1968*

Chrysler Airtemp Groundbreaking, Bowling Green, September 12, 1968*

Consumer Affairs Commission, Frankfort, September 12, 1968

Tradewater River Area Resource Conservation and Development Project Banquet, Pennyrile State Park, Dawson Springs, September 13, 1968*

Opening of the Kentucky Republican Campaign, London, September 14, 1968*

Campbell County Chamber of Commerce, Newport, September 17, 1968

Kiwanis Club, Ashland, September 18, 1968¹

Nixon-Agnew Dinner, Wichita, Kansas, September 19, 1968*

Inauguration of Kentucky Educational Television Network, Lexington, September 23, 1968*

KENTUCKY ASSOCIATION OF PUPIL PERSONNEL WORKERS, Mammoth Cave National Park, September 24, 1968*

LEXINGTON THEOLOGICAL SEMINARY CONVOCATION, Lexington, September 24, 1968*

MIDDLESBORO COMMUNITY MEETING, Middlesboro, September 25, 1968*

DANIEL BOONE STAMP DEDICATION, Frankfort, September 25, 1968[1]

KENTUCKY ASSOCIATION OF SOIL AND WATER CONSERVATION DISTRICTS, Cumberland Falls State Park, Corbin, September 26, 1968

KENTUCKY ASSOCIATION OF THE CHAMBER OF COMMERCE EXECUTIVES, Louisville, September 27, 1968

YOUNG REPUBLICANS RALLY, Elk Grove, Illinois, September 28, 1968

FLORIDA REPUBLICAN WOMEN'S FEDERATION LUNCHEON, Fort Lauderdale, Florida, October 1, 1968

REPUBLICAN RALLY, Savannah, Georgia, October 1, 1968

SPINDLETOP RESEARCH BOARD OF DIRECTORS MEETING, Lexington, October 2, 1968

UPPER CUMBERLAND EDUCATION ASSOCIATION, Barbourville, October 4, 1968

THIRD DISTRICT EDUCATION ASSOCIATION, Bowling Green, October 4, 1968

NATIONAL INSTITUTE ON NATURAL RESOURCES LAW, Louisville, October 8, 1968*

KENTUCKY INDUSTRIAL DEVELOPMENT COUNCIL, Louisville, October 8, 1968*

WINNERS' DINNER, Louisville, October 9, 1968[1]

BEAUTIFICATION EXECUTIVE COMMITTEE (delivered by William Nash), Frankfort, October 10, 1968

REPUBLICAN RALLY, Poplar Bluffs, Missouri, October 14, 1968

NATIONAL COUNTY AGENTS CONFERENCE, Louisville, October 14, 1968*

FEDERAL RESERVE MEETING, Lexington, October 16, 1968[1]

DEPARTMENT OF ECONOMIC SECURITY BUILDING DEDICATION, Somerset, October 16, 1968

DINNER FOR SENATOR TOWER, Lexington, October 17, 1968[1]

REPUBLICAN RALLY, Lafayette, Indiana, October 17, 1968[1]

HAMILTON MINE DEDICATION, ISLAND CREEK COAL COMPANY, Madison-ville, October 18, 1968*

REPUBLICAN FUND-RAISING DINNER FOR BOB SIMMONDS, Bowling Green, October 18, 1968[1]

DEDICATION OF EASTERN KENTUCKY REHABILITATION CENTER (delivered by Press Secretary Larry Van Hoose), Paintsville, October 18, 1968

KENTON COUNTY REPUBLICAN MEN'S CLUB, Covington, October 19, 1968

INAUGURATION OF DR. HARRY SPARKS, Murray State University (delivered by E. G. Adams), Murray, October 21, 1968

KENTUCKY CRIME COMMISSION, Frankfort, October 25, 1968

"KEEP THE BALL ROLLING," OSHEL FOR CONGRESS RALLY, Carbondale, Illinois, October 26, 1968[1]

BLANDING-KIRWAN TOWERS DEDICATION, University of Kentucky, Lexington, October 26, 1968

REPUBLICAN RALLY, Seaford, Delaware, October 29, 1968

KENTUCKY SCIENCE AND INDUSTRY PROCUREMENT CONFERENCE (delivered by Commerce Commissioner Paul W. Grubbs), Louisville, October 30, 1968

OHIO VALLEY IMPROVEMENT ASSOCIATION, Cincinnati, Ohio, October 31, 1968

CONFEDERATE SOLDIERS' HISTORICAL MARKER DEDICATION, Glasgow, November 11, 1968

VETERANS' DAY ADDRESS, Frankfort, November 11, 1968

WORLD TRADE CONFERENCE DINNER, Louisville, November 12, 1968[1]

LIVESTOCK SALES PAVILION DEDICATION, Louisville, November 12, 1968

LINCOLN SCHOOL CONVOCATION, Lincoln Ridge, November 14, 1968*

HORSE CAVE CHAMBER OF COMMERCE, Horse Cave, November 14, 1968[1]

UNIVERSITY OF KENTUCKY DEVELOPMENT COUNCIL, Frankfort, November 15, 1968

KENTUCKY AGRICULTURAL DEVELOPMENT COMMISSION, Frankfort, November 15, 1968

KENTUCKY FARM BUREAU FEDERATION, Louisville, November 18, 1968

BUSINESSMEN'S LUNCHEON, CHEMICAL BANK OF NEW YORK, New York, New York, November 20, 1968*

LOUIE B. NUNN APPRECIATION DAY, Maysville, November 21, 1968

REPUBLICAN GOVERNORS' CONFERENCE, Palm Springs, California, December 6, 1968*

FORTUNE MAGAZINE DINNER, Louisville, December 9, 1968

CHRISTMAS TREE LIGHTING, Frankfort, December 15, 1968

ADDRESS TO THE CHURCH OF THE ASCENSION, Frankfort, December 15, 1968

CHARITY DINNER, West Liberty, December 16, 1968[1]

GREATER LOUISVILLE AUTOMOBILE DEALERS ASSOCIATION, Louisville, December 16, 1968

OWENSBORO CIVIC CLUBS LUNCHEON, Owensboro, December 17, 1968

STUDENT ADVISORY COMMISSION, Frankfort, January 7, 1969

LOUISVILLE PERSONNEL ASSOCIATION, Louisville, January 13, 1969*

KENTUCKY COMMITTEE ON NATIONAL WILDLIFE WEEK, Frankfort, January 14, 1969

KENTUCKY UTILITIES, Lexington, January 22, 1969*

STATE OF THE COMMONWEALTH ADDRESS, KENTUCKY PRESS ASSOCIATION, Louisville, January 24, 1969*[2]

OPENING CONVOCATION, CENTRE COLLEGE SESQUICENTENNIAL, Danville, January 25, 1969

GLASGOW-BARREN COUNTY CHAMBER OF COMMERCE, Glasgow, January 27, 1969

DRUG ABUSE SEMINAR, Frankfort, January 27, 1969*

LEXINGTON JAYCEES OUTSTANDING YOUNG MAN BANQUET, Lexington, January 28, 1969*

TENNESSEE-TOMBIGBEE WATERWAY AUTHORITY, Louisville, February 3, 1969

GLASGOW AREA INDUSTRIAL GROUP, Glasgow, February 5, 1969[1]

THE TURNPIKE AUTHORITY OF KENTUCKY, TOLL ROAD REVENUE BONDS SERIES OF JANUARY 1969, New York, New York, February 6, 1969*[2]

INTRODUCTION OF GERALD FORD, LINCOLN CLUB BANQUET OF KENTUCKY, Louisville, February 8, 1969

YOUNG REPUBLICAN LEADERSHIP DEVELOPMENT SEMINAR, Louisville, February 8, 1969

LINCOLN DAY BANQUET, Knoxville, Tennessee, February 18, 1969

ANNUAL BROTHERHOOD MEETING OF THE MEN'S CLUBS OF HIGHLAND PRESBYTERIAN CHURCH AND ADATH ISRAEL TEMPLE, Louisville, February 19, 1969

FIRST CHRISTIAN CHURCH BROTHERHOOD DINNER, Frankfort, February 20, 1969

BOONE COUNTY LINCOLN DAY DINNER (delivered by Tom Emberton), Florence, February 21, 1969

KENTUCKY JAYCEES OUTSTANDING YOUNG MEN BANQUET, Louisville, February 22, 1969[1]

GLASGOW AREA INDUSTRIAL GROUP MEETING, Glasgow, March 5, 1969*

MT. STERLING-MONTGOMERY COUNTY CHAMBER OF COMMERCE, Mt. Sterling, March 10, 1969

EARL RUBY TESTIMONIAL DINNER, Louisville, March 11, 1969[1]

DANVILLE-BOYLE COUNTY MANAGEMENT ASSOCIATION, Danville, March 18, 1969[1]

KENTUCKY VILLAGE REVISIT, Lexington, March 19, 1969*

J. U. KEVIL MENTAL HEALTH AND MENTAL RETARDATION CENTER DEDICATION, Mayfield, March 21, 1969*

YOUNG AND ADULT FARMER RECOGNITION BANQUET, Hopkinsville, March 21, 1969*

WOODMEN OF THE WORLD LIFE INSURANCE SOCIETY BANQUET, Louisville, March 24, 1969

TO REPRESENTATIVES OF LOCAL POLICE DEPARTMENTS, Frankfort, March 24, 1969

KENTUCKY SCHOOL BOARDS ASSOCIATION CONVENTION, Louisville, March 25, 1969*

KENTUCKY JAYCEES OUTSTANDING YOUNG MAN BANQUET, Louisville, March 25, 1969

KENTUCKY CHAMBER OF COMMERCE, Louisville, March 26, 1969

"CHALLENGE FROM PRESIDENT NIXON," TELEVISION SEMINAR, Louisville, March 26, 1969*

KENTUCKY MEDICAL ASSOCIATION, Lexington, March 26, 1969*

TO THE COMMITTEE ON PUBLIC WORKS, UNITED STATES HOUSE OF REPRESENTATIVES, EXTENSION OF THE APPALACHIAN REGIONAL DEVELOPMENT ACT, Washington, D.C., March 27, 1969*

REPUBLICAN KICK-UP DINNER FOR LINWOOD HOLTON, Richlands, Virginia, March 29, 1969[1]

MURRAY STATE UNIVERSITY ANNUAL PARENTS HONORS DAY, Murray, March 30, 1969

KENTUCKY DENTAL ASSOCIATION, Louisville, March 31, 1969[1]

UNIVERSITY OF KENTUCKY BASKETBALL BANQUET, Lexington, April 1, 1969

INDUSTRIAL APPRECIATION WEEK, Louisville, April 1, 1969

TO THE SUBCOMMITTEE ON LABOR OF THE SENATE COMMITTEE ON LABOR AND PUBLIC WELFARE, UNITED STATES SENATE, COAL SAFETY LEGISLATION, Washington, D.C., April 1, 1969*

SPINDLETOP RESEARCH BOARD OF DIRECTORS MEETING, Lexington, April 14, 1969

AMERICAN SOCIETY OF CIVIL ENGINEERS, Louisville, April 14, 1969

GOVERNOR'S BREAKFAST, KENTUCKY CHAMBER OF COMMERCE, Louisville, April 16, 1969

BLUE GRASS SCHOOL DEDICATION, Lexington, April 17, 1969

KENTUCKY YOUTH ASSEMBLY, Frankfort, April 18, 1969

LEITCHFIELD CHAMBER OF COMMERCE, Leitchfield, April 18, 1969[1]

STATE GOVERNMENT AND HIGHER EDUCATION SEMINAR, Rough River State Park, Falls of Rough, April 19, 1969*

TO LIGHT A CANDLE FOR DECENCY, TEENS FOR DECENCY RALLY, Cincinnati Gardens, Cincinnati, Ohio, April 20, 1969*

NATIONAL ASSOCIATION OF ATTORNEY GENERALS' SOUTHERN REGIONAL CONFERENCE, Lexington, April 21, 1969[1]

DANVILLE ALL-AMERICAN CITY CELEBRATION, Danville, April 22, 1969*

KENTUCKY FEDERATION OF WOMEN'S CLUBS, Louisville, April 23, 1969

KENTUCKY HOSPITAL ASSOCIATION, Louisville, April 23, 1969

REPUBLICAN GOVERNORS' CONFERENCE WELCOME ADDRESS, Lexington, May 1, 1969*

REPUBLICAN GOVERNORS' CONFERENCE, ACCEPTANCE OF POOR PEOPLE'S MULE, Lexington, May 1, 1969*

CAMPAIGN COMMITTEE ADDRESS, REPUBLICAN GOVERNORS' CONFERENCE, Lexington, May 2, 1969

KENTUCKY BROADCASTERS ASSOCIATION SPRING CONVENTION, Louisville, May 6, 1969[*][2]

UNIVERSITY OF KENTUCKY FELLOWS RECOGNITION DINNER, Spindletop, Lexington, May 8, 1969[*][2]

KENTUCKY EDUCATIONAL TELEVISION DEDICATION, Lexington, May 9, 1969[*]

EATON, YALE, AND TOWNE COMPANY GROUNDBREAKING, Henderson, May 14, 1969

PARIS-BOURBON COUNTY CHAMBER OF COMMERCE, Paris, May 14, 1969[1]

STATE GOVERNMENT AND HIGHER EDUCATION SEMINAR, Cumberland Falls State Park, Corbin, May 17, 1969

LOUISVILLE CHAPTER, NATIONAL ASSOCIATION OF ACCOUNTANTS, Louisville, May 20, 1969

GOVERNOR'S INNOVATIVE EDUCATION AWARDS DINNER, Frankfort, May 21, 1969[*][2]

INTERSTATE 65 DEDICATION, Park City, May 21, 1969[*]

ELFUN SOCIETY MEETING, Owensboro, May 28, 1969[1]

OWENSBORO INDUSTRIAL MANAGEMENT CLUB, Owensboro, May 28, 1969[1]

ADVISORY COUNCIL FOR VOCATIONAL EDUCATION AND MANPOWER DEVELOPMENT AND TRAINING, Frankfort, May 28, 1969

FRANKFORT HIGH SCHOOL COMMENCEMENT, Frankfort, May 29, 1969

REGIONAL CRIME COUNCILS, Frankfort, June 2, 1969

MURRAY STATE UNIVERSITY COMMENCEMENT, Murray, June 2, 1969[*][2]

KENTUCKY SCHOOL FOR THE BLIND COMMENCEMENT, Louisville, June 5, 1969

WESTERN KENTUCKY UNIVERSITY COMMENCEMENT, Bowling Green, June 6, 1969

KOSAIR TEMPLE SPRING CEREMONIAL, Louisville, June 7, 1969[1]

ANNUAL BOONE DAY CELEBRATION, Frankfort, June 7, 1969

LINCOLN MEMORIAL UNIVERSITY COMMENCEMENT, Harrogate, Tennessee, June 8, 1969

COUNCIL OF STATE GOVERNMENTS DEDICATION, Lexington, June 9, 1969

KENTUCKY STATE BAR ASSOCIATION, Louisville, June 12, 1969

KENTUCKY FEDERATION OF REPUBLICAN WOMEN, Frankfort, June 12, 1969

GOVERNOR'S CONSERVATION ACHIEVEMENT AWARDS, Lexington, June 13, 1969[1]

KENTUCKY LIONS EYE RESEARCH INSTITUTE DEDICATION, Louisville, June 14, 1969[1]

KENTUCKY MOUNTAIN CLUB, Lexington, June 17, 1969[*2]

COLLEGE REPUBLICANS NATIONAL COMMITTEE, BIENNIAL AWARDS BANQUET, Chicago, Illinois, July 8, 1969[*2]

KENTUCKY REGENTS CLUB DINNER, Fort Thomas, July 10, 1969

FIFTY-FIRST ANNUAL AMERICAN LEGION CONVENTION, Owensboro, July 11, 1969[*]

BARREN RIVER STATE PARK LODGE GROUNDBREAKING, Barren River State Park, Lucas, July 11, 1969

INTERSTATE 71 DEDICATION, La Grange, July 15, 1969

OMAHA WOODMEN LIFE INSURANCE SOCIETY NATIONAL CONVENTION, San Francisco, California, July 21, 1969

KIWANIS-ROTARY LUNCHEON, Hopkinsville, July 22, 1969

HARRISON COUNTY GOVERNOR'S PICNIC, Cynthiana, July 23, 1969[1]

JUVENILE COURT JUDGES CONFERENCE, Louisville, July 24, 1969

ROPER CORPORATION GROUNDBREAKING, Williamsburg, July 25, 1969

DAN C. IRWIN REUNION OF THE SURVIVORS OF BATAAN AND CORREGIDOR, Sarasota, Florida, August 2, 1969

CLASSIC GOLF TOURNAMENT TROPHY PRESENTATION, Frankfort, August 15, 1969

OPENING OF THE KENTUCKY STATE FAIR, Louisville, August 15, 1969[*2]

HIRAM LODGE #4 F. AND A. M., Frankfort, August 18, 1969[1]

DANIEL BOONE PARKWAY GROUNDBREAKING, London, August 18, 1969

STUDENT SEMINAR, Frankfort, August 24, 1969[*2]

TO CONSUMER AFFAIRS COMMITTEE, Senate Chamber, Frankfort, August 27, 1969

KENTUCKY CRIME COMMISSION BANQUET, Louisville, August 28, 1969

EULOGY OF CHIEF JUSTICE MORRIS C. MONTGOMERY, Lawrenceburg, September 5, 1969[*]

BLUEGRASS PERSONNEL ASSOCIATION, Lexington, September 8, 1969

MAYSVILLE COMMUNITY COLLEGE DEDICATION, Maysville, September 12, 1969

CONFERENCE ON COAL WORKERS' PNEUMOCONIOSIS, Lexington, September 13, 1969

TO THE FINANCE COMMITTEE, UNITED STATES SENATE, LEGISLATION ON THE HORSE INDUSTRY, Washington, D.C., September 22, 1969*[2]

KENTUCKY MUNICIPAL LEAGUE LUNCHEON, Louisville, September 23, 1969

ELIZABETHTOWN COMMUNITY COLLEGE BUILDINGS DEDICATION, Elizabethtown, September 24, 1969

LARUE COUNTY LIBRARY DEDICATION, Hopkinsville, September 24, 1969

EULOGY OF JUDGE E. P. SAWYER, Louisville, September 25, 1969*

COMMEMORATION OF FIRST SHIPMENT FROM CONTROL DATA CORPORATION (delivered by Commerce Commissioner Paul W. Grubbs), Campton, September 25, 1969

BOONE COUNTY REPUBLICAN EXECUTIVE COMMITTEE DINNER, Burlington, September 26, 1969*

SCOTTSVILLE ROTARY CLUB, Scottsville, September 26, 1969[1]

MUD RIVER WATERSHED PROJECT DEDICATION, Russellville, September 27, 1969[1]

APPOINTMENT OF ARMIN WILLIG AS JEFFERSON COUNTY JUDGE, Louisville, September 29, 1969

KENTUCKY COUNCIL ON CRIME AND DELINQUENCY, Louisville, September 29, 1969*

CENTRAL ZONE MEETING, GARDEN CLUB OF AMERICA, Louisville, September 30, 1969[1]

STATE PROPERTY AND BUILDINGS COMMISSION, Frankfort, September 30, 1969

KENTUCKY ASSOCIATION OF SOIL AND WATER CONSERVATION, Kentucky Dam Village, Gilbertsville, October 1, 1969*

AMERICAN AUTOMOBILE ASSOCIATION TRAFFIC SAFETY MEETING (delivered by Public Safety Commissioner William O. Newman), Somerset, October 2, 1969[1]

RADIO-TV SEMINAR LUNCHEON, Frankfort, October 3, 1969

STUDENT PROGRAM ON KENTUCKY ENTERPRISE CONFERENCE, Transylvania College, Lexington, October 4, 1969

TENNESSEE-TOMBIGBEE WATERWAY DEVELOPMENT AUTHORITY, Tampa, Florida, October 6, 1969

Kentucky Industrial Development Council Site-Seeing Tour, Fort Mitchell, October 6, 1969[1]

Pennyrile Parkway Dedication, Nortonville, October 9, 1969

Republican Fish Fry, Mt. Vernon, October 10, 1969[1]

Prayer Breakfast, Frankfort, October 10, 1969*[2]

Citizens Conference of Kentucky State Courts, Lexington, October 10, 1969

Western Kentucky University College Republicans, Bowling Green, October 14, 1969

Louisville Suburban Association of Life Underwriters, Louisville, October 16, 1969*[2]

United Cerebral Palsy of the Bluegrass Executive Board Luncheon, Frankfort, October 16, 1969

Kentucky Coal Association, Lexington, October 17, 1969*

National Audubon Society Board of Directors, Lexington, October 17, 1969[1]

Republican Rally, Holton for Governor, Pennington Gap, Virginia, October 18, 1969[1]

Republican Rally, Holton for Governor, Gate City, Virginia, October 18, 1969[1]

Appalachian Industries Training Center Dedication, Vanceburg, October 20, 1969[1]

Grand Lodge of Kentucky F. & A. M., Louisville, October 21, 1969[1]

Grand Chapter, Order of the Eastern Star, Louisville, October 27, 1969

To House Committee on Education and Labor, United States House of Representatives, Washington, D.C., November 6, 1969

Veterans' Day, Frankfort, November 11, 1969

New Circle Road Dedication, Lexington, November 24, 1969*[2]

Council of State Governments Dinner, Lexington, November 24, 1969*

Faultless Caster Company Groundbreaking, Hopkinsville, November 25, 1969

Daviess County Medical Society, Owensboro, November 25, 1969[1]

KENTUCKY REGIONAL LIBRARY FOR THE BLIND AND PHYSICALLY HANDI-
CAPPED DEDICATION (delivered by Press Secretary Larry Van Hoose),
Frankfort, November 26, 1969

PRELEGISLATIVE CONFERENCE, Kentucky Dam, Gilbertsville, December
1, 1969*

YMCA BANQUET, Frankfort, December 2, 1969

YMCA CORNERSTONE LAYING, Frankfort, December 2, 1969

AMERICAN AUTOMOBILE ASSOCIATION TRAFFIC SAFETY MEETING, Lexington, December 4, 1969

FRANKLIN COUNTY EXTENSION CENTER DEDICATION, Frankfort, December
6, 1969*

KENTUCKY ASSOCIATION OF SCHOOL ADMINISTRATORS, Louisville, December 14, 1969

RUBELLA CONFERENCE, Frankfort, December 16, 1969*

STATE OF THE COMMONWEALTH ADDRESS, Frankfort, January 6, 1970*

BUDGET MESSAGE, Frankfort, January 7, 1970*[4]

FRANKFORT-FRANKLIN COUNTY CHAMBER OF COMMERCE, Frankfort, January 14, 1970[1]

CONSUMER PROTECTION, Frankfort, January 20, 1970*[3, 4]

EULOGY OF SENATOR GEORGE M. PLUMMER, Vanceburg, January 20,
1970*[2]

LINCOLN CLUB OF KENTUCKY, Louisville, February 6, 1970[1]

REPUBLICAN RALLY FOR LUTHER K. PLUMMER, South Shore, February 7,
1970

REPUBLICAN FUND-RAISING DINNER, Pekin, Illinois, February 12, 1970

UNIVERSITY OF KENTUCKY ANIMAL SCIENCES BUILDING GROUNDBREAKING,
Lexington, February 17, 1970

GENERAL OBLIGATION BOND ISSUE, Frankfort, March 2, 1970*[4]

EARLE B. COMBS RECOGNITION DINNER, Richmond, March 10, 1970

SPECIAL EDUCATION, Frankfort, March 11, 1970*[4]

EDUCATIONAL REFORM, Frankfort, March 11, 1970*[4]

3. Speech text was obtained from the *Journal of the Senate of the Commonwealth of Kentucky, 1970*.

4. Speech text was obtained from the *Journal of the House of Representatives of the Commonwealth of Kentucky, 1970*.

WELFARE REFORM, Frankfort, March 11, 1970*[4]

VOTING AND GOVERNMENTAL REFORMS, Frankfort, March 11, 1970*[4]

GOOD FRIDAY SERVICES, Frankfort, March 27, 1970

INDUSTRY APPRECIATION LUNCHEON, Louisville, April 2, 1970

ELFUN SOCIETY, Louisville, April 6, 1970*[2]

EMERGENCY RADIO NETWORK DEDICATION, Slade, April 7, 1970

SPINDLETOP RESEARCH BOARD OF DIRECTORS MEETING, Lexington, April 20, 1970

KENTUCKY CHILDREN'S HOME (delivered by Administrative Assistant Mrs. Jewel Hamilton), Louisville, April 24, 1970

MOTHER OF THE YEAR DINNER, Cumberland Falls State Park, Corbin, April 27, 1970[1]

FRANKFORT ROTARY CLUB, Frankfort, April 29, 1970

NATIONAL TURF WRITERS ASSOCIATION, Louisville, April 29, 1970

THOROUGHBRED BREEDERS OF KENTUCKY, Louisville, April 30, 1970

LAW DAY ADDRESS, Broadcast Statewide over Kentucky Educational Television, Lexington, May 1, 1970

ADDRESS CONCERNING UNIVERSITY OF KENTUCKY CAMPUS DISORDER, Lexington, May 6, 1970*[2]

AMERICAN PUBLIC WORKS ASSOCIATION, Frankfort, May 12, 1970

AMERICAN AUTOMOBILE ASSOCIATION TRAFFIC SAFETY MEETING, Louisville, May 13, 1970

PRESENTATION OF J. GRAHAM BROWN PORTRAIT, Frankfort, May 21, 1970*

LILY TULIP PLANT DEDICATION, Bardstown, May 22, 1970

KENTUCKY MILITARY INSTITUTE COMMENCEMENT, Lyndon, May 24, 1970

DEDICATION OF LAKE BARKLEY STATE PARK LODGE, Lake Barkley State Park, Cadiz, May 25, 1970*[2]

FRANKFORT HIGH SCHOOL COMMENCEMENT, Frankfort, May 28, 1970*[2]

KENTUCKY LEAGUE OF SPORTSMEN, Owensboro, June 5, 1970

KENTUCKY FEDERATION OF REPUBLICAN WOMEN, Cumberland Falls State Park, Corbin, June 11, 1970*

3M PLANT DEDICATION, Cynthiana, June 12, 1970

YMCA FUND-RAISING LUNCHEON, Frankfort, June 15, 1970

ASSOCIATION OF THE UNITED STATES ARMY, DANIEL BOONE CHAPTER, Fort Knox, June 15, 1970

SOMERSET-PULASKI COUNTY CHAMBER OF COMMERCE, Somerset, June 16, 1970

TECUMSEH PRODUCTS COMPANY GROUNDBREAKING, Somerset, June 16, 1970[1]

REDEDICATION OF CHANDLER ISLAND, Burnside State Park, Somerset, June 16, 1970*

KENTUCKY PEACE OFFICERS ASSOCIATION, Frankfort, June 17, 1970

CHESAPEAKE AND OHIO BRIDGE DEMOLITION, Covington, June 18, 1970*

NORTHERN KENTUCKY STATE COLLEGE PROGRESS DINNER, Fort Mitchell, June 18, 1970

KENTUCKY YOUNG REPUBLICANS CONVENTION, Lexington, June 21, 1970

FEDERAL-MOGUL CORPORATION GROUNDBREAKING, Princeton, July 10, 1970

TENNESSEE-TOMBIGBEE WATERWAY AUTHORITY, Fort Walton Beach, Florida, July 13, 1970*[2]

MIDWESTERN GOVERNORS' CONFERENCE, Columbus, Ohio, July 21, 1970*[2]

JEWISH HOSPITAL ADDITION GROUNDBREAKING, Louisville, July 22, 1970

GROUNDBREAKING FOR CENTRAL KENTUCKY ANIMAL DISEASE DIAGNOSTIC LABORATORY, Lexington, July 30, 1970*

PADUCAH ROTARY CLUB, Paducah, August 5, 1970

THIRD KENTUCKY CONFERENCE ON VOCATIONAL EDUCATION, Louisville, August 12, 1970*

LINCOLN CLUB, Louisville, August 19, 1970

OPENING, KENTUCKY STATE FAIR, Louisville, August 20, 1970

KINCAID LAKE STATE PARK DEDICATION, Kincaid Lake State Park, Falmouth, August 27, 1970

CHICAGO 500 LUNCHEON, Chicago, Illinois, August 28, 1970*

STRIP MINING RESEARCH CONFERENCE, Frankfort, September 3, 1970

AMERICAN AUTOMOBILE ASSOCIATION TRAFFIC SAFETY MEETING, Bowling Green, September 8, 1970

APOLLO CAPSULE EXPOSITION, Frankfort, September 11, 1970

REPUBLICAN FUND-RAISING DINNER, Scottsville, September 11, 1970[1]

O'Tucks Banquet, Hamilton, Ohio, September 12, 1970[1]

Sons of the American Revolution, Louisville, September 17, 1970

Southern Governors' Conference, State Governments and the Fiscal Crisis, Biloxi, Mississippi, September 22, 1970

Southern Governors' Conference, Biloxi, Mississippi, September 22, 1970[*2]

Educational Institute for Teenage Volunteers, Lexington, September 26, 1970[1]

Robert B. Begley Building Dedication, Eastern Kentucky University, Richmond, September 26, 1970

Industrial Site-Seeing Tour Kick-Off Dinner, Louisville, September 28, 1970

American Standard Air Pollution Control Facility Dedication, Louisville, September 29, 1970

Kentucky Council of Cooperatives, Frankfort, October 1, 1970

Louisville Downtown Rotary Club, Louisville, October 1, 1970

Apple Day Festival, Paintsville, October 3, 1970

Mobile Police Training Unit Announcement, Paris, October 6, 1970

Grayson Reservoir State Park Announcement, Grayson Reservoir State Park, Carter County, October 7, 1970[*]

Pikeville College Founders' Day Convocation, Pikeville, October 8, 1970

Pikeville College Founders' Day Luncheon, Pikeville, October 8, 1970[1]

Testimony, Public Hearing on Relocation of U.S. 23, Pikeville, October 8, 1970

Kentucky Regents' Club, Fort Thomas, October 8, 1970[1]

Rally for Senator Ralph Tyler Smith, Mt. Carmel, Illinois, October 13, 1970[1]

Rally for Senator Ralph Tyler Smith, Mt. Vernon, Illinois, October 13, 1970[*]

Stamping Ground Birthday Celebration, Stamping Ground, October 15, 1970

Rally for Gerald Gregory, Lexington, October 16, 1970

LAYMAN'S MESSAGE, FIRST CHRISTIAN CHURCH, Georgetown, October 18, 1970

IRVINE-RAVENNA KIWANIS CLUB, Irvine, October 19, 1970

REGION SIX HIGH SCHOOL TRAFFIC SAFETY CONFERENCE, Lexington, October 20, 1970*

OCCUPATIONAL HEALTH CONFERENCE, Louisville, October 22, 1970

NATIONAL-SOUTHWIRE ALUMINUM COMPANY DEDICATION, Hawesville, October 23, 1970

KATENKAMP INDUSTRIES DEDICATION, Annville, October 23, 1970

RALLY FOR CONGRESSMAN WILLIAM WAMPLER, Grundy, Virginia, October 23, 1970

REPUBLICAN DINNER, Huntington, West Virginia, October 24, 1970

RALLY FOR JUDGE HOMER NEIKIRK, Greensburg, October 27, 1970

JOINT CONFERENCE OF THE KENTUCKY COUNCIL ON CRIME AND DELINQUENCY AND THE KENTUCKY WELFARE ASSOCIATION, Louisville, October 30, 1970*

DRUG AWARENESS TOUR, Louisville, Lexington, Owensboro, Paducah, Bowling Green, Covington, Ashland, Hazard and London, November 4-5, 1970

WOLFE COUNTY NEIGHBORHOOD FACILITY CORNERSTONE LAYING, Campton, November 6, 1970

NATURAL BRIDGE STATE PARK ASSOCIATION, Natural Bridge State Park, Slade, November 6, 1970

VIETNAM NATIONAL MEMORIAL DEDICATION, Louisville, November 11, 1970

AGNEW APPRECIATION BANQUET, Washington, D.C., November 12, 1970*

KENTUCKY FARM BUREAU, Louisville, November 17, 1970*

NATIONAL ASSOCIATION OF STATE AUDITORS, COMPTROLLERS, TREASURERS, AND LEGISLATIVE AUDITORS, Louisville, November 17, 1970[1]

AMERICAN STANDARD PLANT DEDICATION, Paintsville, November 18, 1970*

ASHLAND COMMUNITY COLLEGE DEDICATION, Ashland, November 18, 1970*

COUNCIL OF STATE GOVERNMENTS, Las Vegas, Nevada, November 20, 1970

CAMP NELSON BRIDGE GROUNDBREAKING, Garrard County, November 23, 1970

LEXINGTON JAYCEES AND CHAMBER OF COMMERCE, Lexington, November 24, 1970*

AMERICAN AUTOMOBILE ASSOCIATION TRAFFIC SAFETY MEETING (delivered by Public Safety Commissioner William O. Newman), Paducah, December 2, 1970[1]

SPECIAL SESSION ON DRUG ABUSE, Louisville, December 3, 1970*

CHRISTMAS TREE LIGHTING, Frankfort, December 6, 1970

THIRD ANNIVERSARY PARTY OF THE INAUGURATION OF GOVERNOR LOUIE B. NUNN, Louisville, December 12, 1970*

CONSTRUCTION INDUSTRY SAFETY SEMINAR (delivered by Highways Commissioner B. E. King), Louisville, December 17, 1970

AUDUBON PARKWAY DEDICATION, Hebbardsville, December 18, 1970

ILLINOIS INSTITUTE OF TECHNOLOGY COMMENCEMENT, Chicago, Illinois, December 22, 1970

BOWLING GREEN CHAMBER OF COMMERCE, Bowling Green, January 8, 1971

CONGREGATION OF THE FIRST CHRISTIAN CHURCH FELLOWSHIP DINNER, Louisville, January 10, 1971*[2]

LEBANON CHAMBER OF COMMERCE, Lebanon, January 12, 1971

STATE OF THE COMMONWEALTH ADDRESS, KENTUCKY PRESS ASSOCIATION, Louisville, January 22, 1971*

METROPOLITAN LOUISVILLE JOB BANK DEDICATION, Louisville, January 22, 1971

AMERICAN LEGION SOUTHERN AREA CONFERENCE ON CHILDREN AND YOUTH, Louisville, January 22, 1971

PRESENTATION OF DEED TO BOYD COUNTY FISCAL COURT, Catlettsburg, January 25, 1971

AMERICAN AUTOMOBILE ASSOCIATION TRAFFIC SAFETY MEETING, Ashland, January 25, 1971*[2]

CONFERENCE OF APPALACHIAN GOVERNORS, White Sulphur Springs, West Virginia, February 5, 1971*[2]

LINCOLN CLUB, Louisville, February 6, 1971[1]

To the Committee on Public Works, United States Senate, Extension of the Appalachian Regional Development Act, Washington, D.C., February 9, 1971[*2]

Midwinter Meeting of the National Governors' Conference, Washington, D.C., February 24, 1971[*2]

Extraordinary Session of the Kentucky General Assembly, Frankfort, February 25, 1971[*]

Lincoln Banquet, Ashland, February 25, 1971

Kentucky College Republican Convention, Lexington, February 27, 1971

Lexington General Agents and Managers Association, Lexington, March 4, 1971

National Guard Association of Kentucky, Louisville, March 6, 1971

Morehead Chamber of Commerce, Morehead, March 10, 1971

Kentucky School Board Association, Louisville, March 16, 1971

Governor's Conference on Exceptional Children, Frankfort, March 17, 1971[*]

Somerset Community College Dedication, Somerset, March 22, 1971

Association of the United States Army, Kentucky-Tennessee Chapter, Fort Campbell, March 22, 1971

Crusade versus Crime Luncheon, Louisville, March 29, 1971[*]

Groundbreaking for Northern Kentucky State College, Covington, March 31, 1971[*]

Governor's Reception Banquet and Ball, Southgate, March 31, 1971[1]

Ohio Valley Improvement Association, Nashville, Tennessee, April 1, 1971

Johnson Service Company Dedication, Georgetown, April 2, 1971

Kentucky Public Health Association, Louisville, April 6, 1971[*]

Sigma Delta Chi, Louisville, April 6, 1971

Industry Appreciation Luncheon, Louisville, April 7, 1971[1]

London Ministerial Association Easter Week Services, London, April 7, 1971[1]

Glasgow Rotary Club, Glasgow, April 8, 1971[1]

Bourbon County Soil and Water Conservation District Cooperators' Dinner, Paris, April 8, 1971[*]

GREENVILLE ROTARY CLUB, Greenville, South Carolina, April 13, 1971

RUSSELLVILLE-LOGAN COUNTY CHAMBER OF COMMERCE, Russellville, April 15, 1971

KENTUCKY MOTHERS' ANNUAL AWARDS LUNCHEON, Louisville, April 17, 1971

SOMERSET AERONAUTICAL TRAINING CENTER DEDICATION, Somerset, April 17, 1971

PULASKI COUNTY REPUBLICAN WOMEN'S CLUB, Somerset, April 17, 1971[1]

INTRODUCTION OF PRESIDENT RICHARD M. NIXON, REPUBLICAN GOVERNORS' CONFERENCE, Williamsburg, Virginia, April 19, 1971[*2]

GENERAL TELEPHONE SHAREHOLDERS MEETING, Lexington, April 21, 1971[1]

KENTUCKY BAR ASSOCIATION, Louisville, April 21, 1971[1]

SPINDLETOP RESEARCH APPRECIATION LUNCHEON HONORING PRINCIPAL CONTRIBUTORS AND GOVERNOR AND MRS. LOUIE B. NUNN, Lexington, April 23, 1971[*]

COMMITTEE FOR FORT THOMAS, Fort Thomas, April 27, 1971[1]

HONORABLE ORDER OF KENTUCKY COLONELS, Louisville, April 30, 1971[1]

MERCER COUNTY CHAMBER OF COMMERCE, Harrodsburg, May 6, 1971

DON JENKINS DAY, Morgantown, May 11, 1971

ELIZABETHTOWN COMMUNITY COLLEGE COMMENCEMENT, Elizabethtown, May 11, 1971

SOUTHEASTERN ASSOCIATION OF RAILROAD AND UTILITIES COMMISSIONERS, Louisville, May 13, 1971[*]

KENTUCKY FEDERATION OF BUSINESS AND PROFESSIONAL WOMEN'S CLUBS, Lexington, May 14, 1971[1]

CONTINENTAL CONVEYOR AND EQUIPMENT COMPANY PLANT LOCATION ANNOUNCEMENT, Salyersville, May 15, 1971

SOUTHERN WATER RESOURCES CONFERENCE, Louisville, May 20, 1971[1]

GOVERNOR'S INNOVATIVE EDUCATION AWARDS CEREMONY, Frankfort, May 20, 1971

ESTILL COUNTY HIGH SCHOOL DEDICATION, Irvine, May 21, 1971

KENTUCKY STATE LIONS CONVENTION, Lexington, May 22, 1971[1]

CALVARY COLLEGE COMMENCEMENT, Blackey, May 26, 1971

GOVERNOR'S ENVIRONMENTAL CONFERENCE, Natural Bridge State Park, Slade, May 27, 1971[*]

KENTUCKY DAIRY ASSOCIATION, Glasgow, June 1, 1971[1]

INTERLAKE STEEL CORPORATION GROUNDBREAKING, Newport, June 3, 1971

SOUTHERN POLICE INSTITUTE COMMENCEMENT, Louisville, June 4, 1971

GRADUATION REVIEW AND BATTALION COMMENCEMENT, Fort Campbell, June 4, 1971

UNIVERSITY OF LOUISVILLE MEDICAL SCHOOL COMMENCEMENT, Louisville, June 6, 1971*

MADISONVILLE AREA VOCATIONAL SCHOOL HEALTH OCCUPATIONS BUILDING DEDICATION, Madisonville, June 7, 1971

KENTUCKY FEDERATION OF REPUBLICAN WOMEN, Lake Barkley State Park, Cadiz, June 9, 1971*

KENTUCKY MOTOR TRANSPORT ASSOCIATION, Lake Barkley State Park, Cadiz, June 12, 1971

KENTUCKY LEAGUE OF SPORTSMEN, Cave City, June 12, 1971

ECONOMIC DEVELOPMENT ADMINISTRATION, Shakertown, Pleasant Hill, June 15, 1971*

GIRLS' STATE, Frankfort, June 18, 1971

KENTUCKY WHITE HOUSE CONFERENCE ON AGING, Lexington, June 22, 1971*

NATIONAL ASSOCIATION OF UNIVERSITY AND COLLEGE ATTORNEYS, Louisville, June 24, 1971

PINE MOUNTAIN BOYS CAMP DEDICATION, Pine Mountain Boys Camp, Harlan County, June 30, 1971*

POKE SALLET FESTIVAL, Harlan, June 30, 1971*

LOUISVILLE JAYCEES, Louisville, July 1, 1971[1]

REPLY TO "ONE MAN'S OPINION," Louisville, July 7, 1971*[2]

SUMMER INTERN AND STUDENT ASSISTANT SEMINAR, Frankfort, July 8, 1971

BIG BONE LICK STATE PARK GROUNDBREAKING, Big Bone Lick State Park, Union, July 12, 1971

I-64 RIVERSIDE EXPRESSWAY DEDICATION, Louisville, July 13, 1971

REPUBLICAN ATTORNEYS' ORGANIZATION, Louisville, July 13, 1971[1]

JESSE STUART LODGE DEDICATION, Greenbo Lake State Park, Greenup, July 14, 1971

PINE MOUNTAIN STATE PARK FACILITIES DEDICATION (delivered by Parks Commissioner Shirley Palmer-Ball), Pineville, July 14, 1971[1]

BUCKHORN LAKE STATE PARK FACILITIES DEDICATION (delivered by Parks Commissioner Shirley Palmer-Ball), Buckhorn, July 14, 1971[1]

MADISONVILLE COMMUNITY COLLEGE GROUNDBREAKING, Madisonville, July 15, 1971

HOPKINS COUNTY UNIVERSITY OF KENTUCKY ALUMNI ASSOCIATION, Madisonville, July 15, 1971[1]

WHITNEY M. YOUNG, JR., RESIDENTIAL MANPOWER CENTER DEDICATION, Simpsonville, July 16, 1971*[2]

MIDWESTERN GOVERNORS' CONFERENCE, Sioux City, Iowa, July 20, 1971*

GOLF COURSE DEDICATION, Lake Barkley State Park, Cadiz, August 4, 1971

LEGEMAN TRACT DEDICATION, Audubon State Park, Henderson, August 4, 1971

BARREN RIVER STATE PARK DEDICATION, Barren River State Park, Lucas, August 4, 1971*

INTERNATIONAL BANANA FESTIVAL, Fulton, August 13, 1971[1]

THE JOCKEY CLUB, Saratoga Springs, New York, August 15, 1971*

ANNOUNCEMENT OF EXPANSION OF FLORIDA TILE INDUSTRIES, INC., Lawrenceburg, August 18, 1971*

OPENING OF THE KENTUCKY STATE FAIR, Louisville, August 19, 1971*

DEDICATION OF BUILDINGS AT KENTUCKY STATE COLLEGE (delivered by Finance Commissioner Albert Christen), Frankfort, August 24, 1971*

FORTY-FIFTH ANNIVERSARY CELEBRATION OF BETHANY CHILDREN'S HOME, Bethany, August 27, 1971

HARLAN APPALACHIAN REGIONAL HOSPITAL FACILITIES DEDICATION, Harlan, August 29, 1971

KENTUCKY-TENNESSEE KIWANIS CLUBS, Lexington, August 30, 1971*

WE BELIEVE (IN BIG-TIME FOOTBALL AT THE UNIVERSITY OF KENTUCKY) BANQUET, Lexington, August 31, 1971

REPUBLICAN RALLY, Louisville, September 9, 1971[1]

TOM SAWYER STATE PARK DEDICATION, Louisville, September 10, 1971

REPUBLICAN FUND-RAISING DINNER, Louisville, September 10, 1971[1]

TESTIMONY CONCERNING THE FEDERAL COAL MINE HEALTH AND SAFETY ACT OF 1969, Lexington, September 16, 1971[*2]

WHITE HALL DEDICATION, Richmond, September 16, 1971[*]

BLUEGRASS REGIONAL MENTAL HEALTH-MENTAL RETARDATION BOARD, Lexington, September 16, 1971

REPUBLICAN RALLY, Levi Jackson State Park, London, September 18, 1971[*]

CLAY WADE BAILEY BRIDGE GROUNDBREAKING, Covington, September 20, 1971

NORTHERN KENTUCKY CHILDREN'S EVALUATION CENTER GROUNDBREAKING, Crittenden, September 20, 1971

NORTHERN KENTUCKY STATE COLLEGE CIVIC CENTER GROUNDBREAKING, Covington, September 20, 1971

CEREBRAL PALSY SCHOOL ADDITION DEDICATION, Louisville, September 27, 1971

BURLEY AND DARK LEAF EXPORTERS ASSOCIATION, Louisville, September 28, 1971[*]

FORT GAY BRIDGE ANNOUNCEMENT, Louisa, September 30, 1971

KENTUCKY COUNCIL OF COOPERATIVES, Louisville, October 1, 1971

REPUBLICAN FUND-RAISING RALLY, Elizabethtown, October 4, 1971[1]

KENTUCKY WELFARE ASSOCIATION, Lexington, October 6, 1971

REPUBLICAN FUND-RAISING RALLY, Harrodsburg, October 7, 1971[1]

DR. THOMAS WALKER STATE PARK REDEDICATION, Dr. Thomas Walker State Park, Barbourville, October 8, 1971

REPUBLICAN RALLY, Lexington, October 11, 1971[1]

ASHLAND CIVIC CLUBS, Ashland, October 13, 1971[1]

REPUBLICAN RALLY, Bowling Green, October 13, 1971[1]

CONSERVATION CONGRESS, Lexington, October 14, 1971

GENERAL ASSEMBLY OF CHRISTIAN CHURCHES, Louisville, October 15, 1971[1]

REPUBLICAN RALLY, Paintsville, October 18, 1971[1]

KIWANIS CLUB, Bardstown, October 19, 1971[1]

REPUBLICAN RALLY, Paducah, October 20, 1971[1]

HANDICAPPED PARK ANNOUNCEMENT, Lexington, October 21, 1971

INTERSTATE MINING COMPACT COMMISSION, Lexington, October 21, 1971*

SOMERSET BY-PASS OPENING, Somerset, October 22, 1971

DEDICATION OF SOMERSET COMPREHENSIVE TRAINING CENTER, Somerset, October 22, 1971*

GRAYSON RESERVOIR STATE PARK ANNOUNCEMENT, Grayson, October 25, 1971

GREEN RIVER STATE PARK ANNOUNCEMENT, Campbellsville, October 25, 1971

FORT BOONESBOROUGH STATE PARK ANNOUNCEMENT, Fort Boonesborough, October 26, 1971

FRANCIS ASBURY CONVOCATION, Wilmore, October 26, 1971

DANIEL BOONE PARKWAY DEDICATION, Manchester, October 28, 1971

CENTRAL KENTUCKY ANIMAL DISEASE DIAGNOSTIC LABORATORY DEDICATION, Lexington, October 28, 1971

CLOSING OF KENTUCKY VILLAGE, Lexington, October 28, 1971*

NATIONAL GUARD ARMORY DEDICATION, Lexington, October 28, 1971

GREEN HILLS SCHOOL DEDICATION, Bledsoe, October 29, 1971

REPUBLICAN RALLY, Betsy Layne, October 29, 1971[1]

REPUBLICAN RALLY, Williamsburg, October 30, 1971[1]

REPUBLICAN RALLY, Somerset, October 30, 1971[1]

REPUBLICAN RALLY, Edmonton, October 30, 1971[1]

JESSAMINE COUNTY JUNIOR HIGH SCHOOL AND HATTIE C. WARNER ELEMENTARY SCHOOL DEDICATION, Nicholasville, October 31, 1971

SOUTHERN GOVERNORS' CONFERENCE, Atlanta, Georgia, November 9, 1971*

SALUTE TO THE PRESIDENT DINNER, Washington, D.C., November 9, 1971*

LEXINGTON ROTARY CLUB, Lexington, November 11, 1971*

MOUNTAIN PARKWAY PLAQUE PRESENTATION HONORING GOVERNOR BERT T. COMBS, Campton, November 16, 1971

KENTUCKY TURNPIKE PLAQUE PRESENTATION HONORING GOVERNOR LAWRENCE WETHERBY, Shepherdsville, November 16, 1971

REPUBLICAN GOVERNORS' CONFERENCE, French Lick, Indiana, November 17, 1971*

KENESETH ISRAEL SYNAGOGUE DEDICATION, Louisville, November 21, 1971

FRANKFORT OPTIMIST CLUB, Frankfort, November 23, 1971

DEDICATION OF LAND AND BUILDINGS, SOUTH UNION SHAKER COLONY, Auburn, November 28, 1971

VALEDICTORY ADDRESS, Frankfort, December 7, 1971*2

INDEX

www.ingramcontent.com/pod-product-compliance
Lightning Source LLC
Chambersburg PA
CBHW020642110726
47901CB00001B/20